OBJECT-ORIENTED PROGRAMMING
C++ SIMPLIFIED

OBJECT-ORIENTED PROGRAMMING C++ SIMPLIFIED

By

HARI MOHAN PANDEY

Assistant Professor

Computer Engineering Department

NMIMS University

Mumbai

(Maharashtra)

UNIVERSITY SCIENCE PRESS

(An Imprint of Laxmi Publications Pvt. Ltd.)

An ISO 9001:2008 Company

BENGALURU • CHENNAI • COCHIN • GUWAHATI • HYDERABAD

JALANDHAR • KOLKATA • LUCKNOW • MUMBAI • RANCHI • NEW DELHI

BOSTON (USA) • NAIROBI (KENYA)

OBJECT-ORIENTED PROGRAMMING C++ SIMPLIFIED

Printed and bound in India
Typeset at ABRO Enterprises, Delhi
First Edition: 2015
ISBN 978-93-81159-50-7

PUBLISHED IN INDIA BY

UNIVERSITY SCIENCE PRESS
(An Imprint of Laxmi Publications Pvt.Ltd.)

An ISO 9001:2008 Certified Company
113, GOLDEN HOUSE, DARYAGANJ,
NEW DELHI - 110002, INDIA
Telephone : 91-11-4353 2500, 4353 2501
Fax : 91-11-2325 2572, 4353 2528
www.laxmipublications.com info@laxmipublications.com

Branches

✆	Bengaluru	080-26 75 69 30	
✆	Chennai	044-24 34 47 26,	24 35 95 07
✆	Cochin	0484-237 70 04,	405 13 03
✆	Guwahati	0361-254 36 69,	251 38 81
✆	Hyderabad	040-27 55 53 83,	27 55 53 93
✆	Jalandhar	0181-222 12 72	
✆	Kolkata	033-22 27 43 84	
✆	Lucknow	0522-220 99 16	
✆	Mumbai	022-24 91 54 15,	24 92 78 69
✆	Ranchi	0651-220 44 64	

C—
printed at : Repro Knowledgecast Limited, Thane

Contents

Preface

This book "***OBJECT-ORIENTED PROGRAMMING C++ SIMPLIFIED***" is a comprehensive, hands-on guide to C++ programming but one that doesn't assume you've programmed before. (People familiar with earlier programming or another structured programming language will, of course, have an easier time and can move through the early chapters quickly.)

Soon, you will write sophisticated programs that take full advantages of C++'s exciting and powerful object-oriented nature. You will start as a beginner and when you have finished this book, you will have moved far along the road to C++ mastery. I have tried hard to cover at the least the fundamentals of every technique that a C++ professional will need to master.

I have also made sure to stress the new ways of thinking needed to master C++ programming, so even experts in more traditional programming languages can benefit from this book. I have taken this approach because trying to force C++ into the framework of older programming languages is ultimately self-defeating, you can't take advantage of its power if you continue to think within an older paradigm.

To make this book even more useful, there are extensive discussions of important topics left out of most other introductory books. There are whole chapters on objects, including non-trivial examples of building your own objects with C++. When I teach you process of inheritance at that time I have introduced you to develop C++ code on behalf of inherited diagrams. There is a chapter for input-output manipulators which shows you number of functions used in C++ for input/output control. In the same chapter I teach you about manipulator and ways to develop your own manipulator. There is a whole chapter for miscellaneous new features of C++. There is also a chapter on exception handling. The book has also dealt about keeping file information through the chapter File Handling. It also has chapters for Standard Template Library and for the String Class and a whole chapter for showing the hidden secrets of C++. The book also includes lots of examples with step-by-step explanation and an extensive discussion of sorting and searching techniques and lots of tips and tricks. In sum, unlike many of the introductory books out there, I not only want to introduce you to a topic, but I go into it in enough depth that you can actually use the techniques for writing practical programs.

Now a confession: My original goal was to make this book a "**one-stop resource**", but, realistically, C++ has gotten far too big and far too powerful for any one book to do this. Nonetheless, if you finish this book, I truly believe that you will be in a position to begin writing commercial-quality C++ programs! True mastery will take longer. I have tried to give suggestions that can take you to next level.

• HOW THIS BOOK IS ORGANIZED

The subject matter of this book is divided into **15 chapters (including chapter 0)**. Each chapter has been written and developed with immensely simplified programs **(except chapter 1, which is foundation chapter for various programming methodology)** which will clear the core concepts of the C++ language. The book **"OBJECT ORIENTED PROGRAMMING C++ SIMPLIFIED"** has been written specially for those students who are tyro in the field of programming. Inside the book you will find numerous programs instead of just code snippet to illustrate even the basic concept. The book assumes no previous exposure to the C++ programming language. It also contains some good programming examples which might be useful for experienced programmers. All the programming examples given in the book have been tested on **VC++ compiler, Turbo C++ 3.0** and **Turbo C++ 4.5 compilers** under **windows** and **DOS**.

Each chapter contains a number of **examples** to explain the theoretical as well as practical concepts. **Every chapter is followed by questions to test the student performance and retentivity**.

Here are short descriptions of the chapters:

Chapter 0: Covers the topics of basic introduction of programming methodology and introduction of OOP like **structured programming** by which one can understand the elementary elements (**sequence structure, Loop or iteration and Decision structure**) of any programming language. The chapter also explains the basic approaches (**Bottom-up** and **Top-down**) and the basic concepts of object-oriented programming too. It gives an idea to programmer to categorise any programming language into **object-oriented or object based language.**

Chapter 1: This chapter gives the details of fundamental aspects of "object oriented design and analysis" and covers the details of **"Grady Booch Approach"**, principles used for OOAD. It flashes the concepts where OOAD fits in software development life cycle.

Chapter 2: In this chapter I have explained the historical development of C++ language. The chapter also gives introductory idea of tokens, variables, data types and basic structure of C++ program. In the same chapter I have explained the method of **compiling** and **executing** the C++ program on **Turbo C++3.0**, **Turbo C++ 4.5 and VC++.**

Chapter 3: This chapter introduces programmers about the behaviour of operators used in C++. Here I have explained the most of the common features applied in C and C++ both, because as we say C++ is super set of C then **operators and expressions** used in C must be implemented with C++ too.

Chapter 4: Covers the **operators used only with C++ and not with C**. Here I have covered the operators like **scope resolution operator, reference variables, bool data type**. This chapter gives idea of **dynamic memory allocation** and operators **new and delete** for dynamic memory allocation in C++.

Chapter 5: Gives the idea of **declaring function (prototyping)**, function of **main ()** function, introduction of **recursion**. It also gives the meaning of **call by reference** and **call by address** and difference between **call by reference** and **call by address**. Here I have explained the functionality of **inline function** and **function overloading** too.

Chapter 6: Gives the introduction of **class and objects** used in C++. Here I have put the comparison of **structure and class**, way of **accessing private data** and given an idea about

passing and returning objects. In this chapter I have given some very crucial elements of C++ like **array of objects, friend function, Static class members and constant member function**. All these concepts play a very important role in software development.

Chapter 7: This chapter covers the behaviours of a **constructor.** Here I show the role of different types of constructor like **default constructor, constructor with parameters, copy constructor.** This chapter also gives the ideas of dynamic constructor and destructor.

Chapter 8: Gives ideas to programmer to **overload different types of operators** used in C++ like, **binary operators, assignment operator, unary operators**. Overloading with the help of **friend function** and rules of overloading any operator and way for **type conversion** too.

Chapter 9: In this chapter we will deal the concept of **inheritance,** different types of inheritance *i.e.,* **single level, multilevel, multiple, hierarchical and hybrid**. Here I have also defined the different visibility modifier with respect to inheritance. Application of **constructor and destructor** in inheritance and concept of **containership** is also defined in the same chapter.

Chapter 10: This chapter gives the way of implementing the concepts like **pointer to objects**, **this pointer**, and way of **binding**, what is **virtual function** and how to work with **virtual function**, rules for **virtual function.** This chapter also gives the comparison of **virtual function** and **pure virtual** function. Also included are the fundamental concepts of **object slicing** and **virtual destructor.**

Chapter 11: Here I have explained the concepts of C++ **stream classes** and **formatted** and **unformatted** input and output operation applied in C++ as well as the concept of **manipulator.**

Chapter 12: This chapter gives the idea of how to handle **file** in C++ programming language and introduces the programmer about the fundamental concepts of **file streams, way of opening and closing file, different modes of opening a text file** in C++. This chapter also gives the approaches to **check end of any file**, **Random access in file**. In the same chapter I have put the introductory ideas of **command line argument** and ways of working with **binary mode** and **error handling mechanism** with file handling.

Chapter 13: Covers the introductory idea of **template programming** *i.e.,* **function template and class template.**

Chapter 14: This chapter deals with basic concepts of **exception handling mechanism and how to handle exception with the help of class,** how to **re-throw** an exception, how to **catch** all exceptions.

Chapter 15: Covers all the experiments given in the syllabus.

Appendix–1 Presents some language-technical elements.

Appendix–2 Discusses the technical questions which are generally asked in technical interviews.

• IMPLEMENTATION NOTE

The language used in this book is "Pure C++" as defined in the C++ standard. Therefore, the examples ought to run on every C++ implementation. The major program fragments in this book were tried using several C++ implementations. Examples using features only recently adopted into C++ didn't compile on every implementation. However, I see no point in mentioning which implementations failed to compile which examples. Such information would soon be out of date because implementers are working hard to ensure that their implementations correctly accept every C++ feature.

• SUGGESTIONS FOR C PROGRAMMERS

The better one knows C, the harder it seems to be to avoid writing C++ in C style, thereby losing some of the potential benefits of C++. Please take a look at Appendix B, which describes the differences between C and C++. Here are a few pointers to the areas in which C++ has better ways of doing something than C has:

1. Macros are almost never necessary in C++. Use `const` or *`enum`* to define manifest constants, `inline` to avoid function-calling overhead, *`templates`* to specify families of functions and types, and *`namespaces`* to avoid name clashes.
2. Don't declare a variable before you need it so that you can initialize it immediately. A declaration can occur anywhere a statement can, in *for-statement* initializers, and in conditions.
3. Don't use *`malloc()`*. The *`new`* operator does the same job better, and instead of *`realloc()`*, try a *`vector`*.
4. Try to avoid *void* *, pointer arithmetic, unions, and casts, except deep within the implementation of some function or class. In most cases, a cast is an indication of a design error. If you must use an explicit type conversion, try using one of the "new casts" for a more precise statement of what you are trying to do.
5. Minimize the use of arrays and C-style strings. The C++ standard library *string and `vector`* classes can often be used to simplify programming compared to traditional C style. In general, try not to build yourself what has already been provided by the standard library.

To obey C linkage conventions, a C++ function must be declared to have C linkage. Most important, try thinking of a program as a set of interacting concepts represented as classes and objects, instead of as a bunch of data structures with functions twiddling their bits.

• SUGGESTIONS FOR C++ PROGRAMMERS

By now, many people have been using C++ for a decade. Many more are using C++ in a single environment and have learned to live with the restrictions imposed by early compilers and first generation libraries. Often, what an experienced C++ programmer has failed to notice over the years is not the introduction of new features as such, but rather the changes in relationships between features that make fundamentally new programming techniques feasible. In other words, what you didn't think of when first learning C++ or found impractical just might be a superior approach today. You find out only by re-examining the basics.

Read through the chapters in order. If you already know the contents of a chapter, you can be through in minutes. If you don't already know the contents, you'll have learned something unexpected. I learned a fair bit writing this book and I suspect that hardly any C++ programmer knows every feature and technique presented. Furthermore, to use the language well, you need a perspective that brings order to the set of features and techniques. Through its organization and examples, this book offers such a perspective.

• EXERCISES

Exercises are found at the ends of chapters. The exercises are mainly of the write a program variety. Always write enough code for a solution to be compiled and run with at least a few test cases. The exercises vary considerably in difficulty, so they are marked with an estimate of their difficulty. The scale is exponential so that if an exercise takes you ten minutes, it might take an hour and it might take a day. The time needed to write and test a program depends more on your experience than on the exercise itself. An exercise might take a day if you first have to get acquainted with a new computer system in order to run it. On the other hand, an exercise might be done in an hour by someone who happens to have the right collection of programs handy.

Any book on programming in C can be used as a source of extra exercises for some introductory chapters. Any book on data structures and algorithms can be used as a source of exercises for some middle chapters for the formation of algorithms.

Acknowledgement

First of all, I would like to say thanks to *"BABA VISVNATH"* for their constant bless in writing this book. As understanding of the study like this is never the outcome of the efforts of a single person, rather it bears the imprint of a number of people who directly or indirectly helped me in completing this book. I would be failing in my duty if I don't say a word of thanks to all those who have offered sincere advice to make this book educative, effective, and pleasurable. I would like to acknowledge **My Father Dr. V. N. Pandey My Mother Smt. Madhuri Pandey, My sisters Ms. Anjana Pandey, Ms. Ranjana Pandey and My brother Mr. Man Mohan Pandey.**

I have immense pleasure in expressing my whole hearted gratitude to **Prof. RR Sedamkar (Associate Dean, MPSTME),** for providing help and guidance during the writing of this book.

I also wish to thank my lots of student whose conceptual queries have always helped me in digging the subject matter deep.

I am thankful to all the employees of **MPSTME, NMIMS University** especially **Mr. Bharat Thodji** and **Mr. Mahendra Joshi** who have been supporting me in all types of Lab activities during the writing of this book.

How can I forget my close buddy **Lecturer Shreedhar Desmukh** who has supported me most of the time during writing of the book? I am also thankful to the librarian of MPSTME at Shirpur **Mr. Anand Gawdekar** who provided each and every good book timely.

—Author

Salient Features of the Book

(*a*) Lucid explanation of OOP concept.

(*b*) Covers C features in nutshell.

(*c*) Emphasis is on new features of C++.

(*d*) Overloaded almost all types of operators.

(*e*) 12 fully explained programs on type conversion.

(*f*) Virtual Functions explored in depth.

(*g*) Covers advance features.

(*h*) Detailed coverage of exception handling and templates.

(*i*) Over 600 thoroughly explained programs.

(*j*) Plenty of exercises to try.

(*k*) Detailed description of file handling with more than 40 thoroughly explained programs.

List of Experiments

OBJECT-ORIENTED PROGRAMMING LAB

1. Program illustrating function overloading feature.
2. Programs illustrating the overloading of various operators:
   Ex: Binary operators, Unary operators, New and delete operators etc.
3. Programs illustrating the use of following functions:
   (*a*) Friend functions (*b*) Inline functions
   (*c*) Static member functions (*d*) Functions with default arguments.
4. Programs to create singly and doubly linked lists and perform insertion and deletion operations.
   Using self referential classes, new and delete operators.
5. Programs illustrating the use of destructor and the various types of constructors (no arguments, constructor, constructor with arguments, copy constructor etc).
6. Programs illustrating the various forms of inheritance:
   Ex. Single, multiple, multilevel, hierarchical inheritance etc.
7. Write a program having student as on abstract class and create many derived classes such as Engg, Science, Medical, etc., from student class. Create their objects and process them.
8. Write a program illustrating the use of virtual functions.
9. Write a program which illustrates the use of virtual base class.
10. Write a program which uses the following sorting methods for sorting elements in ascending order.
    Note: Use function templates
    (*a*) Bubble sort (*b*) Selection sort (*c*) Quick sort.
11. Write a program which illustrates the use of class templates:
    Ex. (*a*) Stack class (*b*) Queue class.
12. Write programs illustrating file handling operations:
    Ex. (*a*) Copying a text file (*b*) Displaying the contents of the file etc.
13. Write programs illustrating the console I/O operations.
14. Write programs illustrating how exceptions are handled (ex: division-by-zero, overflow and underflow in stacks etc.).

CHAPTER 0

INTRODUCTION TO OOPs

STRUCTURED PROGRAMMING

Structured programming (sometimes known as modular programming) is a subset of procedural programming that enforces a logical structure in the programming being written to make it more efficient and easier to understand and modify. Structured programming frequently employes a top-down design model, in which developers map out the overall program structure into separate subsections. A defined function or set of similar functions is coded in a separate modules can be reused in other programs. After a module has been tested individually, it is then integrated with other modules into the overall program structure. Program flow follows a simple hierarchical model that employs looping constructs such as "for", "repeat" and "while". Use of the "Go To" statement is discouraged.

Structured programming was first suggested by Corrado Bohm and Guiseppe Jacopini. The two mathematicians demonstrated that any computer program can be written with just three structures : decision, sequences, and loops.

Coders should break larger pieces of code into shorter subroutines (functions, procedures, methods, blocks, or otherwise) that are small enough to be understood easily. In general, programs should use local variables and take arguments by either value or reference. These techniques help to make isolated small pieces of code easier to understand the whole program at once. PASCAL, Ada, C, are some of the examples of structured programming languages.

Sequence Structure

A sequence structure consists of a single entry and single exit statements *i.e.,* it makes a sequential flow.

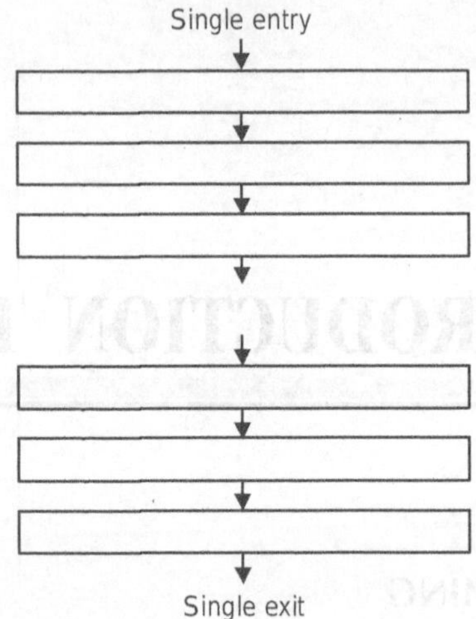

Figure 1. *Implementation of sequence structure.*

Loop or Iteration Structure

The loop consists of number of sequence statements which are executed based on the condition.

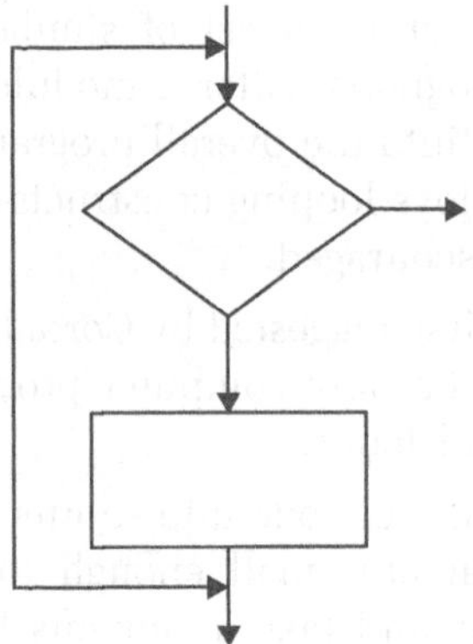

Figure 2. *Implementation of loop or iteration structure.*

Decision Structure

It consists of a condition which may be true or false. Depending upon condition is true or false a different branch is taken and is executed.

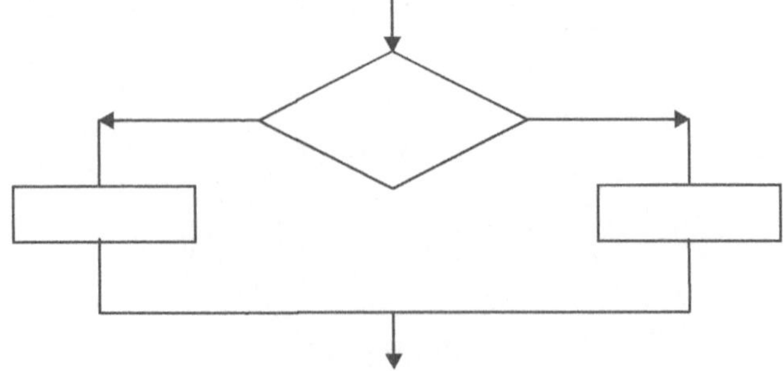

Figure 3. *Implementation of decision structure.*

PROCEDURAL PROGRAMMING

Procedural programming is a programming paradigms based upon the concept of the procedural call. Procedures are also known as routines, subroutines, methods or functions simply contain a series of computational steps to be carried out. Any given procedure can be called at any point during a program's execution including by other procedures or itself. Especially in large, complicated programs, modularity is generally desirable. It can be achieved using procedures that have strictly defined channels for input and output, and usually also clear rules about what types of input and output are allowed or expected. Inputs are usually specified syntactically in the form of arguments and the outputs delivered as return values.

To be considered a procedural, a programming language should support procedural programming by having an explicit concept of a procedure, and syntax to define it. It should ideally support specification of argument types, local variables, recursive procedure calls and use of procedures in separately built program constructs. It may also support distinction of input and output arguments.

C, ALGOL are the classic example of procedural programming languages.

Characteristics of Procedure Oriented Programming

(*a*) Follow top-down approach.

(*b*) Data is given less importance than function.

(*c*) Vulnerability of data is there as functions share global data.

(*d*) Functions manipulate global data, without letting other function to know.

(*e*) Big program is divided into small modules.

(*f*) Algorithms are designed first without bothering about minute details.

PROGRAMMING METHODOLOGY

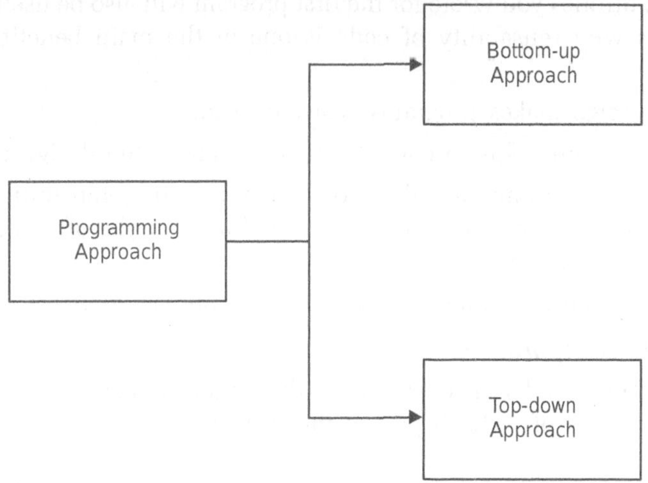

Figure 4. *Different approaches of programming.*

1. Bottom-Up and Top-Down Approaches

Any problem can be dealt with no ways viz top-down or bottom-up. A simple example is given here to illustrate the concept. Sorting an array of numbers involves the following :

(*a*) Comparison

(*b*) Exchange.

At the top level, an algorithm has to be formulated to carry out sorting using the above operations. Once the algorithm is confirmed, then the algorithms for comparison and exchange are formulated, before implementation of the entire algorithm. Therefore in this approach one begins from the top level without bothering about the minute details for implementation to start with.

The bottom-up approach is just the reverse. The lower level tasks are first carried out and are then integrated to provide the solution. In this method lower level structures are carried out. Here the algorithms for exchange and comparison will be formulated before formulating the algorithms for the whole problem.

In any case, dividing the problem into small tasks and then solving each task provides the solution. Therefore, either the top-down or bottom-up methodology has to be adopted for dividing the problem into smaller modules and then solving it. In the top-down methodology, the overall structure is defined before getting into details, but in the bottom-up approach, the details are worked out first before defining the overall structure.

Points about Bottom-Up Approach

1. In bottom-up design individual parts of the system are specified in detail. The parts are then linked together to form larger components, which are in turn linked until a complete system is formed.
2. Bottom-up design yield programs which are smaller and more agile. A shorter program doesn't have to be divided into many components, and fewer components means program which are easier to read or modify.
3. Bottom-up design promotes code reusability. When you write two or more programs, many of the utilities you wrote for the first program will also be useful in the succeeding ones. That's why reusability of code is one of the main benefits of the bottom-up approach.
4. Bottom-up design makes programs easier to read.
5. Working bottom-up helps to clarify your ideas about the design of your program.
6. Bottom-up programming may allow you for unit testing, but until most of the system comes together none of the system can tested as a whole, often causing compilations near the end of the project.
7. An example of programming which uses this approaches is C++ and java.

Points about Top-Down Approach

1. In the top-down model an overview of the system is formulated, without going into detail for any part of it. Each part of the system is then refined by designing it more detail.
2. Each new part may then be refined again, defining it in yet more detail until the entire specification is detailed enough to validate the model.

3. Top-down approaches emphasize planning and a complement understanding of the system. It is inherent that no coding can begin until a sufficient level of detail has been reached in the design of at least some part of the system.
4. Top-down programming is a programming style, the mainstay of traditional procedural languages, in which design begins by specification complex pieces and then dividing them into successively smaller pieces.
5. The technique for writing a program using top-down methods is to write a main procedure that have been coded the program is done.
6. Top-down programming may complicate testing, since nothing executable will even exit until near the end of the project.
7. An example of programming which uses this approach is C and Pascal.

OBJECT-ORIENTED PROGRAMMING

In computer science, Object-oriented Programming OOP for short is a computer programming paradigm.

The idea behind object-oriented programming is that a computer program may be seen as comprising a collection of individual units, or objects, that act on each other, as opposed to a traditional view in which a program may be seen as a collection of functions or simply as a list of instruction to the computer. Each object is capable of receiving messages, processing data, and sending messages to other objects. Each object can be viewed as an independent little machine or actor with a distinct role or responsibility. In order for a language to act as an Object-oriented Programming language it must support three object-oriented features :

1. Polymorphism.
2. Inheritance.
3. Encapsulation.

Together they are called as **PIE** principle.

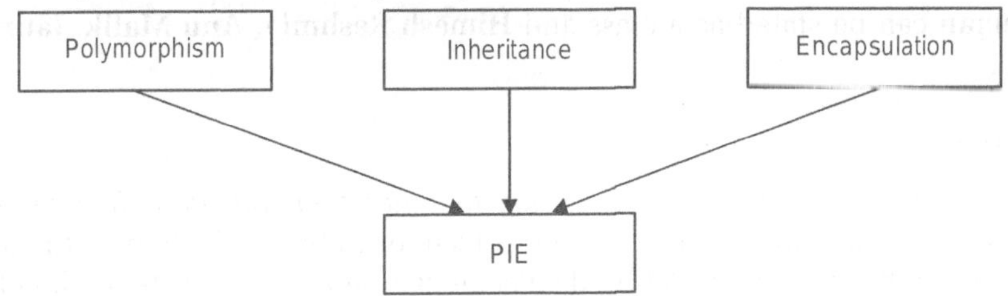

Figure 5. *Shows the PIE principle.*

BASIC CONCEPTS OF OOPs

There are following basic concepts applied in Object-oriented Programming language.

1. Class and Object
2. Encapsulation
3. Abstraction

4. Data Hiding
5. Polymorphism
6. Inheritance
7. Dynamic Binding
8. Message Passing.

1. Class and Object

A class is termed as a basic unit of encapsulation. It's a collection of function code and data which forms the basic of object-oriented programming. A class is an **Abstract Data Type (ADT)** *i.e.*, the class definition only provides the logical abstraction. The data and function defined within the class spring to life only when a variable of type class is created. The variable of type class is created. The variable of type class is called an object which has a physical existence and also known as an instance of class. From one class several objects can be created. Each object has similar set of data defined in the class and it can use functions defined in the class for the manipulation of data.

For example : we can created a class car which have properties like company, model, year of manufacture, fuel type etc., and which may have actions like **acceleration ( ), brake ( )** etc.

Objects are the basic run time entity in a C++ program. All objects are instances of a class. Depending upon type of class an object may represent anything like a person, or mobile, chair, student, employee, book, lecturer, speaker, car, vehicle or anything which we see in our daily life. The state of an object is determined by the data values they are having at a particular instances. Objects occupy space in memory and all objects share same set of data items which are defined when class is created. Two objects may communicate with each other through functions by passing messages.

In layman's terms :

1. **Animal** can be stated as a class and **Lion, Tiger, Elephant, Wolf, Cow**, etc., are its object.
2. **Bird** can be stated as class and **sparrow, Eagle, Hawk, Pigeon** etc., are its objects.
3. **Musician** can be stated as a class and **Himesh Reshmia, Anu Malik, Jatin-Lalit** are its object.

2. Encapsulation

Encapsulation is the mechanism that binds together function and data in one compact form known as class. The data and function may be private or public. Private data/function can only be accessed only within the class. Public data/code can be accessed outside the class. The use of encapsulation hides complexity from the implementation. Linking of function code and data together gives rise to objects which are variables of type class.

3. Abstraction

Abstraction is a mechanism to represent only essential features which are of significance and hides the unimportant details. To make a good abstraction we require a sound knowledge of the problem domain which we are going to implement using **OOP** principle. As an example of the abstraction consider a class **Vehicle**. When we create the **Vehicle** class, we can decide what function code and data to put in the class like vehicle name, number of wheels, fuel type, vehicle type etc., and functions like changing the gear, accelerating/decelerating the vehicle. At this time we are not interested vehicle works like how acceleration, changing gear takes place.

We are also not interested in making more parts of vehicle to be part of the class like model number, vehicle color etc.

4. Data Hiding

Data hiding hides the data from external access by the user. In OOP language we have special keywords like private, protected etc., which hides the data.

5. Polymorphism

If we bifurcated the word Polymorphism, we get "Poly" means many and "Morphism" means form.

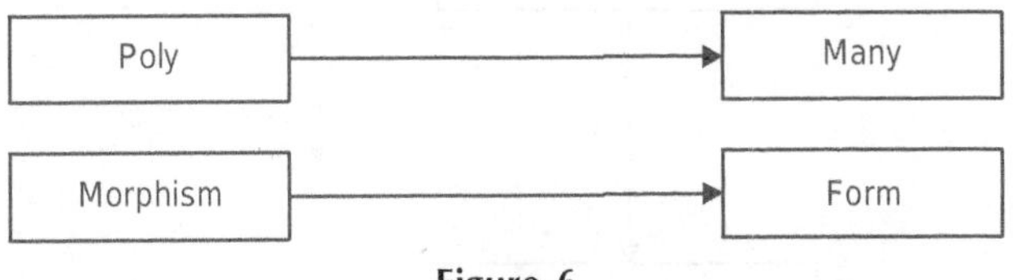

Figure 6

Thus, polymorphism means more than one form. Thus polymorphism provides a way for an entity to behave in several forms. In layman's terms an excellent example of polymorphism is Lord Krishna in Hindu methodology. From programmers point of view polymorphism means "one interface many methods".

It is an attribute that allows one interface to control access to a general class of actions. For example, we want to find out maximum of three numbers; no matter what type of input we pass *i.e.*, integer, float etc. Because of polymorphism we can define three variable versions of the same function with the name max3. Each version of this function takes 3 parameters of the same time *i.e.*, one version of max3 takes 3 arguments of type integer, another takes 3 arguments of type double and so on. The compiler automatically selects the right version of the function depending upon the type of data passed to the function max3. This also termed as function polymorphism or function overloading.

Types of Polymorphism : Polymorphism is of two types which are given below :

1. Compile time polymorphism.
2. Run time polymorphism.

6. Inheritance

Inheritance is the mechanism of deriving a new class from the earlier existing class. The inheritance provides the basic idea of reusability in Object-oriented Programming. The new class inherits the features of the old class. The old class and new class is called (given as pair) base-derived, parent-child, super-sub.

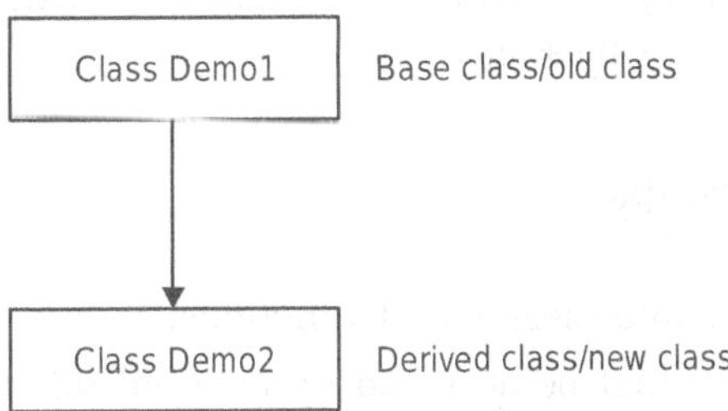

Figure 7. *Demonstration of Inheritance.*

The inheritance supports the idea of classification. In classification we can form hierarchies of different classes each of which having some special characteristics besides some common properties. Through classification a class need only definition those qualities that make it unique within its class.

Examples :

1. As an example at the Top most in the hierarchy we can have a **vehicle class.** All the common features of a vehicle can be put in this class. From this we can drive a new class say **two_wheeler** which contains features specific to two wheeler vehicles only.

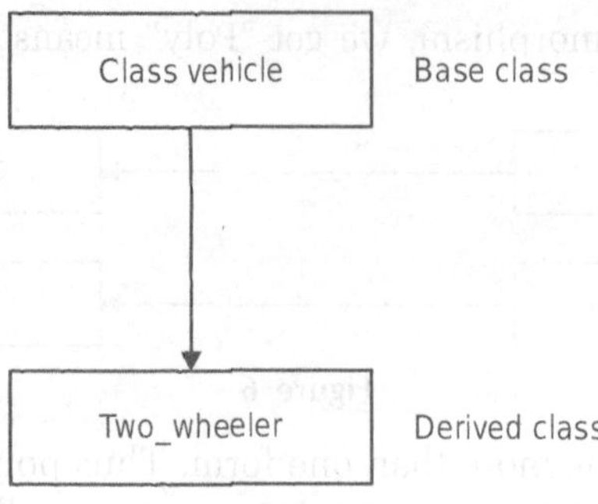

Figure 8

2. As another example we can example of an **engineering college** as the top class with its sub class its various departments like **computer, electronics, electrical** etc. Again the engineering college may have its parent class as the **university** to which it is affiliated.

7. Dynamic Binding

Binding means linking. It is linking of function definition to a function call.

1. If linking of function call to function definition *i.e.,* a place where control has to be transferred is done at compile time, it is known as static binding.
2. When linking is delayed till run time or done during the execution of the program then this type of linking is known as dynamic binding. Which function will be called in response to a function call is find out when program executes.

8. Message Passing

In C++ objects communicate each other by passing messages to each other. A message contains the name of the member function and arguments to pass. In message passing shown below :

```
object. method (parameters);
```

Message passing here means object calling the method and passing parameters. Message passing is nothing but the calling the method of the class and sending parameters. The method is turn executes in response to a message.

CHARACTERISTICS OF OOPs

1. Programs are divided into classes and functions.
2. Data is hidden and cannot be accessed by external functions.
3. Use of inheritance provides reusability of code.

4. New functions and data items can be added easily.
5. Data is given more important than functions.
6. Follows bottom-up approach.
7. Data and function are tied together in a single unit known as class.
8. Objects communicate each other by sending messages in the form of function.

ADVANTAGES OF OOPs

1. Code reusability in terms of inheritance.
2. Object-oriented system can be easily upgraded from one platform to another.
3. Complex projects can be easily divided into small code functions.
4. The principle of abstraction and encapsulation enables a programmer to build secure programs.
5. Software complexity decreases.
6. Principle of data hiding helps programmer to design and develop safe programs.
7. Rapid development of software can be done is short span of time.
8. More than one instance of same class can exist together without any interference.

OBJECT-ORIENTED LANGUAGES

Some of the most popular Object-oriented Programming languages are :

1. C++
2. Java.
3. smalltalk
4. Eiffle.
5. Ruby
6. Delphi
7. Charm++
8. Simula.

OBJECT-BASED LANGUAGES

The language which only concerns with classes and objects and do not have features like inheritance, polymorphism, encapsulation (do not satisfy PIE principle) known as object-based languages. In these types of languages we can create classes and object and can work with them. They are usually having a large numbers of built-in objects of various types. Some of the languages which are object-based are Java script, Visual Basic etc.

INTRODUCTION OF OBJECT-ORIENTED DESIGN

1.1 INTRODUCTION

The aim is to introduce the actual idea, not to give strict and precise definition. Object-orientation is a technique for system modeling. It offers a number of concepts, which are well suited for this purpose. The word 'system' is used here with a wide meaning and can be either a dedicated software system or a system in a wider context (for example, integrated software and hardware system or an organization).

Using Object-orientation as a base, we model the system as a number of objects that interacts. Hence, irrespective of the type of system being modeled, we regard its contents as a number of objects which in one way or another are related our surroundings, for instance, consists of objects, such as people, trees, cars, towns and houses which are in some way related to each other. Thus what the objects model depends on what we wish to represent with our object model. Another model of our surroundings would, perhaps, consists taxation, government and politics as objects. The objects which we include within our model are, therefore, dependent on what the object model is to represent.

People regard their environment in terms of objects. Therefore, it is simple to think in the same way when it comes to designing a model. A model which is designed using an object-oriented technology is often easy to understand, as it can be directly related reality. Thus, with such a design method, only a small semantic gap will exist between reality and the model.

The most prominent qualities of a system designed with an object-oriented method are the following :

1. Understanding of the system is easier as the semantic gap between the system and reality is small.
2. Modifications to the model tend to be local as they often result from an individual item, which is represented by a single object.

This introduction is only an overview and is independent of both the programming language and the development methods used. We shall not give any precise and formal concept definitions, but hope to provide you with a good understanding of these concepts. We shall use the concept and meaning most commonly used within the object-oriented environment.

1.2 OBJECTS

The reality we will describe involves a number of people who perform certain activities. Our task is to try to model this system. We shall see that it is very natural to construct a model, which simulates this reality. (We use 'person' and 'object' in this description to mean the same thing; we actually mean the object that represents the person. As always, one should be careful to separate the reality from the model.)

The word 'object' is misused and is used in nearly all contexts. What we mean by an object is an entity able to save a state (information) and which offers a number of operations (behavior) to either examine or affect this state.

An object is characterized by a number of operations and a state, which remembers the effect of these operations.

An object-oriented model consists of a number of objects; these are clearly delimited parts of the modeled system. Objects usually correspond to real-life entity objects, such as an invoice, a car or a mobile telephone. Each object contains individual information (for example, a car has its registration number).

1.3 CLASS AND INSTANCE

In the system we made, there will be a number of communicating objects. Some of these objects will have common characteristics and we can group the objects according to these characteristics. When we look at the objects in the example, we notice that all three people have similar behavior and information structures. These objects have the same mold or template. Such a group represents a class. In order to describe all objects that have similar behavior and information structure, we can therefore identify and described a class to represent these objects.

A class is a definition, a template or a mold to enable the creation of new objects and is, therefore, a description of the common characteristics of several objects. The objects comprising a certain class have this template in common. As an example, we can view this book. The book you are holding in your hand is an instance of the book. The book description at the publishers represents the class from where instance can be created.

- A class represents a template for several objects and
- Describes how these objects are structured internally.
- Objects of the same class have the same definition both.
- For their operations and for their information structures.

A class is sometimes called the object's type. However, type and a class is not the same thing. As we mentioned above, as abstract data type is definition by set of operations. A type is definition by the manipulations you can do with the type. A class is more than that. You can also look inside a class, for example, to see its information structure. We would therefore rather view the class as one (of possibly many) specific *implementation* of a type.

Using the class concepts, we can associate certain characteristics with a whole group of objects we can consider the class as begin an abstraction that describes all the common characteristics of the objects forming part of the class.

In object-oriented systems, each object belongs to a class. An object that belongs to a certain class is called an instance of the class. We therefore often use objects and instance as synonyms.

An instance is an object created from a class. The class describes the (behavior and information) structure of the instance, while the current state of the instance is defined by the operations performed on the instance.

1.4 POLYMORPHISM

Instances, created from classes, will together provide us with the dynamic behavior that we wish to model. It is when these instances start to communicate with each other that the system's behavior is performed. An instance may know of other instances to which stimuli can be sent. If an instance sends a stimulus to another instance, but does not have to be aware of which class the receiving instance belongs to, we say that we have polymorphism. Polymorphism means, at least in objects-oriented contexts, that the sending instance does not need to now the receiving instance's class and that this class can be any class. **Polymorphism** means that the sender of a stimulus.

- Does not need to know the receiving instance's class.
- The receiving instance can belong to an arbitrary class.

1.5 INHERITANCE

If class B inherits class A, then both the operations and the information structure described in class A will becomes part of class B.

By means of inheritance, we can show similarities between classes and described these similarities in a class, which other classes can inherit. Hence, we can reuse common descriptions. Inheritance is therefore often promoted as a core idea for reuse in the software industry. However, although inheritance, properly used, is a very useful mechanism in many contexts including reuse, it is not a perquisite for reuse.

1.6 OBJECT-ORIENTED ANALYSIS

The purpose of object-oriented analysis, as with all other analysis, is to obtain an understanding of the application : an understanding depending only on the system's functional requirements.

Object-oriented analysis contains, in some order, the following activities :

- Finding the object.
- Organizations the objects.
- Describing how the objects interact.
- Defining the operations of the objects.
- Defining the objects internally.

1.7 FINDING THE OBJECTS

The objects can be found as naturally occurring entries in the application domain. The aim is to find the essential objects, which are to obtain which are to remain essential throughout the system life cycle. Stability also depends on the fact that modifications often begin from some of these items and therefore are local. For example, in a application for controlling for water tank, typically objects would include contained water, regulator, valve and tank.

1.8 CONCEPTUAL MODELING

It has been used in several different contexts since it appeared in the 1970s; example analysis of information management system and organization theory. The aim is to create models of the system or organization to be analyzed. The concepts of conceptual modeling is often used as a synonym for data modeling and is often discussed with structuring and the use of the databases.

1.9 REQUIREMENTS MODEL

The first transformation made is from the requirement specification to the requirement model. The requirements model consists of :

(*a*) A use case model.

(*b*) Interface descriptions.

(*c*) A problem domain model.

The use case model uses actors and use cases. These concepts are simply an aid to defined what exits outside the system (actors) and what should be performed by the system (use case).

1.10 ANALYSIS MODEL

We have seen that the requirements model aims to define the limitations of the system and to specify its behavior. When the requirement model has been developed and approved by the system users or orders, we can start to develop the actual system.

This starts with development of the analysis model. Its model aims to structure the system independently of the actual implementation environment. This means that we focus on the logical structure of the system. It is here that we define the stable, robust and maintainable structure that is also extensible.

1.11 THE DESIGN MODEL

In the construction process, we construct the system using both the analysis model and the requirements, model. First, we create a design model that is a refinement and formalization of the analysis model.

Design emphasizes a *conceptual solution* that fulfils the requirements, rather than its implementation. For example, a description of a database schema and software objects. Ultimately, designs can be implemented. As with analysis, the term is best qualified, a in *object design* or *database design*. Analysis and design have been summarized in the phase *do the right thing (analysis), and do the things right (design).*

1.12 THE IMPLEMENTATION MODEL

The implementation model consists of the annotated source code. The information space is the one that the programming language uses. Note that we do not require an Object-oriented Programming language; the technique may be used with any programming language to obtain an object-oriented structure of the system. However, an Object-oriented-Programming language is desirable since all fundamental concepts can easily be mapped onto language constructs.

1.13 TEST MODEL

The test model is the last model developed in the system development. It describes, simply stated, the result of the testing. The fundamental concepts in testing are mainly the test specification and the test result.

1.13.1 Analysis

Analysis emphasizes an *investigation* of the problem and requirements, rather than a solution. For example, if a new computerized library information system is desired, how will it be used ?

"Analysis" is a broad term, best qualified, as in *requirements analysis* (an investigation of the requirements) or *object analysis* (an investigation of the domain objects).

1.13.2 What is Done in Analysis ?

Two different models are developed in analysis, the requirement model and the analysis model. The real base is the requirement specification and discussions with the prospective users. For example, the system controls a recycling machine for returnable bottles, cans and crates (used in Europe to hold several bottles).

1.13.3 Why Do We have a Construction Process ?

We built our system in the construction phase, based on the analysis model and the requirement's model created during analysis. The construction process lasts until the coding is completed and the code units have been tested. Construction consists of design and implementation.

1.14 OBJECT-ORIENTED ANALYSIS AND DESIGN

Object-oriented technology is built upon a sound engineering foundation, whose elements we collectively call the object model. The object model encompasses the principles of abstraction, encapsulation, modularity, hierarchy, typing, concurrency, and persistence. What is important about the object model is that these elements are brought together in a synergistic way?

Let there be no doubt that object-oriented analysis and design is fundamentally different than traditional structured design approaches. It requires a different way of thinking about decomposition and it produces software architectures that are largely outside the realm of the structured design culture. These differences arise from the fact that structures design methods build upon structure programming whereas object-oriented design builds upon object-oriented programming. Objects-oriented programming means different things to different people.

1.15 THE EVOLUTION OF OBJECT MODEL

The generation of programming languages as we look back upon the relatively briefly yet colorful history of software engineering. We cannot help but notice two sweeping trends. The shift in focus from programming in the small to programming in the large. The evolution of high order programming languages.

1.15.1 Foundations of Object Model

Structured design methods evolved to guide developers who were trying to build complex systems using algorithms as their fundamental building blocks. Similarly object-oriented design methods have evolved to help developers exploit the expressive power of object based and object-oriented programming languages using the class and object as basic building blocks.

Object-oriented analysis and design thus represents an evolutionary development, not a revolutionary one; it does not break with advances from the past, but builds upon proven ones. Unfortunately, most programmers today are formally and informally trained only in the principles of structured design.

1.16 OBJECT-ORIENTED PROGRAMMING

Object-oriented programming is a method of implementation in which programs are organized as cooperative collections of objects, each of which represents an instance of some class, and whose classes are all members of a hierarchy of classes united via inheritance relationships.

Object-oriented programming uses objects, not algorithms, as its fundamental logical building blocks. Each object is an instance of some class. Classes are related to one another via inheritance relationships. A program may appear to be object-oriented, but if any of these elements is missing, it is not an object-oriented program.

It supports objects that are data abstractions with an interface of named operations and a hidden local state.

(*a*) Objects have an associated type (class).

(*b*) Types (classes) may inherit attributes from super types (super classes).

1.17 OBJECT-ORIENTED DESIGN

Object-oriented design is a method of design encompassing the process of object-oriented decomposition and a notation for depicting both logical and physical as well as static and dynamic models of the system under design.

There are two important parts to this definition :

1. Object-oriented design leads to an object-oriented decomposition.
2. It uses different notations to express different models of the logical and physical design of a system, in addition to the static and dynamic aspects of the system.

1.18 OBJECT-ORIENTED ANALYSIS

Object-oriented analysis is a method of analysis that examines requirements from the perspective of the classes and objects found in the vocabulary of the problem domain.

How are OOA, OOD, and OOP related ? Basically, the products of object-oriented analysis serve as the models from which we may start an object-oriented design; the products of object-oriented design can then be used as blueprints for completely implementing a system using object-oriented programming methods.

1.19 ELEMENTS OF OBJECT MODEL

- Procedure oriented Algorithms.
- Object-oriented Classes and objects.
- Logic oriented Goals, often expressed in a predicate calculus.
- Rule oriented If then rules.
- Constraint oriented Invariant relationships.

Each of these styles of programming is based upon its own conceptual framework. Each requires a different mindset, a different way of thinking about the problem. For all things object-oriented the conceptual framework is the object model.

There are four major elements of its model:

(*a*) Abstraction

(*b*) Encapsulation

(*c*) Modularity

(*d*) Hierarchy.

There are three minor elements of the object model :

(*i*) Typing

(*ii*) Concurrency

(*iii*) Persistence.

Object-oriented analysis and design may be the only method we have today that can be employed to attack the complexity inherent in very large systems. In all fairness, however, the use of object-oriented development may be ill-advised for some domains, not for any technical reasons, but for non-technical ones, such as the absence of a suitably trained staff or a good development environment.

1.20 THE ROLE OF OOAD IN THE SOFTWARE LIFE CYCLE

To understand what's right and wrong with OOAD, you need to know where OO methodologies fit into the software life cycle. These methodologies do not replace traditional approaches (such as data flow, process flow, and state transition diagrams); they are important new additions to the toolkit.

According to Donald Firesmith in his book Dictionary of Object Technology (SIGS Books, 1995), analysis is "the development activity consisting of the discovery, modeling, specification and evaluation of requirements," while OO analysis is "the discovery, analysis and specification of requirements in terms of objects with identity that encapsulate properties and operations, message passing, classes, inheritance, polymorphism and dynamic binding." Firesmith also states that OO design is "the design of an application in terms of objects, classes, clusters, frameworks and their interactions."

In comparing the definition of traditional analysis with that of OOAD, the only aspect that is really new is thinking of the world or the problem in terms of objects and object classes. A class is any uniquely identified abstraction (that is, model) of a set of logically related instances that share the same or similar characteristics. An object is any abstraction that models a single thing, and the term "object" is synonymous with instance. Classes have attributes and methods. For an object class named Customer, attributes might be Name and Address, and methods might be Add, Update, Delete, and Validate. The class definition defines the Customer class attributes and methods, and a real customer such as "XYZ Corp." is an instance of the class. If you have different kinds of customers, such as residential customers and commercial customers, you can create two new classes of customers that are descendants of the Customer class. These descendants use inheritance to gain access to all of the Customer class attributes and methods, but can override any of the ancestor attributes and methods, as well as contain any required new attributes and methods.

There are three types of relationships between classes : inheritance, aggregation, and association. Inheritance (also referred to as generalization/specialization) is usually identified by the phrase "is a kind of." For example, Student and Faculty are both a kind of Person and are therefore inherited from the Person class. Aggregation is identified by the phrase "is a part of," as with a product that contains parts. If neither of the first two relationships applies, but the objects are clearly related (for example, an employee is associated with a company), then the relationship is association.

An abstract class is a class that has no instances, and is used only for inheritance. A concrete class is a class that can be instantiated, that is, that can have direct instances.

All of the major OOAD methodologies have a similar basic view of objects, classes, inheritance, and relationships. The drawing notation is slightly different in each; the real differences in the methodologies are more subtle.

When you're choosing a methodology, it is important to consider not only the methodology's features, but also the cost of using it, the types of problems to which it is best suited, its limitations, and the training available. When used in typical initial attempts to develop client/server applications using OOAD methodologies, all of the methodologies suffer from the same basic flaws :

1. An overemphasis on the OO approaches in general, even though another approach might be better for some parts of the problem.

2. An overemphasis on the problem domain object model during the analysis phase.
3. Analysis diagrams and output formats that end users may find difficult to understand.
4. Difficulty in the methodology's ability to describe complex analysis problems.
5. A lack of emphasis on the underlying system architecture.
6. An inability to understand the limitations of either 4GL OO languages or of beginning OO developers.

Every object methodology tells you to start with the object model, not the data model; there are at least four problems with this approach :

1. The data model often exists before the object model.
2. The analyst may rightly be more comfortable building the data model before the object model.
3. A good object model should be able to map to any data model. For me, it is usually a requirement in complex systems that an object's attributes can map to one or more tables in one or more databases.
4. A good abstract object model of the problem domain may not be easy to implement in the chosen language or development tool.

1.21 OOAD METHODOLOGIES

OOAD methodologies fall into two basic types. The ternary (or three-pronged) type is the natural evolution of existing structured methods and has three separate notations for data, dynamics, and process. The unary type asserts that because objects combine processes (methods) and data, only one notation is needed. The unary type is considered to be more object-like and easier to learn from scratch, but has the disadvantage of producing output from analysis that may be impossible to review with users.

Dynamic modeling is concerned with events and states, and generally uses state transition diagrams. Process modeling or functional modeling is concerned with processes that transform data values, and traditionally uses techniques such as data flow diagrams.

1.22 GRADY BOOCH APPROACH

Grady Booch's approach to OOAD is one of the most popular, and is supported by a variety of reasonably priced tools ranging from Visio to Rational Rose. Booch is the chief scientist at Rational Software, which produces Rational Rose. (Now that James Rumbaugh and Ivar Jacobson have joined the company, Rational Software is one of the major forces in the OOAD world).

Booch's design method and notation consist of four major activities and six notations. While the Booch methodology covers requirements analysis and domain analysis; its major strength has been in design. However, with Rumbaugh and Jacobson entering the fold, the (relative) weaknesses in analysis are disappearing rapidly. I believe that Booch represents one of the better developed OOAD methodologies, and now that Rational Rose is moving away from its previous tight link with C++ to a more open approach that supports 4GLs such as PowerBuilder, the methodology's popularity should increase rapidly.

For systems with complex rules, state diagrams are fine for those with a small number of states, but are not usable for systems with a large number of states. Once a single-state transition diagram has more than 8 to 10 states, it becomes difficult to manage. For more than 20 states, state transition diagrams become excessively unwieldy.

Principles of Modeling

The use of modeling has a rich history in all the engineering disciplines. That experience suggests four basic principles of modeling.

1. The choice of what models to create has profound influence on how a problem is attacked and how a solution is shaped.
2. Every model may be expressed at different levels of precision.
3. The best models are connected to reality.
4. No single model is sufficient. Every nontrivial system is best approached through a small set of nearly independent models.

❑❑❑

CHAPTER 2

STARTING WITH C++

2.1 C ++ OVERVIEW

C++ is an object-oriented programming language. It was developed by **Bjarne Stroustrup** at AT & T's bell laboratories in the **Murray Hill. New Jersey, USA** in the early 80's. It's an extension to C with number of new features added. The named C++ came from the increment operator ++ of C as it is considered a super set of C, one version ahead of C, so it was named C++.

The first use of class construct in a programming language occurred in **1967** in the language **Simula** which was derived from **Algol. Bjarne Stroustrup** the inventor of C++, used the language **Simula** in his doctoral research for coding simulation programs he wrote to model computer systems. He found that the **Simula** language was very expressive and permit him to work at a high level of abstraction but when it came time to run the program to get the numerical results he needed for his thesis he found that performance was far too slow and he would never be able to complete his work in time. So, he recoded his programs in C. But he did something very intelligent. In place of hand coding, he wrote a translator program that would take a C–like program with extension for classes and translate to pure C. The result was a language initially called **"C with classes"**, later to become C++. The translator program became the **AT & T's "cfront"** compiler, which would translate C++ to C.**"cfront"** was the first application written in C++.

2.2 C++ CHARACTER SET

A C++ program is a collection of number of instructions written in a meaningful order. Further instructions are made up of keywords, variables, functions, objects etc., which uses the C++ character set defined by C++. It's a collection of various characters, digits and symbols which can be used in a C++ program. It comprises followings :

Table 2.1

S.No.	*Elements of C++ character set*
1.	Upper Case letters : A to Z
2.	Lower Case letters : a to z
3.	Digits : 0 to 9
4.	Symbols (See below table)

Table 2.2 : C++ Character Set

Symbols	*Name*	*Symbols*	*Name*
~	Tilde	>	Greater than
<	Less than	&	Ampersand
|	Or/pipe	#	Hash
>=	Greater than equal	<=	Less than equal
= =	Equal	=	Assignment
!=	Not equal	^	Caret
{	Left brace	}	Right brace
(	Left parenthesis	)	Right parenthesis
[	Left square bracket	]	Right square bracket
/	Forward slash	\	Backward slash
:	Colon	;	Semicolon
+	Plus	–	Minus
*	Multiply	/	Division
%	Mod	,	Comma
‘	Single quote	“	Double quote
>>	Right shift	<<	Left shift
.	Period	_	Underscore

2.3 C++ TOKENS

Smallest individual unit in a C++ program is called C++ token. C++ defined six types of tokens.

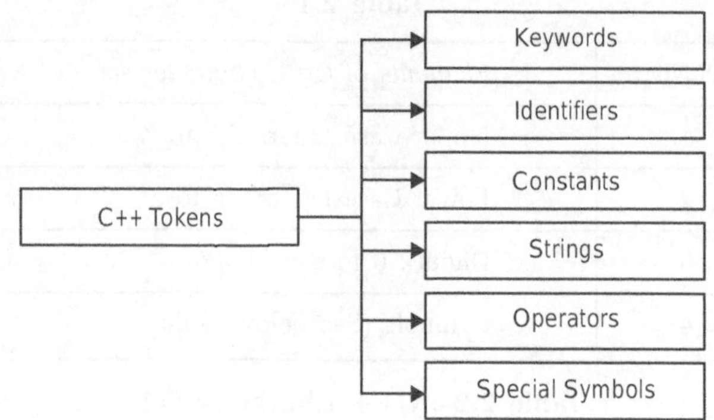

Figure 2.1. *Six types of tokens defined in C++.*

1. Keywords

Keywords are those words whose meaning has already been known to the compiler. That is meaning of each keyword is fixed. You can simply use the keyword for its intended meaning. You cannot change the meaning of keywords. Also you cannot use keywords as names for variables, function, array etc. All keywords are written in small case letters.

There are 63 keywords in C++. Following figure lists all keywords available in C++.

Table 2.3 : C++ keywords

asm	auto	bool	break	cae	catch
char	class	const	const_cast	continue	default
delete	do	double	dynamic_cast	else	enum
explicit	export	extern	false	float	for
friend	goto	if	inline	int	long
mutable	namespace	new	operator	private	protected
public	register	reinterpret_cast	return	short	signed
sizeof	static	static_cast	struct	switch	template
this	throw	true	try	typedef	typeid
typename	union	unsigned	using	virtual	void
volatile	wchar_t	while			

2. Identifier

Identifiers are names given to various program elements like variables, array, functions, structures etc.

- Rules for Writing Identifiers :

Rule 1 : First letter must be an alphabet or underscore.

Rule 2 : From second character onwards any combination of digits, alphabets or underscore is allowed.

Rule 3 : Only digits, alphabets, underscore are allowed. No other symbol is allowed.

Rule 4 : Keywords cannot be used as identifiers.

Rule 5 : For ANSI (American National Standard Institute) C++ maximum length of identifier is 32, but many compiler support more than 32.

Example of valid and invalid identifiers (on the basis of above given rules)

Valid Identifiers :

order_no	name	_err	_123
xyz	radius	a23	int_rate

Invalid Identifiers :

order-no	12name	err	int
x$	s name	hari+45	123

3. Constants

Constants in C++ refer to fixed values that do not change during the execution of a program. There are various types of constants in C++. They are classified into the following categories as given below :

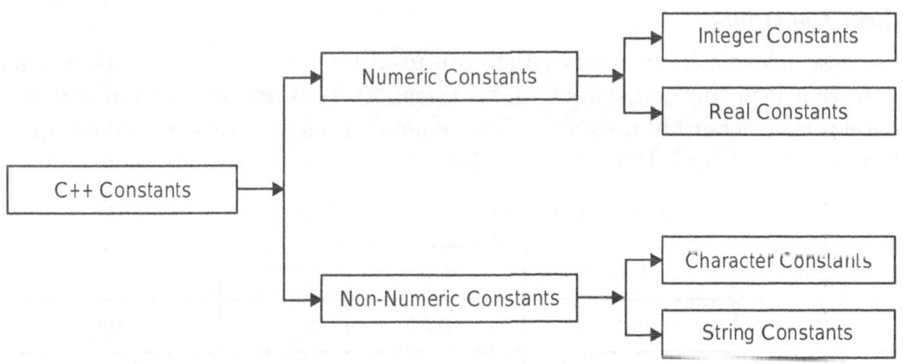

Figure 2.2. *C++ constants.*

(i) Integer Constants

They are of three types :

(*a*) **Decimal Constants :** They are sequence of digits from 0 to 9 without fractional part. It may be negative, positive or zero.

Example : 12, 455, -546, 0 etc.

(*b*) **Octal Constant :** They have sequence of numbers from 0 to 7 and first digit must be 0

Example : 034, 0, 0564, 0123 etc.

(*c*) **Hex Constant :** They have sequence of digits from 0 to 9 and A to F (represents 10 to 15). They start with 0x or 0X.

Example : 0x34, 0xab3, oX3E etc.

(ii) Real Constant

They are the number with fractional part. They also known as floating point constants.

Example : 34.56, 0.67, 1.23 etc.

Real constants can also be represented in exponential or scientific notation which consists of two parts. For example, the number 212.345 can be represented as **2.12345e + 2** where **e + 2** means **10 to the power 2.** Here the portion before the **e** that is **2.12345** is known as **mantissa** and **+2** is the **exponent.** Exponent is always an integer number which can be written either in lower case or upper case.

There may be many more representation of the above given number. I have given just an example of number in scientific notation.

(iii) Single Character Constants

They are enclosed in single quote. They consist of single character or digit.

Example : '4', 'A', '\n' etc.

Character constants have integer value known as ASCII (American Standard Code for Information Interchange) values. For example, ASCII value for A is 65.

(iv) String Constants

They are sequence of characters, digits or any symbol enclosed in double quote.

Example : "hello", "23twenty three","&^ABC". "2.456" etc.

(v) Backslash Constants

C defines several backslash constants which are used for special purpose. They are called so because each backslash constant starts with backslash (\). They are represented with 2 characters whose general form is **\char** but treated as single character. They are also called **escape sequence.** Given below the list of backslash character (escape sequence) character constants :

Table 2.4: Table shows the Backslash Character Constant

S.No.	*BCC*	*Meaning*	*ASCII*
1	\b	Backspace	08
2	\f	Form feed	12
3	\n	New line	10
4	\r	Carriage return	13
5	\"	Double quote	34
6	\'	Single quote	39
7	\ ?	Question mark	63
8	\a	Alert	07
9	\t	Horizontal tab	09
10	\v	Vertical tab	11
11	\0	Null	00

4. Strings

See string constants.

5. Operators

They are discussed in chapters 3 and 4.

6. Special Symbols

They are also known as separator and they are square brackets [], braces { }, parenthesis () etc. They [ ] used in array and known as subscript operator, the symbol () is known as function symbols.

2.4 VARIABLES

A variable is a named location in memory that is used to hold a value that can be modified in the program by the instruction. All variables must be declared before they can be used. They must be declared in the beginning of the function or block (except the global variables). The general form of variable declaration is :

```
data type variable [list];
```

Here list denotes more than one variable separated by commas;

Example :

```
int a;
float b,c;
char p,q;
```

Here **a** is a variable of type int, **b** and **c** are variable of type float, and p, q are variables of type char, int, float and char are data types used in C. The rule for writing variables are same as for writing identifiers as a variables is nothing but an identifier.

C++ allows you to declare variables anywhere in the program. That is unlike C it is not necessary to declare all the variables in the beginning of the program. You can declare wherever you want it to be declares *i.e.*, right on the place where you want to use it. An advantage of this is that sometimes lots of variables are declared in the advance in the beginning of the program and many of them are unreferenced. Declaring variables at the place where they are actually required is handy. You do not need to declare all the variables earlier prior to their use. On the other hand, it is burdensome to look for all the variable declared in the program as variable declaration will be scattered everywhere in the whole program.

C++ also allows you to initialize variable dynamically at the place of use. That is you can write anywhere in the program like this.

```
int x = 23;
float sal = 2345;
char name[ ] = "Hari";
```

This is known as "Dynamic Initialization" of the variables.

An example of declaration and dynamic initialization is given in the dummy program given as :

```
void main()
{
    int x;
    ..............;
    ..............;
    ..............;
    float y,z;
    char str [ ]="hello";
    ..............;
    ..............;
    double d1, d2;
    char s='M';
    ..............;
}
```

2.5 COUNTING TOKENS

1. int a,b,c;

(*i*) int is a keyword (1)

(*ii*) a, b and c variables (3)

(*iii*) comma (,) is operator (2)

(*iv*) ; is delimiter (1)

So, total number of tokens (1 + 3 + 2 + 1= 7)

2. c = a + b – 10;

(*i*) a, b and c variables (3)

(*ii*) +, =, – are operators (3)

(*iii*) ; is delimiter (1)

(*iv*) 10 is integer constant (1)

So, total number of tokens (3 + 3 + 1 + 1 = 8)

2.6 DATA TYPES

C++ defines several data types which can be used under different programming situations like an int data type can be used to represent whole numbers as age of a person, roll number etc. or float data type can be used to represent salary of person, interest rate etc. The basic data types are as shown as follows :

1. Built-in Type

(*a*) Integral Type

(*i*) int

(*ii*) char

(*b*) Floating Types

(*i*) float

(*ii*) double

(*c*) void

(*d*) bool

(*e*) wchar_t

2. User Defined Data Type

(*a*) class

(*b*) struct

(*c*) union

(*d*) enumeration

3. Derived Data Types

(*a*) array

(*b*) function

(*c*) pointer

(*d*) reference

wchar_t is a new data type which supports long characters. The **wchar_t** keyword designates a wide-character type. The **wchar_t** type is defined as an unsigned short (16-bit) data object.

A **wchar_t** constant can be declared by preceding L before it as **L"abc", L'a'**. To use this data type you must include header file **wchar.h.**

2.7 QUALIFIERS

Qualifiers qualify the meaning of data types. Unsigned, signed, short and long are the 4 qualifiers available in C++. The manner in which they are used as follows :

```
signed int x, y, b;
unsigned int p,q;
long int num;
short int n;
```

long int is a data type as mentioned earlier and short int is same as signed int or simply **int** on most of the C++ compilers. Signed qualifier is used where we want to work with both positive and negative values. Unsigned qualifier can be used where we want with only positive values. They can be used only with char and interger data types. The available range increases in positive when we use unsigned say for example, range of signed char or simply char –128 to 127 where as for unsigned char it is 0 to 255. Same holds for int/ or long int. Apart from these two important keywords are also used as qualifiers const and volatile. The const qualifier is used to declare a variable as a constant for example, const int x=10; declare a constant x of type int with constant value. For more about constant see in the next chapter.

2.8 RANGE OF DATA TYPES

Table 2.5 : Data Type and Their Range

S.No.	*Data Type*	*Size(in byte)*	*Range*
1	int or short	2	–32768 to 32767
2	Unsigned int	2	0 to 65535
3	Long int	4	–2147483648 to 2147483647
4	Float	4	3.4e-38 to 3.4e+38
5	Char	1	–128 to 127
6	Unsigned char	1	0 to 255
7	Unsigned long	4	0 to 4294967295
8	Double	8	1.7e-308 to 1.7e+308
9	Long double	10	3.4e-4932 to 3.4e+4932

For the calculation of range of data types we have a fixed formula :

1. For a signed data types if it takes n bits in memory then the range of values a particular variable of this data type can take is

   $$-2^{(n-1)} \text{ to } 2^{(n-1)} - 1$$

   Example : for n=16(int) the range is

   $$-2^{15} \text{ to} 2^{15} - 1$$

   And for char data type n=8 the range is

   $$-2^{7} \text{ to } 2^{7}-1$$

2. For an unsigned data types if it takes n bits in memory then the range of values a particular variables of this data type can take is

   $$0 \text{ to } 2^{n}-1$$

   For example, for n=16 (unsigned short int) the range is 0 to $2^{16}-1$ and for unsigned char data type n=8 the range is 0 to $2^{8}-1$.

2.9 YOUR FIRST C++ PROGRAM

/*PROG 2.1 PRINTS HELLO C++ ON THE SCREEN */

```
#include<iostream.h>
int main()
{
    cout<<" Hello C++";
    return 0;
}
```

OUTPUT :

Hello C++

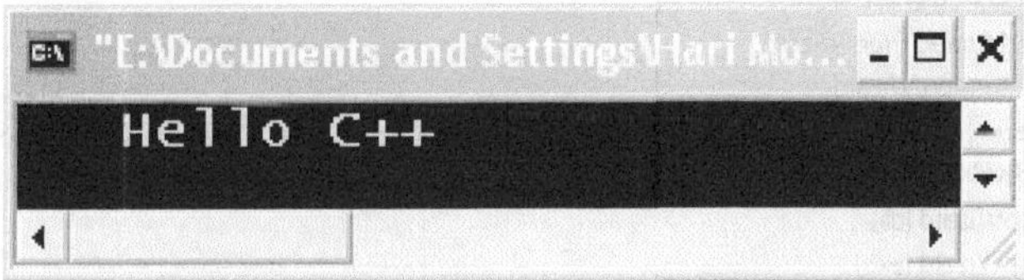

Figure 2.3. *Output screen of program 2.1.*

EXPLANATION: In the first line **#include** is a preprocessor directive, **iostream.h** is a header file which is written enclosed in < and > or in "". **"io"** in **iostream** stands for input output, **.h** stands for header file. The file **iostream.h** has to be included in every C++ program. There may be space between **#include** and **<iostream.h>.** Next line is the function **main ( )** due to symbol ( ) which is known as **function symbol**. This function must be present in every C++ file you make because execution of your C++ program starts from this **main ( ).** **{**is the opening braces for main function and **}** is the closing brace. All the statements, instructions are written inside the **main** function. The **int** before **main** is treated as its **return** type. **cout** is the predefined object of class **iostream_withassign** which is defined in **iostream.h**. The symbol << is an operator known as **put to** or **insertion operator**. The combined effect of **cout<<** is that whatever is written after it is in double quotes is printed onto the screen, so the output. Every statement in a C++ program has to end with; (semicolon). C++ is case sensitive programming language, so whatever you use that is in-built in C++ has to be in lower case. The line **return 0;** is simply for the omission of warning. If you do not write **return 0;** you will not get any error but a warning. The above program can be modified as (with a little change in return type of function **main**).

```
void main()
{
    cout<<"Hello C++";
}
```

2.9.1 Compilation and Execution Process

To run your first program in Windows environment follow the following steps.

1. In the **Visual Studio 6.0** open Microsoft Visual C++ 6.0.
2. In the **IDE** select **new** from file.
3. Under Project tab select option **win 32 Console Application** and give project name say "CPP". Choose location where you want to put your project say D :\. In the project all your files will be saved.

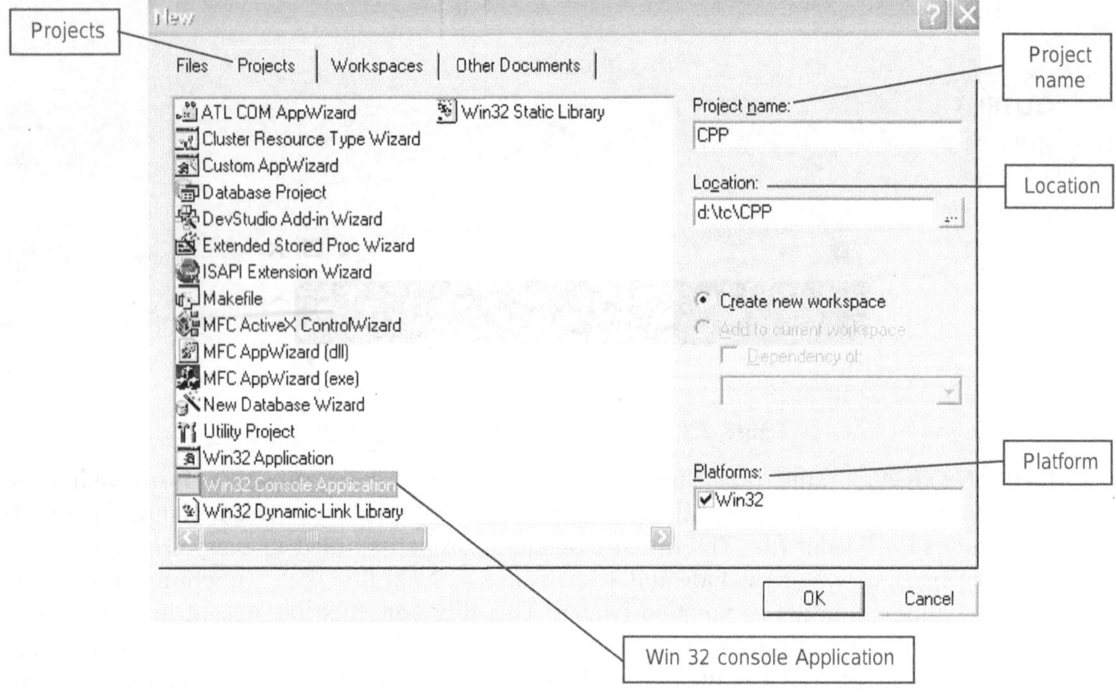

Figure 2.4

4. Click Finish. A new dialog box will appear, simply press OK. At this step you have successfully made a new project CPP under D :\.

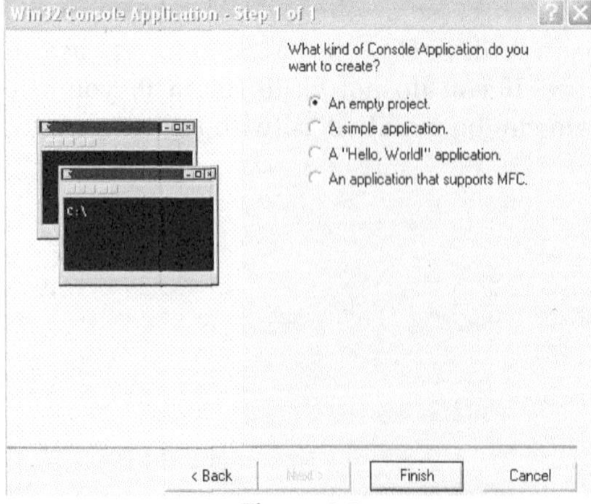

Figure 2.5

5. Now select new from file. Select Files tab and option C++ source file. Give a suitable file name say first. Press OK.

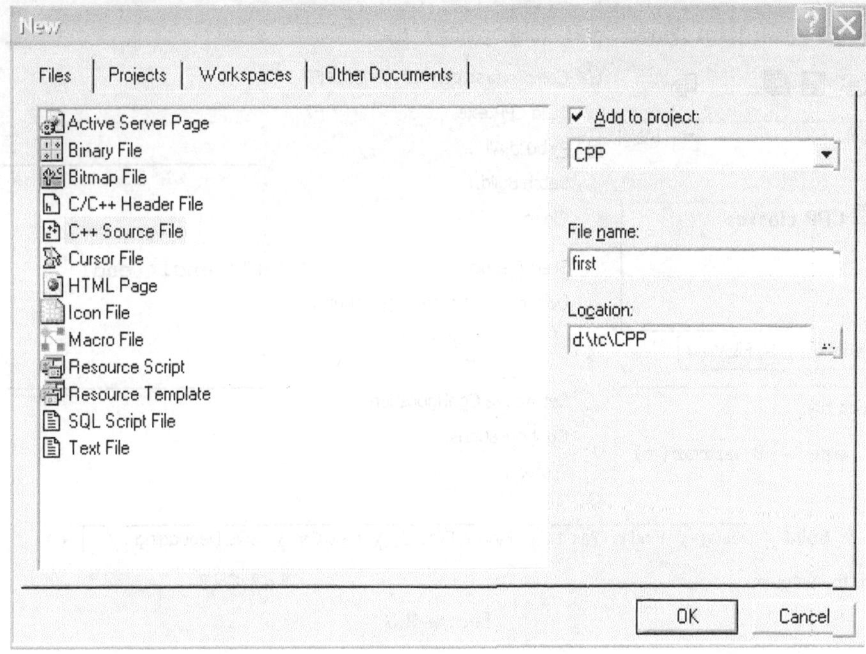

Figure 2.6

6. A new window will appear. Type the above program in the window as it.
7. From the build menu select build CPP.exe option. Assuming no error in the program a new window will appear at the bottom showing 0 error 0 warnings.

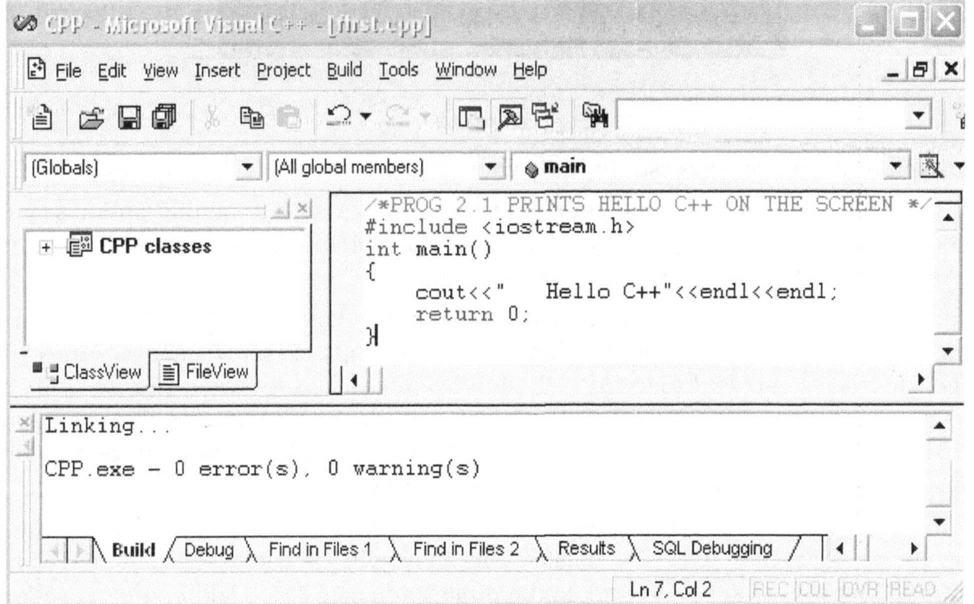

Figure 2.7

8. Now from build menu again select option executes CPP.exe option.

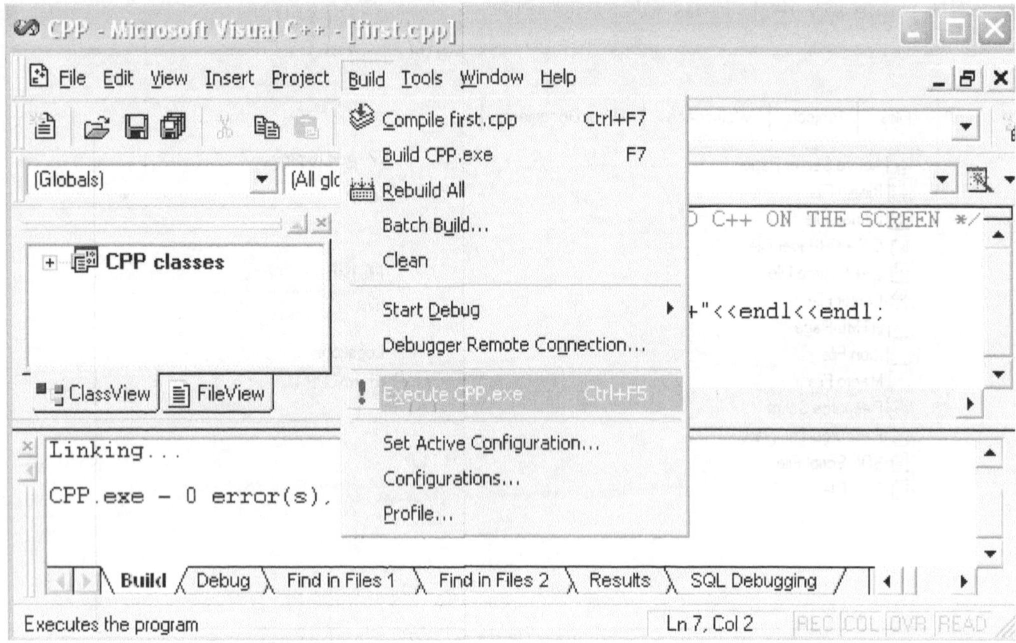

Figure 2.8

9. Next a new console window will appear displaying you the output.

Figure 2.9

10. Voila! You have successfully built your first program in VC++ environment.

In the 7th step before building your program, you can select compile option from build menu too which will compile your program. The build option first compiles the program then make executable, thus combining two steps into one.

Note your file will be visible in the workspace/project window on the left of the main code window. To make a new file simply follow the same steps as shown above. You can have multiple **.cpp** files in the workspace/project window. But make sure when you execute or build using menu option your workspace contains just one file which contains the main function. Otherwise if main function is present in more than one file, linking error will be generated by the Visual C++ compiler as to which file containing main should be executed.

You can simply remove the files from the workspace window by selecting them and pressing delete. The files won't be deleted but they will be removed from the workspace temporarily. When you want them back in the project you can select Add to project option from Project menu.

After a day's work when you want to open your same project simply looks for file with **.dsp** extension whish stands for **data source project**. After wards you can continue making C++ programs.

2.10 STRUCTURE OF A C++ PROGRAM

The general structure of any C++ program is given below. It simply states that a standard C++ program may look like according to various sections presents in the structure.

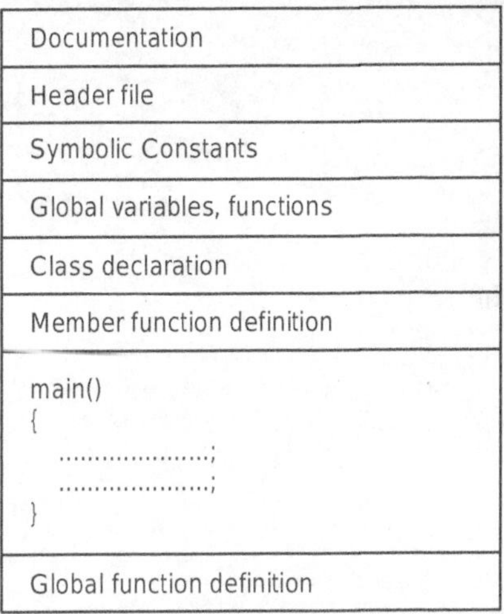

Figure 2.10. *General structure of a C++ program.*

- The first section Documentation is optional and is used to put comments for the program usually the program heading as we have given.
- In second section we include various header files required by our C++ program.
- Symbolic constants and global variable, functions are defined after that if required.
- The class, main building block of C++ programming is declared which consists of declaration of data members and functions. The member function may be declared and defined in the class or they are declared in the class but defined outside the class which is done outside the class declaration.
- The **main()** function must be present in every C++ program. It contains all the statements which are to be executed. Inside this main function we create objects of class created earlier. All statements are put inside the braces and terminate with semicolon.

A full fledge C++ program is given below. Don't worry if you do not understand extra stuff at this point. This is just to give you idea of structure of a C++ program.

```
/*Documentation*/
/* DEMO PROGRAM FOR C++ STRUCTURE, DOES NOT SERVE ANY PURPOSE EXCEPT
DEMONSTRATION */

#include <iostream.h> /*header file inclusion */
#include <iomanip.h>
```

```
int x;float y; char z; /* global variables */
void disp(); /* global function */
/*class declaration starts here */
class demo
{
private :
      int x, y;
public :
      void input(int a, int b);
      void show();
};
/*class declaration ends here */
/*class function definition */
void demo : :input(int a, int b)
{
      x=a;
      y=b;
}
/*class function definition */
void demo : :show()
{
      cout<<"x="<<x<<endl;
      cout<<"y="<<y<<endl;
}
void main() /*main function definiton */
{
      demo d1,d2; //creating objects
      d1.input(10,20);
      ................;
      ................;
      d1.show();
      int num;
      show(); //local function call
}
/*global function definitions */
void show()
{
      cout<<"in show"<<endl;
}
```

2.11 STYLES OF WRITING C++ PROGRAMS

Your first program can be written in two more ways which is rather new style of writing C++ programs. The program you have seen is considered the old style of writing C++ programs. The new style is

```
#include <iostream>
using namespace std;
void main()
{
    cout<<"hello C++"<<endl;
}

or
#include <iostream>
  int main()
 {
  std : :cout<<"hello C++"<<endl;
  return 0;
 }
```

iostream.h is header file and **iostream** is a header file too. The difference is simply that **iostream** provides global **namespace** (refer chapter 13) **std** under which **cout** and **cin** (discussed shortly) are declared. To access **cout** and **cin** you will have to write **std : :cout** and **std : :cin** if **using namespace std** is not written. The return type of function may be **void** or **int**. That does not make your program to contain error. In case of **int** type of **main**, the **main** must return a value. We will be following the old style of writing programs. You may choose any of the style you want, Note the **main** function is nothing to do the old style and new style. It is your choice to use in what manner you want to choose **main** function whether be it old style or new style.

2.12 PROGRAMMING EXAMPLES

/*PROG 2.2 WRITING MULTIPLE STATEMENTS WITH SINGLE COUT */

```
#include <iostream.h>
int main( )
{
    cout<<"Hello NMIMS University"<<endl
      <<"Hello MPSTME Mumbai Campus"<<endl
      <<"Hello MPSTME Shirpur Campus"<<endl;
    return 0;
}
```

OUTPUT :

Hello NMIMS University
Hello MPSTME Mumbai Campus
Hello MPSTME Shirpur Campus

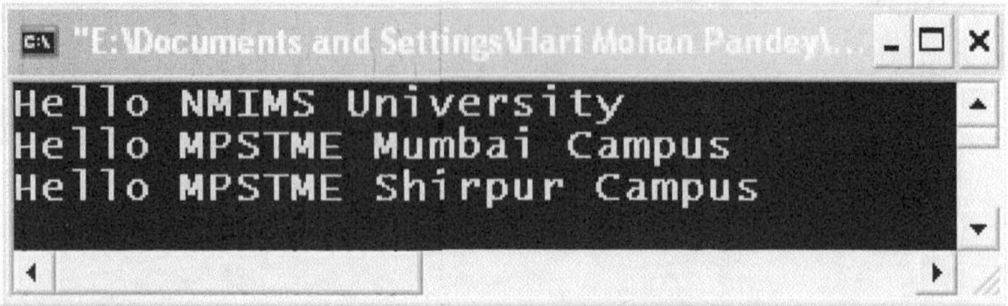

Figure 2.11. *Output screen of program 2.2.*

EXPLANATION : The above program illustrates the fact that multiple statements can be written with a single **cout** and multiple <<operators. The **endl** leaves a line. The semicolon must be put at the end. However, if you do not want to write in the above manner you may write as shown in the next program with multiple **cout** statements.

/* **PROG 2.3 THREE COUT STATEMENT IN A C++ PROGRAM** */

```
#include <iostream.h>
int main()
{
    cout<<"Hello NMIMS University"<<endl;
    cout<<"Hello MPSTME Mumbai Campus"<<endl;
    cout<<"Hello MPSTME Shirpur Campus"<<endl;
    return 0;
}
```

OUTPUT :

Hello NMIMS University
Hello MPSTME Mumbai Campus
Hello MPSTME Shirpur Campus

Figure 2.12. *Output screen of program 2.3.*

EXPLANATION : The program is self-explanatory.

/* PROG 2.4 DISPLAYING DIFFERENT TYPES OF CONTENTS */

```
#include <iostream.h>
void main()
{
    cout<<123<<endl;
    cout<<23.567<<endl;
    cout<<12345678<<endl;
    cout<<'P'<<endl;
    cout<<"Hari"<<endl;
}
```

OUTPUT :

```
123
23.567
12345678
P
Hari
```

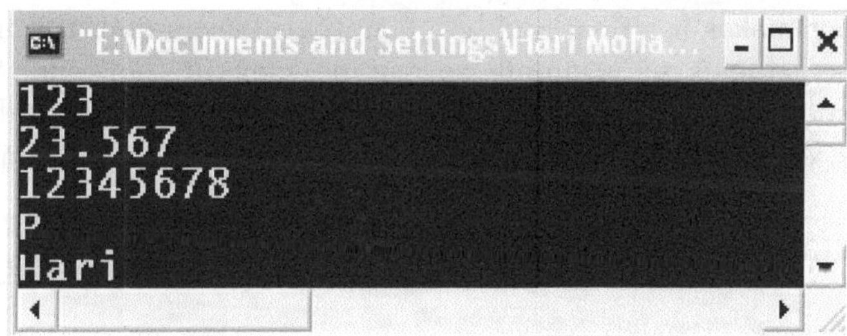

Figure 2.13. *Output screen of program 2.4.*

EXPLANATION : The program simply displays various constants of type **int, char, double, char*** and **char** type. **endl** is built-in manipulator which works similar to '**\n**'. For more about manipulator see chapter 11.

/* PROG 2.5 WORKING WITH VARIABLES VER 1 */

```
#include <iostream.h>
void main()
{
    int x=10;
    float y=2.34f;
    char *s="NMIMS UNIVERSITY";
    cout<<"Value of x :="<< x<<endl;
```

```
    cout<<"Value of y :="<< y<<endl;
    cout<<"Value of s :="<< s<<endl;

}
```

OUTPUT :

```
Value of x :=10
Value of y :=2.34
Value of s :=NMIMS UNIVERSITY
```

```
"E:\Documents and Settings\Hari Mohan Pandey\...
Value of x:=10
Value of y:=2.34
Value of s:=NMIMS UNIVERSITY
```

Figure 2.14. *Output screen of program 2.5.*

EXPLANATION : In the program we have declared and initialized 3 variables **x, y,** and **s** of type **int, float** and **char*** type. Note **y** has the value **2.34f** and not **2.34**. Suffix **f or F** after the floating point number makes it a **float** number. If not written number is considered as **double**. Displaying variables value is very simple as can be seen in the code. Simply write it as **cout<<variable_name**. Again for concatenation simply use <<before and after any variable as **cout<<"x="<<x<<endl;** Variables declared but not initialized contains garbage value.

/*PROG 2.6 WORKING WITH VARIABLES VER 2*/

```
#include <iostream.h>
void main()
{
    int x(10);
    float f(23.34);
    char ch('P');
    cout<<"x="<<x<<endl;
    cout<<"f="<<f<<endl;
    cout<<"ch="<<ch<<endl;
}
```

OUTPUT :

```
x=10
f=23.34
ch=P
```

Figure 2.15. *Output screen of program 2.6*

EXPLANATION : In C++ all built-in data types are treated as classes, like in C they are treated as structures. Here you can assume that int is a class and **x** is an object of it we are initializing **x** by calling the constructor. This is same as writing **int x = 10** but the given notation is called as class constructor notation. Same analogy for **float** and **char** type.

/***PROG 2.7 DYNAMIC INITIALIZATION OF VARIABLES** */

```
#include <iostream.h>
void main()
{
    int num=20;
    cout<<"int num="<<num<<endl;
    double d=23.45;
    cout<<"double d="<<d<<endl;
    char ch='P';
    cout<<"char ch="<<ch<<endl;
    char*s="CPP";
    cout<<"char*s="<<s<<endl;
}
```

OUTPUT :

```
int num=20
double d=23.45
char ch=P
char*s=CPP
```

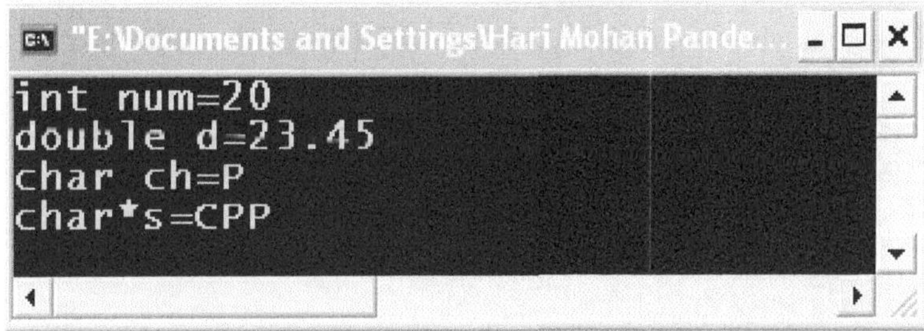

Figure 2.16. *Output screen of program 2.7.*

EXPLANATION : The program demonstrates the fact that variables can be declared and initialized anywhere in the program. Initializing variables dynamically anywhere in the program is known as dynamic initialization.

/* PROG 2.8 WORKING WITH VARIABLES INPUT FROM THE USER */

```
#include <iostream.h>
void main()
{
    int x;
    cout<<"Enter a number"<<endl;
    cin>>x;
    cout<<"You have entered"<<endl;
    cout<<"x :="<<x<<endl;
}
```

OUTPUT :

```
Enter a number
40
You have entered
x :=40
```

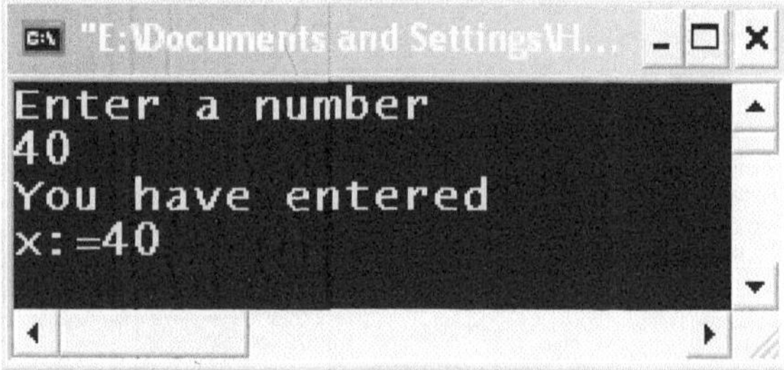

Figure 2.17. *Output screen of program 2.8.*

EXPLANATION : To read a data from keyboard from user we have object **cin**. It represents standard input stream. Its syntax is

```
cin>>var1>>var2>>var2......>>var n
```

The entered values are assigned from left to right *i.e.,* first value is assigned to **var1** and so on. Here we have just one variable **x** of **int** type. We take the input from user in variable x by writing **cin>>x**. The same variable is displayed back using **cout. cin** is an object of **iostream_with assign** class **>>** is known as get from or **extraction operator.**

/*PROG 2.9 INPUT MIX DATA FROM USER */

```
#include <iostream.h>
void main()
{
    int x;
    float y;
    char ch;
    cout<<"Enter an int, char and"
        <<" a float value "<<endl;
    cin>>x>>ch;
    cin>>y;
    cout<<"You entered"<<endl;
    cout<<"Int value x :="<< x<<endl;
    cout<<"float value y :="<< y<<endl;
    cout<<"char value ch :="<< ch<<endl;
}
```

OUTPUT :

```
Enter an int, char and a flaot value
15 h 12.45
You entered
Int value x :=15
float value y :=12.45
char value ch :=h
```

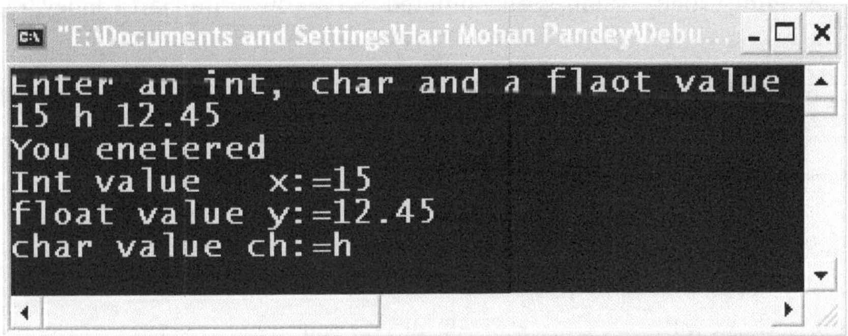

Figure 2.18. *Output screen of program 2.9*

EXPLANATION : In the program we have **3** variables **x** of **int** type, **y** of **float** type and **ch** of **char** type. The **3** variables are not taken by a single **cin** statement as **cin>>x>>ch>>**y. Instead we have taken **int** and **char** type data by writing **cin>>x>>ch** and next data *i.e.*, **float** variable in **y** by writing **cin>>y.**

/*PROG 2.10 TAKING STRING DATA FROM USER */

```
#include <iostream.h>
void main()
{
    char s[15];
    cout<<"Enter your name"<<endl;
    cin>>s;
    cout<<"Hello "<<s<<endl;
}
```

OUTPUT :

```
Enter your name
Hari
Hello Hari
```

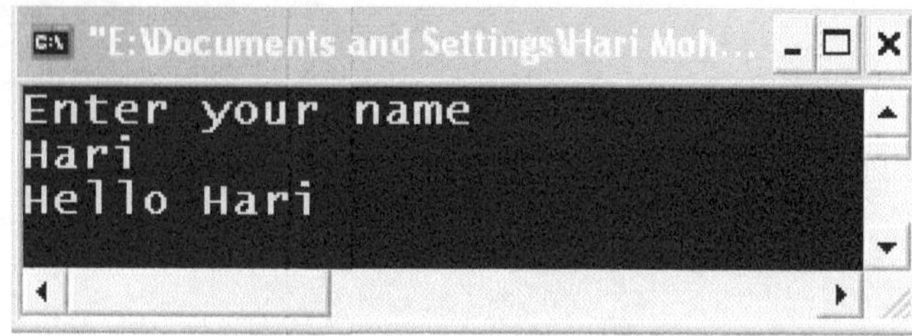

Figure 2.19. *Output screen of program 2.10.*

EXPLANATION : To read a string from user we create a **char** array s of size **15**. Using **cin>>s** we have accepted string **s**. Note **cin** will break at the first white space character in the input string *i.e.,* either space or tab is encountered. So if you write **Hari Pandey**, only **Hari** will be accepted in **s**.

/* PROG 2.11 FINDING LIMITS OF INTEGRAL DATA TYPES */

```
#include <iostream.h>
#include <limits.h>
void main()
{
    cout<<"CHAR_MIN    :=  "<<CHAR_MIN<<endl;
    cout<<"CHAR_MAX    :=  "<<CHAR_MAX<<endl;
    cout<<"INT_MIN     :=  "<<INT_MIN<<endl;
    cout<<"INT_MAX     :=  "<<INT_MAX<<endl;
    cout<<"SHRT_MIN    :=  "<<SHRT_MIN<<endl;
    cout<<"SHRT_MAX    :=  "<<SHRT_MAX<<endl;
    cout<<"LONG_MIN    :=  "<<LONG_MIN<<endl;
    cout<<"LONG_MAX    :=  "<<LONG_MAX<<endl;
```

```
    cout<<"SCHAR_MIN   :=  "<<SCHAR_MIN<<endl;
    cout<<"SCHAR_MAX   :=  "<<SCHAR_MIN<<endl;
    cout<<"UCHAR_MAX   :=  "<<UCHAR_MAX<<endl;
    cout<<"UINT_MAX    :=  "<<UINT_MAX<<endl;
    cout<<"USHRT_MAX   :=  "<<USHRT_MAX<<endl;
    cout<<"ULONG_MAX   :=  "<<ULONG_MAX<<endl;
}
```

OUTPUT :

```
CHAR_MIN   :=  –128
CHAR_MAX   :=  127
INT_MIN    :=  –2147483648
INT_MAX    :=  2147483647
SHRT_MIN   :=  –32768
SHRT_MAX   :=  32767
LONG_MIN   :=  –2147483648
LONG_MAX   :=  2147483647
SCHAR_MIN  :=  –128
SCHAR_MAX  :=  –128
UCHAR_MAX  :=  255
UINT_MAX   :=  4294967295
USHRT_MAX  :=  65535
ULONG_MAX  :=  4294967295
```

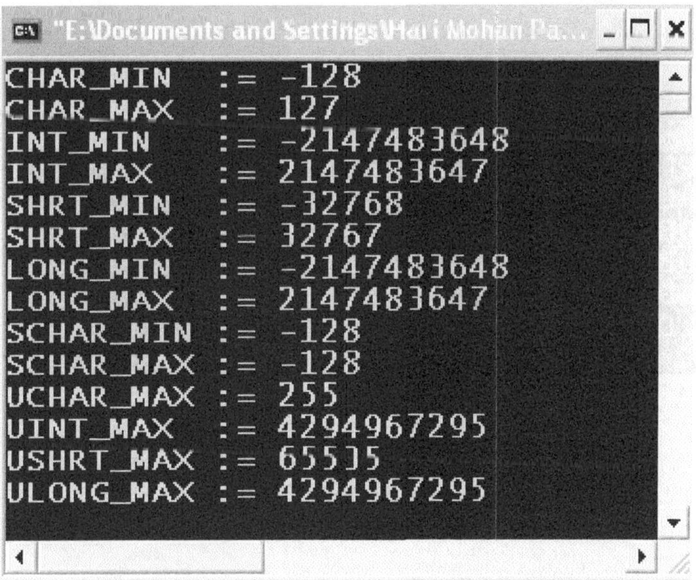

Figure 2.20. *Output screen of program 2.11.*

EXPLANATION : For findings limits of integral data types we have predefined constants stored in the header file **limits.h**. In the program we have used these constants and displayed the range of integral data types. **SHRT** stand for **short**, **UCHAR** for **unsigned char**, **SCHAR** for **signed char** and soon.

/* PROG 2.12 FINDING RANGES OF FLOATING POINT DATA */

```
#include <iostream.h>
#include <float.h>

void main()
{
    cout<<"FLT_MIN   := "<<FLT_MIN<<endl;
    cout<<"FLT_MAX   := "<<FLT_MAX<<endl;
    cout<<"DBL_MIN   := "<<DBL_MIN<<endl;
    cout<<"DBL_MAX   := "<<DBL_MAX<<endl;
    cout<<"LDBL_MIN  := "<<LDBL_MIN<<endl;
    cout<<"LDBL_MAX  := "<<LDBL_MAX<<endl;
}
```

OUTPUT :

```
FLT_MIN   := 1.17549e-038
FLT_MAX   := 3.40282e+038
DBL_MIN   := 2.22507e-308
DBL_MAX   := 1.79769e+308
LDBL_MIN  := 2.22507e-308
LDBL_MAX  := 1.79769e+308
```

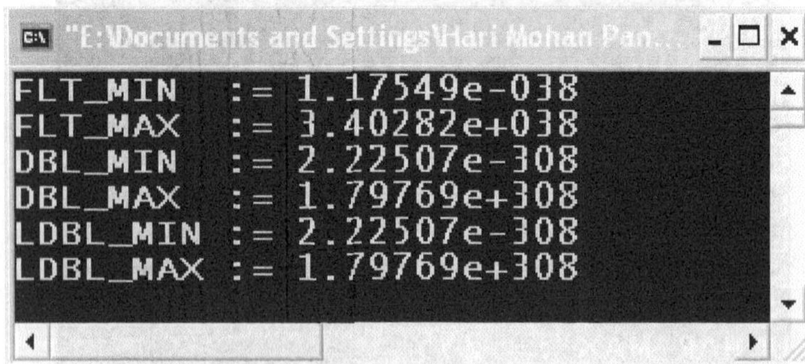

Figure 2.21. *Output screen of program 2.12.*

EXPLANATION : For finding range of floating point data types we have pre defined constant stored in header file **float.h**. In windows **double** and **long double** are treated same.

2.13 PONDERABLE POINTS

1. C++ was developed by Bjarne Stroustrup at AT & T's bell laboratories in the Murray Hill New Jersey, USA in the early 80's.
2. cout is considered standard output stream and used for displaying data onto the screen.
3. cin is considered standard output stream and used for taking data from keyboard.
4. The named C++ came from the increment operator ++ of C as it is considered a super set of C, one version ahead of C, so it was named C++.
5. There are mainly 63 keywords in C++.
6. Smallest individual unit in a C++ program is known as token.
7. cout is an object of ostream_withassign class and cin is an object of istream_withassign class.
8. >> is known as get from or extraction operator and is used with cin.
9. << is known as put to or insertion operator and is used with cout.
10. All C++ program must include basic header file iostream.h.
11. The first application developed in C++ was "cfront".
12. For finding range of integral data types we can us header file limits.h and for finding range of floating point data types we can use header file float.h

    In C++ variables can be declared anywhere in the program. Variables can also be initialized at the place of declaration. This is known as dynamic initialization of variables.

EXERCISE

A. True and False:

1. The extraction operator >> can write characters.
2. cout is an object of ostream class.
3. cin is an object of iostream class.
4. Procedural language is based on objects.
5. // can be used for multiline comment also.
6. volatile keyword cannot be used to declare variables.

B. Fill in the Blanks:

1. The .... declaration specifies that the object can be used between separate translation units.
2. .... is known as exraction operator.
3. .... is known as insertion operator.
4. .... is an object of ostream_withassign class.
5. .... header file must be used in all C++ programs.

C. Answer the Following Questions:

1. What is C++ ? How it evolved ?
2. What is token ? What different types of token are available in C++ ?
3. What is the structure of a C++ program ?
4. What are the various styles of writing a C++ program explain with example ?
5. What are qualifiers ? How they are special ?
6. Discuss all the different types of data types in C++.
7. What is dynamic declaration and dynamic initialization ? What are its advantages and disadvantages ?
8. How does >> and << works ?
9. Explain all the components of the first C++ program.
10. How doe we find out range of data types explain with program ?

D. Brain Drill:

1. Assuming there are 7.481 gallons in a cubic foot, write a program that asks the user to enter a number of gallons, and displays the equivalent in cubic feet.
2. Write a program to generates the following output :

   10

   20

   19

   Use an integer constant for the 10, an arithmetic assignment operator to generate the 20, and a decrement operator to generate the 19.
3. Write a program that displays your favorite poem. Use an appropriate escape sequence for the line breaks.
4. You can convert temperature from degrees Celsius to degree Fahrenheit by multiplying by 9/5 and adding 32. Write a program that allows the user to enter a floating point number representing degree Celsius, and then displays the corresponding degrees Fahrenheit.
5. A library function **islower** takes a single character (a letter) as an argument and returns a non-zero integer if the letter is lowercase, or zero if it is uppercase. This function requires the header file CTYPE.H. Write a program that allows the user to enter a letter, and then displays either zero or non-zero, depending on whether a lowercase or uppercase' letter was entered.
6. On a certain day the British pound was equivalent to $1.487US, the French franc was $0.172, the German deutschemark was $0.584, and the Japanese yen was $0.0095. Write a program that allows the user to enter an amount in dollars, and then displays this value converted to these four other monetary units.

❑❑❑

CHAPTER 3

C FEATURES OF C++

3.1 INTRODUCTION

There are lots of new features in C++ but there are features which are in common in both C and C++. So, even if you do not have any knowledge of C, you can refer this chapter. Most of the features like operators, if-else, loops, goto, arrays etc are discussed in this chapter. Instead of giving separate chapter and increasing the length of the book, I thought better to concentrate on the new features of C++, rather than repeating the same old features of C. The result is this chapter. The chapter gives you a brief overview of all the features which are in C++ but also present in C.

3.2 OPERATORS AND EXPRESSIONS

For performing different kind of operations, various types of operators are required. An operator denotes an operation to be performed on some data that generates some value. For example, plus operator (+) on 2 and 3 generates 5 (2+3=5). Here 2 and 3 are called operands.

Table 3.1 : Operators in C++

S.No.	*Operators*	*Symbols Representation*
1.	Arithmetical	+,-, /, *, %
2.	Logical	&&, ||, !
3.	Relational	>, <, >=, <=, = =, !=
4.	Assignment	=
5.	Increment	++
6.	Decrement	—
7.	Comma	,
8.	Conditional	? :
9.	Bitwise	&, |, ^, !, >>, <<
10.	Special Operator	*sizeof*

Binary Operators

All the operators which require two operands to operate on are known as *binary operators*. For example, as shown in the above table all the arithmetic, relational, logical (except! (NOT) operator), comma, assignment, bitwise (except ~ operator) operators etc., are binary operators.

Example : –2 + 4, 35 > 45, x = 30, 2 & 5.

Unary Operators

Unary operators are those operators which require only one operand to operate on. For example, as shown in the above table increment/decrement,! (NOT), ~ (1's complement operator), sizeof etc., are unary operators. C also provides unary plus and unary minus *i.e.*, +20 and –35. Here + and – are known as unary plus and unary minus operators.

Example : +4, –3, ++x, sizeof (int), sizeof(2.0).

Note : ? : operator is known as ternary operator as it requires three operands to operate on. One before ?, Second after ? and third after :

Expression

Operator together with operands constitutes an expression or a valid combination of constants, variables, and operators forms an expression is usually recognized by the type of operator used with in the expression. Depending upon that you may have integer expression, floating point expression, relational expression etc. You may have different types of operators in an expression which is a mixed mode expression. See the table given below for few examples.

Table 3.2 : Types of Expressions

S.No	*Expression*	*Type of Expression*
1.	2+3*4/6–7	Integer Arithmetic
2.	2.3*4.7/6.0	Real Arithmetic
3.	a>b!=c	Relational
4.	X && 10 || y	Logical
5.	2>3+x && y	Mixed

1. Arithmetic Operators

The various arithmetic operators are shown in the Table

Table 3.3 : Arithmetic Operators

S.No.	*Operator*	*Meaning/ used for*
1.	+	Addition
2.	–	Subtraction
3.	/	Division
4.	*	Multiplication
5.	%	Remainder

First four operators are self-explanatory. The reminder operator can be used only with integers. For all other operators if one of the operands is `float` and second one is `int` then result will be in `float`.

The percentage symbol "%" is used for modulus of a number. `a/b` produces quotient and `a%b` where % is called `remainder operator` produces remainder when `a` is divided by `b`. The mathematical formula behind remainder operator is :

a % b = a – (a / b) * b (where a / b is integer division)

% operator works only with integer operands. Never use `float` operands. C++ does not allow `float` operand with % operator.

/*PROG 3.1 DEMO OF ARITHMETIC OPERATORS */

```
#include<iostream.h>
void main( )
{
int a,b,sum,sub,div,mul,rem;
cout<<"Enter two numbers\n";
cin>>a>>b;
sum=a+b;
sub=a-b;
div=a/b;
mul=a*b;
rem=a%b;
cout<<"Sum of "<<a<<" and "<<b<<" is "<<sum<<endl;
cout<<"Sub of "<<a<<" and "<<b<<" is "<<sub<<endl;
cout<<"Div of "<<a<<" and "<<b<<" is "<<div<<endl;
cout<<"Mul of "<<a<<" and "<<b<<" is "<<mul<<endl;
cout<<"Rem of "<<a<<" and "<<b<<" is "<<rem<<endl;
}
```

OUTPUT :

```
Enter two numbers
35 20
Sum of 35 and 20 is 55
Sub of 35 and 20 is 15
Div of 35 and 20 is 1
Mul of 35 and 20 is 700
Rem of 35 and 20 is 15
```

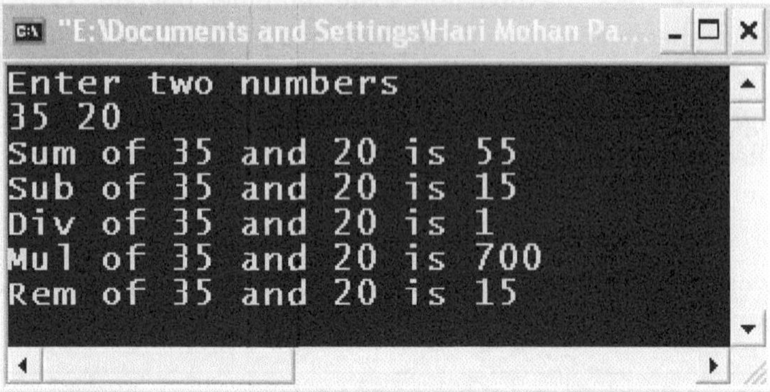
"E:\Documents and Settings\Hari Mohan Pa...
Enter two numbers
35 20
Sum of 35 and 20 is 55
Sub of 35 and 20 is 15
Div of 35 and 20 is 1
Mul of 35 and 20 is 700
Rem of 35 and 20 is 15

Figure 3.1. *Output screen of program.*

EXPLANATION : The program is self explanatory.

/*PROG 3.2 DEMO OF MODULUS(%)OPERATOR*/

```
#include<iostream.h>
void main( )
{
cout<<17<<"/"<<5<<"="<<17/5<<"\t"<<17<<"%"
<<5<<"="<<17%5<<endl;
cout<<-17<<"/"<<5<<"="<<-17/5<<"\t"<<-17
<<"%"<<5<<"="<<-17%5<<endl;
cout<<17<<"/"<<-5<<"="<<17/-5<<"\t"<<17
<<"%"<<-5<<"="<<17%-5<<endl;
cout<<-17<<"/"<<-5<<"="<<-17/-5<<"\t"
<<-17<<"%"<<-5<<"="<<-17%-5<<endl;
}
```

OUTPUT :

```
17/5=3 17%5=2
-17/5=-3 -17%5=-2
17/-5=-3 17%-5=2
-17/-5=3 -17%-5=-2
```

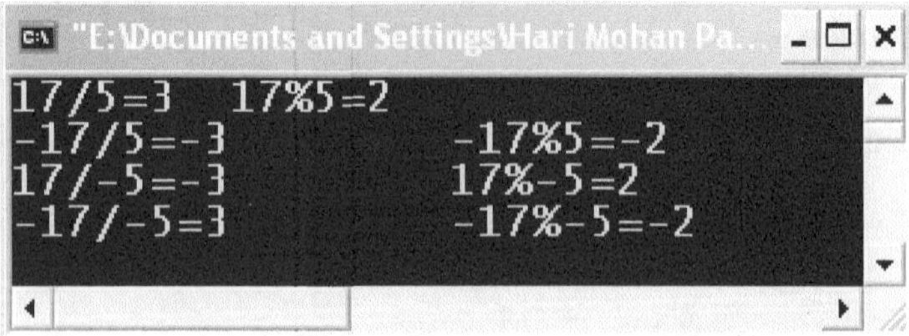
"E:\Documents and Settings\Hari Mohan Pa...
17/5=3 17%5=2
-17/5=-3 -17%5=-2
17/-5=-3 17%-5=2
-17/-5=3 -17%-5=-2

Figure 3.2. *Output screen of program.*

EXPLANATION : In the division operation, sign of quotient depends upon both the operands *i.e.*, follows the rule of mathematics. In remainder operator %. Sign of remainder is determined by sign of numerator or first operator left to %. If is +ve answer will be –ve.

2. Conditional and Relational Operator

Table 3.4 : Relational operators

S.No.	*Operator*	*Meaning/ Used for*
1.	>	Greater than
2.	<	Less than
3.	>=	Greater than equal to
4.	<=	Less than equal to
5.	= =	Equal to
6.	!=	Not equal to

The two symbols ? : together are called ternary or conditional operator. Before? condition is specified with the help of relational operators which may be any one operator as given in Table 3.4. If the condition specified before? is true any expression or statement after? is executed. If condition is false then statement or expression after : (colon) is evaluated. The general syntax is :

```
(Condition)? True part: false part;
```

All relational operators yield Boolean values *i.e.*, true or false. A true value is represented by 1 and false value by 0. In expression any non-zero value is terminated as true value.

/*PROG 3.3 DEMO OF EQUAL(= =) AND TERNARY(? :) OPERATOR*/

```
#include<iostream.h>
void main( )
{
int a=0;
a==0 ?cout<<"a is zero\n" :
cout<<"a is not zero\n";
}
```

OUTPUT :

```
a is zero
```

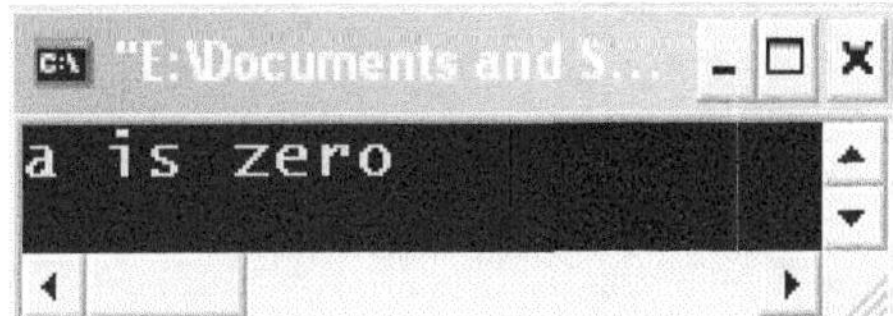

Figure 3.3. *Output screen of program.*

EXPLANATION : ? operator is known as conditional operator (also called ternary operator) works as follows : The condition which is to be checked (here a = =0) written before ? On success of condition the action which is to be performed written after ?. In this case the statement `cout<<"a is zero\n";`. On failure of condition the action which is to be taken written after : In this case the statement `cout<<"a is not zero\n";`. In the condition it is being checked whether value of a is equal to 0 or not. The operator = = is called equality operator. It checks both the operands on either side of it are equal or not. If equal then condition is true else it is false. Try changing value of a and you will get different output.

Note : Conditional operator always works with relational operators.

/*PROG 3.4 DEMO OF RELATIONAL OPERATORS*/

```
#include<iostream.h>
void main( )
{
int a=5,b=6,c,d,e,f,g,h;
c=a>b;
d=a<b;
e=(4!=3);
f=(8>=17);
g=(123<=123);
h=(a==b);
cout<<"value of c= "<<c<<endl;
cout<<"value of d= "<<d<<endl;
cout<<"value of e= "<<e<<endl;
cout<<"value of f= "<<f<<endl;
cout<<"value of g= "<<g<<endl;
cout<<"value of h= "<<h<<endl;
}
```

OUTPUT :

```
value of c= 0
value of d= 1
value of e= 1
value of f= 0
value of g= 1
value of h= 0
```

```
"E:\Documents and Settings\Hari Moh...
value of c= 0
value of d= 1
value of e= 1
value of f= 0
value of g= 1
value of h= 0
```

Figure 3.4. *Output screen of program.*

EXPLANATION : If the condition is true value returned is 1 else 0, so the output. For truth a value of 1 is assumed, for falsity a value of 0 is assumed by C++.

/*PROG 3.5 MAXIMUM OF TWO NUMBER VER 1*/

```
#include<iostream.h>
void main( )
{
 int a,b,c;
 cout<<"Enter the two integer numbers \n";
 cin>>a>>b;
 c=a>b ?a :b;
 cout<<" max of "<<a<<" and "<<b<<" is "<<c<<endl;
}
```

OUTPUT :

```
Enter the two integer numbers
15 20
 max of 15 and 20 is 20
```

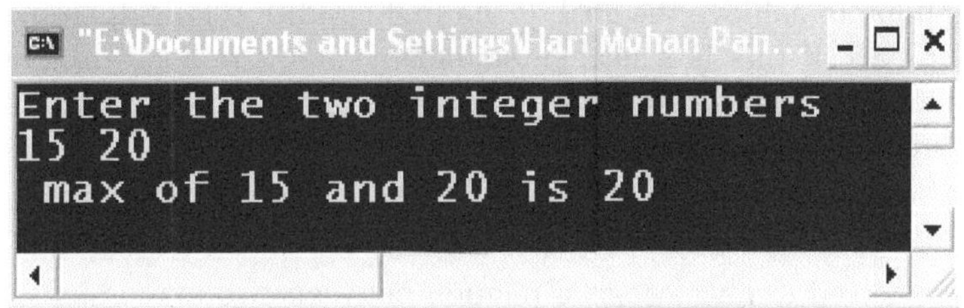

Figure 3.5. *Output screen of program.*

EXPLANATION : If `a` is greater than `b` then `a` is assigned to `c` `else` `b` is assigned to `b`. In any case maximum of two is stored in `c` which is printed by the `cout`. Condition of equality of two numbers is not checked in the program which is shown in the modified program below.

/*PROG 3.6 MAXIMUM OF TWO NUMBERS VER 2*/

```
#include<iostream.h>
void main( )
{
int a,b;
cout<<"Enter two integer numbers \n";
cin>>a>>b;
(a==b) ?cout<<a<<" is equal to "<<b :(a>b) ?cout<<a
<<" is max \n " :cout<<b<<" is max\n";
}
```

OUTPUT :

```
(First run)
Enter two integer numbers
50 50
50 is equal to 50
(Second run)
Enter two integer numbers
50 67
67 is max
```

"E:\Documents and Settings\Hari ...
Enter two integer numbers
50 50
50 is equal to 50

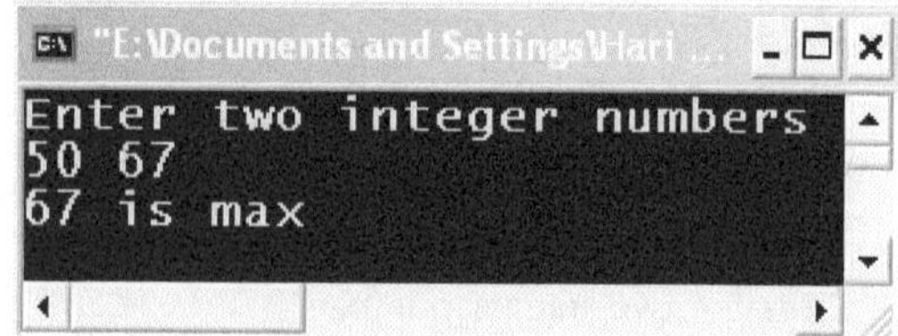

Figure 3.6. *Output screen of first and second run of program.*

EXPLANATION : Observe carefully the above program. Nesting of ternary operator (one inside another) is done to achieve the goal. If the first condition fails, then in the colon (:) part we check whether a>b. If this is true then statement after ? (after a>b) executes *i.e.,* in the failure part of the ternary operator we have one more ternary operator. This is known as nesting of ternary operators.

3. Logical Operators

Logical operators are used to check logical relation between two expressions. Depending upon the truth or falsehood of the expression they are assigned value**1 (true)** and **0(false)**. The expressions may be variables, constants, functions etc. See the table given below :

Table 3.5 : Logical Operators

S.No.	*Symbol*	*Meaning*
1.	&&	AND
2.	||	OR
3.	!	NOT

The && and || are binary operators. For && to return true value both of its operand must yield true value. For || to yield true value at least one of the operand yield true value .The **NOT** (!) operator is unary operator. It negates its operand *i.e.*, if operand is true it convert it into false and vice-versa.

/*PROG 3.7 DEMO OF LOGICAL OPERATOR && (LOGICAL AND) VER 1*/

```
#include<iostream.h>
void main( )
{
int res,a=10,b=20;
res=(a>=10 && b==20);
cout<<"Returned value in res= "<<res<<endl;
}
```

OUTPUT :

```
Returned value in res= 1
```

Figure 3.7. *Output screen of program.*

EXPLANATION : The && is called AND operator. On both of this operator condition is specified. If both conditions are true the returned value is true that is 1 else false value is returned that is 0. In the above program both the conditions in the expression are true so `res` contain 1 as result.

/*PROG 3.8 DEMO OF LOGICAL OPERATOR && (AND)VER 2*/

```
#include<iostream.h>
void main( )
{
int res, a=0,b=2;
res=(a!=0 && b<=2);
```

```
cout<<"Returned value in res= "<<res<<endl;
}
```

OUTPUT :

Returned value in res= 0

Figure 3.8. *Output screen of program.*

EXPLANATION : In the expression the condition before && is false and after && it is true so overall value of the expression is false so a 0 is assigned to `res`.

Logical OR (||)

The operator works with two operands which may be any expression, variable, constant or function. It checks any of its operand returns true value or not. If they it returns true value *i.e.*, a decimal 1. If both of its operands are false, a false value is returned *i.e.*, a decimal 0.

/*PROG 3.9 DEMO OF LOGICAL OR OPERATOR (||)*/

```
#include<iostream.h>
void main( )
{
int res, a= 100, b=120;
res=(a>=100 || b<0);
cout<<"Returned value in res= "<<res<<endl;
}
```

OUTPUT :

Returned value in res= 1

Figure 3.9. *Output screen of program.*

EXPLANATION : The || is called OR operator. On both side of this operator condition is specified. If any of the condition is true the returned value is true that is 1 else 0. In the above program first condition in the expression is true but second is false so **res** contains 1 as result.

Logical NOT (!)

The operator converts a true value into false and vice-versa. Again the operand may be any expression, constant, variable or function.

/*PROG 3.10 DEMO OF LOGICAL OPERATOR !(NOT) VER 1 */

```
#include<iostream.h>
void main( )
{
int res, a=1;
        res=!a;
cout<<"Returned value in res= "<<res<<endl;
}
```

OUTPUT :

```
Returned value in res= 0
```

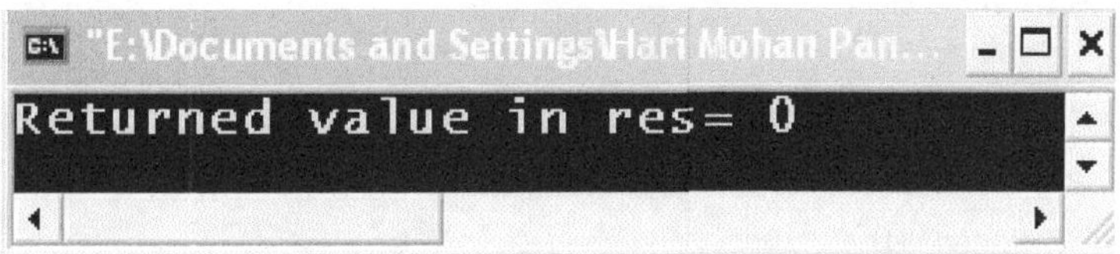

Figure 3.10. *Output screen of program.*

EXPLANATION : The! is called NOT or negation operator. It is an unary operator meaning only one operand is required on it. If operand's value is non-zero it is converted into false value that is 0 and vice-versa. Similarly if a true condition is specified it will be turned into false and vice-versa. Try changing value of a to zero, returned value in res will be 1.

/*PROG 3.11 DEMO OF LOGICAL OPERATOR (NOT ! OPERATOR) VER 2 */

```
#include <iostream.h>
void main( )
{
        int res;
        res=!(10>5 && -4<=1);
        cout<<"returned value in res  := "<< res<<endl;
}
```

OUTPUT :

```
returned value in res  := 0
```

Figure 3.11. *Output screen of program.*

EXPLANATION : Both conditions in && operator are true so whole inner expression is true, after negation the returned value will be 0.

4. Assignment Operator

The = operator is called assignment operator. We have seen several instances of this operator in many of the earlier program. One more use of this operator is the shortening of following types of expressions :

x = x + 1, y = y * (x-5), a = a/10, t = t%10;

In all the above expressions the variable on both side of = operator is same so we can change the above expression in shorter form as follows

x = x + 1 = > x + = 1

y = y* (x-5) = > y* = (x-5)

a = a/10 = > a/ = 10

t = t%10 = > t% = 10

This form **op=** where operator may be any operator is called **compound operator** or **shorthand assignment operator.**

5. Increment Operator (+ +) and Decrement Operator (– –)

The operators ++ is known as increment operator and the operator – –is known as decrement operator. Both are unary operators. The ++ increment the value of its operand by **1** and – decrement the value of its operands by **1.** For example, ++ x becomes 11 (assume x=10 prior to the operation ++x and – –x) and –x becomes 9.

See the program given below for more explanation :

/*PROG 3.12 DEMO OF ++ OPERATOR VER 1*/

```
#include<iostream.h>
void main( )
{
int x;
x=20;
cout<<"Before increment x= "<<x<<endl;
x++;
```

```
cout<<"After increment x= "<<x<<endl;
}
```

OUTPUT :

```
Before increment x= 20
After increment x= 21
```

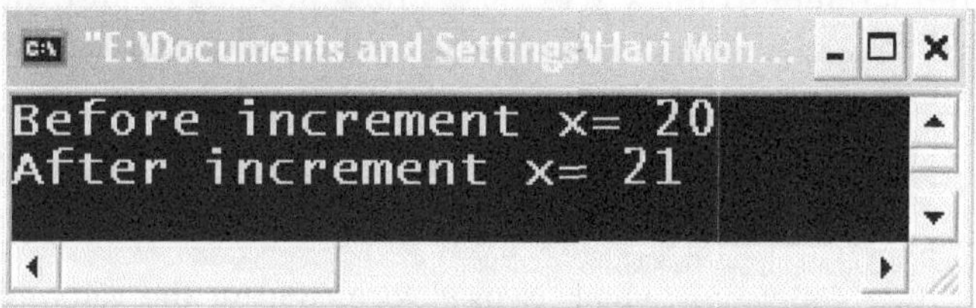

Figure 3.12. *Output screen of program.*

EXPLANATION : The ++ operator is called increment operator. It is an unary operator that is it requires only one operand to operate which increment the value of operand by 1 *i.e.*, x++ is equivalent to x = x+1. If ++ is written before operand *i.e.*, ++x it is known as **pre increment** and if ++ is written after operand *i.e.*, ++x it is known as **post increment.** In the above program we have used post increment operator. Had we have used pre increment the output would be same. For distinction between two check out next two program.

/*PROG 3.13 DEMO OF ++ OPERATOR VER 2*/

```
#include<iostream.h>
void main( )
{
int x,y;
x=20;
y=x++;
cout<<"x="<<x<<"\t"<<"y="<<y<<endl;
}
```

OUTPUT :

```
x = 21 y = 20
```

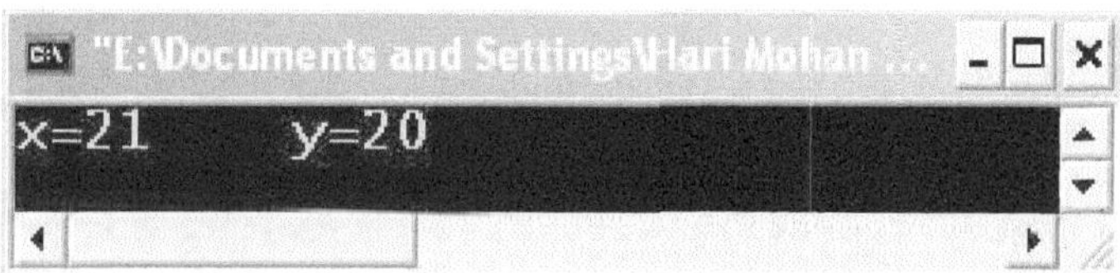

Figure 3.13. *Output screen of program.*

EXPLANATION : In the above program we have used post-increment operator with x and we are assigning the value to y. Due to post increment first x will be assigned to y and x will be incremented by 1 that is y=x++ is equivalent to the following statement :

y = x;

x = x++;

If we write

x = 20;

y = ++x;

Then due to pre-increment first x will be incremented by 1 and the same incremented value will be assigned to y. y=++x is equivalent to the following two statement :

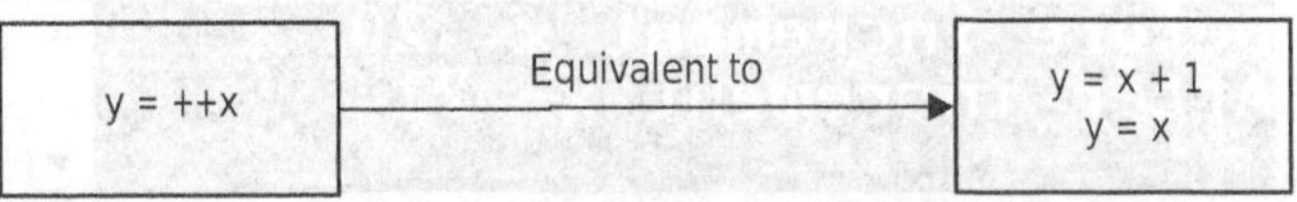

Note : There is only ++ operator which is used to increment the value of the operand by one. There is no such operator as +++ or ++++ which increment the value by 2 or 3.

Similar to increment operator we have decrement operator (– –) which is again may be of two types : pre-decrement operator and post-decrement operator.

/*PROG 3.14 DEMO OF ++ OPERATOR VER 3*/

```
#include<iostream.h>
void main( )
{
int x,y;
x=10;
y=++x;
cout<<"x="<<x<<"\t"<<"y="<<y<<endl;
--x;
cout<<"x="<<x<<endl;
y--;
cout<<"y="<<y<<endl;
x=y++;
cout<<"x="<<x<<"\t"<<"y="<<y<<endl;
y=--x;
cout<<"x="<<x<<"\t"<<"y="<<y<<endl;
x=y++;
cout<<"x="<<x<<"\t"<<"y="<<y<<endl;
}
```

OUTPUT :

```
x=11 y=11
x=10
y=10
```

```
x=10 y=11
x=9 y=9
x=9 y=10
```

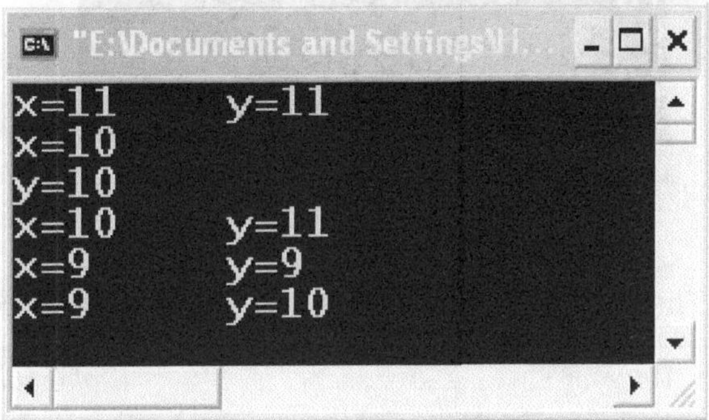

Figure 3.14. *Output screen of program.*

EXPLANATION : For explanation observe the following table :

Statement	*Value of x*	*Value of y*
Y=++x	11	11
– –x	10	11
y– –	10	10
X=y++	10	11
Y=– –x	09	09
X–y I I	09	10

/*PROG 3.15 DEMO OF ++ OPERATOR VER 4*/

```
#include<iostream.h>
 void main( )
 {
 int x;
 x=10;
 cout<<--x<<endl<<++x<<endl<<x<<endl<<x++<<endl
 <<x--<<endl;
 }
```

OUTPUT :

```
10
11
10
9
10
```

Figure 3.15. *Output screen of program.*

EXPLANATION : The output will be determined from right of **cout** statement :

Statement	*Value of x*	*Explanation*
x– –	**10**	**Value of x will be printed then decremented**
x++	**09**	**Value of x will be printed then incremented**
X	**10**	**Value of x will be printed**
++x	**11**	**Value of x will be incremented then printed**
– –x	**10**	**Value of x will be decremented then printed**

So the output is 10 11 10 9 10

6. Bitwise Operators

They are called so because they operate on bits. They can be used for the manipulation of bits. All these operators are extensively used when interfacing with the hardware and for setting of bits in registers of the device. C provides total 6 types of bitwise operators. They are as follows :

Table 3.6 : Bitwise Operators

S.No.	*Operator*	*Meaning/Used for*
1.	&	Bitwise AND
2.	|	Bitwise OR
3.	^	Bitwise XOR
4.	~	One's complement
5.	>>	Right shift
6.	<<	Left shift

For all the following programs we consider only first 4 bits of the number for explanation purpose. So range of possible numbers is –7 to 8 in case of signed numbers (-2^{14} to $-2^{41}-1$) and (0 to $-2^{4}-1$) in case of unsigned numbers. In case you assume **8** bits for the numbers then use full 8 bits for the number even if it can be using 4 bits for example 10 can be written using 4 bits as 1010 and using 8 bits as 00001010.

Bitwise And (&)

It takes two bits as operand and returns the value **1** if both are **1.** If either of them is **0,** the result is **0.**

Table 3.7 : Truth Table of Bitwise AND

First bit	*Second bit*	*Result*
0	0	0
0	1	0
1	0	0
1	1	1

/*PROG 3.16 DEMO OF BITWISE OPERATOR &(BITWISE AND)*/

```
#include<iostream.h>
void main( )
{
int a,b;
a=2;
b=3;
int c=a&b;
cout<<"The value of c :="<<c<<endl;
}
```

OUTPUT :

The value of c : =2

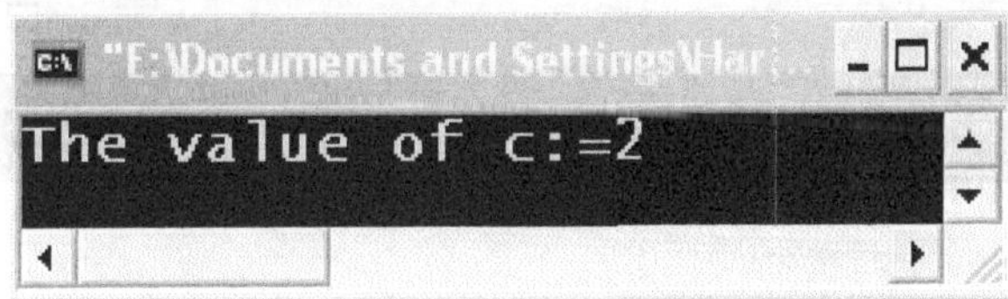

Figure 3.16. *Output screen of program.*

EXPLANATION : Binary values of a=2 is 0010 and b=3 is 0011

Bitwise AND of those values is performed as follows :

```
0 0 1 0
0 0 1 1
-------
0 0 1 0
```

(output in c will be 2 in decimal)

If both bit are **1** output bit will be 1 using **&** operator else **0.**

Bitwise OR (|)

It takes two bits as operand and returns the value **1** if at least one is **1.** If both are **0** only then result is **0** else it is **1.**

Table 3.8 : Truth Table of Bitwise OR

First bit	*Second bit*	*Result*
0	0	0
0	1	1
1	0	1
1	1	1

/*PROG 3.17 DEMO OF BITWISE OPERATOR |(BITWISE OR)*/

```
#include<iostream.h>
void main( )
{
int a,b;
a=12;
b=7;
int c= a|b;
cout<<"The value of c :="<<c<<endl;
}
```

OUTPUT :

The value of c : =15

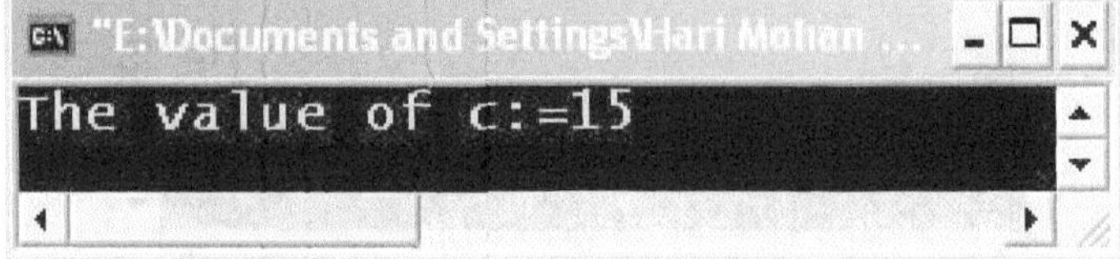

Figure 3.17. *Output screen of program.*

EXPLANATION : Binary value of **a=12 is 1100 and b =7 is 0111**

OR of these two values is performed as follows :

1 1 0 0

0 1 1 1

1 1 1 1 **(output in c will be 15 in decimal)?**

If any of the bit **1** output will be **1** using **OR** operator.

Bitwise XOR (^)

This operator takes at least two bits (may be more than two). If number of **1's** are odd then result is **1** else result is **0.**

Table 3.9 : Truth Table of Bitwise XOR

First bit	*Second bit*	*Result*
0	0	0
0	1	1
1	0	1
1	1	0

/*PROG 3.18 DEMO OF BITWISE OPERATOR ^(XOR)*/

```
#include<iostream.h>
void main( )
{
int a,b;
a=5;b=6;
int c= a^b;
cout<<"The value of c :="<<c<<endl;
}
```

OUTPUT :

The value of c : =3

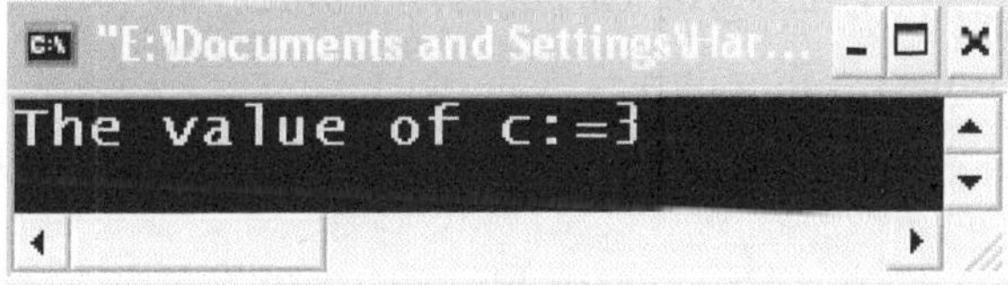

Figure 3.18. *Output screen of program.*

EXPLANATION : Binary values of **a =5 is 0101 and b = 6 is 0110**

XOR of these two values is performed as follows :

0 1 0 1

0 1 1 0

---

0 0 1 1 **(output in c will be 3 in decimal)**

If odd number of 1's are there output will be one otherwise output will be 0 using XOR operator.

1'S Complement (~)

The symbol (~) denotes one's complement. It is a unary operator and complements the bits in its operand *i.e.*, **1** is converted to **0** and **0** is converted to **1.**

/*PROG 3.19 DEMO OF BITWISE OPERATOR ~(1'S COMPLEMENT)*/

```
#include<iostream.h>
void main( )
{
int a,b;
a=5;
b=~a;
cout<<"The value of b :="<<b<<endl;
}
```

OUTPUT :

The value of b : = –6

But the actual answer will be

The value of b := 10

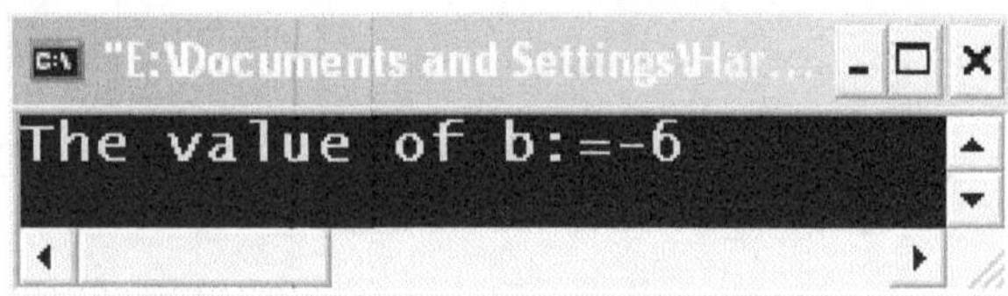

Figure 3.19. *Output screen of program.*

EXPLANATION : Binary value of a = 5 is 0101

In one's complement we invert the bit values *i.e.,* **0** is inverted into **1** and vice-versa. So the output will be :

b= 10 (in binary 1010)

If you get the output **–6** don't get puzzled. What I've said is correct also but the computer has given the answer in 2's complement form?

To reverse check that your answer **10(in decimal)** or **1010(in binary)** is correct read the following matter carefully:

Binary value of 6 → 0110

1's complement of 6 → 1001

2's complement of 6 → 1's complement of 6 +1

1001

0001(1+1= 0 1 and carry 1) 1010 (which is our answer)

Left Shift Operator (<<)

We have seen this operator earlier in almost all programs which is known as insertion or put to operator. The operator is used to shift the bits of its operand. It is written as **x<<num**; which means shifting the bits of **x** towards left by **num** number of times. A new zero is entered in the least significant Bit (LSB) position. (See the programs given below)

/*PROG 3.20 DEMO OF BITWISE OPERATOR <<(LEFT SHIFT) VER 1*/

```
#include<iostream.h>
void main( )
{
int a,b;
a=2;
b=a<<1;
cout<<"The value of b :="<<b<<endl;
}
```

OUTPUT :

```
The value of b : = 4
```

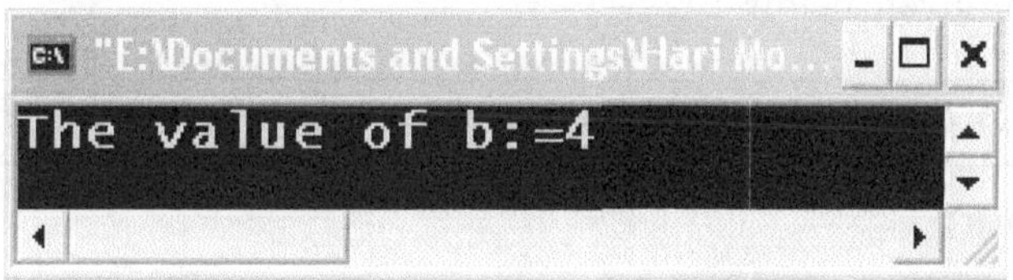

Figure 3.20. *Output screen of program.*

EXPLANATION : a<<1 means shifting the contents of '**a**' towards left by **1** position. If we represent the number **2** in binary as :

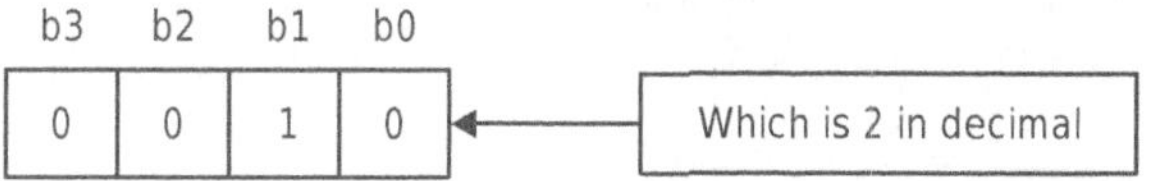

Where **b0** is the first bit from left which is called **Least Significant Bit (LSB)** and **b3** is called **Most Significant Bit (MSB).** Shifting left by **1Bit** position results in **b3** losing its value and taking from b2, b2 getting from **b1** and **b1** form **b0,** a new zero is inserted at **b0.** So the resultant bit pattern will be:

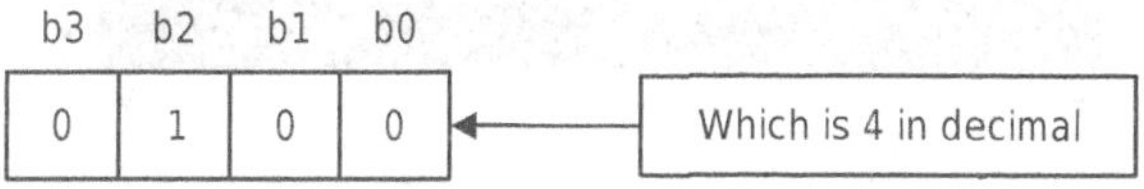

In case you write : a<<2 means shifting the contents of **a** twice towards left.

Original value in **a = 0010**

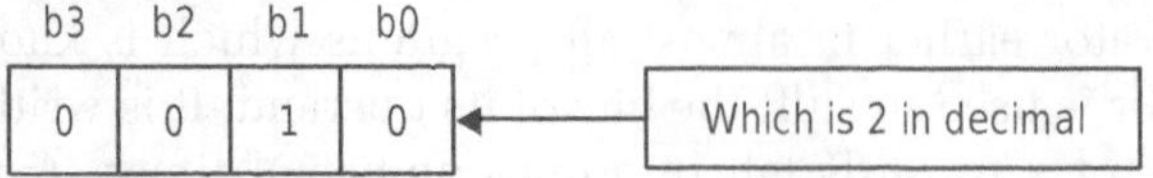

Shifting one

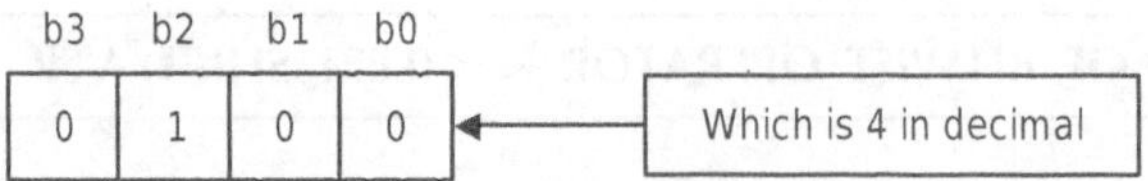

Shifting the value obtained in first step

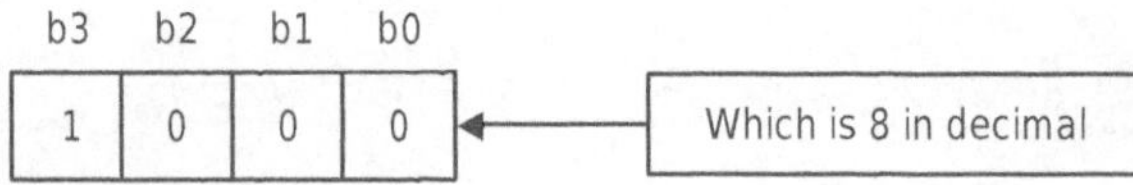

Note : Shifting the bits left once multiplies the number by 2.

Right Shift Operator (>>)

The operator is used to shift the bits of its operand. It is written as **x>> num;** which means shifting the bits of **x** towards right by **num** number of times. A new zero is entered in the **Most significant Bit (MSB)** position.

See the program given below :

/*PROG 3.21 DEMO OF BITWISE OPERATOR >>(RIGHT SHIFT)VER 1*/

```
#include<iostream.h>
void main( )
{
int a=8,b;
b=a>>1;
cout<<"The value of b :="<<b<<endl;
}
```

OUTPUT :

The value of b : = 4

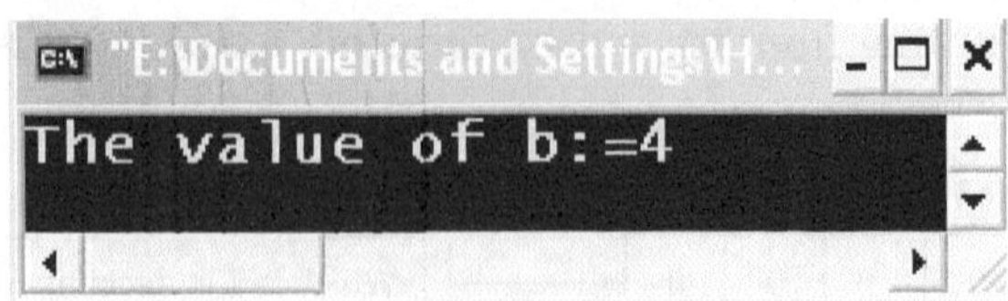

Figure 3.21. *Output screen of program.*

EXPLANATION : a>>**1** means shifting the contents of '**a**' towards right by **1** bit position. If we represent the number **8** in binary as :

b3	b2	b1	b0
1	0	0	0

Shifting right by **1 bit** position results in **b0** losing its value and taking from **b1, b1** getting from **b2** and **b2** from **b1**, new zero is inserted in **b3.** So the resultant bit pattern will be :

b3	b2	b1	b0
0	1	0	0

In case you write a>>2, it means shifting the contents of **'a'** twice toward right

Original value in **a=1000**

b3	b2	b1	b0
1	0	0	0

After shifting once

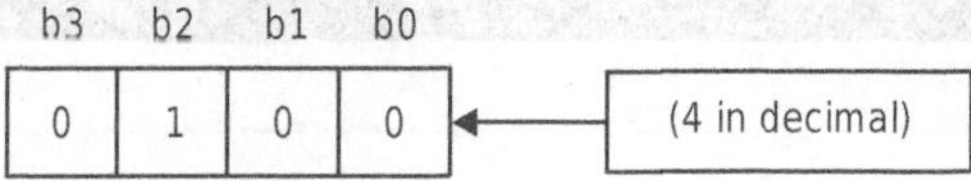

Shifting the value obtained in first step.

b3	b2	b1	b0
0	0	1	0

Which is 2 in decimal and is the final output.

Note : Shifting the bits right once divides the number by 2.

size of Operator

This operator is used to find size in bytes a particular variable of a particular type or a constant takes up in memory. This is the only operator which also works as a function.

/*PROG 3.22 DEMO OF SIZEOF OPERATOR VER 1*/

```
#include<iostream.h>
void main( )
{
short int a;
int b;
float c;
double e;
cout<<"Size of short int variable a :="<<sizeof(a)<<endl;
cout<<"size of int variable       b :="<<sizeof(b)<<endl;
cout<<"Size of float variable     c :="<<sizeof(c)<<endl;
```

```
cout<<"Size of double variable e :="<<sizeof(e)<<endl;
cout<<endl;
}
```

OUTPUT :

```
Size of short int variable a : =2
size of int variable       b : =4
Size of float variable     c : =4
Size of double variable    e : =8
```

```
Size of short int variable a:=2
size of int variable       b:=4
Size of float variable     c:=4
Size of double variable    e:=8
```

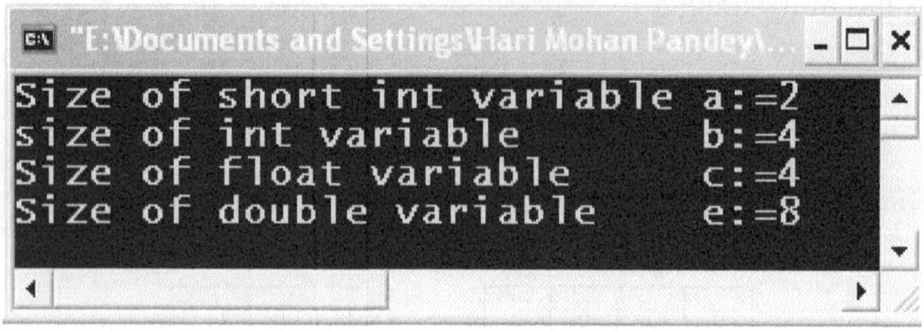

Figure 3.22. *Output screen of program.*

EXPLANATION : The program gives the amount of memory in bytes taken by variables of different types. Size of int variable in Turbo C/C++ is 2 bytes where as in Windows it is of 4 bytes.

/*PROG 3.23 DEMO OF SIZEOF OPERATOR VER 2*/

```
#include<iostream.h>
void main( )
{
cout<<"Size of char constants    : = "<<sizeof('A')<<endl;
cout<<"Size of int variable      : = "<<sizeof(14)<<endl;
cout<<"Size of float variable    : = "<<sizeof(5.6F)<<endl;
cout<<"Size of double variable   : = "<<sizeof(56.78)<<endl;
cout<<endl;
}
```

OUTPUT :

```
Size of char constants  : = 1
Size of int variable    : = 4
Size of float variable  : = 4
Size of double variable : = 8
```

```
Size of char constants  := 1
Size of int variable    := 4
Size of float variable  := 4
Size of double variable:= 8
```

Figure 3.23. *Output screen of program.*

EXPLANATION : Instead of writing variables we have used constants here. The result differs in case of `float` constant. *A character constant is treated as integer and a float constant is treated as double so the output.* If you want a float constant to be treated as float constant not double suffix f or F after `float` constant `sizeof` is called operator because we can write `sizeof` x where x is any variable of any type, whereas we cannot write `sizeof int` or `sizeof float` etc. this results in compilation error. Try your self and see the error.

The Comma (,) Operator

This is most important operator in C yet overlooked by most of the programmers. But understanding how this operator works is must in C. The operator works from left to right and in expressions separated by commas rightmost expression becomes the operand for this operator.

See the example given below :

/*PROG 3.24 DEMO OF COMMA OPERATOR VER 1*/

```
#include<iostream.h>
void main( )
{
int a,b,c,x;
a=5;
b=3;
c=4;
x=2;
x=(a,b,c);
cout<<"The value of x :="<<x<<endl;
}
```

OUTPUT :

```
The value of x : = 4
```

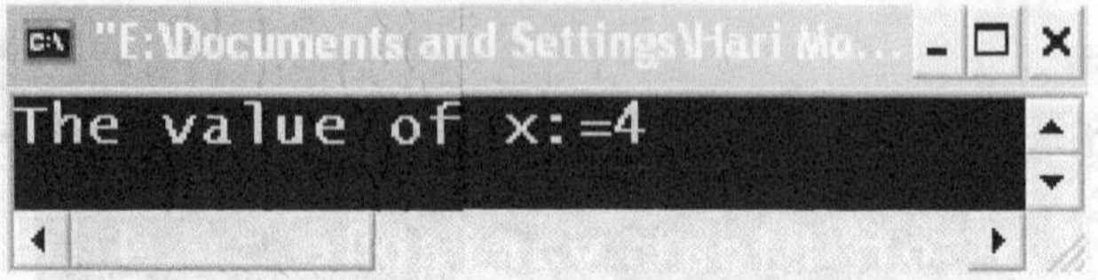

Figure 3.24. *Output screen of program.*

EXPLANATION : The associativity (see next section) of comma operator is from left to right and the rightmost value is given to **x** *i.e.,* value of **c** in the above program.

/*PROG 3.25 DEMO OF COMMA OPERATOR VER 2*/

```
#include<iostream.h>
void main( )
{
int a=2,b=3,c=4,x=2;
x=(c--,c++,++a);
cout<<"The value of x :="<<x<<"\nThe value of c :="
 <<c<<endl;
cout<<endl;
}
```

OUTPUT :

The value of x : = 3

The value of c : = 4

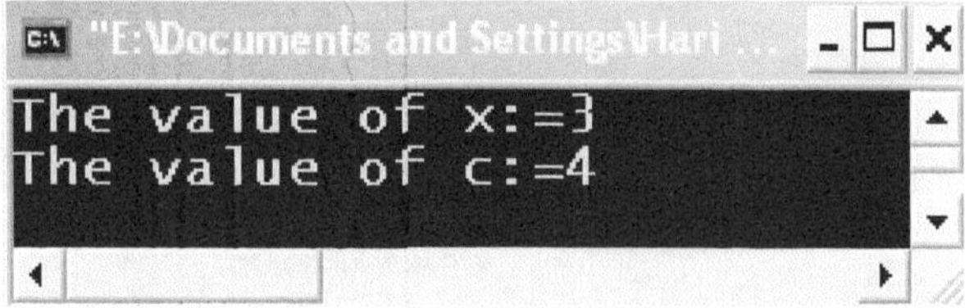

Figure 3.25. *Output screen of program.*

EXPLANATION : As stated earlier comma operators works from left to right. So value of **c** becomes **3** after **c--**, after **c++** it becomes **4** again. Value of '**a**' becomes **3** due to **++a** and this value is assigned to **x**, so the output.

3.3 DECLARING CONSTANTS

A constant is a value which cannot be changed. For example, value of **π (pi) is 22/7 or 3.14** which is a constant. To use constants in our programs C defines mainly three ways of declaring constants. We discuss each of them one by one.

1. Use of #define Directive

#define preprocessor directive can be used to declare a constant. It's general syntax is given as :

```
#define constant_name value
```

There must be at least a single space between `#define` and `constant_name`. For example : `#define PI` **3.14** which declares a constant (actually it is a macro constant) named **PI** with value **3.14.** There should be no assignment operator (=) between **PI** and **3.14.** Each macro constant must be declared on separate line. Macro constants are also known as *symbolic constant as we use string symbols to define constants.*

/*PROG 3.26 DEMO OF CONSTANT #DEFINE*/

```
#define PI 3.14
#define H "hello"
#define DMC "Demo of macro constant"
#include<iostream.h>
 void main( )
 {
 cout<<H<<endl;
 cout<<DMC<<endl;
 cout<<"The value of PI"<<PI<<endl;
 }
```

OUTPUT :

```
hello
Demo of macro constant
The value of PI3.14
```

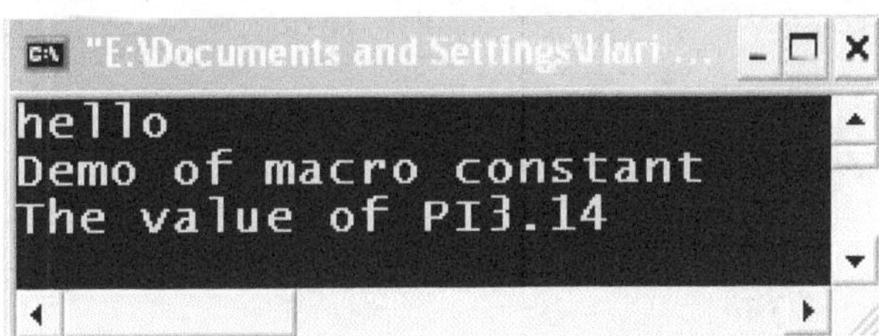

Figure 3.26. *Output screen of program.*

EXPLANATION : We have used three symbolic constants in the program named **PI, H and DMC.** First one (PI) is a float constant and other two are string constants. Before compilation they are processed by a special program called preprocessor which replaces all the occurrences of macro constant by their value. Each macro constant is return in upper case, it is not necessary but to distinguish macro name from variables we declare macro in upper-case and variables in lower-case.

In the above program if we write PI = **PI +1 or PI = 343** *i.e.*, try to change the value of **PI** an error is flashed which states that we cannot change the constant value.

2. Use of Const Keyword to Define Constant

The second way of declaring constant is to use ***const*** keyword. Its syntax is given as follows :

```
const data_type var_name#value;
```

Example :

```
const int x  =  100;
  1    2  3     4
```

1. const ? KEYWORD
2. int ? data type
3. x ? variable
4. 100 ? value

That is **x** as a constant and assign a value **100** to it. Later in the program we cannot change the value of **x.**

/*PROG 3.27 DEMO OF CONST KEYWORD*/

```
#include<iostream.h>
void main( )
{
const int x=100;
const float PI=3.14;
const char*s="constant";
const char c='c';
cout<<"Int constant     X := "<<x<<endl;
cout<<"Float constant   PI := "<<PI<<endl;
cout<<"String constant  s := "<<s<<endl;
cout<<"char constant    C := "<<c<<endl;
}
```

OUTPUT :

```
Int constant     X : = 100
Float constant  PI : = 3.14
String constant s : = constant
char constant   C : = c
```

```
Int constant      X:= 100
Float constant PI:= 3.14
String constant s:= constant
char constant     C:= c
```

Figure 3.27. *Output screen of program.*

EXPLANATION : For string constant we have use **char** pointer variable. Rest is self explanatory.

3. Use of enum to Declare Constant

We understand the use of **enum** with the help of an example :

```
enum my_cons
{
    MIN;
    MID;
    MAX;
};
```

The above declaration creates new data type **my_cons** with the help of **enum** keyword. The declaration statements within { } creates three **int type** constants, **MIN, MID and MAX** which are known as **enumeration constants.** By default the value of **MIN** is **0, MID is 1 and MAX is 2.** As they are constant they cannot be changed inside the program. They can only be of type **int** and **char.** No other type is allowed. Take one more example.

```
enum colors
{
    RED;
    GREEN=25;
    BLUE;
};
```

In this example value of **RED** will be **0, GREEN** will have **25** and **BLUE** will have value **26.** The keyword **enum** is used to create enumeration constants, also known as symbolic constants. After the creation of enumeration constants enumeration type variable can be created for example :

```
enum colors coll, col2;
```

These enumeration variable **col1** and **col2** can be assigned enumeration constants created earlier like :

```
coll = RED; col 2 = BLUE;
```

Although the variables **col 1** and **col 2** can be assigned any integer value but usually they are assigned enumeration constants. That is the following is also valid **col 1=34; col2= 45;**

We give some programming examples.

/*PROG 3.28 DEMO OF ENUMERATION CONSTANTS VER 1*/

```
#include<iostream.h>
void main( )
{
enum colors
{
red, green,blue
};
enum OS
{
dos=1,linux,windows,unix
};
cout<<"red="<<red<<"\tgreen="<<green<<"\tblue="
<<blue<<endl;
cout<<"dos="<<dos<<"\tlinux="<<linux<<"\twindos="
<<windows<<"\tunix="<<unix<<endl;
}
```

OUTPUT :

```
red=0 green=1 blue=2
dos=1 linux=2 windos=3 unix=4
```

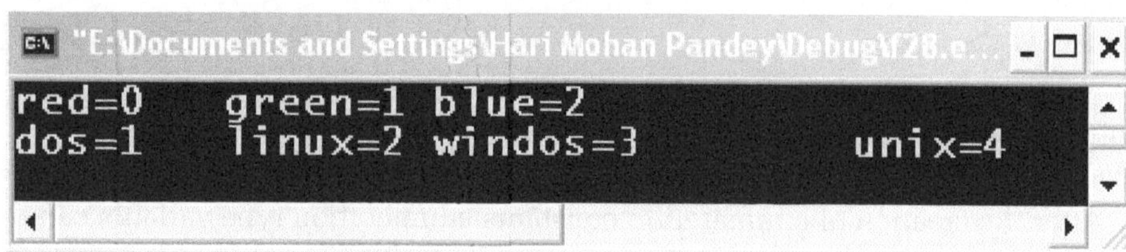

Figure 3.28. *Output screen of program.*

EXPLANATION : The program is self-explanatory. The enumeration constants are basically used in **switch-case** construct.

Note : The following points about enumerators :

- The values of enumerators need not be distinct in the same enumeration type.
- The names of enumerators in different enumeration types must be distinct.
- The names of the enumerators must be different from other normal variables.
- Enumerators are treated only as integer constants by the compiler.

3.4 TYPE CONVERSION

Sometimes in expression we require to convert the data type of a variable or a constant say from `float to int` or `int to float` etc. Two types of conversions C supports :

1. **Implicit type conversion.**
2. **Explicit type conversion.**

1. Implicit Type Conversion

In this type of conversion the compiler internally converts the type depending upon expression without letting user to know. For example, if you write

```
int num = 34.56;
```

Then **num** will be assigned the value **34** not **34.56** is treated as **double** and internal conversion occurs from **double** to **float** and from **float** to **int** and **34** is assigned to the variable **num**.

As another example consider the following code snippet.

```
int a = 10;
float b = 2.5, c;
c = a + b;
```

In the expression ***c* = *a* + *b***, type of ***'a'*** and ***'b'*** is not same. According to size **float** is greater than int so variable ***'a'*** in internally converted into **float** and then addition is performed so the result obtained will also be in **float**.

The conversion is always done from lower data type to higher data type. For example, a **char** can be converted **to** `int, long int, float, double` and `long double`. Similarly, an int can be converted into `float`, `long int` and `long double` and so on.

2. Explicit Type Conversions

In this type of conversion (also known as type **casting**) we explicitly convert the variable's or constant's data type from one to another. For example,

```
int a = 10;
float x = a/3;
```

In the above expression ***x* = *a*/3** both ***x* and 3** are type `int` so output will be 3.000000 and not **3.333333** even though type of ***x*** is `float.` To get the required result we type cast a as float by writing

```
x = (float) a/3;
```

Also we could have written **a/3.0** to get the same result.

3.5 DECISION MAKING : AN INTRODUCTION

Decision making statements are needed to alter the sequence of the statements in the program depending upon certain circumstances. In the absence of decision making statements a program executes in the **serial fashion** statement basis. We have seen examples in the programs given in earlier chapters. In this chapter, we are going to write statements which control the flow of execution on the basis of some decision. Decision can be made on the basis of success or failure of some logical condition. They allow us to control the flow of our program. These conditions can be placed in the program using decision making statements. C language supports the following decision making control statements :

(*a*) The if statement

(*b*) The if-else statement

(*c*) The if-else-if ladder statement

(*d*) The switch –case statement.

All these decision making statements checks the given condition and then executes its **sub block** if the condition happens to be true. On falsity of condition the block is skipped. (**A block is a set of statements enclosed within the opening and closing brace {and}**). All control statement uses a combination of relational and logical operators to form conditions as per the requirement of the programmer.

1. The if Statement

The general syntax of **if** statement is as :

```
if (condition)
{
        Statements;
        Statements;
        Statements;
        ..............;
}
```

The **if** statement is used to execute/skip a block of statements on the basis of truth or falsity of a condition. The condition to be checked is put inside the parenthesis which is preceded by keyword **if.**

/*PROG 3.29 DEMO OF IF STATEMENT */

```
#include<iostream.h>
void main( )
{
int x;
cout<<"Enter the value of x\n";
cin>>x;
if(x>=1000)
{
cout<<"x is greater than or equal to 1000"<<endl;
cout<<"You think high"<<endl;
}
cout<<"X is less than 1000";
}
```

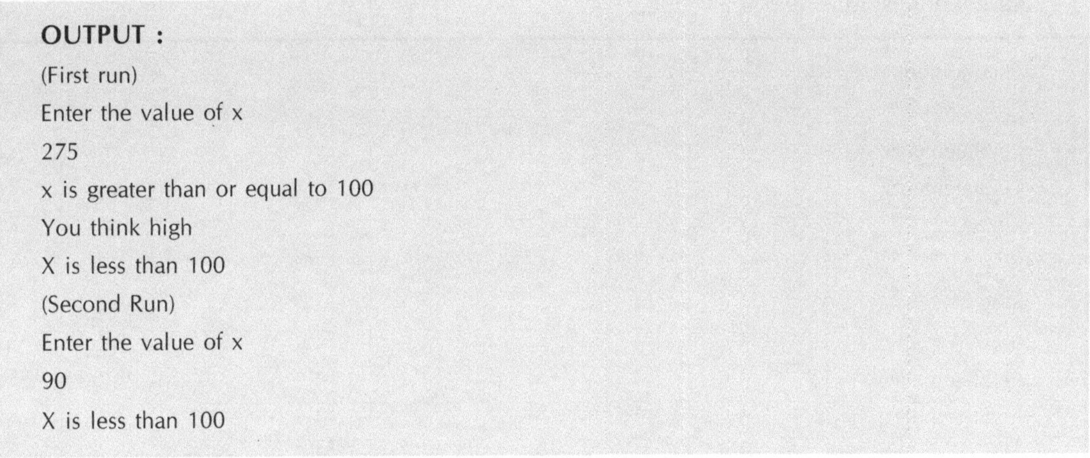

OUTPUT :

(First run)

Enter the value of x

275

x is greater than or equal to 100

You think high

X is less than 100

(Second Run)

Enter the value of x

90

X is less than 100

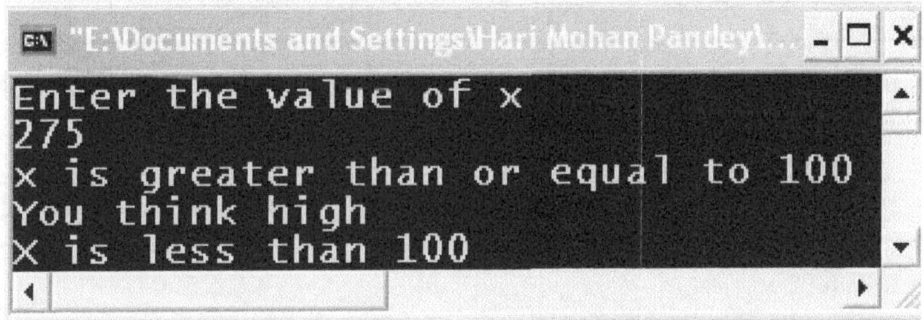

Figure 3.29. *Output screen of first run of program.*

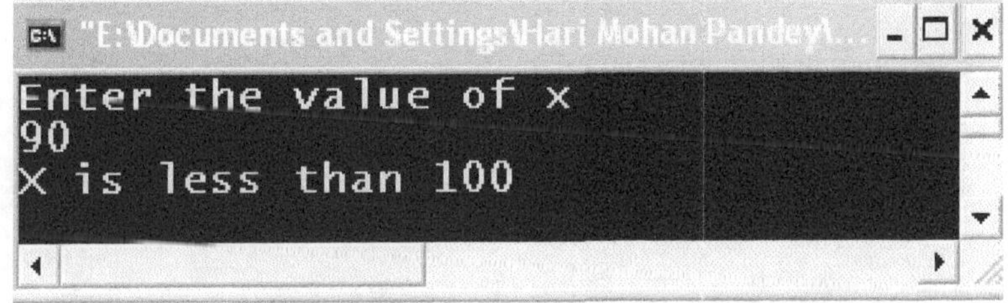

Figure 3.30. *Output screen of second run of program.*

EXPLANATION : You can put any number of statements inside curly braces after `if` and all will be dependent on `if` condition.

Note : 1. if (x) is equivalent to if(x!=0)

2. if (!x) is equivalent to if(x==0)

2. The if-else Statement

In all the above program we didn't write the other side of `if` condition *i.e.*, we didn't take the action when the condition fails. The `if-else` construct allows us to do this.

Its general syntax is :

```
if(condition)
{
   Statements;
   Statements;
   ............;
}
else
{
   Statements;
   Statements;
   ............;
}
```

If the condition within `if` true all the statements within the block following `if` are executed `else` they are skipped and `else` part get executed.

/*PROG 3.30 CHECKING THE NUMBER IS EVEN OR ODD USING IF–ELSE STATEMENT*/

```
#include<iostream.h>
void main( )
{
   int a;
   cout<<"Enter any integer number \n ";
   cin>>a;
   if(a%2==0)
      cout<<"number is even\n";
   else
      cout<<"number is odd\n";
}
```

OUTPUT :

```
(First run)
Enter any integer number
 40
number is even
(Second Run)
Enter any integer number
 17
number is odd
```

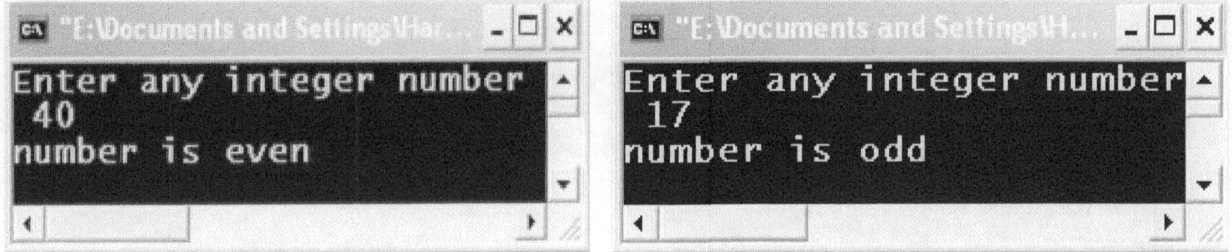

Figure 3.31. *Output screen of first and second run of program.*

EXPLANATION : The priority of **%** is higher than **==**, so **a%2** is compared to **0.** If this is true then the number is even else number is not even. The `else` part executes only when `if` part is false and vice-versa. In the program both `if` and `else` part contains just one statement to be dependent upon them so braces are not needed, however if you put there won't be any harm. The condition could be written in the following manner also :

```
if(num%2!=0)
    printf("number is odd\n");
else
    printf("number is evev\n");
```

/*PROG 3.31 TO CALCULATE GROSS SALARY OF THE PERSON.GIVEN BASIC SALARY(BS) AS INPUT.IF BS IS >5000 DA=555N OF BS AND HRA=15% BS ELSE DA=45% OF BS AND HRA=10% OF BS*/

```
#include<iostream.h>
 void main( )
 {
    float bs,gs,hra,da;
    cout<<"Enter your basic salary"<<endl;
    cin>>bs;
    if(bs<=5000)
    {
      da=(bs*45)/100;
      hra=(bs*10)/100;
    }
      else
      {
         da=(bs*55)/100;
         hra=(bs*15)/100;
      }
      gs=bs+da+hra;
      cout<<"Basic salary is="<<bs<<endl;
      cout<<"HRA is="<<hra<<endl;
```

```
    cout<<"DA is="<<da<<endl;
    cout<<"Gross salary is="<<gs<<endl;
}
```

OUTPUT :

```
Enter your basic salary
8825
Basic salary is=8825
HRA is=1323.75
DA is=4853.75
Gross salary is=15002.5
```

```
"E:\Documents and Settings\Hari Mo...
Enter your basic salary
8825
Basic salary is=8825
HRA is=1323.75
DA is=4853.75
Gross salary is=15002.5
```

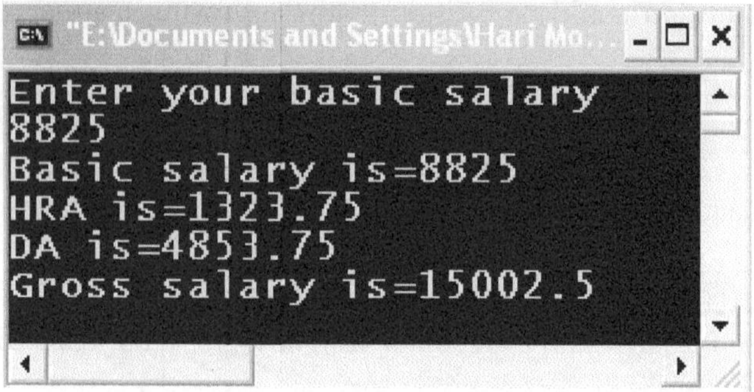

Figure 3.32. *Output screen of program.*

EXPLANATION : We input the basic salary in **bs**. Through **if** condition we check basic salary **bs** against **5000**. Depending upon whether `if` condition is true or false **hra** and **da** are calculated as per the condition specified in the problem.

3. Nesting of if–else's

Nesting of `if-else` means one `if-else` or simple `if` as the part of another `if-else` or simple `if` statement. There may be various syntaxes of nesting of `if-else` we present few of them :

Syntax-1

```
if(condition)
{
    If(condition)
    {
        Statements;
        Statements;
        Statements;
        ............... .
    }
```

```
    else
    {
        Statements;
        Statements;
        Statements;
    }
}
```

In the above case there is no **else** part of the first **if.**

Syntax-2

```
if(condition)
{
    if(condition)
    {
        Statements;
        Statements;
        Statements;
    }
    else
    {
        Statements;
        Statements;
        Statements;
    }
}
else
{
    Statements;
    Statements;
    Statements;
}
```

Syntax-3

```
if(condition)
{
    if(condition)
```

```
        {
            Statements;
            Statements;
            Statements;
        }
        else
        {
            Statements;
            Statements;
            Statements;
        }
}
else
{
        if(condition)
        {
            Statements;
            Statements;
            Statements;
        }

        else
        {
            Statements;
            Statements;
            Statements;
        }
}
```

/* PROG 3.32 TO CHECK WHETHER A YEAR IS LEAP YEAR OR NOT VER 1*/

```
#include<iostream.h>
    void main( )
    {
        int year;
        cout<<"Enter any year\n";
        cin>>year;
        if(year % 100==0)
```

```
        {
            if(year%400==0)
                cout<<"The given year is leap year\n";
        else
                cout<<"The given year is not a leap year\n";
    }
    else
    {
        if(year %4==0)
            cout<<"The given year is leap year\n";
        else
            cout<<"The given year is not a leap year\n";
    }
}
```

OUTPUT :

(First Run)

Enter any year

2000

The given year is leap year

(Second run)

Enter any year

2007

The given year is not a leap year

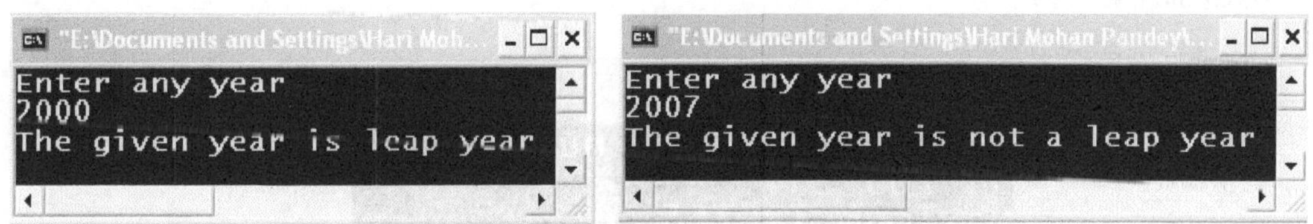

Figure 3.33. *Output screen of first and second run of program.*

EXPLANATION : **A year is leap year if it is completely divisible by 100 and 400 or not divisible by 100 but divisible by 4.** Initially if the **year %100** is zero, the inner `if` checks if the **year %400** is zero. If this is so the year is leap else the year is not leap. If the outer `if` fails its corresponding `else` part executes in which we check **year % 4 ==0,** If this is true the year is leap else year is not leap.

/*PROG 3.33 MAXIMUM OF THREE NUMBERS*/

```
#include<iostream.h>
    void main( )
    {
```

```
        int x,y,z;
        cout<<"Enter the three numbers\n";
        cin>>x>>y>>z;
        if((x==y) &&(y==z))
            cout<<"All three are equal\n";
            if(x>y)
            {
                if(x>z)
            cout<<"Minimum is="<<x<<endl;
                else
            cout<<"Maximum is="<<z<<endl;
            }
    else
    {
        if(y>z)
            cout<<"Maximum is="<<y<<endl;
        else
            cout<<"Maximum is="<<z<<endl;
    }
}
```

OUTPUT :

```
Enter the three numbers
34 765 234
Maximum is=765
```

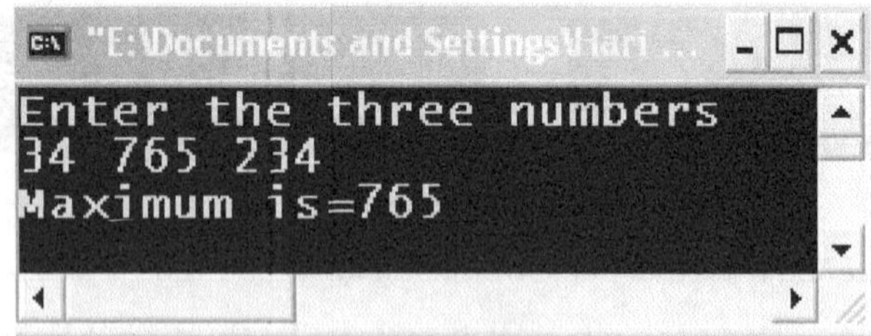

Figure 3.34. *Output screen of program.*

EXPLANATION : If all the numbers are not equal we check **ifa>b**, if this is true it means **a** is greater than **b**, we then check **a>c** if this so then **a** is the greatest else **c** is greatest. If **a>b** is false initially it means **b** is greater than **a b,** we then check whether **b>c,** if this is so then **b** is greatest else **c** is greatest.

4. else-if Ladder

The general syntax of **else-if ladder** is given below :

```
if (condition)
    Statements;
```

```
else if(conditon)
    Statements;
        else if(condition)
            Statements;
            ..................;
            ..................;
```

If the first `if` condition is satisfied, then all its related statements are executed and all other `else-if's` are skipped. The control reaches to first `else-if` only if the first `if` fails. Same for second, third and other `else-if's` depending upon what your program required. **That is out of this else-if ladder only one if condition will be satisfied.**

/*PROG 3.34 TO ARRANGE THREE NUMBERS IN ASCENDING ORDER*/

```
#include<iostream.h>
void main( )
{
    int a,b,c,min,max,mid;
    cout<<"Enter the three number"<<endl;
    cin>>a>>b>>c;
    if(a>b && a>c)
        max=a;
        else if(b>a && b>c)
            max=b;
            else if(c>a && c>b)
                max=c;
    if(a<b && a<c)
        min=a;
        else if(b<a && b<c)
            min=b;
        else if(c<a && c<b)
            min=c;
    mid=(a+b+c)-(min+max);
        cout<<"Number in ascending order"<<min
            <<"\t"<<mid<<"\t"<<max<<endl;
}
```

OUTPUT :

```
Enter the three number
34 57 90
Number in ascending order 34 57 90
```

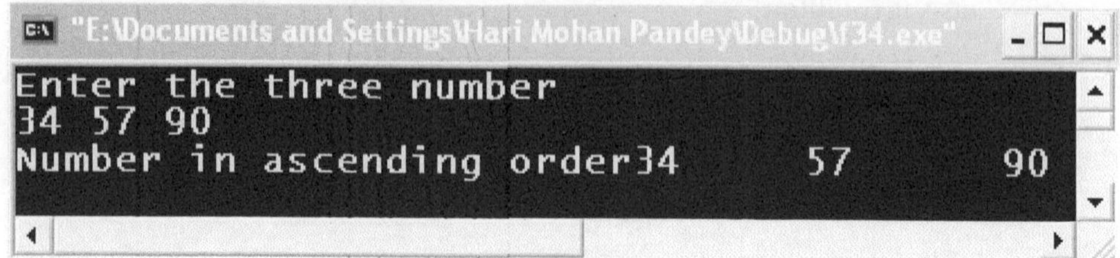

Figure 3.35. *Output screen of program.*

EXPLANATION : In the variable **max** we have stored the maximum among three and in the variable **min** we have stored the minimum among three. The **mid** is calculated by subtracting (**min + max**) from the sum of **a, b, c** *i.e.,* **(a + b + c).**

5. switch-case Statement

Switch-case statement can be used to replace **else-if ladder** construct. Its general syntax is as follows :

```
switch(expression)
{
        case choice1 :
                        statements;
                        break;
        case choice2 :
                        statements;
                        break;
        case choice3 :
                        statements;
                        break;
                        ..............................;
                        ..............................;
        default :
}
```

The **expression** may be any `integer` or `char` type which yield only `char` or `integer` as result. **Choice 1, choice 2, and choice n** are the possible values which we are going to test with the expression. In case none of the values from **choice 1** to **choice n** matches with the values of **expression** the **default** case is executed.

Some Points For switch-case Statements

- The switch statement is a multi-way branch statement.
- If there is a possibility to make a choice from a number of options, this structured selection is useful.

- The switch statement evaluates expression and then looks for its value among the case constant.
- If the value matches with case constant, this particular case statement is executed. If not default is executed.
- Switch, case and default are reversed keywords.
- The break statement used in `switch()` passed control outside the `switch()` block. By mistake if no break statements are given all the cases following it are executed.

/*PROG 3.35 DEMO OF SWITCH-CASE VER 1*/

```
#include<iostream.h>
void main( )
{
int num;
cout<<"Enter 0,1,or 2\n";
cin>>num;
switch(num)
{
case 0 :
        cout<<"U entered zero\n";
        break;
case 1 :
        cout<<"U enetered one\n";
        break;
case 2 :
        cout<<" U entered two\n";
        break;
default :
        cout<<"other than 0,1,or 2\n";
}
}
```

OUTPUT :

```
Enter 0,1,or 2
1
U entered one
```

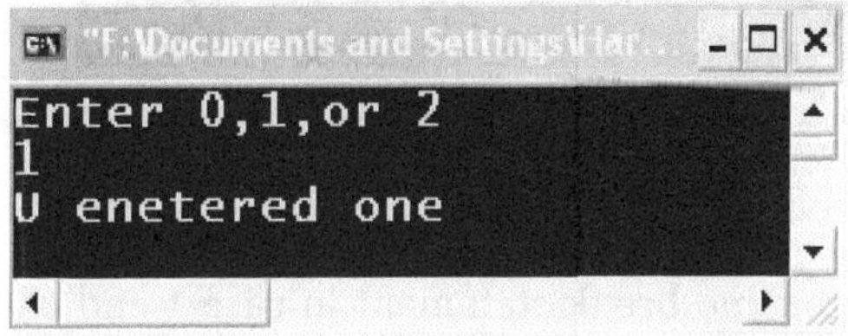

Figure 3.36. *Output screen of program.*

EXPLANATION : The condition to be checked is placed inside `switch` enclosed in parenthesis. The different values against which condition is checked is put using `case` statement. In the first `case` value is checked against `0`. This is similar to writing `if(num = = 0).` The colon : after `case` gets executed. Similarly, if the value of `num` is `zero` then first case matches and all the statement under that `case` gets executed. Similarly, if the value of `num` is `1` second `case` gets executed and same for the rest of the `case` statements. A `break` statement is needed to ignore the rest of the `case` statements and come out from `switch` block in case a match is found. If none of the `case` matches then `default` gets executed. Writing `default` is optional.

/*PROG 3.36 DEMO OF SWITCH-CASE VER 2*/

```
#include<iostream.h>
    void main( )
    {
        int num;
        cout<<"Enter 0,1 or 2\n";
        cin>>num;
        switch(num)
        {
            case 0 : cout<<"U entered zero\n";
                    break;
            case 1 : cout<<"U entered one \n";
            case 2 : cout<<"U eneter two\n";
                    break;
            default :cout<<"Other than 0,1,or2\n";
    }
}
```

OUTPUT :

```
Enter 0,1 or 2
2
U eneter two
```

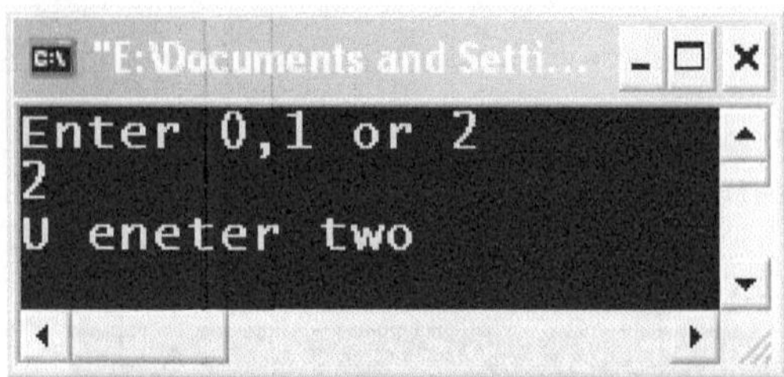

Figure 3.37. *Output screen of program.*

EXPLANATION : There is no **break** statement in **case 1** and **case 2** are assumed to be true so the output. In fact due to the absence of **break** statement in the second **case** rest of the statements are considered part of the second **case** till a **break** is not found. **break** in **case 2**

causes control to come out from `switch`. If break were not in **case 2,** also then **default** would got executed too.

/*PROG 3.37 TO CHECK GIVEN CHARACTER IS VOWEL OR NOT USING SWITCH CASE VER 3*/

```
#include <iostream.h>
#include <ctype.h>
   void main( )
   {
   char ch;
   cout<<"Enter any character \n";
   cin>>ch;
   ch=tolower(ch);
   switch(ch)
   {
       default :
               cout<<"Not a vowel\n";
               break;
       case  'a' :
       case  'e' :
       case  'i' :
       case  'o' :
       case  'u' :
                  cout<<"It's a vowel\n";
   }
}
```

OUTPUT :

```
Enter any character
e
It's a vowel
```

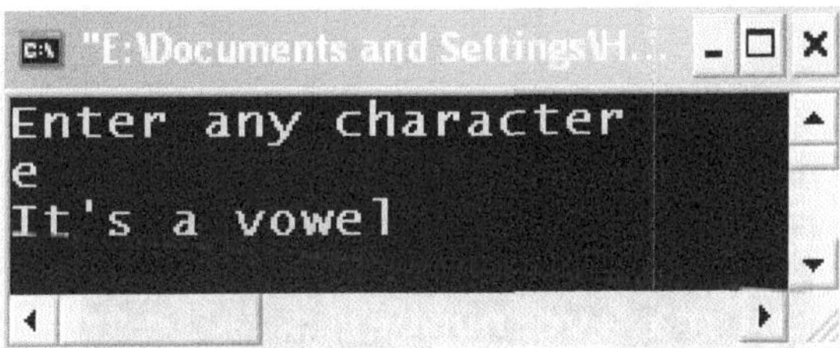

Figure 3.38. *Output screen of program.*

EXPLANATION : We have used inbuilt function tolower to convert a character from uppercase to lowercase. This is than stored back in `ch`. Header file `ctype.h` need to be included. Now whether you input vowel in upper case or lower case it is passed to switch block in lower case which is checked ch for any of the five vowels.

3.6 UNCONDITIONAL BRANCHING USING GOTO

The goto statement is used to transfer control of program from one point to other. In fact it make program control to jump to the statement specified by a lable. This type of **unconditional transfer of control using goto is called branching.** The label must be in the same function in which **goto** is used. The general syntax for goto statement is as follows :

```
goto label;
```

We understand the use of **goto** using a program.

/*PROG 3.38 DEMO OF GOTO VER 1*/

```
#include<iostream.h>
#include<math.h>
void main( )
{
    int x;
    start :
        cout<<"Entera +ve number\n";
        cin>>x;
        if(x<0)
        goto start;
        cout<<"sqrt of number is"<<sqrt(x)<<endl;
}
```

OUTPUT :

```
Entera +ve number
-30
Entera +ve number
40
sqrt of number is 6.32456
```

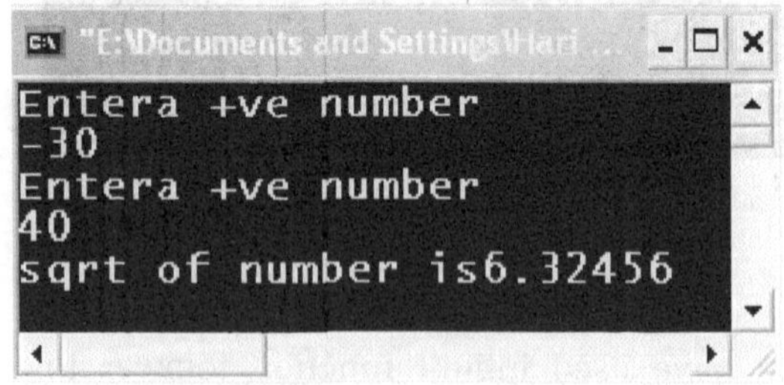

Figure 3.39. *Output screen of program.*

EXPLANATION : The **start** : is terminated as a label. The start is a label name which must be followed by a colon : Any valid identifier name can be taken as label name. When a –ve number is entered `if` condition returns true and control is transferred back to `start` using `goto start;` statement. In the program the jump is backward here the control is being transferred previous to the `goto start;` statement hence it is `backward jump`. If it were ahead of `goto start;` then it would be a `forward jump`.

/*PROG 3.39 LOOP CREATION USING GOTO STATEMENT*/

```
#include<iostream.h>
 void main( )
  {
   int n=0;
   cout<<"Loop starts\n";
   loop :
         n++;
         cout<<"n="<<n<<endl;
         if(n<5)
         goto loop;
         cout<<"Loop Ends\n";
  }
```

OUTPUT :

```
Loop starts
n=1
n=2
n=3
n=4
n=5
Loop Ends
```

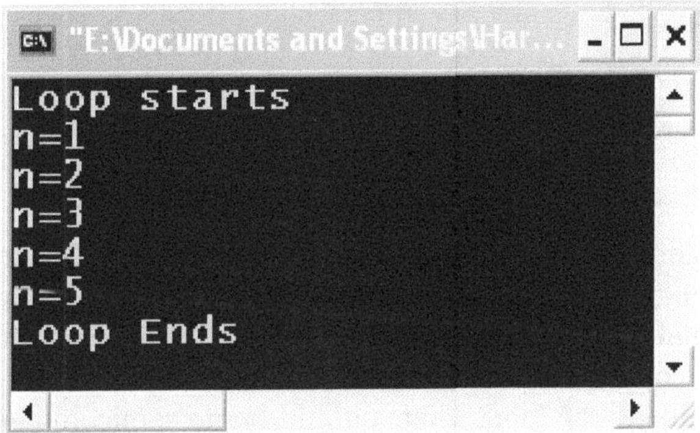

Figure 3.40. *Output screen of program.*

EXPLANATION : Initial value of **n** is **0**. It is incremented at label `loop` and then printed. The value of **n** is checked against **5** using **if.** If **n<5** then control is transferred back to `loop` label *i.e.*, same set of codes are repeated for a finite number of time (here number is 5). This is looping which we have achieved using `goto` and `if`.

3.7 INTRODUCTION TO LOOPING

Looping is a process in which set of statements are executed repeatedly for a finite or infinite number of times. C provides three ways to performs looping by providing three different types of loop. Looping can be called synonymously iteration of repetition. Loops are the most important part of almost all the programming language such as C, C++, java, VB, C#, Delphi etc.

In our practical life we see lots of examples where some repetitive tasks has to be performed like finding average marks of students of a class, finding maximum salary of group of employees, counting numbers etc.

A loop is a block of statements with which are executed again and again till a specific condition is satisfied. C provides three loops to perform repetitive action.

1. while
2. for
3. do-while

To work with any types of loop three things have to be performed :

- Loop control variable and its initialization.
- Condition for controlling the loop.
- Increment / decrement of control variable.

3.7.1 The While Loop

The syntax of the while loop is simple :

```
while (condition)
{
      Statements;
      Statements;
      .......................;
}
```

The statements inside { } is called body of the `while` loop. If no braces are there then only the first statement after `while` is constructed as the body of the `while` loop. All the statements within the body are repeated till the condition specified in the parenthesis in `while` is satisfied. As soon as condition becomes false the body is skipped and control is transferred to the next statement outside the loop. There should be no semicolon after the `while`. We will see what happens when you do so.

/*PROG 3.40 DEMO OF WHILE LOOP (PRINTING NUMBER 1 TO 10) VER 1*/

```
#include<iostream.h>
  void main( )
  {
     int t=1;
     while(t<=10)
     {
        cout<<"t="<<t<<endl;
        t++;
     }
  }
```

OUTPUT :

```
t = 1
t = 2
t = 3
t = 4
t = 5
t = 6
t = 7
t = 8
t = 9
t = 10
```

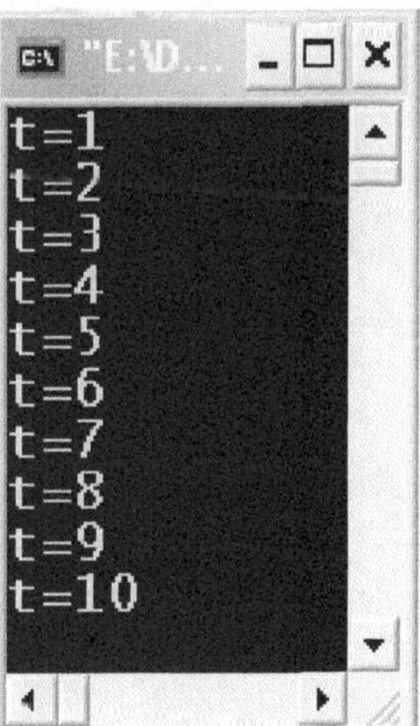

Figure 3.41. *Output screen of program.*

EXPLANATION : In the **while** loop we have stated the condition **t<=10.t** is called loop control variable. Initially value of **t is 1.** This value of **t** is compared with 10 which is true so control reaches into the while loop and printf statesmen within loop executes which prints the value of **t**. Then **t** is incremented by **1** *i.e.,* becomes **2**. Control reaches back to the condition of the while loop which is true. This process continues. When value of **t** becomes **11,** which causes condition in the while loop to becomes false and control comes out of loop. As there is no statement outside the loop so program terminates.

/*PROG 3.41 MAXIMUM OF N ELEMENTS */

```
#include<iostream.h>
  void main( )
  {
    int n,max,t=1,m;
    cout<<"Enter how many numbers\n";
    cin>>n;
    cout<<"Enter the number\n";
    cin>>m;
    max=m;
    while(t<=n-1)
    {
      cout<<"Enter the number\n";
      cin>>m;
      if(max<m)
      max=m;
      t++;
  }
  cout<<"Maximum element is"<<max<<endl;
}
```

OUTPUT :

```
Enter how many numbers
3
Enter the number
10
Enter the number
20
Enter the number
30
Maximum element is 30
```

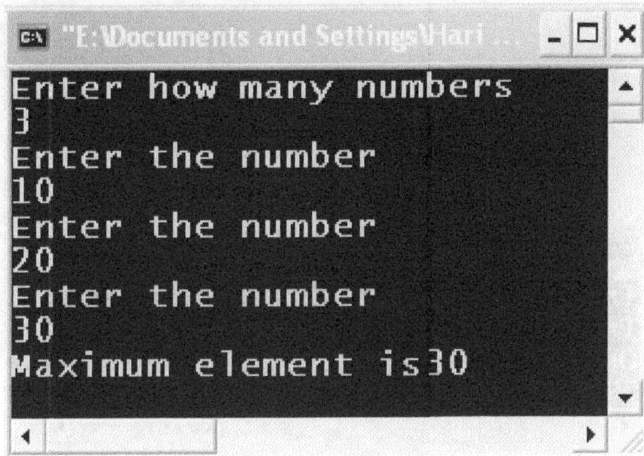

Figure 3.42. *Output screen of program.*

EXPLANATION : Initially numbers of elements are taken is **n**. The first number is taken outside the loop and assumed to be maximum; this number is stored in **max.** Then remaining numbers are taken inside the loop. On each iteration the number is compared with the **max**, if the max is less than number taken then number will be the maximum one. This is checked through if statement. In the end when control comes out from while loop max is displayed.

Break Statement

`Break` statement is used to come out early from loop without waiting for the condition to become false. We have seen one such usage of break in the `switch-case` statements. When the `break` statement is encountered in the `while` loop or any of the loops which will see later, the **control immediately transfers to first statement out of the loop** *i.e.,* **loop is exited prematurely. If there is nesting of loops the *break* will exit only from the current loop containing it.**

Let's write some programs which make use of **break** statement.

```
/*PROG 3.42 DEMO OF BREAK STATEMENT*/

#include<iostream.h>
  void main( )
  {
    int x=1;
    while(x<=5)
    {
    if(x==3)
    break;
    cout<<"Inside the loop x="<<x<<endl;
    x++;
  }
  cout<<"Outside the loopx="<<x<<endl;
}
```

OUTPUT :

Inside the loop x = 1

Inside the loop x = 2

Inside the loop x = 3

Figure 3.43. *Output screen of program.*

EXPLANATION : When **x is** 3 if condition becomes true, the body of the if statement is single break statement so all the statement in the loop following the break are skipped and control is transferred to the first statement after the loop which is printf which prints outside the loop x = 3.

/*PROG 3.43 TO CHECK WHETHER THE NUMBER IS PRIME OR NOT*/

```
#include<iostream.h>
  void main( )
  {
    int num,flag=0,c=2;
    cout<<"Enter the number\n";
    cin>>num;
    while(c<num/2)
    {
      if(num%c==0)
      {
        flag=1;
        break;
      }
      c++;
  }
  if(!flag)
    cout<<"Number is prime\n";
  else
    cout<<"Number is not prime\n";
}
```

OUTPUT :

Enter the number

17

Number is prime

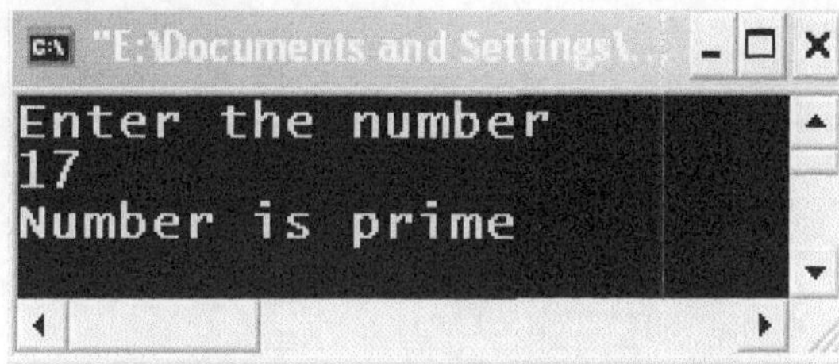

Figure 3.44. *Output screen of program.*

EXPLANATION : **A number is prime if it completely divisible by 1 and itself** *e.g.,* **1, 3, 5, 7, 11, 13, 17, 19, 23 etc.** To check whether a number is prime or not we start from a counter **c=2**(every number divides by 1) continues till **c<=num/2 since no number is completely divisible by a number which is more than half of that number.** For example, **12** is not divisible by **7, 8, 9, 10, 11** which are more than **6.** So we check if the number is divisible by any number**<=num/2** then it cannot not be prime we set **flag =1** and come out from the loop. The **flag** was initialized to **0** in the beginning so **if c%2==0** is true control sets **flag =1** which means number is not prime else **flag** remains zero which means control never transferred to **if** block *i.e.,* number is prime. So outside the loop we check this value of **flag** and prints accordingly.

The Continue Statement

The continue statement causes the remainder of the statements following the continue to be skipped and continue with the next iteration of the loop. So, we can use ***continue*** statement to bypass curtain number of statements in the loop on the basis of some condition given by ***if*** generally.

The syntax of continue statement is simply

```
continue;
```

Lets write a program to illustrate **continue** statement.

/*PROG 3.44 DEMO OF CONTINUE STATEMENT*/

```
#include<iostream.h>
void main( )
{
    int t=0;
    while(t<=10)
    {
        t++;
        if(t%2)
            continue;
        cout<<"t="<<t<<endl;
    }
}
```

OUTPUT :

```
t = 2
t = 4
t = 6
t = 8
t = 10
```

Figure 3.45. *Output screen of program.*

EXPLANATION : When **t** is an odd number `continue` in the body of `if` condition causes loop to continue with next iteration of loop skipping `printf` statement. If number is even the number is simply printed as `continue` itself is skipped.

3.7.2 The For Loop

This is the second loops which are going to examine in this section. The `for` loop is most frequently used by programmers just because of its simplicity. The syntax of `for` loop is given here :

```
for (initialization; condition; increment/decrement)
{
      Statements;
      Statements;
      ..............;
}
```

There are various other syntaxes of `for` **loop** which we will see in a short while.

/*PROG 3.45 DEMO OF FOR LOOP VER 1*/

```
#include<iostream.h>
  void main( )
  {
     int t;
     for(t=1;t<=5;t++)
     cout<<"t="<<t<<endl;
  }
```

OUTPUT :

```
t = 1
t = 2
t = 3
t = 4
t = 5
t = 6
t = 7
t = 8
t = 9
t = 10
```

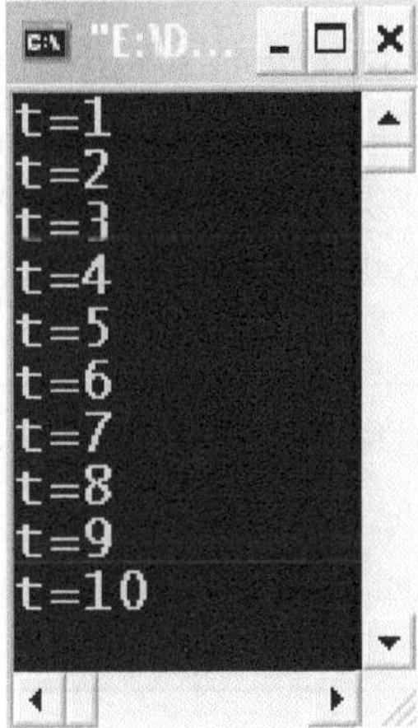

Figure 3.46. *Output screen of program.*

EXPLANATION : The first part of `for` loop **t =1** is the initialization *i.e.*, we are providing an initial value of **1** loop counter **t**. Next statement **t<=10** is the testing condition for which this loop runs if condition is true. The last part is increment of loop works by first making **t = 1** and then checking the condition whether **t<=10** if so it executes the next statement following `for` *i.e.*, `printf`. Recall as there is no braces after `for` loop only first statement is considered the body of the `for` loop. It hen goes to the increment the value of **t**, checks the test condition and executes the `printf`. This continues till the condition **t<=10** is true. As soon as the condition becomes false in this case **t =11** control comes out from loop and program terminates.

There are various syntaxes of writing `for` loop see the next few programs.

```
/*PROG 3.46 FOR LOOP SYNTAX-1 VER 1*/

#include<iostream.h>
void main( )
{
    int t;
```

```
        t = 10;
        for(;t<=100;t+=10)
        cout<<" "<<t;
    }
```

OUTPUT :

10 20 30 40 50 60 70 80 90 100

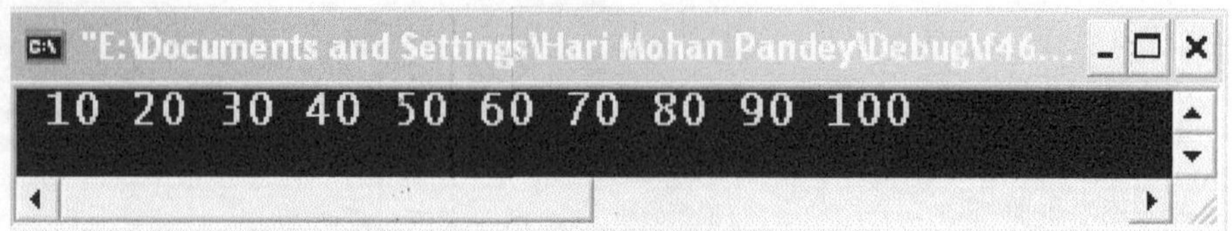

Figure 3.47. *Output screen of program.*

EXPLANATION : In this program we have left the initialization part and have put this before the `for` loop, still semicolon (;) is must in the `for` **loop.**

The general syntax for such type of `for` loop as given in the above program is given below :

```
for (; condition; increment/decrement)
{
    Statements;
}
```

/* PROG 3.47 FOR LOOP SYNTAX2 VER 2*/

```
#include<iostream.h>
void main( )
{
int t;
for(t=1;t<=10;)
{
cout<<" "<<t;
t++;
}
}
```

OUTPUT :

1 2 3 4 5 6 7 8 9 10

Figure 3.48. *Output screen of program 3.47.*

EXPLANATION : In this program we have written within braces. Note braces are must because you are having two statements which we want to make as body of the `for` loop.

The general syntax is given as :

```
for (initialization; condition;)
{
        Statements;
        Increment/decrement;
}
```

/*PROG 3.48 FOR LOOP SYNTAX3 VER 2*/

```
#include<iostream.h>
 void main( )
 {
   int t;
   for(t=1;t<=10;)
   cout<<" "<<t;
   t++;
 }
```

OUTPUT :

1 1 1 1 1 1 1 1 1 1 1 1 1.........................(INFINITE TIMES)

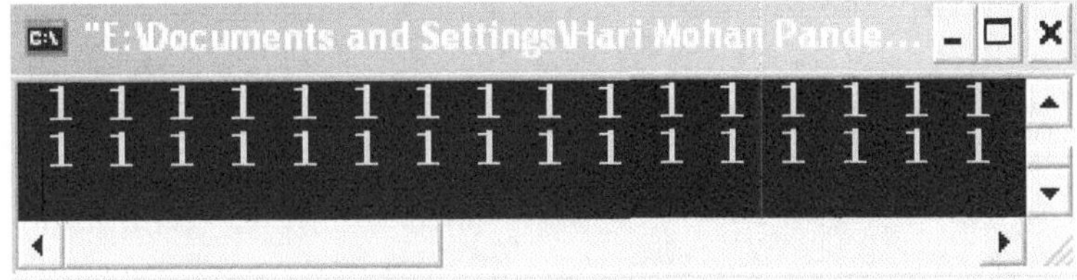

Figure 3.49. *Output screen of program.*

EXPLANATION : As there is no braces after the `for` loop only first statement is assumed as body of the `for` loop and **t++** is not considered as part of the `for` loop so **t<=10** remains true forever, result is `infinite loop`.

/*PROG 3.49 FOR LOOP SYNTAX—4 VER*/

```
#include<iostream.h>
 void main( )
 {
    int t;
    for(t=1;t<=10;)
    cout<<" "<<t++;
 }
```

OUTPUT :

```
1 2 3 4 5 6 7 8 9 10
```

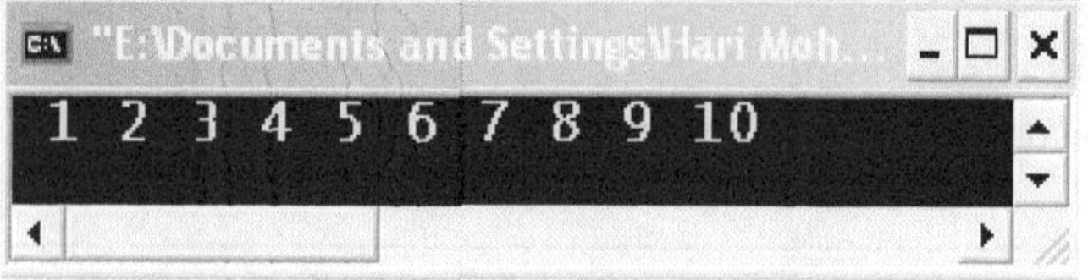

Figure 3.50. *Output screen of program.*

EXPLANATION : Here the mistake done in the above program has been removed. After printing the value of **t** it will be incremented (due to post increment). `for` loop works fine and prints **1 to 10.**

/*PROG 3.50 FOR LOOP SYNTAX–3 VER 1*/

```
#include<iostream.h>
 void main( )
 {
    int t;
    t = 1;
    for(;t<=10;)
    cout<<"t= "<<t++<<endl;
 }
```

OUTPUT :

```
t:= 1 t:= 2 t:= 3 t:= 4 t:= 5 t:= 6 t:= 7 t:= 8 t:= 9 t:= 10
```

```
"E:\Documents and Settings\Hari Mohan Pandey\Debug\f50.exe"
t:= 1 t:= 2 t:= 3 t:= 4 t:= 5 t:= 6 t:= 7 t:= 8 t:= 9 t:= 10
```

Figure 3.51. *Output screen of program.*

EXPLANATION : In this program we have left both unitization and increment/decrement part, still semicolon is necessary on both sides. The general syntax is :

```
initialization;
for (;condition;)
{
        Statements;
        Increment/decrement;
}
```

Nesting of for Loop

Nesting of `for` **loop** is used most frequently in many programming situations and one of the most important usage in displaying various patterns which we will see in the coming programs.

The syntax for nesting of for loop is given here :

```
for(initialization; condition; increment/decrement)
{
        for(initialization; condition; increment/decrement)
        {
                Statements;
        }
        Statements;
}
```

For each iteration of first `for` loop (outer `for` **loop**) inner for loop runs as it is part of the body of outer `for` loop. The inner `for` loop has its own set if statements which executes till the condition for inner `for` loop is true. See numbers of programs given below :

```
/*PROG 3.51 TO PRINT THE FOLLOWING PATTERN, INPUT IS NUMBER OF LINES

1
2 2
3 3 3
4 4 4 4
5 5 5 5 5
*/
#include<iostream.h>
 void main( )
 {
    int line,row,col;
    cout<<"Enter the number of lines"<<endl;
    cin>>line;
    cout<<"The pattern is"<<endl;
    for(row=1;row<=line;row++)
```

```
    {
        for(col=1;col<=row;col++)
        cout<<" "<<row;
        cout<<"\n";
    }
}
```

OUTPUT :

```
Enter the number of lines
4
The pattern is
 1
 2 2
 3 3 3
 4 4 4 4
```

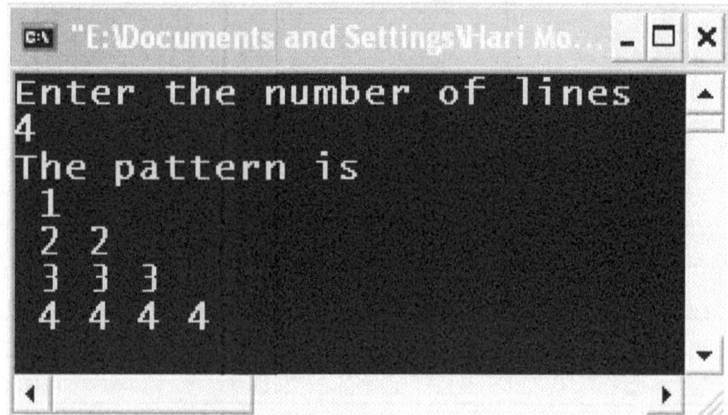

Figure 3.52. *Output screen of program.*

EXPLANATION : We have used two `for` loops in the program. One is to control the number of rows and second is to control number of cols. Initially assume **line =4** so outer `for` loop runs four times. In the first run **row=1** and inner loop runs only once. The **printf("\n")** statement is within the second `for` loop so this leaves new after printing **1.** When control reaches second time inside outer `for` **loop** value of row is 2, inner loop starts again by setting the value of **col = 1,** this time inner loop runs twice printing the value of **row** which is **2** twice. This continues till **row<=4.**

```
/*PROG 3.52 TO PRINT THE FOLLOWING PATTERN, INPUT IS NUMBER OF LINES

1
0 1
1 0 1
0 1 0 1
1 0 1 0 1
   */
```

```
#include<iostream.h>
 void main( )
 {
    int line,row,col;
    cout<<"Enter the number of lines"<<endl;
    cin>>line;
    cout<<"The pattern is"<<endl;
    for(row=1;row<=line;row++)
    {
        for(col=1;col<=row;col++)
           if(row%2==0)
        cout<<!(col%2);
           else
           cout<<(col%2);
        cout<<"\n";
 }
}
```

OUTPUT :

```
Enter the number of lines
4
The pattern is
1
01
101
0101
```

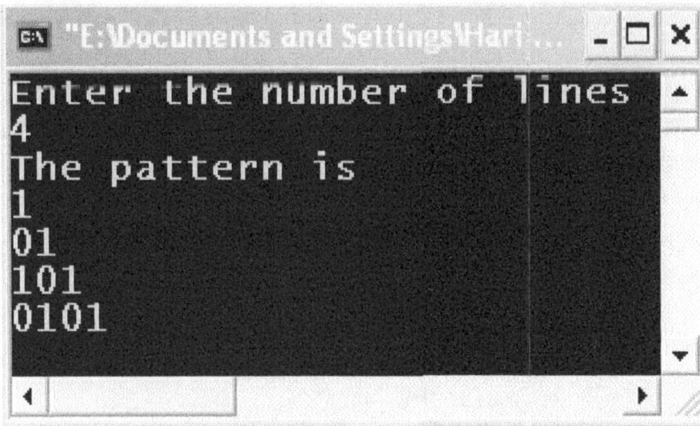

Figure 3.53. *Output screen of program.*

EXPLANATION : Observe the pattern carefully. On even number of lines we have a different pattern and on odd number of line we have a different pattern. On even number of liens *i.e.*, for row=2, 4, 6,..... if we print the complement of col %2 we get the desired pattern. On row=1, 3, 5,...... we simply print the col%2.

3.7.3 do-while Loop

The last loop is the `do-while` loop. Its syntax is as follows :

```
do
{
    Statements;
    Statements;
    Statements;
    ............;
    .............;
} while (condition);
```

It is similar to `while` loop with the difference that condition is checked at the end, instead of checking it at the beginning.

/*PROG 3.53 DEMO OF DO–WHILE LOOP*/

```
#include<iostream.h>
 void main( )
 {
    int t=1;
    do
 {
    cout<<t<<endl;
    t++;
 }while(t<=15);
}
```

OUTPUT :

```
1
2
3
4
5
6
7
8
9
10
```

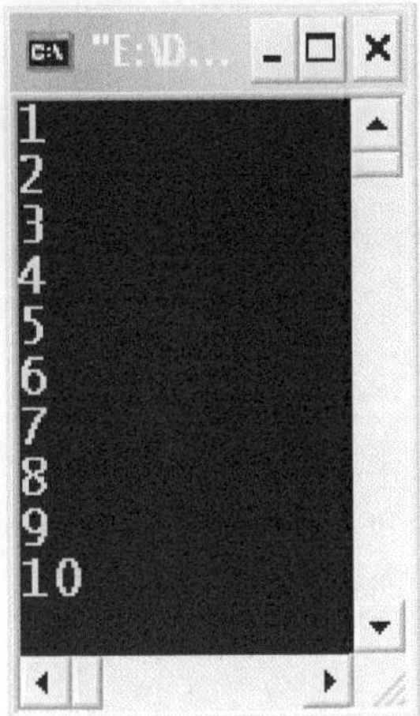

Figure 3.54. *Output screen of program.*

EXPLANATION : The `do-while` loop is similar to the `while` loop with the difference that the condition is checked at the `end`. The loop starts with a `do` following the block and at the end of block the condition is writing using `while`. The `while` is part of the `do-while loop` and it must be terminated by **semicolon;**. Initially the value of **t** is **1** which is printed through **printf** then **t** becomes **2**. At the end of the block the condition is **true**, control transfer back to **do** block and process continues.

Some Important Points Regarding do-while Loop

- **It** is also called **bottom testing loop or exit controlled loop** as condition at the bottom of the loop.
- Regardless of the condition given at the end of block the loop runs at least once.
- The `do-while` loop is mostly used for writing menu driven programs.

/*PROG 3.54 TO FIND NUMBER OF DIGITS IN A GIVEN NUMBER TILL SINGLE DIGIT*/

```
#include<iostream.h>
 void main( )
 {
   int num,r;
   int sum=0,save;
   num=0;
   cout<<"Enter the number\n";
   cin>>num;
   do
   {
     sum=0;
     while(num!=0)
```

```
        {
            r=num%10;
            sum=sum+r;
            num=num/10;
        }
        if(sum>9)
        num=sum;
    } while(num>9);
        cout<<"Sum of digits up to single digit"
            <<"is :="<<sum<<endl;
}
```

OUTPUT :

```
Enter the number
4275
Sum of digits up to single digitis := 9
```

```
"E:\Documents and Settings\Hari Mohan Pandey\Debug\...
Enter the number
4275
Sum of digits up to single digitis:=9
```

Figure 3.55. *Output screen of program.*

EXPLANATION : For example, number is **4275** then sum of digits is **4+2+7+5=18**. As 18 is more than 9 we repeat the process and get the result 1+ 8 = 9. This time answer is in single digit so we stop the process. In the program for finding sum of digits we have used while loop but for sum of digits up to single digit we have used do-while loop. When sum>9, sum is assigned to num and for this num, sum of digits are determined using do-while.

3.8 POINTS TO PONDER

- The assignment operator (=), which has two operands on each side. The value of the right-side operand is assigned to the operand on the left side.
- The arithmetic assignment operators, +=, -=, *=, /=, and %=, which are the combinations of the arithmetic operators with the assignment operator.
- The unary minus operator (–), which returns the negation of a numeric value.
- The two versions of the increment operator, ++. You know that in ++x, the ++ operator is called the pre-increment operator; and in x++, ++ is the post-increment operator.

- The two versions of decrement operator, – –. You have learned that, for example, in – –x, the – –operator is the pre-decrement operator, while in x– –, – – is called the post-decrement operator.
- The six relational operators in C : == (equal to), != (not equal to), > (greater than), < (less than), >= (greater than or equal to), and <= (less than or equal to).
- How to change the type of data by prefixing a cast operator to the data.
- The sizeof operator returns the number of bytes that a specified data type can have. You can use the operator to measure the size of a data type on your machine.
- The logical AND operator (&&) returns 1 only if both its two operands (that is, expressions) are TRUE. Otherwise, the operator returns 0.
- The logical OR operator (||) returns 0 only if both its two operands are FALSE. Otherwise, the operator returns 1.
- The logical negation operator (!) reverses the logical value of its operand.
- There are six bit-manipulation operators : the bitwise AND operator (&), the bitwise OR operator (|), the bitwise XOR operator (^), the bitwise complement operator (~), the right-shift operator (>>), and the left-shift operator (<<).
- The conditional operator (? :) is the only operator in C++ that can take three operands.
- An important task of a program is to instruct the computer to jump to a different portion of the code according to the specified branch conditions.
- The if statement is a very important statement for conditional branching in C++.
- The if statement can be nested for making a series of decisions in your program.
- The if-else statement is an expansion of the if statement.
- The switch statement helps you to keep your program more readable when there are more than just a couple decisions to be made in your code.
- The case and default keywords, followed by a colon (:) and an integral value, are used in the switch statement as labels.
- The break statement can be used to exit the switch construct or a loop (usually, an infinite loop).
- The continue statement is used to let you stay within a loop while skipping over some statements.
- The goto statement enables the computer to jump to some other spot in your computer. Using this statement is not recommended because it may cause your program to be unreliable and hard to debug.
- Looping can be used to perform the same set of statements over and over until specified conditions are met.
- Looping makes your program concise.
- There are three statements, `for`, `while`, and `do-while`, that are used for looping in C++.
- There are three expression fields in the `for` statement. The second field contains the expression used as the specified condition(s).
- The `for` statement does not end with a **semicolon**.
- The empty `for(;;)` statement can be used to form an **infinite loop**.

- Multiple expressions, separated by commas, can be used in the `for` statement.
- There is only one expression field in the while statement, and the expression is used as the specified condition.
- The while statement does not end with a semicolon.
- The `while` **(1)** statement can create an **infinite loop**.
- The `do-while` statement places its expression at the **bottom** of the loop.
- The `do-while` statement does end with a semicolon.
- The **inner loop must finish first before the outer loop resumes its iteration in nested loops.**

EXERCISE

A. True and False :

1. The expression ++ (4+6) is a valid.
2. +++p increment s value of p by 2.
3. A char data type always occupies two bytes in memory.
4. Assignment operation is performed during execution of the program
5. The expression ++(x + y) is a valid one.
6. The one's complement ~ is a binary operator.
7. The assignment a*1=b; is a valid one.
8. The sizeof is a keyword but not a function.
9. The construct `if  a>b;` is correct syntax for `if`.
10. C++ supports `if-else-then` construct.
11. `if(x)` means `if(x=0)`
12. `switch-case` is selective control struct.
13. For decision making in C++ `if-else-endif` is used.
14. `continue` can be used inside `switch-case`.
15. `goto` is used inside `switch-case`.
16. In do-while semicolon is put after the while which is must.
17. In while semicolon is put after while is must.
18. One type of loop can be nested in other type of loop.
19. A continue and break cannot be used together in a loop.
20. Maximum number of initialization that can be put in a for loop is 2 only.
21. A continue statement causes an early exit for the loop.
22. C++ support repeat-until loop.
23. Loops are used for controlling the execution of the program.

B. Fill in the Blanks :

1. The expression **(double (22/7))** yields ....
2. The modulus-operator can be applied only to .... types.

3. Left shifting a number is equivalent to ....
4. The second operator of the operator **%** and / must be ....
5. Assignment operator uses the Associativity of ....
6. The expression (`float` (22/7)) yields ....
7. The symbol for **bitwise AND** is .... and symbol for **logical AND** is ....
8. In C++ there are .... ways to declare constants.
9. **if(!x)** is equal to ....
10. The .... can be placed anywhere in the switch-case statement
11. In switch only .... expression can be used
12. **if** is used for .... in C++.
13. The use of .... should be avoided in programming
14. In else-if ladder only .... condition can be used at a time.
15. For character manipulation functions header file used is ....

C. Answer the Following Questions :

1. Explain different types of operator available in C++.
2. Explain various unary operators in C++.
3. Describe logical operators with their return values.
4. What are the relational operators?
5. Explain ternary operator in C++.
6. What is the difference between '=' and '= ='?
7. Explain the precedence of operators in arithmetic operations.
8. Why bitwise operators are useful? Explain where they are applicable?
9. Why is the need of type conversion?
10. What do you understand by type casting? Give examples of implicit and explicit type casting.
11. What are the uses of comma (,) and conditional (?) operators?
12. What is the difference between division and modular division operations?
13. What are the ASCII codes? List the codes for digits 1 to 9, A to Z and a to z?
14. What are the limitations of switch-case statement?
15. Is it possible to use multiple else with if statement?
16. Can we use multiple default statement in switch-case in C++?
17. Can we put default statement anywhere in the switch-case structure?
18. Give the reason for avoidance of goto statement.
19. Why break statement is essential in switch-case structure? Which other functions or keywords can be used in place of the break statement?
20. Write the use of else and default statements in if ...else and switch case statements respectively.
21. Explain the break and goto with the help of examples.
22. Why use of goto statement is discouraged in programming?
23. What is loop? Why it is necessary in the program?
24. What happens if you create a loop that never ends?
25. What is the difference between (!0) and (!1). How while loop works with these values?

26. Is it possible to nest while loop within for loops?
27. How do you choose between while and for loop?
28. Is it possible to create a for loop that is never executed?
29. Is it possible to use multiple while statement with do statement?
30. Give the syntax of for loop and explain the functionality of for loop?
31. Explain the difference between break and continue. Explain the difference between looping and branching.

D. Brain Drill :

1. Write a program to enter a number (<100 and >15). Display the number in reverse order using % and / operator?
2. Write a program to convert entered temperature from Celsius to Fahrenheit?
3. Write a program to enter a four digit number and find out sum of its digit using % and / operator.
4. Write a program to display number all alphabets (upper and lower) along with their ASCII values.
5. Write a program to enter two numbers and do comparison of them. If first one is greater than find out division of two numbers else find out multiplication of two numbers.
6. Write a program to print whether entered number is even or odd using ternary operator.
7. Write a program to evaluate the expression 2X + 3Y–10. Value for X and Y should be taken from the user side.
8. Write a program to multiply two floating point numbers and print the product as a double in exponential notation.
9. Write a program to complement the bits starting from R and ending at S, of a given number and print the value of the manipulated number in binary, octal and hexadecimal form.
10. Write a program for binary addition with carry of 8 bit numbers.
11. Write a program to shift a number by 4 bits by storing bits to another number. The program should print out the values of the number formed by shifted bits, in decimal and binary forms.
12. Write a program to entered two numbers and find the smallest out of them. Use conditional operator.
13. Write a program to shift the entered numbers by three bits right and display the result.
14. Write a program to shift the entered number by three bits left and display the result.
15. Write a program to check whether a voter is eligible for voting or not? If his/her age is equal to or greater 18 display "Eligible" else display "Not eligible".
16. Write a program to check whether a triangle can be formed with three positive integers supplied.
17. Write a program to check whether a triangle is right-angled or not.
18. Write a program which will find whether a number is divisible by 2,3,4,5 and 6.
19. Write a program in C++ to find out largest of 10 numbers using if and goto only.
20. Write a program in C++ that will read the values of x and evaluate the following function.

$$Y = \begin{cases} 1 & \text{for } x>0 \\ 0 & \text{for } x = 0 \\ -1 & \text{for } x < 0 \end{cases}$$

21. Write a program to calculate the amount of the bill for the following jobs.
    (*a*) Scanning and hardcopy of a passport photo ₹ 5.
    (*b*) Scanning and hardcopies (more than 10) ₹ 3.

22. Write a program to calculate bill of Internet browsing. The conditions are given below:
    (*a*) 1 Hour – ₹ 20
    (*b*) ½ Hour – ₹ 15
    (*c*) 5 Hours – ₹ 90
23. The owner should enter number of hours spent by customer.
24. Write a program to calculate the sum of remainders obtained by dividing with modular division operations by 2 on 1 to 9 numbers.
25. Suppose you give a dinner party for six guests, but your table seats only four. In how many ways can four of the six guests arrange themselves at the table? Any of the six guests can sit in the first chair. Any of the remaining five can sit in the second chair. Any of the remaining four can sit in the third chair, and any of the remaining three can sit in the fourth chair. (The last two will have to stand) So the number of possible arrangements of six guests in four chairs is 6*5*4*3, which is 360. Write a program that calculates the number of possible arrangements for any number of guests and any number of chairs. (Assume there will never be fewer guests than chair) Don't let this too complicated. A simple for loop should do it.

CHAPTER 4

OPERATORS AND REFERENCES IN C++

4.1 INTRODUCTION

This chapter discuss all the new operators introduced by C++. It also discusses some new features of C++ not supported by C. The operators which are in C and C++ both were discussed in chapter 3. A new feature of C++ "reference" will be discussed. The new operators of C++ are given in the following Table below :

Table 4.1 : New Operators in C++

S.No.	*Operator*	*Meaning*
1.	::	Scope resolution operator
2.	>>	Extraction operator
3.	<<	Insertion operator
4.	:: *	Pointer to member declaration
5.	->*	Pointer to member operator(for dereferencing)
6.	.*	Pointer to member operator(for dereferencing)
7.	new	Dynamic memory allocator
8.	delete	Dynamic memory de-allocator.

We have seen usage of >> and << in almost all the program presented in earlier chapter. So we start our discussion with scope resolution operator.

4.2 SCOPE RESOLUTION OPERATOR

The operator :: is known as scope resolution operator in C++. The operator is used for two purposes :

PURPOSE-1 : For accessing global variables.

PURPOSE-2 : Identifying class members to which class they belong.

We will understand the first one. Second will be discussed when classes are introduced. In C++ block can be created by using **{and}.** Any variable declared within that block is confine within that block only. Now if a variable declared within any block and a global variable having same name, the priority is given to the local variable. What if we want to use the global variable having the same name in the block too ? Scope resolution operator helps in these situations. To access any global variable say **gb** we can write :: gb. Now if we are having a local variable **gb** that variable can be accessed simply by referencing **gb**. That is scope resolution operator :: allow us to use the global version of the variable in case local and global variable having same name.

In case one block is contained within another block and both have the same variable name, priority will be given to inner block. Variables of outer block can be used inside the inner block but reverse is not true.

We present numerous example of use of scope resolution operators given below.

/*PROG 4.1 DEMO OF SCOPE RESOLUTION OPERATOR :: VER 1*/

```
#include<iostream.h>
#include<conio.h>
int num=100;
  void main( )
  {
     int num=30;
     clrscr( );
     cout<<"In main\n";
     cout<<"Local num="<<num<<"\t";
     cout<<"Global num="<< :: num<<endl;
     {
        int num=40;
        cout<<"In block1\n";
        cout<<"Local num="<<num<<"\t";
        cout<<"Global num="<< :: num<<endl;
     }
     {
        int num=50;
        cout<<"In block2\n";
        cout<<"Local num="<<num<<"\t";
        cout<<"Global num="<< :: num<<endl;
  }
  getch ( );
}
```

OUTPUT :

```
In main
Local num=30          Global num=100
In block1
Local num=40          Global num=100
In block2
Local num=50          Global num=100
```

EXPLANATION : The :: as discussed earlier known as scope resolution operator. Any global variable say **gb** can be accessed anywhere in the program by writing :: gb. In the program we have declared num at four places in the program, one is global, second is in main function, third in one block and fourth is in the second block. A block can be created by **{and}**. The variable num of one block can be used only inside that block only but num of main can be used anywhere in the main function. Global num can be accessed by writing :: num. On the basis of this I think it will be easy to figure out the output of the program.

/***PROG 4.2 DEMO OF SCOPE RESOLUTION OPERATOR :: VER 2***/

```
#include<iostream.h>
#include<conio.h>
int num=100;
  void main( )
  {
     int num=30;
     cout<<"In main\n";
     cout<<"Local num  ="<<num<<"\t";
     cout<<"Global num="<< :: num<<endl;
     int copynum=num;
     {
        int num=40;
        cout<<"In block 1\n ";
        cout<<"Local num     ="<<num<<"\t";
        cout<<"Global num    ="<< :: num<<"\t";
        cout<<"num of main  ="<<copynum<<endl;
     }
     {
        int num=50;
        cout<<"In block 2\n";
        cout<<"Local num="<<num<<"\t";
        cout<<"Global num="<< :: num<<"\t";
        cout<<"Num of main="<<copynum<<endl;
     }
```

```
    getch( );
  }
```

OUTPUT :

```
In main
Local num=30        Global   num=100
In block1
Local num=40        Global   num=100
In block2
Local num=50        Global   num=100
In main
Local num=30        Global   num=100
In block 1
Local num=40        Global   num=100   num of main=30
In block 2
Local num=50        Global   num=100   Num of main=30
```

EXPLANATION : In the earlier program we could not use num declared in main in any of the block and local variable num got the priority over num of main. But here we have saved the num of main in a new variable copynum. Now, we can print value of num of main using this copynum variable in any block.

/*PROG 4.3 DEMO OF SCOPE RESOLUTION OPERATOR :: VER 3*/

```
#include<iostream.h>
#include<conio.h>
int num=100;
char *str="I am Global";
 void main( )
 {
   int num=30;
   clrscr( );
   char *str="I am in main\n";
   cout<<str;
   cout<<"Local num="<<num<<"\t";
   :: num= :: num+10;
   cout<<"Global num="<< :: num<<endl;
   cout<<"Global str="<< :: str<<endl;
   {
     int num=40;
     char *str="I am in block1\n";
```

```
        cout<<str;
        cout<<"Local num="<<num<<"\t";
        :: num= :: num*2;
        cout<<"Global num="<< :: num<<"\n";
        cout<<"Global str="<< :: str<<endl;
    }
    {
        int num=50;
        char *str="I am in block 2\n";
        cout<<str;
        cout<<"Local num="<<num<<"\t";
        :: num= :: num/2;
        cout<<"Global num="<< :: num<<"\n";
        cout<<"Global str="<< :: str<<endl;
    }
    getch( );
}
```

OUTPUT :

```
I am in main
Local num =30 Global num=110
Global str =I am Global
I am in block1
Local num =40 Global num=220
Global str =I am Global
I am in block 2
Local num =50 Global num=110
Global str =I am Global
```

EXPLANATION : In the program we have taken a global variable str of char* type along with int num. We have also done arithmetic on global num shown in bold. The rest is simple to understand

/*PROG 4.4 DEMO OF SCOPE RESOLUTION OPERATOR :: VER 4*/

```
#include<iostream.h>
#include<conio.h>
  int g1;
  float g2;
  char g3[10];
  void main( )
  {
```

```
    int g1;
    float g2;
    char g3[10];
    clrscr( );
    cout<<"Enter an int, float and a string for global
       data\n";
    cin>> ::g1>> ::g2>>g3;
    cout<<"Enter an int,float and a string for local
       data\n";
    cin>>g1>>g2>>g3;
    cout<<"Local Data\n";
    cout<<g1<<"\t"<<g2<<"\t"<<"\t"<<g3<<endl;
    cout<< ::g1<<"\t"<< ::g2<<"\t"<< ::g3<<endl;
    getch( );
}
```

OUTPUT :

```
Enter an int, float and a string for global data
234          56.78          Hari
Enter an int, float and a string for local data
456          34.56          Pandey
Local Data
456          34.560001      Pandey
Global Data
234          56.779999      Hari
```

EXPLANATION : Just like we take value in the local variable we can also take values for global variables. In the program we have three global **variables :: g1 and g2** of type int and float and g3 of an array of size **10** of char type. In the main we are having same type and same name for local variable. To differentiate them again we make use **of ::** .

/*PROG 4.5 DEMO OF SCOPE RESOLUTION OPERATOR :: VER 5*/

```
#include<iostream.h>
#include<conio.h>
  int g1;
  g1=123;
  float g2;
  g2=123.45;
  char *g3;
  g3="Global";
  void main( )
  {
```

```
        clrscr( );
        cout<<"Global data\n";
        cout<< :: g1<<"\t"<< :: g2<<"\t"<< :: g3<<endl;
        getch( );
    }
```

OUTPUT :

Multiple Errors

EXPLANATION : global variable must be initialized while declaring. You cannot separate the declaration and initialization of global variable. You will get the **compilation error missing storage class or type specifies.**

/*PROG 4.6 DEMO OF SCOPE RESOLUTION OPERATOR :: VER 6*/

```
#include<iostream.h>
#include<conio.h>
int num=20;
    void main( )
    {
        int num=30;
        clrscr( );
        cout<<"Local num\n";
        cout<<"Value="<<num<<"\t"<<"address="<<&num<<endl;
        cout<<"Global num\n";
        cout<<"Value ="<< :: num<<"\t"<<"Address="<<& :: num<<endl;
        getch( );
    }
```

OUTPUT :

```
Local num
Value =30          address=0x8fdcfff4
Global num
Value =20          Address=0x8fdc00aa
```

EXPLANATION : The program simply demonstrate how we can take address of a global data.

4.3 REFERENCE VARIABLES

Reference variable is a new concept in C++. A reference variable is a variable which can take reference of a previous defined variable or any constant. As an example :

```
int x = 10;
int &refx = x;
```

The line `int & refx = x;` creates a reference variable `refx` which contains reference of variable `x`. Creating a reference for a variable means creating a new name for that variable *i.e.,* in the above case both `refx` and `x` refer to the same memory location. Any changes done on either of these variable `refx or x` reflect back to other variable. Assume initial value of `x is 10;` when we write `x++` and display `refx` we will get `11.` If we now write `refx++` and display the value of `x` we will get `12`. The figure given below that shows that address of memory location is `1020` but it has two name `x` and `refx`. If we now try to print `&x` or `&refx` we will get `1020.`

10

x, refx(1020)

The general syntax for defining a reference variable is :

```
data_type &reference_name = referent;
```

Here **&** is not understood as address operator. For instance **int &** means reference to **int.**

A reference variable must be initialized when it is declared *i.e.,* if you write **int & x**; and later write **x = y** will be invalid.

```
/*PROG 4.7 DEMO OF REFERENCE VARIABLE VER 1*/

#include<iostream.h>
#include<conio.h>
void main( )
{
    int x=10;
    int &refx=x;
    clrscr( );
    refx++;
    cout<<"x="<<x<<endl;
    cout<<"refx="<<refx<<endl;
    getch( );
}
```

OUTPUT :

```
X=11
Refx=11
```

EXPLANATION : The statement int &refx =x; creates a reference variable refx which contains reference of variable x. As mentioned earlier a reference variable has to be initialized. You cannot write int &refx. Creating a reference like creating a new name for the same variable so any changes made in refs occurs in x and vice versa. So the output.

```
/*PROG 4.8 DEMO OF REFERENCE VARIABLE VER 2*/

#include<iostream.h>
#include<conio.h>
```

```
void main( )
{
    float f=23.34;
    float &reff=f;
    char *s="hello";
    char * &refs=s;
    clrscr( );
    reff++;
    cout<<"f="<<f<<"\t"<<"reff="<<reff<<endl;
    f++;
    cout<<"f="<<f<<"\t"<<"reff="<<reff<<endl;
    *s='M';
    cout<<"s="<<s<<"\t"<<"refs="<<refs<<endl;
    *refs='P';
    cout<<"s="<<s<<"\t"<<"refs="<<refs<<endl;
    getch( );
    }
```

OUTPUT :

```
f=24.34 reff  =24.34
f=25.34 reff  =25.34
s=Mello refs  =Mello
s=Pello refs  =Pello
```

EXPLANATION : In the program we have two reference variables : one reff for float variable f and other refs for `char*` variable s. Note how to create reference variable for a string. In the program we change the value of variable f twice. One is through f itself and second is through reference variable reff. As both the name refers to the same location, change s made by one appears to another. The overall effect is increment value of f twice. So the output. As refs contains reference of s, writing *s='M' changes the first character of the string "hello", string becomes "Mello". Again as refs and s refer to same memory location so output "Mello" is printed for both s and res. Next change is made through refs in the string. Next time string s becomes "Pello".

/*PROG 4.9 TAKING REFERENCE OF A REFERENCE VARIABLE VER 1*/

```
#include<iostream.h>
#include<conio.h>
void main( )
{
    char ch     ='p';
    char & rch  =ch;
    char & rch1 =rch;
```

```
clrscr( );
rch++;
cout<<"ch="<<ch<<"\t"<<"rch="<<rch<<"\t"
<<"rch1="<<rch1<<endl;
rch1++;
cout<<"ch="<<ch<<"\t"<<"rch="<<rch<<"\t"
<<"rch1="<<rch1<<endl;
getch( );
}
```

OUTPUT :

```
ch=q    rch=q    rch1=q
ch=r    rch=r    rch1=r
```

EXPLANATION : The statement char &rch=ch; creates a reference rch to ch. diagrammatically this is shown as follows :

Ch, rch

This diagram shows memory cell having the two name ch and rch. In the next statement

char & rch1=rch;

We are creating a reference to rch1 which already was a reference variable. So diagram now becomes :

P

Ch, rch, rch1

That is three different name s refer to the same memory location. The first line of output justifies what I have explained just now. As all three name refer to the same location changes done in rch1 by writing rch1++ will affect the value of ch and rch too. So the second line of output.

/*PROG 4.10 DEMO OF CONSTANT REFERENCE */

```
#include<iostream.h>
#include<conio.h>
void main ( )
{
    int x=10;
    const int & cref=x;
    clrscr( );
    x=20;
    cout<<"cref="<<cref<<endl;
    cref++;// line causes error
```

```
        cout<<"cref="<<cref<<endl;
        getch( );
    }
```

OUTPUT :

Error message

Cannot modify a constant object

EXPLANATION : The statement **const int & cref= x;** creates a constant reference **to x**. The constant reference cannot be changed by any means. As we write **x=20; x** changes; no error is generated and value in cref will be **20**. But when you try to change value of cref you will get compilation error as you cannot modify constant reference.

/*PROG 4.11 TAKING REFERENCE OF A CONSTANT */

```
#include<iostream.h>
#include<conio.h>
    void main( )
    {
        const int x=10;
        int & ref=x;
        clrscr( );
        ref=20;
        cout<<"ref="<<ref<<"\t"<<"x="<<x<<endl;
        getch( );
    }
```

Output :

ref=20 x=10

EXPLANATION : In the program we are taking reference of an `int` constant into `ref`. Through ref we are trying to change value of `x`. This won't be allowed in `visual studio c++` compiler but will work in `Turbo C++.`

/* PROG 4.12 TAKING REFERENCE OF AN ARRAY*/

```
#include<iostream.h>
#include<conio.h>
    void main( )
    {
        int arr[ ]={10,20,30,40,50};
        int (&ptr)[5]=arr;
        int i;
        clrscr( );
        for(i=0;i<5;i++)
```

```
        ptr[i]=i+1;
        cout<<"Array elements \n";
        for(i=0; i<5; i++)
        cout<<arr[i]<<" ";
        cout<<endl;
        getch( );
    }
```

OUTPUT :

```
Array elements
1 2 3 4 5
```

EXPLANATION : We can create an array of reference as shown in the program. Now ptr can be treated as a new name for array arr. Through this new name for array we modify the array and later display the array using arr. We get the modified array elements.

4.4 THE BOOL DATA TYPE

The **bool** data type is a new data type in C++ which is used with Boolean values. We can create variables of type `bool` type which can store any true or false value. Even we can assign integer values to `bool` type variables. Any non zero value is termed as `true` and any `0` value is considered as `false`. Integer value `1` is used to represent `true` and `0` for representing `false`. We can also use keywords true and false for representing `true` and `false` value.

/*PROG 4.13 DEMO OF BOOL DATA TYPE VER 1*/

```
#include<iostream.h>
#include<conio.h>
 void main( )
 {
    int x=20,y=40;
    bool b1,b2,b3,b4,b5;
    clrscr( );
    b1=x;
    b2=y;
    b3=x>y;
    b4=true;
    b5=false;
    cout<<"b1="<<b1<<endl;
    cout<<"b2="<<b2<<endl;
    cout<<"b3="<<b3<<endl;
    cout<<"b4="<<b4<<endl;
    cout<<"b5="<<b5<<endl;
```

```
    getch( );
}
```

OUTPUT :

```
b1=1
b2=1
b3=0
b4=1
b5=0
```

EXPLANATION : Any non zero value is taken as true and 0 value as false for bool data type. In the program we have created 5 variables of bool data types. The output is self-explanatory.

/*PROG 4.14 DEMO OF BOOL DATA TYPE VER 2 */

```
#include<iostream.h>
#include<conio.h>
void main( )
{
    int x=20,y=40,z;
    bool b1,b2,b3;
    clrscr( );
    b1=x+y;
    b2=true + true;
    z=true + true;
    b3=b1+b2+false;
    int bx=b3+b2;
    cout<<"b1 ="<<b1<<endl;
    cout<<"b2 ="<<b2<<endl;
    cout<<"b3 ="<<b3<<endl;
    cout<<"bx ="<<bx<<endl;
    cout<<"z  ="<<z<<endl;
    getch( );
}
```

OUTPUT :

```
b1 =1
b2 =1
b3 =1
bx =2
z  =2
```

EXPLANATION : In the program note that true + true assigned to a bool type variable store 1 in that variable but assigned to an int type variable stores 2. Any arithmetic operation performed on bool type variables result a Boolean value *i.e.*, either true or false.

4.5 THE OPERATOR NEW AND DELETE

When we declare variables, arrays, structure (in definition) etc., the memory for them is allocated at the compile time. This allocation is static allocation. When you declare the array say int a[5] we give the size of array *i.e.,* number of elements. We just cannot take input for x from user during program execution and declare the array by writing int a[x]. Memory for array in the above declaration is allocated at compile time so compiler requires the size of the array. The size once fixed cannot be changed during the program execution. This may sometimes results in wastage of memory when size specified in the beginning is more than actually used in the program.

When you write your C++ program, the program's data and code is stored in the RAM. All the local and global variables used in the program are stored in a fixed area of memory allocated to that program. This are allocated is fixed and remain constant during the execution of the program. The local variable are always stored on the stack and are destroyed automatically as soon as control goes out of scope. Global and static variables are known as load time variables they come into existence at the time of loading of the program. Thus, we can say that global and local variables are efficiently handled by C++ compiler. But the programmer must know the amount of space required for every program.

The technique through which a program can obtain space in the RAM during the execution of the program and not during compilation is called dynamic memory allocation. In this method space for the variables (array, strings, structure etc) is allocated from a free memory region which is known as heap. This area is not fixed in nature and keep changing as the memory is allocated and de-allocated from this region. The entire run time view of memory for a program is given below.

Dynamic memory allocation is the allocation of memory at run time *i.e.,* when program executes then required memory is asked from the user and memory is allocated with the help of operator new.

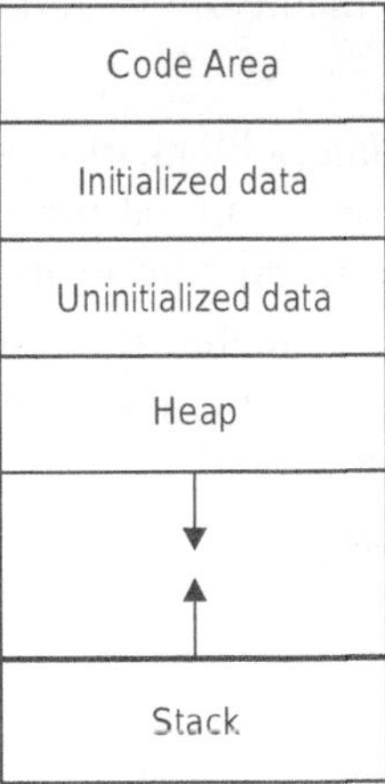

Figure 4.1. *Run time memory area of a C++ program*

Allocation of memory for the variables at run time is known as dynamic memory allocation. The allocated memory can be freed also. For allocation of memory dynamically at run time C++ provides `new` operator. For de-allocation C++ provides delete operator. In C we were having `malloc` and `free` for allocation and de-allocation of memory. Memory allocated using `new` persist till we explicitly destroy it using `delete`. The syntax of using new is simple which is given below :

```
data_type *ptr = new data_type;
```

Here `ptr` is a variable of `data_type`. Memory is allocated by finding the size of `data_type` automatically by the compiler and address of the allocated memory is returned which is stored in `ptr`. Few examples are given as follows :

```
int *ptr = new int;
char *ch = new char;
float *fp = new float;
```

Later we can assign values to the variable created as:

```
*ptr = 34;
*ch = 'p';
*fp = 45.67;
```

We can also initialize the pointer variable while allocating memory using new. See the example given below:

```
int *ptr = new int (10);
cout<<*ptr;            // prints 10
float *fp = new float (34.56);
cout<<*fp;             // prints 34.56
```

We can also create memory dynamically for arrays, strings and even for user defined data types. For creating array of size 10 dynamically of integer type we write as :

```
int *ptr = new int [10];
```

The above statement creates a memory block of size **40** (int in windows takes **4 bytes**) and returns a pointer to the first byte. Now we can treat **ptr** as an array of **10 elements** and can refer any array element as **ptr[i]** or ***(ptr + i)**. We can even create **2D** or **3D** array dynamically.

In case sufficient memory is not available the new operator returns null pointer. Thus prior to work with dynamically allocated variables we can check whether pointer returned by new is not equal to null. This is given as:

```
buff = new char[57000];
if (buff = = null)
{
 code for handling;
}
```

The delete operator can be used to delete memory previously allocated by new operator. For instance if ptr points to memory allocated by new and when this memory is no longer required we can delete it by writing delete ptr;

For deleting a dynamically created array pointed by ptr we can write.

delete [ ] ptr;

/*PROG 4.15 DEMO OF NEW AND DELETE VER 1 */

```
#include<iostream.h>
#include<conio.h>
 void main( )
 {
   int *p=new int;
   *p=20;
   char *ch=new char('p');
   float *fp=new float(2.34);
   cout<<"int value="<<*p<<"\t"<<"Address="<<p<<endl;
   cout<<"charvalue="<<*ch<<"\t"<<"Address value="
   <<(void *)ch<<endl;
   cout<<"Float value="<<*fp<<"\t"<<"Address="<<fp<<endl;
   delete p;
   delete ch;
   delete fp;
   getch( );
 }
```

OUTPUT :

```
Array elements
1 2 3 4 5
int value   =20          Address=0x8f98128e
char value  =p           Address value=0x8f901296
Float value =2.34        Address=0x8f98129e
```

EXPLANATION : In the **program 3.15**, we have created three **dynamic variables** of type **int, char and float** using dynamic memory allocator **new**. Both the syntaxes have been used in the program. Note while displaying address of char type dynamic type casting by **void*** is done. If this is not done than compiler assumes ch is the address of a string and it will start displaying character stored at the memory locations beyond ch till null character is not found. So you may have in output character **P** followed by garbage data. In the end memory allocated dynamically is freed using **delete** operator.

/*PROG 4.16 ALLOCATING MEMORY FOR STRING*/

```
#include<iostream.h>
#include<conio.h>
 void main( )
 {
    int n;
    clrscr( );
    cout<<"Enter the length of your name\n";
    cin>>n;
    char *str=new char[n+1];
    cout<<"Enter you name\n";
    cin>>str;
    cout<<"Hello "<<str<<endl;
    delete str;
    getch( );
 }
```

OUTPUT :

```
Enter the length of your name
8
Enter you name
MADHURI
Hello MADHURI
```

EXPLANATION : In the program 3.16, we are first taking the length of the name from user in variable unknowing this will allow us to determine how much memory to allocate dynamically. The statement `char *str= new char[n+1];` allocates memory dynamically from heap of size `n+1` bytes (`1 for null character`) and returns address of the first byte of allocated memory which is assigned to `char` type pointer `str`. Next string is taken from the user and displaying. In the end memory is freed using `delete`.

/*PROG 4.17 ALLOCATING & DE-ALLOCATING MEMORY DYNAMICALLY FOR ARRAY USING NEW AND DELETE OPERATOR*/

```
#include<iostream.h>
#include<conio.h>
#include<stdlib.h> //for exit ( )
 void main( )
 {
    int i,n;
    clrscr( );
```

```
    cout<<"How many elements you want in array\n";
    cin>>n;
    int* arr=new int[n];
    for(i=0;i<n;i++)
    {
      cout<<"\n Enter arr["<<i<<"] element :";
      cin>>arr[i];
    }
    int ele;
    cout<<"Enter the element you want to search\n";
    cin>>ele;
    for(i=0;i<n;i++)
    {
      if(arr[i]==ele)
      {
        cout<<"Element foun at"<<"index "<<i<<endl;
        exit(0);
      }
    }
    delete arr;
    cout<<"Element does not exist in array\n";
    getch( );
  }
```

OUTPUT :

```
(First run)
How many elements you want in array
10

 Enter arr[0] element :10

 Enter arr[1] element :20

 Enter arr[2] element :30

 Enter arr[3] element :40

 Enter arr[4] element :40

 Enter arr[5] element :50
```

```
 Enter arr[6] element :60

 Enter arr[7] element :70

 Enter arr[8] element :80

 Enter arr[9] element :90
Enter the element you want to search
30
Element foun at index 2

(Second run)
How many elements you want in array
10

 Enter arr[0] element :12

 Enter arr[1] element :13

 Enter arr[2] element :14

 Enter arr[3] element :15

 Enter arr[4] element :16

 Enter arr[5] element :17

 Enter arr[6] element :18

 Enter arr[7] element :19

 Enter arr[8] element :20

 Enter arr[9] element :21
Enter the element you want to search
10
Element does not exist in array
```

EXPLANATION : In the beginning size for the array is taken and stored in `n`. Memory is allocated for this size using statement `int *arr = new int[n];`. From now onwards arr is treated as an array of size `n`. The element to search is taken in the variable `ele`. Using for loop it is checked whether any of the element of the array matches with `ele`. If so we display the position of the element. If element is not in the array, for loop exhausts and in the end we display Element does not exist in **array.**

/* PROG 4.18 DEMO OF ARRAY OF POINTERS AND NEW OPERATOR*/

```
#include <iostream.h>
#include <stdlib.h>

 void main( )
 {
   int n,i;
   cout<<"How many elements you want in array\n";
   cin>>n;
   int*arr=new int [n];
   int **ptr=new int*[n];
   for(i=0;i<n;i++)
   {
     cout<<"\n Enter arr["<<i<<"]element : ";
     cin>>arr[i];
     ptr[i]=&arr[i];
   }
   cout<<"Element\t\t Address\n";
   for(i=0;i<n;i++)
   {
     cout<<*ptr[i]<<"\t\t"<<ptr[i]<<endl;
   }
   delete arr;
   delete [ ] ptr;
 }
```

OUTPUT :

```
How many elements you want in array
5

 Enter arr[0]element : 12

 Enter arr[1]element : 13

 Enter arr[2]element : 14

 Enter arr[3]element : 15
```

```
Enter arr[4]element : 16

Element                 Address

12                      0x8fd20f00
13                      0x8fd20f02
14                      0x8fd20f04
15                      0x8fd20f06
16                      0x8fd20f08
```

EXPLANATION : The statement `int*arr [] = new int [n];` creates an array of size n dynamically. To store addresses of array elements an array of pointers by writing `int **ptr = new int *[n].` In the `for loop` we assign addresses of array element arr of element array ptr. Now, `ptr [0]` and `&ptr [0]` is same. For value `arr [0]` and `*ptr [0]` is same. Using `ptr` array we display address and element of the array arr.

/*PROG 4.19 DYNAMIC MEMORY ALLOCATION FOR 2-D ARRAY */

```
#include <iostream.h>
#include <conio.h>
  void main( )
  {
    int **ptr;
    int i,j;
    int row,col;
    clrscr( );
    cout<<"Enter the number of rows\n";
    cin>>row;
    cout<<"Enter the number of columns\n";
    cin>>col;
    ptr=new int *[row];
    for(i=0;i<row;i++)
      ptr[i]=new int [col];
      int *max= new int [row];
    for(i=0;i<row;i++)
      for(j=0;j<col;j++)
      {
        cout<<"\nEnter ptr["<<i<<"] element : ";
        cin>>*(*(ptr+i)+j);
      }
    cout<<"\n\n Matrix is \n";
    for(i=0;i<row;i++)
```

```
        {
            for(j=0;j<col;j++)
                cout<<ptr[i][j]<<" ";
                cout<<endl;
        }
        for(i=0;i<row;i++)
        {
            max[i]=ptr[i][0];
            for(j=1;j<col;j++)
            {
                if(max[i]<ptr[i][j])
    max[i]=ptr[i][j];
            }
        }
        cout<<"Max of each row is as follows\n ";
        for(i=0;i<row;i++)
            cout<<"Row"<<i+1<<"->"<<max[i]<<endl;
            delete [ ] ptr;
            delete max;
            getch( );
        }
```

OUTPUT :

```
Enter the number of rows
3
Enter the number of columns
3

Enter ptr[0] element : 1

Enter ptr[0] element : 2

Enter ptr[0] element : 3
Enter ptr[1] element : 4

Enter ptr[1] element : 5

Enter ptr[1] element : 6

Enter ptr[2] element : 7
```

```
Enter ptr[2] element : 8

Enter ptr[2] element : 92

 Matrix is
1 2 3
4 5 6
7 8 92
Max of each row is as follows
Row1->3
Row2->6
Row3->92
```

EXPLANATION : To create a `2-D array` dynamically we will have to take a double pointer. Initially the pointer ptr points to memory allocated for `3 rows`. The statement `ptr= new int *[row];` creates an array of pointer of size row. As each of the row will consists of a `1-D array` of `3 elements` so using for loop for the number of row (here 3 in output) we allocated memory for columns (Here 3 in output) using

```
for(i=0; i< row; i++)
ptr[i] = new int [col];
```

We are having three rows here so `ptr[0]` points to first 1-D array. `ptr[1]` points to the second 1-D array and ptr[2] points the third 1-D array. Now, the pointer ptr can be treated as a 2-D array (combination of three 1-D array). To access any of the element we can write say `ptr[i][j] or *(*(ptr+i) +j).`

For finding maximum of each row we have created a dynamic array max of size row. Initially first element of each row is considered as maximum. Then running a `for` loop for each row we find maximum of element of the row.

To delete the `2-D` array we write `delete [] ptr`. This statement first de-allocates memory each row and later deletes pointer itself.

/*PROG 4.20 DYNAMIC ARRAY OF STRINGS */

```
#include <iostream.h>
#include <conio.h>
  void main( )
  {
     int n,i;
     clrscr( );
     cout<<"Enter how many strings \n ";
     cin>>n;
     char **ptr = new char*[n];
     int *len=new int [n];
```

```
    for(i=0;i<n;i++)
    {
       cout<<"\n Enter the length of string no."<<i+1<<endl;
       cin>>len[i];
       cout<<"\nEnter string no."<<i+1<<endl;
       ptr[i]= new char [len[i]+1];
       cin>>ptr[i];
    }
    cout<<"STRING \t\t LENGTH\n";
    for(i=0;i<n;i++)
       cout<<ptr[i]<<"\t\t"<<len[i]<<endl;
       delete len;
       delete [ ] ptr;
       getch( );
 }
```

OUTPUT :

```
Enter how many strings
3
Enter the length of string no.1
6
Enter string no.1
Hari
Enter the length of string no.2
6
Enter string no.2
Ranjana
Enter the length of string no.3
7
Enter string no.3
Manmohan
STRING          LENGTH
Hari               6
Ranjana            6
Manmohan           7
```

EXPLANATION : The statement creates an array of char type pointers **ptr** of size n. ptr[0] will points to first string, ptr[1] to second and so on. Using for loop we first ask the length of the each string in turn. We then allocate memory for each string dynamically using statement ptr[i] = new char [len[i]+1];. After allocation of memory string from user is taken as input and assigned to ptr[i]. In the end we display the string and their length.

4.6 MALLOC VS NEW

There are numbers of differences between the two:

1. **malloc** cannot be overloaded whereas **new** can be.
2. The new operator can be used to create objects.
3. The default return type for malloc is **void** * whereas new returns the appropriate pointer type *i.e.*, int in case of int, float in case of float and pointer to user defined data types when memory is allocated for objects or structures.
4. **new** operator automatically calculates size of object depending upon data type. No need to use **sizeof** operator.

4.7 POINTER MEMBER OPERATORS

There are three operators which are used with pointers to members or pointer to objects. It is advised that you first clear your concepts of class then refer this section. The three operations are :

1. :: * known as pointer to member decelerator.
2. ->* known as pointer to member deference operator (through pointer).
3. .* known as pointer to member dereference operator (through value).

To create a pointer to a member of class :: * operator is used. The general syntax is:

data_type class_name :: *ptr_name =&class_name :: member _name;

For example, for a class demo having an int data member named data, pointer can be declared as :

```
int demo :: * ptr = &demo :: data;
```

To understand it more clearly recall how to create a pointer to an integer and store address of data. We will be written as:

```
int * ptr = &data;
```

Now on the left side of = operator between int and *ptr simply insert demo :: and on the right side of = operator between & and data insert demo :: . What you get ?

```
int demo :: * ptr = &demo :: data;
```

See how it is easy to define pointer to a class member.

After defining pointer ptr it can be used as:

```
demo d;
d.*ptr = 20; // assign value 20 to num of object d.
cout<<d.num<<endl; //display value 20.
```

Once a pointer has been created as shown in the above manner it will be available for all the objects created for the class. Similar to creating pointer for the data member of the class we can also create pointers for the objects also. For a class demo :

demo d;

demo *ptr = &d;

Now data members or functions can be accessed as **ptr -> num or (*ptr). Num**

```
ptr -> input (x), ptr->show()etc.
```

The -> operator is known as pointer to member operator. On the left of this there will always be a pointer.

Just like we create pointer to data member we can also create pointer to member functions of the class. But before telling you how to do it. We see how to create pointer to normal functions which are not member functions of the class. We take two examples:

```
void show ();
int disp(int, float);
```

For creating a pointer to a function we have to note the prototype of the function. In the program the return type of the function is void and function takes no argument. To create the pointer to this type of function we write in this manner.

```
void (*pf) ();
```

Here pf is pointer to function takes no argument. Parenthesis around *pf is must otherwise it will become void *pf(void); which means pf is function which takes no argument and which return an address of type void.

For second function return type is int and function takes two arguments of type int and float. To create a pointer to function of this type we write.

```
int (*pdisp)(int, float);
```

The above declaration tells the compiler that pointer pdisp is a pointer to function which can store address of a function whose return type is int and takes two arguments of type int and float.

Both the pointer to function pointers can be used as :

```
pf = &show ( ); // assigning address of function show
(*pf) ( );      // calls function show using pointer
pdisp =&disp; // assigning address of function disp
int ans=(*pdisp)(20,34.5f);//callfunction disp using pointer.
```

The ampersand (&) is not necessary as name of the function alone represent its address.

Now, assume both the above mentioned functions show and disp are public members of class demo. We now see how to create pointer to these functions of demo class.

We first write for function show. The return type is void and function does not take any argument. Follow the same ways as we did earlier but simply insert the demo :: as.

```
void (demo :: *pf) ( ) = &demo :: show;
```

Similarly for the disp function we write as :

```
int (demo :: &pdisp)(int, float) = &demo :: disp;
```

Now, for an object d of demo class, function can be called as :

```
(d.*pf) ( ); and int ans = (d.*pdisp)(20, 34.56f);
```

/*PROG 4.21 DEMO OF POINTER TO CLASS MEMBERS VER 1*/

```
#include <iostream.h>
#include <conio.h>
  class demo
  {
     public :
        int num;
  };
  void main( )
  {
     int demo :: *ptr=&demo :: num;
     demo d;
     clrscr( );
     d.*ptr = 30;
     cout<<"Number is := "<<d.num<<endl;
     getch( );
  }
```

OUTPUT :

```
Number is : = 30
```

EXPLANATION : The class demo has simply one public member num. In the main we declare pointer ptr of demo class to hold the address of the data member num. Note num being public can be accessed outside the class. If it were private then we would not have used it outside the class.

/*PROG 4.22 DEMO OF POINTER TO CLASS MEMBERS VER 2*/

```
#include <iostream.h>
#include <conio.h>
  class demo
  {
     public :
        int num;
        float f;
        char *str;
  };
  void main( )
  {
     int demo :: *iptr=&demo :: num;
     float demo :: *fptr=&demo :: f;
```

```
    char *demo :: *cptr=&demo :: str;
    demo d;
    clrscr( );
    d.*iptr=30;
    d.*fptr=24.56;
    d.*cptr="Object orinted Programming C++";
    cout<<"num :=  "<<d.num<<endl;
    cout<<"f :=  "<<d.f<<endl;
    cout<<"str :=  "<<d.str<<endl;
    getch( );
}
```

OUTPUT :

```
num := 30
f := 24.559999
str := Object orinted Programming C++
```

EXPLANATION : In the program we have declared pointers to all the data members of the class. Here it is noticeable that the assignment to data members of class has been done using pointers to members as :

d.*iptr =30

d.*fptr = 24.56

d.*cptr="Object Oriented Programming C++"

Later we will display these values using data member's **num, f and str.**

/*PROG 4.23 DEMO OF POINTER TO CLASS MEMBERS VER 3*/

```
#include <iostream.h>
#include <conio.h>
  class demo
  {
     public :
        int num;
  };
     void main( )
     {
        int demo :: *iptr=&demo :: num;
        demo d;
        clrscr( );
        d.*iptr=30;
        cout<<"num :=  "<<d.num<<endl;
```

```
        demo d1;
        d1.*iptr=50;
        cout<<"num := "<<d.*iptr<<endl;
        cout<<"nun :="<<d1.*iptr<<endl;
        getch( );
    }
```

OUTPUT :

```
num := 30
num := 30
nun := 50
```

EXPLANATION : The aim of this program is to simply show that once you have declared a pointer to any member if the demo class that pointer to member will become part of every object created as a separate copy. Here for two different object d and d1 separate copies of iptr is available.

/*PROG 4.24 POINTER TO MEMBER AND POINTER TO OBJECT */

```
#include <iostream.h>
#include <conio.h>
  class demo
  {
     public :
        int num;
  };
  void main( )
  {
     int demo :: *iptr=&demo :: num;
     demo d,*ptr;
     clrscr( );
     ptr=&d;
     d.*iptr=30;
     cout<<"num= "<<d.num<<endl;
     cout<<"num= "<<d.*iptr<<endl;
     cout<<"num= "<<(&d)->num<<endl;
     cout<<"num= "<<(&d)->*iptr<<endl;
     cout<<"num= "<<ptr->num<<endl;
     cout<<"num= "<<(*ptr).num<<endl;
     cout<<"num= "<<(*ptr).*iptr<<endl;
```

```
        cout<<"num=  "<<ptr->*iptr<<endl;
        getch( );
    }
```

OUTPUT :

```
num= 30
num= 30
num= 30
num= 30
num= 30
num= 30
num= 30
num= 30
```

EXPLANATION : In the program we have an object d and a pointer of demo class ptr which hold the address of object d. We also have a pointer to member iptr which hold address of data member's num. Now note the following :

(*a*) As address of num is held by `iptr,` writing num or `*iptr` is same.

(*b*) Address of object `d` is held by `ptr` writing `d` and `*ptr` is same.

(*c*) `num or *iptr` can be access either by object or pointer `ptr` as

(*d*) num or `d.*iptr`; // using object d.

`ptr-> num or ptr ->*iptr;` // using pointer ptr,

As &d is an address we can also write `(&d) -> num and (&d) -> *iptr`. Again as `*ptr and d` is same we can `(*ptr).num` and `(*ptr). *ptr.`

/*PROG 4.25 POINTER TO FUNCTION*/

```
#include <iostream.h>
#include <conio.h>
  void show( );
  int sum(int,int);
  void main( )
  {
     void (*pshow)( );
     int(*psum)(int,int);
     clrscr( );
     pshow=show;
     psum=sum;
        (*pshow)( );
     int x=(*psum)(30,30);
     cout<<"x=  "<<x<<endl;
```

```
        getch( );
    }
        int sum(int x,int y)
        {
            return x+y;
        }
        void show( )
        {
            cout<<"HELLO\n";
        }
```

OUTPUT :

```
HELLO
x= 60
```

EXPLANATION : In the program we have two function show and sum. Inside the main two pointers to functions for show and sum are created. The process is explained earlier. Next we call the function using these pointers.

/*PROG 4.26 POINTER TO MEMBER FUNCTION OF CLASS VER 1*/

```
#include <iostream.h>
#include <conio.h>
  class demo
  {
      public :
      int num;
      void show( );
      int max(int);
  };
  void demo :: show( )
  {
      cout<<"num=  "<<num<<endl;
  }
  int demo :: max(int x)
  {
      if(x>num)
          return x;
      else
          return num;
  }
```

```
void main( )
{
void (demo :: *pshow)( )=&demo :: show;
int (demo :: *pmax)(int)=&demo :: max;
demo d;
clrscr( );
d.num=30;
int x= 60;
cout<<"x= "<<x<<endl;
(d.*pshow)( );
int m=(d.*pmax)(x);
cout<<"max= "<<m<<endl;
getch( );
}
```

OUTPUT :

```
x= 60
num= 30
max= 60
```

EXPLANATION : Read the explanation of the beginning program.

4.8 PONDERABLE POINTS

1. A reference variable is new name for a variable.
2. A block can be created in a program by using {and}.
3. A reference must be initialized when it is declared.
4. All variables declared in the block are considered local to that block and cannot outside the class.
5. A `bool` data type can store logical values true and false. Any nonzero value is considered true and 0 value is considered false.
6. The operator :: is known as scope resolution operator and is used for two purpose :

   Purpose1 :- Accessing global variables and functions

   Purpose2 :- Resolving functions to which class they belong.
7. In c++ memory can be allocated dynamically using operator new and can be de-allocated using delete operator.
8. An array of reference cannot be created but a reference to an array can be created.
9. To delete a pointer `ptr` pointing to memory block allocated by new we can write `delete p`.
10. The operator .* and ->* are known as pointer to member access operator.
11. To delete a 2-D array we have to write [] `ptr`.
12. The operator :: * is known as pointer to member declarator.
13. **delete** can only be used to de-allocate memory previously allocated by **new** operator.

EXERCISE

A. True and False :

1. Array of reference can be created.
2. Size of an array can be altered dynamically.
3. A pointer to a constant can be deleted using delete operator.
4. We can create pointers to a reference variables.
5. The new operator always returns a void pointer.

B. Fill in the Blanks :

1. The .... operator should only be applied to pointers that have been allocated explicitly by the new operator.
2. A .... variable can be accessed using :: operator.
3. A reference type variable must be ....
4. Memory allocation at run time is known as ....
5. .... is known as scope resolution operator.
6. Memory allocation at compile time is known as ....
7. We cannot create .... of reference.

C. Answer the Following Questions :

1. What is the use of scope resolution operator ? Explain with suitable example.
2. What is reference ?
3. What is constant reference ?
4. How the memory is allocated and managed in C++ ?
5. Can we create array of bool data type ?
6. How to create pointer to functions ?
7. How to use bool data type in your C++ program ?
8. Explain how to declare pointer to member of a class ?
9. How the operator new and delete works ?
10. Why new is better than malloc ?
11. Write code for allocating 3-D dynamically using new.

D. Brain Drill :

1. Write a program to allocate memory for 10 string using new and display them.
2. Allocate memory for an array of 10 integers using malloc. After displaying the string de-allocate the memory using delete. Observe what you get ?
3. Write a program to find range of given data type.
4. Allocate memory for a string using new. After displaying the string de-allocate the memory using free. Observe what you get ?
5. Write a class which has two data members. Find maximum of these data members using pointers to member, pointer to object and pointer to functions.
6. Write a program to allocate memory dynamically for a 3-D array. After displaying the array de-allocate the memory using delete.

❑❑❑

CHAPTER 5

FUNCTION IN C++

5.1 INTRODUCTION

A function is a self contained block of code written once for a particular purpose but can be used again and again. A function is a basic entity for C programming language. Even the execution of our program starts from main function. They are the basic building blocks for modular programming.

Depending upon parameters and return type (discussed later) functions are classified into four categories :

(1) No return type and no arguments/parameters.

(2) No returns type but arguments/parameters.

(3) Return type but no arguments/parameters.

(4) Return type with arguments/parameters.

There are numbers of functions which we have used so far like `strlen()`, `strcpy ()`, `exit ()` etc. All these functions are library functions or built-in functions *i.e.,* they are already there in the C++ programming language and we can use them in our programs. Again each of these function belong to one of the categories given below. The limitations of these functions are that their code cannot be known, we can simply use them, and no modification can be done.

All the built-in functions have their prototype or declaration stored in their respective header files. For example, function declaration of strlen and strcpy is stored in header file string.h. The definitions of all the functions *i.e.,* the actual function code (what they do) is stored in compiled form in .obj files and are linked to the program during compilation and linking. The compiled code is stored in .obj file. Thus, we can simply use the built-in functions in our program but we cannot modify them as their code is not available to the programmer.

We can write our own functions depending upon requirements and all those functions will be called user-defined functions as they are defined by the user and be put in any of the categories given above.

One important point to note here is that `main()` is not a library function. It is simply a restriction from C++ compiler that we have to use this function for our programming as execution starts from this function. So, this can be put into the user defined function. Our whole discussion will be totally based on user defined functions.

5.2 FUNCTION DECLARATION/PROTOTYPING

In C++ each function used must be declared first. The declaration of the function is also termed as prototyping. A function prototype tells the compiler three things about a function :

1. **It's name.**
2. **Return type.**
3. **Number of arguments.**

For example : To write a function for `sum` which takes two argument of type `int` and return an int can be written as :

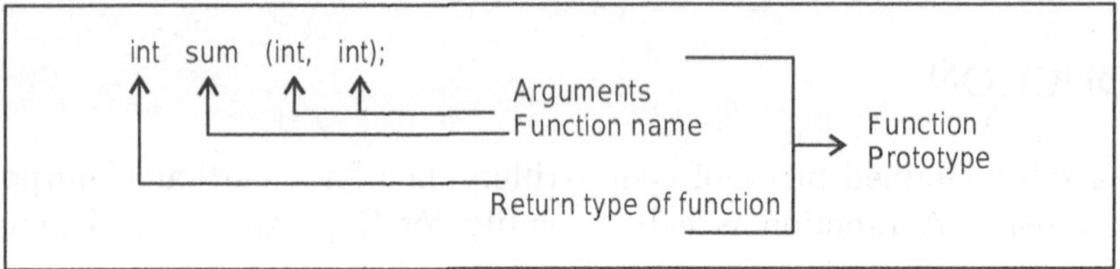

The above statement tells the compiler that sum is a function which accepts two parameters of type int and return type of function is int. We give few example of function.

/*PROG 5.1 DEMO OF FUNCTION VER 1*/

```
#include <iostream.h>
#include <conio.h>
  void main( )
  {
     void show( );
     clrscr( );
     show( );
  }
  void show( )
  {
     cout<<"Hello from show function\n";
  }
```

OUTPUT :

```
Hello from show function
```

EXPLANATION : The line void show ( ) is called declaration or prototype of the function. The general syntax is given above :

void function_name ( );

In the above context void is the return type, **show** is the function name and ( ) after function show indicates that this show function does not take any argument. Whenever you have ( ) after any name then that is a function. Obviously you may have arguments within ( ). Here void means function does not take any arguments and does not return any value. The function declaration must end with semicolon.

Actual working of the function is done by the definition of the function which is :

```
void show( )
{
 cout<<"Hello from show function";
}
```

The function definition starts with the same syntax as given for declaration but it does not end with semicolon and actual work which the function performs written in the form of C++ statements within {}. All the statements within {} of the function is called body of the function.

When we write **show ( )** it means we are calling **show ( )**. Whenever **show ( )** statement is encountered then control is transferred to the body of the function and all statements written the body of the function gets executed. When closing brace of the function is encountered then function return to the next statement after from where the function was called. In C++ every function will be called from some other function. Here we have called show ( ) from within **main ( )**. So **main ( )** is called calling function and **show ( )** is called **called/callee** function.

/*PROG 5.2 WORKING WITH TWO FUNCTIONS*/

```
#include <iostream.h>
#include <conio.h>
  void main( )
  {
     void show( );
     void disp( );
     clrscr( );
     cout<<"In main\n";
     show( );
     disp( );
     cout<<"Back in main\n";
  }
     void show( )
     {
        cout<<"In show function\n";
     }
        void disp( )
        {
        cout<<"In disp function\n";
     }
```

OUTPUT :

```
In main
In show function
In disp function
Back in main
```

EXPLANATION : Here we are working with two functions. Again prototype is given in the beginning. As clear from the output initially first cout in main() is executed then show ( ) is called and cout within show ( ) is executed. When show ( ) returns disp ( ) is called and cout within disp) is executed. When disp() is returned second cout in main () is executed, in the end program terminates.

/*PROG 5.3 DISPLAY OF INTEGER THROUGH FUNCTION VER 1*/

```
#include <iostream.h>
#include <conio.h>
 void main( )
 {
    void show(int);
    int a;
    clrscr( );
    cout<<"Enter a number \n";
    cin>>a;
    show(a);
    cout<<"after function a="<<a<<endl;
 }
    void show(int x)
    {
       cout<<"U entered ="<<x++<<endl;
 }
```

OUTPUT :

```
Enter a number

12

U entered =12

after function a=12
```

EXPLANATION : The declaration void show (int) states that function show does not return any value but accepts an argument/ parameter of int type *i.e.*, an int variable or an int constant will be passed to this function. When we call the function we pass an int value as shown by the statement show (a). Here we are calling the function show and passing a as argument. This is known as call by value as we are calling the function and passing value of the variable a. The a value sent must be collected in some variable in the function definition. We collect this value in variable x. Note the type and number of arguments must match when defining the function. Variable a in the function main is called function show a copy of a is sent which I collected in x. In the function we simply print the value of x. The change in x in function show does not affect the original value of a.

/*PROG 5.4 COMPUTE SQUARE OF FUNCTION AND RETURN USING FUNCTION*/

```
#include <iostream.h>
#include <conio.h>

void main( )
{
    int sqr(int);
    int num, s;

    clrscr( );
    cout<<"Enter the number \n";
    cin>>num;

    s=sqr(num);

    cout<<"num="<<num<<endl;
    cout<<"square of number="<<s<<endl;
}
    int sqr(int x)
    {
        int t;
        t=x*x;
        return t;
    }
```

OUTPUT :

```
Enter the number
2
num=2
square of number=4
```

EXPLANATION : The declaration int sqr(int) tells the compiler that sqr is a function which accepts an argument of type int and the int before function name sqr represent return type of function sqr *i.e.,* an int value will be returned from function sqr through return statement. In the definition/ body of the function we calculate x*x into t and return the value of t through statement return t. When this happens the t returns at the place from where the function sqr was called so the statement s= sqr(num) becomes s=t. If the value of x happens to be 5, t will have 25 when it returns and the same will be assigned to t.

Alternative function definition may be written as :

```
int sqr(int x);
{
 return x*x;
}
```

5.3 THE MAIN FUNCTION IN C++

The main function in C++ must return a value. In C++ we can define function one in two manner as :

```
int main( )
{
   function body;
}

OR

int main(int argc, char **argv);
```

Even you do not define return type of main it does not give any error but compiler simply flashes a warning. To suppress a warning define return type of main and return value from it. You can also write void before main but experts community says that it is a good programming practice to return value from main.

5.4 RECURSION

Recursion is a programming technique in which a function calls itself for a number of times until a particular condition is satisfied. It's a very important technique to understand and once understood many long listing of code can be reduced to a few number of lines. Recursion basically a word mostly used in mathematics to state a new terms in previous term such as :

$$X_{n+1} = X_n + 1 \text{ for } n>=1 \text{and } X_1 = 1$$

Then we can calculate X_2 in terms of X_1, X_3 in terms of X_2 and so on.

When solving a problem through recursion two conditions must be satisfied.

1. The problem must be expressed in recursive manner.
2. There must be a condition which stops the recursion otherwise there would be a stack overflow.

/*PROG 5.5 DEMO OF RECURSION */

```
#include <iostream.h>
#include <stdlib.h>
#include <conio.h>
void main( )
{
    static int t;
    clrscr( );
    if(t==7)
    {
        cout<<"Quit\n ";
        exit(0);
    }
    cout<<endl<<"Hello from main"<<++t;
    main( );
}
```

OUTPUT :

```
Hello from main1
Hello from main2
Hello from main3
Hello from main4
Hello from main5
Hello from main6
Hello from main7
```

EXPLANATION : A static variable persists even when function execution comes to an end and its default initial value is 0. When main ( ) executes for the first time value of t is 0. if condition falls and count after if executes. When control reaches at main ( ) the recursion starts as we are calling main from main. The main starts again for this call with value of t =1. Note static int t; statement is executed only once. cout after if gets executed and main ( ) is called again, this time with value of t=2. This continues until t does not become 5. When t becomes 5, if condition satisfies and recursion stops.

If we do not take t as static in the above program our program will be put into an infinite loop as there will be no condition which stops recursion. As each time main is called a new t will be initialized with a new value, so there will be no effect of incrementing t in the cout statement.

/*PROG 5.6 FACTORIAL OF A NUMBER USING RECURSION*/

```
#include <iostream.h>
void main( )
{
    int fact(int);
    int ans;
    int num;
    cout<<"Enter an integer number \n";
    cin>>num;

    ans=fact(num);

    cout<<"Factorial is"<<ans;
}
    int fact(int n)
    {
        return (n<1 ?1 :n*fact(n-1));
    }
```

OUTPUT :

```
Enter an integer number

5

Factorial is 120
```

EXPLANATION : Assume **n is 4**, now recursion works as :

N	function returns
4	4 * fact (3)
3	4 * (3 * fact (2))
2	4 * (3 * (2 * fact (1)))
1	4 * (3 * (2 * 1))

When recursion starts each call to function **fact** creates new set of variables here only one. Whenever recursion starts the recursive function calls does not executes immediately (in reality function addresses are put). They are saved inside the stack along with the value of variables. *(A stack is a data structure which grows upward from max_limit to 1. Each new item is "pushed" in the stack takes its place above the previously entered item. The items are "popped" out in the reverse order in which they were entered item. That's why they are called LIFO (last in first out).*

This process is called **winding** in the recursion context. When recursion is stopped in the above program when **n becomes 1** and function return the value **1,** *all the function call saved inside the stack are popped out from the stack in the reverse order and get executed i.e., fact (1) returns to fact (2) fact (2) returns to fact (3) and in the end fact (3) returns to fact (4)* which ultimately return to the **main.** This process is called *unwinding.*

5.5 CALL BY REFERENCE

In the earlier chapter, we have studied how to pass value to the function (known as call by value mechanism) and how to pass the variable to the function (known as call by address mechanism). C++ also supports call by reference mechanism in which reference of variable is passing as argument. As variable is passed by reference a new name is generated for the variable passed and whatever changes we perform inside the function, they are actually done on the actual parameter.

For example:

```
void show (int &);      //declaration of function show takes one
                        //argument of int by reference
int x=10;
show(x);  // function call
void show(int & y)      // equalivalent to int & y=x when
                        // function call is made
{
     y=y+10;
}
```

Given below we illustrates few programs which this new features of C++

/*PROG 5.7 REFERENCE VARIABLE AS FUNCTION ARGUMENT VER 1*/

```
#include <iostream.h>
#include <conio.h>

  void main( )
  {
     void change (int &);
     int x=20;

     cout<<"Before calling change \n";
     cout<<"x="<<x<<endl;

     change(x);
```

```
    cout<<"After calling change \n";
    cout<<"x="<<x<<endl;
}
    void change(int & y)
    {
       y++;
    }
```

OUTPUT :

```
Before calling change
x=20
After calling change
x=21
```

EXPLANATION : The declaration `void change (int &);` tells the compiler that change is a function which accepts a parameter of type int by reference and returns nothing. In the main we call the function as `change (x)` and pass `x` by reference. Note in the function call we does not come to know that we are passing value `x` or reference of `x`. This is resolved only when function definition is encountered. In the function definition the statement appears as `int &y= x` *i.e.*, reference of `x` is assigned to `y`. Now `x and y` become one name for the common location. So any changes made in either x or in y become one name for the common location. So any changes made in either x or y actually occurs to the data at location. In the function change we increment the value of y by 1. This change also occurs in x. So, in the main when we display the value of x, 21 will be displayed.

/*PROG 5.8 REFERENCE VARIABLE AS FUNCTION ARGUMENT SWAPPING TWO VALUES VER 1*/

```
#include <iostream.h>
#include <conio.h>

 void main( )
 {
    void swap(int &, int &);
    int x,y;

    cout<<"Enter the two numbers\n";
    cin>>x>>y;

    cout<<"Before calling swap\n";
    cout<<"x="<<x<<"\t"<<"y="<<y<<endl;
    swap(x,y);
    cout<<"After calling swap\n";
```

```
        cout<<"x="<<x<<"\t"<<"y="<<y<<endl;
    }
        void swap(int &rx, int & ry)
        {
            int t;
            t=rx;
            rx=ry;
            ry=t;
        }
```

OUTPUT :

```
Enter the two numbers
23
45
Before calling swap
x=23    y=45
After calling swap
x=45    y=23
```

EXPLANATION : When function show is called as show (a, b) to the compiler it appears as : int & rx = x and int & ry = y. Now any changes done is rx and ry will reflect back to x and y. In the function we are swapping the value of x and y with the help of third variable t. In the main after the function call swapped values of x and y will be displayed.

/*PROG 5.9 REFERENCE VARIABLE AS FUNCTION ARGUMENT SWAPPING TWO VALUES VER 2*/

```
#include <iostream.h>
#include <conio.h>

  void main( )
  {
      void swap(int &, int &);

      int x,y;
      clrscr( );

      cout<<"Enter the two numbers \n";
      cin>>x>>y;

      cout<<"Before calling swap\n";
      cout<<"x="<<x<<"\t"<<"y="<<y<<endl;
```

```
        swap(x,y);

        cout<<"After calling swap\n";
        cout<<"x="<<x<<"\t"<<"y="<<y<<endl;
    }

        void swap(int & rx,int & ry)
        {
            rx=rx+ry;
            ry=rx - ry;
            rx=rx - ry;
        }
```

OUTPUT :

Enter the two numbers

23 45

Before calling swap

x=23 y=45

After calling swap

x=45 y=23

EXPLANATION : The program remains same but the logic to `swap` two values changes. Without using third variable we change the values. Check the logic against any value of `x` and `y`. Take an example for `x=10 and y=5`

x= x + y => x = 10 + 5 => x =15

y = x – y => y = 15 – 5 => y = 10

x = x – y => y = 15 – 10 => x= 5

/*PROG 5.10 REFERENCE VARIABLE AS FUNCTION ARGUMENT SWAPPING TWO VALUES VER 3*/

```
#include <iostream.h>
#include <conio.h>

  void main( )
  {
```

```
    void swap(int &, int &);
    int x,y;

    clrscr( );
    cout<<"Enter the two numbers \n";
    cin>>x>>y;

    cout<<"x="<<x<<"\t"<<"y="<<y<<endl;
    getch( );
}
void swap(int & rx, int &ry)
{
    rx= rx^ry;
    ry=rx^ry;
    rx=rx^ry;
}
```

OUTPUT :

```
Enter the two numbers

23

45

x=23    y=45
```

EXPLANATION : The program uses third method of swapping two variables with the help of bitwise **XOR** operator ^. Take an example for better understanding point of view.

```
Let   a = 5 (0101 in binary)
      b = 7 (0111 in binary)
1.    a = a ^ b (a = 0101 ^ 0111 => a = 0010)
2.    b = a ^ b (b = 0010 ^ 0111 => b = 0101)
3.    a = a ^ b (a = 0010 ^ 0101 => a = 0111)
```

/*PROG 5.11 REFERENCE VARIABLE AS FUNCTION ARGUMENT SWAPPING TWO STRING*/

```
#include <iostream.h>
#include <conio.h>
#include <string.h>
```

```
void main( )
{
   void swap(char* &, char* &);
   char s1[10],s2[10];

   clrscr( );
   cout<<"Enter first name \n";
   cin>>s1;

   cout<<"Enter second name \n";
   cin>>s2;

   cout<<"Before calling swap\n";
   cout<<"s1="<<s1<<"s2="<<s2<<endl;

   swap(s1,s2);

   cout<<"After calling swap\n";
   cout<<"s1="<<s1<<"\t"<<"s2="<<s2<<endl;

   getch( );
}

void swap(char* & rx, char* & ry)
{
   char temp[10];
   strcpy(temp,rx);
   strcpy(rx,ry);
   strcpy(ry,temp);
}
```

OUTPUT :

```
Enter first name

HARI

Enter second name

MOHAN

Before calling swap
```

```
s1=HARI s2=MOHAN

After calling swap

s1=MOHAN s2=HARI
```

EXPLANATION : Similar to swapping two numbers we can swap two strings also. But the string has to copy via built-in string copy function strcpy. Reference to string has been explained earlier.

/*PROG 5.12 TAKING REFERENCE OF A VARIABLE VER 2*/

```
#include <iostream.h>
#include <conio.h>

  void main( )
  {
     void show1(int &);
     void show2(int &);

     int x=10;
     clrscr( );

     show1(x);
     cout<<"x="<<x<<endl;
     getch( );
  }

  void show2(int & z)
  {
     z++;
  }

  void show1(int & y)
  {
     y++;
     show2(y);
  }
```

OUTPUT :

```
x=12
```

EXPLANATION : **x** in **main**, y in show1 and z is show2 all refer to the same memory location and x is incremented twice one in show1 and one is show2. So the output.

/*PROG 5.13 TAKING REFERENCE OF A REFERENCE VARIABLE VER 3 */

```
#include <iostream.h>
#include <conio.h>

void main( )
{
    void show1(int);
    void show2(int &);

    int x=10;
    clrscr( );

    show1(x);

    cout<<"x="<<x<<endl;
    getch( );
}

void show2(int & x)
{
    x++;
}
void show1(int x)
{
    x++;
    show2(x);
}
```

OUTPUT :

```
x=10
```

EXPLANATION : In `show1()` function `x` was passed as value so `x` in `show1` is formal parameter and ++`x` in `show1` does not affect original `x` in `main`. In `show2()` argument is passed by reference but `show2` was called from `show1` and local `x` of `show1` was passed to `show2`. In `show2` incrementing `x` by `1` affect `x` of `show1`.

5.6 CALL BY REFERENCE Vs CALL BY ADDRESS

To compare call by reference and call by address we consider a function change as :

Table : Shows the Difference between Call by Address and Call by Reference

Call By Address	*Call By References*

void change(int *, int *);
void change(int * x, int *y)
{
*x = *x + 10;
*y = *y + 20;
}
int a = 10, b = 20;
change (&a, &b);
	void change (int &, int &);
	void change(int & x, int & y)
	{
	x = x + 10;
	y = y + 20;
	}
	int a =10, b=20;
	change(a,b);

Let CBA ⟶ CALL BY ADDRESS

CBR ⟶ CALL BY REFERENCE

Now, we can see that in **call by address (CBA)** declaration we have to write **int*** and while calling function we write we pass address of variable **a and b** as **change (&a, &b).** In case of **call by reference (CBR),** in the declaration we write **int &** and in calling we write **change (a, b).**

When the function is called in **CBA,** address of **a and b** are passed and new location are created for formal parameters **x and y.** In case of CBR only reference of **a and b** is created *i.e.,* new name for the location **a and b** is created, but no new location is created for **x and y.**

As we can seen from the columns **CBR** approach looks neat and clean as compare to **CBA** approach.

POINTER Vs REFERENCE

(*a*) A reference is a constant pointer. This is not the case with pointer.

(*b*) During function call with reference we write **show (a)** but with pointer we write **show (&a).**

(*c*) We cannot create an array of reference, but array of pointers can be created.

(*d*) A reference has to be initialized when declared. This not the case with pointer.

5.7 RETURN BY REFERENCE

In the normal function call, if function return some value of any type the function call is put on to the right side of assignment operator and variable which stores the value is written on the left hand side. But in C++ a function can return by reference which means that function call can be put on to the left hand side of = operator(assignment operator). As the function by reference we will have to provide some value to it on the right hand side. The general syntax of a function returning by reference is as shown below :

```
return_type & function_name (arguments)
{
    function body;
}
```

Inside the function, the function must not return the reference of any local variable as local variable dies as soon as control goes out of scope. So either you return the reference of any local variable or pass argument to the function by reference. I present few examples for better understanding point of view.

/*PROG 5.14 DEMO OF RETURN BY REFERENCE VER 1*/

```
#include <iostream.h>
#include <conio.h>

  int x;

  int & retref(int p)
  {
     x=x+p;
     return x;
  }
  void main( )
  {
     clrscr( );

     retref(5)=45;

     cout<<"x="<<x<<endl;
     getch( );
  }
```

OUTPUT :

```
x=45
```

EXPLANATION : In return by reference as stated above function call can appear in the left hand side of assignment operator. The program simply demonstrate how to do this. The function retref returns the reference of x which is a global variable. In the function we pass 5. This value 5 is collected in p and function returns reference of x. As function return by reference and a reference has to be initialized so x contains a value 45.

Note: Never return reference of a local variable as local variable dies as soon as control returns from the function and what is the use of value of a variable which no longer exists.

/*PROG 5.15 DEMO OF RETURN BY REFERENCE VER 2*/

```
#include <iostream.h>
#include <conio.h>

int & greater(int & a, int & b)
{
   return a>b ?a : b;
}

void main( )
{
   int x,y;
   clrscr( );
   cout<<"Enter the value of x and y\n";
   cin>>x>>y;

   greater(x,y)=501;

   cout<<"Greater will have reward of 501\n";
   cout<<"x="<<x<<"\t"<<"y="<<y<<endl;

   getch( );
}
```

OUTPUT :

```
Enter the value of x and y

23  45

Greater will have reward of 501

x=23  y=501
```

EXPLANATION : In the program the function greater takes two parameter of type int by reference and return an int by reference. As the function greater by reference we can put this function on the left hand side of **assignment (=) operator**. When the statement **greater(x,y)=501;** executes, the reference parameter x and y in function greater appear as int & a= x and int & b =y. The function finds maximum of a and b and returns reference of maximum value. Here in the program maximum was **y (45)** so function greater returns reference of y. In the **main** the statement replaces as :

y=501; and y gets value 501.

/*PROG 5.16 DEMO OF RETURN BY REFERENCE VER 3*/

```
#include <iostream.h>
#include <conio.h>

#define S 5

int a[S], *p;

  void main( )
  {
     int i;
     int* & fun( );
     int b[S]={1,2,3,4,5};

     clrscr( );
     cout<<"Before calling function\n";
     for(i=0;i<S;i++)
     cout<<a[i]<<" ";
     cout<<endl;
     fun( )=b;
     cout<<"After calling function";
     cout<<endl;
     for(i=0;i<S;i++)
     cout<<p[i]<<"";
     cout<<endl;
     getch( );
  }
 int* & fun( )
 {
   p=a;
   return p;
 }
```

OUTPUT :

```
Before calling function

0 0 0 0 0

After calling function

12345
```

EXPLANATION : The function declaration **int* & fun ( );** tells the compiler that function fun returns a reference to an int type pointer. In the main we are creating an array **b** with **5** values. The array **a** is global and have all its elements initialized to zero. The statement **fun ( ) = b;** calls the function **fun ( )** first. In the function we initially assign the case address of the array **a to p** and return the **p**. In the main **fun ( ) = b;** becomes **p=b** *i.e.,* **p** points to **array b.** Now **p** can be treated as an integer array which prints elements of **b.**

5.8 INLINE FUNCTION

Inline functions are functions which are expanded inline. To make a function inline we simple put keyword inline before the functions definitions. These functions are different from normal functions that in normal function call control is transferred to the place where the actual function definition is written. For example, consider the following dummy code of the program:

```
void main( )
{
   void show( );
   statements;
   statements;
   show( );        //function called here
   statements;     // next statement where function returns
   statements;
}
void show( )
{
   statements;
   statements;
   statements;
}
```

During the execution of the program when function call show is encountered, compiler saves the state of various registers, variables occurred in the program prior to function call show. It also saves the address of the next instruction after the function call show as it has to return to this statement when function show returns. All these are saved onto the stack as stack-frame or activation record. The body of the function show is executed. When the function is about to return, before returning it pops up the various values from the stack-frame and in the end pops the address from where it has to resume. This address is put into the program counter and execution resumes from the statement following function call show.

All these calling the function, saving registers, variables, and return address in stack-frame, popping them back when function returns causes overhead. As these will be done for every function call.

Inline function is not work in the way as explained above manner. They are expanded where they are called. That is the whole body of the inline function is put at the place where function was called. This saves time as there is no control transfer, no saving and popping back from stack-frame. So inline function executes faster than normal function. But at the place of inline function call, the code is expanded. If you have called inline function from 100 places in your program, the code will be expanded 100 places in your program thus increasing program size. So a trade-off between program size and execution efficiency is there. The general syntax of defining the inline functions as:

```
inline return type function_name (parameters)
{
    function definition;
}
```

Some Important Points About Inline Function

1. Inline function is a request to the compiler thus inline function may not work as inline some times. In this regard they differ from macro, which work as macro always.
2. Inline function executes faster than normal function.
3. Strict type checking is performed for variables that are passed as arguments, which is not done in case of macro.
4. Inline function does not produce side effects whereas macro does.
5. All inline functions must be defined prior to their use.
6. Inline function does not work as inline when code contains loops, recursions, goto, switch, static variable etc.
7. They are used where function definition are small so calling cost and overhead for normal functions can be minimized.

/*PROG 5.17 DEMO OF INLINE FUNCTION VER 1*/

```
#include <iostream.h>
#include <conio.h>

inline void show( )
{
  cout<<"Hello from inline show\n";
}

void main( )
{
  clrscr( );
  show( );
  getch( );
}
```

OUTPUT :

Hello from inline show

EXPLANATION : The function show is inline so when it is called in the main it is simply expanded in the main. That is, all the statements written in the function show appear at the place of function call. Here we are having just one cout statement so it appear through we have written cout statement within main itself similar to macro.

/*PROG 5.18 DEMO OF INLINE FUNCTION VER 2*/

```
#include <iostream.h>
#include <conio.h>

inline void show( );

void main( )
{
   show( );
}
inline void show( )
{
   cout<<"Hello from inline show\n";
}
```

OUTPUT :

Hello from inline show

EXPLANATION : An inline function has to be defined before it can be used. But the above program works fine in **Visual Studio C++** compiler. However, in **Turbo C 3.0** on executing the program makes system halts. There is no compilation error in **Turbo C3.0.**

/*PROG 5.19 SQUARE OF A NUMBER USING INLINE FUNCTION VER 1*/

```
#include <iostream.h>
#include <conio.h>

inline int square(int x)
{
   return x*x;
}

void main( )
```

```
{
  int num,snum;

  clrscr( );

  cout<<"Enter a number \n";
  cin>>num;

  cout<<"Square of "<<num<<"is "<<square(num)<<endl;
  getch( );
}
```

OUTPUT :

```
Enter a number
8
Square of 8 is 64
```

EXPLANATION : When the function is called as square (num), the function call is expanded in line as num*num. Rest is easy to understand.

/*PROG 5.20 SQUARE OF A NUMBER USING INLINE FUNCTION VER 2*/

```
#include <iostream.h>
#include <conio.h>
inline int square (int x)
{
  return x*x;
}

void main( )
{
  int s1=square (2+3);
  int s2=square (3*4-5+6/2);
  int s3=square (++s1);

  clrscr( );

  cout<<"s1="<<s1<<endl;
  cout<<"s2="<<s2<<endl;
  cout<<"s3="<<s3<<endl;
```

```
    getch( );
}
```

OUTPUT :

```
s1=26

s2=100

s3=676
```

EXPLANATION : Before expanding the function as function call is encountered compiler first computes the expression written as argument and make a single argument. So square (2+3) first turned into square (5) then expanded, similarly square (3*4-5+6/2) turned into square (10) and finally square (++s1) turned into square (26).

/*PROG 5.21 SQR OF A NUMBER USING MACRO*/

```
#include<iostream.h>
#define SQR(x) (x*x)
#include <conio.h>

void main( )
{
    int s1=SQR(2+3);
    int s2=SQR(3*4–5+6/2);
    int s3=SQR(++s1);

    clrscr( );
    cout<<"s1="<<s1<<endl;
    cout<<"s2="<<s2<<endl;
    cout<<"s3="<<s3<<endl;
    getch( );
}
```

OUTPUT :

```
s1=13
s2=41
s3=156
```

EXPLANATION : The side effect of macro can be seen in the above program. When macro SQR is expanded all three statements appear as :

int s1=2+3*2+3;

int s2= 3*4-5*6/2*3*4-5+6/2;

int s3=++s1 * ++s1;

Now,

s1= 2+6+3=11;

s2= 12-5+3*3*4-5+3;

s2= 12+36+3-10;

s2=41

Due to pre increment twice and same value is used in the expression so **s3= 13 * 13 = 169**.

/*PROG 5.22 FINDING CUBE OF A NUMBER USING INLINE FUNCTION*/

```
#include <iostream.h>
#include <conio.h>

 inline int cube(int x)
 {
   return x*x*x;
 }

 void main( )
 {
   int num;
   clrscr( );

   cout<<"Enter a number \n";
   cin>>num;
   cout<<"Cube of"<<num<<"is"<<cube (num)<<endl;

   getch( );
 }
```

OUTPUT :

```
Enter a number

12

Cube of 12 is 1728
```

EXPLANATION : The program is self-explanatory.

/*PROG 5.23 MAXIMUM OF TWO NUMBERS USING INLINE FUNCTION */

```
#include <iostream.h>
#include <conio.h>

inline int max(int x,int y)
{
  return x>y ? x :y;
}

void main( )
{
  int n1,n2;

  clrscr( );

  cout<<"Enter two numbers \n";
  cin>>n1>>n2;

  int m=max(n1,n2);

  cout<<"Max="<<m<<endl;
  getch( );
}
```

OUTPUT :

```
Enter two numbers
12
45
Max=45
```

EXPLANATION : At the place of function call **max (n1, n2),** function is explained as return x>y ? X : y, value of n1 and n2 is assigned to x and y.

5.9 FUNCTION OVERLOADING

Overloading refers to use of same thing for different purpose. Function overloading refers to creating numbers of functions with the same name which performs different tasks. Function overloading is also known as function polymorphism. Function overloading relieves us from remembering so many functions names with type of arguments they take. In function overloading we can create number of functions with the same name but either number of arguments or type of arguments must be different. We provide few examples:

1. **int sum (int);**
   float sum(float);
   double sum(double);

Here, we have declared three functions with the same name sum. Each function takes just one parameter but all are of different types. That is number of parameters in all overloaded function sum is same but type of parameter is different.

2. **void show(int,int);**
   Void show(int);
   Void show(int,int,int);

Here number of parameters a re not same in show functions but type is same.

3. **void show(int,char);**
   void show (char,int,float);
   void show(int);
   int show(int,int);
   float show(char,char,char);

Here we have a mix of overloaded show functions. Some have same number of arguments but type is different and some have same type of argument but numbers of argument are different.

When we have number of overloaded functions in a program, which function to call is determined by either checking type of argument or number of argument. Note return type does not play any role in function overloading as which function to call is determined by checking type and number of argument a function accepts. When control is transferred to function and function is about to return after execution then return type comes to play.

In function overloading compiler first tries to find an exact match. If exact match is not find then integral promotion/ demotion is used. User defined conversion methods may be used also in case a class object is to be converted to any built-in type or vice-versa.

/*PROG 5.24 DEMO OF FUNCTION OVERLOADING VER 1*/

```
#include <iostream.h>
#include <conio.h>

void main( )
{
  void show(int);
  void show(float);
  void show(char);
  void show(char*);

  int x=10;
  float y=23.45;
  char ch= 'p';
```

```
  char * s="overload";

  clrscr( );
  show(x);
  show(y);
  show(ch);
  show(s);
  getch( );
}

void show(int x)
{
  cout<<"int show x="<<x<<endl;
}

void show(float y)
{
  cout<<"float show y="<<y<<endl;
}

void show(char ch)
{
  cout<<"char show ch="<<ch<<endl;
}

void show(char*s)
{
  cout<<"char *s show s="<<s<<endl;
}
```

OUTPUT :

```
int show x        =10
float show y      = 23.45
char show ch      = p
char *s show s  = overload
```

EXPLANATION : In the program we have functions **show** overloaded **4** times. The function takes a single parameter but each parameter is different in each function as can be seen from the program. In the **main** 4 variable of type **int, char, float and char *** type are generated and **show** is called with these parameters. Each parameter is passed to **show** and **show** is called **4 times**. The compiler depending upon type of argument to function show calls the respective version of the show function *i.e.,* in case of **show(x),** show function of **int** version will be called and so on.

/*PROG 5.25 DEMO OF FUNCTION OVERLOADING VER 2*/

```
#include <iostream.h>
#include <conio.h>

void main( )
{
  void show(int);
  void show(double);

  clrscr( );

  show(23);
  show('p');
  show(2.5f);
  show(3.45);
  getch( );
}

void show(int x)
{
  cout<<"int show x="<<x<<endl;
}

void show(double s)
{
  cout<<"double show s="<<s<<endl;
}
```

OUTPUT :

```
int show x=23
int show x=112
int show x=2.5
int show x=3.45
```

EXPLANATION : In the program we have just overloaded function `show` which takes a single parameter of `int and double` respectively. In function call `show (23), int` version of show is called as `23` is an integer. In function call `show ('p'), int` version of `show` is called why ? The compiler searches for an overloaded `show` function which takes a parameter of type `char`, but it fails as there is no such overloaded function we have written. So it does integral promotion from char to integer and calls the `int` version of `show` function displaying `ASCII` value of `'p'`. Similarly in function call `show (2.5f)`, compiler look for an overloaded function `show` which takes `float` type argument. If fails and overloaded function `show` with `double` type value is called.

/*PROG 5.26 DEMO OF FUNCTION OVERLOADING VER 3*/

```
#include <iostream.h>
#include <conio.h>

void main( )
{
  void show(float);
  void show(double);

  clrscr( );

  show(23);
  show(2.5f);
  show(3.45);

  getch( );
}

void show(float x)
{
  cout<<"float show x="<<x<<endl;
}

void show(double s)
{
  cout<<"double show s="<<s<<endl;
}
```

OUTPUT :

ERROR

'show' : ambiguous call to overloaded function

EXPLANATION : The function call `show (23)` is ambiguous as there is no overloaded function `show` which takes an `int` type of value. Now compiler is in dilemma whether to call overloaded `float` version of show or overloaded `double` version of `show` as can be converted to `float` as well as to `double`.

/*PROG 5.27 DEMO OF FUNCTION OVERLOADING VER 4*/

```
#include <iostream.h>
#include <conio.h>

void main( )
{
   void show(int);
   void show(float);

   clrscr( );
   show('p');
   show(3.45);

   getch( );
}
 void show(float x)
 {
   cout<<"float show x="<<x<<endl;
 }

 void show(int s)
 {
   cout<<"int show s="<<s<<endl;
 }
```

OUTPUT :

Error

'show' : ambiguous call to overloaded function

EXPLANATION : The error is clear as we have not defined an overloaded function `show` for the `double data type`. When function call `show (3.45)` is encountered compiler look for an overloaded function show which takes a single parameter of `double` type. But the error is not what we are thinking. The function call `show ('p')` calls the `int` version of `show`. In the function call `show (3.45)` as overloaded show for `double` data type was not written, `int` or `float` version of `show` can be called. Deciding this confuses the compiler and it generates the error. One more example of demotion is given.

/*PROG 5.28 DEMO OF FUNCTION OVERLOADING VER 5*/

```
#include <iostream.h>
#include <conio.h>
```

```
void main( )
{
  void show(int);
  clrscr( );
  show(5.47f);
  show(3.45);
  getch( );
}

void show(int s)
{
  cout<<"int show s="<<s<<endl;
}
```

OUTPUT :

```
int show s=5
int show s=3
```

EXPLANATION : Demotion takes place from `float to int` in function call `show (5.47f)` and from `double to int` in function call `show (3.45)`.

/*PROG 5.29 DEMO OF FUNCTION OVERLOADING VER 6*/

```
#include <iostream.h>
#include <conio.h>

void main( )
{
  void show(float);
  void show(char);

  clrscr( );
  show(4.76f);
  show(345);
  getch( );
}
void show(char x)
{
  cout<<"Char show x="<<x<<endl;
}
```

```
void show(float s)
{
  cout<<"int show s="<<s<<endl;
}
```

OUTPUT :

Error

'show' : ambiguous call to overloaded function.

EXPLANATION : As there is no overloaded `int` version of `show`, the compiler is in confusion whether to demote `int` or `char` and call version of `show` or promote `int` to `float` and `call float`.

/*PROG 5.30 FUNCTION OVERLOADING MAX OF TWO NUMBERS */

```
#include <iostream.h>
#include <conio.h>

void main( )
{
  int x,y, intmax;
  float f1,f2,fmax;
  char ch1,ch2,chmax;

  int max2(int,int);
  float max2(float,float);
  char max2(char,char);

  clrscr( );
  cout<<"Enter two integers \n";
  cin>>x>>y;

  cout<<"Enter two floats\n";
  cin>>f1>>f2;
  cout<<"Enter two chars \n";
  cin>>ch1>>ch1;

  intmax=max2(x,y);

  fmax=max2(f1,f2);

  chmax=max2(ch1,ch2);
```

```
  cout<<"Max of two int is "<<intmax<<endl;
  cout<<"Max of two float is "<<fmax<<endl;
  cout<<"Max of two char is"<<chmax<<endl;

  getch( );
}
int max2(int x,int y)
{
  return(x>y ?x :y);
}

float max2(float x,float y)
{
  return(x>y ?x :y);
}

char max2(char x,char y)
{
  return(x>y ?x :y);
}
```

OUTPUT :

```
Enter two integers
123 567
Enter two floats
12.34
56.78
Enter two chars
a g
Max of two int is 567
Max of two float is 56.78
Max of two char is g
```

EXPLANATION : We have in the program three over of function `max2` which takes two parameters of type `int, char, and float` and returns the maximum of two numbers. Depending upon type of parameter appropriate version of `max2` function is called.

5.10 FUNCTION WITH DEFAULT ARGUMENTS

In C ++ it is possible for a function not to specify all its arguments. Some of the arguments may be specified their default values at the time of declaring the function. When a function having default argument is called, compiler checks for the number and type of argument as well as was not specified during the function call, default value of that argument is assumed. In case we provide a new value, default argument is overridden.

For example :

void show (int x, int y = 20);

The function show takes two argument of int type out of which second argument from left is default. In case function is called as show (10), default value of y *i.e.,* 20 is assumed. If function is called as show (10,100) than default value of y *i.e.,* 20 is overridden. It is possible not to provide even the formal parameter names during function declaration *i.e.,* we may declare the above function show as

void show (int, int = 20);

In a function with default argument, if one argument is default, all successive arguments must be default. We cannot provide default values in the middle of the arguments or towards left side. We provide few examples:

1. void fun(int x, int y = 20, int z=35);
2. void fun(int x, int y = 30, int z);
3. void fun(int x = 45, int y);

Out of three examples given only 1 is valid and 2 and 3 are invalid. In the 2 middle argument is default and the next argument z is not default. In the 3 first argument is default and next argument is not default.

/*PROG 5.31 DEMO OF FUNCTION WITH DEFAULT ARGUMENT VER 1*/

```
#include <iostream.h>
#include <conio.h>

void main( )
{
 void show(int x=10);

 clrscr( );

 cout<<"Called show with argument 20\n";
 show(20);

 cout<<"Called show without argument \n";
 show( );

 getch( );
}
void show(int y)
```

```
{
 cout<<"Argument to show was"<<y<<endl;
}
```

OUTPUT :

Called show with argument 20

Argument to show was20

Called show without argument

Argument to show was10

EXPLANATION : The function show takes just one argument of type int which is a default argument. Note default argument has to be specified in the function declaration. Writing it in function definition is optional. In the function call `show (20)`, the default argument is overridden and y takes the value `20`. In the function call `show()` as no argument was specified, the compiler assumes default value `10` for `y`. Note argument name is declaration and definition are different, they may be same. Note function declaration can be written in the following manner too:

```
void show (int=10);
```

/*PROG 5.32 DEMO OF FUNCTION WITH DEFAULT ARGUMENTS VER 2*/

```
#include <iostream.h>
#include <conio.h>

void main( )
{
 void show(char* s="Good Morning");
 clrscr( );
 show( );

 show("Good Evening");
 getch( );
}
void show(char *s)
{
 cout<<"Argument to show was"<<s<<endl;
}
```

OUTPUT :

Argument to show was Good Morning

Argument to show was Good Evening

EXPLANATION : The program is similar to previous one with the difference that we have taken default parameter of `char *` type.

/*PROG 5.33 DEMO OF FUNCTION WITH DEFAULT ARGUMENT VER 3*/

```
#include <iostream.h>
#include <conio.h>
void main( )
{
  void show(int, int =30);

  clrscr( );

  show(20);

  show(23,34);

  getch( );
}

void show(int q,int r)
{
  cout<<"Argument to show was\n";
  cout<<"q="<<q<<"\t r="<<r<<endl;
}
```

OUTPUT :

```
Argument to show was
q=20 r=30
Argument to show was
q=23 r=34
```

EXPLANATION : In the function call **show (20), 20** is passed to **q** and **r** takes default value **20.** In the function call **show (23, 34) q** takes value **23** and default parameter is overridden so **r** takes value **34.**

/*PROG 5.34 DEMO OF FUNCTION WITH DEFAULT ARGUMENT VER 4*/

```
#include <iostream.h>
#include <conio.h>

void main( )
```

```
{
  void show(int =20,int =30, int =40);

  clrscr( );

  show(1,2,3);
  show(1,2);
  show(1);
  show( );

  getch( );
}

void show(int p,int q,int r)
{
  cout<<"Argument to show was\n";
  cout<<"p="<<p<<"\tp="<<q<<"\tr="<<r<<endl;
}
```

OUTPUT :

```
Argument to show was

p=1        p=2        r=3

Argument to show was
p=1        p=2        r=40

Argument to show was

p=1        p=30       r=40

Argument to show was

p=20       p=30       r=40
```

EXPLANATION : In the function show all three parameters are default. In the function call **show (1, 2, 3)** all three default parameters are overridden and **1, 2, 3** assigned to **p, q, r** respectively. In the function call **show (1, 2)** the two parameters (from left) are overridden and **r** takes default value. Similar analogy applies to rest of the **show** statements.

/*PROG 5.35 DEMO OF FUNCTION WITH DEFAULT ARGUMENTS VER 5*/

```
#include <iostream.h>
#include <conio.h>

void main( )
{
  void show(int p=20,int q,int r=40);

  clrscr( );

  show(1,2,3);
  show(1,2);
  show(1);
  show( );
  getch( );
}
void show(int p, int q, int r)
{
  cout<<"Argument to show was \n";
  cout<<"p="<<p<<"\tq="<<q<<"\tr="<<r<<endl;
}
```

OUTPUT :

Error
Missing default parameter for parameter 2

EXPLANATION : In the function when one argument is default, all argument following the default argument must be argument. In the function call show (1), 1 is assigned to p and default value 20 is overridden, but parameter 2 was not default so a value has to be given. So the compiler generates error.

/*PROG 5.36 DEMO OF FUNCTION WITH DEFAULT ARGUMENTS, FINDING BONUS FOR AN EMPLOYEE*/

```
#include <iostream.h>
#include <conio.h>
void main( )
{
  void incr(float & sal, float bonus_pr=10);
  float s;
```

```
clrscr( );

cout<<"Enter the salary \n";
cin>>s;

if(s>=5000)
incr(s,15);
else
incr(s);

cout<<"Salary with bonus="<<s<<endl;
getch( );
}

void incr(float & sal, float bonus_pr)
{
sal = sal*(1+bonus_pr/100);
}
```

OUTPUT :

```
Enter the salary
7000
Salary with bonus=8050
```

EXPLANATION : The function **incr** finds new salary after adding bonus to the original salary. If salary is **<5000** we provide a bonus of **10%** of **sal** else we provide bonus of **15%** of salary.

5.11 PONDERABLE POINTS

1. Based on the nature of creation there are two categories of function : **built-in and user-defined.**
2. For all the built-in functions (also called library functions) prototype is stored in the header files and compiled code (which we cannot see) is stored in **.Obj file** form in special files called library. One library may contain number of compiled functions.
3. The functions which are predefined and supplied along with the compiler are known as *built-in function.*
4. The function **main( )** can appear only once in a C program, because execution commences from the first statement in the **main ( )** function. If there is more than one **main( )** function, there will be a confusion while commencing the execution.

5. A function that performs no action is known as dummy function. It is a valid function. Dummy function may be used as a place- holder, which facilitates adding new functions later on. For example:

   void dummy ( ) { }

6. Advantages of recursion :

   (*a*) Easier understand the program logic.

   (*b*) Helpful in implementing recursively defined data structure.

   (*c*) Compact code can be written.

7. Use of return statement helps in early exiting from a function apart from returning a value from a function.
8. C++ permits three ways to pass argument to function : call by value, call by address and call by reference.
9. Passing an argument by reference does not create new memory location, where passing an argument by address or by value creates memory location.
10. For every function used in C++, prior declaration is must.
11. Function prototyping, declaration or signature all is same thing.
12. Function declaration tells the compiler three things : function name, types and number of argument it takes, return type of the function.
13. A function expanded in line is known as inline function.
14. Use of inline function makes execution of program faster but increases program size.
15. Inline function is better than macro as they produce no side effects and type checking is performed for the arguments.
16. When function return by reference, function call can be placed on the left hand side of = (assignment) operator.
17. Function overloading is the creation of number of function with the same name but they differ either in type of argument or number of arguments.
18. There is no limit on how many functions can be overloaded in a program.
19. Return type does not serve any purpose in function overloading.
20. In C++ a function can have default arguments which are used when not all the parameters are supplied to the function.
21. In a function with default argument, when one argument is default, then all successive arguments (towards right) must be default.

EXERCISE

A. True and False :

1. Inline keywords makes function inline which is request to the compiler.
2. Inline function may or may not work as inline.
3. Inline function speed up the execution but increases program size.
4. C++ allows a function to have multiple numbers of arguments.
5. Calls to inline functions are always expanded by the compiler.

6. Call by reference is better than call by address.
7. bool data type can have float type of arguments.

B. Answer the Following Questions :

1. What is function prototyping ? What does it tell about a function ?
2. How main is declared in C++ ?
3. What is recursion ? Why do we need it ?
4. Explain the concept of inline functions.
5. How inline function is different from macro ?
6. What are the advantages of inline functions ?
7. What is function overloading ?
8. What is the difference between function overloading and function overriding ?
9. What is the difference between call be value/address/ reference ?
10. Write difference between pointers and reference.
11. What is the advantage of passing default argument to functions ?
12. How many values can be returned from a function ?
13. Where is function returned type specified ?
14. Here is a function :

```
int times2(int a)
{
        return (a*2);
}
```

    Write a main( ) program that includes everything necessary to call this function.
15. In what unusual place can you use a function call when a function returns a value by reference ?
16. What is the significance of empty parenthesis in a function declaration ?
17. What is the purpose of using argument names in a function declaration ?

C. Brain Drill :

1. Write a program to return more than one value from function using reference variable.
2. Write an inline function to display lines of different patterns.
3. Write a C++ program to arrange a list of names in ascending order using an array of pointers to strings.
4. Write a program in C++ to find the area and perimeter of a circle using pointers.
5. Write a program to accept a float number through the keyboard. Calculate the square of the number. Separate the float number into integer and fractional part. Individually calculate the square of an integer and fractional part and add them in another variable. Compare the two squares obtained.
6. Write a program to list all the strings whose initials starts with a given input character using function and pointer.
7. Write a program to find kth element in an array of strings *i.e.*, string whose length is maximum.
8. Write a function to find power of a given number like pow ( ) function.
9. Write a program to display only integer portion of the given floating point number without typecasting ?

10. Write a program using function to round up and round down the floating point number.
11. Write a function called swap ( ) that interchanges two int values passed to it by the calling program. (Note that this function swaps the values of the variables in the calling program, not those in the function) You will need to decide how to pass the arguments. Create a main( ) program to exercise the function.
12. Write a function that, when you call it, displays a message telling how many times it has been called : "I have been called 3 times", or whatever. Write a main( ) program that calls this function at least 10 times. Try implementing this function in two different ways. First, use external variables to store the count. Second, use a local static variable. Which is more appropriate ? Why can't you use an automatic variable ?
13. Raising a number n to a power p is the same as multiplying n by itself p times. Write a program called power( ) that takes a double value for n and an int value for p, and returns the result as a double value. Use a default argument of 2 for p, so that if this argument is omitted, the number n will be squared. Write a main( ) function that gets values from the user to test this function.
14. Write a function called **zeroSmaller(**) that is passed two int arguments by reference and then sets the smaller of the two numbers to 0. Write a **main(**) program to exercise this function.
15. Write a function that takes two Distance values as arguments and returns the larger one. Include a main( ) program that accepts two Distance values from the user, compares them, and displays the larger.

❑❑❑

CHAPTER 6

CLASS AND OBJECTS IN C++

6.1 WORKING WITH CLASS

The most remarkable feature of C ++ is a class. The *class binds together data and methods which work on data. The class is an abstract data type (ADT) so creation of class simply creates a template.* The general syntax of creating a class in C++ is given below:

```
class class_name
{

     public :
             data & function;
     private :
             data & function;
     protected :
             data & function;
};
```

The class is a keyword. Following this keyword class, class_name represents name of the class. The class name must obey rules of writing identifier as class_name is nothing but an identifier. The class is opened by opening brace} and closed by closing brace}. The class definition/declaration must end with semicolon. Inside the class we define the data members and member functions. They may be defined either public, private or in protected mode. There are three different types of mode :

1. **public**
2. **private**
3. **protected.**

The mode is also known as visibility modifier or access specifier. Data members and functions declared under the public mode can be used inside and outside the class. Private data members and functions can be used only inside the class. Protected data member and function also can only be used inside the class. Protected data member and function also can only used inside the class only but serve a different purpose which you will study in inheritance.

The data member of class are used inside the member functions of the class. Data members are declared inside the class but used in the member functions of the class. Usually the data members are private and member functions are public. So data members can only be used inside the functions of the class. This is to safeguard private data from external access.

If no visibility mode is written the default visibility mode private is assumed for the class.

The declaration of a class alone does not serve any purpose. To make use of the class we need to create variable of type class. A variable of class type is known as an object. The class is loaded into memory when first object of the class is created. Creation of object creates memory space for the object which depends upon size of the data members of the class. For each object separate copy of the data members is created. But only one copy of the member function is created which is shared by the entire object.

The objects call member functions of the class using operator dot (.) operator. Which is known as period or membership operator?

Before a member function can work on to the data member of the class, they must be initialized by calling a function which provides initial values to the data member of the class.

Let's take a practical example of class now.

/*PROG 6.1 DEMO OF CLASS AND OBJECT VER 1*/

```
#include <iostream.h>
#include <conio.h>
class demo
{
  private :
     int cx,cy;
  public :
     void input_data(int x,int y)
     {
        cx=x;
        cy=y;
     }
   void show_data( )
     {
     cout<<"cx="<<cx<<"\t"<<"cy="<<cy<<endl;
     }
};
void main( )
{
```

```
    demo d1;
    clrscr( );
    d1.input_data(10,20);
    d1.show_data( );
    getch( );
}
```

OUTPUT :

```
cx=10 cy=20
```

EXPLANATION : A class is created using **keyword class** followed by class name. The class name follows the rules of writing **identifiers**. Inside the class **demo** we have two variables **cx** and **cy** of type **integer.** The **private** and **public** are known as **visibility modifier** or **access specifier**. Each visibility modifier must end with **: (colon).** All the variables, function etc. declared under **private** a visibility modifier bear that prototype of visibility modifier. Here **cx** and **cy** written under private so they become private. If we do not write **private,** they are also considered as private is the default access level in a class. The function **input_data** takes two parameters of type int and returns nothing as **void** is the return type. The function **show_void** display the two data members' **cx and cy**. Note the two functions are defined within the class. We can also declare them inside the class and defined outside the class. **The class declaration has to end with semicolon.**

In the **main** the statement **demo.d1;** creates a variable of class **demo** type. Not we do not have to write class **demo.d1;**. The variable **d1** of class **demo** type is known as an instance of **class demo or an object**. The creation of an object allocates memory depending upon the size of the class which is the sum of size of data members. Functions do not add to the size of the class or object. Here a memory of **8 bytes** will be allocated for the **object d1.** Functions are given memory when a class is loaded into the memory.

All **public members (data + functions)** can be accessed in the main with the help of object using **dot (.) operator** which is also known as **membership operator or period**. Through statement **d1.input_data (10, 20)** we are calling the function **input_data** and passing two int constant **10 and 20**. They are collected in the formal parameters **x and y** and then assigned to **cx and cy**. Now **cx and cy** can be used in all the functions of **demo**. Whenever you are working with the **class & object**, the first thing you need to perform is to assign values to data members of class through function. You cannot initialize them directly in the class. As **cx and cy** through **cout.** Note as **cx and cy** are **private** they can only be accessed inside the member function of the class and not anywhere. Usually we make data members as **private** function as public while designing a class. All the functions defined inside the class are treated as **inline**.

/*PROG 6.2 DEMO OF CLASS AND OBJECT VER 2*/

```
#include <iostream.h>
#include <conio.h>
class demo
{
  private :
```

```
    int cx, cy;
  public :
    void input_data(int,int);
    void show_data( );
};
void demo : :input_data(int x,int y)
{
  cx = x;
  cy = y;
}
void demo : :show_data( )
{
  cout<<"cx="<<cx<<"\t"<<"cy="<<cy<<endl;
}
void main( )
{
  demo d1;
  clrscr( );
  d1.input_data(10,40);
  d1.show_data( );
  getch( );
}
```

OUTPUT :

```
cx=10 cy=40
```

EXPLANATION : In the program we have declared the function inside the class and defined outside the class. When we define a function outside a class, `scope resolution operator(::)` has to be used with the function to tell the compiler to which class the function belongs. The declaration of function was `void show_data();` to define this function outside the class we first present the general syntax:

```
return_type class_name : : function_name(arguments/parameters)
{
    function code;
}
```

Here `return_type` is `void`, class name is `demo` and function name is `show_data` and it takes no arguments so we define:

```
return_type
|     class_name
|     |        function_name
|     |        |
v     v        v
void demo : : show_data ( )
{
   cout<<"cx="<<cx<<"\t"<<"cy="<<cy<<endl;
}
```

This notation of associating a class name with function using : : is a must. It allows us to have two functions with the same name in two different classes. Then to resolve them we have to use : : operator.

6.2 PROGRAMMING EXAMPLES (PART-1)

/*PROG 6.3 DEMO OF CLASS AND OBJECT VER 3 */

```
#include <iostream.h>
#include <conio.h>

class demo
{
private :
   int cx,cy;
public :
   void input_data( );
   void show_data( );
};

void demo : :input_data( )
{
   cout<<"Enter the value of cx and cy \n";
   cin>>cx>>cy;
}

void demo : :show_data( )
{
   cout<<"cx="<<cx<<"\t"<<"cy="<<cy<<endl;
}
```

```
void main( )
{
   demo d1;
   d1.input_data( );
   d1.show_data( );
   getch( );
}
```

OUTPUT :

```
Enter the value of cx and cy
12
56
cx=12 cy=56
```

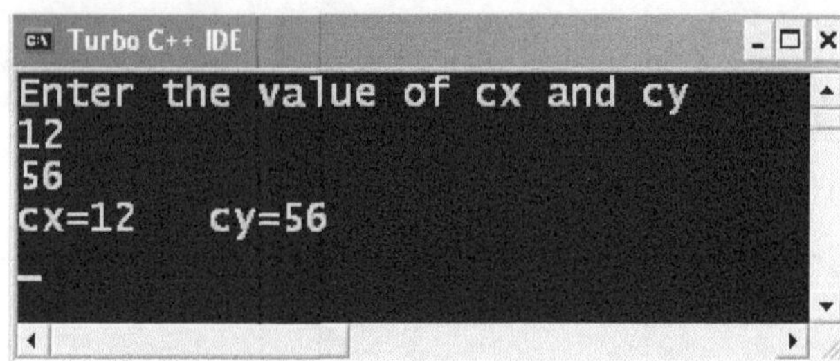

FIGURE 6.1. *Output Screen of Program.*

EXPLANATION : In the earlier two programs, we assigned the values to **cx** and **cy** through formal parameters **x** and **y**. Here, we have changed the function `input_data` completely. Inside the function we take two values from keyboard and store them directly into `cx` and `cy`. Thus the function does not take any argument.

/* PROG 6.4 STUDENT CLASS & OBJECT DEMO */

```
#include <iostream.h>
#include <string.h>
#include <conio.h>
class student
{
   char sname[10];
   int sage;
   char sclass[10];
public :
   void getdata (char[ ], int, char[ ]);
   void showdata( );
};
```

```
void student : :getdata(char sn[10], int a, char sc[10])
{
  strcpy(sname, sn);
  sage =a;
  strcpy(sclass, sc);
}
void student : :showdata( )
{
  cout<<"Name=\t"<<sname<<endl;
  cout<<"Age=\t"<<sage<<endl;
  cout<<"Class=\t"<<sclass<<endl;
}
void main( )
{
  student s1, s2;
  char st[10];
  int sa;
  char scls[10];
  clrscr( );
  cout<<"Enter data for student 1\n";
  cin>>st>>sa>>scls;
  s1.getdata(st,sa,scls);
  cout<<"Enter for student 2\n";
  cin>>st>>sa>>scls;
  s2.getdata(st,sa,scls);
  cout<<"\n\t Student 1\n\n";
  s1.showdata( );
  cout<<"\n\t Student2\n\n";
  s2.showdata( );
  getch( );
}
```

OUTPUT :

```
Enter data for student 1
Hari 21 Third
Enter for student 2
Ravi 24 forth

 Student 1

Name= Hari
```

```
Age= 21
Class= Third

 Student2

Name= Ravi
Age= 24
Class= forth
```

EXPLANATION : In the student class we have three data members : **sname, sage, sclass** and two member function. One for inputting the data and second for displaying the data. In the main we have created two objects s1 and s2. As size of class is **24 bytes** so two memory blocks of **24 bytes** each are allocated for **s1 and s2** and both having their different copy of each data members. We input values for these data members in local variables and call functions getdata and ***showdata*** for both the object. Note string data has to be assigned through strcpy function. You cannot write **sname = sn** in function get

/* PROG 6.5 FINDING FACTORIAL OF A NUMBER */

```
#include <iostream.h>
#include <conio.h>

class Fact
{
        int num;
public :
        void input(int x)
        {
            num = x;
        }
        void getfact( );
};

void Fact : :getfact( )
{
            long int f = 1;
            short i;
            for(i=1;i<=num;i++)
                f=f*i;
            cout<<"Factorial of"<<num<<" is "<<f<<endl;
}
```

```
void main( )
{
        int n;
        clrscr( );
        Fact obj;
        cout<<"ENTER THE NUMBER :=";
        cin>>n;
        obj.input(n);
        obj.getfact( );
        getch( );
}
```

OUTPUT :

```
(FIRST RUN)

ENTER THE NUMBER :=8
Factorial of8 is 40320

(SECOND RUN)
ENTER THE NUMBER :=6
Factorial of6 is 720
```

EXPLANATION : The factorial of number say 5 is calculated by multiplying 5*4*3*2*1 or by multiplying 1*2*3*4*5 which will be 120. The class Fact uses function getfact to find factorial of a number which is assigned to data member num through input function. The function getfact works as follows:

Initially **f is 1**. We run the loop from **1** to ***num***, it may be from **num to 1** also. In each iteration value of **f** is multiplied by **i** and stored back in **f** which is used in the next iteration. For better understanding lets take **num = 4.**

S1	i = 1	f = 1 * 1	=> 1
S2	i = 2	f = 1 * 2	=> 2
S3	i = 3	f = 2 * 3	=> 6
S4	i = 4	f = 6 * 4	=> 24

/* PROG 6.6 FINDING THE REVERSE OF A NUMBER */

```
#include <iostream.h>
#include <conio.h>

class Revnum
{
```

```
    int num;
  public :
    void input(int x)
    {
      num =x;
    }
    int getnum( )
    {
      return num;
    }
    long int getrev( );
  };

  long int Revnum : :getrev( )
  {
      int save = num, r, rev = 0;
      while (save!=0)
      {
        r = save % 10;
        rev = rev*10 + r;
        save = save/10;
      }
      return rev;
    }

  void main( )
  {
    Revnum obj;
    int x;
    clrscr( );
    cout<<"ENTER THE NUMBER";
    endl(cout);
    cin>>x;
    obj.input(x);
    cout<<"reverse of "<<obj.getnum( )
   <<" is "<<obj.getrev( )<<endl;
    getch( );

  }
```

OUTPUT :

```
ENTER THE NUMBER
5678
reverse of 5678 is 8765
```

EXPLANATION : The class Reverse computes reverse of the number. Input is passed through input function. The function getrev calculates the reverse of the number and returns it. The save variable is used as at the end of while loop save becomes zero and num remains safe. The logic is explained below in the step by step manner.

S1 save = 3456	r = 3456 % 10 = 6	rev = 0*10 + 6	= 6	save = 3456/10 =345
S2 save = 345	r = 345 % 10 = 5	rev = 6*10 + 5	= 65	save = 345/10 = 34
S3 save = 34	r = 34 % 10 = 4	rev = 65*10 + 4	= 654	save = 34 /10 = 3
S4 save = 3	r = 3 % 10 = 3	rev = 654*10 +3	= 6543	save = 3/10 = 0

As save is 0 so conditions inside the while loop is false and control comes out of the loop. The reverse number in variable rev which is returned to the main and is printed.

/* PROG 6.7 CHECKING NUMBER IS PALINDROME */

```
#include <iostream.h>
#include <conio.h>

class Palin
{
   int num;
public :
   void input(int x)
   {
      num = x;
   }
   int getnum( )
   {
      return num;
   }
   int checkpalin( );
};

int Palin : :checkpalin( )
   {
      int save = num, r, rev = 0;
      while(save!=0)
```

```
    {
        r=save%10;
        rev = rev*10 + r;
        save = save/10;
    }
    if(rev == num)
        return 1;
    else
        return 0;
  }
void main( )
{
  Palin obj;
  int x;
  clrscr( );
  cout<<"Enter the number to be checked for palindrome\n";
  cin>>x;
  obj.input(x);
  if(obj.checkpalin( )==1)
     cout<<obj.getnum( )<<"is palindrome\n";
  else
     cout<<obj.getnum( )<<"is not palindrome\n";
  getch( );
}
```

OUTPUT :

```
(FIRST RUN)

Enter the number to be checked for palindrome
4554
4554is palindrome

(SECOND RUN)

Enter the number to be checked for palindrome
4567
4567is not palindrome
```

EXPLANATION : *A number is called palindrome if on reversing it is equal to the original number for e.g., 121,3223, 656 etc.* To check whether an enetered number is palindrome or not simply reverse the number and compare with the original number but as we have seen in the program to reverse a number, the original number becomes zero when control comes out from the loop. So we save the original number in a variable before starting processing, in the above program it is in the `save` variable. If the number is palindrome function `checkpalin` return `'1' (true)` which is checked inside the `main` result is displayed.

/* PROG 6.8 CHECKING PERFECTNESS OF A NUMBER */

```
#include <iostream.h>
#include <conio.h>

class perfect
{
  int num;
public :
  void input(int x)
  {
    num=x;
  }
  void check_perfect( )
  {
    int sum = 0, t;
    for(t=1;t<=num/2;t++)
    {
      if(num%10==0)
        sum=sum+t;
    }
    if(sum==num)
      cout<<"NUMBER :="<<num<<"IS PERFECT"<<endl;
    else
      cout<<"NUMBER :="<<num<<"IS NOT
 PERFECT"<<endl;
  }
};
void main( )
{
  perfect obj;
  int x;
  cout<<"ENTER THE NUMBER TO BE CHECKED FOR
 PERFECTNESS"<<endl;
  cin>>x;
  obj.input(x);
  obj.check_perfect( );
```

```
    getch( );
}
```

OUTPUT :

```
(FIRST RUN)

ENTER THE NUMBER TO BE CHECKED FOR PERFECTNESS
28
NUMBER :=28 IS PERFECT

(SECOND RUN)

ENTER THE NUMBER TO BE CHECKED FOR PERFECTNESS
5
NUMBER :=5IS NOT PERFECT
```

EXPLANATION : *A number is called perfect if sum of its factor is equal to the number it self for e.g., 6, its factor are 1,2,3 and sum of its factor is 6 which is equal to the number 6 so it is a perfect number.* Similarly 28 is a perfect number. In the function `check_perfect`, in the `while` loop we initialize `sum to 1` and run loop for `num/2` as for any number say `t` which is more than `num/2`, `num%t` won't be zero(excluding num it self).

/*PROG 6.9 TO CHECK WHETHER A NUMBER IS ARMSTRONG OR NOT */

```
#include <iostream.h>
#include <math.h>
#include <conio.h>

class Armstrong
{
  int num;
public :
  void input(int x)
  {
     num=x;
  }
  void checkAS( );
};
void Armstrong : :checkAS( )
  {
     int save = num, count = 0, newnum = 0, r;
     while(num!=0)
```

```
        {
          num = num /10;
          count++;
        }
        num = save;
        while(save!= 0)
        {
          r = save%10;
          newnum = newnum +pow(r, count);
          save = save/10;
        }
        if(newnum==num)
          cout<<"Number := "<<num<<"is Armstrong\n";
        else
          cout<<"Number"<<num<<"is not Armstrong\n";
      }

    void main( )
    {
      Armstrong obj;
      int x;
      clrscr( );
     cout<<"Enter the number to be checked for
     Armstrong \n";
      cin>>x;
      obj.input(x);
      obj.checkAS( );
      getch( );
    }
```

OUTPUT :

(FIRST RUN)

Enter the number to be checked for Armstrong

153

Number := 153is Armstrong

(SECOND RUN)

Enter the number to be checked for Armstrong

150

Number 150 is not Armstrong

EXPLANATION : A number is called Armstrong if sum of count number of power of each digit is equal to the original number.

For example, to check **153** is Armstrong number or not we see that number of digits are 3 then $\mathbf{1^3 + 5^3 + 3^3 => 1 + 125 + 27 = 153}$ which is equal to the original number so number 153 is Armstrong.

Let's see a four digit number **1634.** Number of digits is **4**

So $\mathbf{1^4 + 6^4 + 3^4 + 4^4 => 1 + 129 + 81 + 25 = 1634}$

So, function `checkAS` proceeds as follows. First find out number of digits, before doing this `save` the number in the '`save`' variable. Now number of digits are stored in the `count` variable. Now number of digits are stored in the `count` variable. `Num` is `0` now so copy the value from '`save`' to '`num`'. '`pow`' is a library function whose prototype is given in a header file `math.h`. It returns number to the power where first argument is number and second is the power for example `pow(2,3)` give 23=8,`pow(3,2)` gives 32=9. As return type of `pow` function is double I have type casted it to act as integer.

Now here I have put the steps of second loop are as follows :

Initially num = 153 newnum = 0 count = 3

S1 num = 153%10 = 3 newnum = 0 + pow(3,3) = 0+27 = 27 num = 153/10 = 15

S2 num = 15%10 = 5 newnum = 27 + pow(5, 3) = 27+125 = 152 num = 15/10 = 1

S3 num = 10%10 = 1 newnum = 152+pow(1,3) = 152+1 = 153 num = 1/10=0

As '**newnum**' contains **153** which is compared with the original number stored in '**save**'. We get output **153** is Armstrong number.

/* **PROG 6.10 GENERATION OF FIBONACCIN SERIES** */

```
#include <iostream.h>
#include <conio.h>

class Fibbo
{
  int term;
public :
  void input(int x)
  {
     term = x;
  }
  void gen_ser( )
  {
     int c, a=0,b=1, t;
     cout<<"fibbonaci series is \n";
     cout<<a<<" " <<b;
     for(t=1;t<=term-2;t++)
```

```
        {
            c= a+b;
            a=b;
            b=c;
            cout<<" "<<c;
        }
        cout<<endl;
    }
};

void main( )
{
    Fibbo obj;
    int x;
    clrscr( );
    cout<<"Enter the number of terms \n";
    cin>>x;
    obj.input(x);
    obj.gen_ser( );
    getch( );
}
```

OUTPUT :

(FIRST RUN)

```
Enter the number of terms
7
fibbonaci series is
0 1 1 2 3 5 8
```

(SECOND RUN)

```
Enter the number of terms
8
fibbonaci series is

0 1 1 2 3 5 8 13
```

EXPLANATION : Fibonacci series is a series in which each new term is the sum of previous two terms. Initially we assume two terms are **0 and 1** so next term will be **0 + 1 = 1**, next term will be **1 + 1 = 2** and so on. So, Fibonacci series is **0, 1, 1, 2, 3, 5, 8, 13, 21, 34,........**

The number of terms for the series is taken as input. In the function ***gen_ser*** we first display the two terms using '**a**' and '**b**'. In the '***for***' loop we calculate ***c = a + b*** and put value of '**b**' into '**a**' and transfer new value computed in '**c**' to '**b**' for next iteration. We then display '**c**'. This continues till **t<= term – 2.**

/*PROG 6.11 USE OF ENUM AS CLASS MEMBER */

```
#include <iostream.h>
#include <conio.h>
class demo
{
public :
   enum
   {
      RED,
      GREEN,
      BLUE,
      YELLOW,
      WHITE
   };
};

void main( )
{
   clrscr( );
   cout<<demo : :RED<<endl;
   cout<<demo : :GREEN<<endl;
   cout<<demo : :BLUE<<endl;
   cout<<demo : :YELLOW<<endl;
   cout<<demo : :WHITE<<endl;
   getch( );
}
```

OUTPUT :

```
0
1
2
3
4
```

EXPLANATION : Similar to other data members of basic data type `int, float, char` etc, we can have enumerators as our class members. The enumeration constant can directly be accessed (if public) in the main using class name with `scope resolution` operator.

It can also be accessed using an object say '**d**' as follows :

```
demo d;
cout<<d.RED<<endl;
cout<<d.GREEN<<endl;
cout<<d.BLUE<<endl;
cout<<d.YELLOW<<endl;
cout<<d.WHITE<<endl;
```

/*PROG 6.12 DEMO OF STRUCTURE AS A MEMBER OF CLASS VER 1 */

```
#include <iostream.h>
#include <conio.h>

class person
{
   char name[15];
   int age;
   float sal;
   struct address
   {
      char hno[15];
      char street[15];
      char city[15];
      char state[15];
   }addr;

public :

   void input( )
   {
      cout<<"ENTER THE PERSON NAME\n";
      cin>>name;
      cout<<"ENTER THE AGE\n";
      cin>>age;
      cout<<"ENTER SALARY\n";
      cin>>sal;
      cout<<"ENTER THE HOUSE NUMBER \n";
      cin>>addr.hno;
      cout<<"ENTER THE STREE NUMBER \n";
      cin>>addr.street;
```

```
        cout<<"ENTER THE CITY\n";
        cin>>addr.city;
        cout<<"ENTER THE STATE\n";
        cin>>addr.state;
    }
    void show( )
    {
        cout<<"NAME :="<<name<<endl;
        cout<<"AGE :="<<age<<endl;
        cout<<"SALARY :="<<sal<<endl;
        cout<<"ADDRESS :="<<addr.hno<<","<<addr.street<<endl;
        cout<<"\t"<<addr.city<<","<<addr.state<<endl;
    }

};

void main( )
{
    person p;
    clrscr( );
    p.input( );
    cout<<"\n\t PERSON DETAILS\n\n";
    p.show( );
    getch( );
}
```

OUTPUT :

```
ENTER THE PERSON NAME
Hari

ENTER THE AGE
24

ENTER SALARY
26000

ENTER THE HOUSE NUMBER
s17/127

ENTER THE STREE NUMBER
23
```

```
ENTER THE CITY
Varanasi

ENTER THE STATE
UP

            PERSON DETAILS

NAME :=Hari
AGE :=24
SALARY :=26000
ADDRESS :=s17/127,23
            varanasi,UP
```

EXPLANATION : The program demonstrates how we can have structure as a member of a class. The class ***person*** has one structure named address whose members are ***hno (house number), street, city,*** and ***state***. After the structure declaration we have created a variable of type structure ***'addr'*** which becomes now member of class ***person***. Note in the ***main*** we have accessed all the members of structure address with this '**addr**' data member of the class.

/* PROG 6.13 DEMO OF STRUCTURE AS A MEMBER OF CLASS VER 2*/

```
#include <iostream.h>
#include <string.h>
#include <conio.h>

class person
{
  char name[15];
  int age;
  float sal;

public :

  struct
  {
     char hno[15];
     char street[15];
     char city[15];
     char state[15];
  }addr;
```

```
    void input(char s[ ], int a, float f)
    {
        strcpy(name, s);
        age=a;
        sal=f;
    }
    void show( )
    {
        cout<<"Name="<<name<<endl;
        cout<<"Age="<<age<<endl;
        cout<<"Salary="<<sal<<endl;
        cout<<"Address :="<<addr.hno<<","<<addr.street<<endl;
        cout<<"\t"<<addr.city<<","<<addr.state<<endl;
    }
};

void main( )
{
    person p;

    clrscr( );

    p.input("HARI",24,15000);
    strcpy(p.addr.hno,"s17/127");
    strcpy(p.addr.street,"23");
    strcpy(p.addr.city,"Varanasi");
    strcpy(p.addr.state,"UP");

    cout<<"\n\t PERSON DETAILS\n\n";

    p.show( );
    getch( );
}
```

OUTPUT :

```
        PERSON DETAILS

Name=HARI
Age=24
Salary=15000
```

```
Address : =s17/127,23
        Varanasi,UP
```

EXPLANATION : In the earlier program the structure were given name address, it was not necessary so here we have removed the name. Also we have made structure as `public` so we can show you how to use it outside the class using an object of class `person`. The three data members `name, age and sal` are `private` so we initialize them using function input. The members of structure are initialized in the `main` using an object of `person` class as :

```
strcpy(p.addr.hno,"s17/127");
strcpy(p.addr.street,"23");
strcpy(p.addr.city,"Varanasi");
strcpy(p.addr.state,"UP");
```

Note : First addr is accessed using object p then member of structures are accessed using dot operator.

6.3 STRUCTURE IN C++

We have learned that for a class default access specifier is **private** *i.e.,* if no access mode is given all data members and functions are considered as **private**. A structure in C++ is similar to class with the difference that default access specifier for a structure is **public**. Other than this there is no difference in structure and classes in C++. Given below in the left column a class is written and on the right column corresponding structure is written. Note for a **class** we didn't specify **private** specifier for the data members as default mode is private. Similarly, for the structure class we didn't specify **public** specifier for the member function as default mode is public.

Table : Shows the Difference between Class and Structure

Simple Demo Class	*Corresponding Structure*

Class demo
{
int x;
int y;
public :
void input(int a,int b)
{
x = a;
y = b;
}
void show( )
{
	struct demo
	{
	void input(int a,int b)
	{
	x=a;
	y=b;
	}
	void show( )
	{
	cout<<"x="<<x<<endl;
	cout<<"y="<<y<<endl;
	}

```
        cout<<"x ="<<x<<endl;
        cout<<"y ="<<y<<endl;
    }
};
```

```
    private :
        int x;
        int y;
};
```

6.4 ACCESSING PRIVATE DATA

We declared data as **private** so that it is only accessible inside the function of the class and other external functions cannot use the **private** data. But sometimes we require that **private** data is accessible outside the class. One way is to make them **public**, but this will defy the principle of **data hiding**. The other solution is to create **public** member functions which return the **private** data members. This is the way which is usually employed for accessing **private** data. Similarly to **private** data you can have private member functions of the class. They cannot be called from outside the class.

Let's have an example to understand how to access private data.

```
/*PROG 6.14 ACCESSING PRIVATE DATA OUTSIDE THE CLASS VER 1*/

#include <iostream.h>
#include <conio.h>

class demo
{
    int num;
public :
    void fun( )
    {
        num=20;
    }
    int getnum( )
    {
        return num;
    }
};
void main( )
{
    demo d;
    clrscr( );
    d.fun( );
    cout<<"num is "<<d.getnum( )<<endl;
    getch( );
}
```

OUTPUT :

num is 20

EXPLANATION : In the program we have a class demo which has a private data member num. In the main when we call the function fun by an object d of class demo, the num is initialized to 20. In order to access this value of num outside the class we have written a public member function getnum() which returns the value of num. As the type of num is int we have kept the written type of function getnum as int. In the main when this function is called as d.getnum(), num is returned from the function getnum. Thus, we have accessed private data member outside the class.

/* PROG 6.15 ACCESSING PRIVATE DATA OUTSIDE THE CLASS VER 2*/

```
#include <iostream.h>
#include <conio.h>
#include <string.h>

class Person
{
   char name[15];
   char sex;
   float sal;

public :

   void input(char n[ ], char s, float f)
   {
      strcpy(name, n);
      sex = s;
      sal = f;
   }

   char * getname( )
   {
      return name;
   }

   char getsex( )
   {
      return sex;
   }
```

```
    float getsal( )
    {
       return sal;
    }

};

void main( )
{
    Person p;

    clrscr( );

    p.input("MANMOHAN",'M',15000);
    cout<<"NAME :="<<p.getname( )<<endl;
    cout<<"Sex :="<<p.getsex( )<<endl;
    cout<<"Salary :="<<p.getsal( )<<endl;

    getch( );
}
```

OUTPUT :

```
NAME : =MANMOHAN
Sex : =M
Salary : =15000
```

EXPLANATION : This time for accessing private data members name, 'sex' and 'sal' we have written three public member functions getname, getsal and getsex which return value of 'name', 'sal' and 'sex' respectively. Note depending upon type of data member we return from public member functions we have set the return type.

/*PROG 6.16 COMPARING SALARY OF TWO EMPLOYEE'S */

```
#include <iostream.h>
#include <conio.h>
#include <string.h>
class Emp
{
    char ename[15];
    float sal;

public :
```

```
    void input(char n[15], float s)
    {
       strcpy(ename, n);
       sal = s;
    }

    float getsal( )
    {
       return sal;
    }

    char * getname( )
    {
       return ename;
    }
};
void main( )
{
    Emp e1;
    clrscr( );
    e1.input("HARI", 26000);
    Emp e2;
    e2.input("VIJAY",30000);
    if(e1.getsal( )>e2.getsal( ))
       cout<<e1.getname( )<<" 's salary is higher \n";
    else
       cout<<e2.getname( )<<" 's salary is higher \n";
    getch( );
}
```

OUTPUT :

VIJAY 's salary is higher

EXPLANATION : The class `Emp` has two data members' `ename` and `sal`. We wish to compare salary of two employees. We initially assign the name and salary to both the employee's which are represented by two object `e1` and `e2`. The two data members are `private` we cannot use them inside the `main`. Writing them `public` will defy the purpose of data hiding so we have made `public` member function `getsal` and `getname` which returns the values of these data member. In the `if` condition `e1.getsal()` returns the salary of object `e1` and `e2.getsal()` returns the salary of `e2`. The salary is compared and appropriate result is displayed.

6.5 PROGRAMMING EXAMPLE (PART-2)

```
/*PROG 6.17 DEMO OF ARRAY WITHIN CLASS, INPUT AND DISPLAY */

#include <iostream.h>
#include <conio.h>
#define S 5 // condition compilation (MACRO)
class demo_Arr
{
   int arr[S];

public :

   void input( )
   {
      for(int i = 0; i<S; i++)
      {
         cout<<"\n Enter arr["<<i<<"]element :=";
         cin>>arr[i];
      }
   }

   void show( )
   {
      cout<<"ARRAY ELEMENTS ARE \n";
      for(int i =0; i<S;i++)
         cout<<"arr["<<i<<"] :="<<arr[i]<<endl;
   }

};

void main( )
{
   demo_Arr obj;

   clrscr( );

   obj.input( );
   obj.show( );
   getch( );
}
```

OUTPUT :

```
Enter arr[0]element :=10
Enter arr[1]element :=11
Enter arr[2]element :=12
Enter arr[3]element :=13
Enter arr[4]element :=14

ARRAY ELEMENTS ARE
arr[0] :=10
arr[1] :=11
arr[2] :=12
arr[3] :=13
arr[4] :=14
```

EXPLANATION : Working with arrays in class is simple as can be seen from the above program. We declare array of size `S` as private data member of class `demo_Arr`. Through `'input'` we take elements from the user and store into array `'arr'`. With the help of `'show'` function we display the array values. Initialization and construction of dynamic array is shown in the next chapter through constructor.

/*PROG 6.18 SORTING OF ARRAY ELEMENTS */

```
#include <iostream.h>
#include <conio.h>
#define S 5
class demoArr
{
  int arr[S];
public :
  void input( )
  {
    for(int i=0;i<S;i++)
    {
      cout<<"\nEnter arr["<<i<<"]element :=";
      cin>>arr[i];
    }
  }
  void show( )
  {
    cout<<"\nARRAY ELEMENTS ARE GIVEN HERE \n";
    for(int i=0;i<S;i++)
```

```
            cout<<"arr["<<i<<"] :="<<arr[i]<<endl;
        }
        void sort( )
        {
          int i,j,t;
          for(i=0;i<S;i++)
            for(j=i+1;j<S;j++)
              if(arr[i]>arr[j])
              {
                t=arr[i];
                arr[i]=arr[j];
                arr[j]=t;
              }
              show( );
        }
};
void main( )
{
    clrscr( );
    demoArr obj;
    obj.input( );
    obj.show( );
    cout<<"SORTED ARRAY IS SHOWN HERE\n";
    obj.sort( );
    getch( );
}
```

OUTPUT :

```
Enter arr[0]element :=45
Enter arr[1]element :=23
Enter arr[2]element :=90
Enter arr[3]element :=15
Enter arr[4]element :=67

ARRAY ELEMENTS ARE GIVEN HERE
arr[0] :=45
arr[1] :=23
arr[2] :=90
arr[3] :=15
arr[4] :=67
```

```
SORTED ARRAY IS SHOWN HERE
ARRAY ELEMENTS ARE GIVEN HERE
arr[0] :=15
arr[1] :=23
arr[2] :=45
arr[3] :=67
arr[4] :=90
```

EXPLANATION : Sorting means arrangement of array elements in either ascending order or descending order. In the program we sort the array in ascending order.

In order to understand the logic behind the program we take 5 elements of array and trace the logic as :

Initial

arr [0]	arr [1]	arr [2]	arr [3]	arr [4]
4	0	3	1	2

For i = 0, inner for loop runs for j = 1to j = 4 and it compares a[0] with all other elements of the array *i.e.,* a[1], a[2], a[3] and a[4]. If any of the element is greater than a[0] then both the elements are swapped . For example, a[0] is 4 and a[1] is 0 if condition turns out to be true then a[0] and a[1] are swapped. Now array becomes :

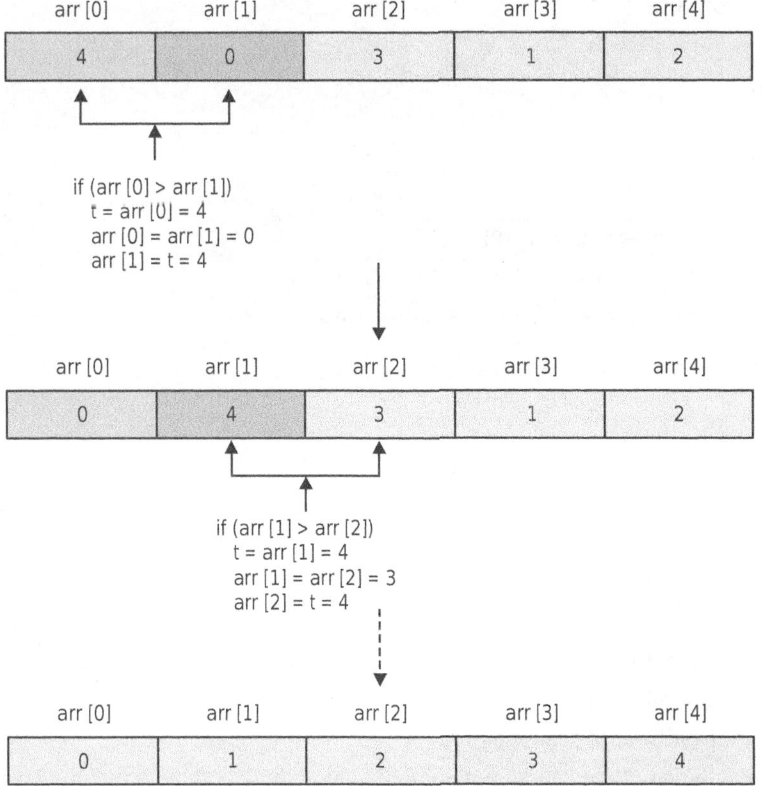

Figure 6.2. *Implementation Logic of Sorting.*

So, after the end of the inner for loop array will be look like as shown in above figure, that is second smallest number is at the second place in the array. So, when the outer loop finishes the array will be sorted in ascending order.

/* PROG 6.19 REVERSING ARRAY ELEMENTS */

```
#include <iostream.h>
#include <conio.h>
#define S 5

class demoArr
{
    int arr[S];

public :

    void input( )
    {
        for(int i=0;i<S; i++)
        {
            cout<<"\n ENTER ARRAY["<<i<<"] element :=";
            cin>>arr[i];
        }
    }

    void show( )
    {
        cout<<"ARRAY ELEMENTS ARE \n";
        for(int i = 0; i<S; i++)
            cout<<"arr["<<i<<"] :="<<arr[i]<<endl;
    }

    void reverse( )
    {
        int i,j;
        for(i=0;i<S;i++)
            for(j=i+1;j<S;j++)
            {
                arr[i]=arr[i]+arr[j];
                arr[j]=arr[i]-arr[j];
                arr[i]=arr[i]-arr[j];
            }
```

```
        show( );
    }

};

void main( )
{
 clrscr( );
  demoArr obj;
  obj.input( );
  obj.show( );
  cout<<"REVERSE";
  obj.reverse( );
  getch( );
}
```

OUTPUT :

```
 ENTER ARRAY[0] element :=12
 ENTER ARRAY[1] element :=13
 ENTER ARRAY[2] element :=14
 ENTER ARRAY[3] element :=15
 ENTER ARRAY[4] element :=16

ARRAY ELEMENTS ARE

arr[0] :=12
arr[1] :=13
arr[2] :=14
arr[3] :=15
arr[4] :=16

REVERSE ARRAY ELEMENTS ARE

arr[0] :=16
arr[1] :=15
arr[2] :=14
arr[3] :=13
arr[4] :=12
```

EXPLANATION : In the earlier program of sorting swapping of two array elements was done on the basis of comparison. If we remove this if condition the two elements will be swapped on conditional basis and when one inner loop finishes top elements will be stored at the bottom of the array.

/*PROG 6.20 DEMO OF 2-D WITHIN CLASS */

```
#include <iostream.h>
#include <conio.h>
#define R 2
#define C 3

class demo_arr
{
  int arr[R][C];
public :
  void input( )
  {
     int i,j;
     for(i=0;i<R;i++)
        for(j=0;j<C;j++)
        {
           cout<<"\n Enter
           arr["<<i<<"]["<<j<<"]element :=";
           cin>>arr[i][j];
        }
  }
  void show( )
  {
     int i,j;
     cout<<"Array elements are \n";
     for(i=0;i<R;i++)
     {
        cout<<"Row "<<i+1<<"->\t";
        for(j=0;j<C;j++)
           cout<<arr[i][j]<<"\t";
        cout<<endl;
     }
  }
};
void main( )
{
 clrscr( );
  demo_arr obj;
  obj.input( );
```

```
    obj.show( );
    getch( );
}
```

EXPLANATION : We have simply defined a 2-D array arr of size R by C. Through input function we take elements in the array and through show we display the element.

/*DEMO 6.21 SORTING OF EACH ROW OF 2-D ARRAY WITHIN CLASS */

```
#include <iostream.h>
#include <conio.h>
#define R 2
#define C 4
class demo_arr
{
  int arr[R][C];

public :

  void input( )
  {
      int i,j;
      for(i=0;i<R;i++)
          for(j=0;j<C;j++)
          {
              cout<<"\nENTER arr["<<i<<"]["<<j<<"]
 ELEMENT :=";
              cin>>arr[i][j];
          }
  }

  void sort( )
  {
      int i, j, k, t;
      for(i=0;i<R;i++)
      {
          for(j=0;j<C;j++)
              for(k=j+1;k<C;k++)
                  if(arr[i][j]>arr[i][k])
                  {
                      t=arr[i][j];
```

```
                arr[i][j]=arr[i][k];
                arr[i][k]=t;
            }
        }
        show( );
    }

    void show( )
    {
        int i,j;
        cout<<"ARRAY ELEMENTS ARE \n";
        for(i=0;i<R;i++)
        {
            cout<<"ROW "<<i+1<<"->\t";
            for(j=0;j<C;j++)
                cout<<arr[i][j]<<"\t";
            cout<<endl;
        }
    }
};
void main( )
{
    clrscr( );

    demo_arr obj;
    obj.input( );
    obj.show( );
    cout<<"SORTED ARRAY ELEMENTS ARE \n";
    obj.sort( );
    getch( );
}
```

OUTPUT :

```
ENTER arr[0][0]ELEMENT :=12

ENTER arr[0][1]ELEMENT :=45

ENTER arr[0][2]ELEMENT :=89

ENTER arr[0][3]ELEMENT :=11
```

```
ENTER arr[1][0]ELEMENT :=17

ENTER arr[1][1]ELEMENT :=19

ENTER arr[1][2]ELEMENT :=10

ENTER arr[1][3]ELEMENT :=26

ARRAY ELEMENTS ARE

ROW 1-> 12      45      89      11
ROW 2-> 17      19      10      26

SORTED ARRAY ELEMENTS ARE

ARRAY ELEMENTS ARE

ROW 1-> 11      12      45      89
ROW 2-> 10      17      19      26
```

EXPLANATION : The logic of sorting a 1-D array was presented earlier. Now assuming each row of a 2-D array as a 1-D array sorting has been done. The second and third loop together performs the sorting and the outer loop does this for all the rows.

/* PROG 6.22 SUM OF DIAGONAL ELEMENTS OF A SQUARE MATRIX */

```
#include <iostream.h>
#include <conio.h>
#define R 3
#define C 3

class sqr_mat
{
   int arr[R][C];
public :
   void input( );
   int diag_sum( );
   void display( );
};

void sqr_mat : :input( )
```

```
{
        int i,j;
        for(i=0;i<R;i++)
         for(j=0;j<C;j++)
         {
        cout<<"\nEnter arr["<<i<<"]["<<j<<"]elements :=";
                cin>>arr[i][j];
        }
}

int sqr_mat : : diag_sum( )
{
        int i,j,sum = 0;
        for(i=0;i<R;i++)
        {
           for(j=0;j<C;j++)
               if(i==j)
                   sum+=arr[i][j];
        }
        return sum;
   }
void sqr_mat : :display( )
   {
        int i, j;
        cout<<"Matrix is \n";
        for(i=0;i<R;i++)
        {
           for(j=0;j<C;j++)
               cout<<arr[i][j]<<"\t";
           cout<<endl;
        }
   }

void main( )
{
   clrscr( );
   sqr_mat obj;
   obj.input( );
   obj.display( );
   cout<<"Sum of diagonal elements is"
  <<obj.diag_sum( )<<endl;
```

```
    getch( );
}
```

OUTPUT :

```
Enter arr[0][0]elements :=1

Enter arr[0][1]elements :=2

Enter arr[0][2]elements :=3

Enter arr[1][0]elements :=4

Enter arr[1][1]elements :=5

Enter arr[1][2]elements :=6

Enter arr[2][0]elements :=7

Enter arr[2][1]elements :=8

Enter arr[2][2]elements :=9
Matrix is
1       2       3
4       5       6
7       8       9
Sum of diagonal elements is 15
```

EXPLANATION : A 2-D array where number of row and number of column is same is termed as square matrix. The diagonal elements as those elements of array where row number and column number is equal. Say **[0,0], [1,1] and [2,2]** and so on. To find out the sum of diagonal elements we compare **'i'** and **'j'** and where they are same we add **arr[i][j]** to **sum**. This is done in the function **diag_sum( )**.

/*PROG 6.23 DEMO OF STRING, FINDING LENGTH VER 1 */

```
#include <iostream.h>
#include <conio.h>
class demo_str
{
    char str[12];
    int len;
```

```
public :

  void input( )
  {
     cout<<"ENTER A STRING :=";
     cin>>str;
  }

  void find_len( )
  {
     int i=0;
     while(str[i++]!=0);
     len=i;
  }

  void show( )
  {
     cout<<"String :="<<str<<endl;
     cout<<"Length :="<<len<<endl;
  }
};
void main( )
{
  demo_str str;
  clrscr( );
  str.input( );
  str.find_len( );
  str.show( );
  getch( );
}
```

OUTPUT :

```
ENTER A STRING :=Hari Mohan
String :=Hari
Length :=5
```

EXPLANATION : A string is nothing but an array of character terminated by `null character '\0'`. We have three function `input`, `find_len` and `show`. The function input takes input from the user and store the string in the variable `str`. The function `find_len` finds the length of the string control variable `i`, till `str[i]!=0`. The body of the `while` loop is simple the null statement. In the end when loop terminates `'i'` is assigned to `len`. Through show we display `str` and `len`. From the output you can conclude that `cin` stops at the very first white space character and `"hari"` including space where it stopped is assigned to `str`.

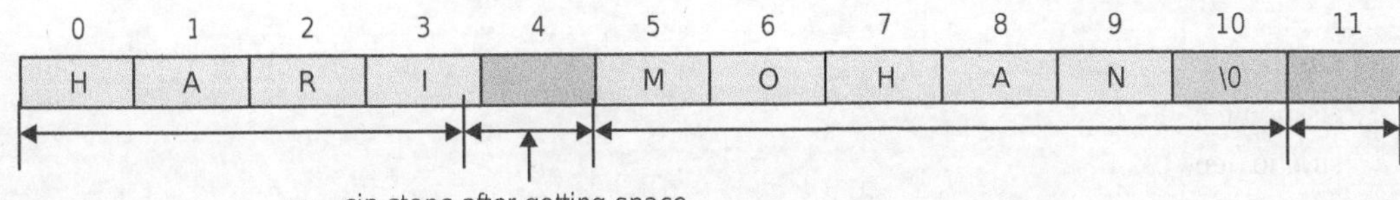

Figure 6.3. *Logical Implementation of cin statement.*

For getting the whole string scanned see the next program.

/* PROG 6.24 DEMO OF STRING, FINDING LENGTH OF STRING VER 2*/

```
#include <iostream.h>
#include <conio.h>

class demostr
{
   char str[12];
   int len;

public :

   void input( )
   {
      cout<<"Enter a string \n";
      cin.getline(str,12);
   }

   void find_len( )
   {
      int i=0;
      while(str[i++]!=0);
      len = i;
   }
   void show( )
   {
      cout<<"String :="<<str<<endl;
      cout<<"Length :="<<len<<endl;
   }

};
void main( )
{
   demostr str;
```

```
    clrscr( );
    str.input( );
    str.find_len( );
    str.show( );

    getch( );
}
```

OUTPUT :

```
Enter a string
Hari Mohan
String :=Hari Mohan
Length :=11
```

EXPLANATION : The function `getline` scans the whole line till the enter key is pressed or `max 19` characters are scanned first. The function scans even the `white space` character like `space, tab`, etc. This time the whole string is scanned and output is what we expected.

/* PROG 6.25 CHANGING CASE OF STRING CHARACTERS */

```
#include <iostream.h>
#include <conio.h>
#include <ctype.h>
class demo_str_case
{
    char str[12];

public :

    void input( );
    void change_case( );

};
void demo_str_case : :input( )
{
        int i=0;
        cout<<"ENTER A STRING \n";
        char ch;
        ch=cin.get( );
        while(i<12)
        {
            str[i]=ch;
            if(ch=='\n'|| i==11)
```

```
            {
               str[i] = '\0';
               break;
            }
            ch  =cin.get( );
            i++;
        }
    }
    void demo_str_case : :change_case( )
    {

     int i=0;
          char ch;
          while(str[i]!=0)
          {
            if(islower(str[i]))
            {
               ch  =str[i]-32;
               cout.put(ch);
            }

            else  if(isupper(str[i]))
            {
               ch  =  str[i]+32;
               cout.put(ch);
            }

            else
               cout.put(str[i]);
            i++;
          }

    }
    void main( )
    {
      demo_str_case str;
      clrscr( );
      str.input( );
      cout<<"STRING IN CHAGE CASE"<<endl;
      str.change_case( );
      getch( );
    }
```

OUTPUT :

```
ENTER A STRING
Hari Mohan
STRING IN CHAGE CASE
hARI mOHAN
```

EXPLANATION : In the function input we are taking the input character by character with the help of **cin.get( )** function accepts one character at a time from keyboard. The maximum size of out char array **str** is **12** so we run a **while** loop using one control variable **'i'** becomes **19** then we come out from the loop. But before that we assign null character to **str[i]** to denote end of string. In the function ***change_case*** we check each character of the string **str** for lower case by macro **islower**, and for upper case by using macro **isupper**, courtesy **ctype.h.** If the character is in lower case we subtract **32** from the character and if the character is in upper case we add **32** to it. If the character is other than alphabet we display it as it is.

/*PROG 6.26 REVERSE A STRING */

```
#include <iostream.h>
#include <string.h>
#include <conio.h>

class string
{
  char str [20];
  int len;
public :
  void input( )
  {
    cout<<"Enter a string \n";
    cin.getline(str,20);
    len=strlen(str);
  }
  char* reverse( )
  {
    int i,j;
  char* rev = new char[len+1] // Dynamic memory
 // allocation
    for(i=len-1,j=0,i>=0,j<len;i--,j++)
      rev[j]=str[i];
    rev[j]='\0';
    return rev;
  }
};
```

```
void main( )
{
   string obj;
   clrscr( );
   obj.input( );
   cout<<"Reverse string is\n";
   cout<<obj.reverse( )<<endl;
   getch( );
}
```

OUTPUT :

```
Enter a string
NMIMS
Reverse string is
SMIMN
```

EXPLANATION : Logic to reverse the string is quite simple. We take the last character from the end and put it at the starting position of the new reverse string. Then we decrement the counter for original and increment for reverse string (*i.e.*, j++ and i––in this case). As we are reversing the string character by character basis we will have to add null character when copying finishes. Note the function space for reverse string has been allocated dynamically from the length of the original string.

/* PROG 6.27 CHECK STRING FOR PALINDROME */

```
#include <iostream.h>
#include <string.h>
#include <conio.h>

class string
{
   char str[20];
   int len;

public :

   void input( )
   {
      cout<<"Enter a string \n";
      cin.getline(str,20);
      len=strlen(str);
   }
```

```
    char* reverse( )
    {
        int i,j;
        char* rev= new char[len+1];
        for(i=len-1,j=0;i>=0,j<len;i--,j++)
            rev[j]=str[i];
        rev[j]='\0';
        return rev;
    }

    void checkpalin( )
    {
        if(strcmp(reverse( ),str)==0)
            cout<<"String is palindrome\n";
        else
            cout<<"String is not palindrome\n";
    }
};
void main( )
{
    string obj;
    clrscr( );
    obj.input( );
    cout<<"Reverse string is \n";
    cout<<obj.reverse( )<<endl;
    obj.checkpalin( );
    getch( );
}
```

OUTPUT :

(FIRST RUN)

```
Enter a string
HARI
Reverse string is
IRAH
String is not palindrome
```

(SECOND RUN)

```
Enter a string
MADAM
Reverse string is
MADAM
String is palindrome
```

EXPLANATION : A string is called *palindrome* if it is same on reversal *i.e.*, peep, sos etc. We have simply reversed the string and checked whether the original and reverse are the same using `strcmp` function. Note function reverse has been called in the checkpalin function. The function `strcmp` compares two strings and if both are equal it `returns 0`.

/* PROG 6.28 DEMO OF ARRAY OF STRING */

```
#include <iostream.h>
#include <string.h>
#include <conio.h>
#define S 5

class string
{
   char str[S][15];

public :
   void input( )
   {
      for(int i=0;i<S;i++)
      {
         cout<<"Enter a string \n";
         cin.getline(str[i],15);
      }
   }

   void show( )
   {
      for(int i=0;i<S;i++)
      cout<<str[i]<<endl;
   }

};

void main( )
{
```

```
    string obj;
    getch( );
    obj.input( );
    cout<<"String are \n";
    obj.show( );
    getch( );
}
```

OUTPUT :

```
Enter a string
hari
Enter a string
vijay
Enter a string
mohan
Enter a string
ranjana
Enter a string
anjana
String are
hari
vijay
mohan
ranjana
anjana
```

EXPLANATION : `char str[S][15]` denotes an array of 5 string each can have maximum `14 characters`. We take input using for loop in each string `(str[0], str[1], ....str[4])` and display the same using function `show()`.

6.6 PASSING AND RETURNING OBJECT

Similar to returning and passing arguments to function of basic type like int, char, double, float, char* etc. we can pass objects of class to functions and even return objects from functions. To pass object we have simply write in the declaration of function, the base name whose objects we will be passing. Similarly for returning an object we will have to write class name as return type. For example for a function show which takes an object of demo class type and return an object of demo class we write the declaration as :

demo show(demo);

/*PROG 6.29 DEMO OF PASSING OBJECTS TO FUNCTION VER 1*/

```
#include <iostream.h>
#include <conio.h>
class demo
{
int num;
public :
   void input(int x)
   {
   num=x;
   }
   void copy(demo);
   void show( )
   {
   cout<<"num="<<num<<endl;
   }
};
void demo : :copy (demo d)
{
num=d.num;
}
void main( )
{
demo d1,d2;
clrscr( );
d1.input(20);
d2.copy(d1);
cout<<"Object d1\n"<<endl;
d1.show( );
cout<<"Object d2\n";
d2.show( );
getch( );
}
```

OUTPUT :

```
Object d1
num=20
Object d2
num=20
```

EXPLANATION : The declaration `void copy(demo);` tells the compiler that copy is a function which takes an object of class `demo` type and returns nothing. The function is defined outside the class but you can define inside the class too. In the `main d1` calls the function copy and pass the `object d2` as argument. This `object d2` is passed through call by mechanism and is copied to formal argument d inside the function copy. Copying an object to another object involves copying all data members. Here `d.num` inside function copy represents `num` of `object d1` in the `main` and `num` alone is num for object who called the function here it is `d2`. So `num` of `d1` is assigned to num of `d2`. In the end both `num` are displayed by a call to `show`.

/* PROG 6.30 DEMO PASSING OBJECT AS ARGUMENT VER 2 */

```
#include <iostream.h>
#include <conio.h>
#include <string.h>

class employee
{
   float sal;
   char name[10];

public :

   void input(float s, char n[ ])
   {
      sal=s;
      strcpy(name,n);
   }

   void comp_sal(employee temp);
};

void employee : : comp_sal(employee temp) // object as argument
{
   if(temp.sal>sal)
      cout<<temp.name<<" 's salary is higher "
  <<" than " <<name<<" 's salary"<<endl;
   else
      cout<<name<<"'s salary is higher "
  <<" than "<<temp.name<<" 's salary\n";
}

void main( )
{
```

```
    employee e1, e2;

    e1.input(10000.275,"Hari");
    e2.input(11000.0,"Ravi");
    e1.comp_sal(e2);

    getch( );
}
```

OUTPUT :

Ravi 's salary is higher than Hari 's salary

EXPLANATION : The declaration `void comp_sal (employee temp);` tells the compiler that `comp_sal` is a function which takes an object of class employee type and returns nothing. The function compares the salary of two employee's. In the `main` object `e1` calls the function `comp_sal` and passes object `e2` as argument. The object `e2` is passed call by value and all data members of `e2` is copied to object `temp`. In the function salary is compared and result is displayed.

/* PROG 6.31 DEMO OF PASSING OBJECT AS ARGUMENT VER 3 */

```
#include <iostream.h>
#include <string.h>
#include <conio.h>
class time
{
    int hours;
    int minutes;
    int secs;

public :

    void input_time(int hh, int mm, int ss)
    {
        hours=hh;
        minutes = mm;
        secs = ss;
    }

    void comp_time(time);
};
```

```
void time : :comp_time(time temp)
{
   long int t1, t2;
   t1=hours*60*60+minutes*60+secs;
   /* calling by object of the class */
   t2=temp.hours*60*60+temp.minutes*60+temp.secs;
   if(t1>t2)
       cout<<"FIRST TIME DURATION (IN SECOND)"<<t1<<"\n
  IS GREATER THAN SECOND (IN SECONDS)"
  <<t2<<endl;
   else
       cout<<"SECOND TIME DURATION (IN SECOND)"<<t2<<"\n
  IS GREATER THAN FIRST (IN SECONDS)"
  <<t1<<endl;
}

void main( )
{
 clrscr( );
   time time1, time2;
   time1.input_time(5,34,45);
   time2.input_time(4,78,50);
   time1.comp_time(time2);    //object of class as
                              // argument here
       getch( );
}
```

OUTPUT :

```
FIRST TIME DURATION (IN SECOND)20085
 IS GREATER THAN SECOND (IN SECONDS)19130
```

EXPLANATION : The class time has **3 data members : hours, minutes and secs** which stores **hour, minutes** and **second** respectively. In the **main** we create two objects **time1** and **time2** for the class time and assign input values to **hours, minutes and secs** by calling the function **input_time** function for both the objects. The function **comp_time** compares two time durations by converting the time into seconds and stores in temporary variables **t1** and **t2**. It than compares **t1** and **t2** and display result accordingly.

/*PROG 6.32 RETURING OBJECT AS ARGUMENT VER 1 */

```
#include <iostream.h>
#include <conio.h>
```

```
class demo
{
   int num;

public :

   void input(int x)
   {
      num = x;
   }

   demo copy( );

   void show( )
   {
      cout<<"num="<<num<<endl;
   }
};

demo demo : :copy( )
{
   demo temp;
   temp.num = num;
   return temp;
}

void main( )
{
   clrscr( );
   demo d1, d2;

   d1.input(20);
   d2=d1.copy( );

   cout<<"Object d1\n";

   d1.show( );

   cout<<"Object d2\n";
   d2.show( );
```

```
    getch( );
}

OUTPUT :
Object d1

num=20

Object d2

num=20
```

EXPLANATION : The declaration democopy() tells the compiler that the function copy doesn't take any argument and returns an object of type demo. Note how the function is defined outside the class :

```
demo demo : :copy( )
{
        demo temp;
        temp.num = num;
        return temp;
}

In the line demo demo : :copy( )
```

In the demo is the return type and demo: :copy specifies that copy is a function of demo class Inside the function we create a temporary object temp. Inside this object temp's num data member we assign num of object d1 actually who called the function copy in the main as d2=d1.copy(). When function copy returns object temp it is assigned to d2 as d2=temp which copies num of temp to num of d2.

```
/*PROG 6.33 DEMO OF PASSING OBJECT AS ARGUMENT AND RETURNING OBJECT AS ARGUMENT */

#include <iostream.h>
#include <string.h>
#include <conio.h>
class time
{
  int hours;
  int minutes;
  int secs;
```

```
public :

   void input_time(int hh,int mm, int ss)
   {
      hours=hh;
      minutes=mm;
      secs=ss;
   }

  time sum_time(time,time);

  void show_time(char*s)
  {
    cout<<s<<endl;
    cout<<"Hours :="<<hours<<"\t"<<"Minutes :="<<minutes
   <<"\t"<<"Seconds :="<<secs<<endl;
  }

  };

  time time : :sum_time(time A, time B)
  {
    int h,m,s;
    time temp;
    s=A.secs+B.secs;
    m=A.mlnutes+B.minutes+s/60;
    h=A.hours+B.hours+m/60;
    temp.secs = s%60;
    temp.minutes = m%60;
    temp.hours = h;
    return temp;
  }


  void main( )
  {
   clrscr( );
    time time1, time2, time3;

    time1.input_time(3,35,45);
    time2.input_time(4,56,45);
```

```
    time3=time3.sum_time(time1,time2);

    time1.show_time("\nTime 1\n");
    time2.show_time("\nTime 2\n");

    time3.show_time("\nSUM OF TWO DURATION IS\n");

    getch( );
}
```

OUTPUT :

```
Time 1

Hours :=3          Minutes :=35          Seconds :=45

Time 2

Hours :=4          Minutes :=56          Seconds :=45

SUM OF TWO DURATION IS

Hours :=8          Minutes :=32          Seconds :=30
```

EXPLANATION : In the program we are finding sum of two durations. The function declaration time `sum_time (time, time);` tells the compiler that `sum_time` is a function which takes two `arguments(objects)` of class time type. In this main we initialize data member's hours, minutes and secs of two objects `time1` and `time2` by calling function `input_time`. In the statement

```
time3=time3.sum_time (time1, time2);
```

`time3` calls the function `sum_time` and passes `time1` and `time2` as argument. Inside the function `sum_time` first we calculate number of `seconds, minutes and hour's` variables `s, m` and `h` and from them we actually assign values to data members of `temp` objects. In the end of this `temp` object is returned and assigned to `time3` in the `main.`

6.7 ARRAY OF OBJECT

Similar to array of any basic data types we can create array of object of any class. This comes handy when we want to process say salary of number of employees, Processing accounts of persons, records of students etc. In all these situation array of objects makes our work easier and makes processing faster. For a class say demo which contains two data members dx and dy of int type array of objects is created as :

demo arr[5];

This creates an array of objects of size 5. The first object is referred by `arr[0]`, second by `arr[1]` and so on. The data members of object `arr[0]` can be accessed as `arr[0].dx` and `arr[0].dy`. As we have just two data members dx and dy of int type inside the class, the size of any object of this demo class will be of `8 bytes`. So, size of array will be `8*5=40`. Each object will be places at a distance of `8 bytes` in the memory as show :

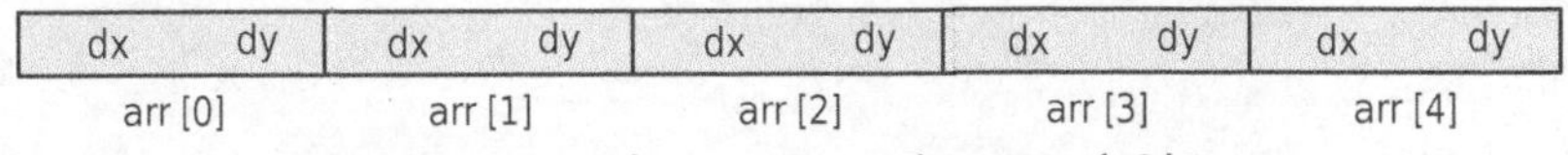

Figure 6.4. *Implementation of Array of Object.*

/*PROG 6.34 DEMO OF ARRAY OF OBJECTS */

```
#include <iostream.h>
#include <conio.h>
#define S 5

class Point
{
  int px;
  int py;
  public :
  void input(int x,int y)
  {
   px=x;
   py=y;
  }
  void show( )
  {
   cout<<"("<<px<<","<<py<<")"<<endl;
  }
};

 void main( )
 {
  Point ptarr[S];
  int i;
  clrscr( );
  for(i=0;i<S;i++)
  ptarr[i].input(234+i*2,254+i*3);
  cout<<"Points are \n";
  for(i=0;i<S;i++)
  ptarr[i].show( );
```

```
    getch( );
  }
```

OUTPUT :

```
Points are
(234,254)
(236,257)
(238,260)
(240,263)
(242,266)
```

EXPLANATION : The class Point store **x** and **y** coordinates of a point. Inside the **main** we have created an array ptarr of size 5 of class type Point. This is similar to creating 5 objects with different name. The array ptarr is an object array of class Point type. ptarr [0] denotes first object, ptarr[1] denotes second object and so on. In the main we call input function for all the objects using for loop a pass arbitrary points to function. Each object will be having different points as data members for each object are unique. Later we display the points of each using show and for loop.

/* PROG 6.35 DISPLAYING EMP NAME AND SALARY USING ARRAY OF OBJECT */

```
#include <iostream.h>
#include <conio.h>
#define S 4

class Emp
{
  char ename[15];
  float sal;

public :
  void input( );
  void show( );
};

void Emp : :input( )
{
  cout<<"Enter the employee name \n";
  cin.getline(ename,15);
  cout<<"Enter salary\n";
  cin>>sal;
  cin.ignore( );
}
```

```
void Emp : :show( )
{
  cout<<ename<<"\t"<<sal<<endl;
}
void main( )
{
  Emp earr[S];
  int i;
  clrscr( );
  for(i=0;i<S;i++)
     earr[i].input( );
  cout<<"Employee Details\n";
  cout<<"\n NAME \t SALARY\n";
  for(i=0;i<S;i++)
     earr[i].show( );
  getch( );
}
```

OUTPUT :

```
Enter the employee name
hari
Enter salary
26000
Enter the employee name
Deshmukh
Enter salary
20000
Enter the employee name
Vivek
Enter salary
21000
Enter the employee name
Malvika
Enter salary
25000
Employee Details

 NAME        SALARY
Hari         26000
Deshmukh     20000
Vivek        21000
Malvika      25000
```

EXPLANATION : The class `Emp` stores information about employee. It has just two data members `ename` and `sal`. Through function input we take employee name and salary directly in data member's `ename` and `sal`. The use of `cin.ignore( )` `flushes` the input buffer. This is equivalent to `fflush(stdin) in C`. In the `main` we create an array of `Emp` object by the name `earr` of size `S`. Through `for` loop and input function we take data for all the `4 object` elements of array `earr` and later display them using `for` and `show`.

/* PROG 6.36 STUDENTS MERIT LIST */

```
#include <iostream.h>
#include <conio.h>
#define S 4

class student
{
  char sname[15];
  int m1, m2, m3;
  float per;

public :

  void input( );
  void show( );
  float getper( );
};

void student : :input( )
{
  cout<<"ENTER THE NAME OF STUDENT"<<endl;
  cin.getline(sname,15);
  cout<<"ENTER THE MARKS IN THREE SUBJECTS"<<endl;
  cin>>m1>>m2>>m3;
  per=(m1+m2+m3)/3.0;
  cin.ignore( );
}
void student : :show( )
{
  cout<<sname<<"\t"<<per<<endl;
}

float student : :getper( )
{
```

```
    return per;
  }

  void main( )
  {
    student sarr[S],temp;
    int i,j;
    clrscr( );
    for(i=0;i<S;i++)
       sarr[i].input( );
    for(i=0;i<S;i++)
       for(j=i+1;j<S;j++)
          if(sarr[i].getper( )<sarr[j].getper( ))
          {
             temp=sarr[i];
             sarr[i]=sarr[j];
             sarr[j]=temp;
          }
          cout<<"STUDENT MERIT LIST\n";
          cout<<"\nNAME \t Per(%)\n";
          for(i=0;i<S;i++)
             sarr[i].show( );
          getch( );
  }
```

OUTPUT :

```
ENTER THE NAME OF STUDENT
Kashap
ENTER THE MARKS IN THREE SUBJECTS
70
78
90
ENTER THE NAME OF STUDENT
Maskara
ENTER THE MARKS IN THREE SUBJECTS
80
67
78
ENTER THE NAME OF STUDENT
Vishnukant
ENTER THE MARKS IN THREE SUBJECTS
```

```
70
80
76
ENTER THE NAME OF STUDENT
Manish
ENTER THE MARKS IN THREE SUBJECTS
64
79
90

STUDENT MERIT LIST

Kashap          79.333336
Maskara         77.666664
Vishnukant      75.333336
Manish          75
```

EXPLANATION : The class student has `5` data members : `sname, m1, m2, m3 and per`. For storing marks in three subjects we have `m1, m2, m3`. For storing percentage we have `per` and for name we have `sname`. We assume all marks are from `100`. (Though no checking has been done through if). In the function input after taking marks we find the percentage and store them in `per`. In the `main` we are performing sorting on the basis of percentage as we generating the merit list of the students. As `per` is `private` we have made a `public` member function `getper` which returns `per`. In the `main` sorting is done on this function getper basis. Note whole object has been swapped while sorting is being done. For that we have taken a temporary object `temp.` Later we have displayed the merit list using `show` and `for` loop.

6.8 FRIEND FUNCTION

A friend function is totally a new concept in C++. As the name implies it will be a friend someone. We can make a function as a friend of a class and can allow that friend function to access private and public data members of that class. **Friend functions are mostly used where two or more classes want to share a common function**. We present a number of points about friend functions.

1. First of all **friend** is keyword. A friend function is created by placing the keyword **friend** in the function declaration but not in function definition. Exception is if you declare and define at the same place.
2. A **friend** function is a **friend** of the class in which it is declared.
3. A **friend** function is not a member function of the class and cannot be called from any object of the class using **dot** operator.
4. A **friend** function can have full access to the **public, private** and **protected** data member of the class to which it is a **friend.**

5. The arguments of **friend** functions are usually objects of the class to which it is a **friend.**
6. A **friend** function not being a member function of class is called as a normal function.
7. A **friend** function can be **friend** of more than one class.
8. A function of one class can be a **friend** of another class.
9. We can have whole class as a **friend** of another class
10. We use **friend** function usually with multiple classes but can used with single class also.
11. A **friend** function can be declared in the **public or private** visibility mode without affecting its meaning.
12. There can be any number of **friend** functions of a class.

The general syntax of creating a **friend** function as a **friend** class is :

```
class demo
{
 data members :
 public :
 members functions;
// friend function declaration
friend data_type function_name (parameters);
};
data_type function_name (parameters)
//definition
{
 function definition;
}
```

Now, let's have some programs which make use of friend keyword.

/*PROG 6.37 DEMO OF FRIEND FUNCTION WITH SINGLE CLASS VER 1*/

```
#include <iostream.h>
#include <conio.h>
class demo
{
  int fx;
  public :
  void inputf(int x)
 {
 fx=x;

 }
```

```
friend int findsqr(demo);
};
int findsqr(demo d)
{
  return d.fx * d.fx;
}
void main( )
{
  demo F;
  clrscr( );
  F.inputf(30);
  cout<<"Square is="<<findsqr(F);
  getch( );
}
```

OUTPUT :

Square is=900

EXPLANATION : The declaration friend `int findsqr (demo);` inside the class tells the compiler that function `findsqr` is a `friend` of class `demo`. This is done with the help of `friend` keyword. As function `findsqr` is a `friend` of the class `demo`, it can accept object of class `demo` and using `dot membership` can access `public and private` members of class `demo`. Note the function is defined outside the class without using `scope resolution operator (: :)` as function does not belong to the base class rather it is a `friend of demo class`. In the function definition the `friend` keyword is not present. Note in the `main` value of `30` is assigned to the data member `fx` for object `F`. Later the function `findsqr` is called without using dot operator with object `F`, instead object `F` is passed to the function `findsqr` through call by value mechanism. The object `F` is copied to `d` and function `findsqr` finds square of `fx` and returns to the main.

/*PROG 6.38 DEMO OF FRIEND FUNCTION WITH SINGLE CLASS VER 2*/

```
#include <iostream.h>
#include <conio.h>
#include <string.h>
class demo
{
  char str[15];
  public :
  void inputf(char s[ ])
{
  strcpy(str,s);
}
```

```
    friend char* toupper(demo d)
    {
      static char temp[15];
      strcpy(temp,strupr(d.str));
      return temp;
    }
};
    void main( )
    {
      demo F;
      clrscr( );
      F.inputf("hari mohan");
      cout<<"String in upper case \n";
      cout<<toupper(F);
      getch( );
    };
```

OUTPUT :

```
String in upper case
HARI MOHAN
```

EXPLANATION : This is another example of `friend` function with single class. Note the function is declared and defined in the class itself. This can be done as function `toupper` is `friend` of `demo class` only. In the `friend` we use a `static char array temp` of size `15`. We convert the original string (data member) `str` to uppercase using built-in string function `strupr` and copy it to `temp`. As we cannot return address of the local variable (`local variable die when control goes out of block`) we have declared array `temp as static.`

The above two programs could have been written with the use of **friend** function by simply writing the function within the class as their part. The real use of **friend** is visible where we have more than one class and we want **friend** function to be **friend** of both the class(in case of two class) so data members of both the classes can be accessed and processing can be done in the **friend** function.

/*PROG 6.39 FINDING MAXIMUM OF TWO DATA OF TWO DIFFERENT CLASS WITH FRIEND FUNCTION*/

```
#include <iostream.h>
#include <conio.h>
class second;
class first
{
   int fx;
```

```
    public :
    void inputf(int x)
  {
    fx=x;
  }
  friend void findmax(first,second);
};
class second
{
    int sx;
    public :
    void inputs(int x)
  {
  sx = x;
  }
  friend void findmax(first,second);
};
void findmax(first A, second B)
{
    if(A.fx>B.sx)
    cout<<A.fx<<"of class first is greater than "<<B.sx<<"of
    class second\n";
    else
    cout<<B.sx<<"of class second is greater than"<<A.fx<<"of
    class first\n";
}
 void main( )
  {
    first F;
    second S;
    clrscr( );
    F.inputf(40);
    S.inputs(70);
    findmax(F,S);
    getch( );
  }
```

OUTPUT :

70of class second is greater than40of class first

EXPLANATION : This is the real example where `friend` serves its purpose. The statement in the beginning of the program class second is forward declaration as we are performing class second in the `friend` function declaration and at that point class `second` was not created. Note the friend function is declared in both the class which tells the compiler that it is a `friend` of both the class `first` and `second`. It accepts an object of class `first` argument and `second` argument is an object of class `second` type. The function definition is given outside the classes. In the main we call the function `findmax` and pass two objects `A and B` of class `first` and `second`.

/* PROG 6.40 SWAPPING OF TWO CLASS DATA USING FRIEND FUNCTION */

```
#include <iostream.h>
#include <conio.h>

class second;                        // global declaration of class
class first
{
   int fx;

public :

   void inputf(int x)
   {
      fx=x;
   }

   void showf( )
   {
      cout<<"fx :="<<fx<<endl;
   }

   friend void swap(first &, second &);   //declaration of
                                          //friend function
};

class second
{
   int sx;

public :
   void inputs(int x)
   {
      sx=x;
   }
```

```
    void shows( )
    {
      cout<<"sx="<<sx<<endl;
    }
    friend void swap(first &, second &);   //declaration of
                                           //friend function
};

void swap(first &A, second &B)    //definition of friend of
                                  //friend function
{
    int t;
    t=A.fx;
    A.fx=B.sx;
    B.sx=t;
}
void main( )
{
    first F;
    second S;
    clrscr( );
    F.inputf(20);
    S.inputs(40);
    cout<<"Before swapping \n";
    F.showf( );
    S.shows( );
    swap(F,S);
    cout<<"AFTER SWAPPING \n";
    F.showf( );
    S.shows( );
    getch( );
}
```

OUTPUT :

```
Before swapping
fx :=20
sx=40
AFTER SWAPPING
fx :=40
sx=20
```

EXPLANATION : In the program we are swapping the data members of two classes **first** and **second** using friend function. The function is a Friend of both the classes and accepts **first** argument of class type first and **second** argument of class type second, both by reference. If we do not pass argument by reference then swapping will be done on local variables of type class first and class second. So changes won't be reflected back to object **F** and **S** in **main.**

/* PROG 6.41 FUNCTION OF ONE CLASS FRIEND OF ANOTHER CLASS */

```
#include <iostream.h>
#include <conio.h>

class second;
class first
{
        int num;

public :

        void input_first( )
        {
                num=20;
        }
        void show(second);
};

class second
{
        int num;

public :

        void input_second(int x)
        {
                num==x;
        }
        friend void first : :show(second);

};
void first : :show(second s)
{
        cout<<"NUM OF CLASS FIRST :="<<num<<endl;
        s.input_second(num*num);
```

```
        cout<<"NUM OF CLASS SECOND :="<<s.num<<endl;
}

void main( )
{
        first f;
        clrscr( );
        f.input_first( );
        second s;
        f.show(s);
        getch( );
}
```

OUTPUT :

```
NUM OF CLASS FIRST :=20
NUM OF CLASS SECOND :=400
```

EXPLANATION : In the program we want to create a function in class `first` which will be friend of class `second`. As function will be friend of class we can have object of class `second` in the function of the `first` class. In the class first we want function `show` to be friend of class `second`. As function show takes a parameter of class `second`, we have to make forward declaration of class `second` prior to defining class `first`.

The line

class second; does the same

Note the declaration of this function `show` in class `second`.

```
friend void first : : show (second);
```

The line tells the compiler that a function show of class first (due to `first : :show`) which returns nothing (`void`) and which takes an argument of class type second by value is a `friend second class`.

As function `show` is friend of class `second, private` members functions of `second` class can be used in `show` function only through objects using dot operator. But as the function show is of class `first, private` data members of class `first` can be used directly. In the main the function is called using an object of class first and passes an object of class `second`. In the function `num* num` (num is of class first) is assigned to num of class second object using a call to function `input_second`.

```
/*PROG 6.42 WHOLE CLASS AS A FRIEND OF ANOTHER CLASS VER 1*/

#include <iostream.h>
#include <conio.h>
```

```
class second;
class first
{
public :
   void silly( )
   {
      cout<<"IN SILLY OF FIRST CLASS "<<endl;
   }
   friend class second;
};
class second
{
public :
   void show(first s)
   {
      s.silly( );
   }
};
void main( )
{
   clrscr( );
   second s;
   first f;
   s.show(f);
   getch( );
}
```

OUTPUT :

IN SILLY OF FIRST CLASS

EXPLANATION : The line `friend class second;` is written in the class `first` which tells the compiler that class `second` is a friend of class `first` which has a meaning of that all the functions of class `second` we can pass object of class `first` type and use data members and function of class `first` using `dot` operator. In the `show` function of class `second` we pass an object of class `first` and call function `silly` of `first class`.

/* PROG 6.43 WHOLE CLASS AS A FRIEND OF ANOTHER CLASS VER 2 */

```
#include <iostream.h>
#include <conio.h>

class second;
```

```
class first
{
public :

   void fun( )
   {
      cout<<"IN FUN OF FIRST"<<endl;
   }
   friend class second;
};

class second
{
   first fri; // OBJECT OF CLASS FIRST
public :
   void show_of_second( )
   {
      fri.fun( );
   }
};
void main( )
{
   clrscr( );
   second s;
   s.show_of_second( );
   getch( );
}
```

OUTPUT :

IN FUN OF FIRST

EXPLANATION : Here we have created an object of class `first` as member of class `second`. Note in the `main` no need to create an object of class `first`. When `s.show_of_second` executes it calls the `fun( )` function from with in `show_of_second` by using its data members `fri` which is an object of class `first`.

Note : The above program will work without making class **first** as **friend** of class **second**. But without making **friend** you cannot access any **private** data of class of the class **first** in class **second**.

```
/* PROG 6.44 WHOLE CLASS AS A FRIEND OF ANOTHER CLASS VER 3 */

#include <iostream.h>
#include <conio.h>
class second;
class first
{
   int num;

public :

   void first_fun( )
   {
      cout<<"IN FIRST_FUN OF FIRST \n";
      num =30;
   }
   friend class second;
};

class second
{
public :
   void show1(first & s)
   {
      s.first_fun( );
   }

   void show2(first s)
   {
      cout<<"num :="<<s.num<<endl;
   }
};
void main( )
{
   second s;
   first f;
   clrscr( );
   s.show1(f);
   s.show2(f);
   getch( );
}
```

OUTPUT :

```
IN FIRST_FUN OF FIRST
num :=30
```

EXPLANATION : In the function `show1` we pass object `f` by reference. So `s` in function `show1` and `f` in `main` are same. In the function we call `first_fun` function which sets the value of `num` to `30`. Later when we call function `show2` and pass object `f` by value the same value of `num` is displayed.

6.8.1 Demerits of Friend Function

1. **Friend** function cannot access the class members and functions directly, they need to have a class object which using dot can call the members of the class.
2. Creating friend classes and functions defy the idea of encapsulation and create exception in the ways of data hiding.
3. Usages of many friend functions some times make you think to redesign your program.
4. **Friend** functions are conceptually messy and potentially lead to spaghetti-code situations as numerous friend functions muddy the clear boundaries between classes.

6.9 STATIC CLASS MEMBERS

Static variables are those variables which persist even after control returns from the functions. In terms of static members as class members they are the members which are one for a class and not one for an object. We know that functions of which belong to class only. Static members can be either functions or static data. They are also known as class variables as they belong to whole of the class.

6.9.1 Static Member Functions

Let's discuss static function first. Note several points about static member's functions :

1. Static functions are functions which are made static by placing keyword static before function definition in side the class.
2. All static function of class must be defined inside the class. You cannot separate the declaration and definition of a static member function.
3. Static functions are one for class and you can call them as.
4. In a static function only static data members, other static variables or other static function can be used.
5. Though static member function is called using class name with : : operator. It can be called explicitly using objects of the class.

/*PROG 6.45 DEMO OF STATIC FUNCTION VER 1*/

```
#include <iostream.h>
#include <conio.h>
```

```
class demo
{
  public :
  static void show( )
  {
  cout<<"Demo of static function\n";
  }
};
 void main( )
 {
  clrscr( );
  demo : :show( );
  getch( );
 }
```

OUTPUT :

Demo of static function

EXPLANATION : As mentioned earlier a static function which is one for all objects and which is called by using : : with class name. In the program we have defined a static function show which is called in the main using class name as `demo::show()`.

/*PROG 6.46 DEMO OF STATIC FUNCTION VER 2*/

```
#include <iostream.h>
#include <conio.h>
class demo
{
  public :
  static void show ( )
  {
  cout<<"Demo of static function \n";
  }
};
 void main( )
 {
  clrscr( );
  demo d1;
  demo : :show( );
  d1.show( );
  getch( );
 }
```

OUTPUT :

Demo of static function

Demo of static function

EXPLANATION : It was mentioned that static function are part of the class and not part of the every object. But a static function can be called using an object too. The program demonstrates this fact.

/*PROG 6.47 DEMO OF STATIC FUNCTION VER 3*/

```
#include <iostream.h>
#include <conio.h>

 class demo
 {
  public :
  static void show( )
 {
  cout<<"Demo of static function \n";
 }
 void disp( )
 {
  show( );
 }
};

void main( )
{
  clrscr( );
  demo d1;
  d1.show( );
  getch( );
}
```

OUTPUT :

Demo of static function

EXPLANATION : Program simple. We have a non static function which call a static function.

```
/* PROG 6.48 DEMO OF STATIC FUNCTION VER 4 */

#include <iostream.h>
#include <conio.h>

class demo
{

public :

    static void show( )
    {
        cout<<"DEMO OF STATIC FUNCTION"<<endl;
        show1( );
    }

    void show1( )
    {
        cout<<"HELLO FROM SHOW FUNCTION"<<endl;
    }
};

void main( )
{
    demo : :show( );
    getch( );
}
```

OUTPUT :

'demo : :show' : illegal call of no-static member function

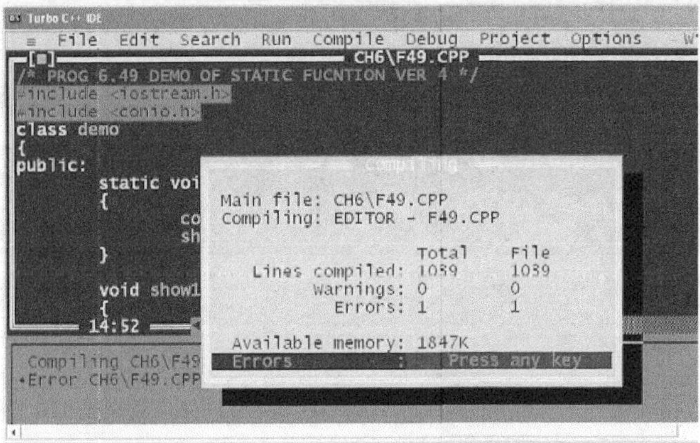

Figure 6.5. *Error message after compiling the program.*

EXPLANATION : In `static` function only `static` function can be used. `show1` function begins no-static cannot be called from show function so the error.

/*PROG 6.49 DEMO OF STATIC FUNCTION VER 5*/

```
#include <iostream.h>
#include <conio.h>

class demo
{
public :

    static void show( );
};

static void demo : :show( )
{
    cout<<"HELLO FROM STATCI SHOW \n";
}

void main( )
{
    demo : :show( );
    getch( );
}
```

OUTPUT :

ERROR : 'show' :'static' should not be used on member function defined at file scope.

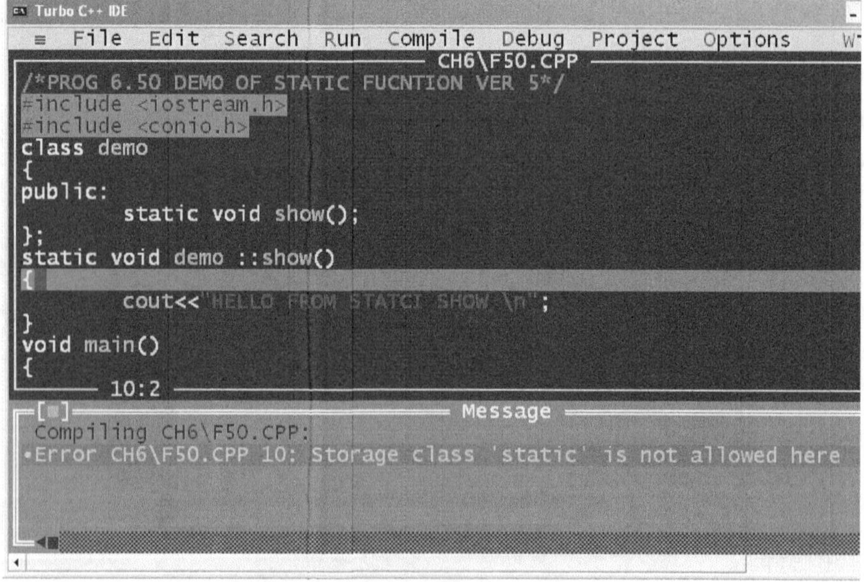

Figure 6.6 *Error message on turbo C++ IDE.*

EXPLANATION : Static member function must be declared and defined inside the class. They cannot be defined outside the class so the error.

6.9.2 Static Data Members

We know that whenever an object is created separate copies of data members are created for each object. But in case of static data members only one copy of static data members is available which is shared among all the objects created. Note several points the about static data members :

1. They are created by placing static keyword before variable declaration.
2. All static variables are declared inside the class but are initialized outside the class as :

   data_type class_name : : static_variable =value;
3. If value is not given they are initialized to zero.
4. There is one single copy of the static data member is created which is shared among all objects. Changes made by one object on a static data members is created which is shared among all objects.
5. The lifetime of a static variable is the entire program.
6. They are used when you have to keep one value common to whole class.

For an example consider the class declaration.

```
class demo
{
    static int s;
    int ns;
};
demo d1, d2,d3;
```

Assume value of **s** is **1** and value of ns for **d1, d2 and d3 is 20, 30, 40** respectively

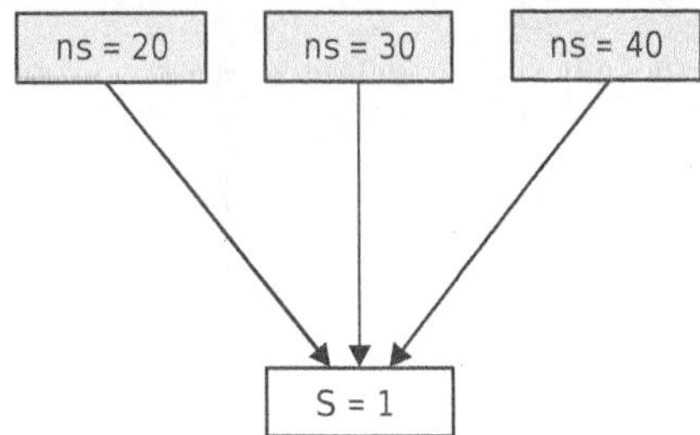

One for class, common to all objects

As clear from the figure that ns is separate for each data object and s is common for all objects.

```
/*PROG 6.50 DEMO OF STATIC VARIABLE*/

#include <iostream.h>
#include <conio.h>
```

```
class stat_demo
{
  static int s;
  static float f;
  static char *str;
  static char ch;

 public :
  static void show( )
 {
  cout<<"s="<<s<<endl;
  cout<<"f="<<f<<endl;
  cout<<"str="<<str<<endl;
  cout<<"ch="<<ch<<endl;
  }
};

 int stat_demo : :s=20;
 float stat_demo : :f=234.567;
 char* stat_demo : :str="static";
 char stat_demo : :ch='S';

 void main( )
 {
  clrscr( );
  stat_demo : :show( );
  getch( );
 }
```

OUTPUT :

```
s=20
f=234.567001
str=static
ch=S
```

EXPLANATION : In the program there are 4 `static` variables : `s of type int, f of type float, str of type char* and ch of type char.` A static variable is declared inside the class but defined outside the class as explained earlier. In the program for example we initialized static `int s` as :

int stat_demo : : s = 20

Where int is the type of static variable, `stat_demo` is class and s is name of static variable, 20 is the initial value of the static variable s. These are displayed int eh static function show.

/*PROG 6.51 STATIC AND NON STATIC VARIABLE VER 1*/

```
#include <iostream.h>
#include <conio.h>

class demo
{
  static int s;
  int ns;
  public :
  void input(int x)
 {
  ns= x;
 }
 void show( )
 {
  cout<<"ns="<<ns<<endl;
  cout<<"s="<<s<<endl;
 }
};
int demo : :s=20;
 void main( )
 {
  demo d1;
  clrscr( );
  d1.Input(10);
  d1.show( );
  getch( );
 }
```

OUTPUT :

```
ns=10
s=20
```

EXPLANATION : In the program there is one static variable s and one non static variable **ns**. Non static variable **ns** is initialized through input function with value **10** and static variable is initialized to value **20**. In the non static function show we display these two values.

/*PROG 6.52 STATIC AND NON STATIC VARIABLE VER 2*/

```
#include <iostream.h>
#include <conio.h>
```

```
class demo
{
  static int s;
  int ns;
  public :
  void input(int x)
 {
  ns = x;
 }
 static void show( )
 {
  cout<<"ns="<<ns<<endl;
  cout<<"s="<<s<<endl;
 }
};
 int demo : :s=20;
 void main( )
 {
  clrscr( );
  demo d1;
  d1.input(10);
  d1.show( );
  getch( );
 }
```

OUTPUT :

Error : illegal reference to data member 'demo' : : ns' in a static member function.

EXPLANATION : `static` data members can be used in static as well as non static functions. But in `static` functions only `static` members or other `static` variables can be used. In the `show` function which is static we are using non static data members ns so compiler flashes the error.

6.10 CONSTANT MEMBER FUNCTION

A constant member function is a member function of class which is made constant by placing keyword const at the end of function declaration and definition both. The main property of const member function is that you cannot modify the values of data members as we may get the compilation error.

The general syntax of a constant member function is, assume this is inside the class.

```
return_type func_name ( ) const
{
  Body of the function;
}
```

If declared in class defined outside the class, it will look like as :

```
return_type func_name ( ) const; //declaration
return_type class_name ( ) : : func_name ( ) const
{
  function definition;
}
```

We present below few examples to make your concepts better.

/*PROG 6.53 DEMO OF CONSTANT MEMBER FUNCTION VER 1*/

```
#include <iostream.h>
 class demo
 {
  int num;
  public :
  void input (int x)
 {
   num=x;
 }
 void change ( )const
 {
   num=num*10;
 }
};
 void main( )
 {
  demo d;
  d.input(20);
  d.change( );
 }
```

OUTPUT :

Error : cannot modify a const object

EXPLANATION : The change is a constant member function. The value of **num** after the input function call for object **d is 20.** This value **20** of **num** cannot be changed inside the constant member function change. Inside the function we have written **num=num*10** which will store **100** into **num**, but due to this expression in constant member function change compiler flashes error.

/*PROG 6.54 DEMO OF CONSTANT MEMBER FUNCTION VER 2*/

```
#include <iostream.h>
#include <conio.h>
class demo
{
    int num;
    public :
    void input(int x)
    {
    num=x;
    }
  void change(int x)const;
  void show( )
  {
    cout<<"num="<<num<<endl;
  }
};
  void demo : : change (int x) const
  {
    ((demo*)this)-> num=x;
  }
  void main( )
  {
    clrscr( );
    demo d;
    d.input (10);
    d.show( );
    d.change(20);
    d.show( );
    getch( );
  }
```

OUTPUT :

```
num=10
num=20
```

EXPLANATION : The expression `((demo*)this) ->num=x;` is the only way to change the value of any data member inside constant member function. The `this` pointer is built-in pointer which stores the address of the current object here of `object d`. In the expression we have type casted it to `demo*` type. Though it should not be necessary but more removing this `demo*` causes compiler to generate error.

EXERCISE

A. True and False :

1. Pointer can point to structure also.
2. All the class elements are public by default.
3. A static function must be declared as public, not as private or protected.
4. A friend function can be friend to other class also.
5. The default access specifier for C++ struct and C++ class is same.
6. The size of an object is sum of its data members and functions of the class.
7. A structure just like class can have functions and data in C++.
8. A structure creates memory space in memory.
9. Static members can be accessed through objects of the class.
10. Private members of a class are accessible to its functions and friend functions only.
11. C++ provides private, protected visibility modifier.
12. When a program is executed, objects interact by sending messages to each other.
13. Array of an instance cannot be created.
14. A class whose objects can be created is known as concrete class.
15. Pointer to function does not store the addresses of the functions.
16. While calculating the size of objects, functions size is considered.
17. All structure elements are private by default.

B. Answer the Following Questions :

1. What do you understand by return by reference?
2. What is the difference between a structure and class?
3. How enums are used inside the class?
4. What is the significance of a class?
5. What are static data members and static functions?
6. What are class variables?
7. What are friend functions? How it is used?
8. Write characteristics of friend function.
9. How can we make member function of one class as a friend of another class?
10. How we can make whole class as a friend of another class?
11. How do we initialize static data member of a class?
12. What are the demerits of using friend function?
13. How can we pass and return an object to/from function?

14. What is constant member function?
15. How can we initialize array of objects?

C. Brain Drill :

1. Write a function that takes two Distance (structure) value as arguments and returns the larger one. Include a main program that accepts two Distance values from the user, compare them and display the larger.
2. Define a class fract whose object represent rational numbers (*i.e.*, fractions). Inside integer data members numr and denr for storing a numerator and a denominator respectively. Provide a constructor and member function eval_fract() for evaluating the value of the rational number, invert() for inverting the rational number, print() for printing the rational number in the form numr/denr(for example, 22/7). Also provide access functions get_numr and get_denr for returning the values of the private data members. Include a member function reduce_fract(), that reduces the fraction numr/denr to lowest term. For example, the fraction 54/90 is stored as the object 3/5. Invoke these member functions in the main () module to test them with suitable data.
3. Assume that an object has a name being accessed by the pointer. Write a program using reference variable for interchanging the names of two objects.
4. Write a program using to declare private data member and function. Also declare public member function. Read and display the data using private function.
5. Write a program to declare a class with two integers. Read values using member functions. Pass the object to another member function. Display the difference between them.
6. Create a class that imitates part of the functionality of the basic data type int. Call the class Int (not different spelling). The only data in this class is an int variable. Include member functions to initialize an Int to 0, to initialize it to an int value, to display it (it looks just like an int), and to add two Int values.

   Write a program that exercise this class by creating two initialized and one uninitialized Int values, adding these two initialized values ad placing the response in the uninitalized value, and then displaying this result.
7. Create a class that includes a data member that holds a "serial number" for each object created from the class. That is, the first object created will be numbered 1, the second 2 and so on.

   To do this, you will need another data member that records a count of how many object have been created so far. (This member should apply to the class as a whole; not to individual objects. What keyword specifies this?) Then, as each object is created, its constructor can examine this count member variable to determine the appropriate serial number for the new object.

   Add a member function that permits an object to report its own serial number. Then write a main () program that creates three objects and quires each one about its serial number. They should respond **I am object number 2**, and so on.
8. Create a class time that has separate int member data for hours, minutes and seconds. One constructor should initialize this data to 0, and another should initialize it to fixed values. Another member function should display it, in 11:59:59 format. The final member function should add two objects of type time passed as arguments.

   A main program should create two initialized time objects (should they be const?) and one that is not initialized. Then it should add the two initialized values together, leaving the result in the third time variable. Finally, it should display the value of this third variable. Make appropriate member functions const.

CHAPTER 7

WORKING WITH CONSTRUCTOR AND DESTRUCTOR

7.1 INTRODUCTION

A constructor is a special member function whose name is same as the name of its class in which it is declared and defined. The purpose of the constructor is to initialize the objects of the class. The constructor is called so because it is used to construct the objects of the class. We present small example of constructor and later illustrate its various features :

/*PROG 7.1 DEMO OF CONSTRUCTOR */

```
#include <iostream.h>
#include <conio.h>

class demo
{
public :
    demo( )
    {
    cout<<"Hello from constructor \n";
    }
};

void main( )
{
  clrscr( );
  demo d;
  getch( );
}
```

OUTPUT :

Hello from constructor

EXPLANATION : The name of class is demo and the following declaration

```
demo( )
{
 cout<<" Hello from constructor \n";
}
```

demo is a constructor of the class as the name of the function is the name of the class. Note the following features of the constructor.

1. The constructors are always declared in the public section. If declared in the private section then objects are can only be created inside the member functions but serve no purpose.
2. They are invoked automatically when objects of the class are created. The declaration demo d; creates an object d which automatically calls the constructor of the class and prints Hello from constructor.
3. They do not have any return type not even void so they cannot return any value.
4. Constructors cannot be inherited, but they can be called from the constructors of derived class.
5. Constructors are used to construct the object of the class.
6. The constructor with no argument is known as default constructor of the class. The default constructor for the class demo will be demo : demo( )
7. Constructors which take arguments like a function takes are known as parameterized constructor.
8. There is no limit of the number of constructors declared in a class but they all must conform to rules of function overloading.
9. Constructor can have default arguments.
10. Addresses of constructors cannot be taken.
11. Constructors cannot be virtual.
12. Constructor make implicit calls to operators new and delete in case memory allocation and de-allocation is to be performed.

The other way to write the above program would be :

```
#include <iostream.h>
Class demo
{
  public :
  demo( ); // declaration
};
```

```
demo : :demo ( ) // definition
{
   cout<<"Hello from constructor \n";
}
void main( )
{
   demo d;
}
```

In all the other programs which we have seen earlier, the objects were created using constructor but we didn't create constructor in the program. Take my words behind every object creation constructor is required. Then who was creating the objects in the entire program where we have made usage of classes and objects ? The answer is simple. When you do not create any constructor in the class, the compiler provides the default constructor for the class. That constructor is known as default constructor or do-nothing constructor. The sole purpose of this constructor is to construct the objects for the class.

7.2 CONSTRUCTOR WITH PARAMETERS

Constructor are similar to functions but they have the name as class name so similar to functions which takes argument we can have constructor which can take arguments. The constructor which takes parameters is known as parameterized constructor. Again depending upon type of arguments and number of arguments they may be overloaded. An example of this is given below :

/*PROG 7.2 DEMO OF PARAMETERIZED CONSTRUCTOR WITH INTEGER DATA*/

```
#include <iostream.h>
#include <conio.h>
class demo
{
   int a,b;
   public :
   demo( )
   {
      a=b=0;
      cout<<"Zero argument constructor called\n";
      show( );
   }
   demo(int x, int y)
   {
```

```
        a=x;
        b=y;
        cout<<"Two argument constructor called\n";
        show( );
    }
    demo(int x)
    {
        a=b=x;
        cout<<"One argument constructor called\n";
        show( );
    }
        void show( )
        {
        cout<<"a="<<a<<"\tb="<<b<<endl;
        }
    };
    void main( )
    {
       clrscr( );
       demo d1;
       demo d2(10,20);
       demo d3(30);
       getch( );
    }
```

OUTPUT :

```
Zero argument constructors called
a=0       b=0
Two argument constructor called
a=10      b=20
One argument constructor called
a=30      b=30
```

EXPLANATION : In the program given above we have **3** constructors in the class. The class has two private data members of **int** type. When statement **demo d1** executes it call the default constructor of the **class demo** and assign a **0** value to both **a and b**. When statement **demo d2 (10, 20)** executes it calls the constructor demo which takes two arguments of int type. The first argument **10** is assigned to formal parameter **x** and second argument **20** is assigned to formal parameter **y**. From **x and y** they are assigned to **a and b** respectively. When **demo d3 (30)** executes, it calls one argument constructor of int type and assign **30** to **x,** which is further assigned to **a and b**. Note show is called from within all the constructors.

7.3 IMPLICIT AND EXPLICIT CALL TO CONSTRUCTOR

Constructor can be called implicitly or explicitly. For example for the above program just explained. All three calls to 3 different constructors were implicit.

```
demo d1;
demo d2 (10, 20);
demo d3 (30);
```

- In implicit call we simply write the class name and then object name (in case of default constructor) or pass parameters but does not use the constructor name is any manner.
- In explicit call to constructor we explicitly call the constructor by writing its name and passing argument if any. For the above implicit call to constructors explicit calls would be :

```
demo d1 = demo( );
demo d2 = demo (10,20);
demo d3 = demo (30);
```

Note on the left side of assignment operator object is created and on the right hand side constructor is called explicitly.

Even when you called a constructor for an object implicitly you can call it explicitly in case you want to provide values to data members or want to modify the values like :

demo d1(10);

Both **a and b** gets the value 10. Later you can write if you want **d1 = demo (100, 200);** which makes **a =100 and b =200.**

```
/*PROG 7.3 DEMO OF PARAMETERIZED CONSTRUCTOR WITH STRING DATA */

#include <iostream.h>
#include <string.h>
#include <conio.h>

class string
{
 char str[20];
 public :
   string( );
   string (char s[ ]);
   void show( );
};
 string : :string( )
 {
```

```
    strcpy (str,"Hari");
    cout<<"Default constructor called\n";
  }
  string : : string(char s[ ])
  {
    strcpy(str,s);
    cout<<"One argument constructor called\n";
  }
  void string : :show( )
  {
    cout<<"string is"<<str<<endl;
  }
  void main( )
  {
    clrscr( );
    string s1;
    s1.show( );
    s1=string("Vijay");
    s1.show( );
    string s2=string("Manmohan");
    s2.show( );
    string s3("Ranjana");
    s3.show( );
    getch( );
  }
```

OUTPUT :

```
Default constructor called
string is Hari
One argument constructor called
string is Vijay
One argument constructor called
string is Manmohan
One argument constructor called
string is Ranjana
```

EXPLANATION : In the case string we have two constructors; one is default and second is one argument constructor. In the execution of statement string s1 default constructor is called which result in printing on the screen.

Default constructor called.

And assign value `"Hari"` to `str` of object `s1`. When the statement `s1= string ("Vijay");` executes one argument constructor is called which results in printing on the screen.

One argument constructor called and assigns value "vijay" to str of object s1. The old value "Hari" is removed.

Same explanation applies to statement string s2 =string ("Manmohan"); and for string s ("Ranjana");

Observe that in the first part the value of str for the object s1 was "Hari" but after the statement s1 ("Vijay").

/*PROG 7.4 FACTORIAL OF A NUMBER, FACTORIAL OF 6 IS 6*5*4*3*2*1=720*/

```
#include <iostream.h>
#include <conio.h>
class fact
{
  int fa;
  int num;
  public :

   fact( )
   {
     fa = 1;
     cout<<"Enter the number \n";
     cin>>num;
   }

   int find_fac( )
   {
     int i;
     for(i=1;i<=num;i++)
     fa=fa*i;
     return fa;
   }

   void show( )
   {
     cout<<"The factorial of"<<num<<"is"<<find_fac( )<<endl;
   }

 };

 void main( )
 {
  clrscr( );
```

```
    fact obj;
    obj.show( );
    getch( );
}
```

OUTPUT :

```
Enter the number
6
The factorial of6is720
```

EXPLANATION : The program is finding factorial of a number. When statement `fact obj` executes `default constructor` is called. This results in setting `fa =1` and promoting user to enter the number whose factorial he/she want to find out. After taking the number into data member `num` the constructor returns and calls the show function. Inside the function we have called the `find_fac` function which finds the factorial of the number and return to show function.

/*PROG 7.5 SEPARATION OF REAL AND INTEGER PART*/

```
#include <iostream.h>
#include <conio.h>

class convert
{
  float num;
  int intp;
  float realp;
  public :
   convert( )
   { }
   convert(float n)
   {
   num=n;
   }
   void find( )
   {
     intp=int (num);
     realp=num-intp;
     show( );
   }
   void show( )
   {
     cout<<"Number ="<<num<<endl;
```

```
        cout<<"Integer Part="<<endl;
        cout<<"Real Part="<<realp<<endl;
    }
};
void main( )
{
    clrscr( );
    convert A(334.89);
    convert B;
    B=convert(456.87);
    cout<<"\tFirst object\n\n";
    A.find( );
    cout<<"\t\n Second Object \n\n";
    B.find( );
    getch( );
}
```

OUTPUT :

```
First object
Number =334.890015
Integer Part=
Real Part=0.890015
Second Object
Number =456.869995
Integer Part=
Real Part=0.869995
```

EXPLANATION : The program is very simple. We first convert the number num into int by type casting and store it in `intp`. We then later subtract it from the original `num` to find out real part.

In the program the constructor `convert () {}` serves as `empty/default/zero` argument constructor. The default constructor serves nothing special here as it is having empty body. We have seen that we can use this constructor to provide the initial values to the members of the objects of the class. As we have created a one argument constructor we can call the constructor by writing `convert c1 ("334.89"),` but if we want it like

```
convert c1;
c1= convert ("334.89");
```

Then we must have the default constructor as started in the above paragraph. If we do not need to create object by writing convert c1; then there is no need to create the default constructor or empty constructor but once we have written the statement convert c1; then we must have the empty constructor in the program. This is must as in case of no constructor in the class the C++ provides its default implicit constructor to construct the objects. (Remembers no constructor no object). Once we have made constructors in our class of any type and in any number and we create the object by writing convert c1 without creating default constructor, the compiler flashes the error **"default constructor required"**. This constructor is do-nothing constructor and is used to just satisfy the compiler. Try running the program by commenting the default constructor in the program.

/*PROG 7.6 ADDITION AND SUBTRACTION OF TWO COMPLEX NUMBER*/

```
#include <iostream.h>
#include <conio.h>

class complex
{
  float real;
  float imag;
  public :
  complex( )
 {
  real=imag=0;
 }
 complex(float r, float i)
 {
  real=r;
  imag=i;
 }
  friend complex sum(complex, complex);
  friend complex sub(complex, complex);
  friend void show(complex);
};
 complex sum(complex A, complex B)
 {
  complex temp;
  temp.real= A.real+B.real;
  temp.imag= B.imag+A.imag;
  return temp;
 }
 complex sub(complex A, complex B)
 {
  complex temp;
  temp.real=A.real-B.real;
  temp.imag=A.imag-B.imag;
```

```
  return temp;
}
void show(complex C)
{
  cout<<C.real<<"+j"<<C.imag<<endl;
}
void main( )
{
  clrscr( );
  complex c1= complex(2.0,3.0);
  complex c2= complex(3.0,2.0);
  complex c3,c4;
  c3=sum(c1,c2);
  c4=sub(c1,c2);
  cout<<"c1=";
  show(c1);
  cout<<"c2=";
  show(c2);
  cout<<"sum=";
  show(c3);
  cout<<"sub=";
  show(c4);
  getch( );
}
```

OUTPUT :

```
c1=2+j3
c2=3+j2
sum=5+j5
sub=-1+j1
```

EXPLANATION : In the program we have one default constructor and second constructor with 2 parameters of type float. We want to find addition and subtraction of two complex numbers. For that we have written two friend functions sum and sub which takes two arguments of class complex type and return a value of class complex type. We have another function show which takes an object of class complex type as argument. The class has two private data members' real and imag which represents real and imaginary part of a complex number. With the two statements.

```
complex C1=complex (2.0, 3.0);
complex C2= complex (3.0, 2.0);
```

We call the 2 argument constructor and set the real and imaginary part for object C1 and C2. For finding sum of C1 and C2 we call the function sum and pass C1 and C2 as argument as C3 = sum(C1, C2); In the function sum two real part and two imaginary parts are added separately and stored in a temporary array which is returned and assigned to C3. Similarly, subtraction is performed by a call to sub function and subtraction of C1 and C2 is assigned to C4. Later they are displayed by a call to show.

/*PROG 7.7 MULTIPLICATION & DIVISION OF TWO COMPLEX NUMBER*/

```
#include <iostream.h>
#include <conio.h>
class complex
{
  float real;
  float imag;
  public :
  complex( )
 {
  real=imag=0;
 }
 complex(float r, float i)
 {
  real = r;
  imag = i;
 }
 void mul(complex, complex);
 void div(complex,complex);
 void show(char*);
 };
 void complex : :mul(complex A, complex B)
 {
  real = A.real*B.real-A.imag*B.imag;
  imag = A.real*B.imag + A.imag * B.real;
 }
 void complex : :div(complex A, complex B)
 {
  double d;
  d= B.real * B.real+B.imag * B.imag;
  real= (A.real*B.real+A.imag*B.imag)/d;
  imag = (B.real*A.imag-B.imag*A.real)/d;
 }
 void complex : :show(char *s)
 {
```

```
  cout<<s<<endl;
  cout<<real<<"+j"<<imag<<endl;
}
void main( )
{
  clrscr( );
  complex c1=complex(2.0,4.0);
  complex c2=complex(3.0,6.0);
  complex c3,c4;
  c3.mul(c1,c2);
  c4.div(c1,c2);
  c1.show("First Number");
  c2.show("Second Number");
  c3.show("Multiplication");
  c4.show("Division");
  getch( );
}
```

OUTPUT :

```
First Number
2+j4
Second Number
3+j6
Multiplication
-18+j24
Division
0.666667+j0
```

EXPLANATION : Assume two complex numbers are (x1 + j y1) and (x2 + j y2). Here j is called iota and –j is sqrt (–1) so j*j will be –1. Now multiplication will be as :

$$(X1 + j\ y1) * (x2 + j\ y2) = x1x2 + jx1y2 + j\ y1x2 - y1y2$$
$$= (x1x2 - y1y2) + j\ (x1y2 + x2\ y1)$$

For division we write :

$$\frac{(x1 + j\,y1) * (x2 - jy2)}{(x2 + j\,y2) * (x2 - jy2)} = \frac{(x1 * x2 + y1 * y2) + j\,(y1 * x2 - x1 * y2)}{\left(x_2^2 + y_2^2\right)}$$

/* PROG 7.8 CALCULATING SIMPLE INTEREST DEFAULT USING BY DEFAULT */

```
#include <iostream.h>
#include <conio.h>

class Sim_Int
{
    float rate;
    float time;
    float principal;

public :

    Sim_Int( )
    {}
    Sim_Int(float p, float r=8.5, float t = 2.0)
    {
        principal = p;
        rate = r;
        time = t;
    }
    float calc( )
    {
        float temp;
        temp = (principal * rate *time)/100;
        return temp;
    }
    void show( )
    {
        cout<<"Principal := "<<principal<<endl;
        cout<<"Rate :="<<rate<<endl;
        cout<<"Time :="<<time<<endl;
        cout<<"Simple Interest :="<<calc( )<<endl<<endl;
    }
};

void main( )
{
    Sim_Int obj1,obj2;

    clrscr( );
```

```
        obj1 = Sim_Int(10000, 10.0,3);
        cout<<"\t Object1 \n\n";
        obj1.show( );
        obj2=Sim_Int(9000,12.5);
        cout<<"\t Object2\n\n";
        obj2.show( );
        Sim_Int obj3(12000);
        cout<<"\tObject 3 \n\n";
        obj3.show( );

        getch( );
}
```

OUTPUT :

```
        Object1

Principal := 10000
Rate :=10
Time :=3
Simple Interest :=3000

        Object2

Principal := 9000
Rate :=12.5
Time :=2
Simple Interest :=2250

        Object 3

Principal := 12000
Rate :=8.5
Time :=2
Simple Interest :=2040
```

EXPLANATION : The program calculates simple interest by taking `3 input parameters`: `principal, rate` and `interest`. For that we have made two constructors in the class `Sim_Int`: one is default and second which takes 2 default arguments for `rate` and `time`. In the `main` when `obj1 = Sim_Int(10000, 10.0, 3);` executes it calls the 3 arguments constructor of the class and initializes `principal, rate` and `time` data members for object `obj1`. Next `obj1.show` is called which calls the `calc` function within it and displays the simple interest.

When `obj2= Sim_Int(9000,12.5);` executes compiler checks that there is no 2 argument constructor defined in the class but it sees that there is a 3 argument constructor and 2 parameters are defined so it calls the constructor and assigns `9000` to `principal, rate` is overridden by `12.5` and for time default value is taken. Next simple interest is calculated and displayed as explained for object `obj1`.

When `Sim_Int obj3(12000);` executes compiler checks that there is no `1 argument` constructor defined in the class but it sees that there is 3 `argument` constructor and 2 `parameters` are default so it calls the constructor and assigns `12000` to `principal,` for both rate and time default value is taken. Next simple interest is calculated and displayed as explained for object `obj1`.

/* PROG 7.9 STACK SIMULATION USING ARRAY AND CLASS */

```
#include <iostream.h>
#include <stdlib.h>
#include <conio.h>
#define S 10

class stack
{
    int top;
    int st[S];

public :

    stack( )
    {
        top=-1;
    }

    void push(int item)
    {
        if(top==9)
        {
            cout<<"STACK IS FULL"<<endl;
            exit(0);
        }
        st[++top]=item;
        cout<<"ITEM PUSHED"<<endl;
    }

    int pop( )
    {
```

```
        if(top==-1)
        {
            cout<<"STACK IS EMPTY"<<endl;
            exit(0);
        }
        return st[top--];
    }

};
void main( )
{
    stack s;
    int ch, item;
    clrscr( );

    do
    {
        cout<<"STACK DEMO"<<endl<<endl;
        cout<<"1 :- PUSH"<<endl;
        cout<<"2 :- POP"<<endl;
        cout<<"3 :- QUIT"<<endl;
        cout<<"ENTER YOUR CHOICE :=";
        cin>>ch;

        switch(ch)
        {
        case 1 : cout<<"ENTER THE ITEM :=";
            cin>>item;
            s.push(item);
            break;
        case 2 :item =s.pop( );
            cout<<"ITEM POPPED :="<<item<<endl;
            break;
        case 3 :cout<<"GOOD BYE"<<endl;
                exit(0);
            break;
        default :cout<<"ERROR"<<endl;
        }

    }while(ch>=1 && ch <= 3);
    getch( );
}
```

OUTPUT :

```
STACK DEMO

1 :- PUSH
2 :- POP
3 :- QUIT
ENTER YOUR CHOICE :=1
ENTER THE ITEM :=10
ITEM PUSHED

STACK DEMO
1 :- PUSH
2 :- POP
3 :- QUIT
ENTER YOUR CHOICE :=1
ENTER THE ITEM :=20
ITEM PUSHED

STACK DEMO

1 : PUSH
2 : POP
3 : QUIT
ENTER YOUR CHOICE :=1
ENTER THE ITEM :=30
ITEM PUSHED
STACK DEMO

1 : PUSH
2 : POP
3 : QUIT
ENTER YOUR CHOICE :=1
ENTER THE ITEM :=12
ITEM PUSHED

STACK DEMO

1 : PUSH
2 : POP
3 : QUIT
```

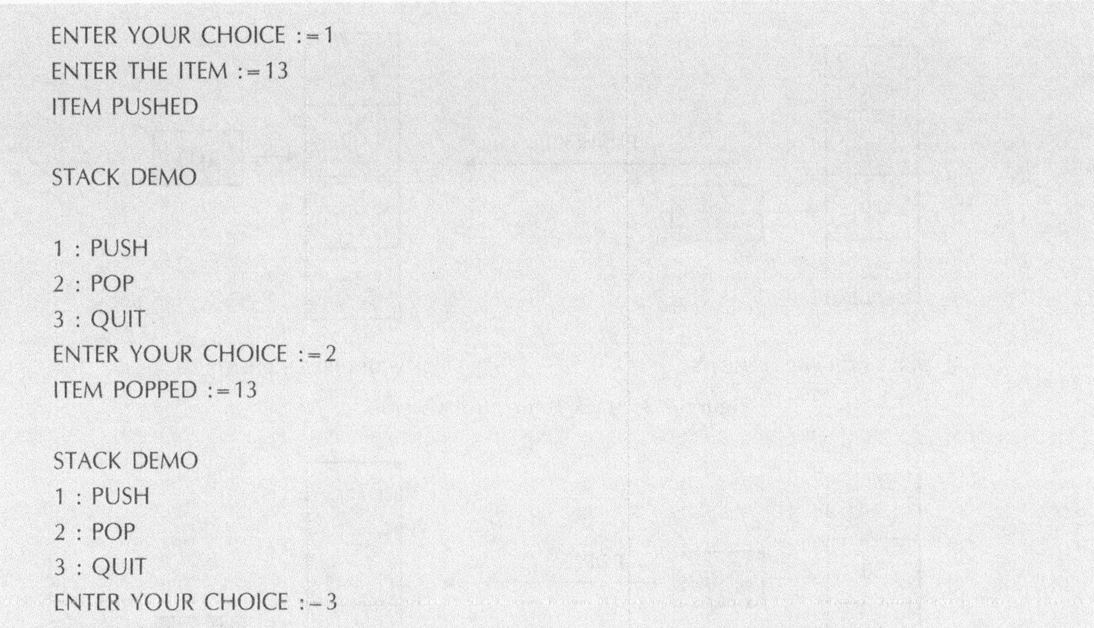

```
ENTER YOUR CHOICE :=1
ENTER THE ITEM :=13
ITEM PUSHED

STACK DEMO

1 : PUSH
2 : POP
3 : QUIT
ENTER YOUR CHOICE :=2
ITEM POPPED :=13

STACK DEMO
1 : PUSH
2 : POP
3 : QUIT
ENTER YOUR CHOICE :-3
GOOD BYE
```

EXPLANATION : The program is simulating stack using array. A stack is a data structure in which last item inserted out first. That's why they are known as **LIFO (last in first out).** Inserting an `'item'` in stack termed as `push` and taking an item out from stack termed as `pop`.

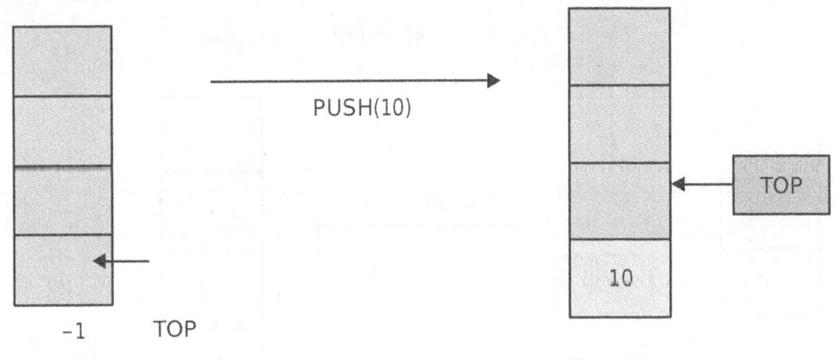

Figure 7.1. *Stack After Push Operation.*

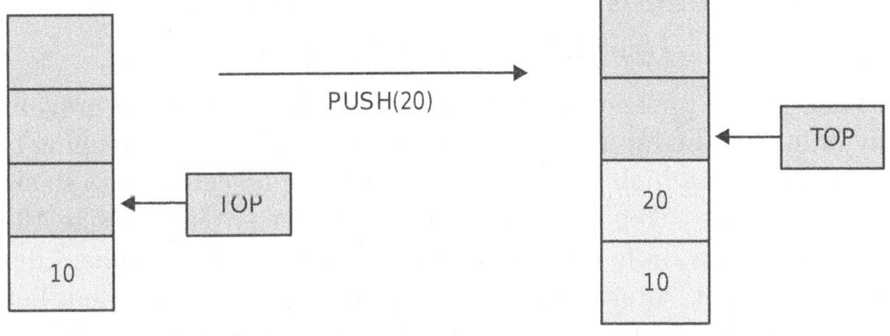

Figure 7.2. *Stack After Push Operation.*

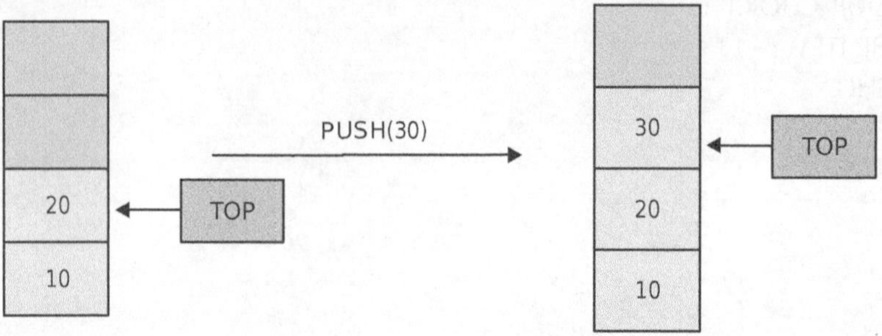

Figure 7.3. *Stack After Push Operation.*

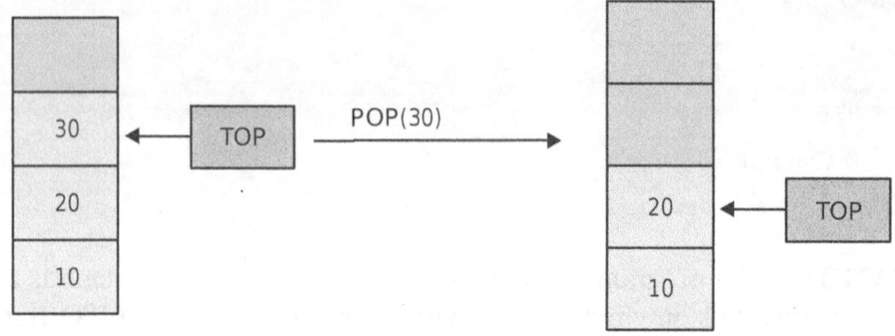

Figure 7.4. *Stack After Pop Operation.*

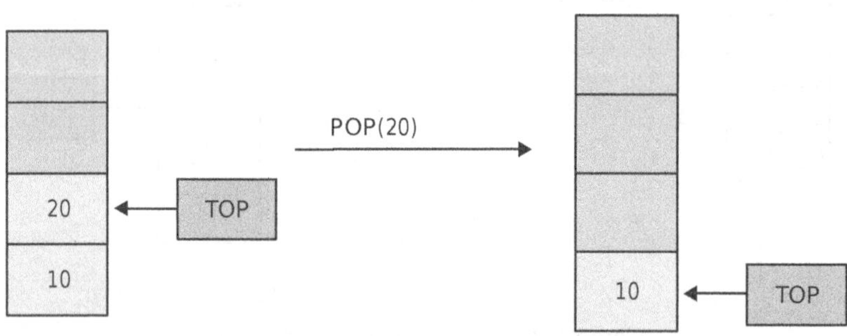

Figure 7.5. *Stack After Pop Operation.*

Only one **item** can be pushed at a time which is added on **top** of previous item pushed. In the same way only one, the top most item can be popped back. For keeping track of top item we have a data member top which is initialized to **–1** when object of class stack is created. The program is simple. We have taken an array as data member of class of size **10** by the name **st** which our stack. When we want to push **item** into this stack st we increment the **top** and assign item to **st** as **st [top] = item**. After each item is pushed **top** is incremented. Before pushing an item we have to check first that we have space for new item in the stack.

This is done as :

```
void push(int item)
        {
                if(top= =9)
                {
                        cout<<"STACK IS FULL"<<endl;
                        exit(0);
                }
```

If **top= =9,** stack is full and we terminate the program.

When an item is popped we take the value at **st[top]** and decrement the **top** by **1** as return **st[top– –].** Before popping an item we check stack is empty or not. This is done as follows :

```
if(top= =-1)
{
        cout<<"STACK IS EMPTY"<<endl;
        exit(0);
}
```

If **top= = –1**, stack is empty and we terminate the program.

/*PROG 7.10 QUEUE SIMULATION USING ARRAY AND CLASS */

```
#include <iostream.h>
#include <conio.h>
#include <stdlib.h>
#define S 5

class queue
{
    int front;
    int rear;
    int que[S];

public :

    queue( )
    {
        front = rear = -1;
    }

    void insert(int item)
    {
```

```
        if(rear == S-1)
        {
            cout<<"QUEUE IS FULL"<<endl;
            exit(0);
        }
        if(front==-1)
            front=0;
        que[++rear]=item;
        cout<<"ITEM INSERTED"<<endl;
    }
    int del( )
    {
        int item;
        if(front==-1)
        {
            cout<<"QUEUE IS EMPTY "<<endl;
            exit(0);
        }
        item = que[front];
        if(front == rear)
            front=rear=-1;
        else
            front++;
        return item;
    }

};
void main( )
{
    queue s;
    int choice, item;

    clrscr( );

    do
    {
        cout<<"QUEUW DEMO"<<endl;
        cout<<"1 : INSERT(REAR OPERATION)"<<endl;
        cout<<"2 : DELETE(FRONT OPERATION)"<<endl;
        cout<<"3 : QUIT"<<endl;
        cin>>choice;
```

```
        switch(choice)
        {
        case 1 :cout<<"ENTER THE ITEM"<<endl;
            cin>>item;
            s.insert(item);
            break;
        case 2 : item=s.del( );
            cout<<"ITEM DELETED :="<<item<<endl;
            break;
        case 3 : cout<<"HAVE A NICE DAY,GOOD BYE"<<endl;
            exit(0);
            break;
        default : cout<<"WRONG CHOICE!ERROR......."<<endl;
        }
    } while (choice>=1 && choice<=3);
    getch( );
}
```

OUTPUT :

```
QUEUW DEMO
1 : INSERT(REAR OPERATION)
2 : DELETE(FRONT OPERATION)
3 : QUIT
1
ENTER THE ITEM
10
ITEM INSERTED

QUEUW DEMO
1 : INSERT(REAR OPERATION)
2 : DELETE(FRONT OPERATION)
3 : QUIT
1
ENTER THE ITEM
20
ITEM INSERTED

QUEUW DEMO
```

```
1 : INSERT(REAR OPERATION)
2 : DELETE(FRONT OPERATION)
3 : QUIT
2
ITEM DELETED :=10

QUEUW DEMO
1 : INSERT(REAR OPERATION)
2 : DELETE(FRONT OPERATION)
3 : QUIT
3
HAVE A NICE DAY,GOOD BYE
```

EXPLANATION : The program simulates the working of queue using array and class. The `queue` is a data structure with two pointer `front` and `rear`. Whenever a new `item` is added to the queue, `rear` pointer is used. It is incremented by `1`. If it is the first item inserted front also becomes 1. The `front` pointer is used when an item is deleted from queue; `front pointer is decremented by 1`. If it was the last item in the queue front and rear both equal to `0`. The queue is also known as **FIFO (First In First Out)** as items are added always at the end of queue (rear end) and are always deleted from front of the queue.

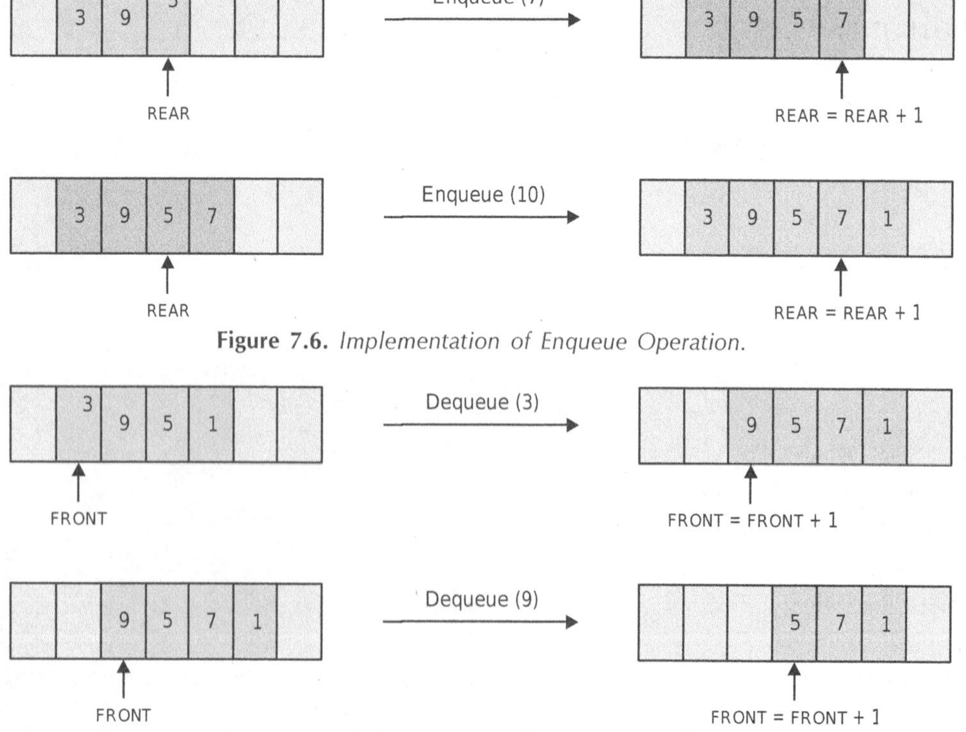

Figure 7.6. *Implementation of Enqueue Operation.*

Figure 7.7. *Implementation of Dequeue Operation.*

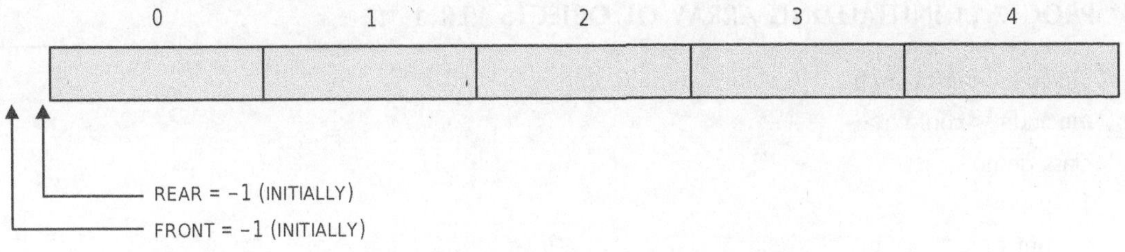

Figure 7.8. *Logical Implementation of Queue at the Beginning.*

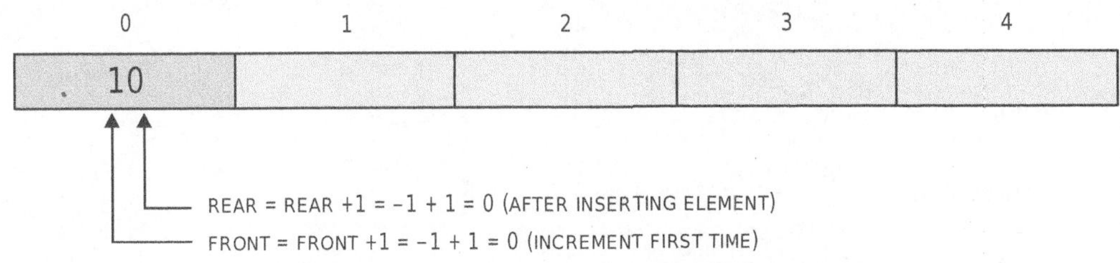

Figure 7.9. *After Applying Enqueue Operation.*

Initially when default constructor is called front and rear are initialized to **–1**. For insertion of item into the queue (implemented as array **que**) **rear** is incremented but it is checked if we have space for the element to be inserted. This is checked as :

```
if(rear == S-1)
        {
                cout<<"QUEUE IS FULL"<<endl;
                exit(0);
        }
```

If item was the first item inserted front was **–1** earlier so it is made to 0. Item is inserted as

```
que [++ rear] = item
```

Pointer rear was also incremented.

For the deletion of item from `que`, front pointer is used. The element in the `que` at the front is returned as `que[front]`. Again before deletion it is checked whether `que` is empty or not as :

```
if(front==-1)
        {
                cout<<"QUEUE IS EMPTY "<<endl;
                exit(0);
        }
```

Now, after deletion if **front** becomes equal to the **rear** (last item deleted) both are assigned value **–1** else **front** is incremented.

/* PROG 7.11 INITIALIZING ARRAY OF OBJECTS VER 1 */

```
#include <iostream.h>
#include <conio.h>
class demo
{
    int num;

public :

    demo(int n)
    {
        num = n;
    }


    void show( )
    {
        cout<<"num="<<num<<endl;
    }

};

void main( )
{
    demo d[ ] = {
                  demo(15),
                  demo(20),
                  demo(45),
                  demo(30),
    };

 clrscr( );

    const int x= sizeof(d)/sizeof(demo);

    for(int i=0;i<x;i++)
        d[i].show( );

    getch( );
}
```

OUTPUT :

```
num=15
num=20
num=45
num=30
```

EXPLANATION : Note how we have initialized array of objects.

```
demo d[ ] = {
                    demo(15),
                    demo(20),
                    demo(45),
                    demo(30),
      };
```

Each **demo(x);** (**x** may have any **int** value) creates an object in array by calling default constructor. The **sizeof(d)** gives total size of array and **sizeof(demo)** gives size of an object. Dividing first by second gives number of objects in the array. Later we display value of **num** for all objects using **show( )** function.

/* PROG 7.12 INITIALIZING ARRAY OF OBJECTS VER 2 */

```
#include <iostream.h>
#include <conio.h>
#include <string.h>

class demo
{
    char name[20];
public :
    demo(char s[20])
    {
        strcpy(name, s);
    }

    void show( )
    {
        cout<<name<<endl;
    }

};
```

```
void main( )
{
    demo d[ ]={

                demo("Prof.RR Sedamkar"),
                demo("Mr.Hari Mohan"),
                demo("Mr.Deshmukh"),
                demo("Mr.Bharat"),
                demo("Mr.Joshi"),
     };

    clrscr( );
    const int x= sizeof(d)/sizeof(demo);

    for(int i=0;i<x;i++)
        d[i].show( );

    getch( );
}
```

EXPLANATION : The program is similar to previous one with the difference that we have used string inseated of integer data.

7.4 COPY CONSTRUCTOR

A copy constructor is used to declare and initialized an object from another object when ever we have statement like `demo d2 = d1` (assume `demo` is class name and `d1` is an already declared object of `demo` class), they make call to copy constructor defined in the class. When we have two objects say `d1` and `d2` and if we write `d2=d1` then this results in copying all members of `d1` to `d2` but does not call `copy constructor`. **This is simply assignment of one object to another of same type,** but when you want to do something more than merely copying one object to another you may use copy constructor. For a class demo, copy constructor is written as :

```
demo (demo &d)
{
        // copy constructor
}
```

For better understanding point of view we present few programs here.

/*PROG 7.13 DEMO OF COPY CONSTRUCTOR VER 1*/

```
#include <iostream.h>
#include <conio.h>

class demo
{
 int data;
 public :
     demo( )
     {
        data =200;
        cout<<"Default constructor is called\n";
     }
     demo(int x)
     {
        data = x;
     }
     demo (demo &d)
     {
        data= d.data;
        cout<<"copy constructor is called\n";
     }
     void show( )
     {
        cout<<"data="<<data<<endl;
     }
 };
 void main( )
 {
     clrscr( );
     demo d1(300);
     demo d2=d1;
     demo d3;
     d3=d2;
     demo d4=demo (d3);
     d1.show( );
     d2.show( );
     d3.show( );
     d4.show( );
     getch( );
 }
```

OUTPUT :

```
copy constructor is called
Default constructor is called
copy constructor is called
data=300
data=300
data=300
data=300
```

EXPLANATION : The declaration and definition

```
demo (demo & d)
{
        data = d.data;
        cout<<"copy constructor is called \n";
}
```

Is a copy constructor. When we write in the **main** function **demo d2 = d1;** copy constructor is called which is as stated above to declare the object d2 and initialize to d1. Here it copy value of data for object d1 to value of data to object d2. The object is passed as reference and not by value *i.e.,* if you write the copy constructor as shown below :

```
demo (demo d)
{
 data = d.data;
 cout<<"copy constructor is called \n";
}
```

The compiler will flash the error message **"illegal copy construor".** The reason behind why an object is always passed by reference and not by value as argument to copy constructor is as follows (assume **&** is not written in copy constructor) : when we write **demo d2=d1**, it will invoke copy constructor and send **d1** as argument to it. When copy constructor receive d1 as argument it will look like demo d=d1, which means to declare and initialize object d from d1 this will again invoke copy constructor. Thus there will be a recursive call and all the system memory will be consumed in the creation of objects. The compiler won't allow this. When we receive pass argument by reference as we do; no copy of the object will be created and only a reference will be passed which avoids creation of object together.

The statement demo d2 (d1) if written will also call copy constructor and initializes object d2 to d1. The process of initializing through a copy constructor is known as copy initialization. Observe that in the above program when we simply write d2 = d1, that does not invoke copy constructor instead calls internally overloaded assignment (=) operator to copy members of d1 and d2 (except pointer members).

Situations Where Copy Constructor will be Called

There are mainly **4 situations** under which a copy constructor will be called:

1. When a new object is initialized to an object of the same class.
2. When an object is passed to a function by value.
3. When an object is returned from a function by value.
4. When the compiler generates a temporary object.

The copy constructor gets called when an object is passed to function or returned from function by value. The compiler always provides a copy constructor when it is not explicitly created in the class. To prove my point we modify the above program and add a friend function which copies data of one object to other and return the object.

See the program given below :

/*PROG 7.14 DEMO OF COPY CONSTRUCTOR VER 2 */

```
#include <iostream.h>
#include <conio.h>

class demo
{
    int data;
    public :

    demo( )
{
    data =200;
    cout<<"Default constructor is called"<<endl;
}
demo(int x)
{
    data = x;
}
demo(demo & d)
{
    data = d.data;
    cout<<"Copy constructor is called"<<endl;
}
friend demo copy(demo d)
{
    demo temp;
    temp.data = d.data;
    return temp;
}
```

```
    void show( )
    {
        cout<<"data = "<<data<<endl;
    }
};

void main( )
{
    clrscr( );
    demo d1(300);
    demo d2= d1;
    demo d3 = copy(d1);
    d1.show( );
    d2.show( );
    d3.show( );
    getch( );
}
```

OUTPUT :

```
Copy constructor is called
Copy constructor is called
Default constructor is called
Copy constructor is called
data = 300
data = 300
data = 300
```

EXPLANATION : In the program we have written a `copy constructor` and a `friend function copy`. The function `copy` takes an object by value as argument, copies the data into another object and returned that object. In the `main` when `demo d1 (300);` executes it calls the one argument constructor and sets data for object `d1 = 200`. When `demo d2 = d1;` executes `copy constructor` is called and `data` for `d2` is equal to `data` for `d1`. Now the important thing to understand. When `demo d3 = copy (d1);` executes, `copy constructor` is called as we have written `demo d3 =`. As we are passing `d1` by value in the `function copy`, `copy constructor` will be called. Inside the function `copy` temporary object `(temp)` is created which is called `default constructor` and in the end we have written the object `temp` by value, `copy constructor` is called again.

If I do a small change as that instead of writing **demo d3 = copy (d1);** we write as :

```
demo d3;
d3 = copy(d1);
```

Sequence of constructor will be called as :

1. For **demo d3, default constructor** will be called.
2. **d1** we are sending by value, **copy constructor** will be called.
3. In the function **demo temp;** causes **default constructor** to be called.
4. **return temp** causes **copy constructor** to be called.

7.5 DYNAMIC INITIALIZATION OF OBJECTS

Dynamic initialization of objects simply means assigning the values to data members of class dynamically by taking the values from the user when program executes. We have examples of this in some of the programs but we were not familiar with the actual term.

Now, given below are few programs which illustrate this concept in details.

/*PROG 7.15 DYNAMIC INITIALIZATION OF OBJECT VER 1*/

```
#include <iostream.h>
#include <conio.h>

class Ipod
{
    int price;
    int capacity;
    public :
    Ipod( )
  {
     cout<<"Enter the price of Ipod"<<endl;
     cin>>price;
     cout<<"Enter the memory capacity in MB"<<endl;
     cin>>capacity;
  }
  void display( )
  {
     cout<<"Price="<<price<<endl;
     cout<<"Capacity="<<capacity<<"MB"<<endl;
  }
};
  void main( )
  {
    clrscr( );
    Ipod ip1;
    ip1.display ( );
```

```
    getch( );
}
```

OUTPUT :

```
Enter the price of Ipod
7500
Enter the memory capacity in MB
1024
Price=7500
Capacity=1024MB
```

EXPLANATION : When the statement `Ipod ip1;` executes `default` constructor of class `Ipod` is called and user is promoted to enter the values for price and capacity for an object `ip1` of `Ipod` type. Each time the program run new values are taken for object `ip1`. Thus initializing objects dynamically.

/*PROG 7.16 DYNAMIC INITIALIZATION OF OBJECTS VER 2*/

```
#include <iostream.h>
#include <conio.h>

class Ipod
{
    int price;
    int capacity;

 public :

    Ipod(int p, int c)
    {
        price= p;
        capacity=c;
    }
    void display( )
    {
        cout<<"Price="<<price<<endl;
        cout<<"Capacity="<<capacity<<"MB"<<endl;
    }
};

void main( )
{
```

```
    int pr, cp;

    clrscr( );

    cout<<"Enter the price of Ipod"<<endl;
    cin>>pr;

    cout<<"Enter the memory capacity in MB"<<endl;
    cin>>cp;

    Ipod ip1= Ipod(pr,cp);
    ip1.display( );

    getch( );
}
```

OUTPUT :

```
Enter the price of Ipod
8000
Enter the memory capacity in MB
1024
Price=8000
Capacity=1024MB
```

EXPLANATION : The program is similar to the previous one with the difference that instead of taking values for data members from constructor, we take values in **main** in local variables and pass these values to two argument constructor of **Ipod** class for initializing **object ip1.**

/*PROG 7.17 DYNAMIC INITIALIZATION OF OBJECTS VER 3*/

```
#include <iostream.h>
#include <string.h>
#include <conio.h>
class mobile
{
    char cname[20];
    char setid[10];
    float price;

public :
```

```
    mobile( )
    {}

    mobile(char s[ ], float p, char cn[ ]="Nokia")
    {
        strcpy(cname, cn);
        strcpy(setid,s);
        price = p;
    }

    mobile(mobile &m)
    {
        strcpy(cname, m.cname);
        strcpy(setid, m.setid);
        price=m.price;
    }

    void show( )
    {
        cout<<"Company :="<<cname<<endl;
        cout<<"Set Id :="<<setid<<endl;
        cout<<"Price :="<<price<<endl;
    }

};
void main( )
{
    char c[20];
    char s[10];
    float p;

    clrscr( );

    cout<<"ENTER THE COMPANY NAME "<<endl;
    cin.getline(c,20);

    cout<<"ENTER THE SET ID AND PRICE "<<endl;
    cin>>s>>p;

    mobile m1, m2;
```

```
    m1=mobile(s,p,c);
    cout<<"ENTER THE SET ID AND PRICE"<<endl;
    cin>>s>>p;

    m2=mobile(s,p);
    mobile m3=m1;

    cout<<"\n \t MOBILE 1 DETAILS "<<endl<<endl;
    m1.show( );

    cout<<"\n\tMOBILE 2 DETAILS "<<endl<<endl;
    m2.show( );

    cout<<"\n\t MOBILE 3 DETAILS"<<endl<<endl;
    m3.show( );

    getch( );
}
```

OUTPUT :

```
ENTER THE COMPANY NAME
Sony Erricson

ENTER THE SET ID AND PRICE
z550i 9000

ENTER THE SET ID AND PRICE
3230 9999

 MOBILE 1 DETAILS

Company :=Sony Erricson
Set Id :=z550i
Price :=9000

 MOBILE 2 DETAILS

Company :=Nokia
Set Id :=3230
Price :=9999
```

```
MOBILE 3 DETAILS
Company :=Sony Erricson
Set Id :=z550i
Price :=9000
```

EXPLANATION : The class `mobile` contains 3 data members for mobile viz `cname`, `setid` and `price`. The object `m1` is dynamically initialized by taking values in 3 local variables and passing to 3 argument constructor of `mobile` class. The default argument value is overridden. The object `m3` gets copy of object `m1` by calling copy constructor when statement mobile `m3 = m1` executes. Note for `mobile` object `m2` only the `price` and `setid` is taken from the user and default value of cname *i.e.*, **"Nokia"** is assumed.

7.6 DYNAMIC CONSTRUCTOR

When in a constructor we create memory dynamically using dynamic memory allocator operator new, then constructor is known as dynamic constructor.

See the given program for better understanding stand point.

/* PROG 7.18 DYNAMIC CONSTRUCTOR, CONSTRUCTING 1-D ARRAY DYNAMICALLY */

```
#include <iostream.h>
#include <conio.h>

class Dyn_arr
{
    int *ptr;
    int size;

public :

    Dyn_arr(int s)
    {
        ptr= new int [size =s];
    }

    void input( );
    void sort( );
    void show( );
};

void Dyn_arr : :input( )
{
```

```
        int i;

        for(i=0;i<size;i++)
        {
            cout<<"\nENTER PTR["<<i<<"]ELEMENT :=";
            cin>>ptr[i];
        }
}

void Dyn_arr : : sort( )
{
        int i,j,t;
        for(i=0;i<size;i++)
            for(j=i+1;j<size;j++)

                if(ptr[i]>ptr[j])
                {
                    t=ptr[i];
                    ptr[i]=ptr[j];
                    ptr[j]=t;
                }
}

void Dyn_arr : :show( )
{
        for(int i=0;i<size;i++)
            cout<<ptr[i]<<" ";
}


void main( )
{
    Dyn_arr obj(5);

    clrscr( );

    obj.input( );

    cout<<"ORIGINAL ARRAY"<<endl;
    obj.show( );
    obj.sort( );
```

```
    cout<<"\n SORTED ARRAY"<<endl;
    obj.show( );

    getch( );
}
```

OUTPUT :

```
ENTER PTR[0]ELEMENT :=12
ENTER PTR[1]ELEMENT :=56
ENTER PTR[2]ELEMENT :=3

ENTER PTR[3]ELEMENT :=90

ENTER PTR[4]ELEMENT :=10

ORIGINAL ARRAY

12 56 3 90 10

 SORTED ARRAY
3 10 12 56 90
```

EXPLANATION : We have seen how to construct 1-D array dynamically in chapter 4. Here when we construct the array dynamically within constructor of the class, the constructor is known as dynamic constructor. The program is very simple. We have pointer data member `'ptr'` of type `'int'`. When the statement `Dyn_arr obj(5);` executes, one argument constructor for class `Dyn_arr` is called and for object `obj` the line `ptr= new int[size = s];` creates which creates a dynamic array of size `5`. The array can now be referred by the name `ptr` and any element of the array can now be accessed as `ptr[i]`, where `'i'` is the index.

/*PROG 7.19 DYNAMIC CONSTRUCTOR, CONSTRUCTING 2-D ARRAY DYNAMICALLY */

```
#include <iostream.h>
#include <conio.h>

class matrix
{
    int **ptr;
    int row,col;
    public :
    matrix(int r, int c);
    void input( );
```

```
    void show( );
}

matrix : :matrix(int r, int c)
{
    row = r; col=c;
    ptr=new int *[row];
    for(int i=0;i<row;i++)
    ptr[i]=new int[col];
}
void matrix : :input( )
{
    int i,j;
    for(i=0;i<row;i++)
    for(j=0;j<col;j++)
  {
    cout<<"\nEnter ptr["<<i<<"]["<<j<<"] element :";
    cin>>ptr[i][j];
  }

  }

  void matrix : ; show( )
  {
    int i,j;
    cout<<"\n Matrix is \n";
    for(i=0;i<row;i++)
  {
    for(j=0;j<col;j++)
    cout<<ptr[i][j]<<"\t";
    cout<<endl;
  }

}

  void main( )
  {
    clrscr( );
    matrix m(3,3);
    m.input( );
    m.show( );
```

```
    getch( );
}
```

OUTPUT :

```
Enter ptr[0][0] element :10

Enter ptr[0][1] element :11

Enter ptr[0][2] element :12

Enter ptr[1][0] element :13

Enter ptr[1][1] element :14

Enter ptr[1][2] element :15

Enter ptr[2][0] element :16

Enter ptr[2][1] element :17

Enter ptr[2][2] element :18

Matrix is

10        11        12
13        14        15
16        17        18
```

EXPLANATION : The construction of dynamic 2-D array was explained in the chapter 4. The same logic is used here but it is put into the class.

/*PROG 7.20 DYNAMIC CONSTRUCTION OF STRING */

```
#include <iostream.h>
#include <conio.h>
#include <string.h>

class string
{
    char *sname;
    int len;
```

```
public :

    string( )
    {
        len=0;
        sname= new char [len + 1];
        *sname = '\0';
    }

    string(char s[ ])
    {
        len=strlen(s);
        sname = new char[len + 1];
        strcpy(sname, s);
    }

    void show( )
    {
        cout<<"STRING IS :="<<sname<<endl;
        cout<<"LENGTH :="<<len<<endl;
        delete sname;
    }

};

void main( )
{
    string s1,s2;
    clrscr( );

    s1=string("HARI");
    s1.show( );

    s2=string("HARI LIKE C++");
    s2.show( );

    getch( );
}
```

OUTPUT :

STRING IS :=HARI

```
LENGTH :=4
STRING IS :=HARI LIKE C++
LENGTH :=13
```

EXPLANATION : In the default constructor we have dynamically created a string of size just 1 character and length is 0. When `s1 = string ("HARI");` executes constructor `string : :string(char s[ ])` is called and `s` contains "HARI"; Inside the constructor first length of `s` is calculated and assigned to `len`. Then we allocated memory dynamically of size `len + 1`. This memory is allocated and returned address of first memory word is assigned to pointer sname. In the function `show` after displaying `len` and `sname`, we delete the `sname` by writing delete `sname` which de-allocates memory pointed by `sname`.

/* PROG 7.21 CONCATENATION OF TWO STRINGS */

```
#include <iostream.h>
#include <string.h>
#include <conio.h>
class string
{
    char *sname;
    int len;
public :
    string( )
    {
        len=0;
        sname = new char [len +1];
        *sname = '\0';
    }

    string(char s[ ])
    {
        len =strlen(s);
        sname =new char[len+1];
        strcpy(sname, s);
    }

    friend string concate(string, string);

    void show( )
    {
        cout<<"String :="<<sname<<endl;
    }
};
```

```
string concate(string A, string B)
{
    string temp;
    temp.len= A.len + B.len +1;
    temp.sname = new char[temp.len+1];
    strcpy(temp.sname, A.sname);
    strcat(temp.sname, " ");
    strcat(temp.sname, B.sname);
    return temp;
}
void main( )
{
    string s1,s2,s3;
    clrscr( );
    s1=string("Hari");
    s1.show( );
    s2=string("Pandey");
    s2.show( );
    s3=concate(s1,s2);
    s3.show( );
    getch( );
}
```

OUTPUT :

```
String :=Hari
String :=Pandey
String :=Hari Pandey
```

EXPLANATION : Here we will explain only the function concate.

```
string concate(string A, string B)
{
        string temp;
        temp.len= A.len + B.len +1;
        temp.sname = new char[temp.len+1];
        strcpy(temp.sname, A.sname);
        strcat(temp.sname, " ");
        strcat(temp.sname, B.sname);
        return temp;
}
```

When line **s3 = concate (s1, s2);** executes **A.sname** is equal to **“Hari”**, **A.len = 4** and **B.sname** is equal to **“Pandey”**, **B.len = 6.**

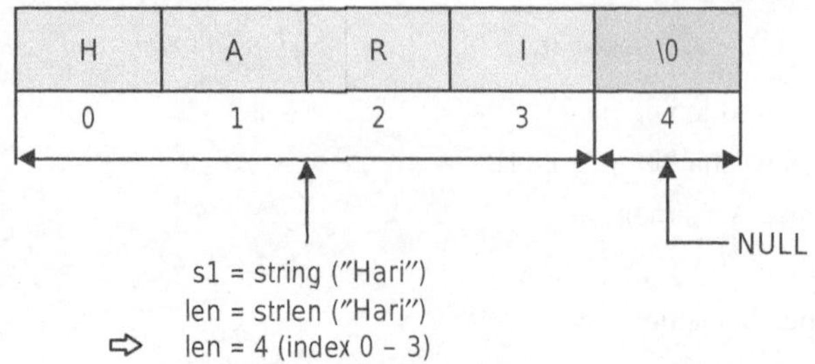

Figure 7.10. *Implementation of length of string by strlen ( ) function.*

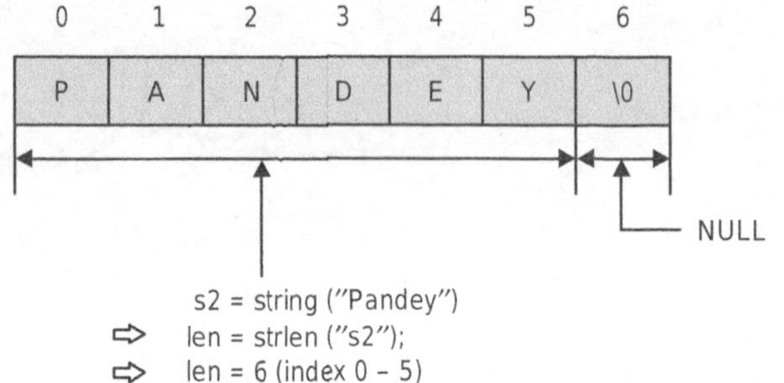

Figure 7.11. *Physical implementation of strlen ( ) function.*

In the function concate first line creates object **temp**. In the next line we sum **A.len, B.len** and **1** extra for adding space between **“Hari”** and **“Pandey”**. Thus **len** of **temp** becomes **4 + 6 + 1 = 11.** The next line allocates memory for **temp.sname**. In the next line **A.sname** *i.e.,* **“Hari”** is copied to **temp.sname** using **strcpy( )** function. Next a space” “is concatenated to temp.sname which contains **“Hari”** at present, using **strcat.** Now **temp.sname** becomes **“Hari”.**

In the next line **B.sname** is concatenated to **temp.sname** using strcat which result in **temp.sname** containing **“Hari Pandey”.** The **temp** object is returned and assigned to **s3**.

A.len = 4

B.len = 6

temp.len = 10 + 1 = 11

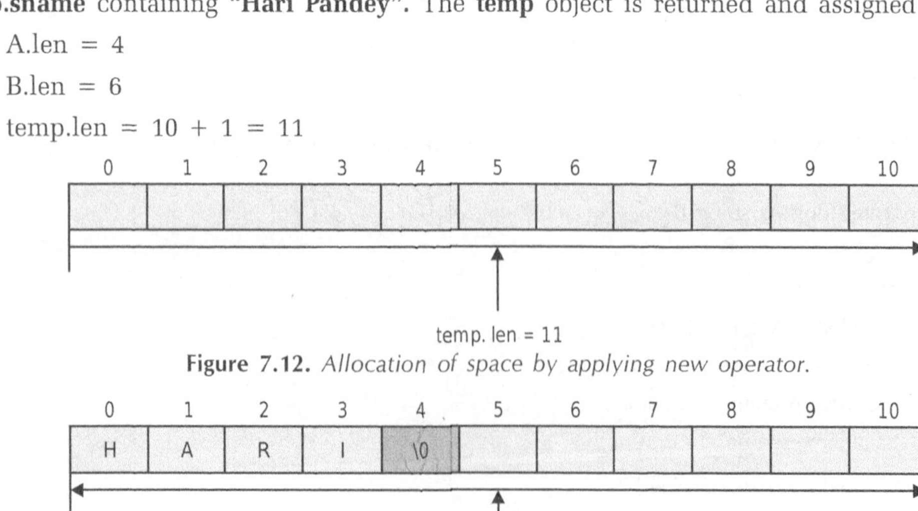

Figure 7.12. *Allocation of space by applying new operator.*

Figure 7.13. *Copying string "Hari" into temp. sname.*

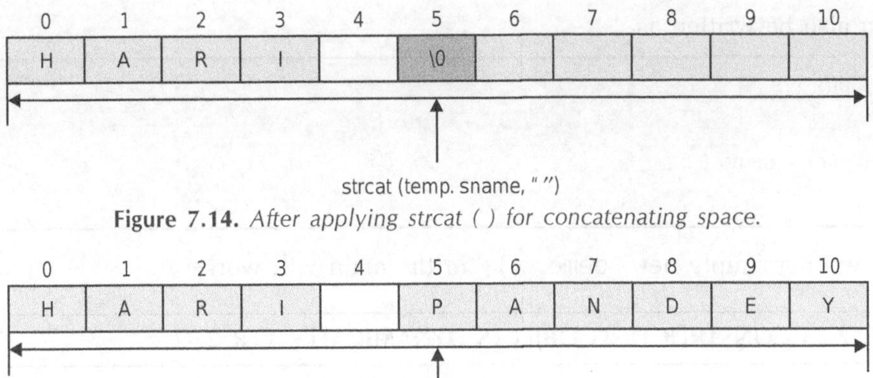

Figure 7.14. *After applying strcat ( ) for concatenating space.*

0	1	2	3	4	5	6	7	8	9	10
H	A	R	I		P	A	N	D	E	Y

s3 = stract (s1, s2)
strcat (temp.sname, B.sname);

Figure 7.15. *After concatenating string1 with string2.*

/*PROG 7.22 CONSTRUCTING OBJECTS DYNAMICALLY */

```
#include <iostream.h>
#include <conio.h>

class demo
{
    public :
    demo( )
    {
    cout<<"Constructor called"<<endl;
    }
};
void main( )
{
    clrscr( );
    demo *ptr=new demo( );
    getch( );
}
```

OUTPUT :

Constructor called

EXPLANATION : The new operator can be used for creating objects dynamically. Creation of pointer does not create objects. For the statement new `demo ( )`, object is constructed by allocating memory from heap and calling the `default constructor` of the class.

It can also be written as :

```
demo *ptr;
{
    ptr= new demo ( );
}
```

Even writing simply `new demo ();` in the main will work.

```
/* PROG 7.23 CONSTRUCTING OBJECTS DYNAMICALLY VER 2 */

#include <iostream.h>
#include <conio.h>

class demo
{
public :
    demo( )
    {
        cout<<"DEFAULT CONSTRUCTOR"<<endl;
    }
    demo (int x)
    {
        cout<<"ONE INT ARGUMENT CONSTRUCTOR"<<endl;
        cout<<"X = "<<x<<endl;
    }
    demo (float f)
    {
        cout<<"ONE FLOAT ARGUMENT CONSTRUCTOR"<<endl;
        cout<<"f :="<<f<<endl;
    }
    demo (int x, char y)
    {
        cout<<"ONE INT AND ONE CHAR ARGUMENT
                CONSTRUCTOR"<<endl;
        cout<<"x :="<<x<<"\t"<<"y :="<<y<<endl;
    }
    demo(char *p)
    {
        cout<<"ONE CHAR* ARGUMENT CONSTRUCTOR"<<endl;
        cout<<"p :="<<p<<endl;
    }
};
```

```
void main( )
{
    clrscr( );
    new demo( );
    new demo(10);
    new demo(10.35f);
    new demo(20,'P');
    new demo("DYNAMIC");
    getch( );
}
```

OUTPUT :

```
DEFAULT CONSTRUCTOR
ONE INT ARGUMENT CONSTRUCTOR
X = 10
ONE FLOAT ARGUMENT CONSTRUCTOR
f :=10.35
ONE INT AND ONE CHAR ARGUMENT CONSTRUCTOR
x :=20 y :=P
ONE CHAR* ARGUMENT CONSTRUCTOR
p :=DYNAMIC
```

EXPLANATION : In the program there are 5 constructors. One is default and the rest are parameterized. In the `main` we call each constructor by creating objects dynamically. Note we have not created pointer variables which represent object like `demo *ptr=new demo ();` this syntax is valid when we want to work with objects later. In the program we are just showing you how to call constructors dynamically that's why we have not stored returned address from any of the new call into the pointer to demo class.

```
/* PROG 7.24 CONSTRUCTING OBJECT DYNAMICALLY */

#include <iostream.h>
#include <conio.h>

class demo
{
public :
    demo( )
    {
        cout<<"DEFAULT CONSTRUCTOR"<<endl;
    }
};
```

```
void main( )
{
    demo *ptr = new demo [5];
    getch( );
}
```

OUTPUT :

```
DEFAULT CONSTRUCTOR
DEFAULT CONSTRUCTOR
DEFAULT CONSTRUCTOR
DEFAULT CONSTRUCTOR
DEFAULT CONSTRUCTOR
```

EXPLANATION : In the program we have created array objects dynamically. The first object is `ptr [0]`, second is `ptr [1]` and so on. For each object creation default constructor is called.

7.7 DESTRUCTOR

A destructor is a member function of the class whose name is same as the name of the class but the preceded with tilde sign (~). The purpose of destructor is to destroy the object when it is no longer needed or goes out of scope. As a very small example of destructor see the program given below :

/*PROG 7.25 DEMO OF DESTRUCTOR VER 1*/

```
#include <iostream.h>
#include <conio.h>

class demo
{
public :
    demo( )
    {
        cout<<"Constructor called\n";
    }
    ~demo( )
    {
        cout<<"Destructor called"<<endl;
    }
};
```

```
void main( )
{
    clrscr( );
    demo d;
    getch( );
}
```

OUTPUT :

```
Constructor called
Destructor called
```

EXPLANATION : When demo d; executes it calls the default constructor of the class and results in printing Constructor called. The scope of object d is the area/place where it is available and in the above program the scope is the whole main function. Being the only statement demo d; in the function main, as soon as compiler finds ending brace of main *i.e.,*} it calls destructor of the class to destroy the object d and prints Destructor called. The code is given as :

```
~demo ( )
{
    cout<<"Destructor called "<<endl;
}
```

is a destructor of the class **demo.**

Features of Destructor

1. The name is same as of class but proceeded with a ~ sign.
2. Destructor is automatically called as soon as an object goes out of scope.
3. Destructor is used to destroy the objects.
4. Once a destructor is called for a object, the object will no longer be available for the future reference.
5. Destructor can be used for housekeeping work such as closing the file, de-allocating the dynamically allocated memory etc. Closing a file in destructor is a good idea as user might forget to close the file associated with object. But as the object goes out of scope destructor will be called and all code written in destructor executes which will always result in closing the file and no data loss may be there. When new is used for allocation of memory in the constructor we must always use delete in the destructor to be allocate the memory.
6. Similar to constructor there is no return type for destructor and that's why they cannot return any value.
7. There is no explicit or implicit category for a destructor. They are always called implicitly by the compiler.
8. Destructor can never take any arguments.

9. Destructor can be virtual.

In our all earlier program destructor can be written. For instance in all our dynamic constructor program destructor can be written for the allocation of memory like.

```
~string( )
{
    delete sname;
}


And


~matrix ( )
{
    delete ptr[ ];
}
```

As one more example of destructor which makes use of block as scope, see the next program given below :

/*PROG 7.26 DEMO OF CONSTRUCTOR VER 2 */

```
#include <iostream.h>
#include <conio.h>

class demo
{
    static int count;

    public :

    demo( )
    {
    cout<<"Object created "<<++count<<endl;
    }
    ~demo( )
    {
    cout<<"Object Destroyed"<<count--<<endl;
    }
};

int demo : :count;
```

```
void main( )
{
    clrscr( );
    cout<<"I am in main \n";
    demo d1;
{
    cout<<"In block 1\n";
    demo d2;
{
    cout<<"In block 2 inside block 1\n";
    demo d3;
}
}
{
    cout<<"In block 3\n";
    demo d4;
}
cout<<"Exiting main\n";
getch( );
}
```

OUTPUT :

```
I am in main
Object created 1

In block 1

Object created 2
In block 2 inside block 1

Object created 3
Object Destroyed3
Object Destroyed2

In block 3

Object created 2
Object Destroyed2
Exiting main
```

EXPLANATION : For keeping track of number of objects created and destroyed we are having `static` data member `count`. This `count` is incremented on object creation in constructor and is decremented on object destruction in destructor. Initially `I'm main` is displayed. When `demo d1` executes it calls default constructor of the `class demo` and `object created 1` is displayed. Next `In block1 displayed.` For `demo d2; Object Created 2` is displayed. Next `In block 2 inside block 1` is displayed. For `demo d3;` calls the `default constructor Object Created 3` is displayed. `Block 2` ends here so destructor for object `d3` will be called which result in displaying `Object Destroyed 2`. Next In `block 3` is printed. The statement `demo d4;` again causes default constructor to be called which displays `Object Destroyed 2`. In the end `Exiting main` is displayed and as `main` is about to terminate, `object d1` created earlier will be destroyed so destructor will be called for `d1` which will display `Object Destroyed 1.`

7.8 PONDERABLE POINTS

1. A constructor is a member function of class whose name is same as the name of the class.
2. A constructor is used to construct the objects of the class. Behind every object creation constructor is involved.
3. A constructor declared as demo ( ) {} is known as default, do-nothing or empty constructor of the class.
4. By default if no constructor is created for the class, C++ provides two default constructors for the class : one is default and second is copy constructor.
5. Constructor can be parameterized and they can take even default values.
6. A constructor never any type.
7. Const and volatile keyword cannot be used with a constructor.
8. A copy constructor is a constructor which is used to copy one object to another.
9. In a copy constructor an argument of class type is passed by reference.
10. When new is used for the allocation of memory for data members of the class in a constructor, the constructor is known as dynamic constructor.
11. A destructor is a member function of the class whose name is same as the name of the class but proceeded with ~ sign.
12. A destructor is used to destroy the object.
13. A destructor is called automatically when an object goes out of scope.
14. A destructor can be called explicitly by an object.
15. Copy constructor is called whenever an object is passed by value to a function or return by value from a function.

EXERCISE

A. True and False :

1. Constructor can be inherited.
2. We can make constructor function as inline.

3. A constructor that accepts no argument is known as do-nothing constructor.
4. A class constructor demo cannot take demo as an argument.
5. Constructors can be overloaded.
6. A destructor must not have argument.
7. Constructor may be private.
8. The destructor and constructor are the only member functions that can be called for a const object.
9. Each class can have exactly one constructor.
10. Declaration of constructor and destructor within a class is mandatory.

B. Answer the Following Questions :

1. What is the difference between constructor overloading and function overloading?
2. What is copy constructor? Why we pass an object by reference to the copy constructor?
3. Under what condition a copy constructor is called?
4. Can we have default argument in the constructors?
5. What is dynamic initialization of objects?
6. What is dynamic destructor? Do you have dynamic destructor?
7. Why an object is passed by reference into the copy constructor?
8. What two different types of constructor C++ provides to a class by default?
9. What is default constructor or do-nothing constructor?
10. What do you understand by an implicit and explicit call to constructor?
11. What is destructor?

C. Brain Drill :

1. Define a class called time that has separate int data members for hours, minutes and seconds. One constructor should initialize these data to 0 and another should initialize them to fixed values. Write a member function to display time in the format 12:28:34. Another member function should add two objects of type time passed as arguments.
2. Write a program to declare global and local objects with the same name. Access member function using both the objects.
3. Define a class named Queue for holding ints and providing function for inserting items at one end and removing items from other end of a queue data structure to be supported by this class. Include a default constructor, a destructor and the usual queue operations: insert ( ), remove ( ), isempty ( ), and isfull ( ). Use array implementation.
4. Define a class of square matrix **N ×N** of integers. Define the necessary constructor/ destructor and other members. Write a program to find the trace (sum of diagonal elements) of a matrix.

❑❑❑

CHAPTER 8

WORKING WITH OPERATOR OVERLOADING

8.1 INTRODUCTION

Operator overloading refers to overloading of one operator for many different purpose. For example, the binary + can be used to add two integer numbers, two float numbers, two structures variables, two union variables or two class objects. Use of operator overloading permits us to see no difference between built-in data types and user defined data types. It is one of the powerful and fascinating features of the C++ which give additional meaning to built-in standard operators like +, –, *, /,>, <, <=, >= etc. Let's see first a small example to give you idea of operator overloading and more concepts will be build later on.

/*PROG 8.1 DEMO OF OPERATOR OVERLOADING, ADDING INTEGER TO OBJECT*/

```
#include<iostream.h>

class demo_op1
{
 private :

    int num;

    public :

    void input( )
    {
        cout<<"Enter the number"<<endl;
        cin>>num;
    }
    void operator +(intx)
```

```
    {
        num=num+x;
    }
    void show( )
    {
        cout<<"The num is "<<num<<endl;
    }
};
void main( )
{
    demo_op1 d1;
    d1.input( );
    d1.show( );
    int x;
    cout<<"Enter the value you want to add\n";
    cin>>x;
    d1+x;
    d1.show( );
}
```

OUTPUT :

```
Enter the number
123
The num is 123
Enter the value you want to add
14
The num is 137
```

EXPLANATION : The syntax of the overloading an operator and writing new overloaded operator function is as follows :

```
return_type operator operator (arguments)
{
    Statements;
    Statements;
    Statements;
}
```

The first word operator is a keyword and must be specified. The second word operator represents the operator which we want to overload *i.e.,* to give a new meaning. It may be +, –, =, = =, >, < etc. Later I will tell you about operators which cannot be overloaded. In the program we have overloaded + operator as given below:

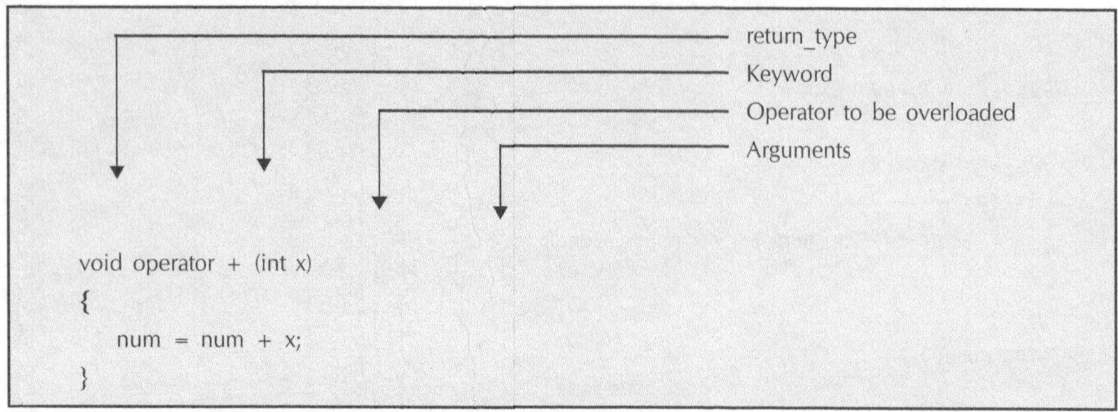

Which accepts an argument of type `int` and returns nothing as return type is `void`. Inside the function we add value of `x` to the `num` of the object. Now see how this function is called from `main`.

The statement **d1+x**; initially interpreted as d1.operator +(x); whenever compiler sees operator like +, –, *, /, ++, – –, etc with variable of user defined data types (here object) it checks whether the operator has been overloaded in the class or not. If not it flashes an error else it calls the appropriate overloaded operator function. As operator function is member function of the class we require some object to call the function so an object is always preceded with the operator which is overloaded and being used in the expression. The argument to be passed is specified as the right operand of the overloaded operator. Here the overall effect of the statement d1+x; is to call the operator function operator + and pass x as argument to it. See how convenient to write d1+x for adding an integer x to object d1 ?

8.2 OPERATOR OVERLOADING WITH BINARY OPERATOR

When overloading binary operator using operator function as class member function, the left side operand must be an object of the class and right side operand may be either a built-in type or user defined type. The other method using friend function will be discussed later on. We present numerous program of overloading binary operators.

/*PROG 8.2 OVERLOADING BINARY + WITH CLASS OBJECTS AS ARGUMENT VER 1*/

```
#include <iostream.h>
#include <conio.h>
class demo_sum
{
    private :
        int num;
        static int count;
    public :
        void input( )
    {
```

```
        cout<<"Enter the number for"<<"Object"<<++count<<"\n";
        cin>>num;
    }
    void operator +(demo_sum temp)
    {
        int x;
        x=num+temp.num;
        cout<<"Sum of two is "<<x<<endl;
    }
    void show( )
    {
        cout<<"The num is"<<num<<endl;
    }
    };
    int demo_sum : :count;
    void main( )
    {
        clrscr( );
        demo_sum d1,d2;
        d1.input( );
        d1.show( );
        d2.input( );
        d2.show( );
        d1+d2;
        getch( );

    }
```

OUTPUT :

```
Enter the number forObject1
23
The num is23
Enter the number forObject2
45
The num is45
Sum of two is 68
```

EXPLANATION : The function

```
void operator + (demo_sum temp)
{
    int x;
    x= num+ temp.num;
    cout<<"sum of two is "<<x<<endl;
}
```

Overloads binary + and accepts an argument of class `demo_sum` type. In the `main` the statement `d1+d2;` is interpreted internally as `d1.operator +(d2)` *i.e.,* `d1` calls the function `d1` and pass `d2` as argument to this overloaded binary + operator function. Inside the function num belongs to objects `d1` (The members of the objects who calls the function, can be inside the function without using object name with dot operator, other syntax using this pointer will be discussed later on) and `d2` is copied to `temp` object so `temp.num` is a copy of `d2.num`. The function finds the sum and displays it.

/*PROG 8.3 OVERLOADING BINARY + WITH CLASS OBJECTS AS ARGUMENT VER 2*/

```
#include <iostream.h>
#include <conio.h>
class demo_sum
{
    private :
        int num;
        static int count;
    public :
     void input( )
     {
        cout<<"Enter the number for object"<<++count<<"\n";
        cin>>num;
     }
  int operator + (demo_sum temp)
  {
     return(num + temp.num);
  }
  void show( )
  {
     cout<<"The num is "<<num<<endl;
  }
};
int demo_sum : :count;
```

```
void main( )
{
    clrscr( );
    demo_sum d1, d2;
    d1.input( );
    d2.input( );
    d1.show( );
    d2.show( );
    int sum=d1+d2;
    cout<<"The sum of two object's num is "<<sum<<endl;
    getch( );
}
```

OUTPUT :

```
Enter the number for object1
23
Enter the number for object2
56
The num is 23
The num is 56
The sum of two object's num is 79
```

EXPLANATION : The program is similar to previous program but instead of displaying the sum in the operator function itself we have returned the sum from function. The function

```
int operator + (demo_sum temp)
{
    return (num + temp.num);
}
```

Overloads the binary **+** and accepts an argument of type **demo_sum**. In the function it finds the sum of two objects **num** and returns it that's why the return type of the function is **int.**

```
/*PROG 8.4 OVERLOADING BINARY + WITH CLASS OBJECTS AS ARGUMENT &
RETURNING OBJECTS */

#include <iostream.h>
#include <conio.h>
class demo_sum
{
    private :
        int num;
```

```
        static int count;
    public :
        void input( )
      {
        cout<<" Enter the number for object"<<++count<<endl;
        cin>>num;
      }
  demo_sum operator +(demo_sum temp)
  {
      demo_sum t;
      t.num = num+ temp.num;
      return t;
  }
  void show( )
  {
      cout<<"The num is "<<num<<endl;
  }
 };
  int demo_sum : :count;
  void main( )
  {
      clrscr( );
      demo_sum d1,d2,d3,d4;
      d1.input( );
      d2.input( );
      d3.input( );
      d1.show( );
      d2.show( );
      d3.show( );
      d4=d1+d2+d3;
      d4.show( );
      getch( );
  }
```

OUTPUT :

```
Enter the number for object1
15
 Enter the number for object2
16
 Enter the number for object3
18
```

```
The num is 15
The num is 16
The num is 18
The num is 49
```

EXPLANATION : The function

```
demo_sum operator + (demo_sum temp)
{
    demo_sum t;
    t.num = num+temp.num;
    return t;
}
```

Overloads binary +, it accepts one argument of type **demo_sum** and returns an object of **demo_sum** type. Returning an object from an overloaded operator function allows us to write expression like **d4 = d1 + d2 + d3 + d4**. See how this expression is evaluated. The usual priority and Associativity rules are follows when determining which sub expression will be evaluated first. Here as only **+** operator is present; evaluation will be done from left to right.

Initially **d1+d2** will be evaluated which is internally interpreted as **d1.operator + (d2)**. In the function a new temporary **object t** is created whose data member **num** contains the sum of **num** of **object d1 and d2** *i.e.,* **31**.The object **t** will be returned and assumes it is **obj (imaginary name assume)** when returned the expression **d4= d1 + d2 + d3** now becomes **d4 = obj + d3** which means **obj** calls the operator function **+** and pass **d3** as argument. Inside the function again sum of **num** of object **obj** and **d3** will be done which will be **31+18** will be stored in the num of temporary object t. In tho last this object will be returned and our expression **d4 = obj + d3** becomes **d4 = t** which copies **num** to the **num** of **d4**.

/*PROG 8.5 OVERLOADING + AND – IN THE SAME PROGRAM */

```
#include <iostream.h>
#include <conio.h>
class demo_sum_sub
{
    private :
        int num;
        static int count1,count2;
    public :
        void input( )
    {
        cout<<"Enter the number for object"<<++count1<<endl;
        cin>>num;
    }
```

```
demo_sum_sub operator +(demo_sum_sub temp)
{
    demo_sum_sub t;
    t.num=num+temp.num;
    return t;
}
demo_sum_sub operator -(demo_sum_sub temp)
{
    demo_sum_sub t;
    t.num=num-temp.num;
    return t;
}
void show( )
{
    cout<<"The num for object"<<++count2<<"is"<<num<<endl;
}
};
int demo_sum_sub : :count1;
int demo_sum_sub : :count2;
void main( )
{
    clrscr( );
    demo_sum_sub d1,d2,d3,d4;
    d1.input( );
    d2.input( );
    d3.input( );
    d1.show( );
    d2.show( );
    d3.show( );
    d4=d1+d2 - d3;
    d4.show( );
    getch( );
}
```

OUTPUT :

```
Enter the number for object1
30
Enter the number for object2
40
Enter the number for object3
35
```

```
The num for object1is30
The num for object2is40
The num for object3is35
The num for object4is35
```

EXPLANATION : The program is similar to previous one but we have overloaded binary – operator together with binary +. As the priority of + and – is same they are evaluated from left to right. Hence first d1+d2 is evaluated where d1 calls overloaded + operator function and pass d2 as argument. Assuming returned object is temp then temp –d3 is evaluated where temp calls the overloaded binary – operator function and pass d3 as argument. The final object returned; again assume obj is assigned to d4.

/*PROG 8.6 OVERLOADING +, -, *, AND / ALL IN ONE */

```
#include <iostream.h>
#include <conio.h>
#include <stdlib.h>
class demo_exp
{
    private :
        float num;
        static count1, count2;
    public :
        void input( )
        {
        cout<<"Enter the number for object"<<++count1<<endl;
        cin>>num;
        }
    demo_exp operator *(demo_exp temp)
    {
        demo_exp t;
        t.num=num*temp.num;
        return t;
    }
    demo_exp operator +(demo_exp temp)
    {
        demo_exp t;
        t.num=num+temp.num;
        return t;
    }
    demo_exp operator -(demo_exp temp)
    {
```

```
        demo_exp t;
        t.num=num-temp.num;
        return t;
    }
    demo_exp operator /(demo_exp temp)
    {
        demo_exp t;
        if(temp.num)
        t.num=num/temp.num;
        else
    {
        cout<<"Division by zero is not allowed"<<endl;
        exit(0);
    }
    return t;
    }
    void show( )
    {
        cout<<"The sum for object"<<++count2<<"is"<<num<<endl;
    }
   };
    int demo_exp : :count1;
    int demo_exp : :count2;
    void main( )
    {
        clrscr( );
        demo_exp d1,d2,d3,d4,d5;
        d1.input( );
        d2.input( );
        d3.input( );
        d4.input( );
        d1.show( );
        d2.show( );
        d3.show( );
        d4.show( );
        d5=d1+d2*d3/d1 - d4;
        d5.show( );
        getch( );
    }
```

OUTPUT :

```
Enter the number for object1
12
Enter the number for object2
13
Enter the number for object3
14
Enter the number for object4
15
The sum for object1is12
The sum for object2is13
The sum for object3is14
The sum for object4is15
The sum for object5is12.166668
```

EXPLANATION : We have overloaded all the 4 binary operation viz +, –, * and /. You can check that code for all the overloaded operation function is same except for the operator symbol. In the division operator function we have checked for denominator to be nonzero. Note overloading of operator does not change their inherent meaning, priority and associativity. So the expression d5 = d1 + d2 * d3 / d1 – d4; is evaluated as (assuming num for objects as shown in the program output) :

As priority of *and/ is higher than +and – and at the same level of priority *and/ are evaluated from left to right so d2 *d3 is evaluated first which internally interpreted as d2.operator *(d3) as explained earlier. Assuming the returned object as temp1 with value of num96 (as 8 *12=96) the expression becomes d5 = d1+temp1/d1-d4. Now temp/d1 will be evaluated where temp1 calling the function operator / and sending d1 as argument. Assuming returned object as temp2 with value of num is 19.2 (as 96/5=19.2) the expression becomes d5=d1+temp2–d4. As priority of + and – is same expression will be evaluated from left to right so next d1 +temp2 will be evaluated where d1 calling the operator function + and sending temp2 as argument. Assuming the returned object as temp3 with value of num 24.2 (as 19.2 + 5 = 24.2) the expression becomes d5=temp3-d4. Now temp3 calls the operator function – and sends d4 as argument. Assuming the returned object as temp4 with value of num 15.2 (as 24.2-9) the expression becomes d5=temp4 and value of num will be assigned to num to object d5.

/*PROG 8.7 OVERLOADING > OPERATOR */

```
#include <iostream.h>
#include <conio.h>
class emp
{
    private :
        int sal;
```

```
    public :
        emp(int s)
      {
        sal=s;
      }
      void operator>(emp temp)
      {
        if(sal>temp.sal)
        cout<<"First employee's salary is higher"<<endl;
        else
        cout<<"Second employee's salary is higher"<<endl;
      }
      void show( )
      {
        cout<<"Salary is "<<sal<<endl;
      }
};
void main( )
{
    clrscr( );
    emp e1=emp(12545);
    emp e2=emp(13458);
    e1.show( );
    e2.show( );
    e1>e2;
    getch( );
}
```

OUTPUT :

```
Salary is 12545
Salary is 13458
Second employee's salary is higher
```

EXPLANATION : In the program we have overloaded the greater than operator **>** which compares the salary of the employees. The statement e1>e2 internally interpreted as e1.operator > (e2) *i.e.*, e1 calls the operator function > sends e2 as argument. In the operator function salary of two objects e1 and e2 is compared and result is displayed accordingly.

8.3 OVERLOADING ASSIGNMENT (=) OPERATOR

We can overload assignment operator if we want to do some extra work other than the simply copy data members from one object to other. The simple copy of two objects can be done as d2=d1. We can also use copy constructor for the same and in this section we are also overloading = operator. Than what is the difference between all three ? Understanding this concept is an important one that's why we have devoted a separate part of this chapter. Consider the program given below :

/*PROG 8.8 OVERLOADING = OPERATOR*/

```
#include <iostream.h>
#include <conio.h>
class demo
{
    int num;
    public :
    demo(int n)
     {
        num=n;
     }
     demo( ){}
     void operator =(demo temp)
     {
        num=temp.num;
        cout<<"hello from ="<<endl;
     }
     void show( )
     {
        cout<<"num="<<num<<endl;
     }
};
void main( )
{
    clrscr( );
    demo d1(20);
    demo d2=d1;
    d1.show( );
    d2.show( );
    getch( );
}
```

OUTPUT :

```
num =20
num =20
```

EXPLANATION : We have studied that statement demo d2=d1 calls copy constructor. Here in the program there is no copy constructor. Compiler provides its default copy constructor for the above operator demo d2=d1. You can also check the output of the program that overloaded that overloaded assignment operator function is not called.

Now add a copy constructor in the program as :

```
demo (demo d1)
{
    num= d.num;
    cout<<"hello"<<endl;
}
```

And run the program again, this time our own constructor is called. The output will be :

```
hello
num=20
num=20
```

Now change the `demo d2=d1;` into `demo d2; d2=d1;` this time `d2=d1` will call the overloaded operator function as `d1.operator = (d2)`. Now if you remove overloaded operator = function, for carrying out `d=d1` compiler simply copies member by member from `d1 to d2` without calling copy constructor.

8.4 OVERLOADING UNARY OPERATORS

Similar to overloading binary operator we can overload unary –, pre and post ++, pre and post – and unary +. In case of overloading binary operators using member function of class left operand is responsible for calling the operator function and right operand was send as argument. In case of unary operator only one operand is there and this operand itself calls the overloaded operator function. Nothing is send as argument to the function. Its general syntax is (defined with the class)

```
return_type operator op ( )
{
    // function code;
}
```

For example, overloading unary – we will be writing.

```
demo operator - ( )
{
    demo temp;
    temp.num = -num;
    return temp;
}
```

It is used as follows :

```
d1=-d; // equivalent to d1 = d.operator - ( );
```

See few programs given below :

/*PROG 8.9 OVERLOADING ++ VER 1*/

```
#include <iostream.h>
#include <conio.h>
class demo
{
      int num;
 public :
      demo( ){}
      demo (int x)
      {
         num=x;
      }
      demo operator ++( )
      {
         demo temp;
         temp.num=num;
         num++;
         return temp;
      }
      void show(char *s)
      {
         cout<<"num of object"<<s<<"="<<num<<endl;
      }
 };
 void main( )
 {
     clrscr( );
     demo d1(20),d2;
     d2=d1++;
     d1.show ("d1");
     d2.show ("d2");
     getch( );
 }
```

OUTPUT :

num of objectd1=21

num of objectd2=20

EXPLANATION : The operator function

```
demo operator ++ ( )
{
    demo temp;
    temp.num=num;
    num++;
    return temp;
}
```

Overloads unary post **++** operator. In the main the expression **d2 = d1++** is equivalent to **d2 = d1.operator ++ ( )**. In the binary operator the left side operand of the operator is responsible for calling the operator function and right side operand is send as argument to the function. But here in unary we have just one operand which calls the operator function and sends no argument. In the overloaded function **++** a temporary object **temp** is created and **num** of this **temp** object gets the value from **num** which represent **num** of object who called the function here it is object **d1**. In the next statement **num** is incremented and **temp** is returned which is assigned to **d1**.We have simply followed the normal working of **post ++** operator *i.e.*, value of **d1** is assigned then it is incremented as if **d1** is an integer. All this is achieved by overloading **++**.

/* PROG 8.10 OVERLOADING ++ VER 2 */

```
#include <iostream.h>
#include <conio.h>

class demo
{
    int num;
public :
    demo( ){}
    demo(int x)
    {
        num = x;
    }
    demo operator ++( )
    {
        demo temp;
        num++;
```

```
        temp.num = num;
        return temp;
    }
    void show(char*s)
    {
        cout<<"NUM OF OBJECT"<<s<<" :="<<num<<endl;
    }
};
void main( )
{
    clrscr( );
    demo d1(30),d2;
    d2 =++d1;
    d1.show("d1");
    d2.show("d2");
    getch( );
}
```

OUTPUT :

```
NUM OF OBJECT d1 :=31
NUM OF OBJECT d2 :=31
```

EXPLANATION : The program is almost same as the previous program with a little difference. In the program we have overloaded `pre ++ operator`. So, in the operator ++ function first num is incremented than assigned to `num` of temporary object. As a result both `d1` and `d2` gets the value `31` for the `num`.

Note in the previous program if you write `d2 = ++d1` then again the same operator ++ function would be called. Then how does the compiler distinguishes between an overloaded `pre++` and `post ++` operator.

See the next program given below :

/* PROG 8.11 OVERLOADING PRE ++ AND POST ++ IN THE SAME PROGRAM */

```
#include <iostream.h>
#include <conio.h>

class demo
{
    int num;
public :
    demo( ){}
```

```
        demo (int x)
        {
            num = x;
        }
        demo operator ++(int)
        {
            demo temp;
            temp.num = num;
            num++;
            return temp;
        }
        demo operator++( )
        {
            demo temp;
            num++;
            temp.num = num;
            return temp;
        }
        void show(char*s)
        {
            cout<<"NUM OF OBJECT"<<s<<" = "<<num<<endl;
        }
};
void main( )
{
        clrscr( );
        demo d1(30),d2,d3;
        d2=d1++;
        d3=++d1;
        d1.show("d1");
        d2.show("d2");
        d3.show("d3");
        getch( );
}
```

OUTPUT :

```
NUM OF OBJECTd1 = 32
NUM OF OBJECTd2 = 30
NUM OF OBJECTd3 = 32
```

EXPLANATION : To distinguishes between an overloaded `pre` and `post ++` an `int` type argument is passed to the overloaded `post ++` operator function. This `int` argument does not serve any purposes except helping compiler to see the difference between a `pre` and `post` ++ operator function when this operator function call implicitly. In the `main` when `d2 = d1++` executes `post++` operator function will be called and in case of `d3 = ++d1; pre++` operator function would be called.

```
/* PROG 8.12 OVERLOADING UNARY - OPERATOR VER 1 */

#include <iostream.h>
#include <conio.h>

class demo
{
    int num;
public :
    demo(int x)
    {
        num=x;
    }
    void operator -( )
    {
        num = num;
    }
    void show( )
    {
        cout<<"num ="<<num<<endl;
    }
};
void main( )
{
    clrscr( );
    demo d1(10);
    cout<<"Before"<<endl;
    d1.show( );
    -d1;
    cout<<"After"<<endl;
    d1.show( );
    getch( );
}
```

OUTPUT :

```
Before
num =10
After
num =10
```

EXPLANATION : In the main the statement `-d1` is equivalent to `d1.operator - ( )`. The initial value of `num` for object `d1` is `10`. When `-d1` executes it call overloaded – operator function which reverse the sign of the `num`. This is the way the unary minus operator works. Note no argument is passed to the function. The function is simply called by the object `d1`.

/* PROG 8.13 OVERLOADING UNARY - OPERATOR VER 2 */

```
#include <iostream.h>
#include <conio.h>
class demo
{
    int num;
public :
    demo( ){}
    demo(int x)
    {
        num=x;
    }
    demo operator -( )
    {
        demo temp;
        temp.num=-num;
        return temp;
    }
    void show(char *s)
    {
        cout<<" Num of object"<<s<<" ="<<num<<endl;
    }
};
void main( )
{
    demo d1(100),d2;
    d2=-d1;
    d1.show("d1");
    d2.show("d2");
```

```
    getch( );
}
```

OUTPUT :

```
Num of object d1 =100
Num of object d2 =-100
```

EXPLANATION : The program is similar to the previous with the change in overloaded operator function – which returns an object of demo class type. In the `main` when `d2 = -d1` executes it becomes internally as `d2 = d1.operator-();` in the function a temp object is created and after reverse sign of num is assigned to `num` of `temp`. This `temp` is returned to `d2` which contains -100 as num of `d1` was 100.

/* PROG 8.14 OVERLOADING UNARY + OPERATOR VER 1 */

```
#include <iostream.h>
#include <conio.h>

class demo
{
    int num;
public :
    demo(int x)
    {
        num=x;
    }
    void operator +( )
    {
        num=num>0 ?num :-num;
    }
    void show( )
    {
        cout<<"num = "<<num<<endl;
    }
};
void main( )
{
    clrscr( );
    demo d1(-100);
    cout<<"Before"<<endl;
    d1.show( );
    +d1;
```

```
    cout<<"After"<<endl;
    d1.show( );
    getch( );
}
```

OUTPUT :

```
Before
num = -100
After
num = 100
```

EXPLANATION : Practically unary + does not serve any purpose *i.e.*, writing `+x` do not affect the value of `x`. But in the program we have overloaded unary operator to make a number positive *i.e.*, work as a function which finds absolute value of the number. In the `main` `+d1` is equivalent to `d1.operator + ()` which calls the operator + function and checks the value of num. If it is positive, we do not change but if is negative we make it positive.

/* PROG 8.15 OVERLOADING UNARY + OPERATOR VER 2 */

```
#include <iostream.h>
#include <conio.h>

class demo
{
    int dx, dy;
public :
    demo(int x,int y)
    {
        dx=x;
        dy=y;
    }
    void operator + ( )
    {
        dx = dx>0 ?dx :-dx;
        dy = dy>0 ?dy :-dy;
    }
    void show( )
    {
        cout<<"dx="<<dx<<endl;
        cout<<"dy="<<dy<<endl;
    }
};
```

```
void main( )
{
    clrscr( );
    demo d1(-10,20);
    cout<<"Before"<<endl;
    d1.show( );
    +d1;
    cout<<"After"<<endl;
    d1.show( );
    getch( );
}
```

OUTPUT :

```
Before
dx=-10
dy=20
After
dx=10
dy=20
```

EXPLANATION: The program is same as the previous one but instead of one data member we have taken two.

```
/* PROG 8.16 OVFRLOADING INDIRECTION OPERATOR '*' */

#include <iostream.h>
#include <conio.h>

class demo
{
    int num;

public :

    demo(int x)
    {
        num=x;
    }
    int operator *( )
    {
```

```
        return num;
    }
};

void main( )
{
    clrscr( );

    demo d1(100);
    cout<<"Value of Object d1 = "<<*d1<<endl;
    getch( );
}
```

OUTPUT :

```
Value of Object d1 = 100
```

EXPLANATION : The `'*'` as `binary operator` is known as multiplication operator but with reference to pointers it is known as `indirection operator`. Overloading indirection operator can make an object to appear as pointer. In the main d1 is an object but `* d1` makes it appear like it is a pointer. In reality it calls operator * as `d.operator *()` which returns the value of num.

8.5 OVERLOADING USING FRIEND FUNCTION

In the programs seen so far we have been overloading number of operators by writing overloaded functions. All the functions were part of the class but we can also overload all operators except few (discussed later) using friend function too. For example, to overload a binary + we declare a function as a class member **function** as :

```
demo operator + (demo A)
```

And in the main we write as d1+d2. As the operator function is a member function of class left side operand must be an object of the class. This is must as internally d1+d2 is treated as d.operator + (d2).

To write the same function using friend

```
friend demo operator + (demo A, demo B);
```

Friend function is not a member function of the class so it cannot be called using an object of the class. So in case of binary + overloaded using friend d1+d2 is interpreted as operator + (d1, d2). That is no object or no operand calls the function and both the operand are send as argument.

Note : In binary operators overloaded using class not using class one argument is passed whereas overloaded using friend two arguments are passed.

Now consider the case of overloading unary ++ operator overloaded using class.

```
demo operator ++( );
```

In main when we write `d2=d1++,` it is internally equivalent to `d2=d1.operator ++ ();`

The same operator ++ overloaded using friend can be written as :

```
friend demo operator ++ (demo d);
```

And **d2 = d1++** is equivalent to **d2 = operator ++ (d1).**

Note : In unary operators overloaded using class no argument is passed whereas overloaded using friend one argument is passed.

Now as we have understood that friend function can be used for overloading operators, questions arises why we need them when we can overload operators using operator function as member function of class. The answer is that in case of expression written as **d1 +d2, d1+20 d1*3**, class operator functions will work but in case of expression like **20 +d1, 10*d1** etc., class operator functions will not work as left operand must be an object of the class. In such situations we can use friend function.

/*PROG 8.17 OVERLOADING BINARY + OPERATOR USING FRIEND VER 1*/

```
#include <iostream.h>
#include <conio.h>
class demo
{
    int num;
    public :
    demo( ){}
    demo(int x)
    {
        num =x;
    }
    friend demo operator +(demo, int);
    void show(char *s)
    {
        cout<<"num of object "<<s<<"="<<num<<endl;
    }
};
demo operator +(demo T, int x)
{
    demo temp;
    temp.num=T.num+x;
    return temp;
}
```

```
void main( )
{
    clrscr( );
    demo d1(100), d2;
    d2=d1+50;
    d1.show("d1");
    d2.show("d2");
    getch( );
}
```

OUTPUT :

```
num of object d1=100
num of object d2=150
```

EXPLANATION : The declaration friend demo operator + (demo, int); tells the compiler that operator + is a friend function of the class which takes two arguments : one of class demo type and second as an int. In the main when d2 = d1+ 50 executes it is interpreted as d2 = operator + (d1, 50). This calls the operator + and passes d1 and 50 by value. Inside the function a temporary object is created which finds sum of T.num. This object is returned to main and assigned to d2.

The overloaded + function could be written as member function of the class.

/*PROG 8.18 OVERLOADING BINARY + OPERATOR USING FRIEND VER 2*/

```
#include <iostream.h>
#include <conio.h>
class demo
{
    int num;
 public :
    demo ( ){}
    demo(int x)
    {
    num=x;
    }
    friend demo operator *(int,demo);
    void show(char *s)
    {
       cout<<"num"<<s<<"="<<num<<endl;
    }
};
```

```
demo operator *(int x,demo T)
{
    demo temp;
    temp.num=x*T.num;
    return temp;
}
void main( )
{
    clrscr( );
    demo d1(200),d2;
    d2=10*d1;
    d1.show("of object d1");
    d2.show("of object d2");
    getch( );
}
```

OUTPUT :

```
num of object d1=200
num of object d2=2000
```

EXPLANATION : In the `main` when `d2=10*d1` executes, it is interpreted as `operator*(10, d1)` and compiler searches an overloaded *function which takes two arguments : as `int` and an object of `demo` class type. As we have overloaded *operator function is called. Inside the function temporary object is created and `temp.num` contains the multiplication of `10 and d1.num`. This object is returned and assigned to `d2`.

/* PROG 8.19 OVERLOADING UNARY OPERATOR - USING FRIEND VER 1 */

```
#include <iostream.h>
#include <conio.h>

class demo
{
    int num;
public :
    demo( ){}
    demo(int x)
    {
        num=x;
    }
    friend demo operator -(demo d)
    {
```

```
        demo temp;
        temp.num=-d.num;
        return temp;
    }
    void show(char *s)
    {
        cout<<"num of object "<<s<<" ="<<num<<endl;
    }
};
void main( )
{
    clrscr( );
    demo d1(100), d2;
    d2=-d1;
    d1.show("d1");
    d2.show("d2");
    getch( );
}
```

OUTPUT :

```
num of object d1 =100
num of object d2 =-100
```

EXPLANATION : The program is similar to the program we have created earlier but here we have overloaded unary operator – using fried function. Compare this and other program in which – is overloaded as class member function.

/*PROG 8.20 OVERLOADING UNARY - USING FRIEDN AND BINARY + USING CLASS */

```
#include <iostream.h>
#include <conio.h>

class demo
{
    int num;
public :
    demo( ){}
    demo(int x)
    {
        num=x;
    }
```

```
        friend demo operator -(demo d)
        {
            demo temp;
            temp.num =-d.num;
            return temp;
        }
        demo operator +(demo d)
        {
            demo A;
            A.num = num + d.num;
            return A;
        }
        void show(char *s)
        {
            cout<<"num of object "<<s<<"="<<num<<endl;
        }
};
void main( )
{
        clrscr( );
        demo d1(100),d2(200), d3;
        d3= - d1 + d2;
        d1.show("d1");
        d2.show("d2");
        d3.show("d3");
        getch( );
}
```

OUTPUT :

```
num of object d1=100
num of object d2=200
num of object d3=100
```

EXPLANATION : Priority of unary – is higher than binary + so in the expression –d1 + d2, d1 calls operator - which return a temporary object A whose num is -100. Next this A object calls overloaded binary + operator function of class demo and send d2 as argument in the following manner : A.operato + (d2). In the operator + function sum of num of temp and d2 is calculated and assigned to num of temporary object A which is returned.

/* PROG 8.21 OVERLOADING >> AND << OPERATOR USING FRIEND VER 1 */

```
#include <iostream.h>
#include <conio.h>

class demo
{
    int dx, dy;
public :
    friend void operator <<(ostream &, demo &);
    friend void operator >>(istream &, demo &);
};
void operator <<(ostream & mycout, demo & d)
{
    mycout<<"dx = "<<d.dx<<"\t"<<"dy = "<<d.dy<<endl;
}
void operator >>(istream & mycin, demo & d)
{
    mycin>>d.dx>>d.dy;
}
void main( )
{
    demo d;
 clrscr( );
    cout<<"Enter the two numbers"<<endl;
    cin>>d;
    cout<<"You entered"<<endl;
    cout<<d;
    getch( );
}
```

OUTPUT :

```
Enter the two numbers
40, 70
You entered
dx = 40 dy = 70
```

EXPLANATION : Object `cout` is considered an object of `ostream` type and `cin` is an object of `istream` type. The operator >> and << are overloaded internally for all basic data types so when you write `cout<<40;` internally it is treated as `cout`.operator <<`(40)`. Similarly when `cin>>x` is written it is treated as `cin.operator >>(x)`. The problem with these operators is that they are overloaded only for basic data types. They are not overloaded for inputting class object using `cin` or displaying class objects using `cout`. For that in the program we have overloaded >> and << operator using `friend`.

Both the operators have been overloaded as :

```
friend void operator <<(ostream &, demo &);
friend void operator >>(istream &, demo &);
```

In the main note we have written as `cin >> d` where `d` is an object of `demo` class. When compiler sees the above input statement it searches an overloaded >> operator function which takes two arguments : one of type `ostream` and second of type `demo` class. When it finds one it calls operator >> function and passes `cout` and `d` by reference. Inside the function >> input values are taken in `dx` and `dy`. Similarly, when `cout<<d` executes overloaded operator << function is called which displays values of `dx` and `dy`.

You can note that with the help of overloading >> and << we are able to treat object as built-in data types and can read and write objects using `cin` and `cout` respectively.

The problem with the above overloaded >> and << functions is that we cannot read or write multiple objects as `cin>>d1>>d2` and `cout<<d1<<d2`. This is so as return type of function is `void`. For achieving the above see the next program given below.

/* PROG 8.22 OVERLOADING >> AND << OPERATOR USING FRIEND VER 2 */

```
#include <iostream.h>
#include <conio.h>
class demo
{
    char name[25];
public :
    friend ostream & operator <<(ostream &, demo &);
    friend istream & operator >>(istream &, demo &);
};
ostream & operator <<(ostream & mycout, demo & d)
{
    mycout<<"name = "<<d.name<<endl;
    return mycout;
}
istream & operator >>(istream & mycin, demo & d)
{
    mycin>>d.name;
    return mycin;
}
void main( )
{
    demo d1,d2;
    clrscr( );
    cout<<"Enter two name"<<endl;
```

```
        cin>>d1>>d2;
        cout<<"You have entered"<<endl;
        cout<<d1<<d2<<endl;
        getch( );
}
```

OUTPUT :

```
Enter two name
Hari
Mohan
You have entered
name = Hari
name = Mohan
```

EXPLANATION : Here we have modified the overloaded operator function >> and << by returning a reference of `ostream` from << and of `istream` from >>. In the `main` when we write `cin>>d1>>d2`, it is called as `operator>> (cin, d1)`. In the function >> after taking data values for object `d1` the function returns reference to `cin` which is used in calling the second object `d2`. Assume returned reference is `cin`, function is called again as `operator>> (cin, d2)`. Same analogy applies to `cout<<d1<<d2`.

/* PROG 8.23 OVERLOADING SUBSCRIPT OPERATOR */

```
#include <iostream.h>
#include <conio.h>

class demo
{
        int *p;
public :
        demo( )
        {
                p=new int [5];
                for(int i=0; i<5; i++)
                        p[i]=i+1;
        }
        int operator [ ](int x)
        {
                return p[x];
        }
};
```

```
void main( )
{
    demo d;
    clrscr( );
    for(int i=0; i<5;i++)
        cout<<d[i]<<" ";
    getch( );
}
```

OUTPUT :

1 2 3 4 5

EXPLANATION : Expression `d[i]` is interpreted internally as `d.operator [ ] (x)`. In each iteration of for loop we call the overloaded operator function [ ] and pass the value of '`i`' which returns the corresponding array elements. Though d was not array but we have made it to be like array by overloading [ ] subscript operator.

/*PROG 8.24 OVERLOADING COMMA (,)OPERATOR */

```
#include <iostream.h>
#include <conio.h>
class demo
{
    int x;
public :
    demo( )
    {}
    demo(int p)
    {
        x=p;

    }
    demo operator,(demo d)
    {
        demo temp;
        temp.x=x;
        return temp;
    }
    void show( )
    {
        cout<<"x="<<x<<endl;
    }
};
```

```
void main( )
{
    clrscr( );
    demo d1(30), d2(50), d3(70), d4;
    d4=(d1,d2,d3);
    d1.show( );
    d2.show( );
    d3.show( );
    d4.show( );
    getch( );
}
```

OUTPUT :

```
x=30
x=50
x=70
x=30
```

EXPLANATION : In the above code `comma (,) operator` has been overloaded. In the default working of comma operator processing is done from `left to right` and right most operand becomes result for the comma operator. So initially `d1` will call the comma operator and send `d2` as argument like `d1.operator,(d2)`. When temporary object return from operator function, it will call again overloaded function, again this time sending `d3` as argument. The final object returnd will be assingned to `d4` which will be `d3`.

/* PROG 8.25 DEMO OF OVERLOADING -> OPERATOR */

```
#include <iostream.h>
#include <conio.h>
#include <string.h>

class demo
{
public :
    demo* operator ->( )
    {
        return this;
    }
    char str[20];
};
```

```
void main( )
{
      demo d;
      clrscr( );
      strcpy(d.str,"MPSTME");
      cout<<d.str<<endl;
      strcpy(d->str,"NMIMS University");
      cout<<d->str<<endl;
      getch( );
}
```

OUTPUT :

```
MPSTME
NMIMS University
```

EXPLANATION : The operator -> allow us to treat object like a pointer. When overloading it is considered as a unary operator. The overloaded -> operator must return address of the current object. The next expression d->str internally treated as :

```
(d.operator -> ( )) str
```

/* PROG 8.26 OVERLOADING OF FUNCTION CALL ( ) OPERATOR */

```
#include <iostream.h>
#include <conio.h>

class demo
{
      int x,y;
public :
      demo( )
      {}
      void operator ( )(int, int);
      void show(char*s)
      {
            cout<<s<<endl;
            cout<<"x="<<x<<endl;
            cout<<"y="<<y<<endl;
      }
};
void demo : :operator ( )(int a, int b)
{
```

```
        x=a;
        y=b;
}
void main( )
{
        demo d1,d2;
        clrscr( );
        d1(20,40);
        d2(35,80);
        d1.show("OBJECT-1");
        d2.show("OBJECT-2");
        getch( );
}
```

OUTPUT :

```
OBJECT-1
x=20
y=40
OBJECT-2
x=35
y=80
```

EXPLANATION : The operator ( ) is known as function call operator we have overloaded it. The overloaded operator function ( ) takes two int argument and returns nothing. In the main when we write `d1 (20, 40)` and `d2 (35, 80)`, they are internally interpreted as :

```
d1.operator ( ) (20, 40);
d2.operator ( ) (35, 80);
```

8.6 RULES OF OPERATOR OVERLOADING

1. Only the operators which are part of the C++ language can be overloaded. No new operator can be created using operator overloading.
2. You can change the meaning of the operator *i.e.*, a + operator can be overloaded to perform multiplication operation or > operator can be overloaded to perform addition operation. But you cannot change the priority of the operators.
3. Any overloaded operator function must have at least one operand which is user-defined type. All of the operands cannot be of basic types. If this is the case than function must be friend function of some class.
4. In case of overloading binary operators left hand side operator must be an object of class when overloaded operator function is a member function of the class.

5. Binary operators overloaded through member function of the class take one argument and overloaded through friend function take two arguments.
6. Unary operators overloaded through member function of the class does not take any argument and overloaded through friend function must take one argument.
7. There are certain operators which cannot be overloaded. They are:

S.No.	*Operators*	*Name of Operator*
1.	: :	Scope resolution operator
2.	.	Dot membership operator
3.	.*	Pointer to member operator
4.	? :	Conditional operator
5.	sizeof	The size of operator

8. There are operators which cannot be overloaded using friend function. They are given as :

S.No.	*Operators*	*Name of Operator*
1.	=	Assignment operator
2.	->	Pointer to member operator
3.	[ ]	Subscript operator
4.	( )	Function call operator.

8.7 TYPE CONVERSION

Many times in programming situations we like to convert one data type into another. Converting data types of a variable into other data type is known as type conversion. We have studied it earlier when we convert int to float, char to int, double to int etc. Compiler also does implicit type conversion. But all we studied involved all built-in types. In this section, we study type conversion with respect to user data type viz. class. We divide the study of type conversion into three parts.

1. **Conversion from Built-in types to class type.**
2. **Conversion from class type to built-in types.**
3. **Conversion from one class type to another.**

1. Conversion from Built-in Types to Class Type

When we want to convert basic built-in types into class types, the simple methods is to define parameterized constructor which takes an argument of basic type which you want to convert to class type. For example, when you want an int to be converted to class type say demo, define a one argument constructor type int in demo class as :

```
demo (int)
{
 constructor body;
}
```

In the **main** we can write **demo d=10**. When compiler we this statement it come to know that both types **demo** and **int** are not compatible so it look for a conversion routine which can convert an **int into demo class** type. When it finds there is a constructor which takes **int** as argument, it calls that constructor, pass the **int value 10** and construct the object and assign to **d.**

Now, I illustrate it more details by some example :

/*PROG 8.27 DEMO OF TYPE CONVERSION INT TO CLASS TYPE */

```
#include <iostream.h>
#include <conio.h>
class demo
{
      int data;
 public :
      demo(int x)
      {
          data=x;
          show( );
      }
      void show( )
      {
          cout<<"data="<<data<<endl;
      }
 };
 void main( )
 {
     int num;
     clrscr( );
     cout<<"Enter the num"<<endl;
     cin>>num;
     demo d=num;
     getch( );
 }
```

OUTPUT :

```
Enter the num
```

```
12
data =12
```

EXPLANATION : For the conversion of basic data type to class, a constructor is created which accepts an argument of that data type. Here, we want to convert an int to class demo type. So we have written one argument int type constructor in the class. When statement demo d= num executes compiler automatically calls this one argument constructor with value num. This value num is assigned to data and show function is called which display the data.

/* PROG 8.28 DEMO OF TYPE CONVERSION char* TO CLASS TYPE */

```
#include <iostream.h>
#include <ctype.h>
#include <string.h>
#include <conio.h>

class demo
{
    char str[20];
public :
    demo(char x[ ])
    {
        strcpy(str,x);
    }
    int countV( )
    {
        int i=0,count=0;
        char ch;
        while(str[i]!=0)
        {
            ch=toupper(str[i]);
            switch(ch)
            {
            case 'A' :
            case 'E' :
            case 'I' :
            case 'O' :
            case 'U' : count++;
            }
            i++;
        }
```

```
                return count;
        }
};
void main( )
{
        demo d="NMIMS University";
        int c =d.countV( );
        clrscr( );
        cout<<"Number of vowels = "<<c<<endl;
        getch( );
}
```

OUTPUT :

Number of vowels = 5

EXPLANATION : For converting a string of `char*` type to class type we have written a one argument constructor which take argument of type `char x[]` (Note `char*` will also do). When `demo d = "NMIMS University";` executes string `"NMIMS University"` is passed to this one argument constructor. The function `countV` is finding the number of vowels in the string using `switch-case`. It checks each character from the string `str` till null character is not encountered. For any of the vowels count is incremented by `1`. In the end when string ends count is returned from function.

/*PROG 8.29 DEMO OF TYPE CONVERSION FLOAT TO CLASS TYPE */

```
#include <iostream.h>
#include <iomanip.h>
#include <conio.h>

class demo
{
        float num;
public :
        demo(float x)
        {
                num = x;
        }
        int int_part( )
        {
                return int (num);
        }
        float real_part( )
        {
```

```
            return (num-int_part( ));
        }
};
void main( )
{

    demo d= 45.56;
    clrscr( );
    cout<<"Integer Part = "<<d.int_part( )<<endl;
    cout<<"RealPart="<<setprecision(2)
        <<d.real_part( )<<endl;
    getch( );
}
```

OUTPUT :

```
Integer Part = 45
Real Part=0.56
```

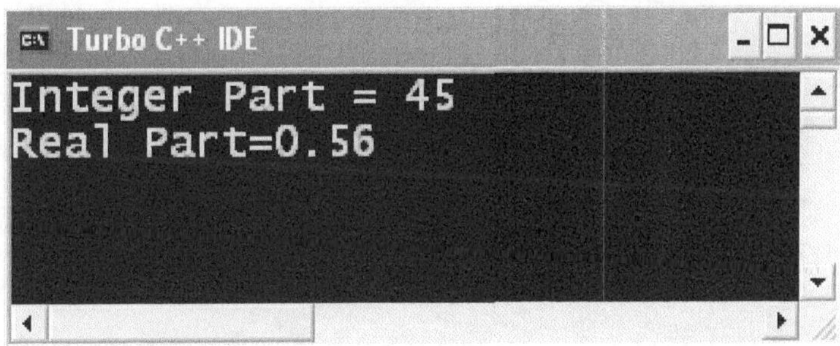

Figure 8.1. *Output screen of program 8.29*

EXPLANATION : When `demo d = 45.56` execute one argument constructor taking `float` type value is called and `num` is assigned the value `45.56`. The function `int_part()` finds the integer portion of the `num` `45.56` by typecasting it to integer which returns `45`. This value is used in the function `real_part()` for finding the fractional part `0.56`. To get the value `0.56` we subtract the integer part returned by `int_part()` function from the original `num`. In the main we have used the manipulator `setprecision` which set the number of digits after the decimal point. Here we want only 2 digits after decimal point. For more about manipulator see the chapter 11.

```
/* PROG 8.30 DEMO OF TYPE CONVERSION LONG INT TO CLASS TYPE */

#include <iostream.h>
#include <conio.h>

class CountDigit
{
```

```
    unsigned long int num;

public :

    CountDigit(unsigned long int x)
    {
        num = x;
    }
    void count( )
    {
        int temp [10]= {0};
        int r,i;
        while(num!=0)
        {
            r=num%10;
            temp[r]++;
            num = num/10;
        }
        cout<<"DIGIT \tFREQ\n";
        for(i=0;i<10;i++)
            cout<< i<<"\t"<<temp[i]<<endl;
    }
};

void main( )
{
 clrscr( );
    CountDigit cd=1234567890;
    cd.count( );
    getch( );
}
```

OUTPUT :

```
DIGIT  FREQ
 0      1
 1      1
 2      1
 3      1
 4      1
 5      1
 6      1
 7      1
 8      1
 9      1
```

EXPLANATION : In the program we are finding the frequency of each digit in the unsigned long int number. When statement `CountDigit cd = 1234567890;` executes one argument constructor which takes an argument of long int type is called and num gets the value `1234567890.` The function `count()`counts the frequency of each digit. For this it uses an array temp `size 10`. The initial value of each element of this array is `0`. In the `while` loop we are extracting the rightmost digit in turn and incrementing the frequency of that number by `1` using `temp` array. For this we have made use of `%` and `/` operator. This continues till number num does not become `zero`. For example, if `r is 0` in the beginning `temp [0]` is incremented by `1`. Next time `temp [9]` is incremented by `1` and so on. The maximum limit of `unsigned long int 4294967295`. Make sure you do not give a number greater that this.

2. Conversion from Class Type to Built-in Types

Here we study reverse of what we have studied in the first part. To convert class type to built-in type the method to be adopted is that simply defined an operator function by the name of data type you want class data type to be converted to. The general syntax is :

```
operator data_type ( )
{

}
```

Here operator is the keyword we have seen earlier and **data_type** is the type in which your class type will be converted to. **The general syntax is :**

```
Operator data_type ( )
{

}
```

Here operator is the keyword we have seen earlier `data_type` in which your class type will be converted. Note there is no return type or argument specified for the function. As the above function will be a member function of the class so you can use any data member or function inside this conversion function. You can do any processing over data member as per your requirement but in the end as function is about to return you must return a value of type `data_type`. For example, assume conversion function is defined in the class `demo` :

```
operator int ( )
{
 int x;
 computing steps;
 return x;
}
```

And in the main it is written `int num = d;` where `d` is an object of `demo` class type. When compiler sees `int num = d;` it comes to know that both types are not compatible so it look for a conversion routine which can convert an object of class `demo` type into an int. It finds operator `int()`. So it calls this conversion function for object `d` implicitly and assigns the return value to `num`.

Check out explanatory examples given below :

/*PROG 8.31 DEMO OF TYPE CONVERSION, CLASS TO INT */

```
#include <iostream.h>
#include <conio.h>
class demo
{
    int num;
public :
    demo(int x)
    {
        num=x;
    }
    operator int( )
    {
        return num*num;
    }
};
void main( )
{
    int k;
    clrscr( );
    cout<<"Enter the number for k :=";
    cin>>k;
    demo d(k);
    int s=d;
    cout<<"Square ="<<s<<endl;
    getch( );
}
```

OUTPUT :

```
Enter the number for k : =15
Square =225
```

EXPLANATION : In the program we have converted an object of `demo` class type into integer type. When the statement `int s=d;` executes compiler searches for a function which can convert an object of `demo` class type to `int` type. As we have written the function `operator int()`, this function is called and executes which returns square of num to the s. the square is then displayed. Inside the `operator int()` you may do whatever you want with the data members of the class but at the end you must return an int type value.

/* PROG 8.32 DEMO OF TYPE CONVERSION, CLASS TO FLOAT */

```
#include <iostream.h>
#include <conio.h>
class circle
{
    float rad;

public :

    circle(float x)
    {
        rad = x;
    }
    operator double( )
    {
        return 3.14 * rad * rad;
    }
};

void main( )
{
    circle d(4.5);
    double area=d;
    clrscr( );
    cout<<"Area of circle = "<<area<<endl;
    getch( );
}
```

OUTPUT :

```
Area of circle = 63.585
```

EXPLANATION : This program is similar to the earlier one. Here we written `operator double` function which will be called automatically when we try to assign an object of `demo` class to a variable of type `double`. The operator `double ( )` uses the `rad` data member and returns area of the circle, which is assigned to variable area of type `double`.

/* PROG 8.33 DEMO OF TYPE CONVERSION, CLASS TO CHAR */

```
#include <iostream.h>
#include <conio.h>
```

```
class Number
{
    int num;
public :
    Number(int x)
    {
        num = x;
    }
    operator char ( )
    {
        if(num<0)
            return 'N';
        else if(num ==0)
            return 'Z';
        else return 'P';
    }
};

void main( )
{
    int n;

    clrscr( );

    cout<<"Enter a number"<<endl;
    cin>>n;

    Number d(n);

    char ch =d;
    switch(ch)
    {
    case 'P' :
        cout<<"POSITIVE"<<endl;
            break;
    case 'N' :
        cout<<"NEGATIVE"<<endl;
            break;
    case 'Z' :
        cout<<"ZERO"<<endl;
            break;
```

```
    }
    getch( );
}
```

OUTPUT :

(First run)

```
Enter a number
23
POSITIVE
```

(Second run)

```
Enter a number
-23
NEGATIVE
```

(Third run)

```
Enter a number
0
ZERO
```

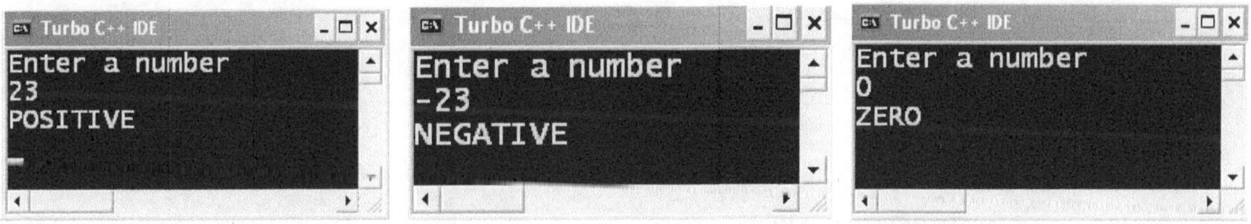

```
Enter a number
23
POSITIVE
```

```
Enter a number
-23
NEGATIVE
```

```
Enter a number
0
ZERO
```

Figure 8.2. *Output screen of first, second and third run of program 8.33*

EXAPLANATION : In the program we arc converting an object of demo class type to char. The function operator `char()` checks num for positive, negative or zero and return `'P', 'N'` and `'Z'` respectively. This returned character is stored in `ch` variable in `main` which is put into the `switch`. Depending upon the value of `ch` appropriate result is displayed.

/* PROG 8.34 DEMO OF TYPE CONVERSION, CLASS TO CHAR* */

```
#include <iostream.h>
#include <conio.h>
#include <string.h>
class Rev
{
    char str[25];
public :
    Rev( )
    {
```

```
        cout<<"ENTER A STRING "<<endl;
        cin.getline(str,25);
    }
    operator char*( );
};

Rev : :operator char*( )
{
    static char s[25];
    strcpy(s,strrev(str));
    return s;
}
void main( )
{
    clrscr( );
    Rev R;
    char *t = R;
    cout<<"Reverse String is "<<t<<endl;
    getch( );
}
```

OUTPUT :

```
ENTER A STRING
NMIMS UNIVERSITY
Reverse String is YTISREVINU SMIMN
```

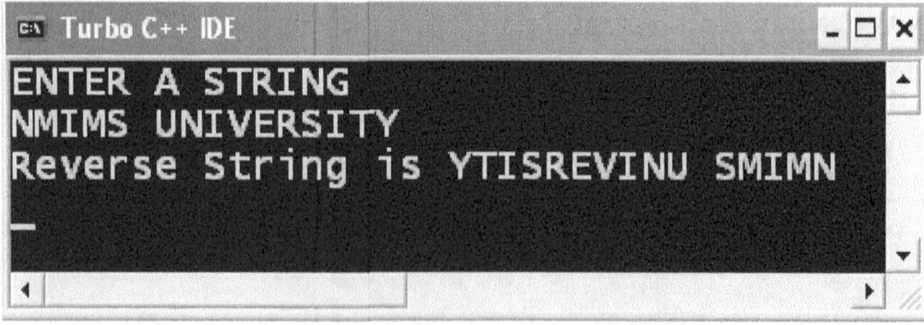

Figure 8.3. *Output screen of program 8.34*

EXPLANATION : `Rev R` creates object `R` by calling default constructor of the class. The default constructor promotes user for the string. Assume string is "`NMIMS UNIVERSITY`". When `char *t=R` executes, function operator `char*()` called automatically. Inside the function we have reversed the string with the help of `strrev` function courtesy `string.h`. Note inside the function we have used static array as return address of a local variable will result in garbage value. The returned reverse string is stored in `t` which is displayed.

3. Conversion from one Class Type to Another

In programming situations when we want to convert object of one class to other class type we can follow either of the two approach we have seen in part one and part two.

Suppose we have a class first second and we want to convert an object of class first type into second type. In the main we will be writing as :

```
first f; second s;
s=f;
```

Note here we want an object f of class to be converted to class second type. In the first method we can write an operator function in the second in the source class (assume source is first and destination is second as we convert from first to second) as :

```
Operator second ( )
{
    function body;
}
```

This operator function must return an object of class second type. In the second method for the same conversion s=f we can write a one argument constructor in the destination class second which takes an object of first class as argument as :

```
second (first fobj)
{
    Constructor body;
}
```

When compiler see **s = f** it automatically look for any conversion routine which can convert an object of first type into second type. As the above constructor was written in the class second it will be called.

/*PROG 8.35 DEMO OF TYPE CONVERSION ONE CLASS TYPE TO ANOTHER CLASS TYPE */

```
#include <iostream.h>
#include <conio.h>
class second
{
    int sx;
 public :
    second( ){}
    second(int x)
    {
    sx=x;
    }
```

```
        int & getsx( )
        {
            return sx;
        }
        void shows( )
        {
            cout<<"sx="<<sx<<endl;
        }
};
class first
{
        int fx;
public :
        first( ){}
        first(int x)
        {
            fx = x;
        }
        operator second( )
        {
            second temp;
            temp.getsx( )=fx*fx;
            return temp;
        }
        void showf( )
        {
            cout<<"fx="<<fx<<endl;
        }
};
void main( )
{
        clrscr( );
        first f(20);
        second s(30);
        cout<<"Before conversion"<<endl;
        f.showf( );
        s.shows( );
        s=f;
        cout<<"After conversion"<<endl;
        f.showf( );
        s.shows( );
        getch( );
}
```

OUTPUT :

```
Before conversion
fx=20
sx=30
After conversion
fx=20
sx=400
```

EXPLANATION : We want to convert an object of class type first to class type second. Here our source class is first and destination class is second. So in the source class first we will have to write function operator `second()` which will return an object of class type second. We have done this in class first. When statement `s=f` executes compiler look for this conversion function. It finds one. In the function we have found square of `fx` and assigned it to the sx of class second. Note `sx` is private so it cannot be accessed in the function `operator second()` which is in class first. As function is in class it cannot be accessed without any problem. To get the `sx` in the operator function second we have returned a reference of `sx` by writing a public member function `getsx` which returns the reference of `sx`. This reference gets the value `fx*fx` and temporary.

/* PROG 8.36 DEMO OF TYPE CONVERSION ONE CLASS TYPE TO ANOTHER CLASS TYPE VER 2 */

```
#include <iostream.h>
#include <conio.h>

class first
{
    int fx;
public :
    first( ){}
    first (int x)
    {
        fx=x;
    }
    int getfx( )
    {
        return fx;
    }
    void showf( )
    {
        cout<<"fx="<<fx<<endl;
    }
};
```

```
class second
{
    int sx;
public :

    second( ){}
    second(int x)
    {
        sx=x;
    }
    second(first obj)
    {
        sx=obj.getfx( )*obj.getfx( );
    }
    void shows( )
    {
        cout<<"sx="<<sx<<endl;
    }
};

void main( )
{
    clrscr( );
    first f(100);
    second s(200);
    cout<<"Before Conversion"<<endl;
    f.showf( );
    s.shows( );
    s=f;
    cout<<"After Conversion"<<endl;
    f.showf( );
    s.shows( );
    getch( );
}
```

OUTPUT :

```
Before Conversion
fx=100
sx=200
After Conversion
fx=100
sx=10000
```

EXPLANATION : The program demonstrates the second method of converting an object of one class type to another class type. Again the source class is first and destination class is second. Here in the constructor conversion method, constructor has to be defined in the destination class. When `s = f` statement executes, constructor or `second(first obj)` is called and f is assigned to obj through call by value mechanism. As constructor is in class second we cannot the private member `fx`. For that we have written public member function `getfx` in class first which return the value of `fx`. The square of `fx` indirectly through `getfx` is assigned to `sx`.

/* PROG 8.37 DEMO OF TYPE CONVERSION ONE CLASS TYPE TO ANOTHER CLASS TYPE */

```
#include <iostream.h>
#include <conio.h>

class first
{
    int fx;
public :

    first( ){}
    first(int x)
    {
        fx=x;
    }
    int getfx( )
    {
        return fx;
    }
    void showf( )
    {
        cout<<"fx="<<fx<<endl;
    }
};

class second
{
    int sx;
public :

    second( ){}
    second(int x)
    {
        sx=x;
    }
    void operato r=(first obj)
```

```
    {
        sx=obj.getfx( )*obj.getfx( );
    }
    void shows( )
    {
        cout<<"sx="<<sx<<endl;
    }
};

void main( )
{
    clrscr( );
    first f(100);
    second s(200);
    cout<<"Before Conversion"<<endl;
    f.showf( );
    s.shows( );
    cout<<"After Conversion"<<endl;
    f.showf( );
    s.shows( );
    getch( );
}
```

OUTPUT :

```
Before Conversion
fx=100
sx=200
After Conversion
fx=100
sx=200
```

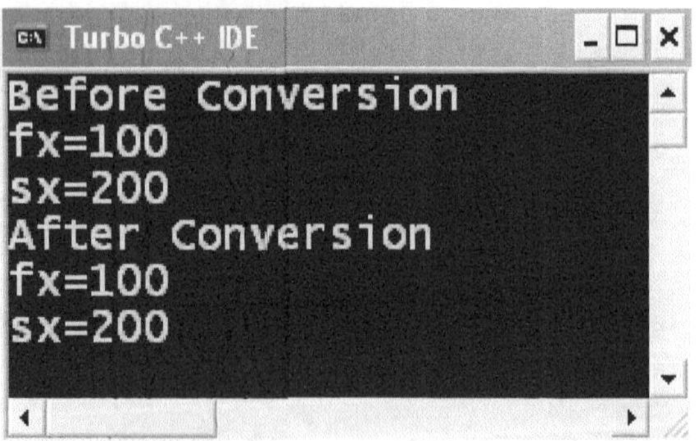

Figure 8.4. *Output screen of the program 8.37*

EXPLANATION : The program demonstrate third way of doing converting an object of one class to another class type. In the destination class `second operator =` function is written which accepts one argument to type first. When the statement `s = f` executes it is internally interpreted as `s.operator = (f).` Rest is self-explanatory.

/* PROG 8.38 TYPE CONVERSION CONVERTING HOUR TO MINUTES AND SECOND */

```
#include <iostream.h>
#include <conio.h>

class Hour
{
    unsigned int hr;

public :

    Hour(unsigned int x)
    {
        hr=x;
    }
    int gethr( )
    {
        return hr;
    }
    void showh( )
    {
        cout<<"Hour="<<hr<<endl;
    }
};
class secmin
{
    unsigned int sec, min;

public :

    secmin( ){}
    secmin(Hour obj)
    {
        min=obj.gethr( )*60;
        sec=min*60;
    }
    void showsm( )
```

```
    {
        cout<<"Mins="<<min<<endl;
        cout<<"Secs="<<sec<<endl;
    }
};
void main( )
{
    clrscr( );

    Hour H(5);
    secmin sm;
    sm=H;

    H.showh( );
    sm.showsm( );
    getch( );
}
```

OUTPUT :

```
Hour=5
Mins=300
Secs=18000
```

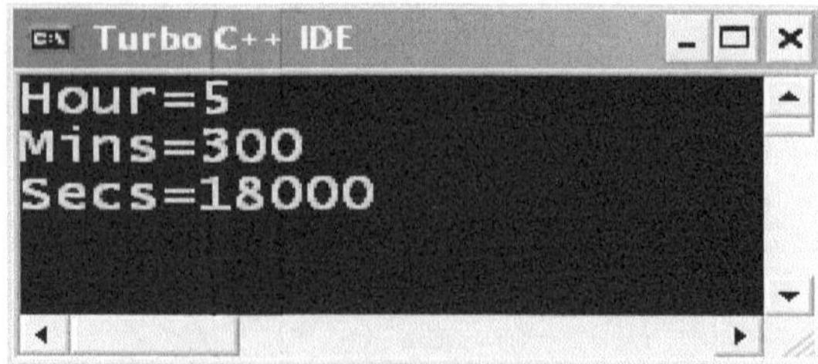

Figure 8.5. *Output screen of program 8.38*

EXPLANATION : The class `Hour` contains one data member `hr` which hold number of hours as input. The class secmin has one constructor which has an object of `Hour` class. When the statement `sm =H` executes constructor of `secmin` class is called and object `H` is passed which is collected in variable `obj`. Inside this constructor minutes and seconds are calculated from the `Hour` class object. Again as `hr` is private, a public member function which returns hr is written.

8.8 PONDERABLE POINTS

1. Operator overloading is mechanism of overloading operators to work with verities of data types including user defined.

2. For overloading operators keyword operator is used in C++.
3. We can overload only existing operator is used in C++.
4. Precedence of operators cannot be changed by operator overloading.
5. Friend keyword can be used for overloading the operators. They are indispensable where left operand is not an object of the class. When overloading binary operator using friend both the operands are passed as argument and when overloading unary operator only single argument is passed to function.
6. We cannot overload following operators :- ? :, .*, ., : : and sizeof.
7. Friend cannot be used to overload =, ->, and [ ] operator.
8. For converting a basic type into class type one argument constructor of that type is created in the class.
9. For converting a class type to any basic type, an operator function by the name of the basic type is created in the class.
10. For converting an object from one class type to another class type, either constructor or operator method can be used.

EXERCISE

A. True and False :

1. Operator in C++ can be overloaded using the function named opt_overload.
2. The operator to be overloaded in C++, must already exist in the language.
3. All operators may be overloaded using friend functions.
4. The assignment operator cannot be overloaded.
5. The compiler won't give any error if* operator is overloaded to be perform summation.
6. A friend function cannot be used to overload the subscript operator [ ].
7. The precedenco of an operator can be changed by overloading it.

B. Answer the Following Questions :

1. What is operator overloading ?
2. Why do need operator overloading ?
3. What is the use of friend in operator overloading ?
4. What is the difference between postfix++ and prefix ++ ?
5. Can we change the precedence of operators using operator overloading ?
6. What are the operator overloading rules ?
7. Which operator cannot e overloaded by using friend ?
8. Which operator we cannot overload ?
9. Why we need type conversion ?
10. Explain two methods of conversion between objects of two different classes.

C. Brain Drill :

1. Consider a class string where each objects contains an array of characters and the length of string. Write member function for

(*a*) Initializing a string object either by a given string constant (*e.g.*,"dsdf") or by an integer indicating maximum size of string to be accommodated or by another string object.

(*b*) Overloading the assignment operator overloading comparison operator = = so that string object may be compared with another string object and a constant string may be compared with other string object.

2. Write C++ program to overload a function named power( ) to allow the calculation of power of both 'int' and 'float' value.

3. Write a program to pass reference of object to operator function and change the contents of object. Use single object as source and destination.

4. Write a program to declare two classes Rupees and Dollar. Declare objects of both the classes and perform conversion between Rupees and Dollar using any of the conversion method.

5. Write a program using a class to convert square to square root and vice-versa. Write conversion methods between objects of two different class.

6. Write a program that substitutes an overloaded += operator for the overloaded + operator. This operator should allow statements like :

```
s1 + = s2;
```

Where s2 is added (concatenated) to s1 and the result is left in s1. The operator should also permits the results of the operation to be used in other calculations, as in

```
s3 = s1 + = s2;
```

7. For math buff only : Create a class Polar that represents the points on the plain as polar coordinates (radius and angle). Create an overloaded +operator for addition of two polar quantities. "Adding" two points on the plain can be accomplished by adding their X coordinates and then adding their Y coordinates. This gives the X and Y coordinates of the "answer". Thus you will need to convert two sets of polar coordinates to rectangular coordinates, and them, and then convert the resulting rectangular representation back to polar.

8. Write a program that incorporates both the bMoney a class and the sterling class. Write conversion operators to convert between bMoney and strling, assuming that one pound (£1.0.0) equals fifty dollars ($50.00). This was the approximate exchange rate in the 19th century when British Empire was at its height and the pound-shillings-pence format was in use. Write a main( ) program that allows the user to enter an amount in either currency, and that then converts it to the other currency and displays the result. Minimize any modification to the existing bMoney and sterling classes.

❑❑❑

CHAPTER 9

WORKING WITH INHERITANCE IN C++

9.1 INTRODUCTION

Inheritance is the mechanism of deriving a new class from an already existing class. Inheritance provides the idea of **reusability *i.e.,* code once written can be used again and again in number of new classes**. The old class and new class is called by the name-pair **base-derived, parent-child, super-sub** etc. The new class can use all or some of the features of the already existing class and can define his own members too.

9.2 TYPES OF INHERITANCE

In general inheritance is of five types:

1. Single level inheritance
2. Multilevel inheritance
3. Multiple inheritances
4. Hierarchical inheritance
5. Hybrid Inheritance

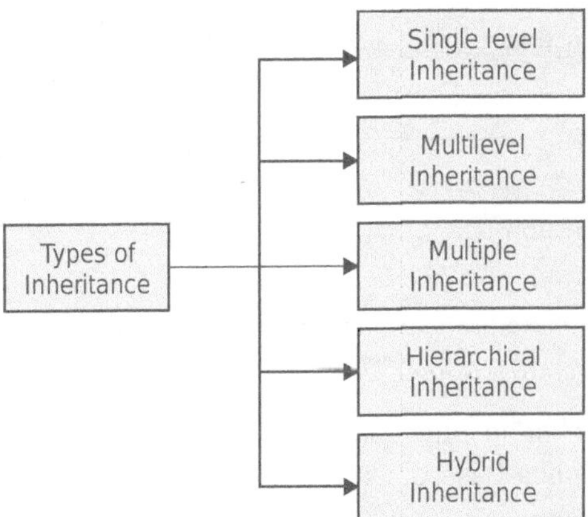

Figure 9.1. *Different types of inheritance*

Again depending upon in which mode we do the above any 5 of the inheritance we can further divide inheritance as :

1. Public Inheritance
2. Private Inheritance
3. Protected Inheritance

The syntax of deriving a new class from an already existing class is shown as :

```
class new_class_name : mode old_class_name
{

};
```

Where class is keyword used to create a class **new_class_name** of new derived class, mode may be **private, public, or protected** or even be absent *i.e.,* be an optional. If mode is not present default mode private is assumed. **Old_class_name** is the name of an already existing class. It may be a user defined or a built-in class.

1. Single Level Inheritance

In single level inheritance we have just one base class and one derived class. It is represented as :

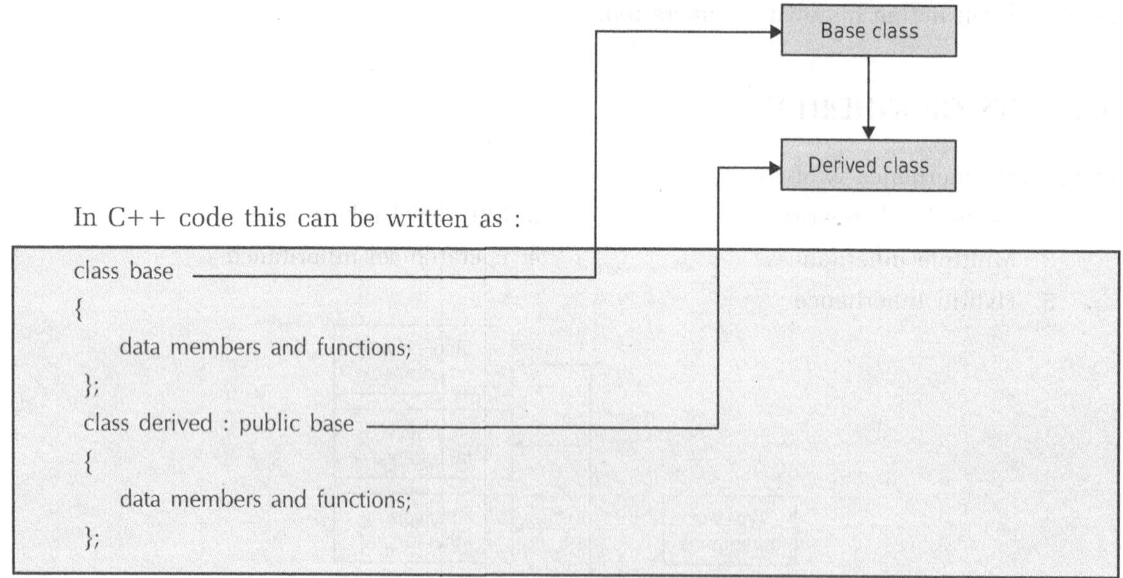

In C++ code this can be written as :

```
class base
{
    data members and functions;
};
class derived : public base
{
    data members and functions;
};
```

2. Multilevel Inheritance

In multiple inheritances we have one base class and one derived at one level. At the next level the derived class becomes base class for the next class and so on. This is as shown on page 395.

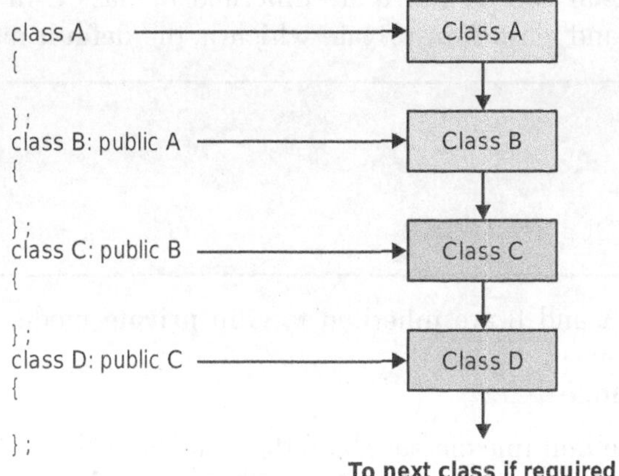

The class A and B together forms one level, class B and class C together forms another level and so on. For a class B, class A is the parent and for class C, class B is the present thus in this inheritance level we can say that A is the grandfather of class C and class C is the grandchild of class A.

3. Multiple Inheritance

In multiple inheritance a child can have more than parent *i.e.*, a child can inherit properties from more than one class. Diagrammatically this is as shown below :

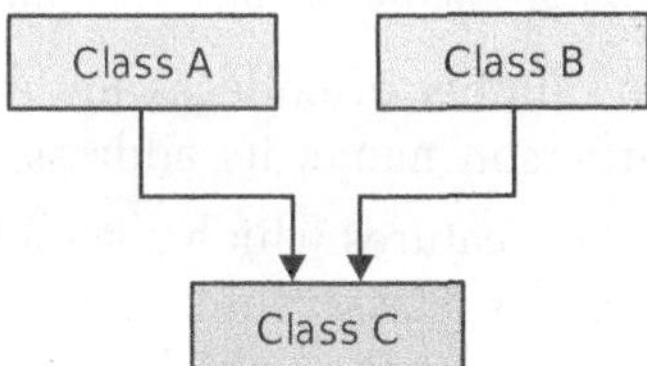

In C++ code for the diagram is given as follows :

```
class A              class B
{                    {

};                   };
class C :   public A,   public B
{

};
```

The mode need not be the same. The **class A** may be inherited in **public** and **class B** in **private** or whatever mode as per the user desired. Note mode has to be specified for both the classes. If you write as :

```
class C :   public A,   B
{

};
```

Than it does not mean both **A** and **B** are inherited in class **C** in **public** mode. The class **A** is inherited in **public** and class **B** in private which is the **default** mode. Again if you write.

```
class C : A,    B
{

};
```

Than both classes A and B are inherited to C in **private** mode.

4. Hierarchical Inheritance

In this type of inheritance multiple classes share the same base class. That is number of classes inherits the properties of one common base class. The derived classes again may become base class for other classes. This is shown as follows :

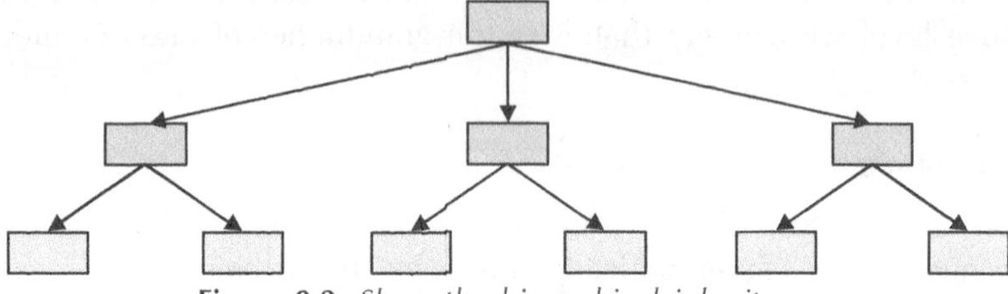

Figure 9.2. *Show the hierarchical inheritance*

For example, a university has number of colleges under its affiliation. Each college may use the university name, the chairperson name, its address, phone number etc.

There are number of properties or features which a vehicle posses. The common properties of all the vehicle may be put under one class vehicle and different classes like two-wheeler, four-wheeler and three-wheeler can inherit the vehicle class.

As another example in an engineering college various departments be termed as various classes which may have one parents class common, the name of engineering college. Again for each department there may be various classes like Lab_staff, Faculty class etc. In C++ code the first level can be seen as follows :

```
class A
{

};

class B : public A  class C :  public A  class D :  public A
{ };                { };                 { };
```

5. Hybrid Inheritance

1. Let's consider the figure as shown below :

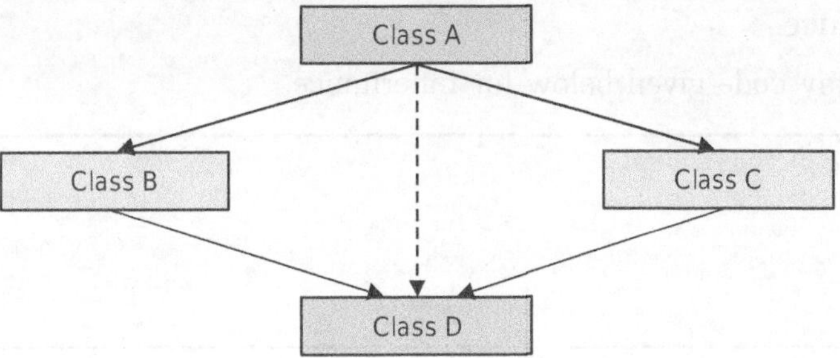

Figure 9.3. *Implementation of hybrid inheritance*

For the first half of the figure, we have hierarchical inheritance as shown by breaking the figure as :

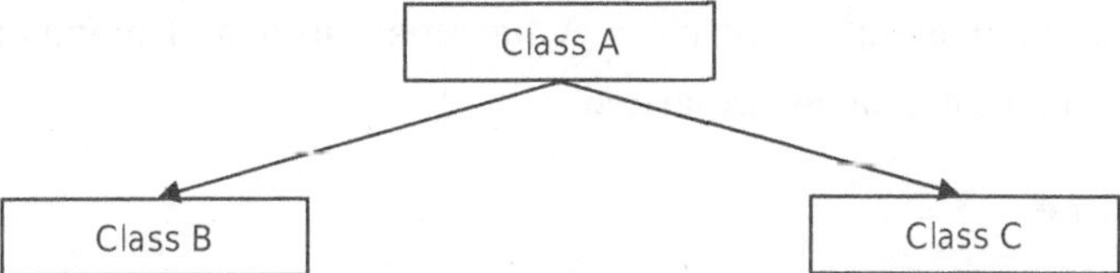

In second half we have multiple inheritance as shown in the figure :

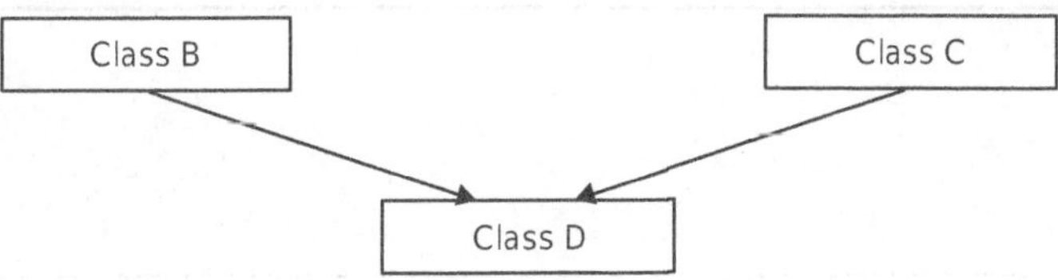

2. The second figure for hybrid inheritance may be viewed as :

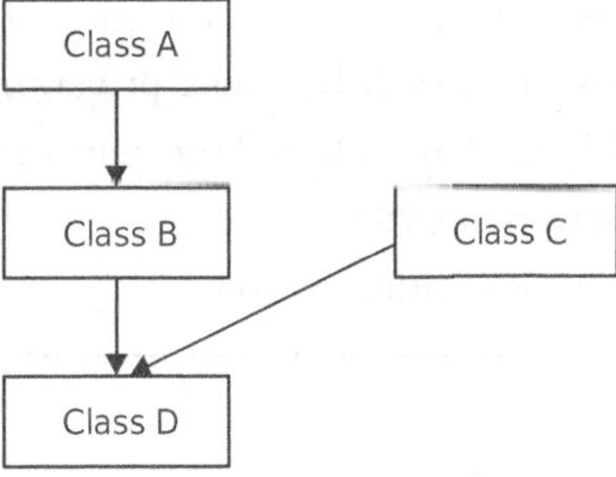

The C++ code may be written as follows :

```
class B :public A
{ };
class D :public B, public C
{


};
```

The inheritance is hybrid as it involves multilevel and multiple inheritance.

9.3 PUBLIC, PRIVATE AND PROTECTED INHERITANCE

1. Public Inheritance

Consider the dummy code given below for inheritance.

```
class B : public A
{

};
```

The line class B : public A tells the compiler that we are inheriting class A in class B in public followings :

(*a*) All the public members of class A becomes public members of class B.

(*b*) All the protected members of class A becomes protected members of class B.

(*c*) Private members are never inherited.

2. Private Inheritance

Consider the dummy code given below for inheritance :

```
class B : private A
{

};
```

The line **class B : private A** tells the compiler that we are inheriting **class A** in **class B** in private mode. In **private mode** inheritance note the following points :

(*a*) All the **public** members of **class A** becomes private members of the **class B**.

(*b*) All the **protected** members of the **class A** becomes private members of **class B.**

(*c*) **Private** members are never inherited.

The above dummy code can be written as too.

```
class B : A
{

};
```

As the default inheritance mode is **private mode**.

3. Protected Inheritance

Consider the dummy code given below for inheritance :

```
class B : protected A
{

};
```

The line class B : protected A tells the compiler that we are inheriting class A in class B in protected mode. In protected mode inheritance note the following points :

(*a*) All the public members of class A becomes protected members of class B.

(*b*) All the protected members of class A becomes protected members of class B.

(*c*) Private members are never inherited.

Note : A class A is inherited in class B in public mode, all protected members of class A becomes protected for class B. Now if this class B is inherited to some new class C, then these protected members inherited from A will be available from A will be available to class C, in whatever mode you inherit class B to class C.

Initially assumed you inherited class A into class B in private mode, then all protected members of class A becomes private for class B. They can be used inside the class B. But if you inherit class B into new class C then these members won't be available in C as private members are never inherited.

/*PROG 9.1 DEMO OF SINGLE LEVEL INHERITANCE VER 1*/

```
#include <iostream.h>
#include <conio.h>
class super
{
 public :
    void sup_show( )
    {
       cout<<"Hello from show of super"<<endl;
    }
};
class sub :public super
{
};
void main( )
{
    clrscr( );
    sub o1;
    o1.sup_show ( );
    getch( );
}
```

OUTPUT :

```
Hello from show of super
```

EXPLANATION : We have a class super in which a single function sup_show under public mode is defined. The line class sub : public super tells the compiler that sub is a new class and we are inheriting class super in public mode in class sub. This makes super as a parent of class sub. The class sub is also known as derived class super as base class. Under public inheritance all the public members of base class becomes public members of derived class. In the class sub we have not defined any data or function, so it contains only inherited members from class super. In the main we create an object of class second and call the function sup_show which was inherited from class super.

/*PROG 9.2 DEMO OF SINGLE INHERITANCE VER 2*/

```
#include <iostream.h>
#include <conio.h>
class super
{
 public :
     int sup_a;
     void show( )
     {
        cout<<"sup_a="<<sup_a<<endl;
     }
};
class sub :public super
{
};
void main( )
{
     clrscr( );
     sub o1;
     o1.sup_a=20;
     o1.show( );
     getch( );
}
```

OUTPUT :

```
sup_a=20
```

EXPLANATION : In the previous program class super was having just one public member function but here we have declared one public data member sup_a of int type also. Again this class super is inherited by class sub in public mode. So member function show and data member sup_a becomes part of class sub through inheritance. In the main we create an object of class sub and assign value of 20 to data member sup_a and by a call to show function we display it.

/*PROG 9.3 DEMO OF SINGLE LEVEL INHERITANCE VER 3*/

```
#include <iostream.h>
#include <conio.h>
class super
{
    int sup_a;
    public :
        void sup_input(int x)
        {
            sup_a=x;
        }
        void sup_show( )
        {
            cout<<"sup_a="<<sup_a<<endl;
        }
};
class sub :public super
{
};
void main( )
{
    int i;
    clrscr( );
    sub o1;
    cout<<"Enter a data member for class super :=";
    cin>>i;
    o1.sup_input(i);
    o1.sup_show( );
    getch( );
}
```

OUTPUT :

```
Enter a data member for class super : =1345
sup_a=1345
```

EXPLANATION : The `class super` contains one private data member `sup_a` and two public member function `sup_input` and `sup_show` which takes input and assign to `sup_a` and display the value of show respectively. When this `class sub` in public mode only the public data members are copied and they become public in derived class too as explained earlier. But remember private data members are never inherited so `sup_a` is not copied to class `sub`. In the `main` we call the two function `sup_input` and `sup_show` through an object of class `sub`.

/*PROG 9.4 DEMO OF SINGLE LEVEL INHERITANCE VER 4*/

```
#include <iostream.h>
#include <conio.h>
class super
{
    int sup_a;
public :
    void sup_input(int x)
    {
        sup_a = x;
    }
    void sup_show( )
    {
        cout<<"sup_a="<<sup_a<<endl;
    }
};
class sub :public super
{
    int sub_a;
    public :
        void sub_input(int x)
    {
        sub_a=x;
    }
    void sub_show( )
    {
        cout<<"sub_a="<<sub_a<<endl;
    }
};
void main( )
{
    int i,j;
    clrscr( );
    sub o1;
    cout<<"Enter the data member of super class i :=";
    cin>>i;
    cout<<"Enter the data member of sub class j :=";
    cin>>j;
    o1.sup_input(i);
    o1.sub_input(j);
```

```
    o1.sup_show( );
    o1.sub_show( );
    getch( );
}
```

OUTPUT :

```
Enter the data member of super class i : =123
Enter the data member of sub class j : =134
sup_a=123
sub_a=134
```

EXPLANATION : In all the earlier programs the class sub was empty. But here we have one private data member's sub_a and two functions for input and show. After inheriting class super in class sub, the class sub has total 4 public members' functions :

⇒ **Two of it's own**

⇒ **And two inherited from class super.**

The class sub also has one private data member sub_a. In the main all 4 functions are called by an object of sub class.

/*PROG 9.5 DEMO OF SINGLE LEVEL INHERITANCE VER 5 */

```
#include <iostream.h>
#include <conio.h>
class super
{
    int sup_a;
    public :
        void sup_input(int x)
        {
            sup_a=x;
        }
        void sup_show( )
        {
            cout<<"sup_a="<<sup_a<<endl;
        }
};
class sub :public super
{
    int sub_a;
    public :
        void sub_input(int x)
```

```
        {
            sup_input(x*2);
            sub_a=x;
        }
        void sub_show( )
        {
            sup_show( );
            cout<<"sub_a="<<sub_a<<endl;
        }
};
void main( )
{
    int i;
    clrscr( );
    sub o1;
    cout<<"Enter the data member :=";
    cin>>i;
    o1.sub_input(i);
    o1.sub_show( );
    getch( );
}
```

OUTPUT :

```
Enter the data member : =145
sup_a=290
sub_a=145
```

EXPLANATION : In the `main` we have called only the functions of sub class. The function `sup_input` is called from `sub_input` with a value `x*2` as argument. Similarly sup_show is called from class `sub`. So, when `sub_input` is called from `main` with value of `'i'` of `int` type, it is collected in variable `x` and the function of base class `sup_input` is called with value `2*145 (290)`, where it is assigned to `sup_a` of `super class`. When control returns `sup_input` function the value `x` is assigned to `sub_a.` When `sup_show` is called, it calls `sup_show` first in its body. When the function `sup_show` returns after displaying the value of `sup_a`, the function `sup_show` displays the value of `sub_a.`

/* **PROG 9.6 DEMO OF SINGLE LEVEL INHERITANCE VER 6** */

```
#include <iostream.h>
#include <conio.h>

class super
{
```

```
    int sup_a;
public :
    void sup_input( )
    {
        cout<<"ENTER THE VALUE FOR SUP_A"<<endl;
        cin>>sup_a;
    }
    void sup_show( )
    {
        cout<<"Sup_a="<<sup_a<<endl;
    }
};
class sub :public super
{
    int sub_a;
public :
    void sub_input( )
    {
        sup_input( );
        cout<<"Enter the value for sub_a"<<endl;
        cin>>sub_a;
    }
    void sub_show( )
    {
        sup_show( );
        cout<<"Sub_a="<<sub_a<<endl;
    }
};
void main( )
{
    clrscr( );
    sub obj;
    obj.sub_input( );
    obj.sub_show( );
    getch( );
}
```

OUTPUT :

```
ENTER THE VALUE FOR SUP_A
34
Enter the value for sub_a
45
Sup_a=34
Sub_a=45
```

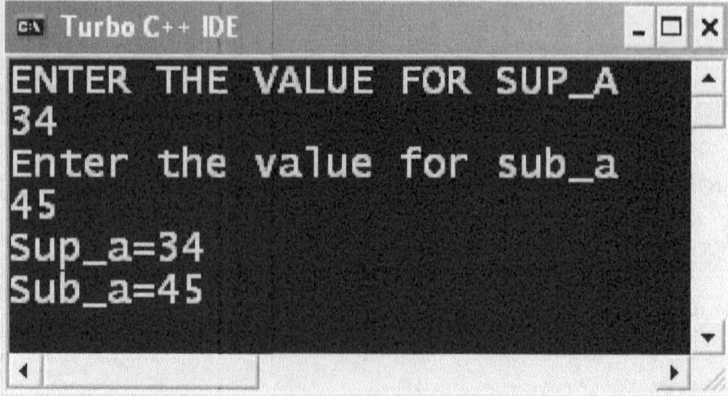

Figure 9.4. *Output screen of the program 9.6*

EXPLANATION : The program is similar to previous one with the a change that in the input functions for both the class we have taken input from the user through keyboard instead of assigning the fixed value to data members.

/*PROG 9.7 DEMO OF SINGLE LEVEL INHERITANCE VER 7 */

```
#include <iostream.h>
#include <conio.h>

class super
{
    int sup_a;
public :
    void sup_input(int x)
    {
        sup_a=x;
    }
    void sup_show( )
    {
        cout<<"sup_a="<<sup_a<<endl;
    }
};
class sub :public super
{
    int sub_a;
    public :
        void sub_input(int x, int y)
        {
            sup_input(y);
            sub_a=x;
        }
```

```
        void sub_show( )
        {
            sup_show( );
            cout<<"sub_a = "<<sub_a<<endl;
        }
};

void main( )
{
    clrscr( );
    sub obj;
    obj.sub_input(20,50);
    obj.sub_show( );
    getch( );
}
```

OUTPUT :

```
sup_a=50
sub_a = 20
```

EXPLANATION : In the previous program we manipulated the value of `x` and passed this value to input function of class supper. But here in the `sub_input` function we have taken two inputs : one for super class and one for itself. Either value can be used in either manner. Here when `sub_input` function is called with the `20` and `50`, they are collected in `x` and `y`. In the function `sub input` the value of `y` is passed to function `sup_input` and value of `x` is assigned to `sub_a`. Later we display the values using `sub_show` function.

/* PROG 9.8 DEMO OF SINGLE LEVEL INHERITANCE VER 8 */

```
#include <iostream.h>
#include <conio.h>
class super
{
    int sup_a;
public :
    void input(int x)
    {
        sup_a=x;
    }
    void show( )
    {
```

```
        cout<<"sup_a="<<sup_a<<endl;
    }
};
class sub :public super
{
    int sub_a;
public :
    void input(int x)
    {
        sub_a=x;
    }
    void show( )
    {
        cout<<"sub_a="<<sub_a<<endl;
    }
};
void main( )
{
    clrscr( );
    sub obj;
    obj.input(40);
    obj.show( );
    getch( );
}
```

OUTPUT :

```
sub_a=40
```

EXPLANATION : Here both the classes have same function signatures so priority is given to derive class. So input and show of derived class will be called.

/* PROG 9.9 DEMO OF SINGLE LEVEL INHERITANCE VER 9 */

```
#include <iostream.h>
#include <conio.h>
class super
{
protected :
    void show( )
    {
        cout<<"Hello from super"<<endl;
    }
};
```

```
class sub :public super
{
};
void main( )
{
    clrscr( );
    sub obj;
    obj.show( );
    getch( );
}
```

OUTPUT :

ERROR :'show' cannot access protected member declared in class 'super'

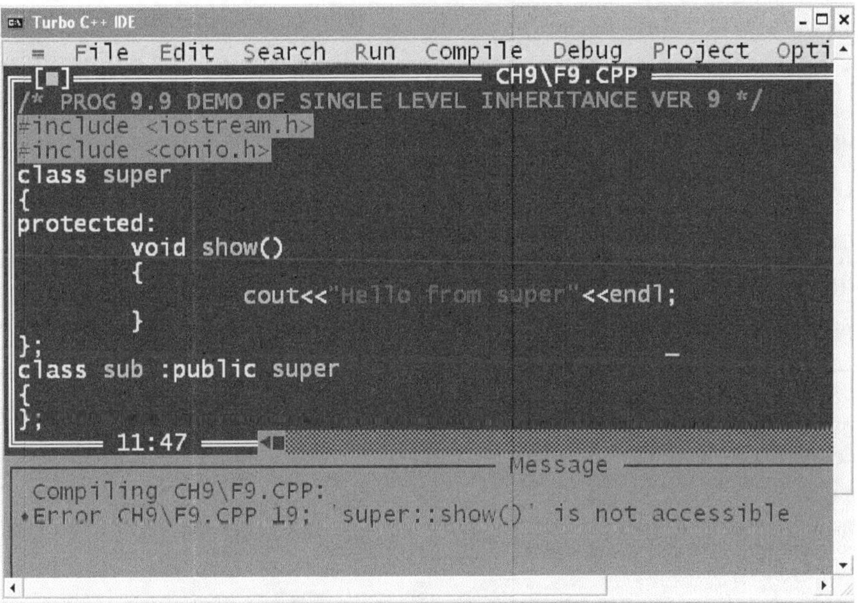

Figure 9.5. *Showing error message*

EXPLANATION : In public inheritance protected members of base are inherited in derived class and remains protected. Protected members cannot be used outside the class similar to private members. So, the error.

/* PROG 9.10 DEMO OF SINGLE LEVEL PRIVATE INHERITANCE VER 1*/

```
#include <iostream.h>
#include <conio.h>

class super
{
```

```
public :
    void sup_show( )
    {
        cout<<"Hello from super"<<endl;
    }
};
class sub :private super
{
};
void main( )
{
    clrscr( );
    sub obj;
    obj.sup_show( );
    getch( );
}
```

OUTPUT :

ERROR :'sup_show' cannot access public member declared in class 'super'.

EXPLANATION : In private inheritance all public members (data & function) becomes private for the derived class. As `sup_show` of class super becomes private in the sub class it cannot be accessed outside the class.

/* PROG 9.11 DEMO OF SINGLE LEVEL PRIVATE INHERITANCE VER 2 */

```
#include <iostream.h>
#include <conio.h>
class super
{
public :
    void sup_show( )
    {
        cout<<"Hello from super"<<endl;
    }
};

class sub :private super
{
public :
    void sub_show( )
    {
```

```
        sup_show( );
        cout<<"Hello from sub"<<endl;
    }
};

void main( )
{
    clrscr( );
    sub obj;
    obj.sub_show( );
    getch( );
}
```

OUTPUT :

Hello from super
Hello from sub

EXPLANATION : The inherited function `sup_show` becomes private in the class `sub`. The class `sub` defines its own function `sub_show`. As `sup_show` is private in the class `sub` it can be called inside any member function of class `sub`. In the `main` when we call `sub_show` through an object of class `sub`. The function definition first call the `sup_show` function of `super` class and executes its own body.

/*PROG 9.12 DEMO OF SINGLE LEVEL PRIVATE INHERITANCE VER 3 */

```
#include <iostream.h>
#include <conio.h>

class super
{
    int num;
};

class sub :super
{
public :
    void sub_show( )
    {
        cout<<"num="<<num<<endl;
    }
};
```

```
void main( )
{
    clrscr( );
    sub obj;
    obj.sub_show( );
    getch( );
}
```

OUTPUT :

ERROR :'super : :num' cannot access private member declared in class 'super'

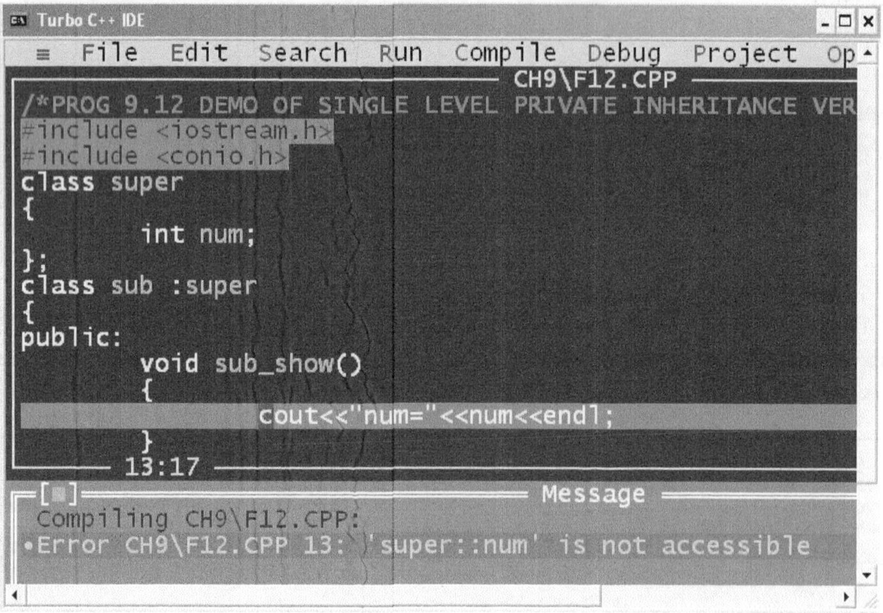

```
Turbo C++ IDE
 ≡  File  Edit  Search  Run  Compile  Debug  Project  Op
                          CH9\F12.CPP
/*PROG 9.12 DEMO OF SINGLE LEVEL PRIVATE INHERITANCE VER
#include <iostream.h>
#include <conio.h>
class super
{
        int num;
};
class sub :super
{
public:
        void sub_show()
        {
                cout<<"num="<<num<<endl;
        }
        13:17
[■]                          Message
 Compiling CH9\F12.CPP:
•Error CH9\F12.CPP 13: 'super::num' is not accessible
```

Figure 9.6. *Showing the compilation error during the execution of the program*

EXPLANATION : If no access specifier is specified than by default all members of a class are private, so num is private. Again mode of inheritance is given while inheriting class super in sub, so default mode private is assumed *i.e.,* the following statement :

```
class sub : super
```

Is equivalent to

```
class sub :private super
```

As `private` members are never inherited, accessing `num` in the following `sub_show` procedure error.

/*PROG 9.13 DEMO OF SINGLE LEVEL PRIVATE INHERITANCE VER 4 */

```
#include <iostream.h>
#include <conio.h>

class super
{
protected :
    int num;
    void input(int x)
    {
        num = x;
    }
};
class sub :super
{
public :
    void sub_show( )
    {
        input(100);
        cout<<"num="<<num<<endl;
    }
};
void main( )
{
    clrscr( );
    sub obj;
    obj.sub_show( );
    getch( );
}
```

OUTPUT :

```
num=100
```

EXPLANATION : In the `super` class `num` and function input is protected. In the class sub we are inheriting class super in private mode. In private mode all protected members of base class become private for the derived class and they can only be used inside the member functions of the derived class and not outside *i.e.,* in the `main`. In the `main` when `obj.sub_show( );` executes it call the function `sub_show`, in side input with value `100` is called which assigns value of `100` to `num`. Later we display this value of `num`.

/* PROG 9.14 DEMO OF SINGLE LEVEL PROTECTED INHERITANCE VER 1 */

```
#include <iostream.h>
#include <conio.h>

class super
{
public :
    void show( )
    {
        cout<<"hello from super"<<endl;
    }
};
class sub :protected super
{
};

void main( )
{
    clrscr( );
    sub obj;
    obj.show( );
    getch( );
}
```

OUTPUT :

ERROR :'show' cannot access public member declared in class 'super'

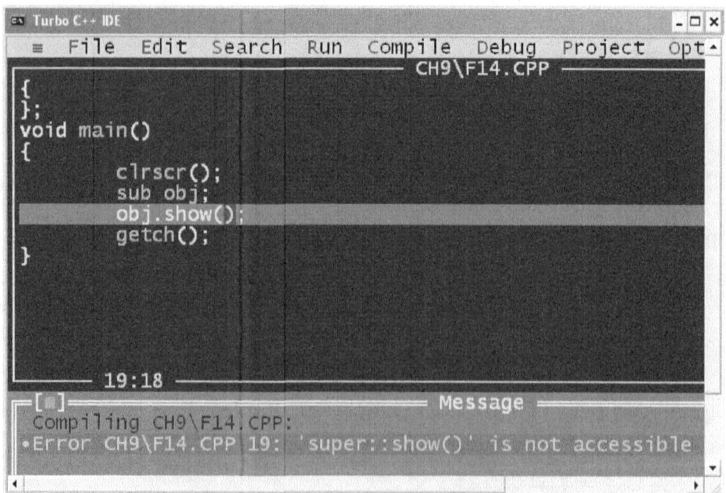

Figure 9.7. *Compile time error during the execution of program 9.14*

EXPLANATION : In class sub we are inheriting class super in protected mode. So, all public members of class super become protected for the class sub and protected members can only be accessed inside the member functions of the class. So, the error.

/* PROG 9.15 DEMO OF SINGLE LEVEL PROTECTED INHERITANCE VER 2 */

```
#include <iostream.h>
#include <conio.h>

class super
{
    void show( )
    {
        cout<<"hello from super"<<endl;
    }
};

class sub :protected super
{

};

void main( )
{
    clrscr( );
    sub obj;
    obj.show( );
    getch( );
}
```

OUTPUT :

ERROR : 'show' cannot access private member delared in class 'super'

EXPLANATION : Private members are never inherited. So we cannot access show in main and any of the member function of the derived class. That's why the above error.

/*PROG 9.16 DEMO ACCESSING PRIVATE MEMBERS IN PRIVATE INHERITANCE */

```
#include <iostream.h>
#include <conio.h>
class super
{
    int num;
```

```
public :
      void input(int x)
      {
            num = x;
      }
      int getnum( )
      {
            return num;
      }
};
class sub :super
{
public :
      void show( )
      {
            input(50);
            cout<<"The square of num is"
                  <<getnum( )*getnum( )<<endl;
      }
};

void main( )
{
      clrscr( );
      sub obj;
      obj.show( );
      getch( );
}
```

OUTPUT :

The square of num is 2500

EXPLANATION : The variable `num` is `private` in class `super`. The class `sub` inherits class `super` in `private` mode so `num` won't be accessible in class `sub`. Then how can we use `num` in class `sub` ? The solution is simple which we have seen earlier. We make a function in `public` mode which returns in the value of `num`. We have made function `getnum` which returns the value of `num`. Through this `getnum` we can easily compute the square of the `num`.

/* PROG 9.17 ACCESSING PRIVATE MEMBERS IN PRIVATE INHERITANCE AND MODIFYING THEM */

```
#include <iostream.h>
#include <conio.h>
```

```
class super
{
    int num;
public :
    void input(int x)
    {
        num=x;
    }
    int &getnum( )
    {
        return num;
    }
    void super_show( )
    {
        cout<<"Num in class super is"<<num<<endl;
    }
};
class sub :super
{
public :
    void show( )
    {
        input(50);
        cout<<"Num in class sub is"<<getnum( )<<endl;
        getnum( )=getnum( )*getnum( );
        super_show( );
    }
};
void main( )
{
    clrscr( );
    sub obj;
    obj.show( );
    getch( );
}
```

OUTPUT :

```
Num in class sub is 50
Num in class super is 2500
```

EXPLANATION : Whenever we want to modify the `private` members of the base class we must have a `public` member function in `base class` which returns reference of `private` data members. As `getnum` return the reference of `num` it can be put on the left side of assignment operator (=). Inside the function `show` we modify the value of `num` using getnum on the left side of =, and assigning `getnum()* getnum()` which stores `2500` into `num`. As we got reference of `num` through `getnum` this change of value occurs in the `num`. So, when `supper_show` is called it displays this value of `num` as `2500`.

/*PROG 9.18 FINDING AREA AND VOLUME USING INHERITANCE VER 1 */

```
#include <iostream.h>
#include <conio.h>
class Area
{
 protected :
     int length, width;
 public :
     void inputa( )
     {
         cout <<"Enter the lenght :=";
         cin  >>length;
         cout <<endl<<"Enter the width :=";
         cin  >>width;
     }
 };
 class volume :public Area
 {
     int height;
     public :
         void inputv( )
     {
         inputa( );
         cout<<"Enter the height :=";
         cin>>height;
     }
     void show( )
     {
         cout<<"Length ="<<length<<endl;
         cout<<"Width  ="<<width<<endl;
         cout<<"Area   ="<<length*width<<endl;
         cout<<"Height="<<height<<endl;
```

```
        cout<<"Volume="<<length*width*height<<endl;
    }
};
void main( )
{
    clrscr( );
    volume v;
    v.inputv( );
    v.show( );
    getch( );
}
```

OUTPUT :

```
Enter the lenght : =12
Enter the width : =13
Enter the height : =14
Length  =12
Width   =13
Area    =156
Height  =14
Volume =2184
```

EXPLANATION : In the class `Area` we have two `protected` data members `length` and `width`. Function `inputa()` takes input from keyboard into these data items directly. The class `Volume` inherits class `Area` in the `public` mode. This class `Volume` contains one data member `height`. The class calculates `area` by using the inherited data members `length` and `width` and with the aid of `height` with `length and width finds volume`. Note we have called only the derived class function `inputv()` inside the `main`. This function in turns calls `inputa()` of the `area` class and takes input from keyboard. The function show calculates `area and volume` and displays.

/* PROG 9.19 FINDING AREA AND VOLUME USING INHERITANCE VER 2 */

```
#include <iostream.h>
#include <conio.h>

class Area
{
    int l, w;
public :
    void input_A(int x,int y)
    {
        l=x;
```

```
        w=y;
    }
    int get_l( )
    {
        return l;
    }
    int get_w( )
    {
        return w;
    }
};

class Volume :public Area
{
    int h;
public :
    void input_V(int x, int y, int z)
    {
        input_A(x,y);
        h=z;
    }
    void show( )
    {
        cout<<"Length :   = "<<get_l( )<<endl;
        cout<<"Width :    = "<<get_w( )<<endl;
        cout<<"Area :     = "<<get_l( )*get_w( )<<endl;
        cout<<"Height :   = "<<h<<endl;
        cout<<"Volumen := "<<get_l( )*get_w( )*h<<endl;
    }
};

void main( )
{
    clrscr( );
    Volume v;
    v.input_V(5,10,15);
    v.show( );
    getch( );
}
```

OUTPUT :

```
Length :   = 5
Width :    = 10
Area :     = 50
Height :   = 15
Volumen : = 750
```

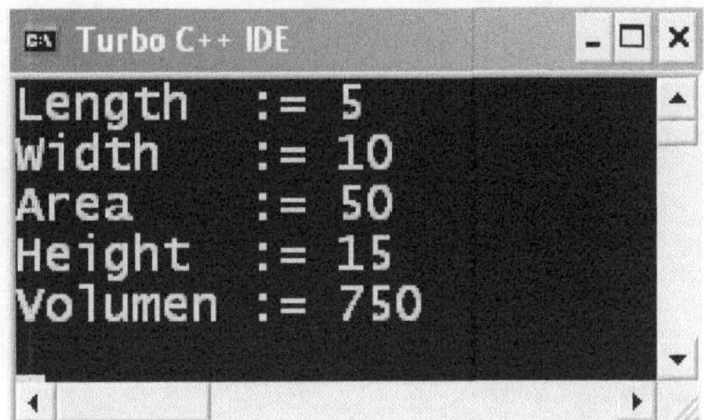

Figure 9.8. *Output screen of program 9.19*

EXPLANATION : In the earlier program length and width in the class. `Area` was `protected` and through `public` inheritance we could use them in class `Volume`. But here both the data members are `private` so we cannot make use of these data members in the derived class `Volume` as `private` members are never inherited. For that we have created two `public` member function `get_l` and `get_w` which returns `length` and `width` respectively. In the `main` we create an object `v` of class `Volume` and call the function `input_V` with three arguments `5, 10` and `15.` These three values are collected in the formal parameters `x,` `y` and `z` respectively. The first two values `x` and `y` are passed to the `input_A` function of class `Area` where they are assigned to `length` and `width`. Later we find out the area and volume by making use of `get_l` and `get_w` function.

/* PROG 9.20 DEMO OF TWO LEVEL INHERITANCE VER 1 */

```
#include <iostream.h>
#include <conio.h>
class first
{
public :
    void show_f( )
    {
        cout<<"Hello from first"<<endl;
    }
};
class second :public first
{
public :
    void show_s( )
    {
        cout<<"Hello from second"<<endl;
    }
};
class third : public second
{
public :
```

```
    void show_t( )
    {
        show_f( );
        show_s( );
        cout<<"Hello from third"<<endl;
    }
};

void main( )
{
    clrscr( );
    third t;
    t.show_t( );
    getch( );
}
```

OUTPUT :

```
Hello from first
Hello from second
Hello from third
```

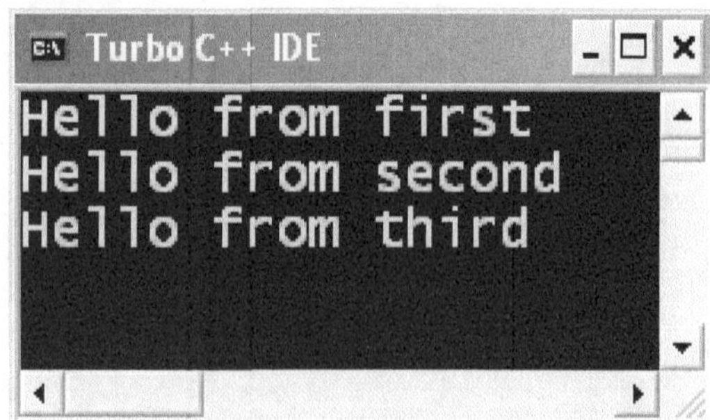

Figure 9.9. *Output screen of program 9.20*

EXPLANATION : The above program demonstrate `2 level of inheritance`. The class `first` is the `base class (parent class)` for class `second (child class)` and class second is the `base class (parent class)` for `class third (child class)`. In turn class `first` is the grandfather of class `third (grand child)`. In `show_t` function of class `third` `show_s` is inherited directly from class second but `show_f` is inherited indirectly from class first through class `second`.

/*PROG 9.21 FINDING MAXIMUM OF THREE CLASS'S DATA */

```
#include <iostream.h>
#include <conio.h>
class first
```

```
{
    protected :
        int fa;
    public :
     void input_f( )
     {
        cout<<"Enter the value for fa :=";
        cin>>fa;
     }
};
 class second :public first
 {
    protected :
        int sa;
    public :
        void input_s( )
     {
        input_f( );
        cout<<"Enter the value for sa :=";
        cin>>sa;
     }
};
class third :public second
{
    protected :
        int ta;
    public :
        void input_t( )
     {
        input_s( );
        cout<<"Enter the value for ta :=";
        cin>>ta;
     }
     void show( )
     {
        cout<<"Data of class first fa :    ="<<fa<<endl;
        cout<<"Data of class second sa :="<<sa<<endl;
        cout<<"Data of class third ta :    ="<<ta<<endl;
     }
```

```
    int max( )
    {
        int t1,t2;
        t1=fa>sa ?fa :sa;
        t2=ta>t1 ?ta :t1;
        return t2;
    }
};
void main( )
{
    clrscr( );
    third t;
    t.input_t( );
    t.show( );
    cout<<"Max is "<<t.max( )<<endl;
    getch( );
}
```

OUTPUT :

```
Enter the value for fa : =123
Enter the value for sa : =567
Enter the value for ta : =234
Data of class first fa : =123
Data of class second sa : =567
Data of class third ta : =234
Max is 567
```

EXPLANATION : In all the three classes data members are `protected`. In `main` when `input_t` of class third is called by an object `t`, it first calls function `input_s` of class second. The function `input_s` in turn call the function `input_f` of class first. As `second` is the base class of class `third` and first is the base class of `second`, data memebers `fa` and `sa` can be used inside the member functions of class `third`. Though how of class `third` we display these data members. The function `max` of class third finds maximum of these `three` data members using ternary operator and return the max value which is displayed in the main.

9.4 MULTIPLE INHERITANCE

Multiple inheritance has been explained in the beginning of the chapter. Recall in a multiple inheritance graph, the derived classes may have a number of direct base classes.

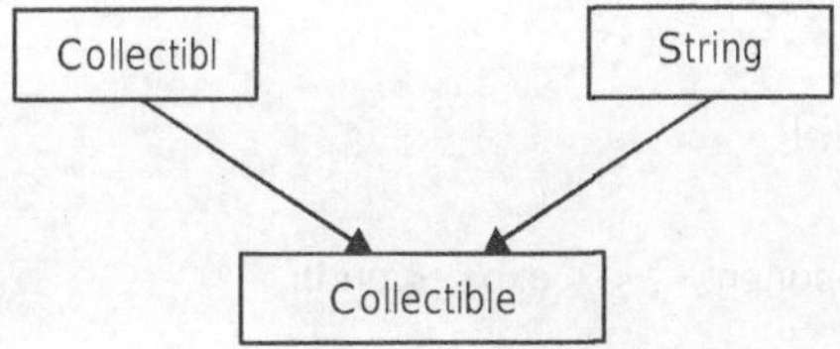

The diagram in the figure shows a class, **collectible String**. It is like a **Collectible** (something that can be contained in a collection). It is like a String. Multiple inheritance is a good solution to this kind of problem (Where a derived class has attributes of more than one class) because it is easy to form a **Collectible Customer, Collectible** Windows, and so on. If the properties of either class are not required for a particular application, either class can be used alone or in combination with other classes. Therefore, given the hierarchy depicted in figure as a basic, you can form noncollection strings and collectibles that are not strings. This flexibility is not possible using single inheritance. We present few examples for better understanding point of view.

/*PROG 9.22 FINDING POWER FROM BASE AND EXPONENT*/

```
#include <iostream.h>
#include <conio.h>
#include <stdlib.h>
class base
{
    protected :
        int ba;
    public :
        void input_base( )
            {
                cout<<"Enter the base :=";
                cin>>ba;
            }
            void show_base( )
            {
                cout<<"base :="<<ba<<endl;
            }
};
class exponent
{
    protected :
        int exp;
    public :
        void input_exp( )
            {
                cout<<"Enter the exponent :=";
                    cin>>exp;
```

```
        }
        void show_exp( )
        {
            cout<<"exponent="<<exp<<endl;
        }
};
class power :public base, public exponent
{
    int po;
    public :
     void input( )
        {
          input_base ( );
           input_exp( );
        };
        void show( )
        {
            show_base( );
            show_exp( );
            int i;
            po=1;
            for(i=1;i<=exp;i++)
            po=po*ba;
            cout<<"power :="<<po<<endl;
          }
};
void main( )
{
    clrscr( );
    power o1;
    o1.input( );
    o1.show( );
    getch( );

}
```

OUTPUT :

```
Enter the base : =5
Enter the exponent : =3
base :       =5
exponent =3
power :      =125
```

EXPLANATION : The program is simple. In the `base class` we have a data member `ba` which represent base and in the class `exponent` we have a data member `exp` which represent `exponent`. These two classes are inherited by class power which has two function input and show. In the input of this class the base and exponent is called. In the show function we find the power using for loop and display the result.

/*PROG 9.23 FINDING TOTAL MARKS FROM INTERNAL AND EXTERNAL MARKS */

```
#include <iostream.h>
#include <conio.h>
#include <stdlib.h>
class Internal
{
protected :
    int i_marks;
public :
     void input_im( )
     {
        cout<<"Enter internal marks :=";
        cin>>i_marks;
        if(!(i_marks>=0 && i_marks<=60))
        {
            cout<<"Invalid Marks";
            exit(0);
        }
     }
     void show_im( )
     {
        cout<<"Internal marks :="<<i_marks<<endl;
     }
};
class External
{
protected :
    int e_marks;
public :
    void input_em( )
    {
       cout<<"Enter external marks :=";
       cin>>e_marks;
       if(!(e_marks>=0 && e_marks<=60))
       {
```

```
            cout<<"Invalid Marks";
            exit(0);
        }
    }
    void show_em( )
    {
        cout<<"External marks :="<<e_marks<<endl;
    }
};
class Total :public Internal, public External
{
    int total_marks;
public :
    void input( )
    {
        input_im( );
        input_em( );
    }
    void show( )
    {
        show_im( );
        show_em( );
        total_marks = i_marks;
        cout<<"Total Mrks :="<<total_marks<<endl;
    }
};
void main( )
{
    clrscr( );
    Total tm;
    tm.input( );
    tm.show( );
    getch( );
}
```

OUTPUT :

```
Enter internal marks : =56
Enter external marks : =35
Internal marks : =56
External marks : =35
Total Marks :    =91
```

EXPLANATION : For student's **internal marks** we have a class **Internal** and for student's external marks we have a **class External**. The internal marks must be between **0 to 60** and external marks must be between **0 to 40.** These two classes are inherited by class total which finds the total marks and display all three marks :

(*a*) Internal

(*b*) External and

(*c*) Total

Note here that **i_marks and e_marks** are protected so that can be used inside the total class. They can be modified by the class total. So ideally **i_marks and e_marks**. Try to make use of this and create a new program yourself.

→ Resolving Ambiguity

In multiple inheritance when two base classes having same name for their functions and data, ambiguity arises when they are used in the derived class. For example, consider the two classes **A and B** having same function signature for function named show like **void show ( ).** Both the classes are inherited in the third **class C**. Now how **class C** can use show of **A** class and show of **B** class individually. Simply accessing show function in class **C** creates confusion as to which show we want to refer; show of **class A** or show of **class B**. In these situations we can use the scope resolution operator with class names to functions for accessing the function of individual class. Thus inside the member functions of **class C** we can access show of class A as **A : : show( )** and show of class **B as B : : show**. If function show is also defined in the class C and all show are public then they can access in the **main** using an object of **C** class as :

```
C o1;
O1.A : :show( );     //calls show of A class
O1.B : :show( );     //calls show of B class
O1.show( );          // calls show of C class
```

See the example given below :

/*PROG 9.24 RESOLVING AMBIGUITY IN MULTIPLE INHERITANCE */

```
#include <iostream.h>
#include <conio.h>
class A
{
protected :
    int num;
public :
    void show( )
    {
        cout<<"show of A\n";
        cout<<"num of A="<<num<<endl;
    }
};
```

```
class B
{
protected :
    int num;
public :
    void show( )
    {
       cout<<"show of B\n";
       cout<<"num of B="<<num<<endl;
    }
};
class C : public A, public B
{
    int num;
public :
C( )
{
    A : :num=20;
    B : :num=30;
    num=40;
}
void show( )
{
    cout<<"Show of C"<<endl;
    cout<<"num of C="<<num<<endl;
}
};
void main( )
{
    clrscr( );
    C o1;
    o1.A : :show( );
    o1.B : :show( );
    o1.show( );
    getch( );
}
```

OUTPUT :

```
show of A
num of A=20
show of B
```

```
num of B=30
Show of C
num of C=40
```

EXPLANATION : In the program we have three classes : A, B and C. In all the classes we have a data member num of int type and function show with same signature. The num of A and B are accessed in the class C as A : : num and B : :num even though they are not static members. In the main the show of A and B classes are accessed with an object o1 of class C as :

O1.A : : show( );

O1.B : : show ( );

9.5 HIERARCHICAL INHERITANCE

This type of inheritance was explained in the earlier sections of this chapter. When number of classes have a direct access to one common class, then this type of inheritance is visible. The main base class can be modified alone if required and all derived classes will see that effect. Here, we present two example of this type of inheritance.

/*PROG 9.25 DEMO OF HIERARCHICAL INHERITANCE VER 1*/

```
#include <iostream.h>
#include <conio.h>
#include <string.h>

class University
{
protected :
    char uname[40];
public :
    University( )
    {
        strcpy(uname,"NMIMS University Mumbai");
    }
};
class college1 :public University
 {
    char cname[50];
public :
    college1( )
    {
        strcpy(cname, "MPSTME Shirpur Campus");
    }
```

```
    void show_college1( )
    {
        cout<<"College Name : ="<<cname<<endl;
        cout<<"Affiliated to :    ="<<uname<<endl;
    }
};
class college2 :public University
{
    char cname [50];
public :
    college2( )
    {
        strcpy(cname,"R C Patel");
    }
    void show_college2( )
    {
        cout<<"College Name  ="<<cname<<endl;
        cout<<"Affiliated to :  ="<<uname <<endl;
    }
};
void main( )
{
    clrscr( );
    college1 c1;
    c1.show_college1( );
    college2 c2;
    c2.show_college2 ( );
    getch( );
}
```

OUTPUT :

```
College Name : =MPSTME Shirpur Campus
Affiliated to :   =NMIMS University Mumbai
College Name    =R C Patel
Affiliated to :   =NMIMS University Mumbai
```

EXPLANATION : The program is so simple. We have university class which has just data member, a `char` array of `40` characters named `uname`. This class is inherited by two classes' `college1` and `college2`. The two classes display their name and the university to which they are affiliated.

/*PROG 9.26 DEMO OF HIERARCHICAL INHERITANCE VER 2*/

```
#include <iostream.h>
#include <conio.h>

class Father
{
    float amount;
public :
    Father( )
    {
        amount=50000;
    }
    float getamount( )
    {
        return amount;
    }
};

class Son1 :public Father
{
    float amount_son1;
    float total;
public :
    Son1( )
    {
        amount_son1=30000;
    }
    void show( )
    {
        cout<<"\tGot from father := "
            <<getamount( )<<endl;
        cout<<"\tOwn Investment := "
            <<amount_son1<<endl;
        total = getamount( ) + amount_son1;
        cout<<"\tTotal Investment := "<<total<<endl;
    }
};
class Son2 : public Father
{
    float amount_son2;
```

```
        float total;
    public :
        Son2( )
        {
            amount_son2=40000;
        }
        void show( )
        {
            cout<<"\tGot from father := "
                <<getamount( )<<endl;
            cout<<"\tOwn Investment := "
                <<amount_son2<<endl;
            total = getamount( )+ amount_son2;
            cout<<"\tTotal Investment := "<<total<<endl;
        }
    };

    void main( )
    {
        clrscr( );
        Son1 S1;
        cout<<"\t++++++Son 1+++++++"<<endl;
        S1.show( );
        Son2 S2;
        cout<<"\t******Son 2*******"<<endl;
        S2.show( );
        getch( );
    }
```

OUTPUT :

```
++++++Son 1+++++++
Got from father : = 50000
Own Investment : = 30000
Total Investment : = 80000
******Son 2*******
Got from father : = 50000
Own Investment : = 40000
Total Investment : = 90000
```

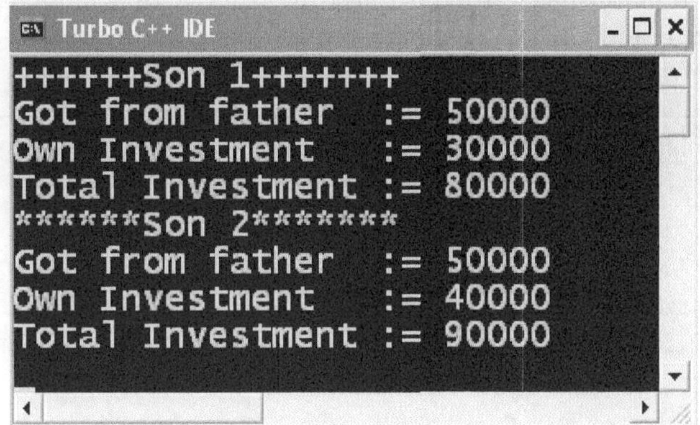

Figure 9.10. *Output screen of the program*

EXPLANATION : The father helps `Son1` and `Son2` in starting their business. So, both the classes `Son1` and `Son2` inherit `Father Class` and rest is self-explanatory.

9.6 VIRTUAL BASE CLASS

Consider the situation where we have one **class A**. This **class A** is inherited by two other classes **B and C.** Both these classes are inherited in a new **class D**. This is as shown in figure given below. In dummy code form this is shown below :

```
class A
{
};
class B :public A              class C   :   public A
{                                {
};                               };
class D      :public C, public B
{
};
```

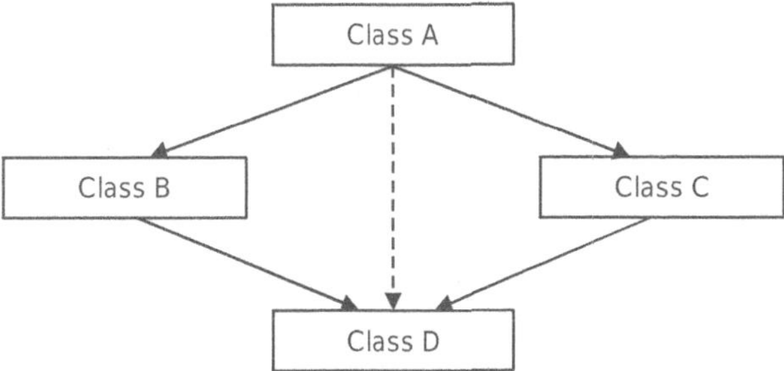

As can be seen from the figure that data members/ functions of class A are inherited twice to class D. One through class B and second through class C. When any data/ function members of class A is accessed by an object of class D, ambiguity arises as to which data/function members would be called ? One inherited through B or the other inherited through C. This confuses compiler and it flashes error message. To resolve this ambiguity when class A is inherited in both class B and class C, it is declared as virtual base class by placing the keyword virtual as :

```
Class B : virtual public A          class C : public virtual A
{                                   {

};                                  };
```

Note : virtual can be written before or after the public. Now only one copy of data/function member will be copied to class C and class B and class A becomes virtual base class.

Virtual base classes offer a way to save space and avoid ambiguities in class hierarchies that uses multiple inheritances. When a base class is specified as a virtual base, it can act as an indirect base more than once without duplication of its data members. A single copy of its members is shared by all the base classes that use it as a virtual base.

See the following example given below :

/*PROG 9.27 DEMO OF VIRTUAL BASE CLASS VER 1*/

```
#include <iostream.h>
#include <conio.h>
class A
{
public :
    int a;
    A( )
    {
        a=100;
    }
};
class B :public virtual A
{
};
class C :virtual public A
{
};
class D : public B, public C
{

};
void main( )
{
    clrscr( );
```

```
    cout<<" a="<<(new D)->a<<endl;
    getch( );
}
```

OUTPUT :

a=100

EXPLANATION : The `class A` has just one data member `a` which is `public`. This class is virtually inherited in `class B` and `class C`. Now `class B` and `class C` becomes virtual base and no duplication of data member `a` is done. In the `main` we display the value of a using a pointer.

/* PROG 9.28 DEMO OF VIRTUAL BASE CLASS VER 2 */

```
#include <iostream.h>
#include <conio.h>

class A
{
public :
    void show( )
    {
        cout<<"hello from show of A"<<endl;
    }
};
class B :public virtual A
{
};
class C :virtual public A
{
};
class D : public B, public C
{
};
void main( )
{
    clrscr( );
    D obj;
    obj.show( );
    getch( );
}
```

OUTPUT :

hello from show of A

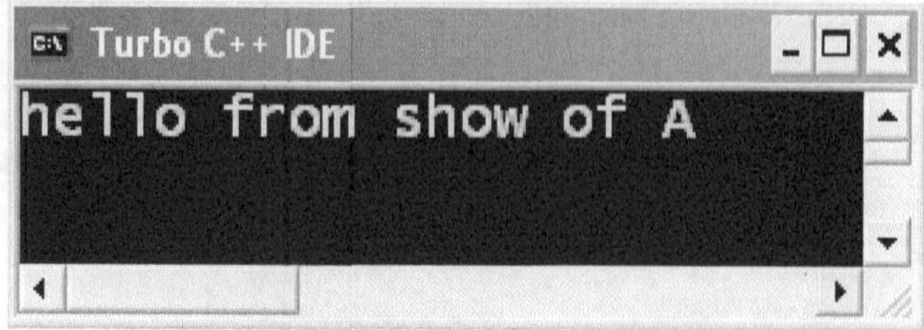

Figure 9.11. *Output screen of program 9.27*

EXPLANATION : In the previous program we were having just one public data member a and here we are having a single public member function show. Rest is simple to understand.

/* PROG 9.29 GENERATING STUDENT REPORT, ELEMENTARY PROGRAM DEVELOPED BY STUDENTS */

```
#include <iostream.h>
#include <conio.h>
#include <stdlib.h>
class student
{
    char sname [20];
    int rollno;
public :
    void input_st( )
    {
        cout<<"Enter student name"<<endl;
        cin.getline(sname,20);
        cout<<"Enter the roll number"<<endl;
        cin>>rollno;
    }
    void show_st( )
    {
        cout<<"\tName :="<<sname<<endl;
        cout<<"\tRoll number :="<<rollno<<endl;
    }
};
class Subject :public student
{
    char subject[25];
public :
    void input_sub( )
    {
        input_st( );
```

```
        cin.ignore( );
        cout<<"Enter the subject name"<<endl;
        cin.getline(subject,25);
    }
    void show_sub( )
    {
        show_st( );
        cout<<"\tSubject="<<subject<<endl;
    }
};
class Internal :virtual public Subject
{
    char subject[25];
protected :
    int i_marks;
public :
    void input_im( )
    {
        cout<<"Enter internal marks (0 to 20)"<<endl;
        cin>>i_marks;
        if(!(i_marks>=0 && i_marks<=20))
        {
            cout<<"Invalid Marks"<<endl;
            exit(0);
        }
    }
    void show_im( )
    {
        cout<<"\tInternal marks="<<i_marks<<endl;
    }
};
class External :virtual public Subject
{
protected :
    int e_marks;
public :
    void input_em( )
    {
        cout<<"Enter External marks (0 to 80)"<<endl;
        cin>>e_marks;
        if(!(e_marks>=0 && e_marks<=80))
```

```
        {
            cout<<"Invalid Marks"<<endl;
            exit(0);
        }
    }
    void show_em( )
    {
        cout<<"\tExternal Marks="<<e_marks<<endl;
    }
};
class Total :public Internal, public External
{
    int total_marks;
public :
    void input( )
    {
        input_sub( );
        input_im( );
        input_em( );
    }
    void show( )
    {
        show_sub( );
        show_im( );
        show_em( );
        total_marks = i_marks + e_marks;
        cout<<"\tTotal Marks="<<total_marks<<endl;
    }
};
void main( )
{
    clrscr( );
    Total tm;
    tm.input( );
    cout<<"\n\t ++++++++++Student Report++++++++\n"<<endl;
        tm.show( );
    getch( );
}
```

OUTPUT :

```
Enter student name
Hari Pandey
Enter the roll number
1001
```

```
Enter the subject name
OOP In C++
Enter internal marks (0 to 20)
18
Enter External marks (0 to 80)
75

        ++++++++++Student Report++++++++
        Name :=Hari Pandey
        Roll number :=1001
        Subject=OOP In C++
        Internal marks =18
        External Marks =75
        Total Marks    =93
```

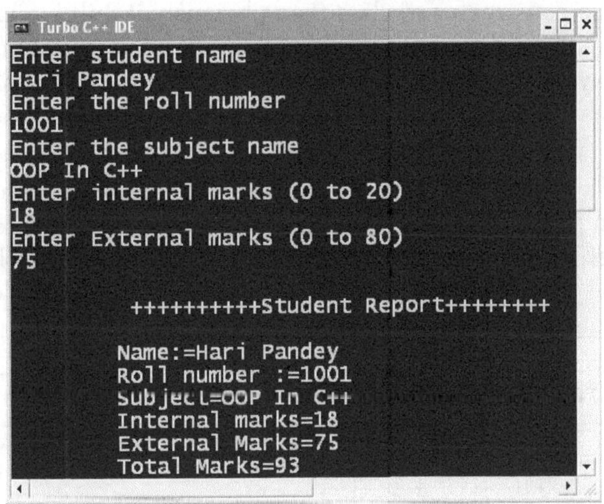

Figure 9.12. *Output screen of the program 9.28*

EXPLANATION : First we show you how the classes in the program are related.

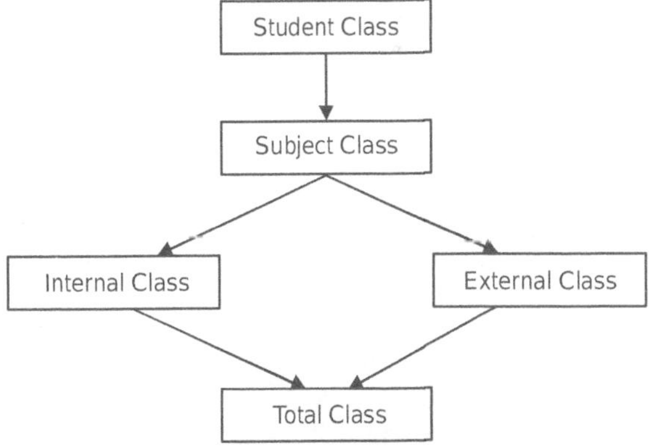

The student class has two private data members sname and **rollno** two **public** member function : **input_st** and **show_st**. This **student** class is inherited by class subject which has just one data member subject and two function **input_sub** and **show_sub**. The function for input and display the student name and roll number are called in the function of this class. The class subject is inherited by class **Internal** and **External** which we have seen earlier. Note both the classes inherit the class Subject in **virtual** public mode so only one copy of data members of class **Subject** will be available in class Total and no ambiguity will arise. Trace the program step wise. It is very simple to understand.

9.7 CONSTRUCTOR AND DESTRUCTOR IN INHERITANCE

When constructors are present both in base and derived classes then how they are called, how values are passed from derived class to base class? That we will see in this section. Assume a small example of single level inheritance in which **class A** is inherited by **class B**. Both the classes have their **default constructors**. When an object of **class B** is created, it calls the constructor of **class B,** but as this **class B** has got **A** as its parent **class**, constructor of **class A** will be called first, then constructor of class then obviously it will be using the data members from base class. Now without calling the constructor of **base class**, data members of base class, unexpected results may follow. Calling a constructor of **base class** first allows base class to properly set up its data members of that they can be used by derived classes.

In case of destructor in inheritance, destructor of derived class is **called first** and then destructor of base class is called. This is so as it is possible that if we call destructor of base class first, destructor might be working with data memebers of base class. So, destroying them in base class has an effect of working with the data members that no longer exist. Compiler won't allow this. That's why destructor class call as first so that it can do its works finishing with any of the data members of class base and do its own cleaning.

/*PROG 9.30 CONSTRUCTOR IN SINGLE LEVEL INHERITANCE VER 1 */

```
#include <iostream.h>
#include <conio.h>
class first
{
public :
    first( )
    {
        cout<<"Hello from con of first"<<endl;
    }
};
class second : first
{
public :
    second( )
    {
```

```
        cout<<"Hello from con of second"<<endl;
    }
};
void main( )
{
    clrscr( );
    second s;
    getch( );
}
```

OUTPUT :

Hello from con of first
Hello from con of second

EXPLANATION : When statement **second s** executes it calls the **default constructor** of **second** class. But as class **first** is base class for **second** constructor of base class is called first, then constructor of derived class is called. So the output is as shown. Note constructors are called implicitly of both the classes by the compiler.

/*PROG 9.31 CONSTRUCTOR IN SINGLE LEVEL INHERITANCE VER 2 */

```
#include <iostream.h>
#include <conio.h>

class first
{
public :
    first( )
    {
        cout<<"Hello from con of first"<<endl;
    }
};

class second :public first
{
public :
    second( ) :first( )
    {
        cout<<"Hello from con of second"<<endl;
    }
};
```

```
void main( )
{
      clrscr( );
      second s;
      getch( );
}
```

OUTPUT :

```
Hello from con of first
Hello from con of second
```

EXPLANATION : Here when default constructor of class second is called. The class second default constructor explicitly calls the constructor of class first. Though this is not necessary as we have seen in the program, but this is another way of calling the constructor of base class.

/* PROG 9.32 CONSTRUCTOR & DESTRUCTOR IN SINGLE LEVEL INHERITANCE VER 1 */

```
#include <iostream.h>
#include <conio.h>

class first
{
public :

      first( )
      {
            cout<<"Hello from con"<<endl;
      }
      ~first( )
      {
            cout<<"Bye Bye from des of first "<<endl;
      }
};
class second : public first
{
public :

      second( ) :first( )
      {
            cout<<"Hello from con of second"<<endl;
      }
```

```
~second( )
    {
        cout<<"Bye Bye from des of second"<<endl;
    }
};

void main( )
{
    clrscr( );
    second s;
    getch( );
}
```

OUTPUT :

Hello from con
Hello from con of second
Bye Bye from des of second
Bye Bye from des of first

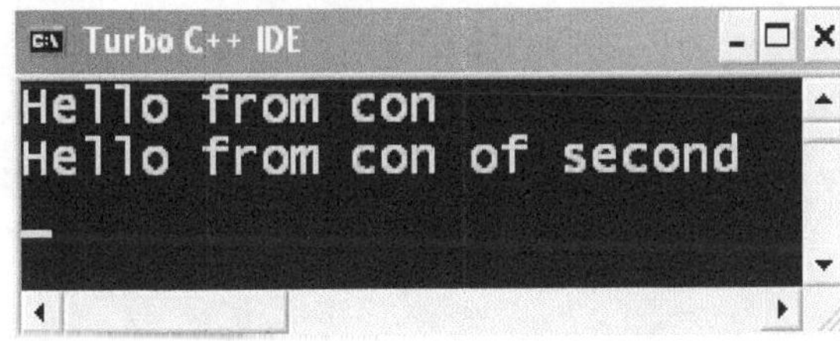

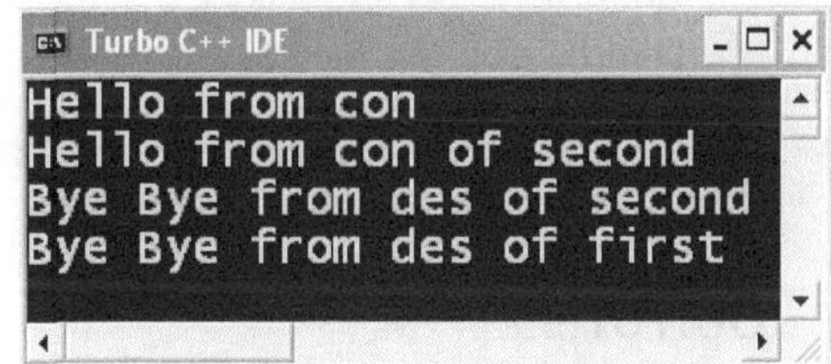

Figure 9.13. *Output screen of program after pressing (Ctrl + F9) and after pressing (Alt + F9)*

EXPLANATION : Destructors are called in the reverse order of constructor. So, destructor of second class will be called first then destructor of first class will be called.

/*PROG 9.33 CONSTRUCTOR IN TWO LEVEL INHERITANCE VER 1*/

```
#include <iostream.h>
#include <conio.h>

class first
{
    public :
        first( )
    {
        cout<<"Hello from con of first"<<endl;
    }
};
```

```
class second :public first
{
public :
    second ( ) : first( )
    {
        cout<<"Hello from con of second "<<endl;
    }
};
class third : second
{
 public :
    third( ) :second ( )
    {
        cout<<"Hello from con of third"<<endl;
    }
};
void main( )
{
    clrscr( );
    third t;
    getch( );
}
```

OUTPUT :

```
Hello from con of first
Hello from con of second
Hello from con of third
```

EXPLANATION : When statement `third t;` executes it calls default constructor of its own class. But before falling into the code default constructor it must call constructor of class `second` which is the base class for class `third`. In the class `second` default constructor, default constructor of class first is called as class first is the base class for class second. So the output as shown above :

/* PROG 9.34 CONSTRUCTOR IN MULTIPLE INHERITANCE VER 1 */

```
#include <iostream.h>
#include <conio.h>

class first
{
public :
```

```
    first ( )
    {
        cout<<"Hello from con first"<<endl;
    }
};
class second
{
public :
    second( )
    {
        cout<<"Hello from con of second"<<endl;
    }
};
class third :second, first
{
public :
    third( )
    {
        cout<<"Hello from con of third"<<endl;
    }
};
void main( )
{
    clrscr( );
    third t;
    getch( );
}
```

OUTPUT :

```
Hello from con of second
Hello from con first
Hello from con of third
```

EXPLANATION : In multiple inheritance constructors of which base class is called determine from the fact that which class was inherited first. Here in the class third, class first and second is inherited as :

class third : second, first

So, constructor of class second will be called first and constructor of first will be called after that. Note if constructor of third class is written as :

```
third ( ) : first( ), second ( )
{
cout<<"Hello from con of third"<<endl;
}
```

Then also constructor of **second** class will be called, followed by constructor of **first** class.

/* PROG 9.35 DEMO OF PARAMETERIZED CONSTRUCTOR IN INHERITANCE VER 1 */

```
#include <iostream.h>
#include <conio.h>
class first
{
    int fa;
public :
    first (int x)
    {
        fa = x;
        cout<<"Con of first called";
    }
    void fshow( )
    {
        cout<<"fa ="<<fa<<endl;
    }
};
class second : public first
{
    int sa;
public :
    second(int a, int b) :first(a)
    {
        sa=b;
        cout<<endl<<"Con of second called"<<endl;
    }
    void sshow( )
    {
        fshow( );
            cout<<"sa="<<sa<<endl;
    }
};
```

```
void main( )
{
      clrscr( );
      second s(10,20);
      s.sshow( );
      getch( );
}
```

OUTPUT :

```
Con of first called
Con of second called
fa =10
sa =20
```

EXPLANATION : When statement `second s (10, 20);` object `s` calls the parameterized constructor of class second and passes parameters `10` and `20`. Inside the constructor they are assigned to `a` and `b`. Before entering into the body of constructor, `first (a)` calls the constructor of class `first` and passes `a` as argument. Inside the class `first` it is assigned to `fa` and `con` of `first` called is displayed. When control enters into the constructor and assigns `b` to `sa`. When `sshow` of class `second` is called, it first calls the `fshow` of class `first`.

/*PROG 9.36 DEMO OF PARAMETERIZED CONSTRUCTOR IN INHERITANCE VER 2*/

```
#include <iostream.h>
#include <conio.h>
class first
{
      int fa;
public :
      first (int x)
      {
            fa=x;
            cout<<" Con of first called"<<endl;
      }
      void fshow( )
      {
            cout<<"fa="<<fa<<endl;
      }
};
class second :public first
{
      int sa;
```

```
public :
    second (int a) : first (a%10), sa(a/10)
    {
        cout<<"Con of second called"<<endl;
    }
    void sshow( )
    {
        fshow( );
        cout<<"sa="<<sa<<endl;
    }
};

void main( )
{
    clrscr( );
    second s(234);
    s.sshow( );
    getch( );
}
```

OUTPUT :

```
Con of first called
Con of second called
fa=4
sa=23
```

EXPLANATION : The program is same in the previous but here we have not taken two arguments for the constructor of class `second`. In the earlier version of this program, by counting the number of arguments in both the classes we chose to keep number of arguments in the constructor of derived class `second`. But here we just take one argument in the constructor of class `second` `234` which `s` collected in formal parameter `a`. From this constructor of `second` class, constructor of `first` class is called passing `a%10` as argument and `a/10` is assigned to `sa` of class second.

/*PROG 9.37 DEMO OF PARAMETERIZED CONSTRUCTOR IN INHERITANCE VER 3 */

```
#include <iostream.h>
#include <conio.h>
#include <string.h>
class first
{
    int fa;
```

```
public :
    first(int x)
    {
        fa=x;
        cout<<"Con of first called"<<endl;
    }
    void fshow( )
    {
        cout<<"fa="<<fa<<endl;
    }
};
class second
{
    int sa;
    float sb;
public :
    second(int a, float b) :sa(a),sb(b)
    {
        cout<<"Con of second called"<<endl;
    }
    void sshow( )
    {
        cout<<"sa="<<sa<<endl;
        cout<<"sb="<<sb<<endl;
    }
};
class third :public first, public second
{
    char str[10];
public :
    third(char*s, int x, int y, float z) :first(x),
        second(y,z)
    {
        strcpy(str,s);
        cout<<"Con of third called"<<endl;
    }
    void tshow( )
    {
        fshow( );
        sshow( );
```

```
        cout<<"str="<<str<<endl;
    }
};
void main( )
{
    clrscr( );
    third t("Welcome",10,20,34.5f);
    t.tshow( );
    getch( );
}
```

OUTPUT :

```
Con of first called
Con of second called
Con of third called
fa=10
sa=20
sb=34.5
str=Welcome
```

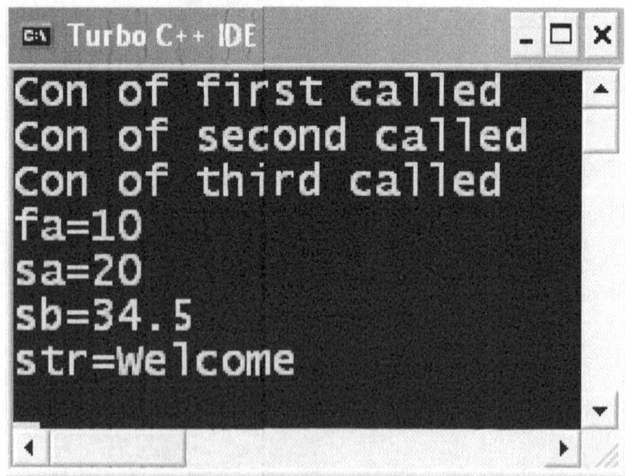

Figure 9.14. *Output screen of program 9.36*

EXPLANATION : When statement `third t ("Welcome", 10, 20, 34.5f);` executes, parameterized constructor of class `third` is called and `("Welcome", 10, 20, 34.5f)` are passed. Inside the constructor of `t` they are collected in formal parameter `s, x, y` and `z` respectively. From the constructor of class `third` constructor of class `first` is called with `x` an assignment. In the class `first` this `x` is assigned to `fa` and cout displays `Con of first called`. Control comes back to constructor of class `third` which now calls constructor of class second passing parameters `y` and `x`. Inside the constructor of class second they are assigned to `sa` and `sb` and `Con of second called` is displayed. When control returns to constructor of class third, it enters into its body and assigns `s` to `str` and displays `Con of third called`.

9.8 CONTAINERSHIP

We can create object of one class into another and that object will be a member of the class. This type of relationship between classes is known as **has_a** relationship as one class contains object of another class. The inheritance which we have seen till now is considered **kind_of** or **is_a** relationship.

/*PROG 9.38 DEMO OF CONTAINERSHIP VER 1*/

```
#include <iostream.h>
#include <conio.h>
class first
{
    public :
        void showf( )
        {
        cout<<"Hello from first"<<endl;
        }
};
class second
{
    first f;
    public :
    second( )
{
    f.showf( );
}
};
void main( )
{
    clrscr( );
    second s;
    getch( );
}
```

OUTPUT :

Hello from first

EXPLANATION : In the `class second` we have an object of `class first`. This is another type of inheritance we are witnessing. This type of inheritance is known as `has_a` relationship as we say that class second has an object of class first as it s member. Form this object f we call the function of `class first`.

/*PROG 9.39 DEMO OF CONTAINERSHIP VER 2*/

```
#include <iostream.h>
#include <conio.h>

class first
{
    private :
        int num;
    public :
        void showf( )
        {
        cout<<"Hello from first"<<endl;
        cout<<"num="<<num<<endl;
        }
        int &getnum( )
        {
        return num;
        }
};
class second
{
    first f;
    public :
    second( )
    {
     f.getnum( )=20;
     f.showf( );
    }
};
void main( )
{
    clrscr( );
    second s;
    getch( );
}
```

OUTPUT :

```
Hello from first
num=20
```

EXPLANATION : With the help of containership we can only use `public` data members/ function of the class but not `protected or private`. In the `first class` we have returned the reference with the help of `getnum` function. In the default constructor of `class second` we assign value of `20 to num` of first class by calling the function getnum. Then we show if we call to `showf`.

/* PROG 9.40 DEMO OF CONTAINERSHIP VER 3 */

```
#include <iostream.h>
#include <conio.h>

class first
{
private :
     int num;
public :
     void showf( )
     {
          cout<<"Hello from first"<<endl;
          cout<<"num="<<num<<endl;
     }
     int &getnum( )
     {
          return num;
     }
};

class second
{
     first f;
public :
     second( )
     {
          f.getnum( )=200;
          f.showf( );
     }
};

void main( )
{
     clrscr( );
     second s;
     getch( );
}
```

OUTPUT :

```
Hello from first
num=20
```

EXPLANATION : With the help of containership we can only use public data member/ function of the class but not protected or private. In the first class we have returned the reference with the help of getnum function. In the default constructor of class second we assign value of 200 to num of first class by calling the function getnum. Then we show if by c call to showf.

9.9 PONDERABLE POINTS

1. Inheritance is the mechanism of deriving new class from an existing class. The old class and new class is known as in pair : super-sub, base-derived, parent-child.
2. In heritance provides the idea of reusability. Code once written can be used again and again in several different classes.
3. C++ provides support for : single level and multilevel inheritance, multiple inheritance, hierarchical inheritance, hybrid inheritance.
4. Private member are never inherited.
5. Virtual base class is used to avoid duplicity of data members into the target derived class.
6. In an inheritance hierarchy constructor of base class is called first, then constructor of derived class is called.
7. In an inheritance hierarchy destructor class is called first, then destructor of base class is called.
8. Containership allows us to use object of one class as a member of other class. This type of containership provides the idea of has_a relationship or nesting of classes.

EXERCISE

A. True and False :

1. Public variables can be accessed from anywhere in the program.
2. Inheritance helps in maintenance of code.
3. A derived class is often called sub-class because it represents a subset of its base class.
4. A pointer to base class can point to an object of a derived class of that base class.
5. If no constructor is specified for a derived class, then object of derived class will use constructor in the base class.
6. An object of derived class cannot access public members of the base class using dot operator.
7. In multiple inheritances, all the constructors are invoked in the reverse of derivation and destructor are invoked in the same order.
8. It is not possible to assign a base class pointer to a derived class object.
9. Sub classes can access protected members of a base class but not private members.
10. When name clash occurs in multiple inheritances, the ambiguity is resolved by using scope resolution operator.
11. A function that is declared as a friend of a base class can be inherited by the derived class.
12. Sub-classes can access private members of a parent class, but not protected members.

13. A protected variable behaves like a private variable within the class but can be inherited as protected in public inheritance.

B. Answer the Following Questions :

1. What is inheritance ? How do we do inheritance in C++ ?
2. Discuss all different types of inheritance C++ supports.
3. What are the main advantages of inheritance ?
4. What is virtual base class ? Why we need it ?
5. Why constructor of derived class calls first than constructor of derived class ?
6. Why destructor of derived class calls first than destructor of base class ?
7. What is the use of protected keyword in inheritance ? Explain.
8. Give an example of hybrid inheritance.
9. Explain the method of resolving ambiguity.

C. Brain Drill :

1. Create a class Country, State, City and Village and arrange them in hierarchical manner.
2. Declare a class Vehicle. From this class derived two_wheeler, three_wheeler and four_wheeler class. Display properties of each type of vehicle using member function of the class.
3. Write a program to declare classes A, B and C. Each class contains one char array as a data member. Apply multiple inheritances. Concatenate strings of class A and B and store it in class C.
4. Imagine a **publishing** company that markets both book and audiocassette versions of its works. Create a class **publication** that stores the title (a **string**) and **price** (type **float**) of publication. From this class derive two classes : **book,** which adds a **page** count (type int); and tape, which adds a playing time in minutes (type float). Each of these three classes should have a **getdata ( )** function to get its data from the user at the keyboard and a **putdata ( )** function to display its data.

   Write a main( ) program to test the book and tape classes by creating instance of them, asking the user to fill in data with getdata( ) and then displaying data with putdata( ).
5. Start with the **publication, book** and **tape** classes of Exercise-4. Add a base class sales that holds an array of three **floats** so that it can record the dollar sales of a particular **publication** for the last three months. Include a **getdata ( )** function to get three sales amounts from the user and a **putdata ( )** function to display the sales figures. After the **book** and **tape** classes so they are derived from both publication and sales. An object of class book or tape should input and output sales data along with its other data. Write a **main ( )** function to create a book object and a tape object and exercise their input/output capabilities.
6. Derive a class called **employee2** from the **employee** class. This new class should add a type **double** data item called **compensation** and, also an **enum** type called **period** to indicate whether the employee is paid hourly, weekly, or monthly. For simplicity you can change the **manager, scientist** and **laborer** classes so they are derived from **employee2** instead of employee. However, note that in many circumstances it might be more in the spirit of OOP to create a separate base class called **compensation** and three new class **manager2, scientist2** and **labour2** and use multiple inheritances to derive these classes from the original **manager, scientist** and **laborer** classes and from **compensation.** This way none of the original classes needs to be modified.

❑❑❑

CHAPTER 10

POINTERS TO OBJECTS AND VIRTUAL FUNCTIONS

10.1 POINTER TO OBJECTS

We have worked with the pointers in the earlier chapters of the book where we worked with pointer to int, char, float and double etc. Similar to pointers to built-in data types we can create pointers to object of class. To create a pointer to an object of class demo we write

```
demo *ptr;
```

Which creates a pointer of type demo class type. Now for an object say d of demo class declared as demo d; we can store address of this object into pointer **ptr** as :

```
ptr = &d;
```

Now any data member or function of demo class can be accessed using pointer as

```
ptr->func_name( ); and ptr->data_member;
```

As the pointer pr contains the address of object d, *ptr denotes object d so we can also write **(*ptr).func_name** and **(*ptr).deat_member;**

We can also create objects dynamically and can store the address into pointer as

```
demo*ptr = new demo;
```

OR

```
demo *ptr;
ptr = new demo;
```

Here, we don't have any object d as in the earlier case. Object will be referred only by pointer pt.

Similarly to pointer to objects we can have a pointer to an array of objects or we can have an array of pointers to objects. To create pointer to an array of objects we can write as :

```
demo d[5];
demo *ptr = d;
```

And dynamically creating an array of object we can write **demo *ptr = new demo [5];** which creates an array of objects of size **5** and returns the base address of this array. The first object will be referred as **ptr [0]**, second as **ptr [1]** and so on. Given below are few examples of what we have studied so far.

/*PROG 10.1 DEMO OF POINTER TO OBJECT VER 1*/

```
#include <iostream.h>
#include <conio.h>

class demo
{
    public :
     void show( )
     {
        cout<<"Hello from show"<<endl;
     }
     void bye_bye( )
     {
        cout<<"BYE BYE"<<endl;
     }
};

void main( )
{
    clrscr( );
    demo d;
    demo*ptr;
    ptr=&d;
    ptr->show( );
    ptr->bye_bye( );
    getch( );
}
```

OUTPUT :

```
Hello from show
BYE BYE
```

EXPLANATION : The statement `demo *ptr;` creates a pointer `ptr` of class `demo` type which can store address of an object of `class demo`. We have created an `object d` of `demo` class and address of this `object d` we have assigned to pointer `ptr` as `ptr = &d.` Whenever we have pointer to an object we can access data members and function using pointer to member operator `->.` Now we have `4 different` ways to call functions of `demo` class using object `d` and pointer `ptr.`

(*a*) d.show( );

(*b*) (&d)->show( );

(*c*) Ptr->show( );

(*d*) (*ptr).show( );

From the above it is clear that &d and ptr is same and **d** and ***ptr** is same. The line

demo *ptr;

ptr = &d;

Can be combined as **demo *pt = &d;**

/*PROG 10.2 DEMO OF POINTER TO OBJECTS VER 2*/

```
#include <iostream.h>
#include <conio.h>

class demo
{
    public :
     void show( )
     {
        cout<<"Hello from show"<<endl;
     }
     void bye_bye( )
     {
        cout<<"BYE BYE"<<endl;
     }
};

void main( )
{
    clrscr( );
    demo *ptr= new demo;
    ptr->show( );
    ptr->bye_bye( );
    getch( );
}
```

OUTPUT :

```
Hello from show
BYE BYE
```

EXPLANATION : The program is similar to previous one with a little difference of just two statements. We have replaced the previous three statements which are given as :

demo d;

demo *ptr;

ptr = &d;

by a single statement demo *ptr = new demo;. Here an object of demo class is created dynamically and returns address is stored in the pointer ptr. Rest is same as explained earlier but note here we have just pointer ptr to refer to an object as object was created dynamically we can refer to dynamically created object by storing its address in a pointer of compatible type. We cannot refer it by name as we had in previous program by d.

/*PROG 10.3 DEMO OF POINTER TO OBJECT VER 3*/

```
#include <iostream.h>
#include <conio.h>
class demo
{
    int dx,dy;
    public :
     demo(int x,int y)
     {
        dx=x;
        dy=y;
     }
     void show( )
     {
        cout<<"dx :="<<dx<<endl;
        cout<<"dy :="<<dy<<endl;
     }
};
void main( )
{
    clrscr( );
    demo *ptr=new demo(10,20);
    (*ptr). show( );
    getch( );
}
```

OUTPUT :

```
dx :=10
dy :=20
```

EXPLANATION : The line `new demo(10,20);` creates a dynamic object by calling the constructor of `demo` class which takes two `int` parameters and returns the address of the dynamically created object which is stored in the pointer. Next we call the function show using `*ptr`.

/*PROG 10.4 DEMO OF POINTER TO OBJECTS VER 4*/

```
#include <iostream.h>
#include <conio.h>
#include <string.h>
#define S 6

class demo
{
      char name [30];
public :
      demo( ){}
      demo(char *s)
      {
         strcpy(name,s);
      }
      void show( )
      {
         cout<<"Name :="<<name<<endl;
      }
};
void main( )
{
      clrscr( );
      demo *ptr=new demo [S];
      demo *temp = ptr;
      int i;
      char s[30];
      for(i=0;i<S;i++)
      {
         cout<<"Enter a number"<<endl;
         cin.getline(s,30);
         ptr[i]=demo(s);
      }
      cout<<"The names are"<<endl;
      for(i=0;i<S;i++)
         temp++->show( );
      delete []ptr;
      getch( );
}
```

OUTPUT :

```
Enter a number
Vijay Nath Pandey
Enter a number
Madhuri Pandey
Enter a number
Anjana Pandey
Enter a number
Man Mohan Pandey
Enter a number
Hari Mohan Pandey
Enter a number
Ranjana Pandey
The names are
Name : =Vijay Nath Pandey
Name : =Madhuri Pandey
Name : =Anjana Pandey
Name : =Man Mohan Pandey
Name : =Hari Mohan Pandey
Name : =Ranjana Pandey
```

EXPLANATION : In the program we have created a pointer to an array of object which is created dynamically in the statement `demo * ptr = new demo [S];` The address of array is saved in temporary variable `temp` as `demo *temp = ptr;` In the `for` loop we take names from the user in `string s` and initialize each dynamically created object using statement

ptr[i] = demo (s);

The entered names are displayed back using for loop as :

```
for(i=0;i<S;i++)
 temp++ -> show( )
```

Initially we assigned `ptr to temp` and now we make use of it. As `temp` contains address of the first object, initially `show` is called for the first object then `temp` is incremented as `temp++`, now `temp` points to the second object and `show` for second object is displayed and so on.

We could simply make use of `ptr` for calling the `show` functions. Why did we take another pointer `temp` ? The answer is simple. If we had used pointer `ptr` for displaying names by a call to show in the end would be pointing somewhere else in the memory and not to the base address of the array. Through it would be ok for this program but if you have to make use of `ptr` later some where in the program then you would not be getting object using `ptr`.

/*PROG 10.5 INITIALIZING ARRAY OF OBJECTS DYNAMICALLY */

```
#include <iostream.h>
#include <conio.h>
```

```
#include <string.h>

class demo
{
    char *name;
public :
    demo( ){}
    demo(char*s)
    {
        name =new char[strlen(s)+1];
        strcpy(name,s);
    }
    void show( )
    {
        cout<<"Name="<<name<<endl;
    }
};
void main( )
{
    demo*ptr[ ]={
                    new demo("Hari Mohan Pandey"),
                    new demo("Man Mohan Pandey"),
                    new demo("Vijay"),
                    new demo("Ranjana"),
     };
    cout<<"The names are"<<endl;
    const int S =sizeof(ptr)/sizeof(demo);
    for(int i=0;i<S;i++)
    {
        ptr[i]->show( );
        delete ptr[i];
    }
    getch( );
}
```

OUTPUT :

```
The names are
Name=Hari Mohan Pandey
Name=Man Mohan Pandey
Name=Vijay
Name=Ranjana
The names are
```

```
Name=Hari Mohan Pandey
Name=Man Mohan Pandey
Name=Vijay
Name=Ranjana
```

EXPLANATION : The following code

```
demo*ptr [ ]={
                    new demo("Hari Mohan Pandey"),
                    new demo("Man Mohan Pandey"),
                    new demo("Vijay"),
                    new demo("Ranjana"),
};
```

Creates four objects dynamically by using `new` operator and calling one argument constructor of `char * type` dynamically. The addresses of each object thus created are stored in the `ptr` array. The `ptr` is an array of objects; `ptr [0]` gives first objects whose data member name has value `"Hari Mohan Pandey"`, `ptr [1]` gives second objects whose data member name has value `"Man Mohan Pandey"` and so on. In the `main` size of `ptr` gives `16` as each pointer is of `4 bytes` long and we have `4` such pointers. The `sizeof (demo)` gives `4` bytes as we have just one pointer variable name data member by a call to show we `delete` the objects created dynamically explicitly by writing `delete ptr[i]`. Note `delete ptr` or `delete [] ptr` won't work.

10.2 THE THIS POINTER

The this pointer is a special pointer which is a built-in pointer. It is a keyword. It stores the address of current object in context. That is the current object which can be referred using this pointer anywhere in the class. The this pointer can be used only inside the class *i.e.*, only inside the member function of the class and cannot be used outside the class. The this pointer is a constant pointer. For an object of say class demo, type of this pointer will be demo* const this. For an object of say class temp, type of this pointer will be temp *const this. When a non static member's function is called for an object, the address of the object is passed as a hidden argument to the function. For example, the following function call

myDate.setMonth (3);

Can be interpreted this ways :

SetMonth (&myDate, 3);

The object's address is available from within the member function as the this pointer. It is legal, through unnecessary, to use this pointer when referring to members of the class. The expression (*this) is commonly used to return the current object from a member function.

→ Important Points About this Pointer

(*a*) It is an implicit pointer used by the system.

(*b*) It stores the address of the current object in reference.

(c) It is a constant pointer to an object.

(d) The object pointed to by the 'this' pointer can be de-referenced and modified.

(e) It can only be used within non static functions of the class.

(f) The this pointer is non modifiable, assignment to this are not allowed.

/*PROG 10.6 DEMO OF this POINTER VER 1*/

```
#include <iostream.h>
#include <conio.h>
#include <string.h>
class Item
{
    char iname[10];
    int icode;
    float iprice;
public :
    Item(char iname[10], int icode, float iprice)
    {
        strcpy(this->iname,iname);
        this->icode = icode;
        (*this).iprice = iprice;
    }
    void show( )
    {
        cout<<"Item Details"<<endl;
        cout<<"Name  ="<<this ->iname <<endl;
        cout<<"Code  ="<<(*this).icode <<endl;
        cout<<"Price  ="<<this->iprice<<endl;
    }
};
void main( )
{
 clrscr( );
    Item I1("Mouse",301,280);
    I1.show( );
    getch( );
}
```

OUTPUT :

```
Item Details
Name=Mouse
Code =301
Price =280
```

EXPLANATION : As explained earlier `this` pointer stores the address of current object in context. In the `main` when object `I1` is created by a call to constructor, `this` pointer is storing the address of object `I1.` Inside the constructor you can note that names of formal parameters and data members are same, then how could we assign say value of formal parameter `icode` to data member's `icode` ? We can't write `icode =icode`. Here the use of `this` pointer come into picture. We know that this pointer is in the function representing `object I1` so writing `this -> icode` represent data members of class for object `I1` and `icode` refers to formal parameter. As this is a pointer we will have to use pointer to member operator `->` with data members or we can use dot operator with `(*this)`. Note writing this is totally optional in the above program but just to give you feel how this pointer can be used we have written this program.

/*PROG 10.7 DEMO OF this POINTER VER 2*/

```
#include <iostream.h>
#include <conio.h>

class demo
{
public :
    demo( )
    {
        cout<<"Default constructor is called"<<endl;
        cout<<"Address of current object="<<this<<endl;
    }
};
void main( )
{
    clrscr( );
    demo d1;
    cout<<"Address of object d1 in main="<<&d1<<endl;
    demo d2;
    cout<<"Address of object d2 in main="<<&d2<<endl;
    getch( );
}
```

OUTPUT :

```
Default constructor is called
Address of current object      =0x8fd5fff4
Address of object d1 in main=0x8fd5fff4
Default constructor is called
Address of current object      =0x8fd5fff2
Address of object d2 in main=0x8fd5fff2
```

EXPLANATION : Initially this pointer contains the address of object d1. So writing this in constructor and writing &d1 displays the same address. When object d2 is the current object this pointer stores the address of current object d2 so writing this in construct and writing &d2 displays the same address.

/*PROG 10.8 DEMO OF this POINTER VER 3*/

```
#include <iostream.h>
#include <conio.h>
class Emp
{
    float sal;
public :
    Emp( )
    {}
    Emp(float s)
    {
        sal=s;
    }
    Emp compare(Emp);
    void show(char *s)
        {
            cout<<s<<" "<<sal<<endl;
        }
    };
    Emp Emp : :compare(Emp E)
    {
        if (this -> sal>E.sal)
            return *this;
        else
            return E;

    }
    void main( )
    {
     clrscr( );
        Emp E1(9500), E2(14000), E3;
        E3=E1.compare(E2);
        E1.show("Sal is=");
        E2.show("Sal is=");
        E3.show("Max sal=");
        getch( );
    }
```

OUTPUT :

```
Sal is= 9500
Sal is= 14000
Max sal= 14000
```

EXPLANATION : In the program salary of object `E1` is `9500` and `E2` is `14000`. This is initialized by calling the one argument constructor. When the statement `E3=E1.compare (E2);` executes `E1` calls the function compare and pass `E2` as argument by value. As `E1` has called the function `E1` is the current object and this pointer is storing the address of object `E1`. Thus object `E1` and `*this` is same. In the function compare as this point to `E1`, the expression this `-> sal` represent `sal of E1`. It could simply be written as `sal` only. Now if `this ->sal` is greater than `E.sal (actually sal of E2)` current object `*this` is returned `else` object `E` is returned.

The alternative code for compare function can be written as :

1.
```
Emp Emp : :compare(Emp E)
{
    Emp temp;
    if (sal>E.sal)
        temp.sal=sal;
            else
                temp.sal=E.sal;
                    return temp;
}
```

2.
```
Emp Emp : :compare(Emp E)
{
    if(this-> sal> E.sal)
        return Emp(this->sal);
            else
                return Emp(E.sal);
}
```

10.3 WHAT IS BINDING IN C++ ?

Binding is the process of linking the function call with the place where the function definition is actually written. So that when a function call is made, it can be ascertained where the control has to be transferred. Binding is also termed as linking. Binding is of two types :

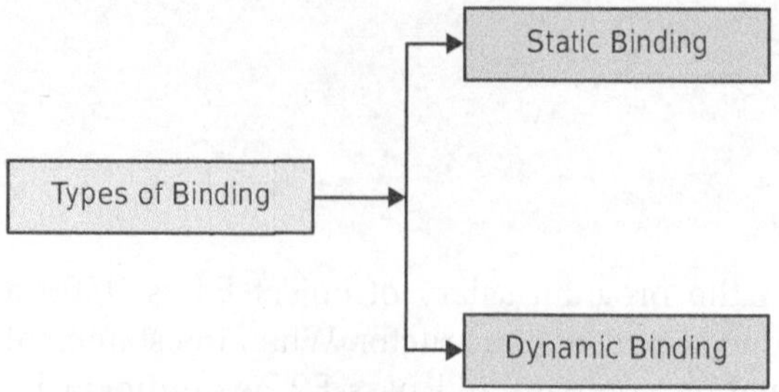

Figure 10.1. *Types of binding in C++*

When it is known at compile time which function will be called in response to a function call, binding is known as static binding, compile time or early binding. Static binding is called so before program executes it is fixed that a particular function be called in response to a function call. Each time program executes same function will be called. As the linking is done early to the execution of the program executes same function will be called. As the linking is done at compile time it is known as compile time binding.

When it is not certain that which function is called in response to a function call, binding is delayed till program executes. At run time the decision is taken as to which function is called in response to a function call. This type of binding is known as late binding, runtime binding or dynamic binding. Dynamic binding is based purely on finding the address of pointers and as addresses are generated during run time or when time run or when program executes, this type of binding is known as run-time or execution time binding.

One form of polymorphism we have seen earlier : compile time polymorphism, which is of two types :

(*a*) Function polymorphism/overloading.

(*b*) Operator Overloading.

Another type of polymorphism we are going to study here is run-time polymorphism in which at run-time it is decided that which function is to be called by checking the pointer and checking the contents of pointers. It is necessary in situations where we have two functions with the same name in both derived class and base class. At run time it will be decided using pointer and objects as to which function of which class is to be called. In C++ run-time polymorphism is implemented using virtual function which is our next topic of discussion.

10.4 VIRTUAL FUNCTIONS

A virtual function is a member function that you except to be redefined in derived classes. When you refer to a derived class object using a pointer or a reference to the base class, you can call a virtual function for that object and execute the derived class's version of the function.

Virtual function is a function which is declared virtual by placing keyword virtual before the function definition/declaration. The virtual function is usually defined in the base classes and is overridden in the derived class. The derived classes as per its requirements override the virtual function and provide the virtual the coding specific to that class only. The derived class is free to decide whether it wants to override the virtual function defined in the base class or to override it. Virtual function behaves like any other member function but they show their importance when accessed via pointers of base class. They are the basis for implementing run-time polymorphism in C++.

The virtual keyword is needed only in the base class's declaration of the function, any subsequent declaration in derived classes are virtual by default.

The derived class's version of a virtual function must have the same parameter list and return type as those of the base class. If these are different, the function is not considered a redefinition of the virtual function. A derived virtual function cannot differ from the original only by return type.

Before delving into the virtual function practically lets first see few examples of pointer to derived class objects.

/*PROG 10.9 DEMO OF POINTER TO DERIVED CLASS OBJECTS VER 1*/

```
#include <iostream.h>
#include <conio.h>

class first
{
public :
    void show( )
    {
        cout<<"Hello from show of first class"<<endl;
    }
};
class second :public first
{
public :
    void show( )
    {
        cout<<"hello from show of second class "<<endl;
    }
};
void main( )
{
        clrscr( );
    first *ptr;
    first f;
    second s;
    ptr=&f;
    ptr->show( );
    ptr=&s;
    ptr->show( );
    getch( );
}
```

OUTPUT :

Hello from show of first class

Hello from show of first class

EXPLANATION : In the program there are `two` classes `first and second`. The `first class` is the `base class` and `second class` is the `derived class` whose parent is the `first class`. The signature of function `show` is same in both the class. In the `main` we create a pointer `ptr` of type `first.` Initially we assign address of object `f` of class `first` and call `show` function. As pointer is of `first` class and address of object `first` class is stored in the `ptr`, function of class `first` is called. Later in the same pointer `ptr` we assign the address of object of class `second` and call function. As class `second` is the derived class for class first and class `first` is the `base class` for class `second;` in a pointer of `base class first` type we can assign the address of an object of `derived class second`. Again the `base class show` *i.e.,* `show` of class `first` is called.

The concept to build here is that in the absence of virtual keyword (discusses later) if we have pointer of base class then regardless of address of object of what type is stored in the pointer, base class version of function is called.

/*PROG 10.10 DEMO OF POINTER TO DERIVED CLASS OBJECTS VER 2*/

```
#include <iostream.h>
#include <conio.h>
class first
{
public :
    void show( )
    {
        cout<<"Hello from show of first class"<<endl;
    }
};
class second :public first
{
public :
    void show( )
    {
        cout<<"Hello from show of second class "<<endl;
    }
};
void main( )
{
    clrscr( );
    first *ptr;
    first f;
    second s;
```

```
    ptr=&f;
    ptr->show( );
    ptr=&s;
    ((second*)ptr)->show( );
    getch( );
}
```

OUTPUT :

Hello from show of first class
Hello from show of second class

EXPLANATION : In the statement `((second*) ptr) ->show ( );` we have typecast pointer `ptr` to behave like pointer of `class second` type temporarily. So it calls the `derived class` version of `show` *i.e.,* function `show` of `second class` is called.

Now you have understood how in the pointer of `base class` we can store the address of `derived class` object. But functions of only `base class` can be called in case function of base class is `overridden` in the `derived class`. Note you cannot store address of base class object in a pointer of derived class.

Let's now see the pratical examples of virtual functions.

/*PROG 10.11 DEMO OF VIRTUAL FUNCTION VER 1*/

```
#include <iostream.h>
#include <conio.h>
class first
{
public :
    virtual void show( )
    {
        cout<<"Hello from show of first class"<<endl;
    }
};
class second :public first
{
public :
    void show( )
    {
        cout<<"Hello from show of second class"<<endl;
    }
};
void main( )
{
```

```
        clrscr( );
        first *ptr;
        first f;
        second s;
        ptr  =&f;
        ptr- >show( );
        ptr  =&s;
        ptr- >show( );
        getch( );
    }
```

OUTPUT :

Hello from show of first class

Hello from show of second class

EXPLANATION : In the class `first` function `show` is `virtual.` When `virtual` keyword precedes the function definition and the same function is `overridden` in the `derived class` lets see what happens when we call them as we did in the earlier program. Initially `ptr` contains the address of `object f` which is of type `class first`. When `ptr-> show()` executes run time system does not check the type of pointer instead it checks what type of object's address the pointer contains. Here pointer `ptr` is storing the address of `object f` which is of `first class` so function call `ptr->show()` calls the `show` function of `first class`. In the second case we have `ptr` storing the address of object of `class second`. Again the C++ run time system checks the contents of `ptr` and at this time `ptr` contains the address of object of class `second` the function call `ptr->show()` calls the `show` function of `class second`.

The concept to build here is that when virtual keyword is present, function is called by checking the contents of pointer of the base class and not by checking the type of pointer.

/*PROG 10.12 DEMO OF VIRTUAL FUNCTION VER 2*/

```
#include <iostream.h>
#include <conio.h>

class first
{
public :
    virtual void show( )
    {
        cout<<"Hello from show of first class"<<endl;
    }
    void display( )
    {
        cout<<"Hello from display of first class"<<endl;
```

```
	}
};
class second :public first
{
public :
	void show( )
	{
		cout<<"Hello from show of second class"<<endl;
	}
	void display( )
	{
		cout<<"Hello from display of second class"<<endl;
	}
};

void main( )
{
	clrscr( );
	first *ptr;
	first f;
	second s;
	ptr=&f;
	ptr->show( );
	ptr->display( );
	ptr=&s;
	ptr->show( );
	ptr->display( );
	getch( );
}
```

OUTPUT :

```
Hello from show of first class
Hello from display of first class
Hello from show of second class
Hello from display of first class
```

EXPLANATION : The function `show` is virtual and is overridden in the derived class `second`. The function display is not `virtual` in the `base class first`. So in the `main` after the statements

```
ptr=&f;
ptr->show( );
ptr-> display( );
```

show() of class first is called and display of class first is also called. When the following statement executes as :

```
ptr = &s;
ptr ->show( );
ptr -> display ( );
```

show of class second is called as show is virtual in the class second and by checking the contents of pointer ptr function will be called. As display is not virtual in the base first, function will be called by checking the type of pointer so display of class first will be called.

10.5 WORKING OF A VIRTUAL FUNCTION

We have seen how the function called at run time depending upon type of object stored in the base class pointer in case of virtual functions. What ever we have learnt seems quite easy to understand but how things happen internally is yet to understand. Here, we will discuss how actual function is called at run time.

Whenever a virtual function is created in a class, a **VTABLE (virtual table)** is created for that class and for all classes that inherit this class. Inside the VTABLE addresses of all virtual functions are stored. If any derived class overrides the virtual functions defined in the base class, address of derived class function is written to the VTABLE of the derived class. If derived class does not override the virtual function then address of virtual function of base class is put inside the VTABLE.

A special pointer called **vptr (called virtual pointer)** points to the first entry of the **VTABLE.** When function is called from a base class pointer compiler checks the contents of the pointer. The contents will be the address of the object base or derived. From this object address, address of VPTR is obtained. Once address of VPTR is known appropriate function can be called from VTABLE for that class.

But whenever I have given in the above is totally maintained by the compiler internally. You need not worry about how this is done internally. But you must know VPTR and VTABLE and how virtual function is called.

/*PROG 10.13 DEMO OF VIRTUAL FUNCTION VER 3*/

```
#include <iostream.h>
#include <conio.h>
class first
{
public :
    virtual void show( )
    {
        cout<<"Hello from show of first class"<<endl;
    }
    virtual void display( )
    {
```

```
        cout<<"Hello from display of first class"<<endl;
    }
    void fun( )
    {
        cout<<"Hello from fun of first"<<endl;
    }
};
class second :public first
{
public :
    void show( )
    {
        cout<<"Hello from show of second class"<<endl;
    }
    void fun( )
    {
        cout<<"Hello from fun of second class"<<endl;
    }
};
class third :public first
{
public :
    void display( )
    {
        cout<<"Hello from display of third class"<<endl;
    }
    void fun( )
    {
        cout<<"Hello from fun of third class"<<endl;
    }
};

void main( )
{
    clrscr( );
    first *ptr;
    first f;
    second s;
    third t;
    ptr= &f;
    ptr->show( );
```

```
    ptr->display( );
    ptr->fun( );
    ptr=&s;
    ptr->show( );
    ptr->display( );
    ptr->fun( );
    ptr=&t;
    ptr->show( );
    ptr->display( );
    ptr->fun( );
    getch( );
}
```

OUTPUT :

```
Hello from show of first class
Hello from display of first class
Hello from fun of first
Hello from show of second class
Hello from display of first class
Hello from fun of first
Hello from show of first class
Hello from display of third class
Hello from fun of first
```

EXPLANATION : The explanation is based on the basis of VPTR and VTABLE. The function show and display is virtual in class first and fun is not virtual. The class second only overrides fun and show. The class third overrides display and fun. The VTABLE for all three classes is as shown below. Note the addresses of different functions in the VTABLE. The VTABLE for the class first need no explanation. The class second overrides virtual function show but does not override display so in the VTABLE for second class address of show of second class and address of display of first class is put. Similarly for the VTABLE of class third address of show of first class and address of display of third class is put. For all three VTABLE a separate VPTR is present.

In the code shown above when ptr contains the address of object f, compiler from the contents of ptr, find out the addresses of VPTR of class first and functions of class first are called.

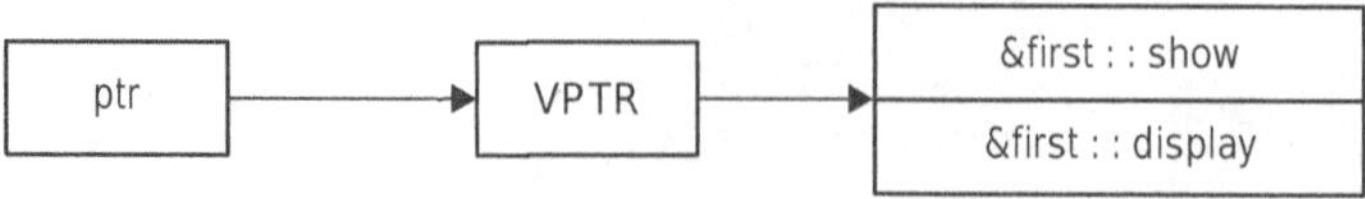

When **ptr** contains the address of **object s**, compiler from the contents of **ptr**, find out the address of **VPTR** of class second and function from **VTABLE** of second gets called.

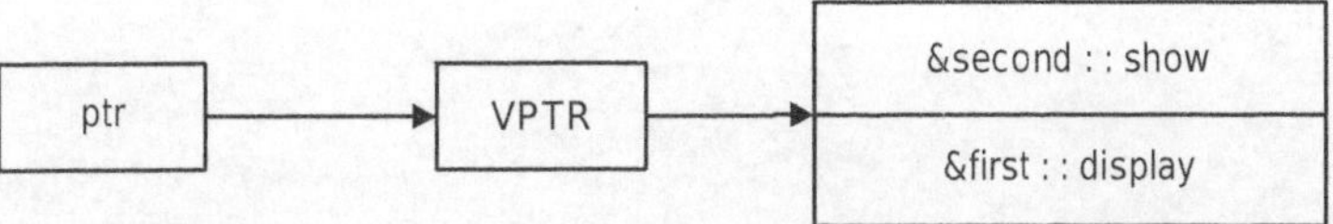

When ptr contains the address of object t, compiler from the contents of ptr, find out the address of VPTR of class third and functions from VTABLE of third gets called.

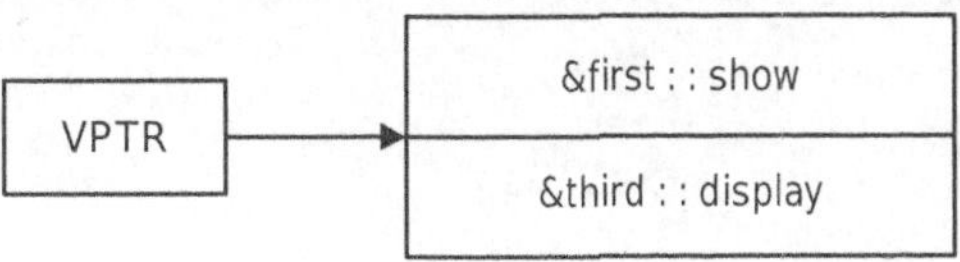

Note fun was not virtual in the first class so regardless of what the pointer ptr contains fun of first will be called.

/*PROG 10.14 DEMO OF VIRTUAL FUNCTION VER 3 */

```
#include <iostream.h>
#include <conio.h>
class first
{
public :
    virtual void show( )
    {
        cout<<"Hello from show first class"<<endl;
    }
    void display( )
    {
        cout<<"Hello from display of first class"<<endl;
    }
};
class second :public first
{
};
void main( )
{
    clrscr( );
    first *ptr;
    first f;
    second s;
    ptr=&f;
    ptr->show( );
    ptr->display( );
    ptr=&s;
    ptr->show( );
```

```
        ptr->display( );
        getch( );
    }
```

OUTPUT :

```
Hello from show first class
Hello from display of first class
Hello from show first class
Hello from display of first class
```

EXPLANATION : When the functions are not present in the derived class regardless of virtual keyword or not, base class version of functions are called. So the output.

/*PROG 10.15 DEMO OF VIRTUAL FUNCTION VER 4*/

```
#include <iostream.h>
#include <conio.h>
class first
{
public :
    virtual void show( )
    {
        cout<<"Hello from show of first class"<<endl;
    }
    virtual void display( )
    {
        cout<<"Hello from display of first class"<<endl;
    }
    void fun( )
    {
        cout<<"Hello from fun of first"<<endl;
    }
};
class second :public first
{
public :
    virtual void show( )
    {
        cout<<"Hello from show of second class"<<endl;
    }
    virtual void fun( )
    {
```

```
        cout<<"Hello from fun of second class"<<endl;
    }
};
void main( )
{
    clrscr( );
    first *ptr;
    first f;
    second s;
    ptr=&f;
    ptr->show( );
    ptr->display( );
    ptr->fun( );
    ptr=&s;
    ptr->show( );
    ptr->display( );
    ptr->fun( );
    getch( );
}
```

OUTPUT :

```
Hello from show of first class
Hello from display of first class
Hello from fun of first
Hello from show of second class
Hello from display of first class
Hello from fun of first
```

EXPLANATION : In the following statements it is clear that all the functions of `class first` will be called :

```
ptr=&f;
ptr->show( );
ptr->display( );
ptr->fu( );
```

Writing the function virtual again when overriding in the derived class `second` makes function virtual for the next class if this class is inherited. `show` was virtual in the `first` class and is overridden in the second class so `show` of second class will be called. `fun` was not virtual in the `first` class so fun of class `first` will be called. The function `display` is present only in the class `first` so obviously it will be called. So the output.

/*PROG 10.16 DEMO OF VIRTUAL FUNCTION VER 5 */

```
#include <iostream.h>
#include <conio.h>
class first
{
public :
    virtual void show( )
    {
        cout<<"Hello from show of first class"<<endl;
    }
};
class second :public first
{
public :
    void show( )
    {
        cout<<"Hello from show of second class"<<endl;
    }
};
class third :public first
{
public :
    void show( )
    {
        cout<<"Hello from show of second class"<<endl;
    }
    void fun( )
    {
        cout<<"Hello from fun of third class"<<endl;
    }
};
void main( )
{
    clrscr( );
    first *ptr;
    first f;
    second s;
    third t;
    ptr=&f;
    ptr-> show( );
```

```
    ptr->fun( ); //line 1
    ptr=&s;
    ptr->show( );
    ptr->fun( ); //line 2
    ptr=&t;
    ptr->show( );
    ptr->fun( ); //line 3
    getch( );
}
```

OUTPUT :

ERROR IN THE PROGRAM

EXPLANATION : The function fun is not present in the first class. So the line 1, 2 and 3 causes error in the program.

/*PROG 10.17 DEMO OF VIRTUAL FUNCTION VER 6*/

```
#include <iostream.h>
#include <conio.h>
class first
{
public :
    void show( )
    {
        cout<<"Hello from show of first class"<<endl;
    }
};
class second : public first
{
public :
    virtual void show( )
    {
        cout<<"Hello from show of second class"<<endl;
    }
};

class third :public second
{
public :

    void show( )
```

```
    {
        cout<<"Hello from show of third class"<<endl;
    }
};
void main( )
{
    clrscr( );
    first *fptr;
    first f;
    second s, *sptr;
    third t;
    fptr=&f;
    fptr->show( );
    fptr=&s;
    fptr->show( );
    sptr=&s;
    sptr->show( );
    sptr=&t;
    sptr->show( );
    getch( );
}
```

OUTPUT :

```
Hello from show of first class
Hello from show of first class
Hello from show of second class
Hello from show of third class
```

EXPLANATION : The function `show` is not virtual in the class `first` and `first` is the `base class` for `class second`. So the statement

```
fptr=&s;
fptr->show( );
```

Executes `show` of class `first` will be called. The `class second` is the base class for `class third`. In `class second show` is virtual and this `show` in class `third` is overridden. In the statement

```
sptr=&s;
sptr->show( );
```

`sptr` contains the address of second class object so function `show` of class second is called. In the following statements as :

```
sptr=&t;
sptr->show( );
```

`sptr` contains the address of object of `class third`. As show is virtual in the class `second` so function of class `third` will be called.

10.6 RULES FOR VIRTUAL FUNCTION

There are some rules for using virtual functions. You must keep these rules in your mind when you are dealing with virtual functions failing which compiler may flash errors. The rules are :

1. They cannot be declared outside the class *i.e.*, must be member of some class.
2. They can be called using object pointers and even using objects but actual works can be seen only with pointers.
3. They cannot be declared as static.
4. Virtual constructor is not possible but we can have virtual destructor.
5. A virtual function can be friend to another class.
6. Making a virtual function in base class is simply a choice for the derived class. The derived class may or may not override virtual function of the base class.
7. In the absence of virtual keyword, the function to be invoked is determined by the type of pointer. The compiler does not check what type of object is stored in the pointer.
8. When virtual keyword is present, functions are called on the basis of which type of object pointer hold in it.
9. Never use ++ or -- operator on pointer of base class pointer to get the next object of derived class. It will only forward/backward the pointer relative to its own class type.
10. Pointers follow the hierarchy of inheritance and pay regards to the older. That is, we can store in a pointer of base class address of any derived class object, but in a pointer of derived class we cannot store object of first class.

10.7 PURE VIRTUAL FUNCTION AND ABSTRACT CLASS

A pure virtual function is a function which has its body set to 0 *i.e.*, the pure virtual function does not have any body. A function declared in a way as shown :

```
virtual void set ( ) =0;
```

is known as pure virtual function. Here = 0 does not mean that function show is equal to 0. It simply means that the virtual function show has no body. The pure virtual function act as an interface and any class which inherits the class in which pure virtual function is present, has to provide the implementation for the function show.

Any class which contains at least a pure virtual function is termed as an abstract class. An abstract class is a class whose objects cannot be created. As its objects cannot be created, this class has to be inherited by some other class. The derived class must define the implementation of all the pure virtual function presents in the class. If the derived class does not define all the pure virtual function than derived class also becomes abstract class. It is not necessary that all functions in an abstract class must be pure virtual. An abstract class may have other virtual or non-virtual functions, data members which may be used by the objects of derived classes. As said earlier objects of an abstract class cannot be created but pointers and references of an abstract class can be created.

The concept behind abstract class is to force derived classes to redefine pure virtual functions as per their requirements and features they posses.

/*PROG 10.18 DEMO OF PURE VIRTUAL FUNCTION VER 1*/

```
#include <iostream.h>
#include <conio.h>

class first
{
public :
    void virtual show( )=0;
};
class second :public first
{
public :
    void show( )
    {
        cout<<"show of second class"<<endl;
    }
};
void main( )
{
    first *ptr=new second;
    ptr->show( );
    getch( );
}
```

OUTPUT :

```
show of second class
```

EXPLANATION : The declaration `void virtual show()=0;` tells the compiler that **show** is a **pure virtual function** as function show has no body. In other way body is equal to **0.** This makes class first as **abstract class** whose objects cannot be created but pointer & references can be. Any class which inherits an abstract class has to provide the definition of function show. The class `second` inherits class first and provide the definition for show. In the main we create a pointer of first and in it assign the address of dynamically created object of second class. Later we call function show. Show of class **second** will be called.

/*PROG 10.19 DEMO OF PURE VIRTUAL FUNCTION VER 2*/

```
#include <iostream.h>
#include <conio.h>
class first
{
public :
```

```
    void virtual show( )=0;
};
class second :public first
{
public :
    void show( )
    {
        cout<<"Show of second"<<endl;
    }
};
class third :public first
{
};
void main( )
{
    first *ptr=new second;
    ptr->show( );
    ptr=new third; // line causes error
    ptr->show( );
}
```

OUTPUT :

ERROR MESSAGE
Cannot create instance of abstract class 'third'

EXPLANATION : The class first has one pure virtual function show, so class first becomes abstract class. The class second inherits class first and provides implementation of function show. The class third also inherits function first but does not provide implementation of show, so class third becomes abstracts class. In the main we are trying to create object of third class which is an abstract class. This causes error as we cannot create object of an abstract class.

/*PROG 10.20 DEMO OF PURE VIRTUAL FUNCTION VER 3*/

```
#include <iostream.h>
#include <conio.h>
class first
{
public :
    void virtual show( )=0;
};
class second :public first
{
```

```
public :
    void show( )
    {
        cout<<"Show of second"<<endl;
    }
};
class third :public first
{
public :
    void show( )
    {
        cout<<"Show of third"<<endl;
    }
};
void main( )
{
    clrscr( );
    second s;
    third t;
    int i;
    first *ptr[]={&s,&t};
    for(i=0;i<2;i++)
        ptr[i]->show( );
    getch( );
}
```

OUTPUT :

```
Show of second
Show of third
```

EXPLANATION : Both class `second` and class `third` provides the implementation for `pure virtual` function `show`. In the `main` we create an object of class `second s` and an object of class `third t`. We create an array of pointers of class `first` type and in it store the addresses of object `s` and object `t`. As class `first` is the `base class` for both classes `second` and class `third`, we can do the following operation :

```
first *ptr [ ] = {&s, &t};
```

In the for loop when `i=0` we have the expression `ptr[0]->show` as `ptr[0]` contains the address of `second` class object so show of `second` class is called. When `i=1` we have the expression `ptr[1] ->show` as `ptr[1]` contains the address of `third` class object so `show` of `third` class is called.

/*PROG 10.21 DEMO OF PURE VIRTUAL FUNCTION VER 4*/

```
#include <iostream.h>
#include <conio.h>
class first
{
public :
    void virtual show( )=0;
};
class second :public first
{
public :
    void show( )
    {
        cout<<"Show of second"<<endl;
    }
};
class third :public first
{
public :
    void show( )
    {
        cout<<"Show of third"<<endl;
    }
};
void main( )
{
    clrscr( );
    second s;
    third t;
    int i;
    first & fref1=s;
    first & fref2=t;
    fref1.show( );
    fref2.show( );
    getch( );
}
```

OUTPUT :

```
Show of second
Show of third
```

EXPLANATION : The program is similar to previous one with the difference that instead of pointer we have created two reference variables of class `first` type and in them assigned the reference object of class `second` and class `third` as shown below :

```
first & fref1 =s;
first & fref2 = t;
```

So when `fref1.show ();` executes show of class second is called and when `fref2.show ();` executes `show` of class `third` is called.

/*PROG 10.22 DEMO OF PURE VIRTUAL FUNCTION VER 5 */

```
#include <iostream.h>
#include <conio.h>

class first
{
public :
      void virtual show( )=0;
      void disp( )
      {
          cout<<"Display of first"<<endl;
      }
      virtual void silly( )
      {
 cout<<"Silly of first"<<endl;
      }
};

class second :public first
{
public :
      void show( )
      {
          cout<<"Show of second"<<endl;
      }
      void disp( )
      {
          cout<<"Display of second"<<endl;
      }
};

class third : public first
{
```

```
public :
    void show( )
    {
        cout<<"Show of third"<<endl;
    }
    void silly( )
    {
        cout<<"silly of third"<<endl;
    }
};

void main( )
{
    clrscr( );
    second s;
    third t;
    int i;
    first *ptr[ ]={&s,&t};
    for(i=0;i<2;i++)
    {
        ptr[i]->show( );
        ptr[i]->silly( );
        ptr[i]->disp( );
    }
    getch( );
}
```

OUTPUT :

```
Show of second
Silly of first
Display of first
Show of third
silly of third
Display of first
```

EXPLANATION : The program demonstrates the fact that apart from creating a **pure virtual function** to make a class as an abstract, **we may write simply ordinary function also in an abstract class**. In the class first there are three functions :

(*a*) **show( )** which is **pure virtual function**,

(*b*) **disp ( )** which is an **ordinary function**

(*c*) **silly ( )** which is a **virtual function**.

The class **second** provides implementation of function **show** and overriding function **disp.**

The class **third** also provide implementation of function **show** and overrides **silly** function which was in **class first.**

In the **main** we assign addresses of object of class **second** and class **third** to an array of pointer of first class as :

first *ptr [ ] = (&s, &t};

In the **for** loop for **i=0; ptr[0]** refers to an object of **second** class type now for the following function calls.

ptr[0]->show( );

ptr[0]->silly( );

ptr[0]->disp ( );

show of class **second** will be called as it is quite obvious from the code. **Silly** was **virtual** in class first and was not overridden in class second so silly of class first will be called. **disp** was not overridden in class **second** and **disp** was not virtual in class first, so **disp** of class **first** will be called.

Now for **i = 1, ptr[1]** refers to an object of **third** class type. For the following function calls

ptr[1] ->show( );

ptr[1]->silly( );

ptr[1]->disp( );

show of class **third** will be called as it is quite obvious from the code. **silly** was **virtual** in classs **first** and was overridden in class **third**, so silly of class **third** will be called. **disp** was not overridden in class **third** and **disp** was not virtual in class first, so **disp** of class **first** will be called.

/*PROG 10.23 FINDING FLYING STATUS OF VARIOUS INSECTS */

```
#include <iostream.h>
#include <conio.h>

class Insect
{
public :
    virtual void flystatus( )=0;
};
class Cockroach :public Insect
{
public :
    void flystatus( )
    {
        cout<<"Cockroach can fly"<<endl;
    }
};
```

```
class Termite :public Insect
{
public :
    void flystatus( )
    {
        cout<<"Termite cannot fly"<<endl;
    }
};
class Grasshopper :public Insect
{
public :
    void flystatus( )
    {
        cout<<"Grasshopper can fly"<<endl;
    }
};
class Ant : public Insect
{
public :
    void flystatus( )
    {
        cout<<"Ant cannot fly"<<endl;
    }
};
void main( )
{
    clrscr( );
    Insect *ptr[4];
    ptr[0]=new Cockroach;
    ptr[1]=new Termite;
    ptr[2]=new Grasshopper;
    ptr[3]=new Ant;
    for(int i=0;i<4;i++)
        ptr[i]->flystatus( );
    getch( );
}
```

OUTPUT :

```
Cockroach can fly
Termite cannot fly
Grasshopper can fly
Ant cannot fly
```

EXPLANATION : The class **Insect** declares one **pure virtual function flystatus**. Any class which inherits this class has to redefine this function and tell his/her flying status *i.e.*, whether he/she can fly or not. This class **Insect** is inherited by **4 different** classes viz **Cockroach, Termite, Grasshopper and Ant**. Each class does provide implementation of function **flystatus**. In the **main** function we create an array of pointer **ptr** of class **Insect** type. In each location of this array we assign dynamically created objects of various derived classes as shown :

```
ptr[0]=new Cockroach;
ptr[1]=new Termite;
ptr[2]=new Grasshopper;
ptr[3]=new Ant;
```

In the **for** loop when we call **flystatus** function using this pointer array **ptr**, respective **flystatus** fuctions of each class is called.

/*PROG 10.24 TO FIND THE COLOR OF VEGETABLE AND WHERE THEY GROW */

```
#include <iostream.h>
#include <conio.h>

class Vegetable
{
public :
    virtual void color( )=0;
    virtual void wh_grow( )=0;
};
class Spanich :public Vegetable
{
public :
    void color( )
    {
        cout<<"Color of spinach is green"<<endl;
    }
    void wh_grow( )
    {
        cout<<"Spinach grows above ground"<<endl;
    }
};
class Potato :public Vegetable
{
public :
    void color( )
    {
        cout<<" Color of Potato is white"<<endl;
    }
```

```
    void wh_grow( )
    {
        cout<<"Potato grows underground"<<endl;
    }
};
class Onion :public Vegetable
{
public :
    void color( )
    {
        cout<<"Color of Onion is red "<<endl;
    }
    void wh_grow( )
    {
        cout<<"Onion grows underground"<<endl;
    }
};
class Tomato :public Vegetable
{
public :
    void color( )
    {
        cout<<"Color of Tomato is red"<<endl;
    }
    void wh_grow( )
    {
        cout<<"Tomato grows above ground"<<endl;
    }
};
void main( )
{
    clrscr( );
    Vegetable *ptr[4];
    ptr[0]=new Spanich;
    ptr[1]=new Potato;
    ptr[2]=new Onion;
    ptr[3]=new Tomato;
    for(int i=0;i<4;i++)
    {
        ptr[i]->color( );
        ptr[i]->wh_grow( );
```

```
    }
    getch( );
}
```

OUTPUT :

```
Color of spinach is green
Spinach grows above ground
Color of Potato is white
Potato grows under ground
Color of Onion is red
Onion grows under ground
Color of Tomato is red
Tomato grows above ground
```

EXPLANATION : The class vegetable declares two pure virtual functions. The function color is for finding the color of the vegetable and wh_grow for finding where the vegetable grows underground or above ground. Any class which inherits the Vegetable class has to redefined these functions and tell what the color of vegetable is and where it grows. This class Vegetable is inherited by 4 different classes viz Spinach, Potato, Onion and Tomato. Each class does provide implementation of both the functions. In the main we create an array of pointer of ptr of class Vegetable type. In each location of this array we assign dynamically created objects of various derived classes as shown :

ptr[0]=new Spanich;

ptr[1]=new Potato;

ptr[2]=new Onion;

ptr[3]=new Tomato;

/*PROG 10.25 CHECKING WHETHER SWEET CONTAINS MAWA AS ITS MAIN INGREDIENT */

```
#include <iostream.h>
#include <conio.h>

class Sweet
{
public :
    virtual void mawastatus( )=0;
};
class Burfi :public Sweet
{
public :
    void mawastatus( )
    {
```

```
        cout<<"Burfi has mawa as one of its main ingredient"<<endl;
    }
};
class Kajukatli :public Sweet
{
public :
    void mawastatus( )
    {
        cout<<"Kajukatli does not have mawa as one of its main ingredient"<<endl;
    }
};
class Jalebee :public Sweet
{
public :
    void mawastatus( )
    {
        cout<<"Jalebee does not have mawa as one of its main ingredient"<<endl;
    }
};
class Rasgulla :public Sweet
{
public :
    void mawastatus ( )
    {
        cout<<"Rasgulla does not have mawa as one of its main ingredient "<<endl;
    }
};
void main( )
{
    clrscr( );
    Burfi B;
    Kajukatli k;
    Jalebee J;
    Rasgulla R;
    Sweet *ptr[4]={&B,&k,&J,&R};
    for(int i=0;i<4;i++)
    {
        ptr[i]->mawastatus( );
    }
    getch( );
}
```

OUTPUT :

```
Burfi has mawa as one of its main ingredient
Kajukatli does not have mawa as one of its main ingredient
Jalebee does not have mawa as one of its main ingredient
Rasgulla does not have mawa as one of its main ingredient
```

EXPLANATION : The class **Sweet** declares one **pure virtual** function **mawastatus**. Any classs which inherits this class has to redefine this function and tell whether they contain mawa as one of its main ingredients. This class **Sweet** is inherited by **4 different** class viz **Burfi, Kajukatli, Jalebee and Rasgulla**. Each class does provide implementation of function **mawastatus**. In the **main** we create an array of pointer **ptr** of class **Sweet** type. We also create an object of the **4 derived classes**. In the pointer array **ptr**, we assign the addresses of theses objects.

```
Burfi B;
Kajukatli k;
Jalebee J;
Rasgulla R;
Sweet *ptr[4]={&B,&k,&J,&R};
```

In the **for** loop when we call the function **mawastatus** using the pointer **array ptr**, respective **mawastatus** function of each class is called.

10.8 OBJECT SLICING

Object slicing is a process of removing off the derived portion of the object when an object of derived class is assigned to a base class object. Only the base class data are copied to derived class object. Consider the following two classes :

```
class A
{
public :
    int Ax, Ay;
};
class B :public A
{
public :
    int Bx;
};
```

Through inheritance public **data members Ax and Ay** of class **A** are copied to class **B**. When in the **main** we write as :

```
B b1; A a1;
a1=b1;
```

Only the data members of object **b1** which were inherited from **class A** are assigned to **object a1.** The data member **Bx** of object **b1** is not copied. That is we say that **object b1** was sliced off.

/*PROG 10.26 DEMO OF OBJECT SLICING VER 1*/

```
#include <iostream.h>
#include <conio.h>

class demo
{
public :
    void show_demo( )
    {
        cout<<"Hello from show of demo"<<endl;
    }
};
class der_demo :public demo
{
public :
    void show_der( )
    {
        cout<<"Hello from show of der_demo"<<endl;
    }
};
void main( )
{
    clrscr( );
    demo d1;
    der_demo d2;
    d1=d2;
    d1.show_der( );
    getch( );
}
```

OUTPUT :

ERROR MESSAGE

'show_der' is not a member of 'demo'

EXPLANATION : In the **main** function when an **object d2** of derived class **der_demo** is assigned to an object **d1** of **base class demo**. Only the inherited portion of **base class** is assigned to **d1**. Through function are usually not part of the object but a function of one class can be called from object of that class or from objects of derived class. Here from **d1**, we cannot call the function **show_der** of derived class.

/*PROG 10.27 DEMO OF OBJECT SLICING VER 2*/

```
#include <iostream.h>
#include <conio.h>

class demo
{
public :
    int bx,by;
    demo(int x,int y)
    {
        bx=y;
        by=y;
    }
    demo( ){}
};
class der_demo :public demo
{
public :
    int dx;
    der_demo(int x,int y,int z) :demo(x,y),dx(z)
    {
    }
};
void main( )
{
    clrscr( );
    der_demo d2(10,20,30);
    demo d1;
    d1=d2;
    cout<<d1.bx<<"\t"<<d1.by<<"\t"<<d1.dx;
    getch( );
}
```

OUTPUT :

ERROR MESSAGE

'dx';is not a member of demo

EXPLANATION : The class demo consists of two data members bx and by and der_demo has just one data member dx. When in the main we write d1=d2, only the inherited data members bx and by are assigned to object d1. The data member dx from d2 is not assigned to d1. In the effect object d2 gets sliced. So you cannot call dx from an object of demo class.

10.9 SOME FACTS ABOUT VIRTUAL FUNCTION

/*PROG 10.28 CALLING VIRTUAL FUNCTION EXPLICITLY */

```
#include <iostream.h>
#include <conio.h>

class first
{
public :
    virtual void show( )
    {
        cout<<"In show of first"<<endl;
    }
};
class second :public first
{
public :
    void show( )
    {
        cout<<"In show of second"<<endl;
    }
};
void main( )
{
    clrscr( );
    first f;
    f.show( );
    second s;
    s.show( );
    getch( );
}
```

OUTPUT :

```
In show of first
In show of second
```

EXPLANATION : The basic aim of the program is to simply show that **virtual** functions can be called **explicitly using objects of class**. **virtual** mechanism works only in case of pointers to object.

/*PROG 10.29 PURE VIRTUAL FUNCTION CAN HAVE BODY */

```
#include <iostream.h>
#include <conio.h>
class first
{
public :
    virtual void show( )=0
    {
        cout<<"In show of first"<<endl;
    }
};
class second :public first
{
public :
    void show( )
    {
        cout<<"In show of second"<<endl;
    }
};
void main( )
{
    clrscr( );
    first *ptr=new second;
    ptr->show( );
    getch( );
}
```

OUTPUT :

In show of second

EXPLANATION : The sole aim of this program is to show that a pure virtual function can have body but in no way we can use this body.

/*PROG 10.30 CALLING VIRTUAL FUNCTION FROM CONSTRUCTION VER 1*/

```
#include <iostream.h>
#include <conio.h>

class first
{
public :
```

```
    virtual void silly( )
    {
        cout<<"Hello from silly of first"<<endl;
    }
    first ( )
    {
        silly ( );
    }
};

class second :public first
{
public :
    void silly( )
    {
        cout<<"Hello from silly of second"<<endl;
    }
};
void main( )
{
    clrscr( );
    (new second);
    getch( );
}
```

OUTPUT :

Hello from silly of first

EXPLANATION : In the above program when object of `second` class is created. First constructor of `first` class gets called then constructor of `second` class. In the `first` class we are calling the function `silly` which has been `overridden` in derived class `second`. As derived class second will be constructed when its constructor would be called. Compiler has at this time no idea of `silly` function present in second class. So the `base class` first version of `silly` is called.

/*PROG 10.31 CALLING VIRTUAL FUNCTION FROM CONSTRUCTOR VER 2*/

```
#include <iostream.h>
#include <conio.h>

class first
{
public :
```

```
        virtual void silly( )
        {
            cout<<"Hello from of first"<<endl;
        }
        first( )
        {
            silly( );
        }
};
class second :public first
{
public :
        second( )
        {
            silly( );
        }
        void silly( )
        {
            cout<<"Hello from silly of second"<<endl;
        }
};
void main( )
{
        clrscr( );
        second s;
        getch( );
}
```

OUTPUT :

```
Hello from of first
Hello from silly of second
```

EXPLANATION : Here it is clear from the program that we are calling `silly` function from construtor of both the classes. The `silly` of `first class` is called from constructor of class `first`. As `silly` was defined in the class `second` and is called from its constructor, `silly` of `second` class will be called too. We have simply followed the normal calling of constructor in inheritance.

10.10 VIRTUAL DESTRUCTOR

There is no concept of virtual constructor in C++ but a virtual destructor can be in C++. In the normal call sequence of constructor and destructor, they follows the basic rules which have been discussed earlier *i.e.*, constructor of base class is called first and destructor of derived class calls first even the destructor in the base class is virtual. See the program given below for better understanding point of view.

/*PROG 10.32 DEMO OF VIRTUAL DESTRUCTOR VER 1*/

```
#include <iostream.h>
#include <conio.h>

class first
{
public :
    first( )
    {
        cout<<"First con called"<<endl;
    }
    virtual ~first( )
    {
        cout<<"First des called"<<endl;
    }
};
class second :public first
{
    char *ptr;
public :
    second( )
    {
        ptr=new char[10];
        cout<<"Second con called"<<endl;
    }
    ~second( )
    {
        cout<<"Second des called"<<endl;
        delete ptr;
    }
};
void main( )
{
    clrscr( );
    second s;
    getch( );
}
```

OUTPUT :

```
(First run)
First con called
Second con called
Press (Alt+F5) to see the function of virtual destructor which are given below :
First con called
Second con called
Second des called
First des called
```

EXPLANATION : The output is simple to understand. Note the destructor is virtual but the output is as we expect. Constructor of base class is called first and destructor of derived class is called first.

We have seen earlier that virtual mechanism works only in case of pointers. Same is true with virtual destructor. But before telling you the actual use of virtual destructor we modify the above program as shown below (here constructor are omitted).

/*PROG 10.33 DEMO OF VIRTUAL DESTRUCTOR VER 2*/

```
#include <iostream.h>
#include <conio.h>

class first
{
public :
    ~first( )
    {
        cout<<"first des called"<<endl;
    }
};
class second :public first
{
    char *ptr;
public :
    ~second( )
    {
        cout<<"Second des called"<<endl;
    }
};
void main( )
{
```

```
        clrscr( );
        first *f=new second;
        delete f;
        getch( );
    }
```

OUTPUT :

first des called

EXPLANATION : As pointer `f` is of class first type, only the destructor of `first` class is called. But ideally destructor of `second` class should get called `first`, after that destructor would be called, so that memory for string pointer ptr would be de-allocated. The solution is to make destructor of `class first as virtual`. See the next program.

/*PROG 10.34 DEMO OF VIRTUAL DESTRUCTOR VER 3*/

```
#include <iostream.h>
#include <conio.h>

class first
{
public :
    virtual ~first( )
    {
        cout<<"First des called"<<endl;
    }
};
class second :public first
{
    char *ptr;
public :
    second( )
    {
        ptr=new char [10];
    }
    ~second ( )
    {
        cout<<"Second des called"<<endl;
        delete ptr;
}
};
void main( )
```

```
{
    clrscr( );
    first *f=new second;
    delete f;
    getch( );
}
```

OUTPUT :

```
Second des called
First des called
```

EXPLANATION : In the **main** we have declared a pointer of **type first** and in the pointer we have stored address of an object of class **second**. When **delete ptr** executes, destructor of **second** class is called first then destructor of **first** class is called. This is just because of virtual. If it were not in the first class only the destructor of **first** class would have been called and **ptr** wouldn't be deleted. So this is the **main** use of virtual destructor where you have pointer of **base** class and object stored is of derived class.

10.11 PONDERABLE POINTS

1. A pointer of base class can store address of an object of derived class but reverse is not true.
2. This pointer is a constant pointer which stores the address of the current object.
3. This pointer can only be used inside the non-static member functions of the class.
4. In the absence of virtual keyword, pointer of base class will call only its function no matter address of what type of object is stored inside the pointer.
5. When virtual function is present then function call is made by checking the contents of pointer rather then checking type of pointer.
6. For every class in which virtual function is present and all other classes derived from this class, VTABLE is created.
7. The VTABLE contains addresses of all the virtual function present/inherited in the class. A special pointer vptr points to the VTABLE.
8. A pure virtual function is a function which has no body.
9. For a class to be abstract class, it must have at least one pure virtual function.
10. Pointers and references of an abstract class can be created.
11. Virtual function is the only mechanism to provide-run-time polymorphism in C++.
12. Binding is the linking of function call with the place where function definition is written.
13. When binding is done at compile time it is known as early-binding, compile time binding or static binding.
14. When binding is done at run time it is known as late-binding, runtime binding or dynamic binding.

15. Static binding provides efficiency but less flexible.
16. Dynamic binding provides flexibility but less efficient.

EXERCISE

A. True and False :

1. An abstract class can be instantiated.
2. This pointer points to current object only.
3. A class containing at least one pure virtual function is known as abstract class.
4. A class whose objects cannot be created is known as abstract class.
5. All functions in an abstract base class must be declared as abstract class.
6. Virtual function cannot be overloaded.
7. Polymorphism can be implemented only using virtual functions.

B. Answer the Following Questions :

1. How do create pointer to objects of a class?
2. How can be call member function of derived class when pointer is of base class and virtual keyword is not present ?
3. What is virtual function ?
4. What is VTABLE ?
5. How does virtual function works ?
6. What is this pointer ? What are its main characteristics ?
7. How do we implement run-time polymorphism in C++ ?
8. What is binding ? What is the significance of binding ?
9. What is an abstract class ?
10. What is pure virtual function ? How it is different from all other functions ?
11. Why cannot we create an object of an abstract class ?
12. What is object slicing ?
13. What is the significance of virtual destructor ?
14. Why cannot we have virtual destructor ?
15. Can we call virtual function explicitly without using pointers ?

C. Brain Drill :

1. Suppose that there is an abstract class 'Shape', which is the base class of classes 'Polygon' and 'Circle'. "Polygon" class is the base class from which a class Rectangular is derived. Pure virtual functions compute Area and compute Perimeter are declared in the class Shape. These functions are actually defined in the derived classes "Rectangle" and "Circle". Define the classes "Shape", "Polygon", "Rectangle" and "Circle". Write a global function "ComputeAllArea" as double computeAllArea(Shape*s[100], int numberofShapes).

   The above function computes the total area of all shapes object pointed to by s[0], s[1], ...s[numberOfShapes].

2. Suppose that you need to define classes for employee and manager objects. An employee has a name, an employee code, salary and age. A manager is also an employee. But a manager object contains an additional list of references to employee objects that the manager supervises. An employee object should also contain a reference to his/her manager. A manager can supervises at most 10 employee. It is required to print details of employee or a manager. When information of an employee object is printed, his/her name, salary and age is printed. When information of a manager object is printed, his/her name, salary and age is printed and names of all the employees that he/she supervises are displayed. Define the classes keeping the following in mind :

   (*a*) References to employee objects can be added/deleted from the list of supervised employees in a manager object.

   (*b*) Reference to the manager object can be modified for an employee object.

CHAPTER 11

INPUT-OUTPUT AND MANIPULATORS IN C++

11.1 INTRODUCTION

In all the earlier chapters, we have worked with cin and cout for taking all different types of data as input and displaying them. But, we have not worked with the formatted output *i.e.,* the way we want to print the data onto screen. For managing the input and output operations C++ provides the concept of stream classes. We know that cin is treated as standard input stream and cout as standard output stream classes. We known that cin is treated as standard input streams and cout as standard output streams. A stream is termed as input stream and when data is sent by the program to the output device say screen, the stream termed as output stream. It is quite obvious as we have seen in almost all the C++ programs so far that to take data from keyboard we have cin, which receives data and display s onto the screen. Thus, cin is standard input stream and cout is standard output stream.

We have also said that >> is an extraction operator <<is insertion operator. This is so as cin >> extraction data from input stream from input stream and cout << displays inserts data into output stream. C++ provides numbers of stream classes for the efficient handling input and output and which is our next topic of discussion.

11.2 C++ STREAM CLASSES

In C++ there are number of **streams** classes for defining various streams related with files and for doing input output operations. All these classes are defined in the file **iostream.h**. Figure given below shows the hierarchy of these classes :

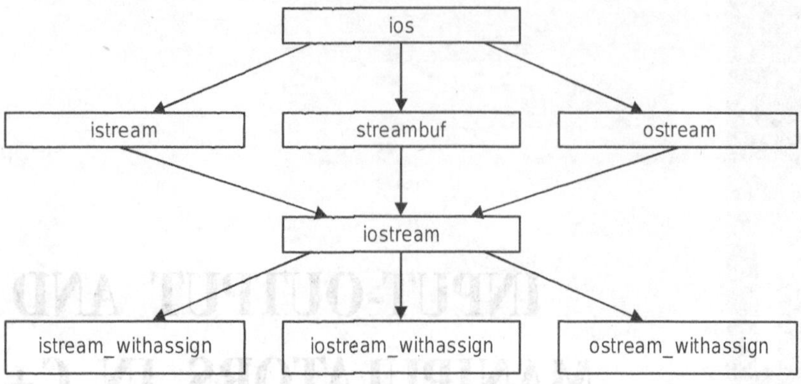

Figure 11.1. *Hierarchy of ios file*

As can be seen from the figure that :

1. **ios** class is the topmost class in the **stream** classes hierarchy. It is the base class for **istream, ostream and streambuf** class.
2. **istream, ostream** serves the base classes for **iostream class**. The class **istream** is used for input and **ostream** for output.
3. Class **ios** is indirectly to **iostream** class using **istream** and **ostream**. To avoid the duplicity of data and member functions of **ios** class, it is declared as virtual **base class** when inheriting **in istream and ostream** as :

```
class istream : virtual public ios
{
};

class ostream :virtual public ios
{
};
```

4. The **_withassign classes** are provided with extra functionality for the assignment operations that's why **_withassign** classes.

After discussing about various stream classes we now understand their purpose and what type of facilities are provided by these **stream classes.**

1. The ios Class

The ios class is responsible for providing all input and output facilities to all other stream classes as it is the topmost class in the hierarchy of stream classes. As we will be seeing later in the chapter, this class provides number of functions for efficient handling of formatted output for strings and numbers.

2. The istream Class

This class is responsible for handling input stream. It provides number of functions for handling **chars, strings and objects, record** etc, besides inheriting the properties from **ios** class. The **istream class** provides the basic capability for sequential and random—access input. An **istream** object has a **streambuf-**derived object attached, and the two classes work together; the istream class does the formatting, and the **streambuf** class does the low-level buffered input. The class provides number of methods for input handling such as **get, getline, read, peek, gcount, ignore, eatwhite, putback etc**. This class also contains overloaded **extraction operator >>** for handling all data types such as **int, signed int, char, long, double, float, long double**. The extraction operator is also overloaded for handling **streambuf and istream** types of objects.

3. istream_withassign Class

The **istream_withassign** class is a variant **istream** that allows object assignment. The predefined object cin is an object of this class and thus may be reassigned at run time to a different **istream** class.

4. ostream_withassign Class

The **ostream_withassign** class is variant of **ostream** that allows object assignment. The predefined object **cout, cerr and clog** are objects of this class and thus may be reassigned at run time to a different **ostream object.**

11.3 UNFORMATTED INPUT/OUTPUT

Until now is all the program with the help of cin and cout we have taking input without making use of any formatting function. Thus, general syntax of using data as input and output is as follows :

```
cin>>data1>>data2>>data3>>.................................>>data n;
cout<<data1<<data2<<data3<<...............................<<data n;
```

Where **data1, data2....** Are variables of **int, char, float** etc.

Here data is scanned as it is input and similarly it is displayed as it. This is because the operator **>> and <<** overloaded for all the basic types like **int, char, unsigned, float** etc.

In case of string data the input breaks at occurrence of very first white space character like tab or space. Similarly for reading **int, float** etc., input must match the type of variable in which you are accepting it.

Before discussing how to format data for input and output we first see few functions for input and output character, scanning and printing strings.

1. The get Function

This function is used to scan a single character from the keyboard. There are two different syntaxes of using get function.

(*a*) void cin.get(char);

(*b*) char cin.get( );

In the first syntax get function takes an argument of type char. This is used as :

```
char x;
cin.get(x);
```

The input character entered from keyboard is taken into the x.

In the second syntax the entered character is returned by the get function. This is used as :

```
char x = cin.get ( );
```

2. The put Function

The function is used to put a single character onto the screen. Its general syntax is given as :

```
void put (char);
```

The character to be displayed is passed as argument to function put. This is used as :

```
char x = 'P';
cout.put(x)
```

We can even pass ASCII values to put function which is converted internally to their character counterpart *i.e.*,

```
count. put (97)
Will display a.
```

3. The getline Function

The syntax of the function is given as :

```
istream& getline (char *pch, int ncount, char delim='\n');
```

We have seen usage of this function in number of program earlier. The function **getline** scans character into the array pch till **nCount-1** has been scanned or delim is encountered, the default is **'\n'**. An example.

```
char str [20];
cin.getline (str, 20,'$');
```

This function scans first 19 character or break at the very first occurrence of '$' character. The function getline scans all white characters like tab, spaces etc. As function returns reference of **istream** type we can write function **getline** as :

```
char s1[10], s2 [10];
cin. getline (s1, 10).getline (s2, 10);
```

4. The write Function

```
ostream & write (const char * pch, int nCount);
```

The function display nCount character from the array pch. For instance.

```
cout.write ("hello", 3);
display : hel
```

As return type of function write is ostream type we can write multiple write statement s to form one as :

```
cout.write ("hello", 5).write ("world", 6);
```

is equal to

```
cout.write ("hello", 5);
cout.write ("world", 6);
```

5. The gcount Function

The prototype is

```
int gcount ( ) const;
```

Returns the number of characters extracted by the last unformatted input function. Formatted extraction operators may call unformatted input functions and thus reset this number.

6. The putback Function

The prototype of the function is given as :

```
istream & putback(char ch);
```

Puts a character back into the input stream. The putback function may fail and set the error state. If ch does not match the character that was previously extracted, the result is undefined.

7. The peek Function

The prototype is given as :

```
int peek ( );
```

Returns the next character without extracting it from the stream. Returns EOF if the stream is end of file.

8. The eatwhite Function

The prototype is given as follows :

```
void eatwhite ( );
```

Extract white spaces from the stream by advancing the get pointer past spaces and tabs.

9. The ignore Function

```
istream & ignore (int nCount =1,int delim=EOF);
```

Extracts and discards up to **nCount** characters. Extraction stops if the delimiter **delim** is extracted or the end of file is reached. If **delim = EOF** (the default), then only the end of file condition causes termination. The delimiter character is extracted.

For all the function from 5 to 9 usages is given in the programs given later.

/*PROG 11.1 DEMO OF INPUTTING A CHARACTER USING get( )*/

```
#include <iostream.h>
#include <conio.h>

void main( )
{
    clrscr( );

    char ch;

    cout<<"Enter a character :=";
    cin.get(ch);

    cout<<"You have entered :="<<ch<<endl;
    getch( );
}
```

OUTPUT :

```
Enter a character : =S
You have entered : =S
```

EXPLANATION : We simply input a character from the user and accept it using **cin.get ( )** function. Later we display the character using **cout.**

/*PROG 11.2 DEMO OF INPUTTING A CHARACTER USING get( ) AND OUTPUT USING put( )*/

```
#include <iostream.h>
#include <conio.h>

void main( )
{
    char ch;
    clrscr( );

    cout<<"Enter a character :=";
    ch=cin.get( );

    cout<<"You entered :=";
    cout.put(ch);
```

```
    getch( );
}
```

OUTPUT :

```
Enter a character : =a
You entered : =a
```

EXPLANATION : Here, we have used the second version of `cin.get()` which returns the character entered by the user. This is stored in `ch`. This character is then displayed back using `cout.put(ch)`

/*PROG 11.3 DEMO OF put( )*/

```
#include <iostream.h>
#include <conio.h>

void main( )
{
    char ch=97;
    clrscr( );
    cout<<"Character is :=";
    cout.put(ch);

    getch( );
}
```

OUTPUT :

```
Character is : = a
```

EXPLANATION : A character can store integers in terms of `ASCII` values of characters. Hence `97` is stored in the character `ch`. When we display it we get character `'a'`.

/*PROG 11.4 DISPLAYING ASCII AND CHARACTER VALUES */

```
#include <iostream.h>
#include <conio.h>

void main( )
{
    char ch;
    clrscr( );
```

```
        for(ch=65;ch<91;ch++)
        {
            cout<<int (ch)<<"-->";
            cout.put(ch)<<"\t";
            ch++;
            cout<<int(ch)<<"-->";
            cout.put(ch)<<endl;
        }

        getch( );
    }
```

OUTPUT :

```
65-->A 66-->B
67-->C 68-->D
69-->E 70-->F
71-->G 72-->H
73-->I 74-->J
75-->K 76-->L
77-->M 78-->N
79-->O 80-->P
81-->Q 82-->R
83-->S 84-->T
85-->U 86-->V
87-->W 88-->X
89-->Y 90-->Z
```

EXPLANATION : In the program we are displaying alphabets in upper-case and their ASCII values too. Note we have type casted character to int thus statement `int(ch)` displays ASCII value of `ch`. But `put` method displays the character value only.

/*PROG 11.5 ENTER A LINE OF TEXT AND DISPLAY IT BACK USING get( ) AND put( ) FUNCTION */

```
#include <iostream.h>
#include <conio.h>

void main( )
{
    char ch;
    clrscr( );
```

```
    cout<<"Enter a line of text"<<endl;
    cin.get(ch);

    while(ch!='\n')
    {
        cout.put(ch);
        cin.get(ch);
    }

    getch( );
}
```

OUTPUT :

```
Enter a line of text
this is NMIMS university
this is NMIMS university
```

EXPLANATION : The first character of line entered is scanned in ch using get method. It is checked whether entered character is \n or not. If it is not we display it on to the screen using put and scan the next character again. As soon as next character scanned in equal to '\n' the while loop terminates. Note the whole line is displayed when you press Enter. The entered data is stored in the input before displaying back to screen.

/*PROG 11.6 ENTER A LINE OF TEXT AND DISPLAY IT BACK USING getline AND cout */

```
#include <iostream.h>
#include <conio.h>
void main( )
{
    char str[50];
    clrscr( );

    cout<<"Enter line of text"<<endl;
    cin.getline(str,50);

    cout<<"You entered "<<endl;
    cout<<str<<endl;

    getch( );
}
```

OUTPUT :

```
Enter line of text
```

```
THE WELL OF PROVIDENCE IS DEEP. IT'S THE BUCKETS WE BRING TO IT THAT ARE SMALL
You entered
THE WELL OF PROVIDENCE IS DEEP. IT'S THE BUCKETS WE BRING TO IT THAT ARE SMALL
```

EXPLANATION : In the earlier program, we were taking input character by character but here whole line is scanned at once using `getline()` function/method. The `getline` scan the line till `\n` (new line) is not pressed or till the first `49` characters have been scanned (second parameter). It scans white space character also like tab, spaces etc.

/*PROG 11.7 ENTER A LINE OF TEXT AND DISPLAY IT BACK USING getline AND write FUNCTION */

```
#include <iostream.h>
#include <conio.h>
#include <string.h>

void main( )
{
    char str[100];
    clrscr( );

    cout<<"======================================="<<endl;
    cout<<"Enter a line of text"<<endl;
    cout<<"======================================="<<endl;
    cin.getline(str,100);

    cout<<"======================================="<<endl;
    cout<<"You have entered"<<endl;
    cout<<"======================================="<<endl;
    cout.write(str,strlen(str));
cout<<"===================================="<<endl;

    getch( );
}
```

OUTPUT :

```
================================================
Enter a line of text
================================================
Life is like an ice-cream. Eat it before it melts
================================================
You have entered
```

```
===============================================================
Life is like an ice-cream. Eat it before it melts
===============================================================
```

EXPLANATION : The write method displays the `str` onto the screen. It takes two parameters :

(*a*) **First one is the string.**

(*b*) **Second one is its length.**

Depending upon the length, that number of characters is displayed.

/*PROG 11.8 DISPLAY PATTERN USING write METHOD */

```
#include <iostream.h>
#include <conio.h>
#include <string.h>

void main( )
{
    char str [20];
    int i,len;
    clrscr( );
    cout<<"========================================"<<endl;
    cout<<"Enter a string"<<endl;
    cout<<"========================================"<<endl;
    cin.getline(str,20);
    len=strlen(str);
    cout<<"========================================"<<endl;
    cout<<"Pattern is"<<endl;
    for(i=1;i<=len;i++)
    {
        cout.write(str,i);
        cout<<endl;
    }
    for(i=len;i>=1;i--)
    {
        cout.write(str,i);
        cout<<endl;
    }
    cout<<endl;
cout<<"========================================"<<endl;
    getch( );
}
```

OUTPUT :

```
===========================================
Enter a string
===========================================
UNIVERSITY
===========================================
Pattern is
U
UN
UNI
UNIV
UNIVE
UNIVER
UNIVERS
UNIVERSI
UNIVERSIT
UNIVERSITY
UNIVERSITY
UNIVERSIT
UNIVERSI
UNIVERS
UNIVER
UNIVE
UNIV
UNI
UN
U
===========================================
```

EXPLANATION : The first **for loop**

```
for(i=1;i<=len;i++)
    {
        cout.write(str,i);
        cout<<endl;
    }
```

Display the pattern as :

```
U
UN
UNI
```

```
UNIV
UNIVE
UNIVER
UNIVERS
UNIVERSI
UNIVERSIT
UNIVERSITY
```

As i varies from 1 to length of the string and this i is used as second argument of method write. Second `for loop`

```
for(i=len;i>=1;i--)
    {
        cout.write(str,i);
        cout<<endl;
    }
```

Display the following pattern as :

```
UNIVERSITY
UNIVERSIT
UNIVERSI
UNIVERS
UNIVER
UNIVE
UNIV
UNI
UN
U
```

As **i** varies from **len-1 to i** decrementing in each iteration.

/*PROG 11.9 DISPLAYING FULL NAME USING write METHOD */

```
#include <iostream.h>
#include <string.h>
#include <conio.h>
void main( )
{
    char fname [20],lname[20];

    cout<<"Enter first name :=";
    cin>>fname;
```

```
    cout<<"Enter the last name :=";
    cin>>lname;

    cout<<"Your full name :=";
    ostream & refcout=cout.write(fname, strlen(fname));

    refcout.write(" ",1);
    refcout.write(lname,strlen(lname));
    cout<<endl;

    getch( );
}
```

OUTPUT :

```
Enter first name : =HARI
Enter the last name : =PANDEY
Your full name : =HARI PANDEY
```

EXPLANATION : The statement given below as :

```
ostream & refcout=cout.write(fname, strlen(fname));
```

First display fname onto the screen and then returns reference of ostream type which is stored in refcout. In the next statement we use this refcout to display lname using write method. The whole of the write statements can be written in the shorter form as :

```
cout.write(fname, strlen (fname))
Write("",1).write (lname,strlen(lname));
```

11.4 FORMATTED INPUT/OUTPUT OPERATIONS

In C++ for formatting input and output we have three methods :

1. Use of functions and flags defined by ios class.
2. Use of manipulators (built-in)
3. User defined manipulators.

1. Use of Functions and Flags Defined by ios Class

A. ios Function and Flags

The class ios provides number of formatting functions for input and output. The most frequently used are listed below :

(*a*) The width ( ) Function

The function is used to set the width *i.e.*, field size for displaying a data value of type numeric or string. The syntax of this is as follows :

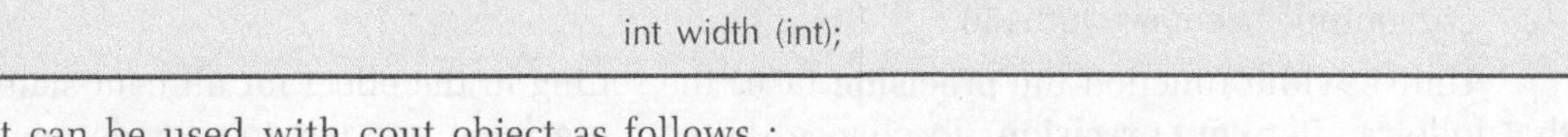

It can be used with cout object as follows :

```
cout.width (5);
cout< <123;
```

		1	2	3

cout . width (5);

Figure 11.2. *Implementation of width function*

For each data value to be printed separate width function has to be used. That is for the following.

```
cout.width(5);
cout< <123;
cout< <45;
```

Only for the first cout statement width is set and not for the second. For printing second cout statement in a width of 5 we will have to write.

```
cout.width(5);
cout< <123;
cout.width(5);
cout< <45;
```

(*b*) The precision Function

The function is used for setting the number of digits to be displayed after a floating point number. Its syntax is :

```
int precision (int);
```

It can be used as :

```
cout.precision (3);
cout< <123.456789;
```

Output displayed is given as :

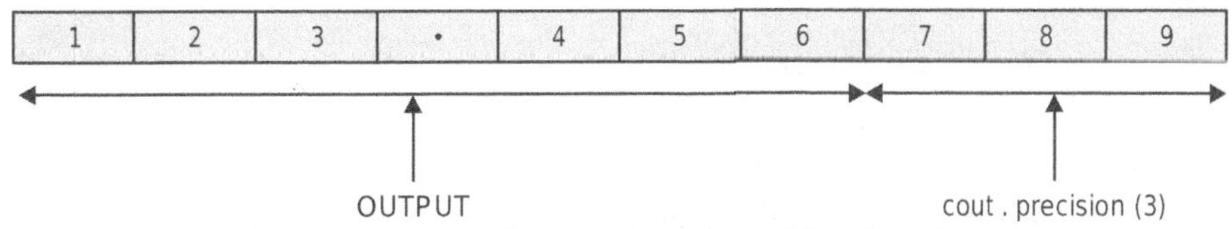

Figure 11.3. *Implementation of precision function*

i.e., output becomes 123.456

Unlike **width** function the **precision** takes the setting in the effect for all cout statements that follows after **cout.precision**. To change the new **precision** one has to provide new value inside **precision** function.

(*c*) The fill Function

The fill function is used to fill the empty spaces in the given field size set by width function. Its syntax is given as :

```
char fill (char);
```

It can be used as :

```
cout.width (10);
cout.fill ('#');
cout<<23456;
```

The output for the above given code snippet is given as :

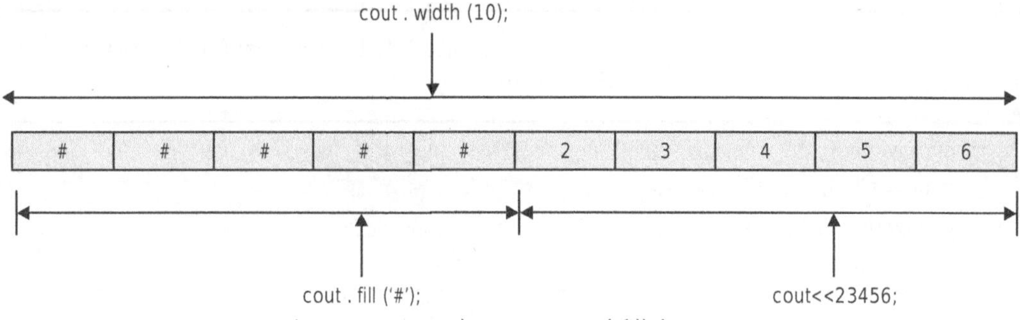

Figure 11.4. *Implementation of fill function*

(*d*) The setf Function

This function is used for setting the various flags for controlling the output such as displaying such as displaying output left justified or right justified, displaying numbers in **decimal, hex, octal**, scientific notation etc. This function is discussed in detail later.

(*e*) The unsetf Function

The function is used for clearing the flags previously set by setf function.

```
/*PROG 11.10 DEMO OF WIDTH FUNCTION VER 1*/

#include <iostream.h>
#include <conio.h>

void main( )
{
    int a = 1234, b = 645, c = 28, d = 8;

    clrscr( );
```

```
    cout<<"===================================="<<endl;
    cout<<"THE DEMO OF width IS GIVEN BELOW"<<endl;
    cout<<"===================================="<<endl;
    cout.width(8);

    cout<<a<<endl;
    cout<<b<<endl;
    cout<<c<<endl;
    cout<<d<<endl;

    cout<<"===================================="<<endl;
    getch( );
}
```

OUTPUT :

```
------------------------------------
THE DEMO OF width IS GIVEN BELOW
====================================
 1234
645
28
8
====================================
```

EXPLANATION : The aim of above program is to demonstrate the basic functionality of width function. When compiler control read the statement **cout.width (8);** it will create a block of **8 cells** and set the value **1234** as right alignment. Other value will be set as usual.

/*PROG 11.11 DEMO OF WIDTH FUNCTION VER 2 */

```
#include <iostream.h>
#include <conio.h>

void main( )
{
    int a= 12345, b = 1234, c =123, d = 12, e=1;
    clrscr( );
    cout<<"========================================"<<endl;
    cout<<"\tTHE PATTERN IS GIVEN AS"<<endl;
    cout<<"========================================"<<end;
    cout.width(8);
```

```
    cout<<a<<endl;
    cout.width(8);

    cout<<b<<endl;
    cout.width(8);

    cout<<c<<endl;
    cout.width(8);

    cout<<d<<endl;
    cout.width(8);

    cout<<e<<endl;
    cout<<"====================================="<<endl;
    getch( );
}
```

OUTPUT :

```
=====================================
THE PATTERN IS GIVEN AS
=====================================
12345
1234
123
12
1
=====================================
```

EXPLANATION : The width function first set the width of 8 characters and then displays the data followed in the width of 8 starting from right justified and left padded. For each data to be printed, separated width has to be set first.

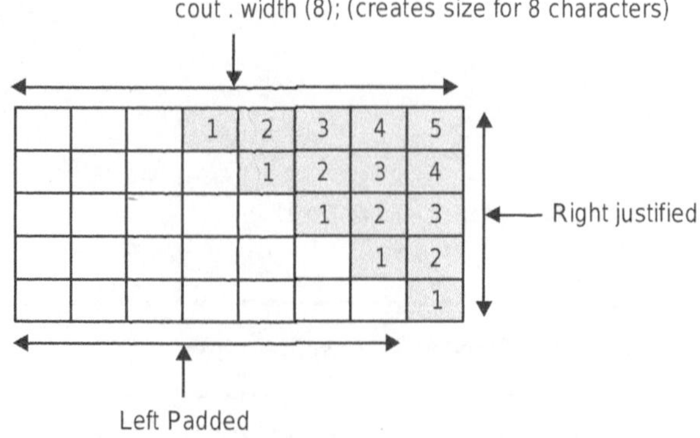

Figure 11.5. *Demo of width function*

/*PROG 11.12 DEMO OF WIDTH FUNCTION VER 2*/

```
#include <iostream.h>
#define S 5
#include <conio.h>

void main( )
{
    int arr[S], i;

    clrscr( );
    cout<<" Enter the "<<S<<"numbers"<<endl;

    for(i=0;i<S;i++)
    {
        cin>>arr[i];
    }

    cout.width(10);
    cout<<"====================================="<<endl;
    cout<<" Number";
    cout<<" Square";
    cout<<endl;
    for(i=0;i<S;i++)
    {
  cout.width(10),
     cout<<arr[i];
     cout.width(10);
     cout<<arr[i]*arr[i];
     cout<<endl;
    }
    cout<<"====================================="<<endl;
    getch( );
}
```

OUTPUT :

```
Enter the 5numbers
47
78
98
99
156
```

```
====================================
      Number      Square
        47          2209
        78          6084
        98          9604
        99          9801
       156         24336
====================================
```

EXPLANATION : For displaying Number and Square as heading we set the width 10. In the for loop for displaying the number and their square same width is set again.

/*PROG 11.13 DEMO OF WIDTH AND FILL FUNCTION TOGETHER */

```
#include <iostream.h>
#include <conio.h>
void main( )
{
    int a = 12345, b = 1234, c= 123, d = 12, e=1;
    clrscr( );
    cout<<"+*+*+*+**+*+*+*+*+*+*+**+*+*+*+*+*+*+*"<<endl;
    cout<<"DEMO OF fill AND width FUNCTION"<<endl;
    cout<<"+*+*+*+*+*+*+*+*+*+*+*+*+*+*+*+*+*+*"<<endl<<endl;
    cout.fill('$');
    cout.width(8);
    cout<<a<<endl;
    cout.width(8);
    cout<<b<<endl;
    cout.width(8);
    cout<<c<<endl;
    cout.width(8);
    cout<<d<<endl;
    cout.width(8);
    cout<<e<<endl;
    cout<<endl<<"+*+*+*+*+*+*+*+*+*+*+*+*+*+*+*+*+*"<<endl;
    getch( );
}
```

OUTPUT :

```
+*+*+*+*+*+*+*+*+*+*+*+**+*+*+*+*+*+*+**+*+*+*+*+*+*
DEMO OF fill AND width FUNCTION
+*+*+*+*+*+*+*+*+*+*+*+*+*+*+*+*+*+*+*+*+*+*+*+*+*+*+*
```

```
$$$12345
$$$$1234
$$$$$123
$$$$$$12
$$$$$$$1
*+*+*+*+*+*+*+*+*+*+*+*+*+*+*+*+*+*+*+*+*+*+*+*+*+*+*+*+*+*+*+*+*+*+*+*+*+*+*+*+*
```

EXPLANATION : If whole of the width allocated is not utilized by the data to be printed, remaining empty spaces can be filled using `cout.fill();` method. The fill function takes a character as argument which acts as a filling character. Once this is set extra spaces will be filled by character specified as argument to fill method.

The output of the above program can be shown diagrammatically as follows :

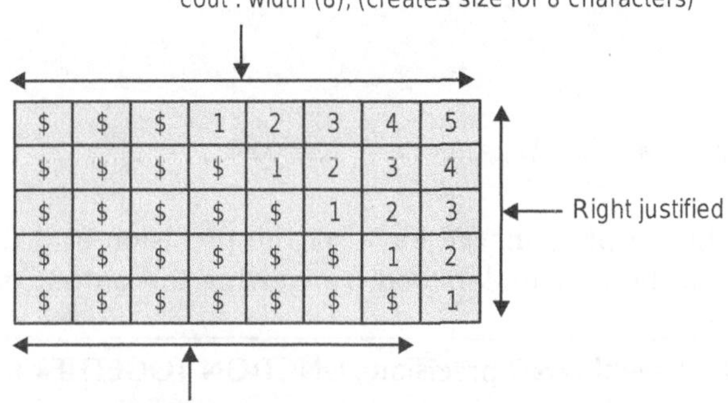

Figure 11.6. *Demo of fill and width function together.*

/*PROG 11.14 DEMO OF PRECISION FUNCTION */

```
#include <iostream.h>
#include <conio.h>

void main( )
{
    clrscr( );

    cout<<"####################################"<<endl;
    cout<<" DEMO OF PRECISION FUNCTION"<<endl;
    cout<<"####################################"<<endl;

    cout.precision (3);
    cout<<"\t"<<123.12345<<endl;

    cout.precision(4);
    cout<<"\t"<<345.656767<<endl;
```

```
    cout.precision(10);
    cout<<"\t"<<22/7.0<<endl;

    cout<<endl;
    cout<<"####################################"<<endl;
    getch( );
}
```

OUTPUT :

```
####################################
 DEMO OF PRECISION FUNCTION
####################################
 123.123
 345.6568
 3.1428571429
####################################
```

EXPLANATION : In the program we have set the precision at 3 different places and all are different. Program can be best understood by viewing the output of the program.

```
/*PROG 11.15 DEMO OF width AND precision FUNCTION TOGETHER IN A SINGLE PROGRAM
*/

#include <iostream.h>
#include <conio.h>
#include <math.h>

#define S 5
void main( )
{
    float arr[S]={34.0, 79.0, 67.0, 33.0, 24.0};
    int i;
    clrscr( );
    cout<<"#$#$#$#$#$#$$#$#$#$#$#$#$#$#$#$#$#$#$"<<endl;
    cout<<"DEMO OF WIDTH AND PRECISION FUNCTION TOGETHER"<<endl;
    cout<<"$#$#$#$#$#$#$#$#$#$#$#$#$#$#$#$#$#$#$"<<endl;
    cout.precision(4);

cout<<endl<<"++++++++++++++++++++++++++++++++++++"<<endl;
    cout.width(8);
    cout<<"Number";
    cout.width(15);
```

```
    cout<<"Square Root"<<endl;
cout<<"++++++++++++++++++++++++++++++++++++++++++++++"<<endl;
    for(i=0;i<S;i++)
    {
        cout.width(5);
        cout<<arr[i];
        cout.width(12);
        cout<<sqrt(arr[i]);
        cout<<endl;
    }
cout<<"++++++++++++++++++++++++++++++++++++++++++++++"<<endl;
    getch( );
}
```

OUTPUT :

```
#$#$#$#$#$#$#$#$#$$#$#$#$#$#$#$#$#$#$#$#$#$#$#$#$#$#
DEMO OF WIDTH AND PRECISION FUNCTION TOGETHER
$#$#$#$#$#$#$#$#$#$#$#$#$#$#$#$#$#$#$#$#$#$#$#$#$#$#
++++++++++++++++++++++++++++++++++++++++++++
Number   Square Root
++++++++++++++++++++++++++++++++++++++++++++
34      5.831
79      8.8882
67      8.1854
33      5.7446
24      4.899
++++++++++++++++++++++++++++++++++++++++++++
```

EXPLANATION : The program is self explanatory.

(*f*) Formatting Using setf Function

The setf function is very important function for printing output in a verity of fashion. Whether it is numeric data or string data. The function stands for setting the flag. There are two different variant of setf.

(*i*) The first syntax of setf is given below as :

```
long setf (long Flags, long Mask);
```

The first statement Flags is number of flags defined in the class ios. Each flag is equivalent of 1 if set. For combining many flag, OR (|) can be used. The second parameter Mask specifies the group to which first parameter belongs. The Mask parameter is also known as bit-field. The table given below shows all types of formatting flags and their corresponding Mask.

Table 11.1 : Formatted Flags Used in C++

S.No.	*Flags*	*Mask*	*Output*
1.	ios : :left	ios : :adjustfield	Left justified
2.	ios : :right	ios : :adjustfield	Right justified
3.	ios : :internal	ios : :adjustfield	Add fill characters after any leading sign or base indication
4.	ios : :scientific	ios : :floatfield	Scientific notation
5.	ios : :fixed	ios : :floatified	Fixed point notation
6.	ios : :doc	ios : :basefield	Output in decimal
7.	ios : :hex	ios : :basefield	Output in hex
8.	ios : :oct	ios : :basefield	Output in octal

(g) The Second Syntax of setf is :

```
long stef (long flags);
```

Function turns on only those format bits that are specified b 1s in flags. It returns a long that contains the previous values of all the flags. These are the flags which are used independently without the use of Mask parameter. The table given below lists all the flags :

Table 11.2 : Formatted Flags Used in C++

S.No.	*Flags*	*Purpose*
1.	ios : :showpoint	Show decimal point and trailing zero for floating-point values.
2.	ios : :showbase	Display numeric constants in a format that can be read by the C++ compiler.
3.	ios : :showpos	Show plus sign (+) for positive values.
4.	ios : :uppercase	Display uppercase A through F for hexadecimal values and E for scientific values.
5.	ios : :skipws	Skip white space on input
6.	ios : :unitbuf	Flush the stream after each insertion.
7.	ios : :stdio	Flush stdout and stderr after each insertion

/*PROG 11.16 DEMO OF FORMATTING FLAGS VER 1*/

```
#include <iostream.h>
#include <conio.h>
void main( )
{
    char s[ ]="Hello";
```

```
    clrscr( );
    cout<<"——————————————————————————"<<endl;
    cout<<"STRING WITHOUT SETTING WIDTH\n";
    cout<<"——————————————————————————"<<endl;
    cout<<s<<endl;
    cout<<endl<<"——————————————————————————"<<endl;
    cout<<"STRING AFTER SETTING WIDTH AND PADDING"<<endl;
    cout<<"——————————————————————————"<<endl;
    cout<<"RIGHT JUSTIFIED"<<endl;
    cout<<"——————————————————————————"<<endl;
    cout.fill('&');
    cout.setf(ios : :right, ios : :adjustfield);
    cout.width(15);
    cout<<s<<endl;
    cout<<"——————————————————————————"<<endl;
    cout<<"LEFT JUSTIFIED"<<endl;
    cout<<"——————————————————————————"<<endl;
    cout.fill('&');
    cout.setf(ios : : left,ios : : adjustfield);
    cout.width(15);
    cout<<s<<endl;
    cout<<"——————————————————————————"<<endl;
    getch( );
}
```

OUTPUT :

```
——————————————————————————
STRING WITHOUT SETTING WIDTH
——————————————————————————
Hello
——————————————————————————
STRING AFTER SETTING WIDTH AND PADDING
——————————————————————————
RIGHT JUSTIFIED
——————————————————————————
&&&&&&&&&&Hello
——————————————————————————
LEFT JUSTIFIED
——————————————————————————
Hello&&&&&&&&&&
——————————————————————————
```

EXPLANATION : For the following settings :

```
cout.fill('&');
    cout.setf(ios : :right, ios : :adjustfield);
    cout.width(15);
```

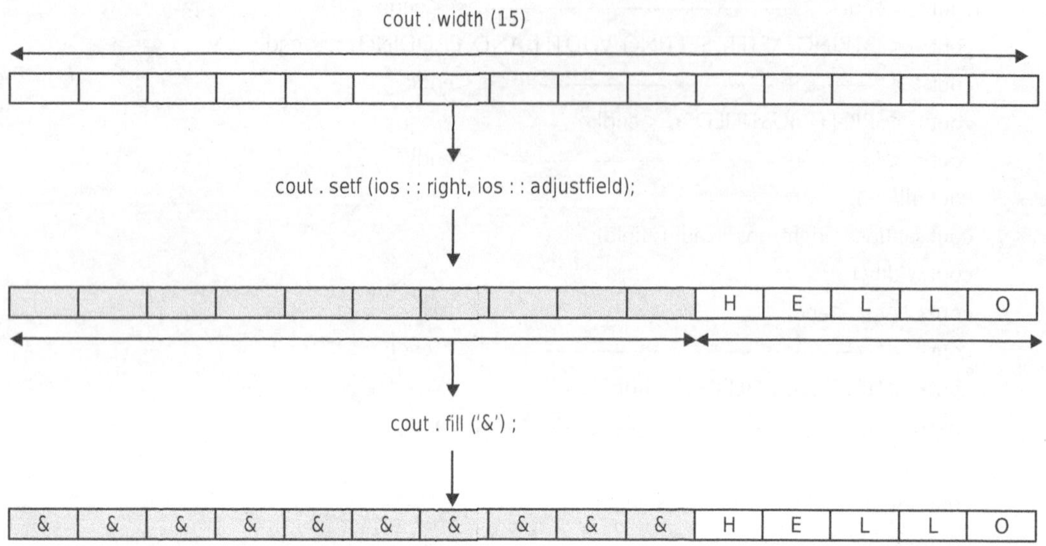

Figure 11.7. *Implementation of ios flags*

Now, by changing **ios :: right to ios :: left** we get the output as :

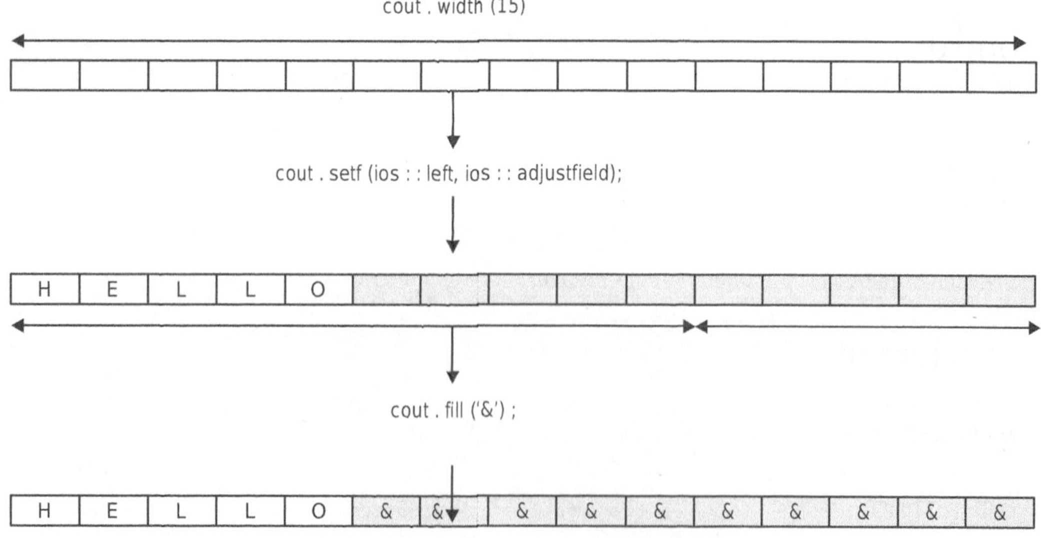

Figure 11.8. *Implementation of ios flags*

/*PROG 11.17 DEMO OF FORMATTING FLAGS VER 2*/

```
#include <iostream.h>
#include <conio.h>

void main( )
{
    clrscr( );
    cout<<"=================================="<<endl;
    cout<<"THE FIRST FORMATTED FLAG"<<endl;
    cout<<"=================================="<<endl;
    cout.fill('+');
    cout.width(10);
    cout.setf(ios : :internal, ios : :adjustfield);
    cout<<-7.89<<endl;
    cout<<"=================================="<<endl;
    cout<<"SECOND FORMATTED FLAG"<<endl;
    cout<<"=================================="<<endl;
    cout.fill('X');
    cout.precision(3);
    cout.width(15);
    cout.setf(ios : :internal,ios : :adjustfield);
    cout.setf(ios : :scientific,ios : :floatfield);
    cout<<-32.43567<<endl;
    cout<<endl<<"=================================="<<endl;
    getch( );
}
```

OUTPUT :

```
==================================
THE FIRST FORMATTED FLAG
==================================
-+++++7.89
==================================
SECOND FORMATTED FLAG
==================================
-XXXXX3.244e+01
==================================
```

EXPLANATION : The program is simple to understand. For the argument ios : :scientific the output is usually compiler dependent. For the following statement :

```
cout.fill('+');
cout.width(10);
cout.setf(ios : :internal, ios : :adjustfield);
cout< <–7.89< <endl;
```

Output displayed is as shown below :

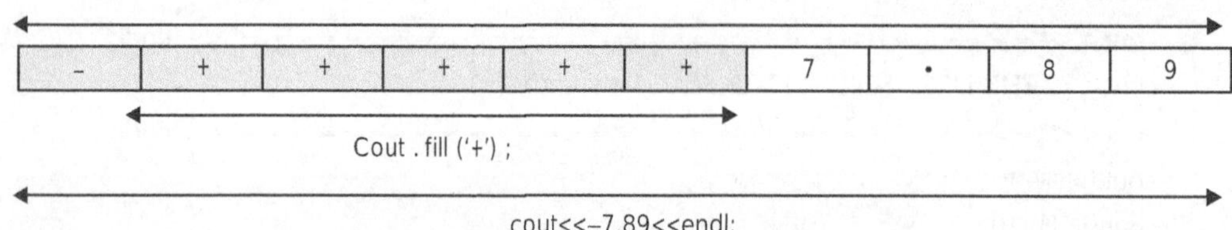

Figure 11.9. *Implementation of flags used in C++*

The following statement used to flash the second formatted flag.

```
cout.fill('X');
cout.precision(3);
cout.width(15);
cout.setf(ios : :internal,ios : :adjustfield);
cout.setf(ios : :scientific,ios : :floatfield);
cout< <-32.43567< <endl;
```

-	X	X	X	X	3	•	2	4	4	C	+	0	0	1

/* PROG 11.18 CONVERTING DECIMAL VALUE INTO OCTAL AND HEX USING FORMATTING FLAGS */

```
#include <iostream.h>
#include <conio.h>
void main( )
{
    int x;
    clrscr( );
    cout< <"——————————————————"< <endl;
    cout< <"ENTER ANY NUMBER IN DECIMAL \n";
    cout< <"——————————————————"< <endl;
    cin> >x;
    cout< <"——————————————————"< <endl;
    cout< <"DECIMAL VALUE IS :";
    cout< <"\n——————————————————"< <endl;
    cout.setf(ios : :dec,ios : : basefield);
    cout< <x< <endl;
```

```
    cout<<"\n--------------------------------"<<endl;
    cout<<"OCTAL VALUE IS :=";
    cout<<"\n--------------------------------"<<endl;
    cout.setf(ios : :oct,ios : :basefield);
    cout<<x<<endl;
    cout<<"\n--------------------------------"<<endl;
    cout<<"HEX VALUE IS :=";
    cout<<"\n--------------------------------"<<endl;
    cout.setf(ios : :hex,ios : :basefield);
    cout<<x<<endl;
    cout<<"\n--------------------------------"<<endl;
    getch( );
}
```

OUTPUT :

```
--------------------------------
ENTER ANY NUMBER IN DECIMAL
--------------------------------
23
--------------------------------
DECIMAL VALUE IS :
--------------------------------
23
--------------------------------
OCTAL VALUE IS : =
--------------------------------
27
--------------------------------
HEX VALUE IS : =
--------------------------------
17
--------------------------------
```

EXPLANATION : Formatting flag

cout.setf (ios : : dec,ios : :basefield);

Used to display integer data into decimal

cout.setf (ios : : oct, ios : : basefield);

Displays integer data into octal

cout.setf (ios : :hex, ios : : basefield);

Displays integer data into hexadecimal

/* PROG 11.19 DEMO OF SHOW POS AND SHOWPOINT FLAGS */

```
#include <iostream.h>
#include <conio.h>
 void main( )
 {
      clrscr( );
      cout.setf(ios : :showpos);
      cout.setf(ios : :showpoint);
      cout.width(8);
      cout.precision(4);
      cout<<125<<endl;
      cout.width(8);
      cout<<23.0<<endl;
      cout.width(8);
      cout<<34.5<<endl;
      cout.setf(ios : :hex,ios : :basefield);
      cout.setf(ios : :uppercase);
      cout<<0x34f<<endl;
      getch( );
 }
```

OUTPUT :

```
 +125
+23.0000
+34.5000
34F
```

EXPLANATION : For the first three cout width of 8 is set. So output appears as :

				+	1	2	5
+	2	3	•	0	0	0	0
+	3	4	•	5	0	0	0

In last cout output appear in **hex** in uppercase due to flag **ios : :uppercase.**

/* PROG 11.20 RETURN TYPE OF WIDTH AND PRECISION FUNCTION */

```
#include <iostream.h>
#include <conio.h>
```

```
void main( )
{
    clrscr( );
    cout.width(10);
    int pw=  cout.width(5);
    cout<<"previous width="<<pw<<endl;
    cout.precision(3);
    int pp=cout.precision(4);
    cout<<"previous precision="<<pp<<endl;
    getch( );
}
```

OUTPUT :

```
previous width=10
previous precision=3
```

EXPLANATION : The `width` and `precision` function returns the previous width and previous precision respectively set earlier and sets the new width and new precision. In the program `pw` contains the previous width set *i.e.,* `10` and `pp` contains the previous `precision` set *i.e.,*`3`.

/*PROG 11.21 DEMO OF PEEK AND IGNORE FUNCTION */

```
#include <iostream.h>
#include <conio.h>

void main( )
{
    clrscr( );
    cout<<"ENTER A STRING"<<endl;
    char ch,x;
    ch=cin.get( );
    while(ch!='\n')
    {
        cout.put(ch);
        x=cin.peek( );
        while(x=='$')
        {
            cin.ignore(1,'$');
            x=  cin.peek( );
        }
        ch=cin.get( );
    }
```

```
        cout<<endl;
        getch( );
    }
```

OUTPUT :

```
Enter a string with $ character embedded
This $ is $$ de$mo$.
This is demo.
```

EXPLANATION : The function `peek()` returns the next character without extracting it from the `stream`. In the program it is enclosed it is checked whether next input character is `'$'`. The function ignore extracts the number of characters n given as first argument (here 1) matching second argument character (here '$'). So whenever next input character in the stream is `'$'` it is ignored. The ignore function extracts the character and discard it. Here one `'$'` character and discard. Here one `'$'` character at a time is discarded.

/* PROG 11.22 DEMO OF putback FUNCTION */

```
#include <iostream.h>
#include <conio.h>

 void main( )
 {
        clrscr( );
        cout<<"ENTER A STRING"<<endl;
        char ch;
        ch=cin.get( );
        while(ch!='\0')
        {
            if(ch=='$')
            cin.putback('&');
            cout.put(ch);
            ch=cin.get( );
        }
        cout<<endl;
        getch( );
 }
```

OUTPUT :

```
ENTER A STRING
This$ is $ de$mo
This$& is $& de$&mo
```

EXPLANATION : The `putback` function puts a character back into the input stream. The character to put back must be character previously extracted. Here character is extracted from the input streams and if extracted character is equal to `'$'` character `'&'` is put back into the input stream.

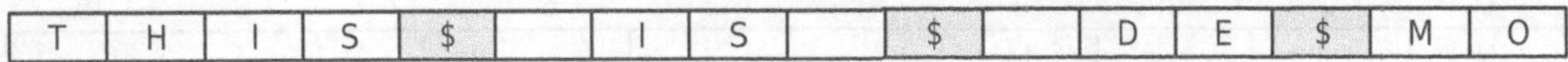

T	H	I	S	$		I	S		$		D	E	$	M	O

Figure 11.10. *Before applying putback function*

When compiler control finds the statements given below then after '$' symbol put '&'.

```
if(ch= ='$')
cin.putback('&');
```

T	H	I	S	$	&	I	S		$	&	D	E	$	&	M	O

Figure 11.11. *After applying putback function*

/*PROG 11.23 DEMO OF gcount( ) FUNCTION */

```
#include <iostream.h>
#include <conio.h>
#include <ctype.h>
void main( )
{
    char str[15];
    clrscr( );
    cout<<"————————————————————"<<endl;
    cout<<"ENTER A STRING HERE";
    cout<<endl<<"————————————————————"<<endl;

    cin.getline(str,15);
    int len;
    len=cin.gcount( );
    cout<<endl<<"————————————————————"<<endl;
    cout<<"LENGTH OF STRING IS :="<<len-1<<endl;
    cout<<"————————————————————"<<endl;
    getch( );
}
```

OUTPUT :

```
————————————————————
ENTER A STRING HERE
————————————————————
MPSTME NMIMS
————————————————————
LENGTH OF STRING IS : =12
————————————————————
```

EXPLANATION : The function gcount returns the number of characters extracted by the last unformatted function is `getline`, `cin.gcount()` returns the number of characters extracted from keyboard by getline function and assigned to `str`. It also count null character so **length-1** is used here.

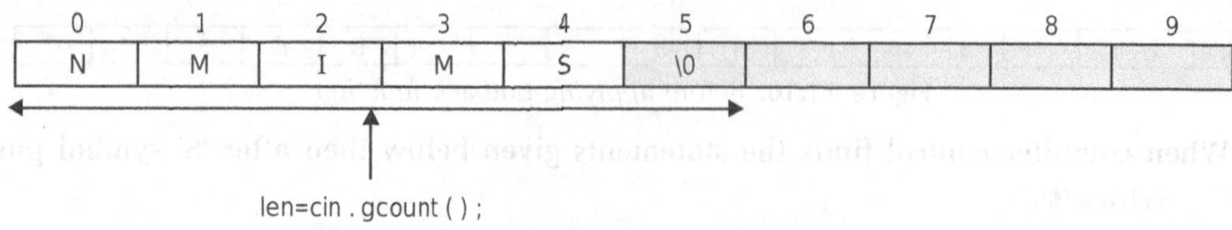

Figure 11.12. *Logical implementation of gcount( )*

The prototype of this function lies in **istream.h (istream : : gcount (member function)).**

/*PROG 11.24 DEMO OF eatwhite FUNCTION */

```
#include <iostream.h>
#include <conio.h>
void main( )
{
    ifstream file("num.txt");
    char ch;
    file.get(ch);
    while(file.eof( )= =0)
    {
        cout.put(ch);
        file.eatwhite( );
        file.get( );
    }
    file.close( );
    getch( );
}
```

OUTPUT :

```
Thisisdemoofeatwhite
```

EXPLANATION : As explained earlier the function eatwhite eats whites spaces like spaces, tabs etc and advances the `get` pointer. Here we assumes that file `num.txt` contains contains `"This is demo of eat white"`. We read the file sequentially character by character using get. Whenever any while space character is found function eatwhite eats it and advances `get` pointer. The output is all characters except space and tab.

/*PROG 11.25 GIVING new NAME TO cout AND cin */

```
#include <iostream.h>
#include <conio.h>
```

```
void main( )
{
    clrscr( );
    ostream print(1);
    istream_withassign scan;
    scan = cin;
    print<<"————————————————"<<endl;
    print<<"ENTER YOUR NAME"<<endl;
    print<<"————————————————"<<endl;
        char str[15];
    scan.getline(str,15);
    print<<endl<<"————————————————"<<endl;
    print<<"HELLO "<<str<<endl;
    print<<endl<<"————————————————"<<endl;
    getch( );
}
```

OUTPUT :

```
————————————————
ENTER YOUR NAME
————————————————
Hari Pandey
————————————————
HELLO Hari Pandey
————————————————
```

EXPLANATION : Here `1` represents standard output stream. We have created an object of ostream class and in it passed `1` as argument. Now print can be treated as `cout`. `cin` is an object of `istream_withassign` so we create an object scan of this type assign cin to it. Now scan can be treated as cin.

11.5 MANIPULATORS

Manipulators are functions which are used to manipulate the input/output formats. Manipulators are of two types :

(*a*) One which take arguments.

(*b*) Second which does not take any argument.

One type of manipulator which we have seen is **endl** which is used to insert new line into stream. All the manipulators which are built-in and which is used to insert new line are defined in the header file **iomanip.h**. The file **iostream.h** provides some manipulators which does not take any argument.

Most of the built-in manipulators are similar to their setf counterpart like **width, precision, fill** etc. The advantage here is that manipulators can directly be put into the stream as :

```
cout<<setw(5)<<123;
cout<<x<<endl;
cout<<hex<<x;
```

All manipulators which do not take any argument are having the following syntax :

```
ostream & mani_name(ostream &)
{
}
```

For example the most commonly used manipulator endl is defined as :

```
ostream endl(ostream &);
```

When we write **cout<<endl;**

It is interpreted internally as **cout.operator<<(endl);**

Again as **endl** takes a reference of **ostream** as argument writing **endl(cout);** is equivalent to writing **cout<<endl;**

Table 11.3 : List of Most Commonly Used Built-in Manipulator

S.No.	*Manipulator*	*Meaning*
1	setw(int n)	Sets the output width of n characters
2.	setfill(char x)	The manipulator sets the stream's fill character
3.	setprecision(int n)	Sets the precision for floating points number
4.	hex	Converts to hexadecimal
5.	oct	Convert to octal
6.	dec	Convert to decimal
7.	left	Left justify, right padding
8.	right	Right justify, left padding
9.	endl	Insert a new line and flush output stream
10.	uppercase	Displays A-F for hex and E for scientific
11.	showpos	To insert a plus sign in a non-negative generated numeric field
12.	scientific	To insert floating-point values in scientific format
13.	fixed	To insert floating-point values in fixed-point format
14.	setiosflags(flags f)	Sets the formatting flags specified by f. setting remains in effect until changed.
15.	resetiosflags(flags f)	Clear the formatting flags specified by f. setting remains in effect until changed.

/*PROG 11.26 DEMO OF BUILT-IN MANIPULATORS VER 1*/

```
#include <iostream.h>
#include <iomanip.h>
#include <conio.h>
void main( )
{
    clrscr( );
    cout<<setw(5)<<345<<endl;
    cout<<setw(5)<<45<<endl;
    cout<<5<<endl;
    cout<<setfill('$')<<setw(10)
<<"hello"<<setw(10)<<345.678<<endl;
    getch( );
}
```

OUTPUT :

```
  345
   45
5
$$$$$hello$$$345.678
```

EXPLANATION : The following two cout statement sets the width 5 and displays the data that follows :

```
cout<<setw(5)<<345<<endl;
    cout<<setw(5)<<45<<endl;
```

		3	4	5
			4	5

Figure 11.13. *Implementation of setw function*

The next cout display 5 as it as no width is set. The next cout statement

```
cout<<setfill('$')<<setw(10)
        <<"hello"<<setw(10)<<345.678<<endl;
```

First sets width **10** and fill character **'$'** for displaying string **"hello"**. Next width of **10** for displaying **345.678**

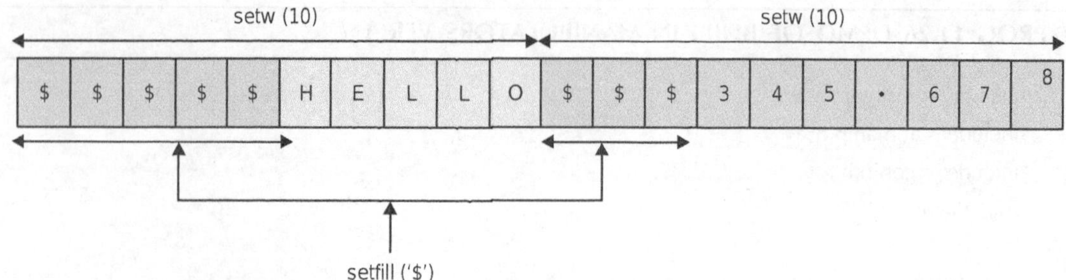

Figure 11.14. *Diagrammatic implementation of built-in manipulators*

/* PROG 11.27 DEMO OF BUILT-IN MANIPULATORS VER 2*/

```
#include <iostream.h>
#include <iomanip.h>
#include <conio.h>

void main( )

{
    int x=456;
    float y = 23.45456;
    char *s="Manipulator";
    clrscr( );
    cout<<"============================="<<endl;
    cout<<"THE DEMO SHOWN BELOW"<<endl;
    cout<<"============================="<<endl;
    cout<<setfill('$')<<setw(15)<<setiosflags(ios : :left)
          <<x<<endl;
    cout<<setfill('*')<<setw(15)<<setiosflags(ios : :left)
          <<setprecision(3)<<y<<endl;
    cout<<setfill('&')<<setw(15)<<setiosflags(ios : :left)
          <<s<<endl;
    cout<<endl<<"============================="<<endl;
    cout<<"DEMO FINISH"<<endl;
    cout<<"============================="<<endl;
    getch( );
}
```

OUTPUT :

```
==========================
THE DEMO SHOWN BELOW
==========================
```

```
456$$$$$$$$$$$$
23.455*********
Manipulator&&&&

============================

DEMO FINISH
============================
```

EXPLANATION : The following cout statement

```
cout<<setfill('$')<<setw(15)<<setiosflags(ios : :left)
        <<x<<endl;
```

Sets the width 15, setfill character to '$' and sets the output left justified which causes value of x to be printed.

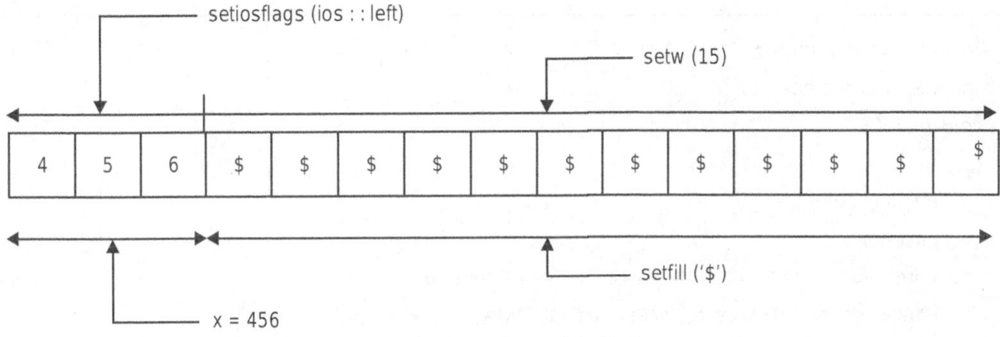

Figure 11.15. *Implementation of built in manipulator*

The next cout statement is given as :

```
cout<<setfill('*')<<setw(15)<<setiosflags(ios : :left)
        <<setprecision(3)<<y<<endl;
```

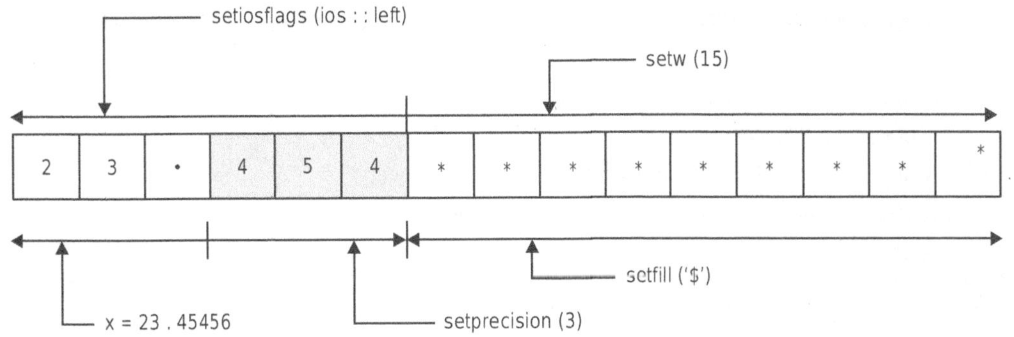

Figure 11.16. *Demo of setprecision and setiosflags (ios : :left)*

The next cout statement

```
cout<<setfill('&')<<setw(15)<<setiosflags(ios : :left)
            <<s<<endl;
```

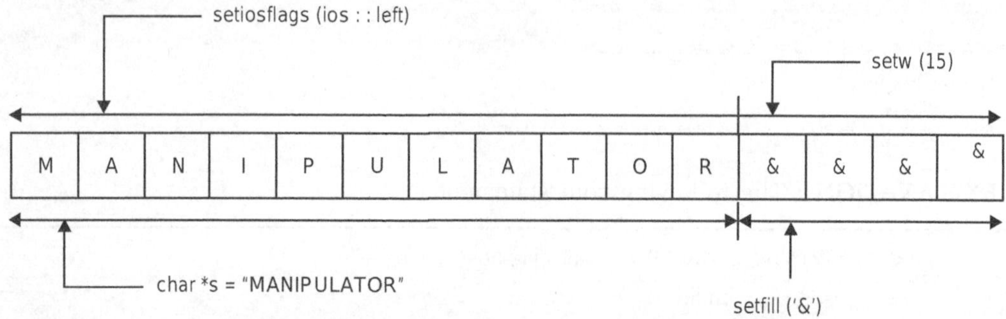

Figure 11.17. *Implementation of manipulator for string.*

/*PROG 11.28 DEMO OF BUILT-IN MANIPULATORS VER 3*/

```
#include <iostream.h>
#include <conio.h>
void main( )
{
    int dec_enter;
    clrscr( );
    cout<<"---------------------------"<<endl;
    cout<<"ENTER ANY NUMBER IN DECIMAL :="<<endl;
    cout<<"---------------------------"<<endl;
    cin>>dec_enter;
    cout<<"---------------------------"<<endl;
    cout<<"DECIMAL VALUE :=";
    cout<<dec<<dec_enter<<endl;
    cout<<"---------------------------"<<endl;
    cout<<"OCTAL VALUE :=";
    cout<<oct<<dec_enter<<endl;
    cout<<"---------------------------"<<endl;
    cout<<"HEXADECIMAL :=";
    cout<<hex<<dec_enter<<endl;
    cout<<"---------------------------"<<endl;
    getch( );
}
```

OUTPUT :

```
---------------------------
ENTER ANY NUMBER IN DECIMAL : =
```

```
----------------------------
35
----------------------------
DECIMAL VALUE : =35
----------------------------
OCTAL VALUE : =43
----------------------------
HEXADECIMAL : =23
----------------------------
```

EXPLANATION : In the above given program the statement `cout<<hex<<dec_enter<<endl;` displays the value of `dec_enter` in hex format. In the same track `cout<<oct<<dec_enter<<endl;` used to display the value of `dec_enter` in octal format.

/*PROG 11.29 DEMO OF BUILT-IN MANIPULATORS VER 4*/

```
#include <iostream.h>
#include <conio.h>

void main( )
{
    int x,y;
    clrscr( );
    cout<<"==========================="<<endl;
    cout<<"ENTER A HEX VALUE"<<endl;
    cout<<"==========================="<<endl;
    cin>>hex>>x;
    cout<<"==========================="<<endl;
    cout<<"HEX VALUE :="<<hex<<x<<endl;
    cout<<"==========================="<<endl;
    cout<<"DEC VALUE :="<<dec<<x<<endl;
    cout<<"==========================="<<endl;
    cout<<"OCTAL VALUE :="<<oct<<x<<endl;
    cout<<"==========================="<<endl;
    getch( );
}
```

OUTPUT :

```
==========================
ENTER A HEX VALUE
==========================
F
```

```
===========================
HEX VALUE : =f
===========================
DEC VALUE : =15
===========================
OCTAL VALUE : =17
===========================
```

EXPLANATION : The program is self explanatory. For better understand point see the explanation of the previous program.

/*PROG 11.30 DEMO OF BUILT-IN MANIPULATORS VER 5*/

```
#include <iostream.h>
#include <conio.h>

void main( )
{
    int oct_enter;
    clrscr( );
    cout<<"====================================="<<endl;
    cout<<"ENTER AN OCTAL VALUE \n";
    cout<<"====================================="<<endl;
    cin>>oct>>oct_enter;
    cout<<"====================================="<<endl;
    cout<<"HEX VALUE :="<<hex<<oct_enter<<endl;
    cout<<"====================================="<<endl;
    cout<<"DEC VALUE :="<<dec<<oct_enter<<endl;
    cout<<"====================================="<<endl;
    cout<<"OCT VALUE :="<<oct<<oct_enter<<endl;
    cout<<"====================================="<<endl;
    getch( );
}
```

OUTPUT :

```
=================================
ENTER AN OCTAL VALUE
=================================
17
=================================
HEX VALUE : =f
=================================
```

```
DEC VALUE : =15
===================================
OCT VALUE : =17
===================================
```

EXPLANATION : See the explanation of the program 11.28.

/*PROG 11.31 DEMO OF BUILT-IN MANIPULATORS VER 5*/

```
#include <iostream.h>
#include <conio.h>

void main( )
{
    clrscr( );
    cout<<"************************";
    endl(cout);
    cout<<"FIRST LINE";
    endl(cout);
    cout<<"************************";
    endl(cout);
    cout<<"SECOND LINE";
    endl(cout);
    cout<<"************************";
    endl(cout);
    cout<<"THIRD LINE";
    endl(cout);
    cout<<"************************";
    endl(cout);
    cout<<"FOURTH LINE";
    endl(cout);
    cout<<"************************";
    getch( );
}
```

OUTPUT :

```
***********************
FIRST LINE
***********************
SECOND LINE
***********************
THIRD LINE
```

```
**********************
FOURTH LINE
**********************
```

EXPLANATION : All the manipulators take an argument of `ostream` by reference so we can pass `cout` as an argument of `endl`. So writing `endl(cout);` works as writing `cout<<endl;`

11.5.1 Creating Your Own Manipulators

Apart from using the built-in manipulators of C++, you can create your own manipulator for whatever purpose you want. For creating your own manipulator which does not take any argument the syntax is as shown earlier :

```
ostream & manip_name (ostream & mycout)
{
        ____________;
        ____________;
        ____________;
        return mycout;
}
```

All user defined manipulator must take an argument by reference of ostream type and return ostream type by reference. As we pass reference of cout when use this manipulator, actual changes done by manipulator occur as if we are working with cout. For example consider a manipulator which emulates double space *i.e.,* when we use it leaves two spaces in the stream and continues.

```
ostream & DS(ostream & mycout)
{
        mycout<<"  ";
        return mycout;
}
```

To use this we can write as **cout<<DS<<"hello"<<DS;**

This first leaves two spaces, prints **"hello"** and then again leaves two spaces. As mentioned earlier the main advantage of manipulators whether user defined or built-in that they can be put into the **cin** and **cout** stream easily using **>>** and **<<**. This advantage of manipulator makes them popular.

We present few program for better understanding point of view.

/*PROG 11.32 CREATING YOUR OWN MANIPULATOR VER 1*/

```
#include <iostream.h>
#include <conio.h>
```

```
ostream & DS(ostream & mycout)
{
    mycout<<" ";
    return mycout;
}

void main( )

{
    clrscr( );
    cout<<"Before Applying manipulator";
    endl(cout);
    cout<<"HELLO";
    endl(cout);
    cout<<"After applying own manipulator";
    endl(cout);
    cout<<DS<<"HELLO"<<DS;
    getch( );
}
```

OUTPUT :

```
Before Applying manipulator
Hello
After applying own manipulator
 HELLO
```

EXPLANATION : In the program the following given statements just used to print **"hello"**

```
cout<<"Before Applying manipulator";
    endl(cout);
    cout<<"HELLO";
```

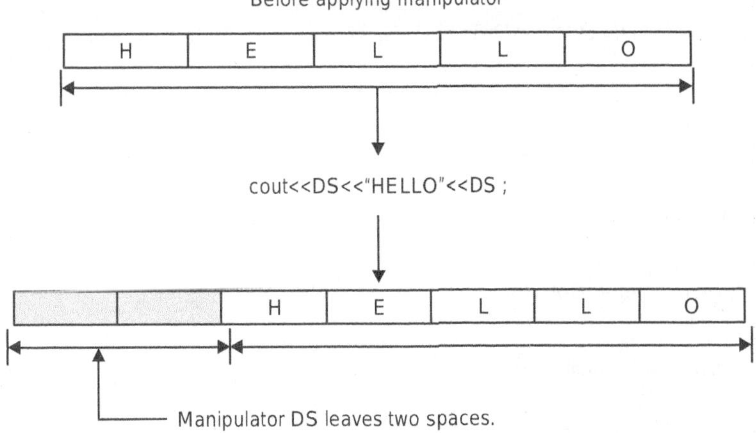

Figure 11.18 : *Logical implementation of user defined manipulator*

/*PROG 11.33 CREATING YOUR OWN MANIPULATOR VER 2*/

```
#include <iostream.h>
#include <conio.h>

/* Manipulator for two spaces */
ostream & DSD(ostream & mycout)
{
    mycout<<" ";
    return mycout;
}
/*Manipulator for three spaces */
ostream & DST(ostream & mycout)
{
    mycout<<" ";
    return mycout;
}
void main( )
{
    clrscr( );
    cout<<"Before Applying manipulator";
    endl(cout);
    cout<<"HELLO";
    endl(cout);
    cout<<"After applying own manipulator DSD";
    endl(cout);
    cout<<DSD<<"HELLO"<<DSD;
    endl(cout);
    cout<<"After applying own manipulator DST";
    endl(cout);
    cout<<DST<<"HELLO"<<DST;
    getch( );
}
```

OUTPUT :

```
Before Applying manipulator
HELLO
After applying own manipulator DSD
 HELLO
After applying own manipulator DST
 HELLO
```

EXPLANATION : This program is very much similar to previous one, only the difference is that in this we have declared one more user defined manipulator for putting three spaces in the beginning the desired string **"HELLO"**. The below shown figure shows the actual implementation of manipulators.

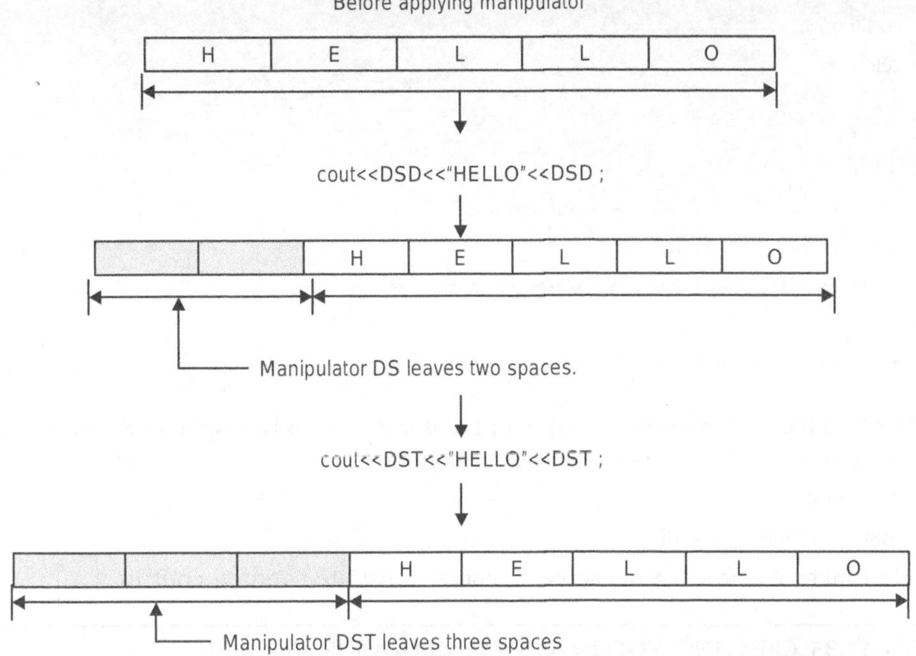

Figure 11.19. *Implementation of more than one user-defined manipulator*

/* PROG 11.34 CREATING YOUR OWN MANIPULATOR VER 3 */

```
#include <iostream.h>
#include <conio.h>
/* CREATION OF MANIPULATOR */
ostream & Rup(ostream & mycout)
{
    mycout<<"Rs ";
    return mycout;
}
void main( )
{
    int money = 8000;
    clrscr( );
    cout<<"==============================";
    endl(cout);
    cout<<"AMOUNT IS SHOWN HERE";
    endl(cout);
```

```
	cout<<"=============================";
	endl(cout);
	cout<<Rup<<money<<"/-"<<endl;
	cout<<"=============================";
	endl(cout);
	getch( );
}
```

OUTPUT :

```
=============================
AMOUNT IS SHOWN HERE
=============================
Rs 8000/-
=============================
```

EXPLANATION : The user defined manipulator Rup simply displays "Rs" where it is used in the cout statement. It can be used in this manner also.

```
Rup (cout);
cout<<money<<endl;
```

As Rup takes a reference of ostream type and we are sending cout in it.

/* PROG 11.35 CREATING YOUR OWN MANIPULATOR VER 4 */

```
#include <iostream.h>
#include <conio.h>
#include <iomanip.h>
ostream & format(ostream & mycout)
{
	mycout<<setw(8)<<setfill('$');
	return mycout;
}

void main( )
{
	int num1 = 1234;
	float num2=35.56;
	char *str ="HELLO";
	clrscr( );
	cout<<format<<num1<<endl;
	cout<<format<<num2<<endl;
	cout<<format<<str<<endl;
	getch( );
}
```

OUTPUT :

```
$$$$1234
$$$35.56
$$$HELLO
```

EXPLANATION : The manipulator format does two things when called with cout, its sets width of 8 and fill character as '$'. For all three data **num1, num2**, and **str** a single call to format sets the width and sets fill character **'$'.** You can use any formatting manipulator as per your requirement and make one as your own manipulator.

/*PROG 11.36 CREATING YOUR OWN MANIPULATOR VER 5*/

```
#include <iostream.h>
#include <conio.h>

/*CREATION OF MANIPULATOR STARTS */

ostream & tab (ostream & mycout)
{
    mycout<<"\t";
        return mycout;
}

ostream & new_line(ostream & mycout)
{
    mycout<<"\n";
    return mycout;
}

ostream & bell_alert(ostream & mycout)
{
    mycout<<"\a";
    return mycout;
}

ostream & ver_tab(ostream & mycout)
{
    mycout<<"\v";
    return mycout;
}

ostream & wel_mssg(ostream & mycout)
```

```
{
    mycout<<"WELCOME";
    return mycout;
}

/* CREATION OF MANIPULATOR FINISH HERE */

void main( )
{
    int a=5,b=6;
    char *name = "hari";
    clrscr( );
    cout<<"————————————————"<<endl;
    cout<<"DEMO OF TAB AND NEW LINE"<<endl;
    cout<<"————————————————"<<endl;
    cout<<a<<tab<<b<<new_line;
    cout<<endl;
    cout<<"————————————————"<<endl;
    cout<<"DEMO OF VERTICAL TAB AND NEW LINE"<<endl;
    cout<<"————————————————"<<endl;
    cout<<a<<ver_tab<<b<<new_line;
    cout<<endl;
    cout<<"————————————————"<<endl;
    cout<<wel_mssg<<name<<new_line;
    cout<<endl;
    cout<<"————————————————"<<endl;
    cout<<"DEMO OF BELL ALERT"<<endl;
    cout<<"————————————————"<<endl;
    cout<<bell_alert<<a<<tab<<bell_alert<<b<<new_line;
    getch( );
}
```

OUTPUT :

```
————————————————————————————
DEMO OF TAB AND NEW LINE
————————————————————————————
5        6
————————————————————————————
DEMO OF VERTICAL TAB AND NEW LINE
————————————————————————————
5
```

```
6
--------------------------------
WELCOME hari
--------------------------------
DEMO OF BELL ALERT
--------------------------------
5       6
```

EXPLANATION : In the program we have created a numbers of manipulator for `tab` for horizontal tab `('\t')`, `new_line` for new line `('\n')`, `ver_tab` for vertical tab `('\v')`, `wel_mssg` for printing welcome, and `bell_alert` for bell alert `('\a')`. Rest statements are self explanatory.

11.6 PONDERABLE POINTS

1. A stream is sequence of bytes.
2. ios is the topmost class in the hierarchy of stream class.
3. The most common stream classes for input and output is istream and ostream.
4. cin is considered as standard input stream as it read data from standard input stream device *i.e.*, keyboard and put into program.
5. cout is considered as standard output stream as its read data from program and put onto the standard output device which is screen.
6. Simple use of input and output with cout and cin with << and >> is termed as unformatted input/output operations.
7. To read a single character from keyboard we have function get and for writing a character onto the screen we have put function.
8. For reading a whole line of text including white space, getline can be used.
9. For setting the various flags for input and output cout.setf can be used.
10. Manipulator are special function which takes a reference of ostream class and return a reference of ostream class.
11. They are better than their counterpart ios formatting functions as they can be put directly into the input and output stream.

EXERCISE

A. Answer the Following Questions :

1. What do you understand by streams ?
2. What is the different type of stream classes C++ provides ?
3. What is formatted and unformatted input/output ?
4. How does cin and cout works with >> and << operator ?
5. What is the importance of self-function ?

6. What are various flags the function self can take ?
7. What is manipulator ?
8. How manipulator is different from ios functions ?
9. How can we create our own manipulator ?

B. Brain Drill :

1. Create an input manipulator say skiptoletter that reads and discards all characters which are not letters. When the first letter is found, the manipulator puts it back into the input stream and returns. Write a suitable main function which illustrates the use of this manipulator.

❑❑❑

CHAPTER 12

FILE HANDLING IN C++

12.1 INTRODUCTION

We all know that **RAM** is a volatile memory and any data stored in **RAM** is lost when PC is turned off. All the program we have seen so far have made use of **RAM**. Any data variable that we define in our program is destroyed when the program execution is over. Also the outputs generated by the program are lost.

One solution may be to take printouts of the program and outputs. They may help up to a certain extent but that is not appropriate for the practical purpose. Therefore in most real word applications data is stored in text files which is stored permanently on to the hard disk, floppy, compact disk or in any other persistent storage media. These files can be read back again, and can be modified also.

A data file is a collection of data items stored permanently in persistent storage area. The **C++** language provides the facility to create these data files, write data into them, read back data, modify them and many more operations. The program data or output can be stored in these files and that persists even after program execution is over. The data can be read whenever necessary and can be placed back into the file after modification. The data remains safe provided storage media does not crash or corrupt.

From permanent storage point of view, a file is a region of memory space in the persistent storage media and it can be accessed using built-in library functions and classes available in header file iostream.h or by the stream calls of the operating systems. High level files are those files which are accessed and manipulated using library functions. For transfer of data they make use of stream. A stream is a pointer to a buffer of memory which is used for transferring the data. In general stream can be assumed as a sequence of bytes which flow from source to destination. An I/O stream may be text stream or binary stream depending upon in which mode you have opened the file. A text stream contains lines of text and the characters in a text stream may be manipulated as per the suitability. But a binary stream is a sequence of unprocessed data without any modification. The standard I/O stream or stream pointers are **cin (for reading), cout (for writing), and cerr (for error).** By default cin represent key board, **stdout** and **stderr** represents monitor **VDU**.

Low-level files makes use of the system-calls of the opening system under which the program is run.

12.2 FILE STREAMS

In C++ there are three main classes for handling disk files input and output. They are :

(*a*) ifstream

(*b*) ofstream

(*c*) fstream

(*a*) The **ifstream** class is an istream derived specialized for disk file input. Its constructors automatically create and attach a **filebuf** buffer object. A file can be created by the constructor method or using the open method of ifstream class. For closing the file close method can be used. **ifstream** can only be used for reading a file.

(*b*) The **ofstream** class is an ostream derivative specialized for disk file output. All of its constructors automatically create and associate a **filebuf** buffer object. A file can be created by the constructor method or using the open method of **ofstream** class. For closing the file close method can be used. **ofstream** can only be used for writing to a file only.

(*c*) The **fstream** class is an iostream derivative specialized for combined disk file input and output. Its constructor automatically create and attach a **filebuf** buffer object. A file can be created by the constructor or method or using the open method of **fstream** class. For closing the file close method can be used. The **fstream** class can be used for reading writing, appending or doing any other operation as well as we will see shortly.

12.3 OPENING AND CLOSING A FILE

For opening a file any of the above discussed file stream can be used. For opening a file for reading only we can use ifstream class as :

(*a*) ifstream rdfile("demo.txt")

The above method creates an object of class ifstream type and attaches it to the file **"demo.txt"**. The file is opened for read only. The object is created by calling the constructor of the class ifstream and passing an argument of char* type which is file name to open. As soon as file is opened for read mode, file pointer is placed at the beginning of the file. We assume that there is no error in opening the file. Error handling will be discussed later on. Assuming the file is opened successfully. We can read from the file as :

```
char str[10];
file>>str;
```

The string read from file (assuming file contains a string "hello") will be stored in the variable **str.** The file can be closed later by calling the close method of the class as :

```
file.close( );
```

Calling close method ensures all data stored in the buffer related to the file will be written to the disk and all links will be broken. Always make a practice of closing a file when you are done with the file.

(*b*) ifstream rdfile;

```
rdfile.open ("demo.txt");
```

This is the second method of opening the file. Here first an object of ifstream class type is created. We then open the file using the open function of the ifstream class.

On the similar ground we can open a file for writing only the ofstream class as :

(*a*) ofstream wrfile("demo.txt");

(*b*) ofstream wrfile;

```
wrfile.open("demo.txt");
```

Explanation for the above methods is similar to the explanation as given for the ifstream class. The data can be written to the file as :

```
wrfile<<"hello";
```

The file can be closed as :

```
wrfile.close ( );
```

The ifstream class and ofstream class are suitable only when we want to read only from file or write only to the file. In situations when we want to perform reading and writing to the same file. There are two ways :

- First is to create two separate objects of ifstream and ofstream class. When writing is done, close the file and open the file for reading using an object of ifstream class.
- The second method is to create just one object of class fstream class and use as :

```
fstream file;
file.open("demo.txt",ios : :out);
//perform writing operation;
file.close( );
file.open("demo.txt",ios : :in);
//perform reading operation;
```

In the open function of **fstream** class, second argument is the file opening mode. The mode **ios : :in** is for reading and **ios : :out** for writing only. The modes are defined as enumeration constants in the class ios so scope resolution operator is used with it. We discuss more modes later in this chapter.

Note that there is no **ios : :in** or **ios : :out** default mode for **fstream** objects. You must specify both modes if your **fstream** object read and write files. We can also have constructor method of **fstream** for creating and opening a file as :

```
fstream file("num.txt"ios : :in);
char str[10];
file>>str;
cout<<str<<endl;
```

Let's have some programming examples first then we will see what other modes we can have for handling the files.

/*PROG 12.1 DEMO OF FILE HANDLING, WRITING TO FILE VER 1*/

```
#include <iostream.h>
#include <fstream.h>
#include <conio.h>

void main( )
{
      clrscr( );
      ofstream fobj("demo.txt");
      fobj<<"FILE HANDLING DEMONSTATION "<<endl;
      fobj.close( );
      getch( );
}
```

OUTPUT :

(BLANK SCREEN)

EXPLANATION : The statement ofstream `fobj("demo.txt");` creates an object of ostream class type named `fobj` and passes file name as `"demo.txt"`. This way of creating file is `called constructor notation` as we are creating and object of `ostream` type by calling the constructor which takes an argument of type `char*` type. After the execution of the above statement a file stream `fobj` is created and linked to the file `"demo.txt"`. Now when you want to write something to the file you can write it as shown with the use of <<operator.

```
fobj<<"FILE HANDLING DEMONSTRATION"<<endl;
```

This writes string "**FILE HANDLING DEMONSTRATION**" to the file "**demo.txt**".

Note **ofstream** class is meant only for writing to the disk files. You cannot read from the file using an object of ofstream. As soon as you open the file using an object of **ofstream** class type, the file is automatically opened in the write mode. That's why no mode was specified while opening the file. If file "**demo.txt**" were already existing its contents will be destroyed and file pointer will be placed at the beginning of the file. If file were not already present it will be created.

/*PROG 12.2 DEMO OF FILE HANDLING, WRITING TO FILE VER 2 */

```
#include <iostream.h>
#include <fstream.h>
#include <conio.h>

void main( )
{
      clrscr( );
      ofstream fobj;
      fobj.open("demo.txt");
```

```
    fobj<<" FILE HANDLING DEMO"<<endl;
    fobj.close( );
    getch( );
}
```

OUTPUT :

(BLANK SCREEN)

EXPLANATION : The program shows the outer method of opening a file for writing only. It simply creates an object of ofstream class type and by using open method opens the file. Rest is same as explained in the previous program. There is one more parameter to the open method which specifies the mode in which we want to open the file. Here mode for writing is ios : :out, but this is optional for ofstream class as by default file is opened for writing only.

/* PROG 12.3 DEMO OF FILE HANDLING, READING FROM FILE VER 1*/

```
#include <iostream.h>
#include <fstream.h>
#include <conio.h>

void main( )
{
    clrscr( );
    ifstream fobj;
    fobj.open("demo.txt");
    char str[30];
    fobj.getline(str,30);
    cout<<"STRING READ FROM FILE"<<endl;
    cout<<str<<endl;
    fobj.close( );
    getch( );
}
```

OUTPUT :

```
STRING READ FROM FILE
 FILE HANDLING DEMO
```

EXPLANATION : The statement ifstream fobj; creates an object of ifstream type name fobj. The class ifstream is meant only for reading only. We open the file using the open method. The file name which we want to open is passed as argument to open method. The open method opens the file demo.txt and links objects fobj to this file. Now this object fobj work as a stream for reading from this file "demo.txt". We read from the file as :

```
fobj. getline(str,30);
```

The above lines read from the file "demo.txt" first 29 characters or number of characters till '\n' is not encountered. The scanned string is stored in str which we display on to the screen using standard output stream cout.

Note the following two lines :

```
ifstream fobj;
    fobj.open("demo.txt");
```

Can be written as :

```
ifstream fobj("demo.txt");
```

As we did for ofstream class.

There is one more parameter to the open method which specifies the mode in which we want to open the file. Here mode for reading is ios : :in, but this is optional for ifstream class as by default file is opened for reading only.

/* PROG 12.4 WRITING PERSON DATA TO FILE */

```
#include <iostream.h>
#include <fstream.h>
#include <conio.h>

void main( )
{
    clrscr( );
    ofstream fobj;
    fobj.open("demo.txt");
    char name[25];
    int age;
    char sex;
    cout<<"ENTER NAME HERE :=";
    cin.getline(name,25);
    cout<<endl<<"ENTER THE AGE AND SEX :=";
    cin>>age>>sex;
    fobj<<name<<endl<<age<<endl<<sex<<endl;
    fobj.close( );
    getch( );
}
```

OUTPUT :

```
ENTER NAME HERE : =HARI MOHAN PANDEY
ENTER THE AGE AND SEX : =24 M
```

EXPLANATION : In the program we have opened a file `demo.txt`. In the file we are putting the details of person viz : `name, age and sex`. We take input from the standard input stream (*i.e.*, from keyboard) and put the scanned data to the file `demo.txt` which is linked to the `fobj` an object of `ofstream` class type. Note after each data item put into the class, a new lie is inserted. This comes handy when we read data from the file.

/* PROG 12.5 READING PERSON DATA FROM FILE */

```
#include <iostream.h>
#include <fstream.h>
#include <conio.h>
void main( )
{
    ifstream fobj;
    fobj.open("demo.txt");
    char name[20];
    int age;
    char sex;
    fobj.getline(name,20);
    fobj>>age>>sex;
    cout<<"Name :="<<name<<"\nAge :="<<age<<"\nSex :="<<sex
        <<endl;
    fobj.close( );
}
```

OUTPUT :

```
Name :=Hari
Age := 25
Sex := M
```

EXPLANATION : Here we opened the file which we created in the previous program. We create three variables : **name, age** and **sex**. The file is opened in read mode using an object of ifstream type named fobj. When we write **fobj.getline (name, 20);** it reads name from the file dem0.txt. After that age and sex from the file in the next statement as :

```
fobj>> age>>sex;
```

This is similar to reading from keyboard using cin but here instead from keyboard we are reading from file.

12.4 FILE OPENING MODES

Table 12.1: File opening modes

S.No.	*Mode*	*Meaning*
1.	ios : :in	Opening file in read mode only
2.	ios : :out	Opening file in write mode only

3.	ios : :app	Opening file in append mode
4.	ios : :trunc	File contents deleted if file already exists
5.	ios : :nocreate	In case file does not exist, open function will fail
6.	ios : :noreplace	Opens the file if file already exits
7.	ios : :binary	Open binary file
8.	ios : :ate	File pointer move to end of file on opening the file.

A brief description of all the modes is as follows :

1. ios : :trunc

If the file already exists, its contents are discarded. This mode is implied if **ios : :out** is specified, and **ios : :ate, ios : :app, and ios : :in** are not specified.

2. ios : :noreplace

If the file already exists, the function fails. This mode automatically opens the files for writing if file does not exist.

3. ios : :binary

Opens the file in binary mode (the default in text mode).

4. ios : :in

The files is opened for input. The original file (if it exists) will not be truncated.

5. ios : :ate

The function performs a seek to the end of file. When the first new byte is written to the file, it is appended to the end, but when subsequent bytes are written, they are written to the current position *i.e.*, any where in the file.

6. ios : :app

The function performs a seek to the end of file. When new bytes are written to the file, they are always appended to the end, even if the position is moved with the **ostream : :seekp** function.

7. ios : :nocreate

If the file does not already exist, the function fails.

8. A file can be opened in more than one mode. Number of modes can be combined using binary OR symbol (|)as :

```
file. open("demo.txt",ios : :in|ios : :out|ios : :binary);
```

/*PROG 12.6 READING AND WRITING THE SAME FILE IN ONE PROGRAM VER 1*/

```
#include <iostream.h>
#include <fstream.h>

void main( )
{
    fstream rw;
```

```
        rw.open("demo1.txt",ios : :out);
        char str[50];

        cout<<"ENTER A STRING"<<endl;
        cin.getline(str,50);

        rw<<str<<endl;

        rw.close( );

        rw.open("demo1.txt",ios : :in);
        rw.getline(str,50);
        cout<<"STRING READ FROM FILE"<<endl;
        cout<<str<<endl;

        rw.close( );
}
```

OUTPUT :

```
ENTER A STRING
Hello pandey
STRING READ FROM FILE
Hello pandey
```

EXPLANATION : Using an object of fstream class we can open the file in both the mode read and write using function open. Initially the file is opened in write mode as :

rw.open("demo1.txt", ios : :out);

The second parameter is file opening flag. The **ios** is a class and out is the property of the class. Together they are written as ios : :out which indicates that we have opened the file **demo1.txt** in write mode. Again if file did not exist already it will be created. If already created them all the contents will be wiped off. A string is taken from the standard input stream and written to the file as **rw<<str<<endl;** file is then closed by calling close method as :

rw.close( );

The file closing clears all buffers related to the file demo1.txt and unlike fie **demo 1.txt** from fstream object **rw.** The file closing is must as pointer advances into the file as characters are written to it so after entering string **str** to the file pointer will be advanced by **sizeof(str)** bytes. To get the pointer beginning to the file and opening it back in reading mode file closing is must.

To read from the file what we have entered just now we open the file again. But this time in read with the help of flag **ios : :in**. This flag open the file **demo1.txt** in read mode. We read the string from the file by writing.

rw.getline(str,50);

Which reads string from file pointer by **rw** and stores the string in **str**. The read string is displayed back to the screen using standard output stream **cout**.

/*PROG 12.7 READING AND WRITING THE SAME FILE IN ONE PROGRAM VER 2 */

```
#include <iostream.h>
#include <fstream.h>
#include <conio.h>
void main( )
{
    fstream rw;
    rw.open("demo1.txt",ios : :out|ios : :in);
    char str[50];
    clrscr( );
    cout<<"Enter a string"<<endl;
    cin.getline(str,50);
    rw<<str<<endl;
    rw.seekg(0,ios : :beg);
    rw.getline(str,50);
    cout<<"String read from file"<<endl;
    cout<<str<<endl;
    rw.close( );
}
```

OUTPUT :

```
Enter a string
MPSTME, NMIMS UNIVERSITY MUMBAI
String read from file
MPSTME, NMIMS UNIVERSITY MUMBAI
```

Figure 12.1. *Output screen of program 12.7*

EXPLANATION : We can open the file in more than one mode by oring the flags using binary OR symbols (|). The statement given as :

```
rw.open("demo1.txt",ios : :out|ios : :in);
```

Open the file **"demo1.txt"** for reading and writing. Initially the file pointer is in the beginning of the file. After reading string from keyboard and writing to the file, the pointer advances to **len** locations where **len** is the length of the string written to the file **demo1.txt**. To read the string back from the file, the pointer must be in the beginning of the file. For that we have used the function seekg (discussed in detail later) takes file pointer to the **0th bytes** (first argument) from beginning (second argument). Now we can read from the file. The string is read and displayed.

/*PROG 12.8 READING AND WRITING MOBILE DETAIL */

```
#include <iostream.h>
#include <fstream.h>
void main( )
{
    fstream rw;
    rw.open("demo2.txt",ios : :out);
    char mcomp[20],model[10];
    float price;
    cout<<"Enter the mobile model"<<endl;
    cin.getline(model, 10);
    cout<<"Enter the mobile company"<<endl;
    cin.getline(mcomp, 20);
    cout<<"Enter the mobile price"<<endl;
    cin>>price;
    rw<<model<<endl<<mcomp<<endl<<price<<endl;
    rw.close( );
    rw.open("demo2.txt",ios : :in);
    rw.getline(model,10);
    rw.getline(mcomp,20);
    rw>>price;
    cout<<"Mobile details read from file"<<endl;
    cout<<"Model :="<<model<<endl;
    cout<<"Company :="<<mcomp<<endl;
    cout<<"Price :="<<price<<endl;
    rw.close( );
}
```

OUTPUT :

```
Enter the mobile model
z550i
Enter the mobile company
Sony
Enter the mobile price
8000
Mobile details read from file
Model :=z550i
Company :=Sony
Price :=8000
```

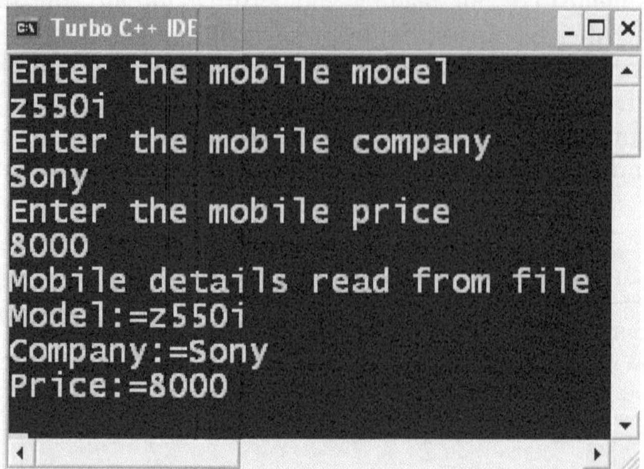

Figure 12.2. *Output screen of program 12.8.*

EXPLANATION : The program is simple. We input detail of mobile from keyboard, write into the file and close the file. We open the file in read mode and read mobile details from the file which is displayed on to the screen.

12.5 CHECKING END OF FILE

When file is opened for reading, data from file can be read as long as file is open and till end of file is not encountered. The end of file can be checked in two ways :

(A) In the first method the file stream objects can be written in the while loop as :

```
while (filestr)
{
read from file pointer by file str;
process data;
}
```

As long as we are reading filestr returns nonzero value. As soon as end of the file is encountered, filestr returns zero and while loop terminates.

(B) The second method which is most frequently used is of finding file using eof ( ) function. The function eof returns zero as soon as there is some data in the file *i.e.*, as long as end of file is not reached. As soon as end of the file reached, eof( ) function returns nonzero value. It can be used with while loop as :

```
While(filestr.eof( ) = =0)        or        while(!file.eof( ))
{
    read from file pointer by filestr;
    process data;
}
```

/*PROG 12.9 DEMO OF EOF FUNCTION AND APPEND MODE */

```
#include <iostream.h>
#include <fstream.h>
#include <conio.h>

void main( )
{
    fstream rw;
    char str[100];
    clrscr( );
    rw.open("demo.txt",ios : :in);
    cout<<"data read from file";
    endl(cout);
    while(rw.eof( )==0)
    {
        rw.getline(str,100);
        cout<<str<<endl;
    }
    rw.close( );
    rw.open("demo.txt",ios : :app);
    cin.getline(str,100);
    rw<<str<<endl;
    rw.close( );
    rw.open("demo.txt",ios : :in);
    cout<<"File with append data \n";
    while(rw.eof( )==0)
    {
        rw.getline(str,100);
        cout<<str<<endl;
    }
    rw.close( );
    getch( );
}
```

OUTPUT :

```
data read from file
This program for checking end of file
Hello C++
File with append data
This program for checking end of file
Hello C++
```

EXPLANATION : The file **demo.txt** is initially opened in read mode. The function **eof returns 0** as long as we are reading from the file. As soon as end of file in reached, function eof returns a non zero value. We read from the file till function **eof returns 0**. In each iteration of the while loop we read a string **str** of maximum **99** characters. As soon as end of file is encountered while loop terminates. We close the file and open the append mode by using **ios : :app** flag. When file is opened in append mode, file pointer is at end of the file. The string is to be appended to the file is taken from user and appended to the file. File is closed again. Next file is opened in read mode and is displayed which shows appended string together with the original contents before appending.

```
/* PROG 12.10 TO READING AND WRITING USING GET AND PUT */

#include <iostream.h>
#include <fstream.h>
#include <stdio.h>
void main( )
{
    fstream rw;
    char ch;
    rw.open("temp.txt",ios : :in|ios : :out);
    cout<<"Enter some data"<<endl;
    cin.get(ch);
    while(ch!=EOF)
    {
        rw.put(ch);
        cin.get(ch);
    }
    rw.seekg(0,ios : :beg);
    while(rw.eof( )==0)
    {
        cout.put(ch);
        rw.get(ch);
    }
    rw.close( );
}
```

OUTPUT :

```
Enter some data
Hari Mohan Pandey faculty in CSE Dept.(Enter F6 or Ctrl+Z)^Z
Hari Mohan Pandey faculty in CSE Dept.(Enter F6 or Ctrl+Z)
```

EXPLANATION : The two functions `put` and `get` allows us to write and read file sequentially. We open the file `temp.txt` for both reading and writing. We prompt user to enter some data. The data is scanned character by character using get and put into the file one character at a time. When user enter `F6` or `Ctrl+Z`, first `while` loop terminates. The pointer is then moved to beginning of the file by writing `rw.seekg(0,ios::beg)`. We now read from file character by character till end of the file does not reach. EOF is a macro defined in the file stdio.h whose ASCII value is 26.

/*PROG 12.11 FILE COPYING USING GET AND PUT */

```
#include <iostream.h>
#include <fstream.h>
#include <conio.h>

void main( )
{
    fstream source, dest;
    char sfile[15], dfile[15];
    char ch;
    clrscr( );
    cout<<"Enter the source file name"<<endl;
    cin>>sfile;
    source.open(sfile,ios : :in);
    cout<<"Enter the destination file name"<<endl;
    cin>>dfile;
    dest.open(dfile,ios : :out);
    while(source.eof( )==0)
    {
        source.get(ch);
        dest.put(ch);
    }
    source.close( );
    dest.close( ),
}
```

OUTPUT :

```
Enter the source file name
Hari.txt
Enter the destination file name
Pandey.txt
```

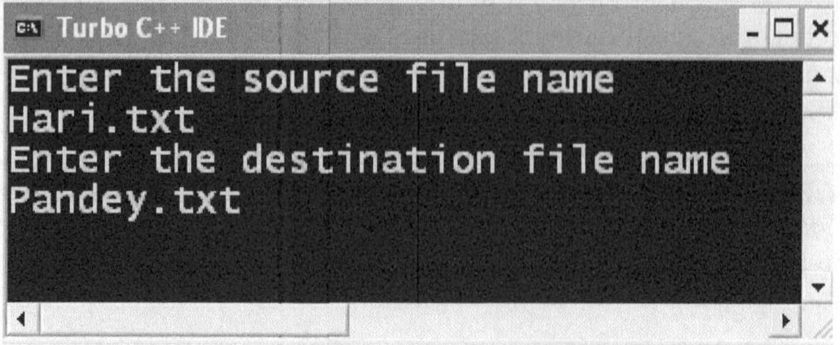

Figure 12.3. *Output screen of program 12.11.*

EXPLANATION : We input source and destination file name from the user. It is assumed that source file exist so we have not put any error checking code in the program. The source file is than opened in read mode and destination file is in write mode. We read one character at a time from source file and put this into destination file. This continues till source file does not come to end. In the end both files are closed.

/* PROG 12.12 WORKING WITH TWO FILES AT A TIME */

```
#include <iostream.h>
#include <fstream.h>
#include <conio.h>

void main( )
{
    fstream f1, f2;
    clrscr( );
    f1.open("names.txt",ios : :out);
    f1<<"Hari"<<endl;
    f1<<"Vijay"<<endl;
    f1<<"Ranjana"<<endl;
    f1.close( );
    f2.open("sname.txt",ios : :out);
    f2<<"Pandey"<<endl;
    f2<<"Nath"<<endl;
    f2<<"Pandey"<<endl;
    f2.close( );
    f1.open("names.txt",ios : :in);
    f2.open("sname.txt",ios : :in);
    char str[15];
    while(f1.eof( )= =0)
    {
        f1.getline(str,15);
```

```
        cout<<str<<" ";
        f2.getline(str,15);
        cout<<str<<endl;
    }
    f1.close( );
    f2.close( );
}
```

OUTPUT :

Hari Pandey

Vijay Nath

Ranjana Pandey

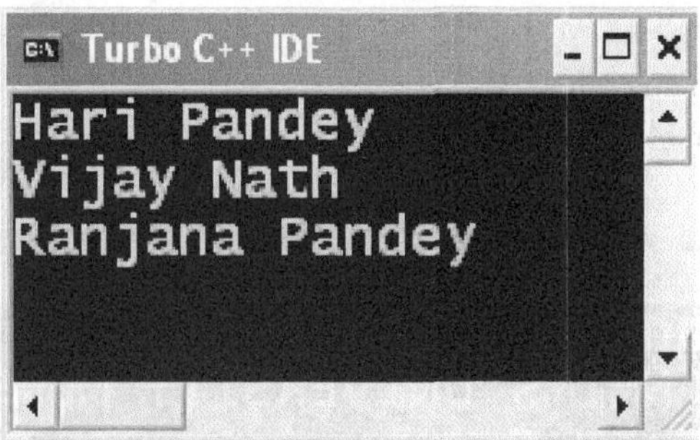

Figure 12.4. *Output Screen of program 12.12.*

EXPLANATION : In the program we have used two files **names.txt** in which we have stored few names and snames.txt in which we have stored surnames. We open the two files simultaneously and display the full name. If end of first is encountered we terminate the program.

/* **PROG 12.13 COUNTING NUMBER OF CHARACTERS IN FILE** */

```
#include <iostream.h>
#include <fstream.h>
#include <conio.h>
void main( )
{
    fstream rw;
    char str[50];
    int count = 0;
    char ch;
    clrscr( );
    rw.open("demo1.txt",ios : :in);
    cout<<"Data read from file"<<endl;
```

```
        rw.get(ch);
        while(rw.eof( )= =0)
        {
                cout.put(ch);
            rw.get(ch);
                count+ +;
        }
        cout< <"Number of character in file := "< <count< <endl;
        rw.close( );
}
```

OUTPUT :

```
Data read from file
MPSTME, NMIMS UNIVERSITY MUMBAI
HANDLING IN C
Number of character in file := 46
```

Figure 12.5. *Output screen of program 12.13.*

EXPLANATION : The program opens the file demo1.txt in read mode. It reads file character by character and increments count in each iteration. Out of while loop, count displays number of character in the file. Note you have to add 4 extra for new line characters if you counter check the output by finding number of characters manually.

12.6 RANDOM ACCESS IN FILE

Random access means reading data randomly from any where in the file. For this purpose we need to set the position of the file pointer first in the file and then read the data. C++ file stream classes provides the following functions for the manipulation of file pointer any where in the file. With the help of these functions we can access data in random fashion.

(*a*) Seekg( )
(*b*) seekp( )
(*c*) tellg( )
(*d*) tellp( )

The function seekg and tellg are used when we are reading from file *i.e.,* when used with the get pointer that's why the suffix g. The function tellp and seekp are used when writing to the file *i.e.,* when put pointer is used that's why the suffix p. The seek (p/g) function moves pointer to the specified position and tell (p/g) gives the position of the current pointer. The most frequently used function is seekg whose syntax is as :

```
istream & seekg (streamoff off, ios : :seek_dir dir);
```

The off is the new offset value and streamoff is a typedef equivalent to long. offset positive means move forwards, –ve means move backwards and 0 means stay at the current position. First byte in the file is at position 0. The dir is the seek diretion. Must be done of the following enumerators :

→ ios : :beg Seek from the beginning of the stream.

→ ios : :cur Seek from the current position in the stream.

→ ios : : end Seek from the end of the stream.

```
ifstream file;
file.seekg(2,ios : :beg)-> Third byte from the beginning.
file.seekg(6,ios : :cur)-> Forward by 6 bytes from current pos.
file.seekg(-5,ios : :cur)->Backwardby 5 bytes from current pos.
file.seekg(-4,ios : :end)-> Backward by 4 bytes from end.
file.seekg(0,ios : :cur)-> stay at the current position.
```

Similar, to seekg you can use seekp for moving pointer within a file which is opened for writing. The function tellg and tellp can be used for finding number of bytes into the file by opening the file and moving pointer to the end of the file. They can be used as :

```
ofstream file("num.txt", ios : :ate);
cout<<file.tellp( )<<endl;
```

When file is opened the pointer will be at the end of the file and tellp will give number of bytes in the file. Similarly, we can use tellg as :

```
ifstream file("num.txt", ios : :in);
file.seekg(0, ios : :end);
cout<<file.tellg( )<<endl;
```

When file is opened for reading, the file pointer will be in the beginning of the file so we have moved pointer to the end of the file using seekg.

Let's have few programs now which uses these function.

/* PROG 12.14 REVERSING FILE CONTENTS */

```
#include <iostream.h>
#include <fstream.h>
#include <conio.h>

void main( )
{
    fstream file;
    int count, x=1;
```

```
        char ch;
        clrscr( );
        file.open("num.txt",ios : :in);
        cout< <"file contents";
        endl(cout);
        while(file.eof( )= =0)
        {
            file.get(ch);
            cout.put(ch);
        }
        endl(cout);
        cout< <"Reversing contents";
        endl(cout);
        file.clear( );
        file.seekg(0,ios : :end);
        count=file.tellg( );
        while(x< =count)
        {
            file.seekg(-x,ios : :end);
            file.get(ch);
            cout.put(ch);
            x+ +;
        }
        cout< <endl;
        file.close( );
        getch( );
}
```

OUTPUT :

```
file contents
Love is blind
I Love programming
Reversing contents
gnimmargorp evoL I
dnilb si evoL
```

EXPLANATION : Initially file is opened in the read mode and displayed. The file then reaches at the end of file and error bit is set. It is must to clear this end of first bit other wise after setting the pointer to last character of the file we won't be able to read from the file. Number of characters in the file is then find out as :

```
file.seekg(0,ios : :end);
count = file.tellg( );
```

Now to display reverse contents of the file we start from 1 and continue till x<= count. We read first character from end when x = 1 as :

```
file.seekg(-x, ios : :end);
file.get(ch);
```

Which is displayed using cout.put(ch). As x increments we have the second character and so on.

/* PROG 12.15 RANDOM ACCESS DEMO, PRINTING NAME "PARI" */

```
#include <iostream.h>
#include <fstream.h>
#include <conio.h>

void main( )
{
    fstream file;
    char ch;
    clrscr( );
    file.open("alpha.txt",ios : :out);
    file<<"ABCDEFGHIJKLMNOPQRST\n";
    file.close( );
    file.open("alpha.txt",ios : :in);
    //file character is at 0 pos
    //16th byte from begining
    file.seekg(15,ios : :beg);
    file.get(ch);
    cout<<ch; //prints P
    //first character from the beginning
    file.seekg(0,ios : :beg);
    file.get(ch);
    cout<<ch; //prints A
    //11th character from end Z at –3, 'R'
    file.seekg(–5,ios : :end);
    file.get(ch);
    cout<<ch; //prints R
    //10th character from current position
    //including current pos 'I'
    file.seekg(-10,ios : :cur);
    file.get(ch);
    cout<<ch; //prints I
```

```
    cout<<endl;
    file.close( );
}
```

OUTPUT :

PARI

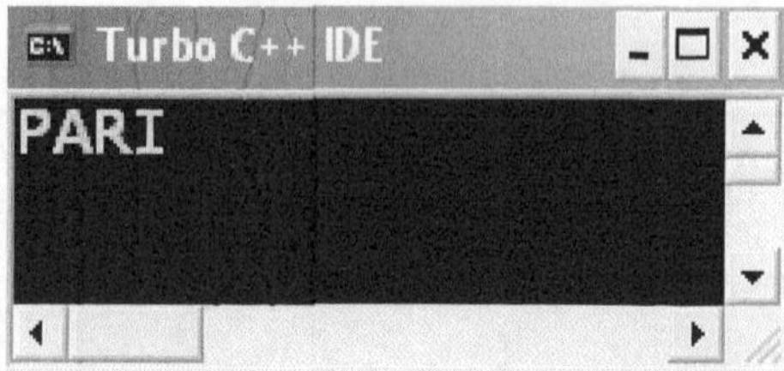

Figure 12.6. *Output screen of the program 12.15.*

EXPLANATION : The program is quite self-explanatory as comments are inserted at appropriate places. When you place \n inside the file as this is done in the program then start counting z from-3 position else count z from position -1 (remove \n).

/*PROG 12.16 COUNTING LINES AND CHARACTERS */

```
#include <iostream.h>
#include <fstream.h>
#include <stdio.h>

void main( )
{
    fstream file;
    int lines=0, count=0;
    char ch;
    file.open("temp.txt",ios : :out);
    cout<<"Enter some text\n";
    cin.get(ch);
    while(ch!=EOF)
    {
        file.put(ch);
        cin.get(ch);
    }
    file.close( );
    file.open("temp.txt",ios : :in);
    while(file.eof( )==0)
    {
        file.get(ch);
```

```
        if(ch = = '\n');
        lines + +;
        count + +;
    }
    cout< <"Number of characters := "< <count-lines-1< <endl;
    cout< <"Number of line :=  "< <lines< <endl;
    file.close( );
}
```

OUTPUT :

```
Enter some text
One
Two
Three
Four
Number of characters =15
Number of lines = 4
```

EXPLANATION : For counting the number of lines we check for **'\n'** and for counting number of characters we **count** all characters in **while** by incrementing **count** in each iteration. In the end when **while** loop terminates **count** will be one more than total number of characters. It also includes number of **'\n'** characters. So in the end of number of characters is displayed as **count-line-1**.

/* PROG 12.17 DEMO OF IOS : :NOCREATE FLAG */

```
#include <iostream.h>
#include <fstream.h>
#include <stdlib.h>
#include <conio.h>

void main( )
{
    fstream file;
    clrscr( );
    file.open("silly",ios : :nocreate);
    if(file.fail( ))
    {
        cout< <"File opening error"< <endl;
        exit(0);
    }
}
```

OUTPUT :

```
File opening error
```

Figure 12.7. *Output screen of the program 12.17.*

EXPLANATION : We have assumed that file `silly` does not exist. The `ios : :nocreate` does not open the file if it already not existing and instead gives error. The error in opening is checked using `file.fail( )` which returns true if there is some error in opening the file. As file does not exist if condition is true so cout displays "`File opening error`" and program terminates.

/* PROG 12.18 READING AND WRITING NUMERIC DATA */

```
#include <iostream.h>
#include <fstream.h>
#include <conio.h>
void main( )
{
    int i;

    clrscr( );

    ofstream file("num.txt");
    for(i=1;i<=10;i++)
        cout<<i<<endl;
    file.close( );
    ifstream file1("num.txt");
    while(1)
    {
        file1>>i;
        if(file1.eof( )!=0)
            break;
        cout<<i<<endl;
    }
    file1.close( );
}
```

OUTPUT :

```
1
2
```

```
3
4
5
6
7
8
9
10
```

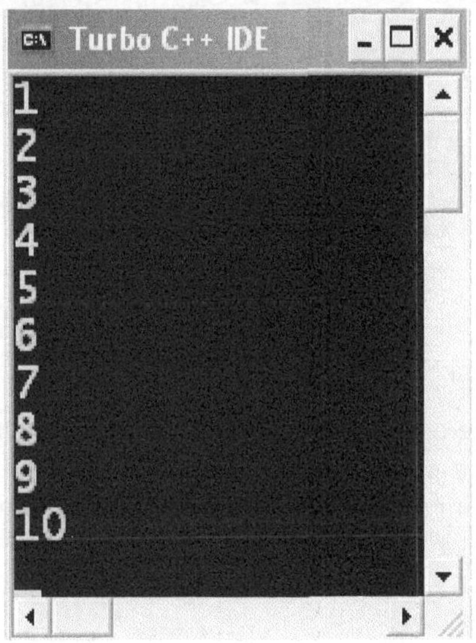

Figure 12.8. *Output screen of program 12.18.*

EXPLANATION : The program is simple. We input 10 numbers into the file and later display it back. Note there is no special function available in C++ for handling numbers using files.

12.7 COMMAND LINE ARGUMENTS

In all the programs we have used so far we have written **main( )** without arguments but in reality **main ( )** does take arguments and also have a return type. The prototype of **main( )** in C++ is given as :

```
int main(int argc, char * argv[ ])
```

or

```
int main(int argc, char ** argv)
```

Number of parameters are passed are collected into the parameter argc which stands for argument count. Value of each argument is stored in string array argv which stands for argument value. All arguments are of string type whether they are int, float or even a character. By default return type of any function if not specified int is assumed that's why int before **main( )** is optional. For better understanding point of view see the following examples.

/*PROG 12.19 DEMO OF COMMAND LINE ARGUMENT */

```
#include <iostream.h>
#include <conio.h>
void main(int argc, char*argv[ ])
{
    int i;
    clrscr( );
    for(i=1;i<argc;i++)
        cout<<"ARGUMENT="<<i<<"\t"<<argv[i]<<endl;
    getch( );
}
```

OUTPUT :

```
ARGUMENT=1 HELLO
ARGUMENT=2 NMIMS
ARGUMENT=3 UNIVERSITY
ARGUMENT=4 MUMBAI
```

EXPLANATION : Type the above program in Visual C++ environment build the program which will make **exe** file by the project name assuming project name is **F19**. Now come at the **DOS prompt** by moving to your project directory. On my laptop the project name was **F19** under **C** :\ so.

```
C :\TC>
C :\TC>F19
C :\TC>F19 HELLO NMIMS UNIVERSITY MUMBAI
```

As shown in below figure :

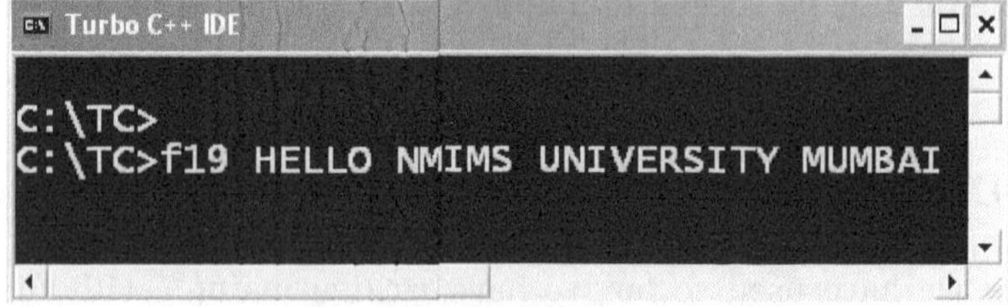

Figure 12.9. *Showing the execution process of the program 12.19.*

When you press **Enter**. You will get the output as shown below :

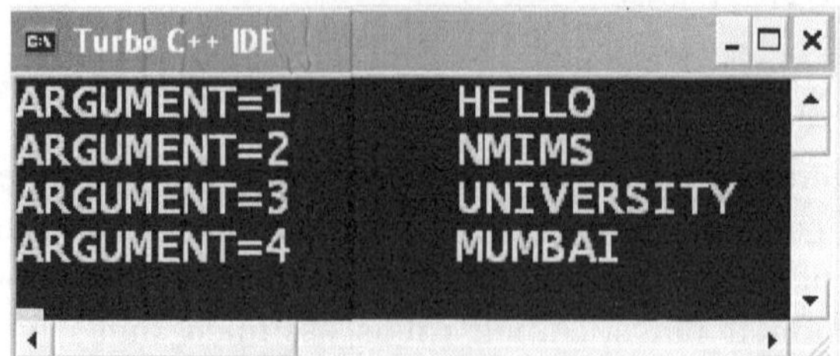

Figure 12.10. *Showing the output screen of the program 12.19.*

Here total number of arguments is **4** stored in **argc** with a space between each command line argument. First argument is the file name itself which we have not printed **F19.exe** is stored in **argv[0]**, second argument **HELLO** is stored in **argv [1]** and so on. The parameter name **argc** and **argv** are not fixed. They may be something else.

/* PROG 12.20 SUM OF COMMAND LINE ARGUMENT */

```
#include <iostream.h>
#include <stdlib.h>
void main(int argc, char **argv)
{
    int i, sum = 0;
    for(i=0;i<argc;i++)
        sum=sum+atoi(argv[i]);
    cout<<"Sum is "<<sum<<endl;
}
```

OUTPUT :

```
C :\TC>F20 1 2 3 4 5 6 7 8 9
Sum is 45
C :\TC>
```

Figure 12.11. *Output screen of program 12.20.*

EXPLANATION : As mentioned in the previous program the argument supplied at command line are by default treated as strings. We run the program as :

F20 1 2 3 4 5 6 7 8 9

Now starting from second argument that 1 each argument is converted into integer with the help of built-in function **atoi** whose prototype is given in file **stdlib.h** and summed up in variable **sum**.

/* PROG 12.21 MAX OF COMMAND LINE ARGUMENTS, FLOAT DATA */

```
#include <iostream.h>
#include <stdlib.h>
```

```
void main(int argc, char **argv)
{
    int i;
    float max, t;
    max= atof(argv[1]);
    for(i=1; i<argc; i++)
    {
        t = atof(argv[i]);
        if(max<t)
            max = t;
    }
    cout<<"max is"<<max<<endl;
}
```

OUTPUT :

```
C :\TC>f21 4.5 6.7 2.34 56.8 78.90
max is78.900002
C :\TC>
```

Turbo C++ IDE

```
C:\TC>f21 4.5 6.7 2.34 56.8 78.90
max is78.900002

C:\TC>
```

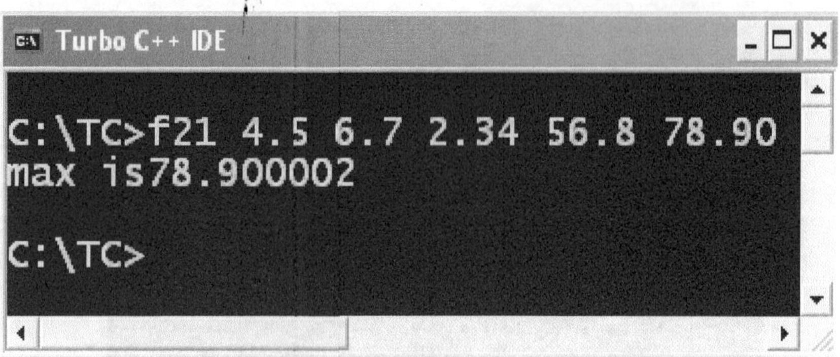

Figure 12.12. *Output screen of program 12.21.*

EXPLANATION : Program is self-explanatory. See previous program's explanation.

/* PROG 12.22 SORTING COMMAND LINE ARGUMENTS */

```
#include <iostream.h>
#include <string.h>

void main(int argc, char **argv)
{
    char *temp;
    int i,j;
    for(i=1;i<argc;i++)
```

```
    {
        for(j=i+1;j<argc;j++)
            if(strcmp(argv[i],argv[j])>0)
            {
                temp=argv[i];
                argv[i]=argv[j];
                argv[j]=temp;
            }
    }
    for(i=1;i<argc;i++)
        cout<<argv[i]<<endl;
}
```

OUTPUT :

```
C :\TC>F22 ONE TWO THREE FOUR
FOUR
ONE
THREE
TWO
```

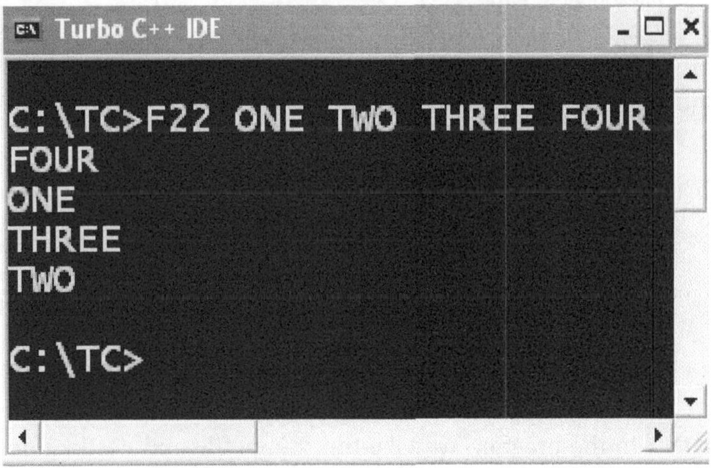

Figure 12.13. *Output screen of program 12.22.*

EXPLANATION : The program is run as

C :\TC>F22 ONE TWO THREE FOUR

As shown in above figure. The logic for sorting the string has been covered in earlier chapter.

/* PROG 12.23 COPYING OF ONE FILE INTO ANOTHER WITH FILE NAMES SUPPLIED AS COMMAND LINE ARGUMENTS */

```
#include <iostream.h>
#include <fstream.h>
#include <stdlib.h>
void main(int argc, char **argv)
{
    fstream f1,f2;
    char ch;
    cout<<argc<<endl;
    if(argc!=3)
    {
        cout<<"Usage :<<filename><source file<dest file>";
        exit(0);
    }
    f1.open(argv[1],ios::in);
    f2.open(argv[2], ios::out);
    if(f1.fail( ))
    {
        cout<<"File opening error";
        exit(0);
    }
    while(f1.eof( )==0)
    {
        f1.get(ch);
        f2.put(ch);
    }
    f1.close( );
    f2.close( );
}
```

EXPLANATION : In the program we take the source file and destination file as command line arguments. If number of arguments are not there we flash an error message. Similarly, if there is error in opening the source file flash error. If all goes well we copy file into destination character by character basis.

12.8 WORKING WITH BINARY MODE

Numeric data including integer and floating point as well as character data, all are treated in terms of character data *i.e.,* string "file" will take 4 bytes in memory, integer number 1245 will take 4 bytes in memory and even 1.23 will take 4 bytes in memory. But as these data stored in disk file they are stored in binary form and in this they are stored as per their type *i.e.*, integer takes 2 bytes, float takes 4 bytes and character takes 1 bytes. So, if reading and writing is done when treating file as text file and it contains lots of numerical data it will require large amount of disk space. For that we can have two functions provided by C++ stream classes read and write which reads and write data in terms of binary. For opening file in binary mode we have the mode ios : :binary. The prototype of both the function is given as :

```
Ostream & write(const char * pch, int nCount);
Istream & read(char * pch, int nCount);
```

The first argument in the write is the address of the character array and second is the number of characters to be written. Similar arguments apply to fread with the difference that it reads instead of writing.

/*PROG 12.24 READING AND WRITING OBJECT VER 1 */

```
#include <iostream.h>
#include <fstream.h>
#include <string.h>
#include <conio.h>
class person
{
    char name[10];
    int age;
public :
    void input(char n[ ], int a)
    {
        strcpy(name, n);
        age=a;
    }
    void show( )
    {
        cout<<"Name =" <<name<<endl;
        cout<<"AGE =" <<age<<endl;
    }
};
void main( )
{
    fstream file;
    clrscr( );
    file.open("obj.txt",ios : :in|ios : :out);
    person d;
    d.input("HARI",24);
    file.write((char*)&d,sizeof(d));
```

```
        file.read((char*)&d,sizeof(d));
        d.show( );
        file.close( );
        getch( );
}
```

OUTPUT :

Name = HARI

AGE = 24

EXPLANATION : The two function write and read work with binary files. Initially we assign values to data members of object d using function input. We then call function write which takes first argument as address of object d *i.e.,* where the write has to perform and second takes size of object. After writing object to the file, reading takes place by read function whose syntax is similar to the write. The object is read and displayed using a call to function show.

/* PROG 12.25 READING AND WRITING OBJECT VER 2 */

```
#include <iostream.h>
#include <fstream.h>
#include <string.h>
#include <conio.h>

class person
{
        char name[10];
        int age;
        char sex;
public :
        void input( )
        {
            cout<<"Enter person name"<<endl;
            cin>>name;
            cout<<"Enter age and sex"<<endl;
            cin>>age>>sex;
        }
        void show( )
        {
            cout<<"Name :="<<name<<endl;
            cout<<"Age :="<<age<<endl;
```

```
        cout<<"Sex :="<<sex<<endl;
    }
};
void main( )
{
    fstream file;
    file.open("obj.txt",ios : :in|ios : :out);
    person d[3];
    int i;

    clrscr( );

    for(i=0;i<3;i++)
    {
        d[i].input( );
        file.write((char*)&d[i],sizeof(d[i]));
    }
    cout<<"Data read from file"<<endl;
    for(i=0;i<3;i++)
    {
        cout<<"\n Person"<<i+1<<"\n";
        file.read((char*)&d[i],sizeof(d[i]));
        d[i].show( );
    }
    file.close( );
}
```

OUTPUT :

```
Enter person name
HARI
Enter age and sex
24 m
Enter person name
MAN
Enter age and sex
26 M
Enter person name
RANJANA
Enter age and sex
23 F
```

```
Data read from file
 Person1
Name :=HARI
Age :=24
Sex :=m
 Person2
Name :=MAN
Age :=26
Sex :=M
 Person3
Name :=  RANJANA
Age :=  23
Sex :=  F
```

EXPLANATION : In the program we have an array of objects **d** of size **3** of class **person** type. We run the **for** loop and take values for data members for all three objects using function input. The objects are then stored in the file using function **read**. In the next **for** loop we read objects from file and display using **write.**

/* PROG 12.26 READING AND WRITING ARRAY */

```
#include <iostream.h>
#include <fstream.h>
#include <conio.h>

void main( )
{
    fstream file;
    int a[10], i;

    clrscr( );

    file.open("arr.txt",ios::in|ios::out);
    for(i=0;i<=9;i++)
        a[i]=i+1;
    file.write((char*)a,sizeof(a));
    cout<<"Array is"<<endl;
    for(i=0;i<=9;i++)
        cout<<endl<<"  "<<a[i];
    cout<<endl;
```

```
    file.close( );
    getch( );
}
```

OUTPUT:

```
Array is
 1
 2
 3
 4
 5
 6
 7
 8
 9
 10
```

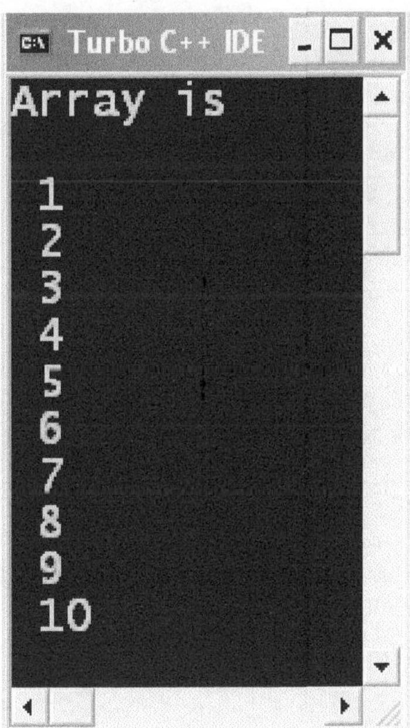

Figure 12.14. *Showing the output screen of program 12.26.*

EXPLANATION : Not only object we can also store array into the file. In the program we have first assigned numbers `1 to 10` into the array a and stored the whole array into the file `arr.txt` by using just one statement `file.write ((char*)a, sizeof(a));` `a` is the `base address` of the array, `sizeof a` gives `40`. We then make all elements to array `a` to zero so that when we read back from file we get the original array. The array is read through `fread` and displayed.

/* PROG 12.27 STUDENT DATA BASE MANAGEMENT */

```
#include <iostream.h>
#include <fstream.h>
#include <stdlib.h>
#include <stdio.h>
#include <conio.h>

class student
{
    char sname[15];
    int c_rno;
    char cls[10];
public :
    void input_data( );
    void show_data( );
    int getcrn( )
    {
        return c_rno;
    }
};
void student : :input_data( )
{
    cout<<"Enter the student name"<<endl;
    cin>>sname;
    cout<<"Enter college roll no and class"<<endl;
    cin>>c_rno>>cls;
}
void student : :show_data( )
{
    cout<<"Name :="<<sname<<"\t";
    cout<<"CRN :="<<c_rno<<"\t";
    cout<<"Class :="<<cls<<endl;
}
void main( )
{
    int ch, crn;
    student st;
    fstream file;
    int found = 0;
    int noc, nor;
```

```
long int move;
clrscr( );
file.open("student.txt",ios : :in|ios : :out|ios : :binary
          |ios : :ate);
do
{
    cout< <"\n Welcome to student Database\n";
    cout< <"1. Add a record\n";
    cout< <"2. View Record \n";
    cout< <"3. Search Record \n";
    cout< <"4. Delete a Record \n";
    cout< <"5. Modify a record \n";
    cout< <"6. Count Records \n";
    cout< <"7. Exit\n";
    cout< <"Enter your choice (1 to 6)\n";
    cin> >ch;
    switch(ch)
    {
    case 1 :st.input_data( );
        file.write((char*)&st, sizeof(st));
        cout< <"Record is added \n";
        file.clear( );
        break;
    case 2 : file.seekg(0,ios : :beg);
        while(file.read((char*)&st, sizeof(st)))
            st.show_data( );
        file.clear( );
        break;
    case 3 :cout< <"Enter the college roll number \n";
        cin> >crn;
        file.seekg(0,ios : :beg);
        while(file.read((char*)&st,sizeof(st)))
        {
            if(st.getcrn( )= =crn)
            {
                cout< <"Record found\n";
                st.show_data( );
                found=1;
            }
        }
        if(found = =0)
```

```
                cout<<"Record does not found \n";
            file.clear( );
            break;
        case 4 :cout<<"Enter the college roll number \n";
            cin>>crn;
            file.seekg(0,ios : :beg);
            while(file.read((char*)&st,sizeof(st)))
            {
                if(st.getcrn( )= =crn)
                {
                    cout<<"Record found \n";
                    found=1;
                    st.show_data( );
                    int ans;
                    cout<<"Are you sure to delete this
                                record (1/0) ?\n";
                    cin>>ans;
                    if(ans= =1)
                    {
                        file.seekg(0,ios : :beg);
                        fstream newf;
newf.open("newstu.txt",ios : :out);
while(file.read((char*)&st,sizeof(st)))
                        {
                            if(st.getcrn( )!=crn)
newf.write((char*)&st,sizeof(st));
                        }
                        file.close( );
                        remove("student.txt");
                        newf.close( );
rename("newstu.txt","student.txt");
file.open("student",ios : :in|ios : :out|ios : :binary
            |ios : :ate);
                        cout<<"Record deleted\n";
                    }
                }
            }
            if(found= =0)
                cout<<"Record does not found\n";
            file.clear( );
            break;
```

```
        case 5 :cout<<"Enter the second record number to
                                modify \n";
            int recno;
            cin>>recno;
            move=(recno-1)*sizeof(st);
            file.seekg(move,ios : :beg);
            cout<<"Please enter new data \n";
            st.input_data( );
            file.write((char*)&st,sizeof(st));
            file.clear( );
            break;
        case 6 : file.seekg(0,ios : :end);
            noc=file.tellg( );
            nor=noc/sizeof(st);
            cout<<"Number of record :="<<nor<<endl;
            break;
        case 7 : cout<<"Bye Bye\a.\a.\a.\a.\a.\a.
                                \a..!\a!\a!"<<endl;
            exit(0);
        }
    }while(ch>=1 && ch<=7);
    getch( );
    }
```

OUTPUT :

```
 Welcome to student Database
1. Add a record
2. View Record
3. Search Record
4. Delete a Record
5. Modify a record
6. Count Records
7. Exit
Enter your choice (1 to 6)
1
Enter the student name
Hari
Enter college roll no and class
12 BTech
Record is added
```

```
Welcome to student Database
1. Add a record
2. View Record
3. Search Record
4. Delete a Record
5. Modify a record
6. Count Records
7. Exit
Enter your choice (1 to 6)
1
Enter the student name
Ravi
Enter college roll no and class
13 MBA
Record is added
Welcome to student Database
1. Add a record
2. View Record
3. Search Record
4. Delete a Record
5. Modify a record
6. Count Records
7. Exit
Enter your choice (1 to 6)
2
Name :=Hari          CRN :=12 Class :=B Tech
Name :=Ravi          CRN :=13 Class :=MBA
Welcome to student Database
1. Add a record
2. View Record
3. Search Record
4. Delete a Record
5. Modify a record
6. Count Records
7. Exit
Enter your choice (1 to 6)
Welcome to student Database
1. Add a record
2. View Record
3. Search Record
4. Delete a Record
```

```
5. Modify a record
6. Count Records
7. Exit
Enter your choice (1 to 6)
7
Bye Bye
```

EXPLANATION : To modify a record we initially reach to the location of that record. The location can be found out as :

```
Loc=(n-1) *sizeof(st);
```

Where `st` is an object of class student and n is the record number.

Then through `seekg` we reach to the loc in the file *i.e.,* beginning of the record which is to e modified. We then accept the new data for the resord and overwrite the exiting record.

The file is opened in `ios : :ate` mode which takes pointer to the end of the file. For moving any where in the file we have to use `seekg.` For accessing file again once end of the file has been set we have cleared it by using clear function which turn off the end of file flag.

To search for a record we ask from the user the college roll no and scan the whole file for the record where `c_rno` matches with the user supplied crn. As `c_rno` is `private` so we have a public member function getcrn which gives college roll number.

For deletion of a record we move all the other records to a temporary file `temp.txt`. We then remove the original file using the built function remove which takes a single argument of `const char*` type, the file name to be removed. We then rename the temporary file temp.txt to the old `student.txt`.

12.9 ERROR HANDLING

When dealing with the file errors might occurs such as :

- File does not exist
- Reading from file which is opened for writing only.
- Path is not valid.
- File already exist etc.

To cope up with all these error we check whether file is opened successfully or what type of error has beem generated.

Some of the error handling functions with their descripton is given below :

1. The good Function

```
SYNTAX : int good( ) const;
```

Returns nonzero values if all error bits are clear. Note that the **good** member function is not simply the inverse of **bad** function.

2. The bad Function

```
SYNTAX : int bad( ) const;
```

Returns a nonzerovalue to indicates a serious I/O error. This is the same as setting the badbit error state. Do not continue I/O operations on the stream is this situtation.

3. The fail Function

SYNTAX : int fail ( ) const;

Returns a nonzero value if any I/O error (not end of file) has occurred. This consdition corresponds to either the badbit or failbit error flag being set. If a call to bad returns 0, you can assume that the error condition is nonfatal and that you can probably continue processing after you clear the flags.

4. The clear Function

SYNTAX : void clear (int nState = 0);

The parameter nState, if 0, then all error bits are cleared, otherwise bits are set according to the following masks(ios enemerators) that can be combined using the bitwise OR (|) operator. The nState parameter must have one of the following values :

-> ios : :goobit No error condition (no bits set).

-> ios : :eofbit End of file reached.

-> ios : :failbit A possibly recoverable formatting or coversion error.

-> ios : :badbit A server I/O error.

The function sets or clear the error-state flags. The rdstate function can be used to read the current error state.

5. The eof( ) Function

SYNTAX : int eof( ) const;

Returns a nonzero value if end of file has been reached. This is the same as setting the eofbit error flag.

6. The rdstate Function

SYNTAX :int rdstate ( ) const;

Returns the current error state as specified by the following masks(ios enumerators).

-> ios : :goobit No error condition (no bits set).

-> ios : :eofbit End of file reached.

-> ios : :failbit A possibly recoverable formatting or coversion error.

-> ios : :badbit A server I/O error or unknown state.

This is shown in the figure given below. The last 4 bits are unused.

The returned value can be tested against a mask with the AND (&) operator, but we do not have to as we can have functions which tells us which bit is set or reset.

7	6	5	4	3	2	1	0
				goodbit	badbit	failbit	eofbit

Figure 12.15. *Error state specified by the masks given above*

/* PROG 12.28 ERROR HANDLING WITH FILES */

```
#include <iostream.h>
#include <conio.h>
#include <fstream.h>
 void main( )
 {
        clrscr( );
        ofstream file("silly.text", ios : :noreplace);
        if(!file)
        {
              cout<<"FILE OPEING ERROR";
              endl(cout);
        }
        cout<<"THE VARIOUS FLAGS SET/ RESET ARE";
        endl(cout);
        cout<<"rdstate="<<file.rdstate( );
        endl(cout);
        cout<<"bad="<<file.bad( );
        endl(cout);
        cout<<"fail="<<file.fail( );
        endl(cout);
        cout<<"good="<<file.good( );
        endl(cout);
        cout<<"eof="<<file.eof( );
        endl(cout);
        getch( );
 }
```

OUTPUT :

```
FILE OPEING ERROR
THE VARIOUS FLAGS SET/ RESET ARE
rdstate=2
bad=0
fail=2
good=0
eof=0
```

EXPLANATION : The file **silly.txt** was existing earlier. The noreplace flashes error if file was existing and we tried to open it for writing. That is using this flag we come to know that file already exist and we do not have to modify the file. The file opeing error occurred so fail will returned a non zero value, good returns 1 only when no error of any type occurs *i.e.*, all the bits are cleared. The bad returns 0 as there is no I/O error. Eof was not reached so eof returns 0. Now checking from the figure, the rdstate will be as :

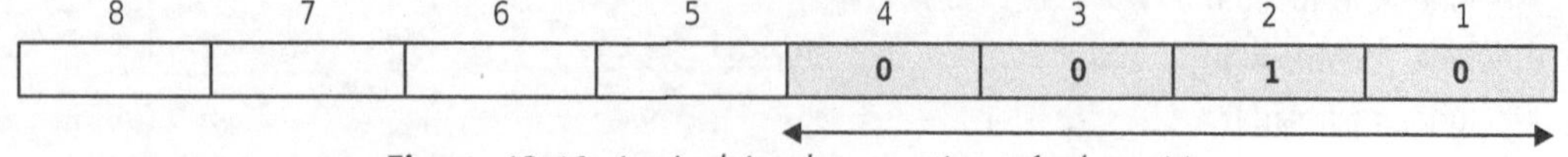

Figure 12.16. *Logical Implementation of rdstate( )*

0010 is decimal 2, so rdstate return 2.

In the program if file was not opened and we try to write to the file then function bad returns true and badbit which indicates file input/output error. This can be cheked again as :

```
file<<"WRITING TO THE FILE"<<endl;
if(!file)
{
    cout<<"WRITING ERROR";
    endl(cout);
}
//check all flags here;
```

/*PROG 12.29 DEMO OF FAIL AND GOOD */

```
#include <iostream.h>
#include <fstream.h>
#include <conio.h>
void main( )
{
    clrscr( );
    ifstream file("num.txt",ios : :nocreate);
    if(file.good( ))
    {
        cout<<"File is opened successfully"<<endl;
        cout<<"good flag :="<<file.good( )<<endl;
    }
    else if(file.fail( ))
    {
        cout<<"Error in opening file \n";
        cout<<"Fail flag :="<<file.bad( )<<endl;
    }
}
```

OUTPUT :

```
File is opened successfully
good flag :=1
```

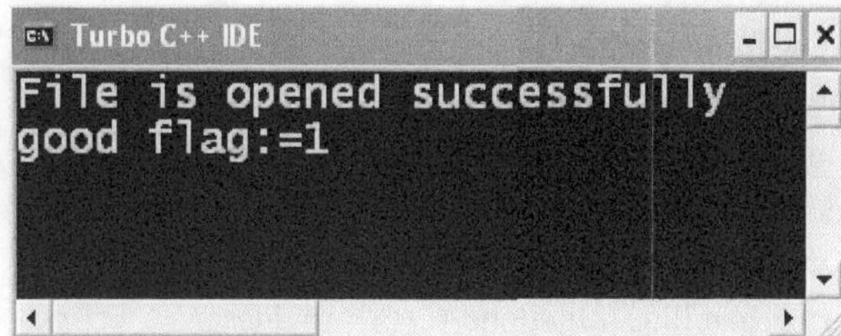

Figure 12.17. *Showing the output screen of the program 12.29.*

EXPLANATION : The program is self-explanatory.

12.10 PONDERABLE POINTS

1. Opening a file links the program with the files. The link is made through an object of any of the file stream classes like fstream, ifstream, ofstream etc., which are defined in header file fstream.h.
2. The files which are accessed using library functions are known as high level files and those by system-calls are known as low level files. System calls are special command to the operating system (OS) and are specified to a particular OS.
3. High level files are also known as stream oriented files and low level files are also known as system oriented files.
4. There are two types of stream in general
   (*a*) Text streams which is a sequence of bytes (lines of tex).
   (*b*) Binary stream which is a sequence of unprocessed bytes.
5. Normally all files are opened and accessed in text mode. For opening a file a binary mode ios : :binary mode has to be specified.
6. For opening file either the constructor method or open function can be used.
7. The various modes like ios : :in, ios : :out, ios : :ate etc., are enumeration constants of ios class.
8. The various functions for handling error are good, bad, clear etc.

EXERCISE

A. True and False :

1. read( ) and write( ) method are used for character input and output.
2. The fstream can only be used for reading the data.
3. The read and write functions are used to read and write objects from/to file.
4. A stream may be connected to more than one file at a time.

B. Answer the Following Questions :

1. What different types of file streams C++ provides ?
2. Why we need fstream. Header file ?

3. What is the advantage of files ?
4. How text file different from binary file ?
5. Discuss function for random access of a file.
6. What are the opening modes ? Explain the purpose of each mode.
7. What are command line arguments ? How do we use them in our program ?
8. How can we read write object from/to file ?
9. What are various error handling functions C++ provides ?
10. What is eof ? How it can detect end of file ?

C. Brain Drill :

1. Write a program that displays on the screen the contents of text file line by line backwards. It should be possible to run your program by providing the file name as a command line argument.
2. Write a C++ class to read an existing file and create another file with all words of the source file stored in reverse order. It is assumed that successive words are separated by one or more white space characters.
3. Write a C++ program to compare contents of two files whose names are supplied through the command line. Display the first line having mismatch along with its number.
4. Write a C++ program to copy the alternate lines in reverse order from a source file to target file with the file names are entered at the command prompt.
5. Write a program that emulates the DOS COPY command. That is, it should copy the contents of a text file (such as any .CPP file) to another file. Invoke the program with two command-line arguments—the source file and the destination file-like this :

   C>copy srcfile.cpp destfile.cpp

   In the program, check that the user has typed the correct number of command-line arguments, and that the files specified can be opened.
6. Write a program that returns the size in bytes of a program entered on the command line :

   C>filesize program.exe
7. In a loop, prompt the user to enter name data consisting of a first name, middle initial, last name, and employee number (type unsigned long). Then, using formatted I/O with the insertion (<<) operator, write these four data items to an ofstream object. Don't forget that strings must be terminated with a space or other white space character. When the user indicates that no more name data will be entered, close the ofstream object, open an ifstream object, read and display all the data in the file, and terminate the program.
8. Create a time class that includes integer member values for hours, minutes, and seconds. Make a member function get_time ( ) that gets a time value from the user, and a function put_time ( ) that displays a time in 12 :59 :59 format. Add error checking to the get_time ( ) function to minimize user mistake. This function should request hours, minutes, and second separately, and check each one for ios error status flags and the correct range. Hours should be between 0 and 23, and minutes and seconds between 0 to 59. Don't input these values as strings and then convert them; read them directly as integers. This implies that you won't be able to screen out entries with superfluous decimal points.

   In main ( ), use a loop to repeatedly get a time vale from the user with get_time ( ) and then display it with put_time ( ), like this :

   ```
   Enter hours : 11
   Enter minutes : 59
   Enter seconds : 59
   Time = 11 :59 :59
   Do another (y/n) ? y
   ```

❑❑❑

CHAPTER 13

TEMPLATE PROGRAMMING

13.1 INTRODUCTION

Template is one of the most important and useful feature of C++ which was added only a few years back. Template provides the idea of generic classes. Use of one function or class that works for all data types is generalization. With the help of templates and functions we can create generic data types and idea leads to generic programming. In the generic programming generic data types are passed as argument to function and classes.

Some facts about templates are given below:

- Template provides the idea of generic classes.
- Use of one function or class that works for all data types is generalization.
- With the help of templates and functions we can create generic data types and this idea leads to generic programming.
- In the generic programming generic data types are passed as argument to function and classes.
- A template is similar to a macro which can work for different types of data.
- A template created for a function so a function works for variety of data types is termed as function template.
- For example a function template max is written which finds maximum of two integer, two floats, two chars etc.
- Similarly, when a template is written for a class so one single class works for variety of data types is turned as class template.

13.2 FUNCTION TEMPLATE

- A function template is created when we write one definition of function which works with different type of data types.
- A function template does not occupy space in memory.

- The actual definition of function template is generated when function is called with specific data type.
- The function template does not result in saving memory.
- Function template simply relieves us from writing same amount of code for different data types.
- The syntax for creating a function template :

```
template <class name>
function definition;
```

Before function definition we write template which is a keyword. In the brackets < and > we write class and any name which serves as the generic type. The name may be a single character or a word (similar to identifier). The name usually written in capital but may be in small case too.

We present below a small example of function template.

/*PROG 13.1 DISPLAYING DIFFERENT TYPES OF VARIABLES WITH THEIR TYPE USING FUNCTION TEMPLATE */

```
#include <iostream.h>
#include <typeinfo.h>

template <class FUNC>
void show(FUNC par)
{
    cout<<"Displaying"<<typeid(par).name( )<<"Parameter\t"<<par <<endl;
}

void main( )
{
    int x=234;
    float y=34.56f;
    double d=3.444456;
    char ch='P';
    char *s= "Template";
    show(x);
    show(y);
    show(d);
    show(ch);
    show(s);
}
```

OUTPUT :

```
Displaying int Parameter 234
Displaying float Parameter 34.56
Displaying double Parameter 3.44446
Displaying char Parameter P
Displaying char * Parameter Template
```

EXPLANATION : The function template is written as :

```
void show(FUNC par)
{
    cout<<"Displaying"<<typeid(par).name( )<<"Parameter\t"<<par
        <<endl;
}
```

The line template<class FUNC> has to be written whenever you want to create either a function template or class template. The name FUNC is generic data type name. It is replaced by the actual data type when a specific data type is used with the function call. The statement typeid(par).name gives the actual data type of the variable as discussed earlier. In the main when the following functions are called, depending upon type of parameter is passed, a separate function definition is generated in the memory.

```
show(x);
show(y);
show(d);
show(ch),
show(s);
```

For example, for show(x) as type of x is int, function definition is generated as (because of function template void show( )FUNC par) :

```
void show(FUNC par)
{
    cout<<"Displaying"<<typeid(par).name( )<<"Parameter\t"<<par
        <<endl;
}
```

Similarly for other data types function definition will be generated. That is for 5 different data types with function template show five different versions of show are generated in the memory. So function template does not save memory. It saves us only from writing repetitive code which works for different type of data.

/* PROG 13.2 TO FIND MAXIMUM OF TWO NUMBER USING FUNCTION TEMPLATE */

```
#include <iostream.h>
#include <conio.h>

template <class FUNC>

FUNC max2(FUNC a, FUNC b)
{
    return (a>b?a :b);
}

void main( )
{
    int x=10,y=20;
    float f1=2.4, f2=4.5;
    char ch1='A', ch2='B';
    clrscr( );
    cout<<"\n Max of two integers "<< x <<" & "<< y
        <<" is\t";
    cout<<max2(x,y);
    cout<<"\n Max of two floats "<< f1 <<" & "<< f2
        <<" is\t";
    cout<<max2(f1,f2);
    cout<<"\n Max of two chars "<< ch1 <<" & "<< ch2
        <<" is\t";
    cout<<max2(ch1,ch2);
    getch( );
}
```

OUTPUT :

```
Max of two integers 10 & 20 is 20
Max of two floats 2.4 & 4.5 is 4.5
Max of two chars A & B is B
```

EXPLANATION : In the program we have written a function template which finds maximum of different data types passed as argument by returning it from the function template. The function template is written as :

```
template <class FUNC>
FUNC max2(FUNC a, FUNC b)
{
    return (a>b ? a :b);
}
```

Here only one generic data type is used but thrice, two times as argument to the function template max2, and third time as return type for the function template max2.

In the main again as function calls are encountered in the main as **max2(x,y), max2(f1,f2),** and **max2(ch1,ch2).** Three different functions from the function template definition are generated and all instances of generic types are replaced by int, float and char respectively in separate function definition.

This is as shown below :

```
int max2(int a, int b)
{
    return (a>b ? a :b);
}
float max2(float a, float b)
{
    return (a>b ? a :b);
}

char max2(char a, char b)
{
    return (a>b ? a :b);
}
```

/* PROG 13.3 SORTING ARRAY ELEMENTS USING FUNCTION TEMPLATE VER 1*/

```
#include <iostream.h>
#define S 5
template<class TYPE>
void sort(TYPE arr[ ])
{
    int i,j;
    for(i=0;i<S;i++)
        for(j=i+1;j<S;j++)
            if(arr[i]>arr[j])
            {
                TYPE t = arr[i];
                arr[i] = arr[j];
                arr[j] = t;
            }
            for(i=0;i<S;i++)
                cout<<arr[i]<<" ";
            cout<<endl;
}
```

```
void main( )
{
    int iarr[S]={1, 34, 56,22, 15};
    float farr[S]={2.3, 1.5, 4.8, 1.3, 5.8};
    char carr[S]={'a','c','e','b','d'};
    cout<<"SORTED INTEGERE ARRAY"<<endl;
    sort(iarr);
    cout<<"SORTED FLOAT ARRAY"<<endl;
    sort(farr);
    cout<<"SORTED CHAR ARRRAY"<<endl;
    sort(carr);
}
```

OUTPUT :

```
SORTED INTEGERE ARRAY
1 15 22 34 56
SORTED FLOAT ARRAY
1.3 1.5 2.3 4.8 5.8
SORTED CHAR ARRRAY
a b c d e
```

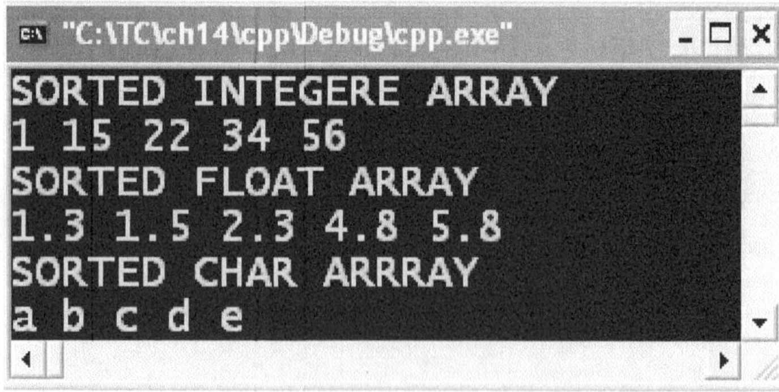

Figure 13.1. *Showing the output screen of program 13.3*

EXPLANATION : This time we have written a function template sort for sorting array of different data types. Logic of sorting has been used earlier with arrays so no need to discusss it again. In the main we have initialized three arrays of type int, float and char. When function sort(iarr), sort(farr) and sort(carr), three different versions of function template are generated and generic type TYPE is replaced by int, float and char respectively. Rest is easy to understand.

/* PROG 13.4 SORTING ARRAY ELEMENTS USING FUNCTION TEMPLATE VER 2*/

```
#include <iostream.h>
#include <typeinfo.h>
#define S 5
```

```
template<class TYPE>
void sort(TYPE arr[ ])
{
    int i,j;
    for(i=0;i<S;i++)
        for(j=i+1;j<S;j++)
            if(arr[i]>arr[j])
            {
                TYPE t=arr[i];
                arr[i]=arr[j];
                arr[j]=t;
            }
}

template<class TYPE>
void input(TYPE arr[ ])
{
    int i;
    cout<<"Enter"<<S<<"
"<<typeid(arr[0]).name( )<<"number"<<endl;
    for(i=0;i<S;i++)
        cin>>arr[i];
}

template<class TYPE>
void show(TYPE arr[ ])
{
    int i;
    for(i=0;i<S;i++)
        cout<<arr[i]<<" ";
    cout<<endl;
}

void main( )
{
    int a1[S];
    input(a1);
    sort(a1);
    cout<<"SORTED ARRAY IS"<<endl;
    show(a1);
    float f[S];
```

```
        input(f);
        sort(f);
        cout<<"SORTED ARRAY IS"<<endl;
        show(f);
}
```

OUTPUT :

```
Enter5 intnumber
10 5 26 17 80
SORTED ARRAY IS
5 10 17 26 80
Enter5 floatnumber
56.8 4.5 2.3 90.634.56
SORTED ARRAY IS
0.56 2.3 4.5 56.8 90.634
```

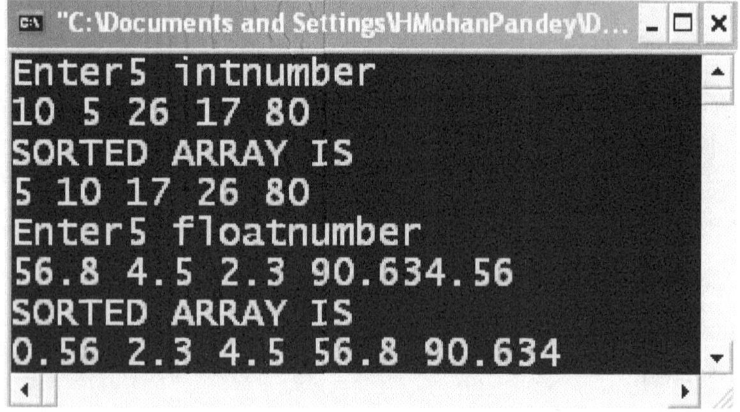

Figure 13.2. *Showing the output screen of program 13.4*

EXPLANATION : In the program we have three function templates :

1. One for inputting array elements.
2. Second for showing the array elements.
3. Third for sorting array element.

As we have array of two different data types, total **2 × 3 = 6** function definition are generated when specific call is made to each function *i.e.,* **3** for integer data type **int : input, show and sort** and **3** for **float** data type. Rest is simple to understand.

/* PROG 13.5 WORKING WITH TWO GENERIC DATA TYPE AT A TIME */

```
#include <iostream.h>
#include <typeinfo.h>
template<class T1, class T2>
```

```
void show(T1 par1, T2 par2)
{
    cout<<typeid(par1).name( )<<" parameter="<<par1<<"\t";
    cout<<typeid(par2).name( )<<" parameter="<<par2<<endl;
}

void main( )
{
    show(14,'B');
    show("NMIMS",35.67);
}
```

OUTPUT :

```
int parameter=14 char parameter=B
char * parameter=NMIMS double parameter=35.67
```

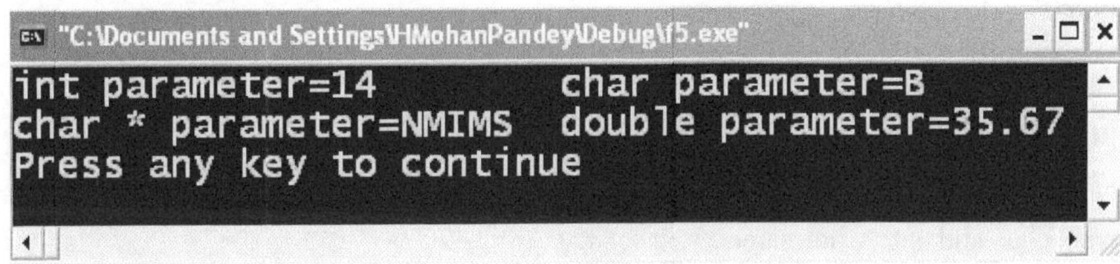

Figure 13.3. *Output screen of program 13.5*

EXPLANATION : In the program we have a function template `show` which takes two generic types as arguments. Note in the following the template keyword both the generic type has been declared as `<class T1, class T2>`. Many more generic types can be declared separating by comma but each must be declared using `class` keyword. In the function template `show` we simply display the type and value of the arguments. As we call `show` twice with the different arguments, two different definition of the function template is created in the memory.

/* PROG 13.6 CHECKING EQUALITY OF DATA TYPE OF TWO VARIABLES USING FUNCTION TEMPLATE VER 1*/

```
#include <iostream.h>
#include <typeinfo.h>
#include <string.h>

template<class T1, class T2>
void equal(T1 x, T2 y)
{
    const char *p1=typeid(x).name( );
    const char *p2=typeid(y).name( );
    if(strcmp(p1,p2)==0)
```

```
        cout<<"Data type"<<p1<<" and "<<p2
            <<" is same "<<endl;
    else
        cout<<"Data type "<<p1<<" and "<<p2
            <<" is not same "<<endl;
}
void main( )
{
    int a =10, b=20;
    float c=23.45;
    char ch = 'A';
    char*s1 = "string", *s2="string";
    equal(a,c);
    equal(ch,b);
    equal(a,b);
    equal(s1,s2);
}
```

OUTPUT :

```
Data type int and float is not same
Data type char and int is not same
Data typeint and int is same
Data typechar * and char * is same
```

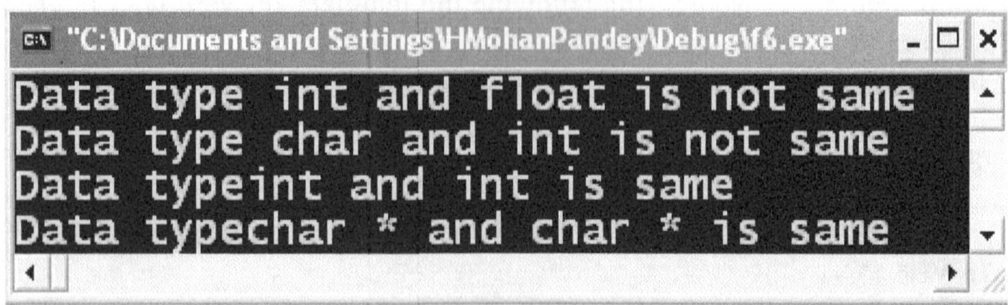

Figure 13.4. *Showing the output of the program 13.6*

EXPLANATION : In the function template we are trying to check whether two generic data types are same or not. This will be checked when an instance of function template is created passing actual type as arguments. For the first call `equal(a,c)` function template is instantiated and a function definition as shown below is created.

```
void equal(T1 x, T2 y)
{
    const char *p1=typeid(x).name( );
    const char *p2=typeid(y).name( );
    if(strcmp(p1,p2)==0)
        cout<<"Data type"<<p1<<" and "<<p2
            <<" is same "<<endl;
    else
        cout<<"Data type "<<p1<<" and "<<p2
            <<" is not same "<<endl;
}
```

typeid(x).name( ) returns the data type as constant string so **p1** stores **"int"** and **p2** stores **"float"**, both as string. Later we compare whether two strings are same or not by comparing them using **strcmp( ).** If strcmp return two data type are same otherwise not same. Same for other call to equal hold.

/* PROG 13.7 CHECKING EQUALITY OF DATA TYPE OF TWO VARIABLES USING FUNCTION TEMPLATE VER 2 */

```
#include <iostream.h>
#include <typeinfo.h>
#include <string.h>

template <class T1, class T2>
void equal(T1 x, T2 y)
{
    const char*p1=typeid(x).name( );
    const char*p2=typeid(y).name( );
    if(strcmp(p1,p2)==0)
        cout<<"Data type "<<p1<<" and "<<p2
            <<" is same"<<endl;
    else
        cout<<"Data type "<<p1<<" and "
            <<p2<<" is not same"<<endl;
}
void main( )
{
    equal(23.45, 23.45);
    equal('A',65);
    equal(2.0, 2.0f);
    equal("str",(int*)"str");
}
```

OUTPUT :

```
Data type double and double is same
Data type char and int is not same
Data type double and float is not same
Data type char * and int * is not same
```

```
"C:\Documents and Settings\HMohanPandey\Debug\f7.exe"
Data type char and int is not same
Data type double and float is not same
Data type char * and int * is not same
Press any key to continue
```

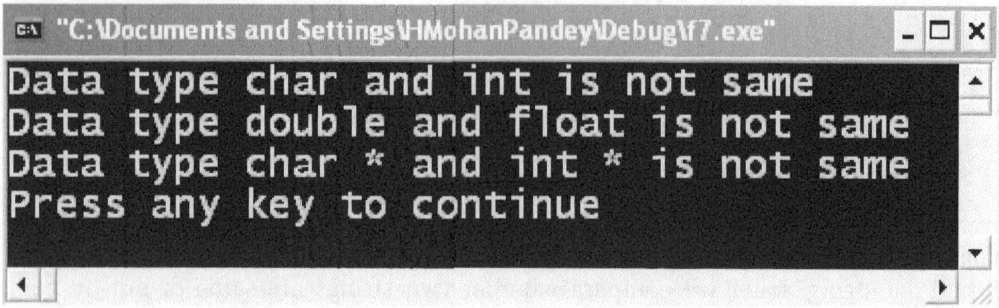

Figure 13.5. *Showing the output of program 13.7*

EXPLANATION : The program is similar to previous program with change in main. In the previous program we declared the variable of different data type and then passed to function equal. But here we are passing them as constants as shown :

```
equal(23.45, 23.45);
equal('A',65);
equal(2.0, 2.0f);
equal("str",(int*)"str");
```

In the first statement shown above both arguments are treated as double. In the second one is of character and second is of integer. In the third first one is of **double** and second is of **float** (due to f). In the fourth call to equal first argument is of type **char*** and second is of type **int*** (explicit type casting). Four different function definitions will be generated.

/* PROG 13.8 TO CHECK EQUALITY OF THREE DATA TYPES USING FUNCTION TEMPLATE */

```
#include <iostream.h>
#include <typeinfo.h>
#include <string.h>

template<class T1, class T2, class T3>
void equal(T1 x, T2 y, T3 z)
{
    const char*p1=typeid(x).name( );
    const char*p2=typeid(y).name( );
    const char*p3=typeid(z).name( );
```

```
        bool b1,b2;
        b1=strcmp(p1,p2);
        b2=strcmp(p2,p3);
        if(!b1&&!b2)
            cout<<"Data type "<<p1<<", "<<p2<<" and "
                <<p3<<" is same"<<endl;
        else
            cout<<"Data type "<<p1<<","<<p2<<" and "
                <<p3<<" is not same"<<endl;
}
void main( )
{
        equal(2,5,6);
        equal(2, 3.5, 'B');
}
```

OUTPUT :

Data type int, int and int is same

Data type int,double and char is not same

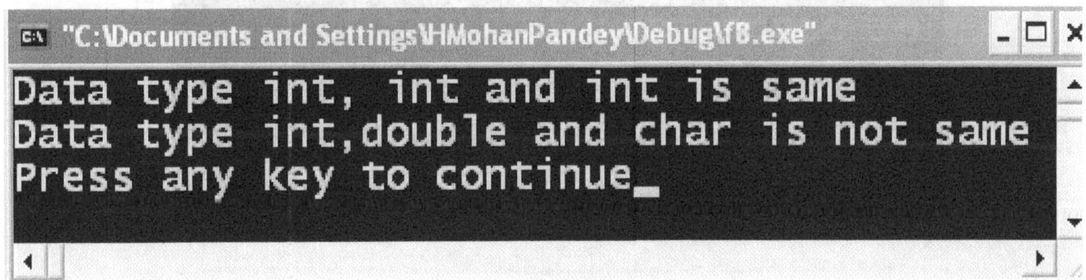

Figure 13.6. *Showing the output screen of the program 13.8*

EXPLANATION : The function template equal checks equality of three data types. In the function template **p1**, **p2** and **p3** contains the data type of arguments in string form. For example, when the function template is instantiated for function call **equal(2, 5, 6)**, p1, p2 and p3 all contains "int". As p1 and p2 is same b1 contains a value 0 or false. Similarly b2 contains value 0 or false. In the if we check if both are not zero (not ! before b1 and b2) using && (logical and). If the if condition is true all three data are same else not.

/* PROG 13.9 MIXING BUILT-IN TYPE WITH GENERIC TYPE VER 1*/

```
#include <iostream.h>
#include <typeinfo.h>

template <class T>
void show(T par, char*s)
```

```
{
    cout<<"*+*+*+*+"<<s<<"*+*+*+*+*+"<<endl;
    cout<<typeid(par).name( )<<" parameter="<<par<<endl;
}

void main( )
{
    show(12,"good Morning");
    show(34.45,"Good Morning");
}
```

OUTPUT :

```
*+*+*+*+good Morning*+*+*+*+*+
int parameter=12
*+*+*+*+Good Morning*+*+*+*+*+
double parameter=34.45
```

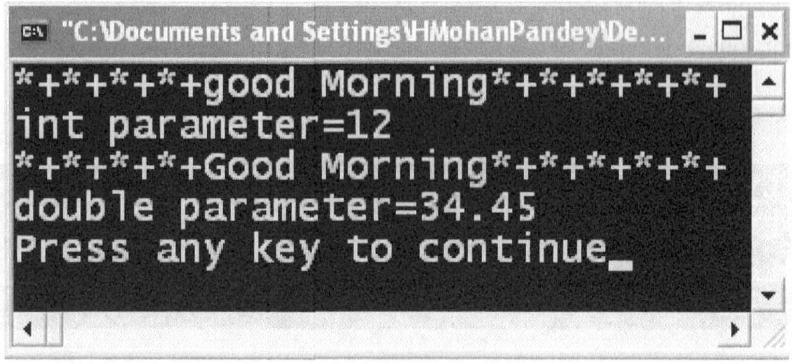

Figure 13.7. *Showing the output of program 13.9*

EXPLANATION : You can fix some of the arguments to the function template as shown above. Here in the fucntion show the first argument may be of any type but second argument is fix which must be of `char*` type. In the similar way you can fix any number of arguments in the function template. But note the fix argument must not be written in the template declaration. Like writing `template <class T, char*s>` will be wrong in the above case. It must be written as function argument.

```
/* PROG 13.10 MIXING BUILT-IN TYPE WITH GENERIC TYPES VER 2 */

#include <iostream.h>
#include <typeinfo.h>
template <class T>
void show(T par, char*s= "Good Morning")
{
```

```
        cout<<"**********"<<s<<"************"<<endl;
        cout<<typeid(par).name( )<<" parameter= "<<par<<endl;
}

void main( )
{
        show(12);
        show(35.46);
}
```

OUTPUT :

```
**********Good Morning************
int parameter= 12
**********Good Morning************
double parameter= 35.46
```

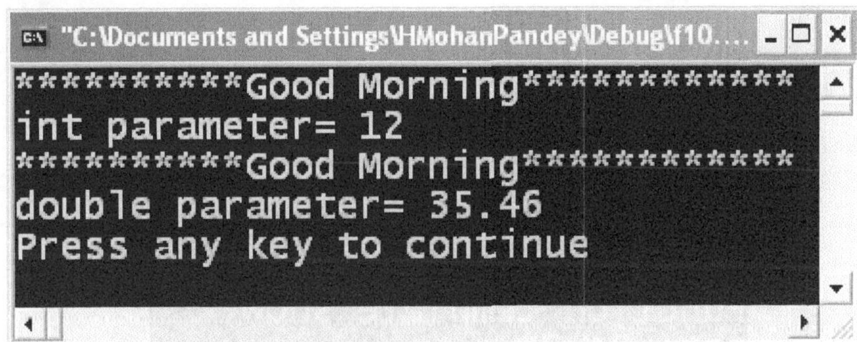

Figure 13.8. *Output screen of program 13.10*

EXPLANATION : The program is similar to previous one but here we have taken second argument to function template show as default argument of `char*` type. Thus, you may have default argument to function template.

/* PROG 13.11 OVERLOADING OF FUNCTION TEMPLATE */

```
#include <iostream.h>
#include <typeinfo.h>
template <class T>
void show(T par)
{
        cout<<"Function template show \n";
        cout<<"par :="<<par<<endl;
}
```

```
void show(char*s)
{
    cout<<"Explicit function show\n";
    cout<<"s="<<s<<endl;
}
void main( )
{
    show(12);
    show(34.78);
    show("Explicit");
}
```

OUTPUT :

```
Function template show
par :=12
Function template show
par :=34.78
Explicit function show
s=Explicit
```

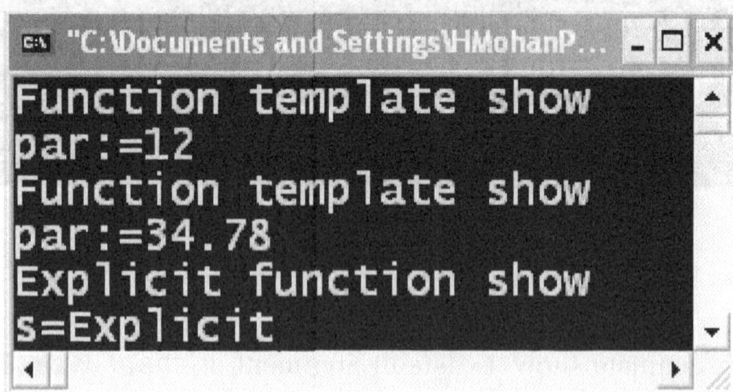

Figure 13.9. *Output screen of program 13.11*

EXPLANATION : When an explicit function is return with the same name as function template for specific data type, explicit function is called first instead of instantiating function template for that specific data type. Here we have function template `show` which has just one argument of generic data type. And we have a function `show` which takes a single argument of `char*` type. When `show("Explicit")` executes, function template is not instantiated but `show(char*)` function is called. For all other types of argument function template will be instantiated.

13.3 CLASS TEMPLATE

Similar to function template we can create class template. The difference is simply that earlier we created template for a function now we will be creating it for class. The class templates are basically used for creating container classes. That is which can contains varieties of objects of any type. For the class templates definition method remains same but instantiation changes.

Take an example :

```
template<class T>
class demo
{
 T x, y;
 public :
 ..............;
 ..............;
};
```

The template class can be instantiated when an object of the class will be created. That is :

```
demo<int>d1;
```

creates an instance of class template demo for integer data type. Similarly

```
demo<float> d2;
```

will create an instance of class template demo for float data type. At this instance there will bo two different demo classes residing in memory. One will be using integer data members and other float data members.

```
/* PROG 13.12 SUM OF TWO NUMBER USING CLASS TEMPLATE */

#include <iostream.h>
#include <conio.h>

template <class PAR>

class demo
{
    PAR n1,n2;
public :
    demo(PAR x, PAR y)
    {
        n1=x;
```

```
            n2=y;
        }
        PAR sum( )
        {
            return(n1+n2);
        }
};

void main( )
{
        clrscr( );
        demo<int>d1(10,20);
        cout<<"Sum="<<d1.sum( )<<endl;
        demo<float>d2(2.4f,4.5f);
        cout<<"Sum="<<d2.sum( )<<endl;
        getch( );
}
```

OUTPUT :

```
Sum=30
Sum=6.9
```

EXPLANATION : A class template is similar to function template with the difference it is used with the class. Here a template class `demo` is written which makes use of generic data type `PAR`. Note template declaration is same as written for the function template. The class templates has two data members `n1` and `n2`, one constructor and function `sum` which finds sum of two data members and returns.

In the `main` note how to do we instantiates a class template. The statement `demo<int>d1(10,20);` instantiates a new class `demo` for `int` data types. All occurrences of `PAR` are replaced by word in the class template. First the class name, then in the brackets < and >, data type is written, `d1(10,20)` creates objects `d1` by calling the two argument constructor of `demo` class. We then find the `sum` of two data members by calling the function `sum`.

The class in the memory will look like this :

```
        class demo
        {
                int n1, n2;
            public :
                        demo (int x, int y)
                        {
                                n1 = x;
                                n2 = y;
                        }
```

```
                    int sum( )
                    {
                        return (n1+n2);
                    }
};
```

Similarly, the statement `demo<float>d2(2.4f,4.5f);` instantites class template for data type `float` and a new `demo` class for `float` data type will be created.

/* PROG 13.13 DISPLAY OF DIFFERENT TYPES OF DATA USING CLASS TEMPLATE VER 1 */

```
#include <iostream.h>
#include <typeinfo.h>

template <class PAR>
class demo
{
    PAR n1,n2;
public :
    demo(PAR x, PAR y)
    {
        n1=x;
        n2=y;
        show( );
    }
    void show( )
    {
        cout<<typeid(PAR).name( )<<"Data\n";
        cout<<n1<<"\t"<<n2<<endl;
    }
};
void main( )
{
    demo<int>d1(10,20);
    demo<float>d2(2.4f,4.5f);
    demo<char>d3('P','T');
    demo<char*>d4("One","Two");
}
```

OUTPUT :

```
intData
10          20
```

```
floatData
2.4       4.5
charData
P T
char *Data
One       Two
```

```
"d:\tc\ch14\Debug\CPP.exe"
intData
10        20
floatData
2.4       4.5
charData
P         T
char *Data
One       Two
```

Figure 13.10. *Output screen of program 13.13*

EXPLANATION : Here, we have a class template which is similar to class template **demo** created in the earlier program with the difference that this class simply accepts and display the data members. In the **main** when **demo<int>d1(10,20);** executes a new **demo** class for **int** data type will be created and all occurrences of **PAR** will be replaced by **int**. Constructor of **demo** class be called and **n1** will have value **10** and **n2** will have **20**. From the constructor we have called function **show** which displays data type of **n1** and **n2** and their values. Similar argument holds for other statements :

```
demo<float>d2(2.4f,4.5f);
demo<char>d3('P','T');
demo<char*>d4("One","Two");
```

/*PROG 13.14 DISPLAY OF DIFFERENT TYPES OF DATA USING CLASS TEMPLATE VER 2*/

```
#include <iostream.h>
#include <typeinfo.h>
template <class T1,class T2>
class demo
{
    T1 n1;
    T2 n2;
public :
    demo(T1 x, T2 y)
```

```
    {
        n1=x;
        n2=y;
        show( );
    }
    void show( )
    {
        cout<<n1<<" is of type"<<typeid(T1).name( )<<endl;
        cout<<n2<<" is of type"<<typeid(T2).name( )<<endl;
    }
    void main( )
    {
        demo<int,float>d1(10,20.54f);
        demo<float,char>d2(2.4f,'H');
        demo<char,char*>d3('M',"NMIMS");
        demo<char*,int>d4("MPSTME",24);
    }
```

OUTPUT :

```
10 is of type int
20.54 is of type float
2.4 is of type float
H is of type char
M is of type char
NMIMS is of type char*
MPSTME is of type char*
24 is of type int
```

EXPLANATION : We can have two different generic data types in the class template similar to function template written as **template<class T1, class T2>.** In the **main** when all **4** statement executes **4** different classes will be created for **4** different argument pairs. For example, when **demo<int, float>d1(10,20.54f);** executes a **new demo** class will be created following the definition of class template **demo** and all occurrence of **T1** will be replaced by **int** and all occurrences of **T2** will be replaced by **float**. The class will look like :

```
class demo
    {
        int n1;
        float n2;
    public :
        demo(int x,float y)
        {
```

```
        n1=x;
        n2=y;
        show( );
    }
    void show( )
    {
        cout<<n1<<" is of type "
            <<typeid(int).name( )<<endl;
        cout<<n2<<" is of type "
            <<typeid(float).name( )<<endl;
    }
};
```

/* PROG 13.15 CLASS TEMPLATE FOR FINDING SUM OF ARRAY ELEMENTS */

```
#include <iostream.h>
#include <typeinfo.h>
#define S 5

template <class TARR>
class demo
{
    TARR arr[S];
public :
    demo( )
    {
        int i;
        cout<<" Enter "<<S<<" "<<typeid(TARR).name( )
            <<"numbers\n";
        for(i=0;i<S;i++)
            cin>>arr[i];
    }
    TARR sum( )
    {
        int i;
        TARR s=0;
        for(i=0;i<S;i++)
            s+=arr[i];
        return s;
    }
};
```

```
void main( )
{
    demo<int>d1;
    cout<<"Sum="<<d1.sum( )<<endl;
    demo<float>d2;
    cout<<"Sum="<<d2.sum( )<<endl;
    demo<<long>d3;
    cout<<"Sum="<<d3.sum( )<<endl;
}
```

OUTPUT :

```
Enter 5 int numbers
2 45 67 34 23
Sum = 169
Fnter 5 float numbers
1.2 3.4 3.3 4.5 5.6
Sum = 18
Enter 5 long numbers
12345
234567
76543
34567
127865
Sum = 485815
```

EXPLANATION : The class template is created for declaring and defining arrays of different types and finding sum of its elements. When **demo<float>d2;** executes a new version of demo class template is instantiated and all prompt user for 5 elements. Numbers are stored in the array and sum is displayed by a call to sum function using object d2. The class will look like as :

```
class demo
{
    float arr[S];
public :
    demo( )
    {
        int i;
        cout<<"Enter "<<S<<" "<<typeid(float).name( )
            <<"numbers\n";
        for(i=0;i<S;i++)
```

```
            cin>>arr[i];
        }
        float sum( )
        {
            int i;
            float s=0;
            for(i=0;i<S;i++)
                s+=arr[i];
            return s;
        }
};
```

/* PROG 13.16 DEMO OF CLASS TEMPLATE, MEMBER FUNCTIONS ARE DEFINED OUTSIDE THE CLASS */

```
#include <iostream.h>
#include <conio.h>

template <class T>

class demo
{
    T num1,num2;
public :
    void input(T x, T y);
    void show( )
    {
        cout<<"num1="<<num1<<"\t";
        cout<<"num2="<<num2<<"\t";
    }
};
template <class T>
void demo <T> : : input(T x, T y)
{
    num1=x;
    num2=y;
}

void main( )
{
    demo<int>d;
```

```
    clrscr( );
    d.input(10,20);
    d.show( );
    getch( );
}
```

OUTPUT :

```
num1=10 num2=20
```

EXPLANATION : The aim of the program is to show that how can we define a function of a class template outside the class. For each function declared in the class template, the definition must contain the first line as :

template<class T>

followed by actual definition of the function with generic type we have done in the program

```
template<class T>
void demo<T> : : input<T x, T y>
{
    num1 = x;
    num2 = y;
}
```

/* PROG 13.17 A SIMPLE LINKED LIST WITHOUT TEMPLATE */

```
#include <iostream.h>
#include <typeinfo.h>
class Linklist
{
    struct node
    {
        int data;
        struct node*next;
    }*start,*save,*temp;
public :
    Linklist( )
    {
        start=NULL;
    }
    void add(int d)
    {
        if(start= =NULL)
```

```
        {
            start=new node;
            start->data=d;
            start->next=NULL;
        }
        else
        {
            temp=new node;
            temp->data=d;
            temp->next=NULL;
            save=start;
            while(save->next!=NULL)
                save=save->next;
            save->next=temp;
        }
    }
    void show( )
    {
        while(start!=NULL)
        {
            cout<<start->data<<"->";
            start=start->next;
        }
    }
};
void main( )
{
    Linklist L;
    L.add(10);
    L.add(20);
    L.add(30);
    L.add(40);
}
```

OUTPUT :

10->20->30->40

EXPLANATION : We create a node for the linked list using structure node which has a data member of type int and a pointer to next node of type struct node named next. Just after the declaration of structure node we create three pointer start, temp and save. The start pointer is for keeping track of starting node of the linked list. temp and save is for temporary purposes. The function add adds a new node to the link list. It checks whether start is NULL; if it is so it makes the first node for the linked list and start points to it. If start is not NULL, then we move to the last node using while loop and save pointer and adds a new node there. Note the node was created earlier pointed by temp pointer. To show the linklist we have show function which displays data of each node.

/*PROG 13.18 A TEMPLATE BASED LINKED LIST */

```
#include <iostream.h>
#include <typeinfo.h>
template <class T>

class Linklist
{
    struct node
    {
        T data;
        struct node*next;
    }*start,*save,*temp;
public :
    Linklist( )
    {
        start=NULL;
    }
    void add(T d)
    {
        if(start= =NULL)
        {
            start=new node;
            start->data=d;
            start->next=NULL;
        }
        else
        {
            temp=new node;
            temp->data=d;
            temp->next=NULL :
            save=start;
            while(save->next!=NULL)
                save=save->next;
            save->next=temp;
        }
    }
```

```
    void show( )
    {
        while(start!=NULL)
        {
            cout<<start->data<<"->";
            start=start->next;
        }
    }
};
void main( )
{
    Linklist<int>L;
    L.add(10);
    L.add(20);
    L.add(30);
    cout<<"\nLinked List of integer\n";
    L.show( );
    Linklist<char>L1;
    L1.add('A');
    L1.add('B');
    L1.add('C');
    L1.add('E');
    cout<<"\n Linked List of charaters \n";
    L1.show( );
    Linklist<char*>L2;
    L2.add("Hari");
    L2.add("Mohan");
    L2.add("Pandey");
    L2.add("Lecturer");
    cout<<"\n Linked list of string \n";
    L2.show( );
    Linklist<float>L3;
    L3.add(123.456f);
    L3.add(34.56f);
    L3.add(456.67f);
    L3.add(4532.895f);
    cout<<"\nLinked list of float \n";
    L3.show( );
}
```

```
OUTPUT :
Linked list of integer
10->20->30->
Linked list of character
A->B->C->E->
Linked list of string
Hari->Mohan->Pandey->Lecturer
Linked list of float
123.456->34.56->456.67->4532.895->
```

EXPLANATION : The program is similar to the previous one with the difference that we have here made a class template which will be instantiated 4 times for different types. That is `L` represent a link list of `integer`, `L1` a linked list of `characters`, `L2` a linked list of strings and `L3` a linked list of `floats`.

/*PROG 13.19 TEMPLATE BASED LINKED LIST WITHOUT USING STRUCTURE AS A NODE */

```
#include <iostream.h>
template <class LIST>
class Linkelist
{
    LIST data;
    linklist*next;
public :
    linklist(LIST num)
    {
        data=num;
        next=NULL;
    }
    void add_node(linklist*node)
    {
        node->next=this;
        this->next=NULL;
    }
    linklist *getnext( )
    {
        return next;
    }
    LIST getdata( )
    {
        return data;
    }
};
```

```
void main( )
{
    linklist<int>LL(1);
    linklist<int>*temp,*link;
    link=&LL;
    int j;
    for(j=2;j<=5;j++)
    {
        temp=new linklist<int>(j);
        temp->add_node(link);
        link=temp;
    }
    temp=&LL;
    cout<<"Linked list is \n";
    for(j=1;j<=5;j++)
    {
        cout<<temp->getdata( )<<"->";
        temp=temp->getnext( );
    }
}
```

OUTPUT :

```
Linked List is
1->2->3->4->5->
```

EXPLANATION : The class linklist contains a pointer data member next of linklist type. These types of classes are known as self-referential classes. The class has one data member data of generic type. The constructor of class template linklist creates first node for the class and assign value of 1 to data and NULL to next. The temporary class type pointer link saves address of the first node represented by LL in the main. Note here each node of the linked list is an object of class linklist. In the for loop for j=2 statements :

```
temp = new linklist<int>(j);
```

Creates a new node with data value 2 and next=NULL. Now this node has to be added at the end of the linked list. For that we call the function add_node and pass link as argument as

```
temp->add_node (link);
```

The new node is temp and this pointer represents the temp inside the function add_node. The link represents the first node. So, in the function add_node next of link node will be sorting address of this new node represented by this pointer and next of this new node will be NULL. The same is done in the function add_node as :

```
node->next=this;
this->next =NULL;
```

In the next statement inside the for loop we have assigned address of the new node to the link, so that when new node is created for j=3, it will be added after the last node. This will continue for j=4 and 5.

To display the node we take the address of first object *i.e.*, &LL into the temp pointer. In the class template we have created two functions which return the next pointer and the data. Initially the data for the first node is displayed then pointer is made to point to next object in the linklist by getting the next pointer. For that we call the function getnext as :

temp = temp->getnext( );

/*PROG 13.20 DEMO OF USER DEFINED TYPES AS TEMPLATE PARAMETERS */

```
#include <iostream.h>

class A
{
public :
    void show( )
    {
        cout<<"Hello from A\n";
    }
};

class B
{
public :
    void show( )
    {
        cout<<"Hello from B \n";
    }
};

template <class T>
class demo
{
    T aa;
public :
    void showd( )
    {
        aa.show( );
    }
};
```

```
void main( )
{
    demo<A>d1;
    demo<B>d2;
    d1.showd( );
    d2.showd( );
}
```

OUTPUT :

```
Hello from A
Hello from B
```

EXPLANATION : In the program instead of basic types for generic types, user defined types will be substituted for generic types. We have two different classes A and B. Both the class has a function show. The class template demo simply has one showd function. In the `main` when we write `demo<A>d1;` then generic type T is replaced by A and when we call `d1.showd` then inside the `showd` function `show` of `class A` is called as function definition of showd is `A.show`. When we write `demo<B>d2;` then generic type T is replaced by B and when we call `d2.show` then inside the `showd` function `show` of `class B` is called as function of `show` is `B.show`.

/* PROG 13.21 CLASS TEMPLATE WITH FIX ARGUMENTS */

```
#include <iostream.h>
#include <typeinfo.h>
template <class TARR, int size>
class demo
{
    TARR arr[size];
public :
    demo( )
    {
        int i;
        cout<<"Enter "<<size<<" "<<typeid(TARR).name( )
  <<"numbers \n";
        for(i=0;i<size;i++)
            cin>>arr[i];
    }
    TARR sum( )
    {
        int i;
        TARR s=0;
        for(i=0;i<size;i++)
```

```
            s+=arr[i];
        return s;
    }
};
void main( )
{
    demo<int, 3>d1;
    cout<<"Sum="<<d1.sum( )<<endl;
    demo<float,4>d2;
    cout<<"Sum="<<d2.sum( )<<endl;
    demo<<long,5>d3;
    cout<<"Sum="<<d3.sum( )<<endl;
}
```

OUTPUT :

```
Enter 3 int numbers
2 45 67
Sum = 114
Enter 4 float numbers
1.2 3.4 3.3 4.5
Sum = 12.4
Enter 5 long numbers
12345
234567
76543
34567
127865
Sum = 485815
```

EXPLANATION : In the program, the class template contains a fixed argument size of type int. In the main when template class is instantiated for different data types, second argument remain fixed which denotes size of the array.

13.4 PONDERABLE POINTS

1. Template is the mechanism which allows us to declare generic classes and functions.
2. Use of one function or class that works for all data types is generalization. With the help of templates and functions we can create generic data types and this idea leads to generic programming. In the generic programming generic data types are passed as argument to function and classes.
3. A template is created using the keyword template followed by generic data type name using keyword class as : - **template<class T>**.

4. Use of template saves us from writing repetitive code for different data types. It does not save any memory space.
5. A function template is instantiated when a particular template function is called with variables or constants of any data type.
6. Both function template and class template can have default arguments.

EXERCISE

A. True and False :

1. Template is used to declare generic classes and functions.
2. Template is frequently used to define container classes.
3. Template and function overloading is related.
4. Template saves memory.

B. Answer the Following Questions :

1. What do you understand by template ?
2. How does a function template works ?
3. How does a class template works ?
4. What is the difference between template and function overloading ?
5. What is the difference between template and macro ?
6. Why do we need template ?
7. What are the disadvantages of using templates ?

C. Brain Drill :

1. Write a program to pass an object to template function and display its members.
2. Write a program to show values of different data types using template and constructor.
3. Write a program using function template to find maximum value stored in the array.
4. Write a program to define template and display the absolute value of int, float and long data type of variable.
5. Give the definition of template class POLY which is to be implemented as a linked list using pointers where each node contains a coefficient, and exponent and a pointer to the next element. Initialize an empty POLY object with no node. Also write code for inserting a node in the list in proper ordered position according to the exponent in the node to be inserted.
6. Write a template function that returns the average of all elements of an array. The arguments to the function should be the array name and the size of the array (type int). In main ( ), exercise the function with arrays of type int, long, double, and char.
7. Create a function called swap ( ) that interchanges the values of the two arguments sent to it. (You will probably want to pass these arguments by reference) Make the function into a template, so it can be used with all numerical data types (char, int, float and so on). Write a main ( ) program to exercise the function with several types.
8. Create a function called amax ( ) that returns the value of the largest element I an array. The arguments to the function should be the address of the array and its size. Make this function into a template so it will work with an array of any numerical type. Write a main ( ) program that applies this function to arrays of various types.

❑❑❑

CHAPTER 14

EXCEPTION HANDLING IN C++

14.1 INTRODUCTION

In C++ errors can be divided into two categories :

1. **Compile time errors and**
2. **Run time errors.**

Compile time errors are syntactic errors which occurs during the writing of the program. Most common examples of compile time errors are missing semicolon, missing comma, missing double quotes, etc. They occurs mainly due to poor understanding of language or writing program without proper concentration to the program.

There are logical errors which are mainly due to improper understanding of the program logic by the programmer. Logical errors cause the unexpected or unwanted output.

Exceptions are runtime errors which a programmer usually does not except. They occurs accidentally which may result in abnormal termination of the program. C++ provides exception handling mechanism which can be used to trap this exception and running programs smoothly after catching the exception.

Common examples of exceptions are division by zero, opening file which does not exist, insufficient memory, violating array bounds, etc.

14.2 BASICS OF EXCEPTION HANDLING

Exception handling is the process to handle the exception if generated by the program at run time. The aim of exception handling is to write code which passes exception generated to a routine which can handle the exception and can take suitable action. Any exception handling mechanism must have the following steps:

Step 1 : Writing exception class (optional).

Step 2 : Writing try block.

Step 3 : Throwing an exception.

Step 4 : Catching and handling the exception thrown.

1. The try Block

The exception is to be thrown to be written in the try block. Whenever an exception is generated in the try block, it is thrown. An exception is an object so we can say that an exception object is thrown. The throw keyword is used for throwing an exception. The usual practice of using the throw statement is as :

```
throw exception;
```

For throwing an exception and simply

```
throw;
```

For re-throwing an exception.

The syntax of try block is as shown :

```
try
{
        statements;
        statements;
        statements;
        throw exception;
}
```

2. The catch Block

An exception thrown by try block is caught by the catch block. A try block must have at least one catch, though there can be many catch block for catching different types of exceptions. A catch block must have a try block prior written which will throw an exception. The catch block is used as :

```
try
{
        statements;
        statements;
        statements;
        throw exception;
}
catch (object or argument)
{
        statements for handling the exception;
}
```

The catch block catches any exception thrown by the try block. If exception thrown matches with the argument or object in the block, the statements written within the catch block and we say that exception thrown by try block was caught successfully by the catch block. After the successful execution of the catch block statements any statements following the catch block will be executed. If argument does not match with the exception thrown, catch couldn't handle it and this may results in abnormal program termination.

14.3 EXCEPTION HANDLING MECHANISM

The try, throw and catch all together provide exception handling mechanism in C++. The exception is generated by the throw keyword which is written in the try block. Any exception generated within this try block is thrown using this throw keyword. Immediately following the try block, catch block is written. As soon as some run time errors occurs an exception is thrown by the try block using throw which informs the catch block that an error has occurred in the try block. This try block is also known as exception generated block. The catch block is responsible for catching the execution thrown by the try block. When try throw an exception, the control of the program passes to the catch block and if argument matches as explained earlier, exception is caught. In case no exception is thrown the catch block is ignored and control passes to the next statement after the catch block.

/*PROG 14.1 DEMO OF EXCEPTION HANDLING */

```
#include <iostream.h>
void main( )
{
    try
    {
        throw"DEMO OF EXCEPTION";
    }
    catch(char*E)
    {
        cout<<"Exception caught="<<E<<endl;
    }
    cout<<"Continue after catch block"<<endl;
}
```

OUTPUT :

```
Exception caught=DEMO OF EXCEPTION
Continue after catch block
```

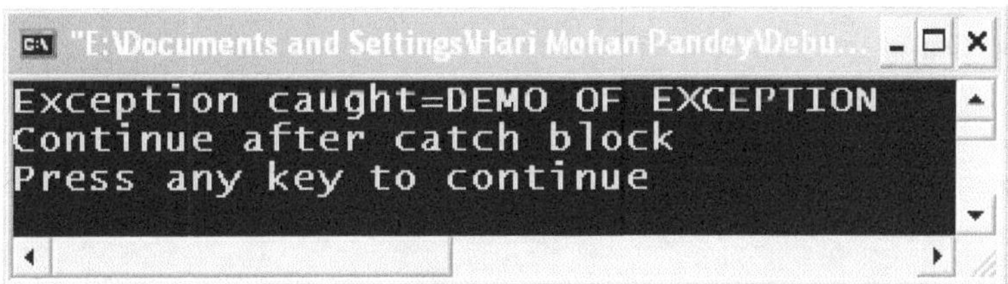

Figure 14.1. *Output screen of program 14.1*

EXPLANATION : This is very basic program which has the sole purpose to demonstrate you, how exception are thrown and caught. All exceptions which are to be thrown must be put inside the try block. Any exception thrown must precede throw keyword. The throw statement is responsible for throwing an exception. Following throw any variable of any built in data type, constants or an object of any class (built-in or user defined) or structure may be present. Any try block must have a corresponding catch block. The exception thrown by the try block is caught by the catch block. Here, we are throwing an exception **"DEMO OF EXCEPTION"** of **char*** type. So inside the **catch ( )** we must have an argument of type **char*** which can catch the exception object **thrown**. Here exception thrown is caught by catch block in variable **E** of **char*** type. The **catch** block then executes and display the output **"Exception caught = DEMO OF EXCEPTION"**. After the execution of statements within catch block program continues with the statements following the **catch** block. If exception thrown is not handled than your program may terminate abnormally leaving all statements after try unexecuted.

14.4 PROGRAMMING EXAMPLES

```
/* PROG 14.2 DEMO OF EXCEPTION HANDLING, CATCHING DIVISION BY ZERO
EXCEPTION */

#include <iostream.h>
void main( )
{
    float x,y;
    cout<<"Enter two numbers\n";
    cin>>x>>y;
    try
    {
        if(y!=0)
            cout<<"Div="<<x/y<<endl;
        else
            throw(y);
    }
    catch(float E)
    {
        cout<<"Caught an Exception \n";
        cout<<"y="<<y<<endl;
    }
    cout<<"Out of try catch block \n";
}
```

OUTPUT :

```
Enter two numbers
35 78
Div=0.448718
Out of try catch block
```

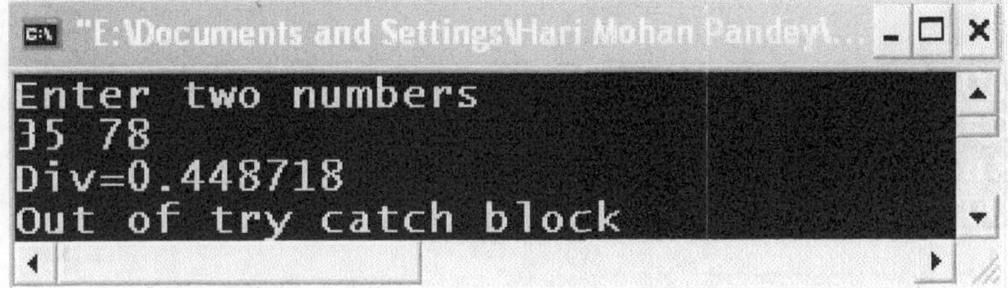

Figure 14.2. *output screen of program 14.2*

EXPLANATION : Here we are performing the division of two numbers within try block. If denominator *i.e.*, **y** is not **0** we carry out division is a normal fashion. But if **y** is **0** we throw an exception, the value of **y**. This expression is caught by the catch block in argument **E**, which handles the exception and display.

/*PROG 14.3 DEMO OF EXCEPTION HANDLING THROWING EXCEPTION int 1-b WHERE a>b */

```
#include <iostream.h>
void main( )
{
    int x,y;
    bool m;
    cout<<"Enter two numbers \n";
    cin>>x>>y;
    m=x>y ?true :false;
    try
    {
        if(m==true)
            cout<<"Subtraction="<<x-y<<endl;
        else
            throw("subtraction not possible");
    }
    catch(char*E)
    {
        cout<<"Caught an Exception\n";
        cout<<E<<endl;
    }
    cout<<"Out of try catch block\n";
}
```

OUTPUT :

```
Enter two numbers
70 90
Caught an Exception
subtraction not possible
Out of try catch block
```

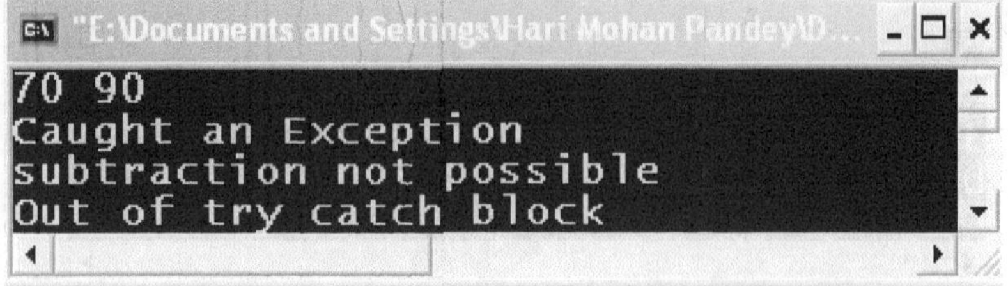

Figure 14.3. *output screen of program 14.3*

EXPLANATION : In the program we are checking if **x>y** if this is so we do the subtraction x-y. If y>x we do not perform subtraction instead we throw an exception "Subtraction not possible". This exception is caught by the catch block in variable E.

/*PROG 14.4 MULTIPLE CATCH STATEMENT WITH SINGLE TRY */

```
#include <iostream.h>
void main( )
{
    int num=10;
    for(num=10;num<=30;num+=10)
    {
        try
        {
            if(num==20)
                throw("GOOD");
            else if(num<20)
                throw num;
            else if (num>20)
                throw 2.25f;
        }
        catch(int E)
        {
            cout<<"Caught int Exception E="<<E<<endl;
        }
        catch(char* E)
        {
            cout<<"Caught string Exception E="<<E<<endl;
        }
        catch(float E)
        {
            cout<<"Caught float Exception E="<<E<<endl;
        }
    }
```

```
    cout<<"Outside try catch block"<<endl;
}
```

OUTPUT :

```
Caught int Exception E=10
Caught string Exception E=GOOD
Caught float Exception E=2.25
Outside try catch block
```


Figure 14.4. *Output screen of program 14.4*

EXPLANATION : We can put multiple catch blocks for a single try in case try block throws different types of exceptions. To demonstrate how we can have multiple catch statements with a single try we have run a for loop from 10 to 30 with increment of 10. Initially value of 'num' is 10 first else if condition is true and num is thrown by the try block. As the type of num is int so the exception thrown is caught by the first catch block which has one argument of type int. This block handles the exception and displays

Caught int Exception E = 10

In the second iteration of for loop value of num is 20, initial if condition is true so throw("GOOD") executes which throws an exception of char* type. This exception is handled by the second catch block which displays

Caught string Exception E = GOOD

In the third iteration of for loop value of num is 30, second else if condition is true so throw 2.25f executes which throws an exception of char* type. This exception is handled by the third catch block which displays

Caught float Exception E = 2.25

/*PROG 14.5 GENERATING EXCEPTION IN FUNCTION, FUNCTION IS IN TRY BLOCK */

```
#include <iostream.h>
void main( )
{
    int x,y;
    void genExp(int, int);
    cout<<"Enter two numbers \n";
    cin>>x>>y;
    try
```

```
    {
        genExp(x,y);
    }
    catch(char*E)
    {
        cout<<"Caught an Exception"<<endl;
        cout<<E<<endl;
    }
    cout<<"Out of try catch block"<<endl;
}
void genExp(int x, int y)
{
    bool m;
    m=x>y ?true :false;
    if(m==true)
        cout<<"Subtraction="<<x-y<<endl;
    else
        throw("Subtraction not possible");
}
```

OUTPUT :

```
(FIRST RUN)
Enter two numbers
50 30
Subtraction=20
Out of try catch block
(SECOND RUN)
Enter two numbers
30 50
Caught an Exception
Subtraction not possible
Out of try catch block
Press any key to continue
```

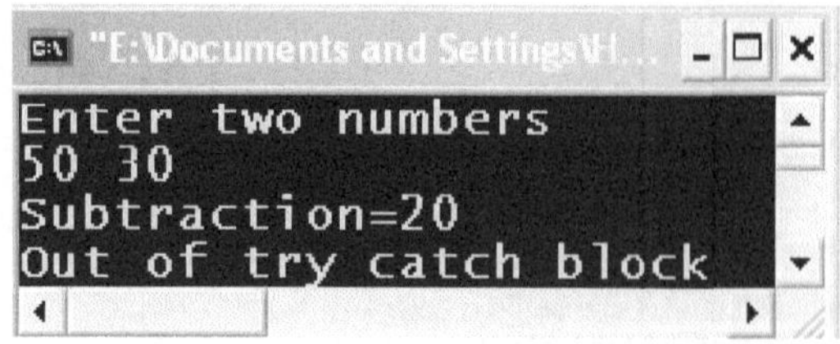

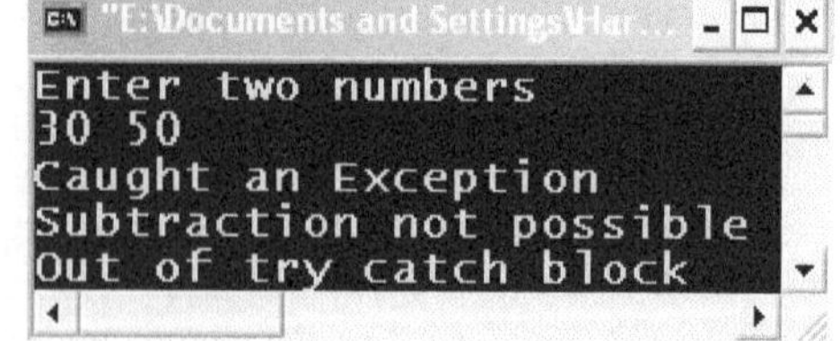

Figure 14.5. *Output screen of program 14.5*

EXPLANATION : The program is similar to the program we have seen earlier with difference that whole of the logic has been put in the function genExp. As function genExp may generate exception it is placed inside the try block. Note the exception is thrown by the function placed in the try block which is caught by the catch block following try.

/*PROG 14.6 CATCHING ARRAY INDEX OUT OF BOUND EXCEPTION */

```
#include <iostream.h>
#define S 5
void main( )
{
    int arr[S]={1,2,3,4,5};
    int idx;
    void show_ele(int[ ],int);
    cout<<"Enter the array index\n";
    cin>>idx;
    try
    {
        show_ele(arr,idx);
    }
    catch(char* E)
    {
        cout<<"Caught an Exception\n";
        cout<<E<<endl;
    }
    cout<<"Out of try catch block \n";
}
void show_ele(int arr[ ],int idx)
{
    if(idx>=0 && idx<S)
        cout<<"Element at"<<idx<<"is"<<arr[idx]<<endl;
    else
        throw("Array index out of bound");
}
```

OUTPUT :

```
(First Run)
Enter the array index
3
Element at3is4
Out of try catch block
(Second Run)
```

```
Enter the array index
8
Caught an Exception
Array index out of bound
Out of try catch block
(First Run)    (Second Run)
```

"E:\Documents and Settings\...
Enter the array index
3
Element at3is4
Out of try catch block

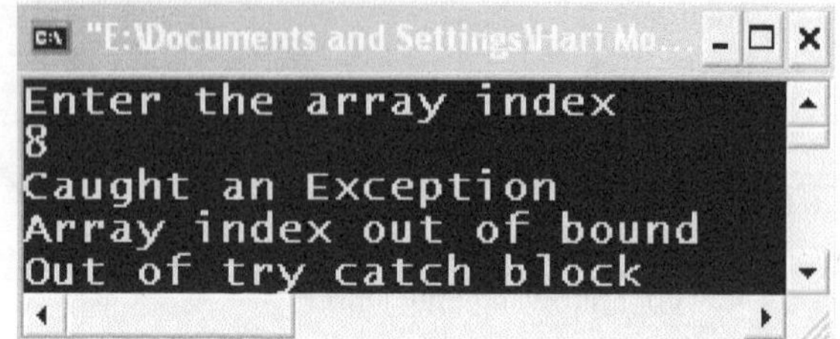

Figure 14.6. *Showing the output screen of program 14.6*

EXPLANATION : The function show_ele displays array element at given index. It takes both array arr and idx as its argument. If idx is within the limit 0 and S we display the array element as arr[idx] else we throw an exception "Array index out of bound". As function show_ele may throw an exception it is put inside the try block. The exception thrown is caught by the catch block and handled.

14.5 EXCEPTION HANDLING WITH CLASS

Until now we have been doing exception handling without using class. We can use exception handling with class too. Even we can throw objects as exception of user defined class types. For throwing an exception of say demo class type within the try block we may write

throw demo( );

See few programs given below :

/* PROG 14.7 EXCEPTION HANDLING WITH SINGLE CLASS */

```
#include <iostream.h>
class demo
{
};
void main( )
{
    try
    {
        throw demo( );
    }
    catch(demo d)
```

```
    {
        cout<<"Caught exception of demo class \n";
    }
}
```

OUTPUT :

Caught exception of demo class

EXPLANATION : The program is very simple example to show how class object can be thrown and caught. In the program we have declared an empty class. In the try block we are throwing an object of demo class type. The try block catches the object and displays the result.

/* PROG 14.8 EXCEPTION HANDLING WITH TWO CLASSES */

```
#include <iostream.h>
class demo1
{
};
class demo2
{
};
void main( )
{
    for(int i=1;i<=2;i++)
    {
        try
        {
            if(i==1)
                throw demo1( );
            else if(i==2)
            throw demo2( );
        }
        catch(demo1 d1)
        {
            cout<<"Caught exception of demo1 class \n";
        }
        catch(demo2 d2)
        {
            cout<<"Caught exception of demo2 class \n";
        }
    }
}
```

OUTPUT :

Caught exception of demo1 class

Caught exception of demo2 class

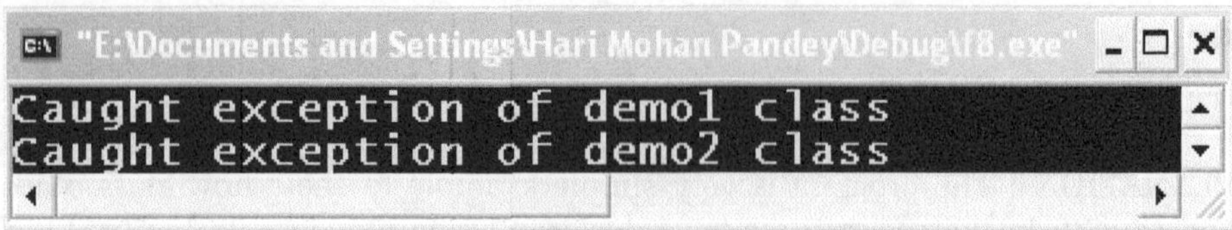

Figure 14.7. *Output screen of program 14.8*

EXPLANATION : In the program we have declared two empty classes' demo1 and demo2. For i=1 object demo1 is thrown and for i=2 an object of demo2 is thrown. For catching object of different classes two catch blocks have been written. Note both catch block must be written inside the for loop.

/* PROG 14.9 EXCEPTION HANDLING WITH NHERITANCE */

```
#include <iostream.h>
class demo1
{
};
class demo2 :public demo1
{
};
void main( )
{
    for(int i=1;i<=2;i++)
    {
        try
        {
            if(i==1)
                throw demo1( );
            else if(i==2)
                throw demo2( );
        }
        catch(demo1 d1)
        {
            cout<<"Caught exception of demo1 class \n";
        }
        catch(demo2 d2)
```

```
        {
            cout<<"Caught exception of demo2 class \n";
        }
    }
}
```

OUTPUT :

Caught exception of demo1 class

Caught exception of demo1 class

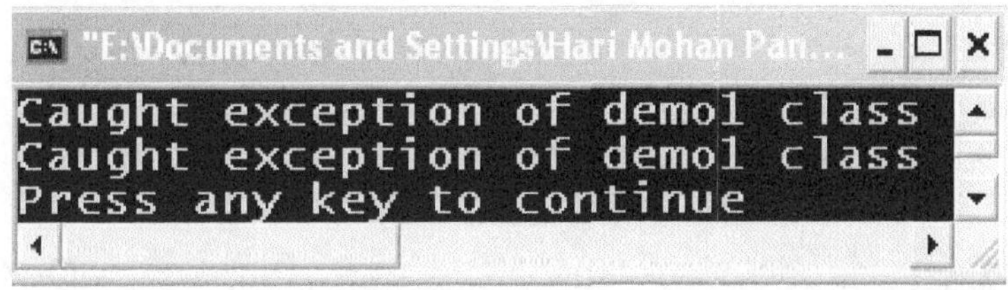

Figure 14.8. *Output screen of program 14.9*

EXPLANATION : The program is similar to previous one but here we have made demo2 as derived class for demo1. Note the catch block for demo1 is written first. As demo1 is base class for demo2 as object thrown of demo2 class will be handled by the first catch block. That's why the output.

/* PROG 14.10 EXCEPTION HANDLING IN CONSTRUCTOR VER 1 */

```
#include <iostream.h>
class demo
{
    int num;
public :
    demo( )
    {
        try
        {
            throw 25;
        }
        catch(int E)
        {
            cout<<"Exception caught \n";
            num=E;
        }
    }
```

```
    void show( )
    {
        cout<<"num="<<num<<endl;
    }
};
void main( )
{
    demo d;
    d.show( );
}
```

OUTPUT :

Exception caught
num=25

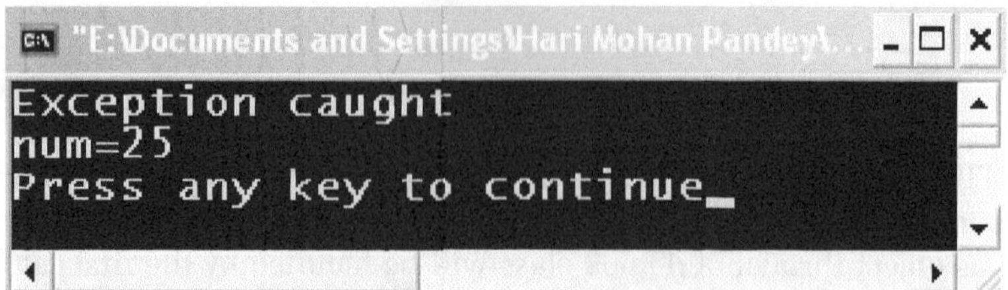

Figure 14.9. *Output screen of the program 14.10*

EXPLANATION : Though we cannot return any value from the constructor but with the help of try catch block we can. The program simply demonstrates how you can do this. In the constructor we throw an int constant 25 which is caught by the catch block. The value thrown 25 is assigned to data member num. This value is displayed by the show function.

/*PROG 14.11 EXCEPTION HANDLING IN CONSTRUCTOR VER 2 */

```
#include <iostream.h>
class demo
{
public :
    demo( )
    {
        try
        {
            throw"hello from constructor";
        }
        catch(char*E)
        {
            cout<<"Exception caught"<<endl;
```

```
            cout<<E<<endl;
        }
    }
};
void main( )
{
    demo d;
}
```

OUTPUT :

Exception caught
hello from constructor

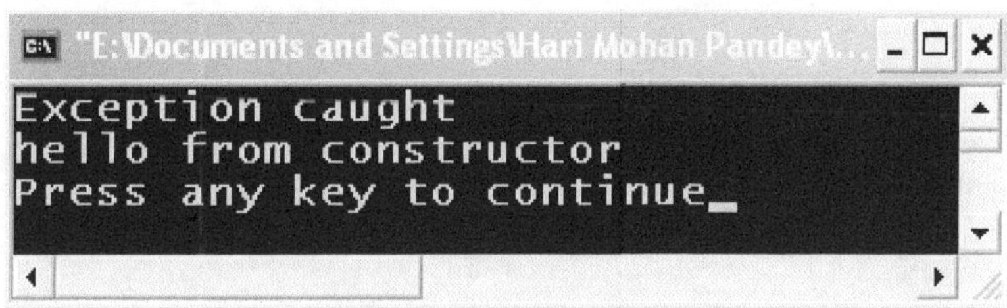

Figure 14.10. *Output screen of program 14.11*

EXPLANATION : Here, we have thrown string object from the constructor. The same object is caught by the catch block.

/*PROG 14.12 EXCEPTION HANDLING IN CONSTRUCTOR VER 3 */

```
#include <iostream.h>
class demo
{
    int num;
public :
    demo(int x)
    {
        try
        {
            if(x==0)
                throw("Zero not allowed");
            num=x;
            show( );
        }
```

```
        catch(char*exp)
        {
            cout<<"Exception caught"<<endl;
            cout<<exp<<endl;
        }
    }
    void show( )
    {
        cout<<"Num="<<num<<endl;
    }
};
void main( )
{
    int n;
    cout<<"Enter a number"<<endl;
    cin>>n;
    demo d(n);
}
```

OUTPUT :

(First Run)

Enter a number

35

Num=35

(Second Run)

Enter a number

0

Exception caught

Zero not allowed

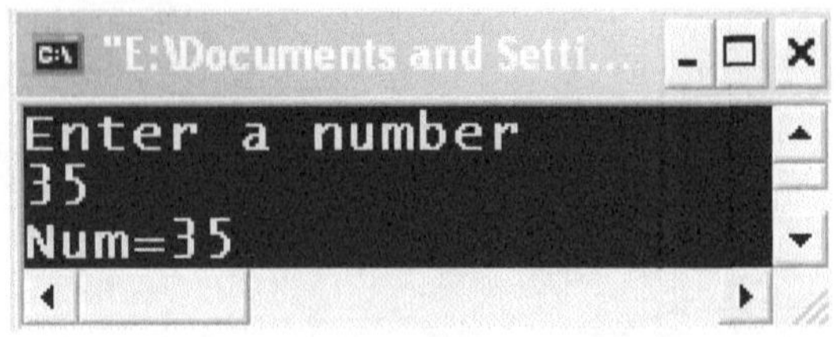

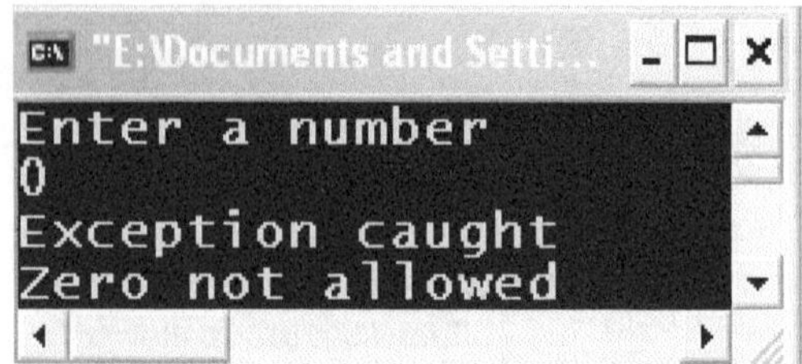

Figure 14.11. *Output screen of program 14.12*

EXPLANATION : Before assigning a value to the data member num it is checked whether value is equal to 0 or not. If not it is assigned to num and displayed by a call to show function. If value is 0 an exception **Zero not allowed** is thrown.

/*PROG 14.13 RE-THROWING AN EXCEPTION VER 1 */

```
#include <iostream.h>
void main( )
{
    try
    {
        try
        {
            throw 20;
        }
        catch(int)
        {
            cout<<"Caught an exception inner catch\n";
            throw;
        }
    }
    catch(int x)
    {
        cout<<"caught an int exception x="<<x<<endl;
    }
}
```

OUTPUT :

```
Caught an exception inner catch
caught an int exception x=20
```

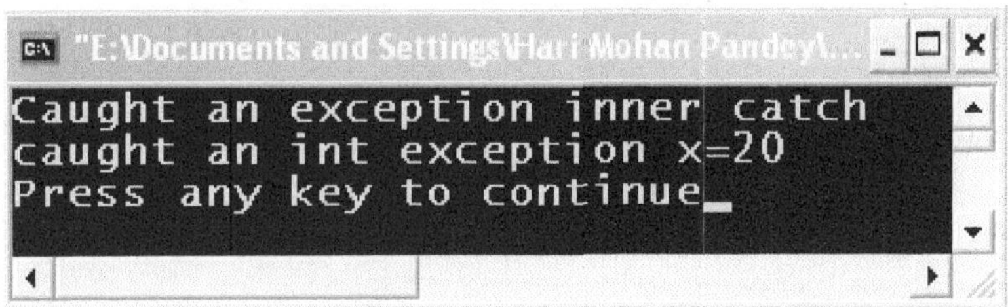

Figure 14.12. *Output screen of program 14.13*

EXPLANATION : When exception is thrown it is caught by the inner catch block. The statement thrown in the next lines causes' exception to be re-thrown exception is passed to the outer catch block which is then executed.

/*PROG 14.14 RE-THROWING AN EXCEPTION VER 2 */

```
#include <iostream.h>
#include <math.h>
void main( )
{
    void check(int x);
    int x;
    cout<<"Enter a +ve number \n";
    cin>>x;
    try
    {
        check(x);
    }
    catch(char*s)
    {
        cout<<"Exception thrown in main \n";
        cout<<s<<endl;
    }
    cout<<"Terminating main \n";
}
void check(int x)
{
    char*str="cannot take square root of -ve numbers \n";
    try
    {
        if(x<0)
            throw str;
        else
            cout<<"square root is"<<sqrt(x)<<endl;
    }
    catch(char*)
    {
        cout<<"Caught exception in function\n";
        cout<<"Rethrowing \n";
        throw;
    }
}
```

OUTPUT :

(First Run)

Enter a +ve number

25

square root is5

Terminating main

(Second Run)

Enter a +ve number

-25

Caught exception in function

Rethrowing

Exception thrown in main

cannot take square root of -ve numbers

Terminating main

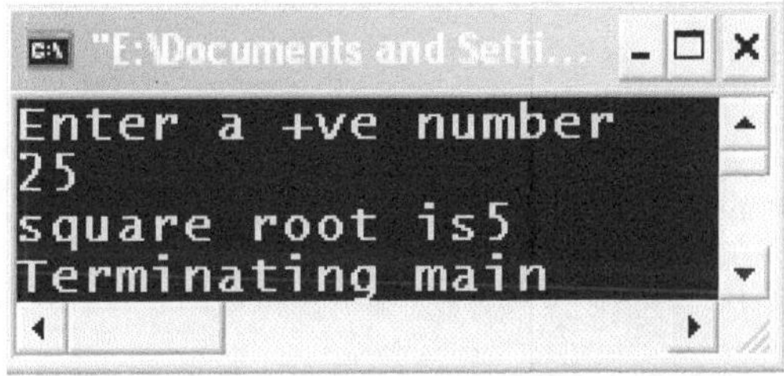

Figure 14.13. *Output screen of first run*

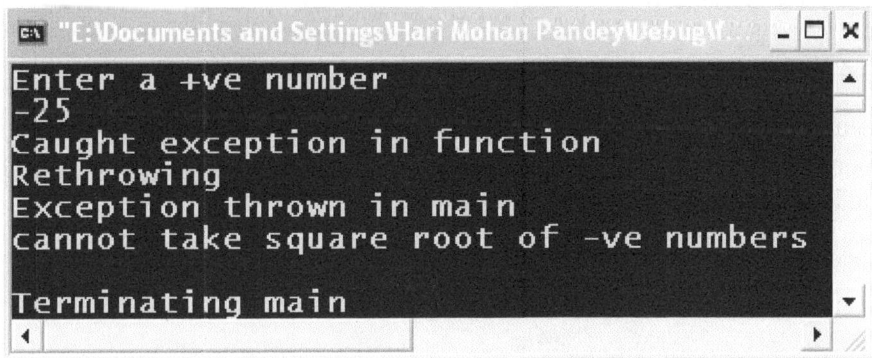

Figure 14.14. *Output screen of second run*

EXPLANATION : In the program within try block function check is called. Inside the check function we have one more try catch block. When a negative number is passed to the check function in the try block within check, exception is thrown. This exception thrown is handled within the catch block external to check. After handling the exception it is re-thrown by using throw keyword. This re-thrown exception is handled by the catch block within main.

14.6 CATCHING ALL EXCEPTIONS

A single catch block can be used for catching all different types of exceptions. This is necessary in situations when we do not know in advance what particular types of exception may be thrown by the try block. In these situations we can write a generic catch block as shown :

```
catch(...)
{
    Statements for handling exceptions;
}
```

Note the catch block has just three dots as its argument. We present an example of usage of this generic catch block.

/*PROG 14.15 CATCHING ALL TYPES OF EXCEPTION WITH A SINGLE CATCH BLOCK VER 1 */

```
#include <iostream.h>
void main( )
{
    int num = 10;
    for(num=10;num<=30;num+=10)
    {
        try
        {
            if(num==20)
                throw("Good");
            else if(num<20)
                throw num;
            else if(num>20)
                throw 2.25f;
        }
        catch(...)
        {
            cout<<"Caught an Exception \n";
        }
        cout<<"Outside try catch block\n";
    }
}
```

OUTPUT :

```
Caught an Exception
Outside try catch block
Caught an Exception
Outside try catch block
Caught an Exception
Outside try catch block
```

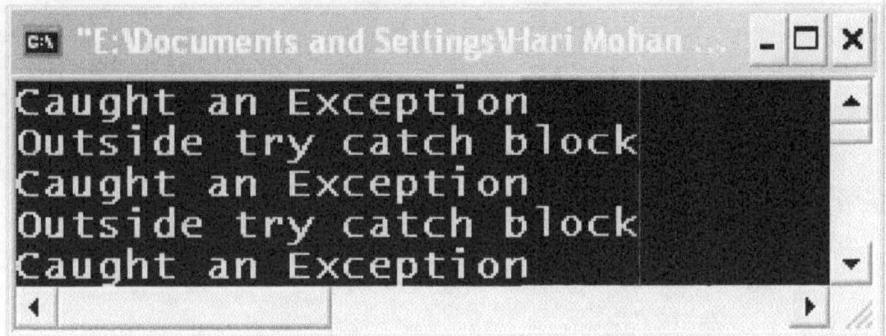

Figure 14.15. *Output screen of program 14.15*

EXPLANATION : As we are having catch (...) block, all exception thrown of any type will be caught by this. On each iteration of for loop an exception of different types is thrown which is caught by catch (...) block.

/*PROG 14.16 CATCHING ALL TYPES OF EXCEPTION WITH A SINGLE CATCH BLOCK VER 2 */

```
#include <iostream.h>
class demo1
{
};
class demo2
{
};
class demo3
{
};
void main( )
{
    int num=10;
    for(num=10;num<=30;num+=10)
    {
        try
        {
            if(num==20)
                throw new demo1( );
            else if(num<20)
                throw new demo2( );
            else if(num>20)
                throw new demo3( );
        }
```

```
        catch(...)
        {
            cout<<"Caught an Exception"<<endl;
        }
        cout<<"Outside try catch block"<<endl;
    }
}
```

OUTPUT :

```
Caught an Exception
Outside try catch block
Caught an Exception
Outside try catch block
Caught an Exception
Outside try catch block
```

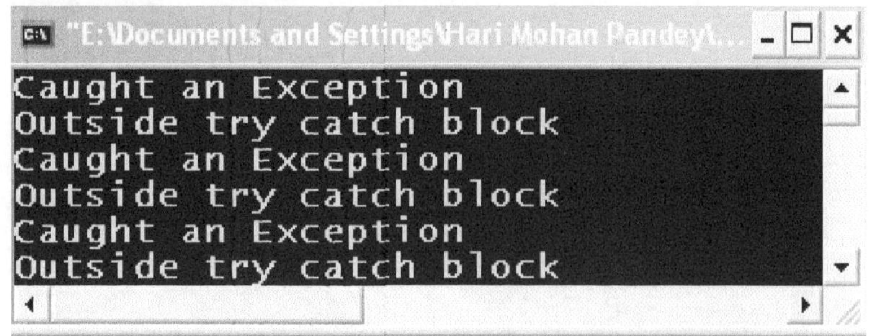

Figure 14.16. *Output screen of program 14.16*

EXPLANATION : The **catch (...)** block can caught exception thrown of user defined classes type. On 3 iteration of loop 3 exception of **demo1, demo2** and **demo3** type are thrown which is caught by **catch (...)** block.

14.7 SPECIFYING EXCEPTION FOR A FUNCTION

We can specify the types of exception for a function to be thrown as a list passed to throw. In this way we can restrict a function to throw only exception specified in the list and not any other types of exception. The general syntax of writing a function which specifies exception to be thrown as :

```
return type function-name(function parameters)
throw (data-types)
{
    function definition;
}
```

In case a function does not want to throw an exception it may leave throw empty like **throw ( )**.

/*PROG 14.17 SPECIFYING AN EXCEPTION */

```
#include <iostream.h>
void demo( ) throw(int,char,char*)
{
    for(int i=0;i<=2;i++)
    {
        try
        {
            switch(i)
            {
            case 0 :throw 123;
                break;
            case 1 :throw 'p';
                break;
            case 2 :throw "NMIMS UNIVERSITY";
                break;
            }
        }
        catch(int x)
        {
            cout<<"Caught an int exception :="<<x<<endl;
        }
        catch(char x)
        {
            cout<<"Caught a char exception :=  "<<x<<endl;
        }
        catch(char* x)
        {
        cout<<"Caught a char* exception :="<<x<<endl;
        }
    }
}
void main( )
{
    demo( );
}
```

OUTPUT :

```
Caught an int exception := 123
Caught a char exception := p
Caught a char* exception := NMIMS UNIVERSITY
```

```
"E:\Documents and Settings\Hari Mohan Pandey\Debug\f17.exe"
Caught an int exception    := 123
Caught a char exception    := p
Caught a char* exception := NMIMS UNIVERSITY
```

Figure 14.17. *Output screen of program 14.17*

EXPLANATION : The statement **void demo ( ) throw (int, char, char*)** specifies that the function **demo** may throw exceptions of type **int, char** and **char*** type. Using **for** loop we throw all specified types of exceptions. All the thrown exceptions are caught by their respective **catch** block.

14.8 PONDERABLE POINTS

1. Exception is run-time error which may occur in the program.
2. An exception if not handled may terminate the program abnormally.
3. To deal with exception, try-catch blocks are used.
4. An exception in programming term is considered an object which is thrown.
5. Any program code or function which may generate exception is placed in the try block. The exception is thrown by using keyword throw.
6. For one try block there may be multiple catch block.
7. An exception can be rethrown in case of nesting of try-catch blocks. To rethrown an exception, we simply write throw;
8. A function can specify what type of exception can be thrown by specifying in the function declaration.
9. Objects of user defined classes as exception can also be thrown.
10. The expression catch (...) can be used to catch all types of exceptions.

EXERCISE

A. True and False :

1. The throw statement can be used for throwing an exception.
2. The "throw" expression creates a pointer to an exception object.
3. Throwing an exception always causes program termination.
4. Code that may generate run time error is placed in catch block.

5. The exception is generated during compilation.
6. A group of catch blocks may be associated with a single try block.

B. Answer the Following Questions :

1. What is exception ?
2. How do we handle exception ?
3. Describe the meaning of try, catch and throw.
4. How do we catch multiple exceptions ?
5. How do we catch all exceptions ?
6. Explain the methodology of try-catch.
7. How can we restrict a function to show only specific types of exceptions ?
8. What if the exception thrown is not caught ?

C. Brain Drill :

1. Write a program to prompt user for entering a number. If number is not event then throw exception.
2. Write a program to accept strings. If any string does not start with capital letter then throw the exception.
3. Write a class queue and with all the necessary function. Whenever queue is empty and delete operation is performed an object of class queue_empty class is thrown. Similarly, whenever the queue is full an exception of queue_full class is thrown. The queur is implemented using array.
4. Write a program in which memory is allocated by new. If enough memory is not available then new returns NULL. Whenever new returns NULL an exception is thrown.
5. Write a program to enter five numbers into array. Whenever a number greater than 100 is taken an exception is thrown.
6. Sometimes the easiest way to use exception is to create a new class of which an exception class is a member. Try this with a class that uses exceptions to handle file errors. Make a class dofile that includes an exception class and member functions to read and write files. A constructor to this class can take the filename as an argument and open a file with that name. You may also want a member function to reset the file pointer to the beginning of the file. Write a main ( ) program that provides the same functionality but does so by calling on members of the dofile class.

CHAPTER 15

OBJECT-ORIENTED PROGRAMMING HAND ON LAB

Experiment-1 : Program illustrating function overloading feature.

/*Program : Illustrating function overloading */

```
#include <iostream.h>
#include <conio.h>

void main( )
{
    void show(int);
    void show(float);
    void show(char);
    void show(char*);

    int x=10;
    float y=23.45;
    char ch= 'p';

    char * s="overload";

    clrscr( );
    show(x);
    show(y);
    show(ch);
    show(s);
    getch( );
}
```

```
void show(int x)
{
    cout<<"int show x="<<x<<endl;
}

void show(float y)
{
    cout<<"float show y="<<y<<endl;
}

void show(char ch)
{
    cout<<"char show ch="<<ch<<endl;
}

void show(char*s)
{
    cout<<"char *s show s="<<s<<endl;
}
```

Output :

```
int show x=10
float show y= 23.45
char show ch = p
char *s show s= overload
```

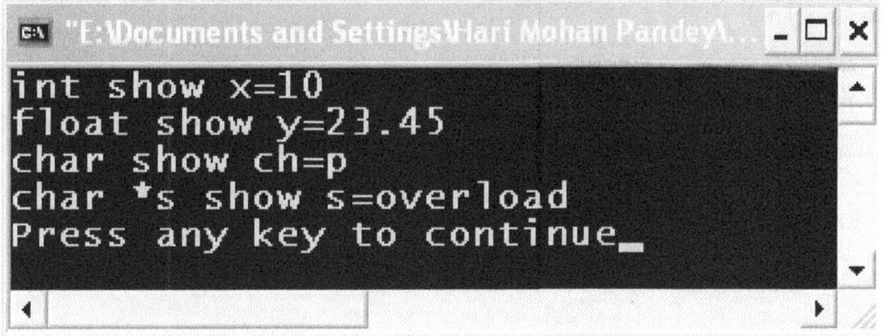

Figure 15.1. *Output screen of the program.*

EXPLANATION : In the program we have functions `show` overloaded 4 times. The function takes a single parameter but each parameter is different in each function as can be seen from the program. In the `main` 4 variable of type `int, char, float and char *` type are generated and `show` is called with these parameters. Each parameter is passed to `show` and `show` is called `4 times`. The compiler depending upon type of argument to function show calls the respective version of the show function *i.e.*, in case of `show(x),` show function of `int` version will be called and so on.

/*Program : Function overloading max of two numbers */

```
#include <iostream.h>
#include <conio.h>

void main( )
{
    int x,y, intmax;
    float f1,f2,fmax;
    char ch1,ch2,chmax;

    int max2(int,int);
    float max2(float,float);
    char max2(char,char);

    clrscr( );
    cout<<"Enter two integers \n";
    cin>>x>>y;

    cout<<"Enter two floats\n";
    cin>>f1>>f2;
    cout<<"Enter two chars \n";
    cin>>ch1>>ch1;

    intmax=max2(x,y);

    fmax=max2(f1,f2);

    chmax=max2(ch1,ch2);

    cout<<"Max of two int is "<<intmax<<endl;
    cout<<"Max of two float is "<<fmax<<endl;
    cout<<"Max of two char is"<<chmax<<endl;

    getch( );
}
int max2(int x,int y)
{
    return(x>y ?x :y);
}
```

```
float max2(float x,float y)
{
    return(x>y ?x :y);
}

char max2(char x,char y)
{
    return(x>y ?x :y);
}
```

Output :

```
Enter two integers
123 567
Enter two floats
12.34
56.78
Enter two chars
a g
Max of two int is 567
Max of two float is 56.78
Max of two char is g
```

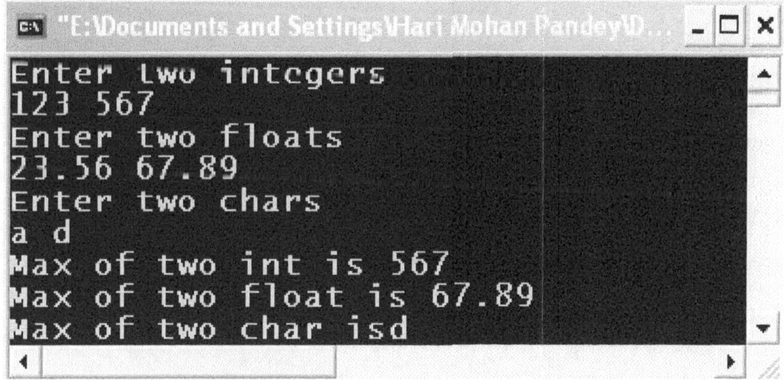

Figure 15.2. *Output screen of program.*

EXPLANATION : We have in the program three over of function `max2` which takes two parameters of type `int, char, and float` and returns the maximum of two numbers. Depending upon type of parameter appropriate version of `max2` function is called.

Experiment-2 Programs illustrating the overloading of various operators. Ex : Binary operators, Unary operators, New and delete operators, etc.

/*Program : Overloading binary + with class objects as argument */

```
#include <iostream.h>
#include <conio.h>
class demo_sum
{
    private :
        int num;
        static int count;
    public :
        void input( )
 {
    cout<<"Enter the number for"<<"Object"<<++count<<"\n";
    cin>>num;
 }
 void operator +(demo_sum temp)
 {
    int x;
    x=num+temp.num;
    cout<<"Sum of two is "<<x<<endl;
 }
 void show( )
 {
    cout<<"The num is"<<num<<endl;
 }
 };
 int demo_sum : :count;
 void main( )
 {
    clrscr( );
    demo_sum d1,d2;
    d1.input( );
    d1.show( );
    d2.input( );
    d2.show( );
    d1+d2;
    getch( );

 }
```

Output :

Enter the number forObject1

23

The num is23

Enter the number forObject2

45

The num is45

Sum of two is 68

```
Enter the number forObject1
23
The num is23
Enter the number forObject2
45
The num is45
Sum of two is 68
```

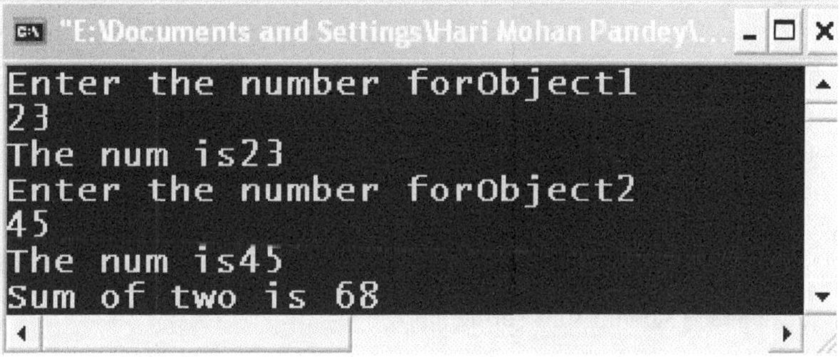

Figure 15.3. *Output screen of program.*

EXPLANATION : The function

```
void operator + (demo_sum temp)
{
    int x;
    x= num+ temp.num;
    cout<<"sum of two is "<<x<<endl;
}
```

Overloads binary **+** and accepts an argument of class **demo_sum** type. In the **main** the statement **d1+d2;** is interpreted internally as **d1.operator +(d2) i.e. d1** calls the function **d1** and pass **d2** as argument to this overloaded binary **+** operator function. Inside the function num belongs to objects **d1** (The members of the objects who calls the function, can be inside the function without using object name with dot operator, other syntax using this pointer will be discussed later on) and **d2** is copied to **temp** object so **temp.num** is a copy of **d2.num.** The function finds the sum and displays it.

/***Program : Overloading + and – in the same program** */

```
#include <iostream.h>
#include <conio.h>
class demo_sum_sub
```

```
{
    private :
        int num;
        static int count1,count2;
    public :
        void input( )
        {
        cout<<"Enter the number for object"<<++count1<<endl;
        cin>>num;
        }
    demo_sum_sub operator +(demo_sum_sub temp)
    {
        demo_sum_sub t;
        t.num=num+temp.num;
        return t;
    }
    demo_sum_sub operator -(demo_sum_sub temp)
    {
        demo_sum_sub t;
        t.num=num-temp.num;
        return t;
    }
    void show( )
    {
        cout<<"The num for object"<<++count2<<"is"<<num<<endl;
    }
};
int demo_sum_sub : :count1;
int demo_sum_sub : :count2;
void main( )
{
    clrscr( );
    demo_sum_sub d1,d2,d3,d4;
    d1.input( );
    d2.input( );
    d3.input( );
    d1.show( );
    d2.show( );
    d3.show( );
    d4=d1+d2-d3;
```

```
        d4.show( );
        getch( );
}
```

Output :

```
Enter the number for object1
30
Enter the number for object2
40
Enter the number for object3
35
The num for object1is30
The num for object2is40
The num for object3is35
The num for object4is35
```

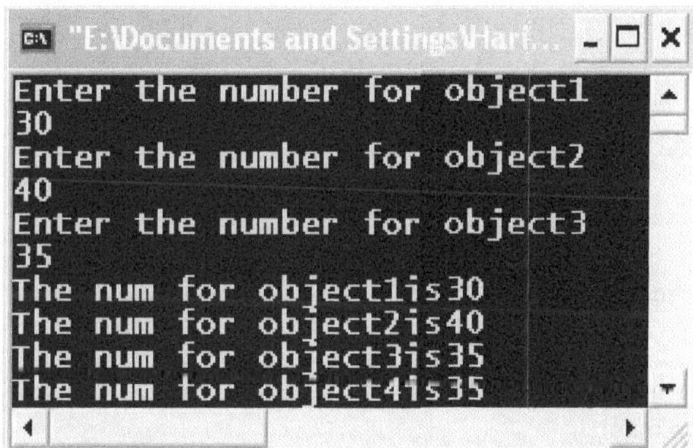

Figure 15.4. *Output screen of program.*

EXPLANATION : The program is similar to previous one but we have overloaded **binary** – operator together with binary **+**. As the priority of **+ and –** is same they are evaluated from left to right. Hence first **d1+d2** is evaluated where **d1** calls overloaded **+** operator function and pass d2 as argument. Assuming returned object is **temp** then temp –d3 is evaluated where temp calls the overloaded binary – operator function and pass d3 as argument. The final object returned; again assume obj is assigned to d4.

/*Program : Overloading +, - , *, and / all in one */

```
#include <iostream.h>
#include <conio.h>
#include <stdlib.h>
class demo_exp
```

```
{
    private :
        float num;
        static count1, count2;
    public :
        void input( )
        {
            cout<<"Enter the number for object"<<++count1<<endl;
            cin>>num;
        }
    demo_exp operator *(demo_exp temp)
    {
        demo_exp t;
        t.num=num*temp.num;
        return t;
    }
    demo_exp operator +(demo_exp temp)
    {
        demo_exp t;
        t.num=num+temp.num;
        return t;
    }
    demo_exp operator -(demo_exp temp)
    {
        demo_exp t;
        t.num=num-temp.num;
        return t;
    }
    demo_exp operator /(demo_exp temp)
    {
        demo_exp t;
        if(temp.num)
        t.num=num/temp.num;
        else
    {
        cout<<"Division by zero is not allowed"<<endl;
        exit(0);
    }
    return t;
    }
```

```
void show( )
{
    cout<<"The sum for object"<<++count2<<"is"<<num<<endl;
}
};
int demo_exp : :count1;
int demo_exp : :count2;
void main( )
{
    clrscr( );
    demo_exp d1,d2,d3,d4,d5;
    d1.input( );
    d2.input( );
    d3.input( );
    d4.input( );
    d1.show( );
    d2.show( );
    d3.show( );
    d4.show( );
    d5=d1+d2*d3/d1-d4;
    d5.show( );
    getch( );
}
```

Output :

```
Enter the number for object1
12
Enter the number for object2
13
Enter the number for object3
14
Enter the number for object4
15
The sum for object1is12
The sum for object2is13
The sum for object3is14
The sum for object4is15
The sum for object5is12.166668
```

```
"E:\Documents and Settings\Hari Mohan Pandey...
Enter the number for object1
12
Enter the number for object2
13
Enter the number for object3
14
Enter the number for object4
15
The sum for object1is12
The sum for object2is13
The sum for object3is14
The sum for object4is15
The sum for object5is12.1667
```

Figure 15.5. *Output screen of program.*

EXPLANATION : We have overloaded all the **4 binary operation viz** +, -, * **and** /. You can check that code for all the overloaded operation function is same except for the operator symbol. In the division operator function we have checked for denominator to be nonzero. Note overloading of operator does not change their inherent meaning, priority and associativity. So the expression **d5 = d1 + d2 * d3 / d1 - d4;** is evaluated as (assuming num for objects as shown in the program output) :

As priority of * **and** / is higher than **+and** – and at the same level of priority ***and** / are evaluated from left to right so **d2 *d3** is evaluated first which internally interpreted as **d2**.operator * **(d3)** as explained earlier. Assuming the returned object as **temp1** with value of **num96** (as **8 *12=96**) the expression becomes **d5 = d1+temp1/d1-d4**. Now **temp** / **d1** will be evaluated where **temp1** calling the function **operator** / and sending **d1** as argument. Assuming returned object as **temp2** with value of **num is 19.2 (as 96/5 = 19.2)** the expression becomes **d5 = d1 + temp2 – d4.** As priority of **+ and** – is same expression will be evaluated from left to right so next **d1 +temp2** will be evaluated where **d1** calling the operator function **+** and sending **temp2** as argument. Assuming the returned object as **temp3** with value of **num 24.2 (as 19.2 + 5 = 24.2)** the expression becomes **d5=temp3-d4.** Now **temp3** calls the operator function – and sends **d4** as argument. Assuming the returned object as **temp4** with value of **num 15.2 (as 24.2-9)** the expression becomes **d5=temp4** and value of **num** will be assigned to **num** to object **d5**.

/* **PROGRAM : OVERLOADING PRE ++ AND POST ++ IN THE SAME PROGRAM** */

```
#include <iostream.h>
#include <conio.h>

class demo
{
    int num;
public :
    demo( ){}
```

```
    demo (int x)
    {
        num = x;
    }
    demo operator ++(int)
    {
        demo temp;
        temp.num = num;
        num++;
        return temp;
    }
    demo operator++( )
    {
        demo temp;
        num++;
        temp.num = num;
        return temp;
    }
    void show(char*s)
    {
        cout<<"NUM OF OBJECT"<<s<<" = "<<num<<endl;
    }
};
void main( )
{
    clrscr( );
    demo d1(30),d2,d3;
    d2=d1++;
    d3=++d1;
    d1.show("d1");
    d2.show("d2");
    d3.show("d3");
    getch( );
}
```

OUTPUT :

```
NUM OF OBJECTd1 = 32
NUM OF OBJECTd2 = 30
NUM OF OBJECTd3 = 32
```

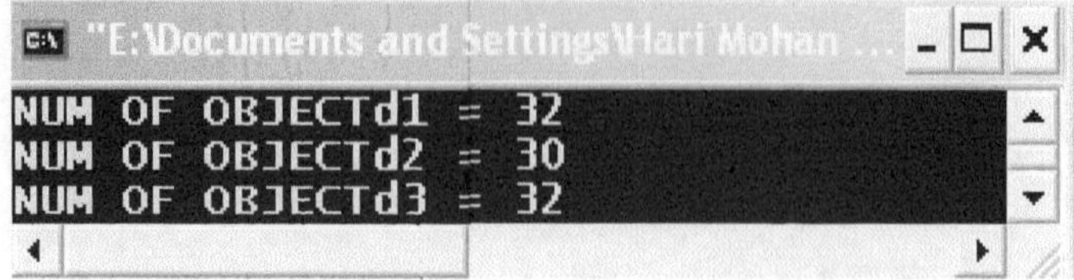

Figure 15.6. *Output screen of program.*

EXPLANATION : To distinguishes between an overloaded `pre` and `post ++` an `int` type argument is passed to the overloaded `post ++` operator function. This `int` argument does not serve any purposes except helping compiler to see the difference between a `pre` and `post ++` operator function when this operator function call implicitly. In the `main` when `d2 = d1++` executes `post++` operator function will be called and in case of `d3 = ++d1; pre++` operator function would be called.

/* PROGRAM : OVERLOADING UNARY - OPERATOR */

```
#include <iostream.h>
#include <conio.h>

class demo
{
    int num;
public :
    demo(int x)
    {
        num=x;
    }
    void operator -( )
    {
        num = num;
    }
    void show( )
    {
        cout<<"num ="<<num<<endl;
    }
};
void main( )
{
    clrscr( );
    demo d1(10);
    cout<<"Before"<<endl;
    d1.show( );
    -d1;
```

```
        cout<<"After"<<endl;
        d1.show( );
        getch( );
}
```

OUTPUT :

```
Before
num =10
After
num =10
```

Figure 15.7. *Output screen of program.*

EXPLANATION : In the main the statement **–d1** is equivalent to **d1.operator – ( )**. The initial value of **num** for object **d1** is **10**. When **–d1** executes it call overloaded – operator function which reverse the sign of the **num**. This is the way the unary minus operator works. Note no argument is passed to the function. The function is simply called by the object **d1.**

/* **PROGRAM : OVERLOADING UNARY + OPERATOR** */

```
#include <iostream.h>
#include <conio.h>

class demo
{
    int num;
public :
    demo(int x)
    {
        num=x;
    }
    void operator +( )
    {
        num=num>0 ?num :-num;
    }
    void show( )
```

```
        {
            cout<<"num = "<<num<<endl;
        }
};
void main( )
{
        clrscr( );
        demo d1(-100);
        cout<<"Before"<<endl;
        d1.show( );
        +d1;
        cout<<"After"<<endl;
        d1.show( );
        getch( );
}
```

OUTPUT :

```
Before
num = -100
After
num = 100
```

Figure 15.8. *Output screen of program.*

EXPLANATION : Practically unary **+** does not serve any purpose *i.e.,* writing **+x** do not affect the value of **x.** But in the program we have overloaded unary operator to make a number positive *i.e.,* work as a function which finds absolute value of the number. In the **main +d1** is equivalent to **d1.operator + ( )** which calls the operator + function and checks the value of num. If it is positive, we do not change but if is negative we make it positive.

Experiment-3 : Programs illustrating the use of following functions :

(*a*) Friend functions

(*b*) Inline functions

(*c*) Static Member functions

(*d*) Functions with default arguments.

/*Program : Finding maximum of two data of two different class with friend function*/

```
#include <iostream.h>
#include <conio.h>
class second;
class first
{
    int fx;
    public :
        void inputf(int x)
        {
            fx=x;
        }
        friend void findmax(first,second);
};
class second
{
    int sx;
    public :
        void inputs(int x)
        {
            sx = x;
        }
        friend void findmax(first,second);
};
void findmax(first A, second B)
{
    if(A.fx>B.sx)
        cout<<A.fx<<"of class first is greater than "<<B.sx<<"of
            class second\n";
    else
        cout<<B.sx<<"of class second is greater than"<<A.fx<<"of
            class first\n";
}
void main( )
{
    first F;
    second S;
    clrscr( );
    F.inputf(40);
    S.inputs(70);
```

```
    findmax(F,S);
    getch( );
}
```

Output :

70 of class second is greater than 40 of class first

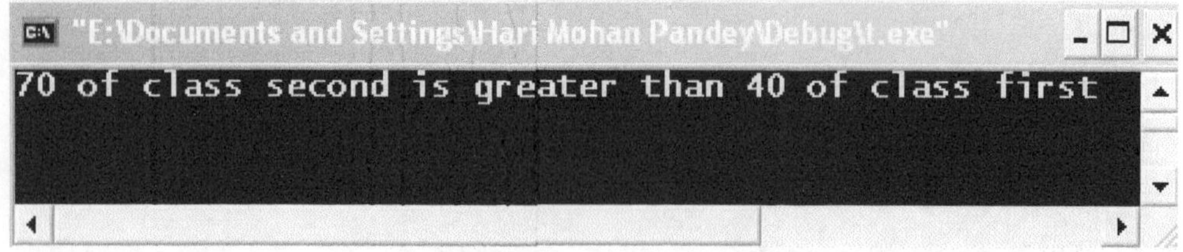

Figure 15.9. *Output screen of program.*

EXPLANATION : This is the real example where **friend** serves its purpose. The statement in the beginning of the program class second is forward declaration as we are performing class second in the **friend** function declaration and at that point class **second** was not created. Note the friend function is declared in both the class which tells the compiler that it is a **friend** of both the class **first** and **second**. It accepts an object of class **first** argument and **second** argument is an object of class **second** type. The function definition is given outside the classes. In the main we call the function **findmax** and pass two objects **A and B** of class **first and second**.

/* PROGRAM : SWAPPING OF TWO CLASS DATA USING FRIEND FUNCTION */

```
#include <iostream.h>
#include <conio.h>

class second;                  // global declaration of class
class first
{
    int fx;
public :

    void inputf(int x)
    {
        fx=x;
    }

    void showf( )
    {
        cout<<"fx :="<<fx<<endl;
    }
```

```
    friend void swap(first &, second &);       //declaration of
                                               //friend function
};
class second
{
    int sx;

public :
    void inputs(int x)
    {
        sx=x;
    }
    void shows( )
    {
        cout<<"sx="<<sx<<endl;
    }
    friend void swap(first &, second &);       //declaration of
                                               //friend function
};

void swap(first &A, second &B)        //definition of friend of
                                      //friend function
{
    int t;
    t=A.fx;
    A.fx=B.sx;
    B.sx=t;
}
void main( )
{
    first F;
    second S;
    clrscr( );
    F.inputf(20);
    S.inputs(40);
    cout<<"Before swapping \n";
    F.showf( );
    S.shows( );
    swap(F,S);
    cout<<"AFTER SWAPPING \n";
    F.showf( );
```

```
    S.shows( );
    getch( );
}
```

OUTPUT :

```
Before swapping
fx :=20
sx=40
AFTER SWAPPING
fx :=40
sx=20
```

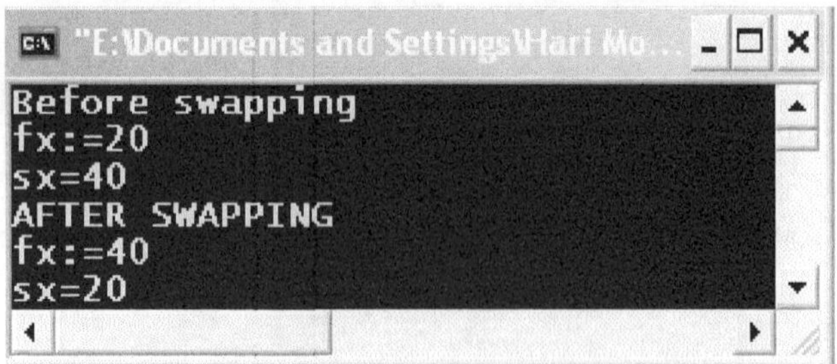

Figure 15.10. *Output screen of program.*

EXPLANATION : In the program we are swapping the data members of two classes **first** and **second** using friend function. The function is a friend of both the classes and accepts **first** argument of class type first and **second** argument of class type second, both by reference. If we do not pass argument by reference then swapping will be done on local variables of type class first and class second. So changes won't be reflected back to object **F** and **S** in **main.**

/***Program : Square of a number using inline function** */

```
#include <iostream.h>
#include <conio.h>
inline int square(int x)
{
    return x*x;
}

void main( )
{
    int num,snum;
    clrscr( );
    cout<<"Enter a number \n";
    cin>>num;
```

```
    cout<<"Square of "<<num<<"is "<<square(num)<<endl;
    getch( );
}
```

Output :

```
Enter a number
8
Square of 8is 64
```

Figure 15.11. *Output screen of the program.*

EXPLANATION : When the function is called as square (num), the function call is expanded in line as num*num. Rest is easy to understand.

/*Program : Maximum of two numbers using inline function */

```
#include <iostream.h>
#include <conio.h>
inline int max(int x,int y)
{
    return x>y?x :y;
}
void main( )
{
    int n1,n2;
    clrscr( );
    cout<<"Enter two numbers \n";
    cin>>n1>>n2;
    int m=max(n1,n2);
    cout<<"Max="<<m<<endl;
    getch( );
}
```

Output :

```
Enter two numbers
12
45
Max=45
```

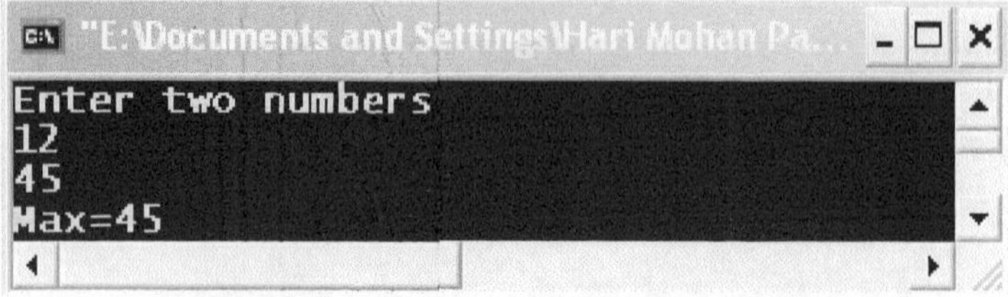

Figure 15.12. *Output screen of program.*

EXPLANATION : At the place of function call **max (n1, n2)**, function is explained as return x>y ? X : y, value of n1 and n2 is assigned to x and y.

/*Program : Demo of static function */

```
#include <iostream.h>
#include <conio.h>
class demo
{
 public :
 static void show( )
 {
    cout<<"Demo of static function\n";
 }
};
 void main( )
 {
 clrscr( );
 demo : :show( );
 getch( );
 }
```

Output :

Demo of static function

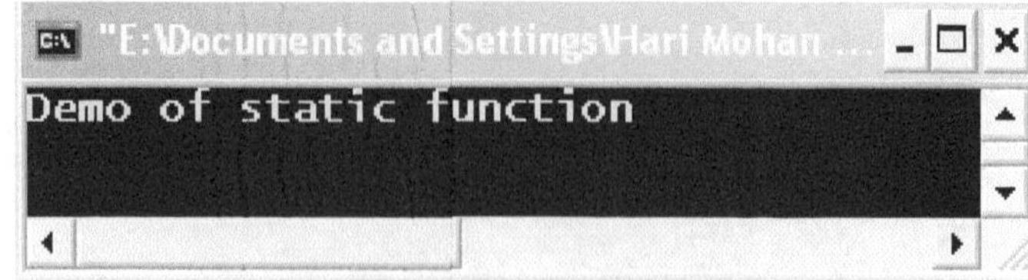

Figure 15.13. *Output screen of program.*

EXPLANATION : As mentioned earlier a static function which is one for all objects and which is called by using : : with class name. In the program we have defined a static function show which is called in the main using class name as **demo : : show ( )**.

/*PROGRAM : DEMO OF STATIC FUNCTION */

```
#include <iostream.h>
#include <conio.h>
class demo
{
public :

    static void show( );
};
static void demo : :show( )
{
    cout<<"HELLO FROM STATIC SHOW \n";
}
void main( )
{
    demo : :show( );
    getch( );
}
```

OUTPUT :

ERROR : 'show' :'static' should not be used on member function defined at file scope.

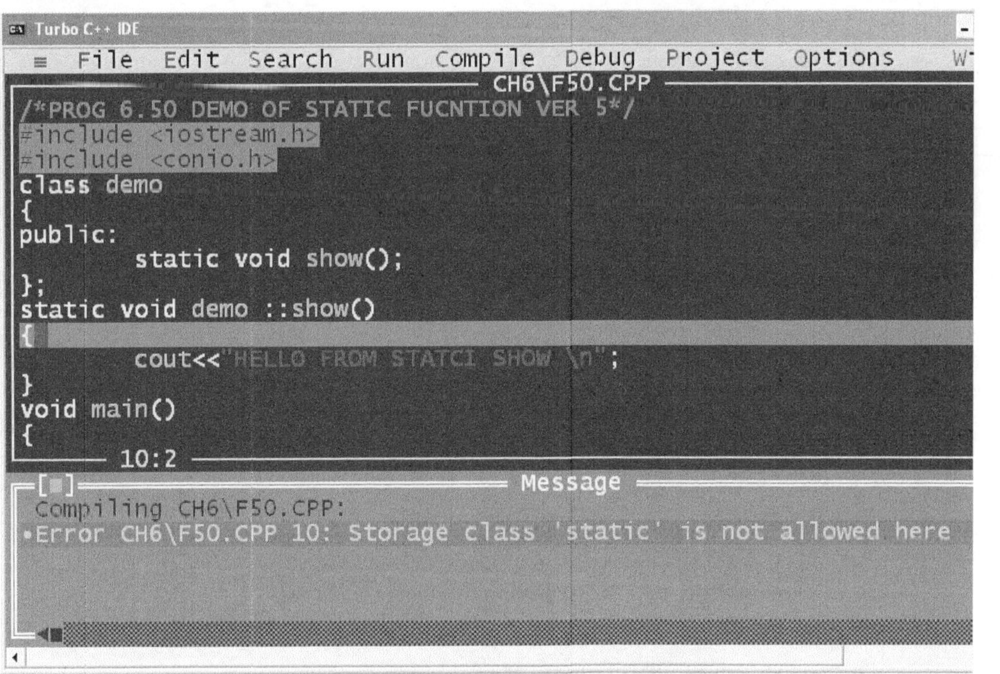

```
Turbo C++ IDE
 ≡  File  Edit  Search  Run  Compile  Debug  Project  Options  W
CH6\F50.CPP
/*PROG 6.50 DEMO OF STATIC FUCNTION VER 5*/
#include <iostream.h>
#include <conio.h>
class demo
{
public:
        static void show();
};
static void demo ::show()
{
        cout<<"HELLO FROM STATCI SHOW \n";
}
void main()
{
10:2
Message
 Compiling CH6\F50.CPP:
•Error CH6\F50.CPP 10: Storage class 'static' is not allowed here
```

Figure 15.14. *Error Message on Turbo C++ IDE.*

EXPLANATION : Static member function must be declared and defined inside the class. They cannot be defined outside the class so the error.

Experiment-4 : Programs to create singly and doubly linked lists and perform insertion and deletion Operations. Using self referential classes, new and delete operators.

/*PROGRAM : TO CREATE AND DISPLAY A LINKED LIST */

```
#include <iostream.h>
struct node
{
    int data;
    node*next;
};
class link_list
{
private :
    node*start;
public :
    link_list( )//constructor
    {
        start=NULL; //initially the list has no node
    }
    void add_data(int i)
    {
        node* new_link=new node; //create a new node;
        new_link->data = i;
        new_link->next=start; //make new node to point to the first node
        start=new_link; //make new node as the first node in the list
    }
    void display( ); //function prototype
};
//function definition display( )
void link_list : :display( )
{
    node*move=start;
    node*temp;
    while(move)
    {
        cout<<move->data<<"->"; //display the data
        temp = move;
        move=move->next; //move to next node
```

```
            delete temp; //delete the displayed node.
        }
        cout<<"NULL\n";
}
void main( )
{
        link_list link;
        cout<<"The elements of the linked list :"<<endl<<endl;
        for(int i=5;i<=10;i++)
            link.add_data(i);
        link.display( );
}
```

OUTPUT :

The elements of the linked list :

10->9->8->7->6->5->NULL

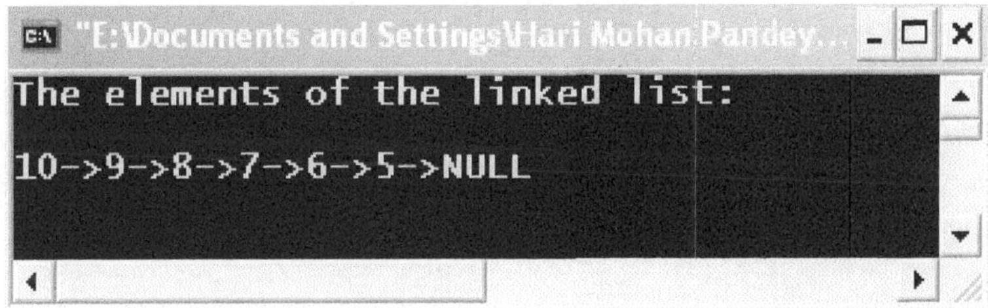

Figure 15.15. *Output screen of program.*

/*PROGRAM : INSERT A NODE AT THE BEGINNING OR AT THE END OF THE LINED LIST */

```
#include <iostream.h>

struct node
{
        int data;
        node*next;
};

class link_list
{
private :
        node*start;
public :
        link_list( )        //constructor
```

```
    {
        start=NULL;        //initially the list has no node
    }
    void create (int i)
    {
        node*new_node = new node; //create a new node;
        new_node->data=i;
        new_node->next=start;  //make new node to point to
                               the first node
            start=new_node;     //make new node as the
                               first node in the list
    }
    void display(int); //function prototype
    void beginning(int data)
    {
        node*new_node=new node;      //create a new node
        new_node->data=data;
        new_node->next=start;  //make new node to point to
 the first node
        start=new_node;
    }
    void end(int); //function prototype
};

//Function definition display( )
void link_list : :display(int delete_node)
{
    node*move=start;
    node*temp;
    while(move)
    {
        cout<<move->data<<"->"; //display the data
        temp=move;
        move=move->next; //move to next node
        if(delete_node)
            delete(temp);
    }
    cout<<"NULL";
}

//function definition end( )
```

```
void link_list : :end(int data)
{
    node*temp=start;
    while(temp->next!=NULL)
        temp=temp->next;
    node*new_node=new node;        //create a new node
    new_node->data=data;
    temp->next=new_node;
    new_node->next=NULL;
}

void main( )
{
    int data, choice;
    link_list link;
    for(int i=5;i<=10;i++)
        link.create(i);
    cout<<"\n\nThe list before any operation is
                performed :\n\n";
    link.display(0);
    cout<<"\n\n Enter the data field value of the node to
                be inserted :=";
    cin>>data;
    cout<<"\n\nEnter the option(1,2) :=";
    cout<<"\n 1. At the beginning",
    cout<<"\n 2. At the end\n";
    cin>>choice;
    switch(choice)
    {
 case 1 :
        link.beginning(data);
         break;
 case 2 :
        link.end(data);
         break;
 default :
    cout<<"Invalid choice entered\n";
    }
    cout<<"\n\n The list after insertion is :\n\n";
    link.display(1);
}
```

OUTPUT :

The list before any operation is performed :

10->9->8->7->6->5->NULL

Enter the data field value of the node to be inserted : =15

Enter the option (1, 2) :=

1. At the beginning
2. At the end

1

The list after insertion is :

15->10->9->8->7->6->5->NULL

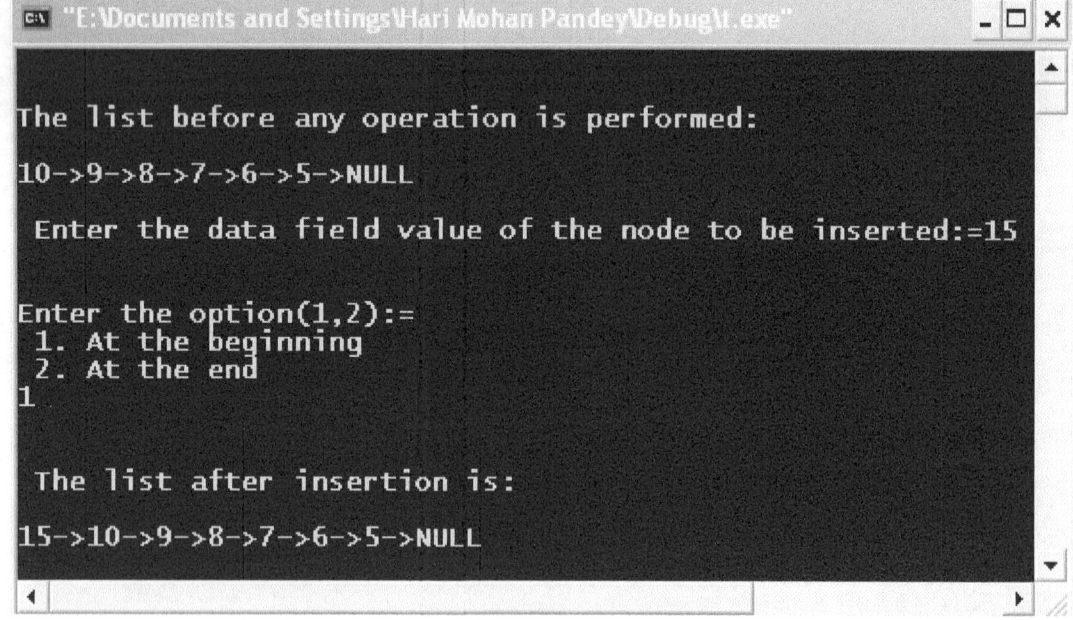

Figure 15.16. *Output screen of program.*

/*PROGRAM : TO INSERT AT THE DESIRED POSITION IN A LINKED LIST */

```
#include <iostream.h>
#include <process.h>      //for exit( ) function
struct node
{
    int data;
    node*next;
};
class link_list
{
```

```
private :
    node*start;
public :
    link_list( ) //constructor
    {
        start=NULL;   //intitially the list has no node
    }
    void create (int i)
    {
        node*new_node=new node;      //create a new node
        new_node->data=i;
        new_node->next=start;        //make new node to point
                                      to the first node
        start=new_node;         //make new node as the first
                                 node in the list
    }
    void display(int);   //function prototype
    void insert(int,int);     //function prototype
};  //end of the class
//function definition display( )
void link_list : :display(int delete_node)
{
    node*move=start;
    node*temp;
    while(move)
 {
    cout<<move->data<<"->";    //display the data
    temp=move;
    move=move->next;  //move to next node
    if(delete_node)
        delete(temp);
 }
 cout<<"NULL";
}
//function definition insert( )
void link_list : :insert(int position,int data)
{
    node*move=start;
    int steps=1;
    while(steps<position-1)
```

```
    {
        move=move->next;
        steps++;
    }
    node*new_node=new node;        //create a new node;
    new_node->data=data;
    if(position==1)          //if node is to be inserted at the
 first place
    {
        new_node->next=start;
        start=new_node;
    }
    else
        new_node->next=move->next;
    move->next=new_node;
}
void main( )
{
    int value,data,choice,position,total=0;
    link_list link;
    cout<<"Enter the elements of the list terminated by
                negative number :\n";
    cin>>value;
    do
    {
        link.create(value);
        total++; //increment with every node inserted;
        cin>>value;
    }
    while(value>=0);
        cout<<"\n\n The list before any operation is
 performed (LIFO) :\n\n";
    link.display(0);
    cout<<"\n\nTotal node :="<<total;
    cout<<"\n\nEnter the porition where node is to be
 inserted :";
    cin>>position;
    if(position<=0||position>total+1) //check for valid
 position
    {
        cout<<"\nWrong position inputted\n";
```

```
        exit(1);
    }
    cout<<"\n\nEnter the value of the node to be
 inserted :=";
    cin>>data;
    link.insert(position, data);
    cout<<"\nThe list after insertion is :\n";
    link.display(1);
}
```

OUTPUT :

Enter the elements of the list terminated by negative number :
10 20 30 40 50 60 -2
 The list before any operation is performed (LIFO) :
60->50->40->30->20->10->NULL
Total node :=6
Enter the position where node is to be inserted :3
Enter the value of the node to be inserted :=90
The list after insertion is :
60->50->90->40->30->20->10->NULL

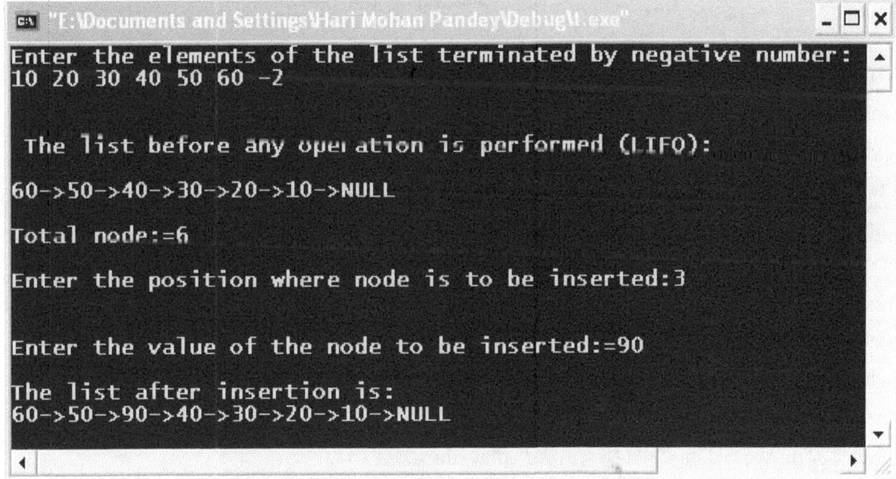

Figure 15.17. *Output screen of program.*

/*PROGRAM : TO DELETE A NODE FROM A LINKED LIST*/

```
#include <iostream.h>
#include <process.h>      //for exit( )function
struct node
```

```
{
    int data;                //data field
    node*next;               //pointer to the next node
};
class link_list
{
private :
    node*start;
public :
    link_list( )             //constructor
    {
        start=NULL;          //initially the list has no node
    }
    void create(int i)
    {
        node*new_node=new node;      //create a new node
        new_node->data=i;
        new_node->next=start;        //make new node to point
                                     to the first node
        start=new_node;              //make new node as the
                                     first node in the list
    }
    void display(int);               //function prototype
    void remove(int);                //function prototype
}; //end of class
//function definition display( )
void link_list : :display(int delete_node)
{
    node*move=start;
    node*temp;
    while(move)
    {
    cout<<move->data<<"->";      //display the data
    temp=move;
    move=move->next;             //move to next node
    if(delete_node)
        delete(temp);
    }
    cout<<"NULL";
}
```

```
//function definition remove( )
void link_list : :remove(int position)
{
    node*move=start;
    int steps=1;
    while(steps<position-1)
    {
        move=move->next;
        steps++;
    }
    if(position==1)     //if to be inserted at the first
                        place
    {
        node*temp=start;
        start=start->next;
        delete(temp);
    }
    else
    {
        node*temp=move->next;
        move->next=move->next->next;
        delete(temp);
    }
}
void main( )
{
    int value, data, choice, number, total=0;
    link_list link;
    cout<<"Enter the element of the list terminated by
            negative number :\n";
    cin>>value;
    do
    {
        link.create(value);
        total++;   /increment with every node inserted
        cin>>value;
    }
    while(value>=0);
    cout<<"\nThe list before any operation is perfomed
        (LIFO) :\n";
    link.display(0);
```

```
    cout<<"\nTotal node :="<<total;
    cout<<"\n\nEnter the number of the node to be
 deleted :=";
    cin>>number;
    if(number<=0||number>total) //check for valid
 position
    {
        cout<<"\n Wrong number inptted";
        exit(1);
    }
    total—;
    link.remove(number);
    cout<<"\n\nThe list after deletion is :\n";
    link.display(1);
    cout<<"\n\nTotal nodes :="<<total;
}
```

OUTPUT :

Enter the element of the list terminated by negative number :

10 20 30 40 50 60 -70

The list before any operation is perfomed (LIFO) :

60->50->40->30->20->10->NULL

Total node :=6

Enter the number of the node to be deleted :=3

The list after deletion is :

60->50->30->20->10->NULL

Total nodes :=5

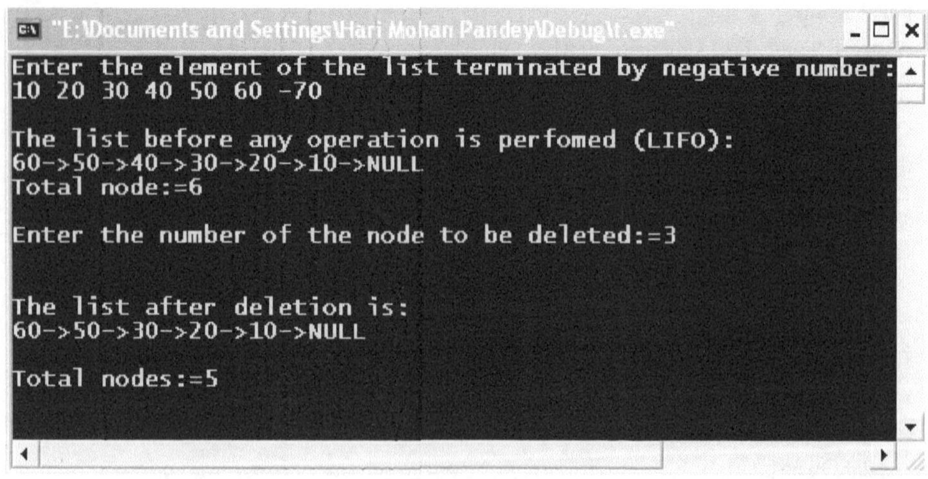

Figure 15.18. *Output screen of program.*

/*PROGRAM : TO CREATE AND TRAVERSE A DOUBLY LINKED LIST */

```
#include <iostream.h>
struct doubly
{
    int data;
    doubly*back;
    doubly*front;
};
class doubly_class
{
private :
    doubly*start;
public :
    doubly_class( )
    {
        start=new doubly;
        start->front=NULL;
        start->back=NULL;
        start->data=-1;        //header node -can contain
                               other information also
    }
    void create( );            //fucntion prototype
    void display( );           //function prototype
};
//function definition create( )
void doubly_class : :create( )
{
    int value;
    doubly* new_node=new doubly;
    new_node=start;
    cout<<"Enter the data terminated by negative
            number :\n";
    cin>>value;
    while(value>=0)
    {
        new_node->front=new doubly;
        new_node->front->back=new_node;
        new_node=new_node->front;
        new_node->data=value;
        new_node->front=NULL;
```

```
        cin>>value;
    }
}
//function definition display( )
void doubly_class : :display( )
{
    cout<<"\n\nTraversing in the forward direction :\n\n";
    doubly*move=start;
    do
    {
        move=move->front;
        cout<<move->data<<"<->";
    }
    while(move->front);
    cout<<"NULL";
    cout<<"\n\n Traversing in the back direction :\n\n";
    do
    {
        cout<<move->data<<"<->";
        move=move->back;
    }
    while(move->back);
    cout<<"NULL";
}
void main( )
{
    doubly_class d_list;    //creation of an object for
                            doubly_class
    d_list.create( );
    d_list.display( );
}
```

OUTPUT :

Enter the data terminated by negative number

20 30 10 40 60 50 -90

Traversing in the forward direction :

20<->30<->10<->40<->60<->50<->NULL

Traversing in the back direction :

50<->60<->40<->10<->30<->20<->NULL

/*PROGRAM : TO INSERT A NODE AT FIRST PLACE IN A DOUBLY LINKED LIST */

```
#include <iostream.h>
struct doubly
{
    int data;
    doubly* back;
    doubly* front;
};
class doubly_class
{
private :
    doubly* start;
public :
    doubly_class( )
    {
        start=new doubly;
        start->front=NULL;
        start->back=NULL;
        start->data=-1;
    }
    void create( );
    void insert_first(int data)
    {
        doubly* temp=new doubly;
        temp->data=data;
        temp->front=start->front;
        start->front->back=temp;
        temp->back=start;
        start->front=temp;
    }
    void display( );
};
void doubly_class : :create( )
{
    int value;
    doubly* new_node=new doubly;
    new_node=start;
    cout<<"\nEnter the data terminated by negative
  number :\n";
    cin>>value;
```

```
        while(value>=0)
        {
            new_node->front=new doubly;
            new_node->front->back=new_node;
            new_node=new_node->front;
            new_node->data=value;
            new_node->front=NULL;
            cin>>value;
        }
    }
    void doubly_class : :display( )
    {
        cout<<"\n\nTraversing in the forward direction :\n\n";
        doubly* move=start;
        do
        {
            move=move->front;
            cout<<move->data<<"<->";
        }
        while(move->front);
        cout<<"NULL";
        cout<<"\n\nTraversing in the back direction :\n\n";
        do
        {
            cout<<move->data<<"<->";
            move=move->back;
        }
        while(move->back);
        cout<<"NULL";
    }
    void main( )
    {
        int value;
        doubly_class list;
        list.create( );
        cout<<"Before any operation :";
        list.display( );
        cout<<"\n\nEnter the data value of the first node :";
        cin>>value;
        list.insert_first(value);
```

```
    cout<<"\nAfter inserting operation :";
    list.display( );
}
```

OUTPUT :

```
Enter the data terminated by negative number :
10 20 30 40 50 60 70 -3
Before any operation :
Traversing in the forward direction :
10<->20<->30<->40<->50<->60<->70<->NULL
Traversing in the back direction :
70<->60<->50<->40<->30<->20<->10<->NULL
Enter the data value of the first node :99
After inserting operation :
Traversing in the forward direction :
99<->10<->20<->30<->40<->50<->60<->70<->NULL
Traversing in the back direction :
70<->60<->50<->40<->30<->20<->10<->99<->NULL
```

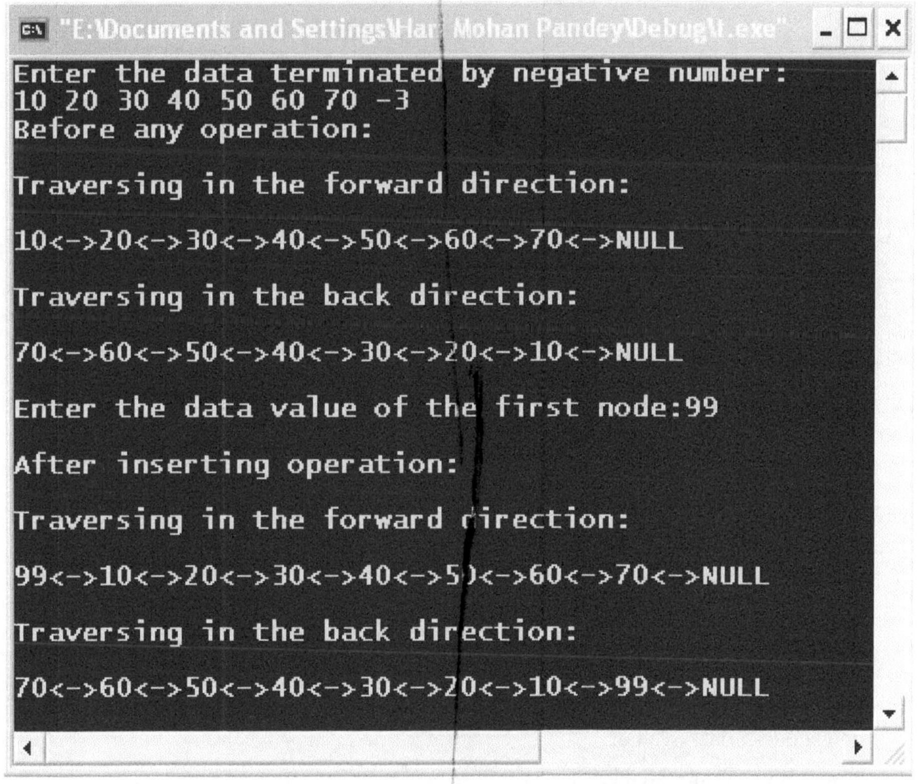

Figure 15.19. *Output screen of program.*

/*PROGRAM :TO INSERT A NODE AT THE END OF A DOUBLY LINKED LIST */

```
#include <iostream.h>
struct doubly
{
    int data;
    doubly* back;
    doubly* front;
};
class doubly_class
{
private :
    doubly* start;
public :
    doubly_class( )
    {
        start=new doubly;
        start->front=NULL;
        start->back=NULL;
        start->data=-1;
    }
    void create( );
    void insert_end(int);
    void display( );
};
void doubly_class : :create( )
{
    int value;
    doubly* new_node=new doubly;
    new_node=start;
    cout<<"\nEnter the data terminated by negative
                number :\n";
    cin>>value;
    while(value>=0)
    {
        new_node->front=new doubly;
        new_node->front->back=new_node;
        new_node=new_node->front;
        new_node->data=value;
        new_node->front=NULL;
```

```
        cin>>value;
    }
}
void doubly_class : :insert_end(int data)
{
    doubly*temp=new doubly;
    temp->data=data;
    doubly*move=start;
    while(move->front)
        move=move->front;
    temp->front=NULL;
    temp->back=move;
    move->front=temp;
}
void doubly_class : :display( )
{
    cout<<"\n\nTraversing in the forward direction :\n\n";
    doubly* move=start;
    do
    {
        move=move->front;
        cout<<move->data<<"<->";
    }
    while(move->front);
    cout<<"NULL";
    cout<<"\n\nTraversing in the back direction :\n\n";
    do
    {
        cout<<move->data<<"<->";
        move=move->back;
    }
    while(move->back!=NULL);
    cout<<"NULL";
}
void main( )
{
    int value;
    doubly_class list;
    list.create( );
    cout<<"\nBefore any operation";
    list.display( );
```

```
        cout<<"\nEnter the data value of the last node :=";
        cin>>value;
        list.insert_end(value);
        cout<<"\nAfter insertion operation";
        list.display( );
}
```

OUTPUT :

```
Enter the data terminated by negative number :
10 20 30 40 50 60 70 80 -3
Before any operation
Traversing in the forward direction :
10<->20<->30<->40<->50<->60<->70<->80<->NULL
Traversing in the back direction :
80<->70<->60<->50<->40<->30<->20<->10<->NULL
Enter the data value of the last node :=145
After insertion operation
Traversing in the forward direction :
10<->20<->30<->40<->50<->60<->70<->80<->145<->NULL
Traversing in the back direction :
145<->80<->70<->60<->50<->40<->30<->20<->10<->NULL
```

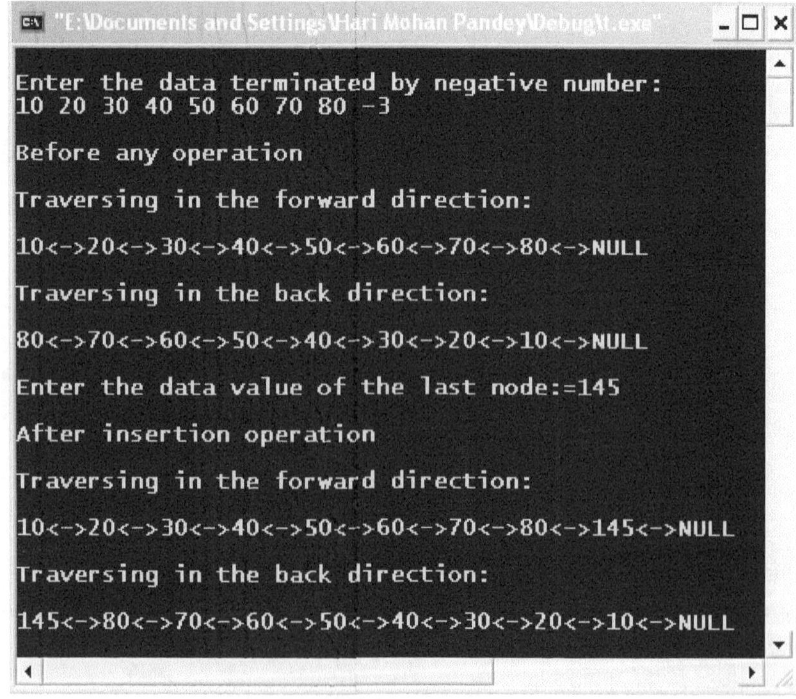

Figure 15.20. *Output screen of the program.*

/*PROGRAM : TO INSERT A NODE AT THE DESIRED POSITION IN A DOUBLY LINKED LIST */

```
#include <iostream.h>
#include <process.h>
struct doubly
{
    int data;
    doubly* back;
    doubly* front;
};
class doubly_class
{
private :
    doubly* start;
    int total;
public :
    doubly_class( )
    {
        start=new doubly;
        start->front=NULL;
        start->back=NULL;
        start->data=-1;
    }
    void create( );
    void insert( );
    void display( );
};
//function definition create( )
void doubly_class : :create( )
{
    int value;
    total=0;
    doubly*new_node=new doubly;
    new_node=start;
    cout<<"\nEnter the data terminated by negative
                number\n";
    cin>>value;
    while(value>=0)
    {
        new_node->front=new doubly;
```

```
            new_node->front->back=new_node;
            new_node=new_node->front;
            new_node->data=value;
            new_node->front=NULL;
            total++;
            cin>>value;
        }
    }
    //function defintion insert( )
    void doubly_class : :insert( )
    {
        int data,position;
        cout<<"\n\nEnter the data value of the node to be
                    inserted :";
        cin>>data;

        cout<<"Enter the position where node is to be
                inserted :";
        cin>>position;
        if(position<=0||position>total+1)
        {
            cout<<"\nInvalid position inputted";
            exit(1);
        }
        doubly* temp=new doubly;
        temp->data=data;
        if(position==1)
        {
            temp->front=start->front;
            temp->back=start;
            if(temp->front)
                start->front->back=temp;
            start->front=temp;
        }
        else
        {
            int steps=1;
            doubly*move=start->front;
            while(steps<position-1)
            {
                move=move->front;
```

```
            steps++;
        }
        temp->front=move->front;
        temp->back=move;
        if(temp->front)
            move->front->back=temp;
        move->front=temp;
    }
    total++;
}
    //function definition display( )
    void doubly_class : :display( )
    {
        cout<<"\nTotal number of nodes :"<<total;
        cout<<"\nTraversing in the forward
                    direction :\n\n";
        doubly*move =start;
        do
        {
            move=move->front;
            cout<<move->data<<"<->";
        }
        while(move->front);
        cout<<"NULL";
        cout<<"\n\nTraversing in the back
                        direction :\n\n";
        do
        {
            cout<<move->data<<"<->";
            move=move->back;
        }
        while(move->back!=NULL);
        cout<<"NULL";
    }
void main( )
{
        int value;
        doubly_class list;
        list.create( );
        cout<<"Before any operation :";
        list.display( );
```

```
        list.insert( );
        cout<<"\nAfter insertion operation :";
        list.display( );
}
```

OUTPUT :

```
Enter the data terminated by negative number
10 20 30 40 50 60 70 80 -8
Before any operation :
Total number of nodes : 8
Traversing in the forward direction :
10<->20<->30<->40<->50<->60<->70<->80<->NULL
Traversing in the back direction :
80<->70<->60<->50<->40<->30<->20<->10<->NULL
Enter the data value of the node to be inserted :150
Enter the position where node is to be inserted :4
After insertion operation :
Total number of nodes :9
Traversing in the forward direction :
10<->20<->30<->150<->40<->50<->60<->70<->80<->NULL
Traversing in the back direction :
80<->70<->60<->50<->40<->150<->30<->20<->10<->NULL
```

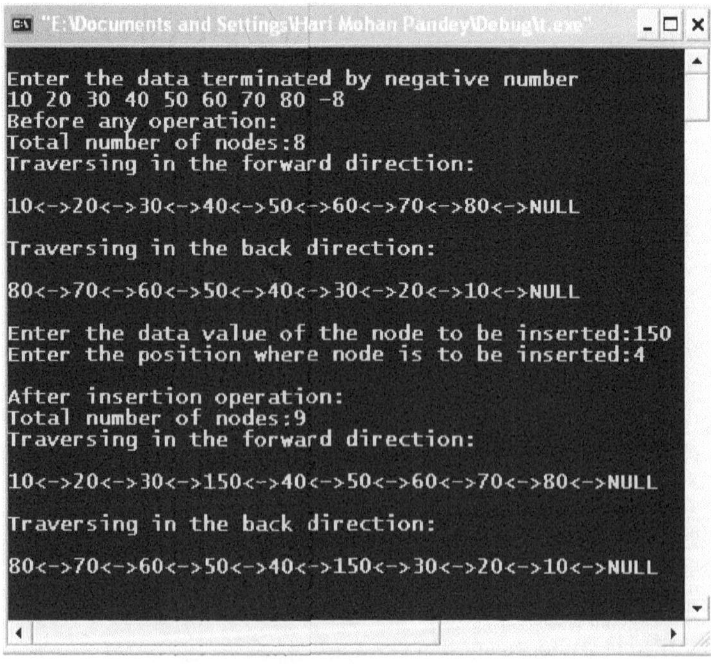

Figure 15.21. *Output screen of the program.*

Experiment-5 : Programs illustrating the use of destructor and the various types of constructors :

1. Constructor with no arguments
2. Constructors with arguments
3. Copy constructor etc.

/*PROGRAM : DEMO OF CONSTRUCTOR NO ARGUMENT */

```
#include <iostream.h>
#include <conio.h>

class demo
{
    public :
        demo( )
        {
            cout<<"Hello from constructor \n";
        }
};

void main( )
{
    clrscr( );
    demo d;
    getch( );
}
```

Output :

Hello from constructor

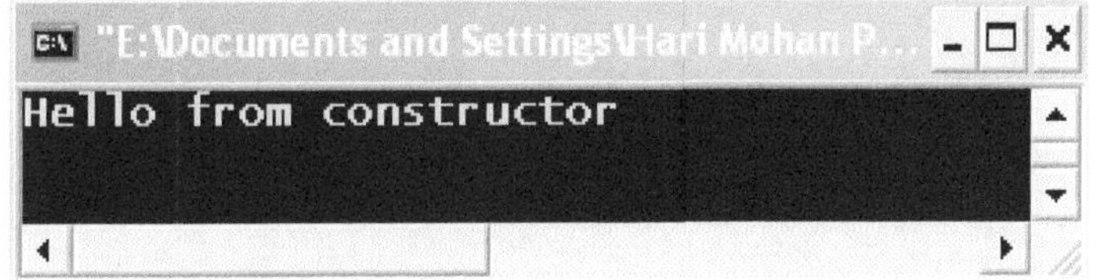

Figure 15.22. *Output screen of program.*

EXPLANATION : The name of class is demo and the following declaration

```
demo( )
{
    cout<<" Hello from constructor \n";
}
```

Demo is a constructor of the class as the name of the function is the name of the class.

/*PROGRAM : DEMO OF PARAMETERIZED CONSTRUCTOR WITH STRING DATA */

```
#include <iostream.h>
#include <string.h>
#include <conio.h>

class string
{
    char str[20];
    public :
        string( );
        string (char s[ ]);
        void show( );
};
 string : :string( )
 {
    strcpy (str,"Hari");
    cout<<"Default constructor called\n";
 }
 string : : string(char s[ ])
 {
    strcpy(str,s);
    cout<<"One argument constructor called\n";
 }
 void string : :show( )
 {
    cout<<"string is"<<str<<endl;
 }
 void main( )
 {
    clrscr( );
    string s1;
    s1.show( );
    s1=string("Vijay");
    s1.show( );
    string s2=string("Manmohan");
    s2.show( );
    string s3("Ranjana");
    s3.show( );
    getch( );
 }
```

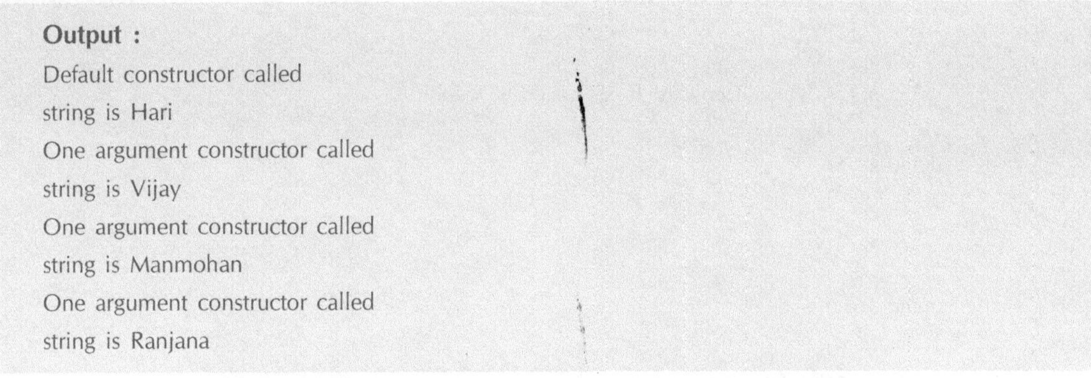

Output :

Default constructor called
string is Hari
One argument constructor called
string is Vijay
One argument constructor called
string is Manmohan
One argument constructor called
string is Ranjana

Figure 15.23. *Output screen of program.*

EXPLANATION : In the case string we have two constructors; one is default and second is one argument constructor. In the execution of statement string s1 default constructor is called which result in printing on the screen.

Default constructor called.

And assign value **"Hari"** to **str** of object **s1**. When the statement **s1= string ("Vijay");** executes one argument constructor is called which results in printing on the screen.

One argument constructor called and assigns value "vijay" to str of object s1. The old value "Hari" is removed.

Same explanation applies to statement string s2 =string ("Manmohan"); and for string s ("Ranjana"); Observe that in the first part the value of str for the object s1 was "Hari" but after the statement s1 (".

/*PROGRAM : DEMO OF COPY CONSTRUCTOR */

```
#include <iostream.h>
#include <conio.h>

class demo
{
        int data;
    public :

        demo( )
```

```
        {
            data =200;
            cout<<"Default constructor is called"<<endl;
        }
        demo(int x)
        {
            data = x;
        }
        demo(demo & d)
        {
            data = d.data;
            cout<<"Copy constructor is called"<<endl;
        }
        friend demo copy(demo d)
        {
            demo temp;
                temp.data = d.data;
                    return temp;
        }
        void show( )
        {
            cout<<"data = "<<data<<endl;
        }
};

void main( )
{
    clrscr( );
    demo d1(300);
    demo d2= d1;
    demo d3 = copy(d1);
    d1.show( );
    d2.show( );
    d3.show( );
    getch( );
}
```

OUTPUT :

```
Copy constructor is called
Copy constructor is called
Default constructor is called
Copy constructor is called
data = 300
data = 300
data = 300
```

```
"E:\Documents and Settings\Hari Mohan P...
Copy constructor is called
Copy constructor is called
Default constructor is called
Copy constructor is called
Copy constructor is called
data = 300
data = 300
data = 300
```

Figure 15.24. *Output screen of the program.*

EXPLANATION : In the program we have written a **copy constructor** and a **friend function copy**. The function **copy** takes an object by value as argument, copies the data into another object and returned that object. In the **main** when **demo d1 (300);** executes it calls the one argument constructor and sets data for object **d1 = 200**. When **demo d2 = d1;** executes **copy constructor** is called and **data** for **d2** is equal to **data** for **d1**. Now the important thing to understand. When **demo d3 = copy (d1);** executes, **copy constructor** is called as we have written **demo d3 =**. As we are passing **d1** by value in the **function copy, copy constructor** will be called. Inside the function **copy** temporary object **(temp)** is created which is called **default constructor** and in the end we have written the object **temp** by value, **copy constructor** is called again.

If I do a small change as that instead of writing **demo d3 = copy (d1);** we write as :

```
demo d3;
d3 = copy(d1);
```

Sequence of constructor will be called as :

1. For **demo d3, default constructor** will be called.
2. **d1** we are sending by value, **copy constructor** will be called.
3. In the function **demo temp;** causes **default constructor** to be called.
4. **return temp** causes **copy constructor** to be called.

Experiment-6 : Programs illustrating the various forms of inheritance :

1. Single Inheritance.
2. Multiple Inheritances.
3. Multilevel Inheritance.
4. Hierarchical inheritance, etc.

/*PROGRAM : DEMO OF SINGLE LEVEL INHERITANCE */

```
#include <iostream.h>
#include <conio.h>
class super
{
        int sup_a;
```

```
    public :
        void sup_input(int x)
        {
            sup_a=x;
        }
        void sup_show( )
        {
            cout<<"sup_a="<<sup_a<<endl;
        }
};
class sub :public super
{
        int sub_a;
    public :
        void sub_input(int x)
        {
            sup_input(x*2);
            sub_a=x;
        }
        void sub_show( )
        {
            sup_show( );
            cout<<"sub_a="<<sub_a<<endl;
        }
};
void main( )
{
    int i;
    clrscr( );
    sub o1;
    cout<<"Enter the data member :=";
    cin>>i;
    o1.sub_input(i);
    o1.sub_show( );
    getch( );
}
```

OUTPUT :

```
Enter the data member : =145
sup_a=290
sub_a=145
```

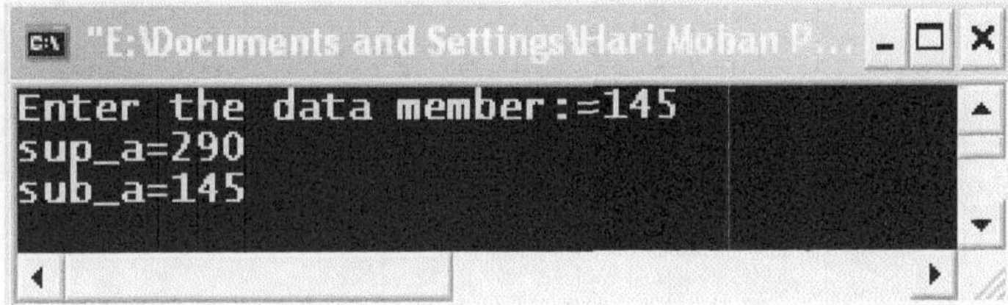

Figure 15.25. *Output screen of the program.*

EXPLANATION : In the **main** we have called only the functions of sub class. The function **sup_input** is called from **sub_input** with a value **x*2** as argument. Similarly sup_show is called from class **sub**. So, when **sub_input** is called from **main** with value of **'i'** of **int** type, it is collected in variable **x** and the function of base class **sup_input** is called with value **2*145 (290)**, where it is assigned to **sup_a** of **super class**. When control returns **sup_input** function the value **x** is assigned to **sub_a**. When **sup_show** is called, it calls **sup_show** first in its body. When the function **sup_show** returns after displaying the value of **sup_a,** the function **sup_show** displays the value of **sub_a**.

/*PROGRAM : DEMO OF MULTILEVEL INHERITENCE FINDING MAXIMUM OF THREE CLASS'S DATA */

```
#include <iostream.h>
#include <conio.h>
class first
{
    protected :
        int fa;
    public :
        void input_f( )
        {
            cout<<"Enter the value for fa :=";
            cin>>fa;
        }
};
class second :public first
{
    protected :
        int sa;
    public :
        void input_s( )
        {
        input_f( );
        cout<<"Enter the value for sa :=";
```

```
            cin>>sa;
        }
    };
    class third :public second
    {
        protected :
            int ta;
        public :
            void input_t( )
            {
            input_s( );
            cout<<"Enter the value for ta :=";
            cin>>ta;
            }
            void show( )
            {
            cout<<"Data of class first fa :="<<fa<<endl;
            cout<<"Data of class second sa :="<<sa<<endl;
            cout<<"Data of class third ta :="<<ta<<endl;
            }
            int max( )
            {
            int t1,t2;
            t1=fa>sa ?fa :sa;
            t2=ta>t1 ?ta :t1;
            return t2;
            }
    };
    void main( )
    {
        clrscr( );
        third t;
        t.input_t( );
        t.show( );
        cout<<"Max is "<<t.max( )<<endl;
        getch( );
    }
```

OUTPUT :

```
Enter the value for fa : =123
Enter the value for sa : =567
Enter the value for ta : =234
Data of class first fa : =123
Data of class second sa : =567
Data of class third ta : =234
Max is 567
```

```
"E:\Documents and Settings\Hari Mohan Pa...
Enter the value for fa:=123

Enter the value for sa:=567

Enter the value for ta:=234

Data of class first fa:=123

Data of class second sa:=567

Data of class third ta:=234
Max is 567
```

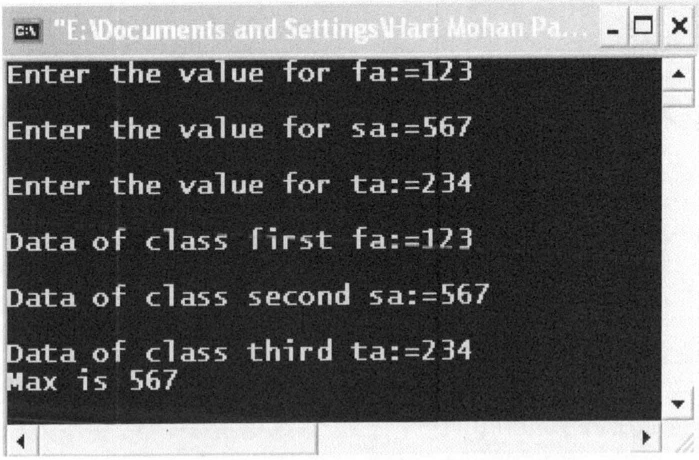

Figure 15.26. *Output screen of program.*

EXPLANATION : In all the three classes data members are **protected**. In **main** when **input_t** of class third is called by an object **t**, it first calls function **input_s** of class second. The function **input_s** in turn call the function **input_f** of class first. As **second** is the base class of class **third** and first is the base class of **second**, data members **fa** and **sa** can be used inside the member functions of class **third.** Though how of class **third** we display these data members. The function **max** of class third finds maximum of these **three** data members using ternary operator and return the max value which is displayed in the main.

/*PROGRAM : DEMO OF MULTIPLE INHERITENCE FINDING TOTAL MARKS FROM INTERNAL AND EXTERNAL MARKS */

```
#include <iostream.h>
#include <conio.h>
#include <stdlib.h>
class Internal
{
protected :
    int i_marks;
public :
    void input_im( )
```

```
        {
            cout<<"Enter internal marks :=";
            cin>>i_marks;
            if(!(i_marks>=0 && i_marks<=60))
            {
                cout<<"Invalid Marks";
                exit(0);
            }
        }
        void show_im( )
        {
            cout<<"Internal marks :="<<i_marks<<endl;
        }
};
class External
{
protected :
        int e_marks;
public :
        void input_em( )
        {
            cout<<"Enter external marks :=";
            cin>>e_marks;
            if(!(e_marks>=0 && e_marks<=60))
            {
                cout<<"Invalid Marks";
                exit(0);
            }
        }
        void show_em( )
        {
            cout<<"External marks :="<<e_marks<<endl;
        }
};
class Total :public Internal, public External
{
        int total_marks;
public :
        void input( )
        {
            input_im( );
```

```
            input_em( );
        }
        void show( )
        {
            show_im( );
            show_em( );
            total_marks = i_marks;
            cout<<"Total Mrks :="<<total_marks<<endl;
        }
};
void main( )
{
        clrscr( );
        Total tm;
        tm.input( );
        tm.show( );
        getch( );
}
```

OUTPUT :

```
Enter internal marks : =56
Enter external marks : =35
Internal marks : =56
External marks : =35
Total Marks : =91
```

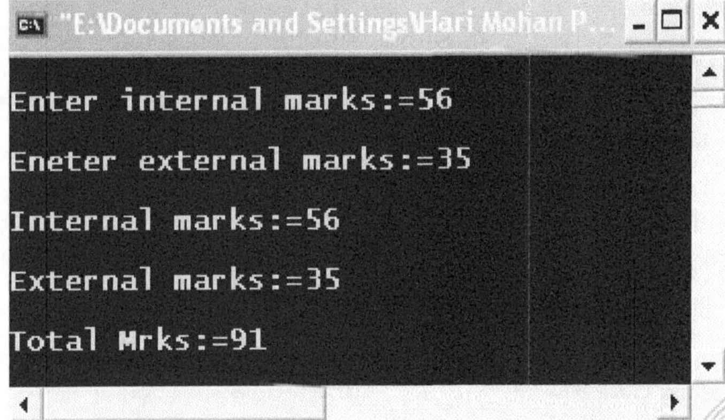

Figure 15.27. *Output screen of the program.*

EXPLANATION : For student's **internal marks** we have a class **Internal** and for student's external marks we have a **class External**. The internal marks must be between **0 to 60** and external marks must be between **0 to 40.** These two classes are inherited by class total which finds the total marks and display all three marks :

(*a*) **Internal**

(*b*) **External and**

(*c*) **Total**

Note here that **i_marks and e_marks** are protected so that can be used inside the total class. They can be modified by the class total. So ideally **i_marks and e_marks**. Try to make use of this and create a new program yourself.

/*PROGRAM : DEMO OF HIERARCHICAL INHERITANCE */

```
#include <iostream.h>
#include <conio.h>
#include <string.h>
class University
{
protected :
    char uname[40];
public :
    University( )
    {
        strcpy(uname,"NMIMS University Mumbai");
    }
};
class college1 :public University
{
    char cname[50];
public :
    college1( )
    {
        strcpy(cname, "MPSTME Shirpur Campus");
    }
    void show_college1( )
    {
        cout<<"College Name :="<<cname<<endl;
        cout<<"Affiliated to :="<<uname<<endl;
    }
};
class college2 :public University
{
    char cname [50];
public :
    college2( )
```

```
    {
        strcpy(cname,"R C Patel");
    }
    void show_college2( )
    {
        cout<<"College Name ="<<cname<<endl;
        cout<<"Affiliated to :="<<uname <<endl;
    }
};
void main( )
{
    clrscr( );
    college1 c1;
    c1.show_college1( );
    college2 c2;
    c2.show_college2 ( );
    getch( );
}
```

OUTPUT :

```
College Name : =MPSTME Shirpur Campus
Affiliated to : =NMIMS University Mumbai
College Name =R C Patel
Affiliated to : =NMIMS University Mumbai
```

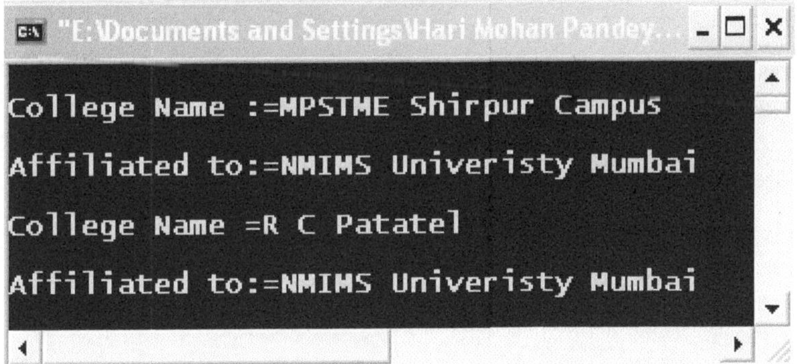

Figure 15.28. *Output screen of program.*

EXPLANATION : The program is so simple. We have university class which has just data member, a **char** array of **40** characters named **uname**. This class is inherited by two classes' **college1** and **college2.** The two classes display their name and the university to which they are affiliated.

Experiment-7 : Write a program illustrating the use of virtual functions.

```
/*PROGRAM : DEMO OF VIRTUAL FUNCTION */

#include <iostream.h>
#include <conio.h>
class first
{
public :
    virtual void show( )
    {
        cout<<"Hello from show of first class"<<endl;
    }
    virtual void display( )
    {
        cout<<"Hello from display of first class"<<endl;
    }
    void fun( )
    {
        cout<<"Hello from fun of first"<<endl;
    }
};
class second :public first
{
public :
    virtual void show( )
    {
        cout<<"Hello from show of second class"<<endl;
    }
    virtual void fun( )
    {
        cout<<"Hello from fun of second class"<<endl;
    }
};
void main( )
{
        clrscr( );
    first *ptr;
    first f;
    second s;
    ptr=&f;
    ptr->show( );
```

```
    ptr->display( );
    ptr->fun( );
    ptr=&s;
    ptr->show( );
    ptr->display( );
    ptr->fun( );
    getch( );
}
```

OUTPUT :

Hello from show of first class
Hello from display of first class
Hello from fun of first
Hello from show of second class
Hello from display of first class
Hello from fun of first

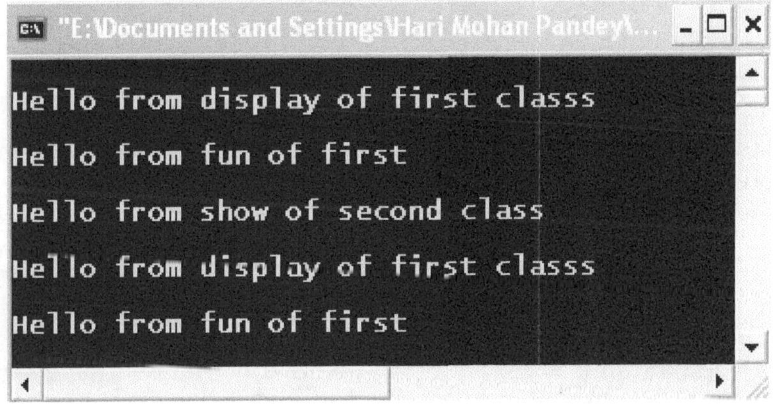

Figure 15.29. *Output screen of program.*

EXPLANATION : In the following statements it is clear that all the functions of **class first** will be called :

```
ptr=&f;
ptr->show( );
ptr->display( );
ptr->fu( );
```

Writing the function virtual again when overriding in the derived class **second** makes function virtual for the next class if this class is inherited. **show** was virtual in the **first** class and is overridden in the second class so **show** of second class will be called. **fun** was not virtual in the **first** class so fun of class **first** will be called. The function **display** is presented only in the class **first** so obviously it will be called. So the output.

Experiment-8 : Write a program which illustrates the use of virtual base class.

/* PROGRAM : GENERATING STUDENT REPORT, ELEMENTARY PROGRAM DEVELOPED BY STUDENTS */

```
#include <iostream.h>
#include <conio.h>
#include <stdlib.h>
class student
{
    char sname [20];
    int rollno;
public :
    void input_st( )
    {
        cout<<"Enter student name"<<endl;
        cin.getline(sname,20);
        cout<<"Enter the roll number"<<endl;
        cin>>rollno;
    }
    void show_st( )
    {
        cout<<"\tName :="<<sname<<endl;
        cout<<"\tRoll number :="<<rollno<<endl;
    }
};
class Subject :public student
{
    char subject[25];
public :
    void input_sub( )
    {
        input_st( );
        cin.ignore( );
        cout<<"Enter the subject name"<<endl;
        cin.getline(subject,25);
    }
    void show_sub( )
    {
        show_st( );
        cout<<"\tSubject="<<subject<<endl;
    }
};
```

```
class Internal :virtual public Subject
{
    char subject[25];
protected :
    int i_marks;
public :
    void input_im( )
    {
        cout<<"Enter internal marks (0 to 20)"<<endl;
        cin>>i_marks;
        if(!(i_marks>=0 && i_marks<=20))
        {
            cout<<"Invalid Marks"<<endl;
            exit(0);
        }
    }
    void show_im( )
    {
        cout<<"\tInternal marks="<<i_marks<<endl;
    }
};
class External :virtual public Subject
{
protected :
    int e_marks;
public :
    void input_em( )
    {
        cout<<"Enter External marks (0 to 80)"<<endl;
        cin>>e_marks;
        if(!(e_marks>=0 && e_marks<=80))
        {
            cout<<"Invalid Marks"<<endl;
            exit(0);
        }
    }
    void show_em( )
    {
        cout<<"\tExternal Marks="<<e_marks<<endl;
    }
};
```

```
class Total :public Internal, public External
{
    int total_marks;
public :
    void input( )
    {
        input_sub( );
        input_im( );
        input_em( );
    }
    void show( )
    {
        show_sub( );
        show_im( );
        show_em( );
        total_marks = i_marks + e_marks;
        cout<<"\tTotal Marks:"<<total_marks<<endl;
    }
};
void main( )
{
    clrscr( );
    Total tm;
    tm.input( );
    cout<<"\n\t ++++++++++Student Report++++++++\n"<<endl;
        tm.show( );
    getch( );
}
```

OUTPUT :

```
Enter student name
Hari Pandey
Enter the roll number
1001
Enter the subject name
OOP In C++
Enter internal marks (0 to 20)
18
Enter External marks (0 to 80)
75
 ++++++++++Student Report++++++++
```

```
Name :=Hari Pandey
Roll number :=1001
Subject=OOP In C++
Internal marks=18
External Marks=75
Total Marks=93
```

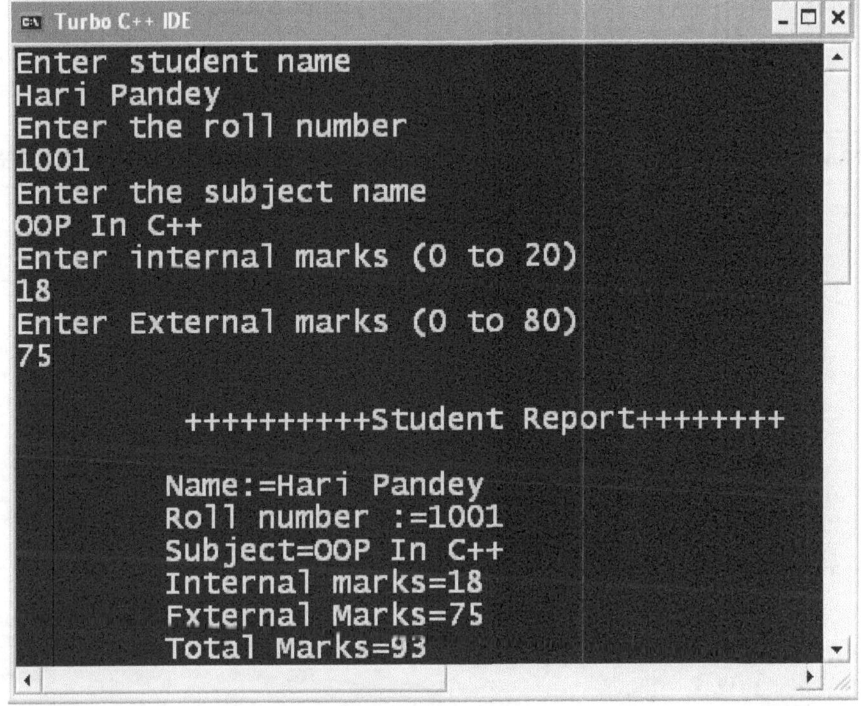

Figure 15.30. *Output screen of the program.*

EXPLANATION : First we show you how the classes in the program are related.

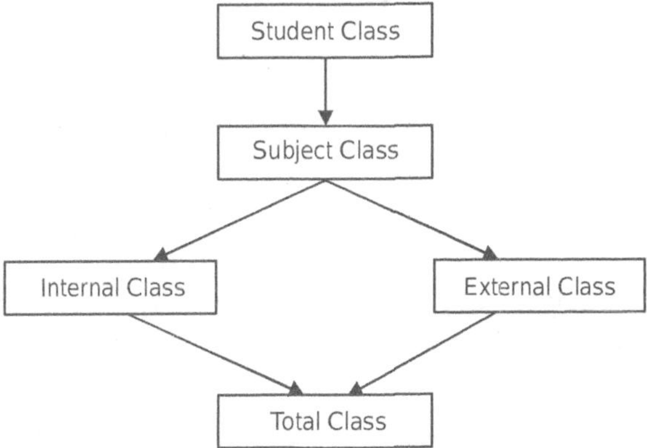

The student class has two private data members sname and **rollno** two **public** member function : **input_st** and **show_st**. This **student** class is inherited by class subject which has just one data member subject and two function **input_sub** and **show_sub**. The function for input and display the student name and roll number are called in the function of this class. The class subject is inherited by class **Internal** and **External** which we have seen earlier. Note both the classes inherit the class Subject in **virtual** public mode so only one copy of data members of class **Subject** will be available in class Total and no ambiguity will arise. Trace the program step-wise. It is very simple to understand.

Experiment-9 : Write a program which uses the following sorting methods for sorting elements in ascending order. Use function templates :

(*a*) Bubble sort

(*b*) Selection sort

(*c*) Quick sort.

/*PROGRAM : (BUBBLE SORT) SORTING ARRAY ELEMENTS USING FUNCTION TEMPLATE */

```
#include <iostream.h>
#include <typeinfo.h>
#define S 5

template<class TYPE>
void sort(TYPE arr[ ])
{
    int i,j;
    for(i=0;i<S;i++)
        for(j=i+1;j<S;j++)
            if(arr[i]>arr[j])
            {
                TYPE t=arr[i];
                arr[i]=arr[j];
                arr[j]=t;
            }
}

template<class TYPE>
void input(TYPE arr[ ])
{
    int i;
    cout<<"Enter"<<S<<"
"<<typeid(arr[0]).name( )<<"number"<<endl;
    for(i=0;i<S;i++)
        cin>>arr[i];
}
```

```
template<class TYPE>
void show(TYPE arr[ ])
{
    int i;
    for(i=0;i<S;i++)
        cout<<arr[i]<<" ";
    cout<<endl;
}
void main( )
{
    int a1[S];
    input(a1);
    sort(a1);
    cout<<"SORTED ARRAY IS"<<endl;
    show(a1);
    float f[S];
    input(f);
    sort(f);
    cout<<"SORTED ARRAY IS"<<endl;
    show(f);
}
```

OUTPUT :

```
Enter5 intnumber
10 5 26 17 80
SORTED ARRAY IS
5 10 17 26 80
Enter5 floatnumber
56.8 4.5 2.3 90.634.56
SORTED ARRAY IS
0.56 2.3 4.5 56.8 90.634
```

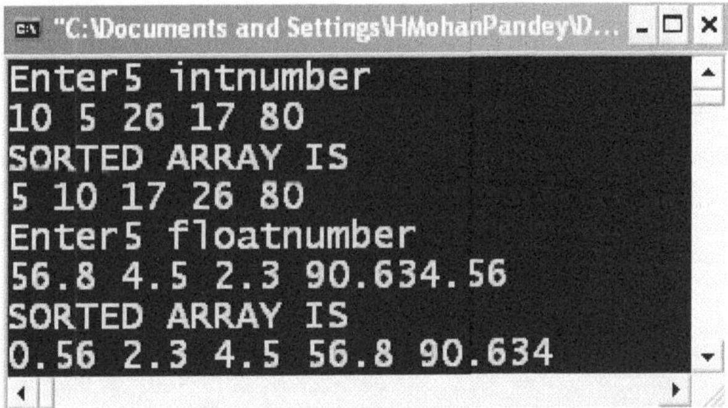

Figure 15.31. *Showing the output screen of program.*

EXPLANATION : In the program we have three function templates :

1. One for inputting array elements.
2. Second for showing the array elements.
3. Third for sorting array element.

As we have array of two different data types, total **2 × 3 = 6** function definition are generated when specific call is made to each function *i.e.,* **3** for integer data type **int : input, show and sort** and **3** for **float** data type. Rest is simple to understand.

/*PROGRAM : SELECTION SORT ASCENDING ORDER */

```
#include <iostream.h>
#define size 20
class array
{
private :
    int i;
    float a[size];
public :
    void enter(int);
    void display(int);
    void selection_sort(int);
};
//definition of the function function enter( )
void array : :enter(int n)
{
    for(i=0;i<n;i++)
        cin>>a[i];
}
//definition of the function display( )
void array : :display(int n)
{
    for(i=0;i<n;i++)
        cout<<a[i]<<" ";
}
//definition of the function selection_sort( )
void array : :selection_sort(int n)
{
    float temp;         //temp is used here for swapping
    int min_index;      //min_index denotes the position of the
                        least element during a pass
    //Now Applying Sorting
```

```
    for(int pass=0;pass<n-1;pass++)
    {
        min_index=pass;
        for(i=pass+1;i<n;i++)
        {
            if(a[i]<a[min_index])
                min_index=i;
        }//innermost for loop
        if(pass!=min_index)
        {
            temp=a[pass];
            a[pass]=a[min_index];
            a[min_index]=temp;
        }
    }//outermost for loop
}
void main( )
{
    array obj;
    int n;
    cout<<"Enter no of elements<<="<<size<<"\n";
    cin>>n;
    cout<<"\nEnter "<<n<<" elements\n";
    obj.enter(n);
    //echo the data
    cout<<"\nGiven array is \n\n";
    obj.display(n);
    obj.selection_sort(n);
    cout<<"\n\n After applying selection sort array
                is :\n\n";
    obj.display(n);
}
```

OUTPUT :

```
Enter no of elements<<=20
6
Enter 6 elements
10 17 23 5 3 89
Given array is
10 17 23 5 3 89
After applying selection sort array is :
3 5 10 17 23 89
```

```
"E:\Documents and Settings\Hari Mohan Pandey\D...
Enter no of elements<<=20
6

Enter 6 elements
10 17 23 5 3 89

Given array is

10 17 23 5 3 89

 After applying selection sort array is:

3 5 10 17 23 89
```

Figure 15.32. *Output screen of program.*

/*PROGRAM : QUICK SORT FOR ASCENDING ORDER */

```
#include <iostream.h>
#define size 20
class array
{
private :
    float a[size];
    int i,low,high,pivot_value, temp;
public :
    void enter(float*,int);
    void display(float*,int);
    void quick_sort(float*,int beg,int end);
};
//definition of the function enter( )
void array : :enter(float a[ ], int n)
{
    for(i=0;i<n;i++)
        cin>>a[i];
}
//definition of the display( )
void array : :display(float a[ ], int n)
{
    for(i=0;i<n;i++)
        cout<<a[i]<<" ";
}
```

```
//definition of the function quick_sort( )
void array : :quick_sort(float arr[ ],int beg, int end)
{
    low=beg;
    high=end;
    pivot_value=arr[(beg+end)/2];
    do
    {
        while(arr[low]<pivot_value)
            low++;
        while(arr[high]>pivot_value)
            high—;
        if(low<=high)
        {
            temp=arr[low];
            arr[low++]=arr[high];
            arr[high—]=temp;
        }
    }while(low<=high);
    if(beg<high)
        quick_sort(arr,beg,high);    //recursive call to
                                      the function
    if(low<end)
        quick_sort(arr,low,end);     //recursive call to
                                      the function
    }
    void main( )
    {
        array obj;
        float a[size];
        int n;
        cout<<"Enter no of elements<="<<size<<"\n";
        cin>>n;
        cout<<"\nEnter "<<n<<" elements\n\n";
        obj.enter(a,n);
        //echo the data
        cout<<"\nGiven array is      \n\n";
        obj.display(a,n);
        obj.quick_sort(a,0,n-1);     //function call
                                      quick_sort
        cout<<"\n\nSorted array is :\n\n";
        obj.display(a,n);
    }
```

OUTPUT :

```
Enter no of elements<=20
6
Enter 6 elements
60 10 30 20 45 25
Given array is
60 10 30 20 45 25
Sorted array is :
10 20 25 30 45 60
```

```
"E:\Documents and Settings\Hari Mohan Pandey\D...
Enter 6 elements
60 10 30 20 45 25
Given array is
60 10 30 20 45 25
Sorted array is:
10 20 25 30 45 60
```

Figure 15.33. *Output screen of the program.*

Experiment-10 : Write programs illustrating file handling operations :

(*a*) Copying a text file

(*b*) Displaying the contents of the file, etc.

/*PROGRAM : READING AND WRITING MOBILE DETAIL */

```
#include <iostream.h>
#include <fstream.h>
void main( )
{
    fstream rw;
    rw.open("demo2.txt",ios : :out);
    char mcomp[20],model[10];
    float price;
    cout<<"Enter the mobile model"<<endl;
    cin.getline(model, 10);
    cout<<"Enter the mobile company"<<endl;
    cin.getline(mcomp, 20);
```

```
    cout<<"Enter the mobile price"<<endl;
    cin>>price;
    rw<<model<<endl<<mcomp<<endl<<price<<endl;
    rw.close( );
    rw.open("demo2.txt",ios : :in);
    rw.getline(model,10);
    rw.getline(mcomp,20);
    rw>>price;
    cout<<"Mobile details read from file"<<endl;
    cout<<"Model :="<<model<<endl;
    cout<<"Company :="<<mcomp<<endl;
    cout<<"Price :="<<price<<endl;
    rw.close( );
}
```

OUTPUT :

Enter the mobile model

z550i

Enter the mobile company

Sony

Enter the mobile price

8000

Mobile details read from file

Model :=z550i

Company :=Sony

Price :=8000

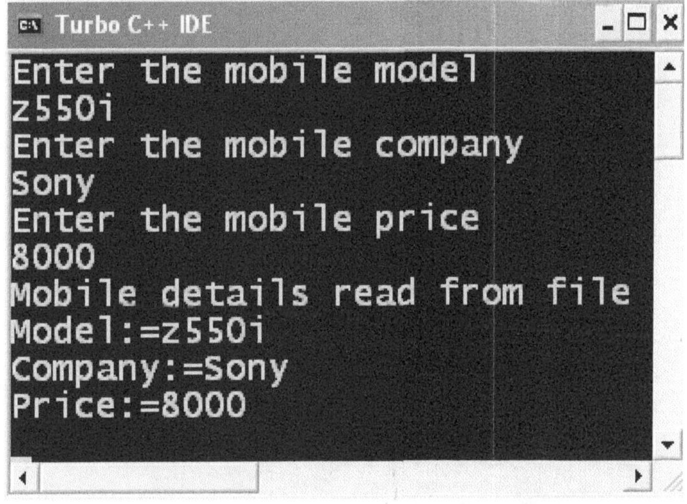

Figure 15.34. *Output screen of program.*

EXPLANATION : The program is simple. We input detail of mobile from keyboard, write into the file and close the file. We open the file in read mode and read mobile details from the file which is displayed on to the screen.

/*PROGRAM : FILE COPYING USING GET AND PUT */

```
#include <iostream.h>
#include <fstream.h>
#include <conio.h>

void main( )
{
    fstream source, dest;
    char sfile[15], dfile[15];
    char ch;
    clrscr( );
    cout<<"Enter the source file name"<<endl;
    cin>>sfile;
    source.open(sfile,ios : :in);
    cout<<"Enter the destination file name"<<endl;
    cin>>dfile;
    dest.open(dfile,ios : :out);
    while(source.eof( )==0)
    {
        source.get(ch);
        dest.put(ch);
    }
    source.close( );
    dest.close( );
}
```

OUTPUT :

```
Enter the source file name
Hari.txt
Enter the destination file name
Pandey.txt
```

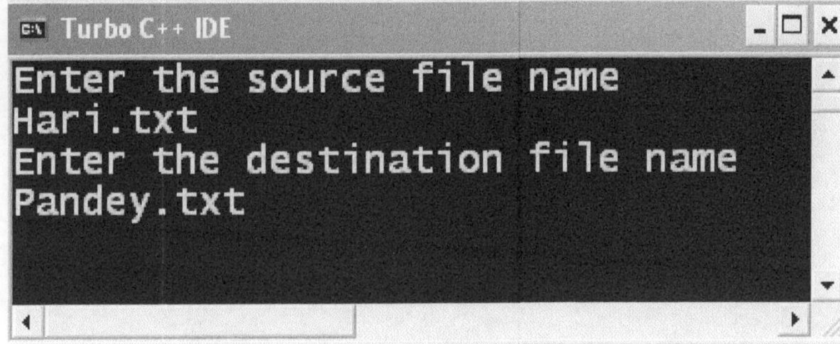

Figure 15.35. *Output screen of program.*

EXPLANATION : We input source and destination file name from the user. It is assumed that source file exist so we have not put any error checking code in the program. The source file is than opened in read mode and destination file is in write mode. We read one character at a time from source file and put this into destination file. This continues till source file does not come to end. In the end both files are closed.

❑❑❑

APPENDIX 1

KEY ELEMENTS USED IN TROUBLE FREE C++

1. **&** has a number of distinct meanings. When it precedes the name of a *variable* without following the name of a *type*, it means "the address of the following variable". For example, & Str means "the address of the variable Str". When & follows a type name and precedes a variable name, it means that the variable being declared is a *reference*—that is, another name for a preexisting variable. In this book, references are used only in *argument lists*, where they indicate that the variable being defined is a new name for the caller's variable rather than a new local variable.
2. **%** is the "modulus" operator, which returns the remainder after dividing its left-hand argument by its right-hand argument.
3. **: :** is the **scope resolution operator**, which is used to tell the compiler the scope of a variable. We can prefix it to the name of a global variable to prevent the compiler from confusing it with a variable of the same name from the standard library. It is also used to specify the *namespace* or *class* of a variable or function, when placed between the *namespace* or *class* name and the variable or function name.
4. **<** is the "less than" operator, which returns the value true if the expression on its left has a lower value than the expression on its right; otherwise, it returns the value false. Also see *operator* < in the index.
5. **<<** is the "stream output" operator, used to write data to an ostream. Also see *operator* << in the index.[1]
6. **<=** is the "less than or equal to" operator, which returns the value true if the expression on its left has the same or a lower value than the expression on its right; otherwise, it returns the value false. Also see *operator* <= in the index.
7. **=** is the assignment operator, which assigns the value on its right to the variable on its left. Also see *operator* = in the index.
8. **==** is the "equals" operator, which returns the value true if the expression on its left has the same value as the expression on its right; otherwise, it returns the value false. Also see *operator* == in the index.

9. **>** is the "greater than" operator, which returns the value true if the expression on its left has a greater value than the expression on its right; otherwise, it returns the value false. Also see *operator* > in the index.
10. **>=** is the "greater than or equal to" operator, which returns the value true if the expression on its left has the same or a greater value than the expression on its right; otherwise, it returns the value false. Also see *operator* >= in the index.
11. **>>** is the "stream input" operator, used to read data from an istream. Also see *operator* >> in the index.
12. **[** is the left square bracket; see *square brackets* for usage.
13. **]** is the right square bracket; see *square brackets* for usage.
14. **[ ]** is used after the delete operator to tell the compiler that the pointer for which delete was called refers to a group of elements rather than just one data item, *e.g.*, when deleting an array of chars. This is one of the few times when we have to make that distinction explicitly rather than leaving it to context.
15. { is the left curly brace; see *curly braces* for usage.
16. } is the right curly brace; see *curly braces* for usage.
17. **!=** is the "not equals" operator, which returns the value true if the expression on its left has a value different from the expression on its right; otherwise, it returns the value false. Also see *operator* != in the index.
18. **&&** is the "logical AND" operator. It produces the result true if the expressions on both its right and left are true; if either of those expressions is false, it produces the result false. However, this isn't the whole story. There is a special rule in C++ governing the execution of the && operator : If the expression on the left is false, then the answer must be false and the expression on the right is not executed at all. The reason for this *short-circuit evaluation rule* is that in some cases you may want to write a right-hand expression that will only be valid if the left-hand expression is true.
19. **++** is the increment operator, which adds 1 to the variable to which it is affixed. **+=** is the "add to variable" operator, which adds the value on its right to the variable on its left.
20. **-=** is the "subtract from variable" operator, which subtracts the value on its right from the variable on its left.
21. // is the comment operator; see *comment* for usage.
22. **||** is the "logical OR" operator. It produces the result true if at least one of the two expressions on its right and left is true; if both expressions are false, it produces the result false. However, there is a special rule in C++ governing the execution of the || operator : if the expression on the left is true, then the answer must be true and the expression on the right is not executed at all. The reason for this *short-circuit evaluation* rule is that in some cases you may want to write a right-hand expression that will only be valid if the left-hand expression is false.
23. A **#define** statement is a *preprocessor directive* that defines a *preprocessor symbol*. While this statement can be used to define constant values for general use, it has been mostly superseded except as part of the *include guard* mechanism.
24. An **#endif** statement is a *preprocessor directive* that terminates a section of conditional code. It is used in this book as part of the *include guard* mechanism.

25. An **#ifdef** statement is a *preprocessor directive* that begins a section of conditional code. It has the opposite effect from the *#ifndef* directive.

26. An **#ifndef** statement is a *preprocessor directive* that tells the preprocessor to check whether a particular *preprocessor symbol* has been defined. If not, the following source code is treated normally. However, if the specified preprocessor symbol has been defined, the following source code is skipped by the rest of the compiler as though it were not present in the source file. The #ifndef statement is used in this book as part of the *include guard* mechanism.

27. An **#include** statement is a *preprocessor directive* that has the same effect as that of copying all of the code from a specified file into another file at the point where the #include statement is written. For example, if we wanted to use definitions contained in a file called xstream.h in the implementation file test.cpp, we could insert the include statement #include "xstream.h" in test.cpp rather than physically copying the lines from the file xstream.h into test.cpp.

28. An **access specifier** controls the access of nonmember functions to the member functions and variables of a class. The C++ access specifiers are public, private, and protected. See *public, private,* and *protected* for details. Also see *friend.*

29. **Access time** is a measure of how long it takes to retrieve data from a storage device, such as a hard disk or RAM.

30. An **algorithm** is a set of precisely defined steps guaranteed to arrive at an answer to a problem or set of problems. As this implies, a set of steps that might never end is not an algorithm in the strictest sense.

31. **Aliasing** is the practice of referring to one object by more than one "name"; in C++, these names are actually *pointers* or *references.*

32. The **aliasing problem** is a name for the difficulties that are caused by altering a shared object.

33. An **application program** is a program that actually accomplishes some useful or interesting task. Examples include inventory control, payroll, and games.

34. An **application programmer** (or *class user*) is a programmer who uses native and class variables to write an application program. Also see *library designer.*

35. An **argument** is a value supplied by one function (the *calling function*) that wishes to make use of the services of another function (the *called function*). There are two main types of arguments : *value arguments,* which are copies of the values from the calling function, and *reference arguments,* which are not copies but actually refer to variables in the calling function.

36. An **argument list** is a set of argument definitions specified in a function declaration. The argument list describes the types and names of all the variables the function receives when it is called by a calling function.

37. An **array** is a group of elements of the same type - for example, an array of chars. The array name corresponds to the address of the first of these elements; the other elements follow the first one immediately in memory. As with a vector, we can refer to the individual elements by their indexes. Thus, if we have an array of chars called m_Data, m_Data[i] refers to the ith char in the array. Also see *pointer, vector.*

38. An **array initialization list** is a list of values used to initialize the elements of an *array*. The ability to specify a list of values for an array is built into the C++ language and is not available for user-defined data types such as the vector.
39. The **ASCII code** is a standardized representation of characters by binary or hexadecimal values. For example, the letter "A" is represented as a char with the hexadecimal value 41, and the digit 0 is represented as a char with the hexadecimal value 30. All other printable characters also have representations in the ASCII code.
40. An **assembler** is a program that translates *assembly language* instructions into *machine instructions*.
41. An **assembly language** instruction is the human-readable representation of a *machine instruction*.
42. **Assignment** is the operation of setting a variable to a value. The operator that indicates assignment is the equal sign, =. Also see *operator* = in the index.
43. An **assignment operator** is a function that sets a preexisting variable to a value of the same type. There are three varieties of assignment operators :
    (*a*) For a variable of a native type, the compiler supplies a *native* assignment operator.
    (*b*) For a variable of a class type, the compiler generates its own version of an assignment operator (a *compiler-generated* assignment operator) if the class writer does not write one.
    (*c*) The class writer can write a member function (a *user-defined* assignment operator) to do the assignment; see *operator* = in the index.
44. An **assignment statement** such as x = 5; is not an algebraic equality, no matter how much it may resemble one. It is a command telling the compiler to assign a value to a variable. In the example, the variable is x and the value is 5.
45. The **auto storage class** is the default *storage class* for variables declared within C++ functions. When we define a variable of the auto storage class, its memory address is assigned automatically upon entry to the function where it is defined; the memory address is valid for the duration of that function.
46. **Automatic conversion** is a feature of C++ that allows an expression of one type to be used where another type is expected. For example, a short variable or expression can be provided when an int expression is expected, and the compiler will convert the type of the expression automatically.
47. A **base class initializer** specifies which base class constructor we want to use to initialize the base class part of a derived class object. It is one of the two types of expressions allowed in a *member initialization list*. Also see *inheritance, constructor*.
48. The **base class part** of a derived class object is an unnamed component of the derived class object whose member variables and functions are accessible as though they were defined in the derived class, so long as they are either *public* or *protected*.
49. A **batch file** is a text file that directs the execution of a number of programs, one after the other, without manual intervention. A similar facility is available in most operating systems.
50. A **binary** number system uses only two digits, 0 and 1.

51. A **bit** is the fundamental unit of storage in a modern computer; the word *bit* is derived from the phrase *binary digit*. Each bit, as this suggests, can have one of two states : 0 and 1.

52. A **block** is a group of statements considered as one logical statement. It is delimited by the curly braces, {and}. The first of these symbols starts a block, and the second one ends it. A block can be used anywhere that a statement can be used and is treated exactly as if it were one statement. For example, if a block is the controlled block of an if statement, all of the statements in the block are executed if the condition in the if is true, and none is executed if the condition in the if is false.

53. A **bool** (short for Boolean) is a type of variable whose range of values is limited to true or false. This is the most appropriate return type for a function that uses its *return value* to report whether some condition exists, such as *operator* <. In that particular case, the return value true indicates that the first argument is less than the second, while false indicates that the first argument is not less than the second.

54. A **break statement** is a loop control device that interrupts the processing of a loop whenever it is executed within the controlled block of a loop control statement. When a break statement is executed, the flow of control passes to the next statement after the end of the controlled block.

55. A **buffer** is a temporary holding place where information is stored while it is being manipulated.

56. **Buffering** is the process of using a buffer to store or retrieve information.

57. A **byte** is the unit in which data capacities are stated, whether in RAM or on a disk. In most modern computers, a byte consists of eight bits.

58. A **C function** is one that is inherited from the *C library*. Because C does not have a number of features that have been added in C++, such as *function overloading* and *reference arguments*, C functions must often be called in different ways from those we use when calling a C++ function.

59. The **C standard library** is a part of the C++ standard library. It consists of a collection of functions that were originally written for users of the C programming language. Because C++ is a descendant of C, these functions are often still useful in C++ programs.

60. The **C++ standard library** is a collection of code defined by the ISO (International Standards Organization), that must be included with every standards-compliant compiler. Unfortunately, as of this writing, there are no completely standards-compliant compilers. The types defined in the standard library include the *vector* and *string* classes that we have used either directly or indirectly throughout this book, as well as hundreds of other very useful types and functions.

61. A **C string** is a sequence of characters referred to by a *char** pointer. Do not confuse this with the C++ *string class*.

62. A **C string literal** is a literal value representing a variable number of characters. An example is "This is a test.". C string literals are surrounded by double quotes ("). The name of this data type indicates its origin in C, which did not have a real string type such as the C++ string. While these two types have some similarities, they behave quite differently and should not be confused with one another.

63. A **cache** is a small amount of fast memory where frequently used data is stored temporarily.
64. **Call**; see *function call* or *call instruction*.
65. A **call instruction** is an *assembly language* instruction used to implement a *function call*. It saves the *program counter* on the stack and then transfers execution from the *calling function* to the *called function*.
66. A **called function** is a function that starts execution as the result of a *function call*. Normally, it returns to the *calling function* via a *return statement* when finished.
67. A **calling function** is a function that suspends execution as a result of a *function call*; the *called function* begins execution at the point of the function call.
68. The **carriage return** character is used to signal the end of a line of text. Also see *newline* in the index.
69. A function is said to be **case-sensitive** if upper- and lower-case letters are considered to be distinct.
70. A function is said to be **case-insensitive** if upper- and lower-case letters are considered equivalent. See *less_nocase* in the index.
71. To **catch** an *exception* means to handle an interruption in the normal flow control of a program, usually due to an error condition. An exception is generated via a *throw* statement, and can be caught in a function that has directly or indirectly called the function that threw the exception. The catch keyword is used in conjunction with *try*, which specifies a block of code to which a specific catch statement or statements may be applicable. A catch can specify the type of exceptions that it will handle, or can use "..." to specify that it will handle any and all exceptions.
72. A **char** is an *integer variable* type that can represent either one character of text or a small whole number. Both *signed* and *unsigned* chars are available for use as "really short" *integer variables*; a signed char can represent a number from -128 to +127, whereas an unsigned char can represent a number from 0 to 255. (In case you were wondering, the most common pronunciation of char has an "a" as in "married", while the "ch" sounds like "k". Other pronunciations include the standard English pronunciation of "char" as in overcooking meat, and even "car" as in "automobile".)
73. A **char*** (pronounced "char star") is a pointer to (*i.e.*, the memory address of) a char or the first of a group of chars.
74. **cin** (pronounced "see in") is a predefined *istream*; it gets its characters from the keyboard.
75. A **class** is a *user-defined* type; for example, std : :string is a class.
76. A **class designer** is a programmer who designs classes. Also see *application programmer*.
77. A **class implementation** tells the compiler how to implement the facilities defined in the *class interface*. It is usually found in an implementation file, which the compiler assumes has the extension .cpp.
78. A **class interface** tells the user of the class what facilities the class provides by specifying the class's public member functions. The class interface also tells the compiler what data elements are included in objects of the class, but this is not logically part of the interface. A class interface is usually found in a *header file* - that is, one with the extension .h.

79. The **class membership operator**, : :, indicates which class a function belongs to. For example, the full name of the default constructor for the string class is string : :string().
80. **class scope** describes the visibility of *member variables* - that is, those defined within a class. A variable with this scope can be accessed by any *member function* of its class; its accessibility to other functions is controlled by the *access specifier* in effect when it was defined in the *class interface*.
81. A **comment** is a note to yourself or another programmer; it is ignored by the compiler. The symbol // marks the beginning of a comment; the comment continues until the end of the line containing the //. For those of you with BASIC experience, this is just like REM (the "remark" keyword) - anything after it on a line is ignored by the compiler.
82. **Compilation** is the process of translating source code into an object program, which is composed of machine instructions along with the data needed by those instructions. Virtually all software is created by this process.
83. A **compiler** is a program that performs compilation.
84. A **compiler-generated function** is supplied by the compiler because the existence of that function is fundamental to the notion of a *concrete data type*. The compiler will automatically generate its own version of any of the following functions if they are not provided by the creator of the class : the *assignment operator*, the *copy constructor*, the *default constructor*, and the *destructor*.
85. A **compiler warning** is a message from the compiler informing the programmer of a potentially erroneous construct. While a warning does not prevent the compiler from generating an *executable program*, a wise programmer will heed such warnings, as they often reveal hazardous coding practices.
86. **Compile time** means "while the compiler is compiling the source code of a program".
87. **Concatenation** is the operation of appending a string to the end of another string. Also see *operator* + in the index.
88. A **concrete data type** is a class whose objects behave like variables of native data types. That is, the class gives the compiler enough information that objects of that class can be created, copied, assigned, and automatically destroyed at the end of their useful lifetimes, just as native variables are.
89. A **console mode program** is a program that looks like a DOS program rather than a Windows program.
90. The keyword **const** has two distinct meanings as employed in this book. The first is as a modifier to an argument of a function. In this context, it means that we are promising not to modify the value of that argument in the function. An example of this use might be the function declaration string& operator = (const string& Str);. The second use of const in this book is to define a data item similar to a variable, except that its value cannot be changed once it has been initialized. For this reason, it is mandatory to supply an initial value when creating a const. An example of this use is const short x = 5;.
91. A **constructor** is a *member function* that creates new objects of a (particular) class type. All constructors have the same name as that of the class for which they are constructors; for example, the constructors for the string class have the name string. A constructor that takes only one required argument is also a *conversion function*.

92. A **continuation expression** is the part of a for statement computed before every execution of the controlled block. The block controlled by the for will be executed if the result of the computation is true but not if it is false. See *for statement* for an example.
93. The **continue** keyword causes execution of a for loop to continue to the next iteration without executing any further statements in the current iteration.
94. A **controlled block** is a block under the control of a loop control statement or an if or else statement. The controlled block of a loop control statement can be executed a variable number of times, whereas the controlled block of an if or else statement is executed either once or not at all.
95. **Controlled statement**; see *controlled block.*
96. A **conversion function** is a *member function* that converts an object of its class to some other type, or vice versa. Also see *implicit conversion.*
97. A **copy constructor** makes a new object with the same contents as an existing object of the same type.
98. **cout** (pronounced "see out") is a predefined ostream; characters sent to it are displayed on the screen.
99. **CPU** is an abbreviation for Central Processing Unit. This is the "active" part of your computer, which executes all the *machine instructions* that make the computer do useful work.
100. The **curly braces** {and} are used to surround a *block.* The compiler treats the statements in the block as one statement.
101. A **cursor** is an abstract object that represents the position on the screen where input or output will occur next.
102. **Data** refers to the pieces of information that are operated on by programs. Originally, "data" was the plural of "datum"; however, the form "data" is now commonly used as both singular and plural.
103. A **day number** is an integer value representing the number of days between two dates.
104. A **debugger** is a program that controls the execution of another program so that you can see what the latter program is doing.
105. **Debugging** is the art of finding and eradicating errors (**bugs**) from your program. One of the best ways of debugging a program is to try to explain it to someone else in great detail. If you don't see your error, the other person almost certainly will!
106. A **dedicated register** is a register such as the *stack pointer* whose usage is predefined rather than determined by the programmer, as in the case of *general registers* such as eax.
107. A **default argument** is a method of specifying a value for an argument to a function when the user of the function doesn't supply a value for that argument. The value of the default argument is specified in the declaration of the function.
108. A **default constructor** is a *member function* that is used to create an object when no initial value is specified for that object. For example, string : :string() is the default constructor for the string class.
109. The **default** keyword is used with the switch statement to specify an action to be performed when none of the case statements match the selection expression of the switch.

110. The **delete** operator is used to free memory previously used for variables of the *dynamic storage class*. This allows the memory to be reused for other variables.

111. **Derived class** : see *inheritance*.

112. A **destructor** is a *member function* that cleans up when an object expires; for an object of the auto storage class, the destructor is called automatically at the end of the block where that object is defined.

113. A **digit** is one of the characters used in any positional numbering system to represent all numbers starting at 0 and ending at one less than the base of the numbering system. In the decimal system, there are ten digits, '0' through '9', and in the hexadecimal system, there are sixteen digits, '0' through 9 and 'a' through 'f'.

114. A **double** is a type of *floating-point variable* that can represent a range of positive and negative numbers, including fractional values. These numbers can vary from approximately 4.940656e - 324 to approximately 1.79769e + 308 (and 0), with approximately 16 digits of precision.

115. **Dynamic memory allocation** is the practice of assigning memory locations to variables during execution of the program by explicit request of the programmer.

116. Variables of the **dynamic storage class** are assigned memory addresses at the programmer's explicit request. This storage class is often used for variables whose size is not known until run time.

117. **Dynamic type checking** refers to checking the correct usage of variables of different types during execution of a program rather than during compilation.

118. **Dynamic typing** means delaying the determination of the exact type of a *variable* until *run time* rather than fixing that type at *compile time*, as in *static typing*. Please note that dynamic typing is not the same as *dynamic type checking*; C++ has the former but not the latter.

119. An **element** is one of the variables that make up a *vector* or an *array*.

120. The keyword **else** causes its *controlled block* to be executed if the condition in its matching *if* statement turns out to be false at run time.

121. An **empty stack** is a stack that currently contains no values.

122. **Encapsulation** means hiding the details of a class inside the *implementation* of that class rather than exposing them in the *interface*. This is one of the primary organizing principles of *object-oriented programming*.

123. An **end user** is the person who actually uses an application program to perform some useful or interesting task. Also see *application programmer, library designer*.

124. The Enter key is the key that generates a *newline* character, which tells an *input* routine that the user has finished entering data.

125. **Envelope** class; see *manager/worker idiom*.

126. An **enum** is a way to define a number of unchangeable values, which are quite similar to *consts*. The value of each successive name in an enum is automatically incremented from the value of the previous name (if you don't specify another value explicitly). The term enum is short for "enumeration", which is a list of named items.

127. An **exception** is an interruption in the normal flow of control in a program. When a function encounters an error condition, it can "throw an exception" to notify any

calling function that wishes to handle this problem that it has occurred. If none of the calling functions handles the exception via a *catch* statement, the program will terminate.

128. Executable; see *executable program.*

129. An **executable program** is a program in a form suitable for running on a computer; it is composed of *machine instructions* along with data needed by those instructions.

130. The **explicit** keyword tells the compiler not to call a specified constructor unless that constructor has been called explicitly. This prevents such a constructor from being called to perform an *implicit conversion.*

131. The keyword **false** is a predefined value representing the result of a conditional expression whose condition is not satisfied. For example, in the conditional expression x < y, if x is not less than y, the result of the expression will be false.

132. A **fencepost error** is a logical error that causes a loop to be executed one more or one fewer time than the correct count. A common cause of this error is confusing the number of elements in a *vector* or *array* with the index of the last element. The derivation of this term is by analogy with the problem of calculating the number of fence sections and fenceposts that you need for a given fence. For example, if you have to put up a fence 100 feet long and each section of the fence is 10 feet long, how many sections of fence do you need ? Obviously, the answer is 10. Now, how many fenceposts do you need ? 11. The confusion caused by counting fenceposts when you should be counting segments of fence (and vice versa) is the cause of a fencepost error. To return to a programming example, if you have a vector with 11 elements, the index of the last element is 10, not 11. Confusing the number of elements with the highest index has much the same effect as that of the fencepost problem. This sort of problem is also known, less colorfully, as an *off-by-one error.*

133. Field; see *manipulator.*

134(*a*). A **float** is a type of *floating-point variable* that can represent a range of positive and negative numbers, including fractional values. These numbers can vary from approximately 1.401298e - 45 to approximately 3.40282e + 38 (and 0), with approximately 6 digits of precision.

134(*b*). A **floating-point variable** is a C++ approximation of a mathematical "real number". Unlike mathematical real numbers, C++ floating-point variables have a limited range and precision depending on their types. See the individual types *float* and *double* for details.

135. A **for** statement is a *loop control statement* that causes its *controlled block* to be executed while a specified logical expression (the *continuation expression*) is true. It also provides for a *starting expression* to be executed before the first execution of the controlled block and for a *modification expression* to be executed after every execution of the controlled block. For example, in the for statement for (i = 0; i < 10; i ++), the initialization expression is i = 0, the continuation expression is i < 10, and the modification expression is i ++.

136. A **form-feed** character, when sent to a printer, causes the paper to be advanced to a new page.

137. The **free store** is the area of memory where variables of the *dynamic storage class* store their data.

138. The keyword **friend** allows access by a specified *class* or *function* to *private* or *protected* members of a particular class.

139. A **function** is a section of code having a name, optional *arguments*, and a *return type*. The name makes it possible for one function to start execution of another one via a *function call*. The arguments provide input for the function, and the return type allows the function to provide output to its *calling function* when the return statement causes the *calling function* to resume execution.

140. A **function call** (or *call* for short) causes execution to be transferred temporarily from the current function (the *calling function*) to the one named in the function call (the *called function*). Normally, when a called function is finished with its task, it returns to the calling function, which picks up execution at the statement after the function call.

141. A **function declaration** tells the compiler some vital statistics of the function : its name, its *arguments*, and its *return type*. Before we can use a function, the compiler must have already seen its function declaration. The most common way to arrange for this is to use a *#include* statement to insert the function declaration from a *header file* into an *implementation file*.

142. **Function header**; see *function declaration*.

143. **Function overloading** is the C++ facility that allows us to create more than one function with the same name. So long as all such functions have different *signatures*, we can write as many of them as we wish and the compiler will be able to figure out which one we mean.

144. A **general register** is a register whose usage is determined by the programmer, not predefined as with dedicated registers such as the *stack pointer*. On an Intel CPU such as the 486 or Pentium, the 16-bit general registers are **ax, bx, cx, dx, si, di,** and **bp**; the 32-bit general registers are **eax, ebx, ecx, edx, esi, edi,** and **ebp**.

145. A **get pointer** holds the address of the next byte in the input area of an *istream* - that is, where the next byte will be retrieved if we use >> to read data from the stream.

146. **Global scope** describes the visibility of variables defined outside any function; such variables can be accessed by code in any function. It also describes the visibility of functions defined outside any class.

147. The **global namespace** is a name for the set of identifiers visible to all functions without a class or namespace name being specified. Adding identifiers to the global namespace should be avoided when possible, as such identifiers can conflict with other similar identifiers defined by other programmers.

148. A **global function** is a function that has *global scope*.

149. A **global variable** is a variable that has *global scope*.

150. **Hardware** refers to the physical components of a computer - the ones you can touch. Examples include the keyboard, the monitor, and the printer.

151. A **header file** is a file that contains *class interface* definitions and/or *global* function declarations. By convention, header files have the extension .h.

152. **Hex** is a shortened form of hexadecimal.

153. A **hexadecimal** number system has sixteen digits, '0' through '9' and 'a' through 'f'.

154. An **identifier** is a user-defined name; both function names and variable names are identifiers. Identifiers must not conflict with keywords such as if and for; for example, you cannot create a function or a variable with the name for.
155. An **if** statement is a statement that causes its *controlled block* to be executed if the logical expression specified in the if statement is true.
156. An **ifstream** (pronounced "i f stream") is a *stream* used for input from a file.
157. **Implementation**; see *class implementation*.
158. An **implementation file** contains *source code statements* that are turned into *executable code* by a *compiler*. In this book, implementation files have the extension .cpp.
159. An **implicit conversion** is one that occurs without the programmer's explicit request. Also see *explicit*.
160. **Include**; see #include statement.
161. An **include guard** is a mechanism used to prevent the same class definition from being included in the same source code file more than once.
162. To **increment** a variable means to add 1 to its value. This can be done in C++ by using the increment operator, ++.
163. An **index** is an expression used to select one of a number of elements of a *vector* or an *array*. It is enclosed in square brackets ([ ]). For example, in the expression a[i+1], the index is the expression i+1.
164. An **index variable** is a variable used to hold an index into a *vector* or an *array*.
165. **Inheritance** is the definition of one class as a more specific version of another previously defined class. The newly defined class is called the *derived* (or sometimes the child) class, while the previously defined class is called the *base* (or sometimes the parent) class. In this book, we use the terms *base* and *derived*. The derived class inherits all of the *member variables* and *regular member functions* from the base class. Inheritance is one of the primary organizing principles of *object-oriented programming*.
166. **Initialization** is the process of setting the initial value of a *variable* or *const*. It is very similar to *assignment* but not identical. Initialization is done only when a variable or const is created, whereas a variable can be assigned to as many times as desired. A const, however, cannot be assigned to at all, so it must be initialized when it is created.
167. **Input** is the process of reading data into the computer from the outside world. A very commonly used source of input for simple programs is the keyboard.
168. **Instruction**; see *machine instruction*.
169. An **int** (short for *integer*) is a type of *integer variable*. While the C++ language definition requires only that an int be at least as long as a short and no longer than a long, with most current C++ compilers this type is equivalent to either a short or a long, depending on the compiler you are using. A 16-bit compiler, such as Borland C++ 3.1, has 16-bit (2-byte) ints that are the same size as shorts.
170. An **integer variable** is a C++ representation of a whole number. Unlike mathematical integers, C++ integers have a limited range, which varies depending on their types. See the individual types char, short, int, and long for details. The type bool is sometimes also considered an integer variable type.
171. **Integral type** : see *integer variable*.

172. **Interface**; see *class interface*.

173. **Interface file**; see *header file*.

174. **Internal polymorphism**; see *polymorphic object*.

175. **I/O** is an abbreviation for "input/output". This refers to the process of getting information into and out of the computer. See *input* and *output* for more details.

176. **Iostream** is the name of the *header file* that tells the compiler how to compile code that uses predefined stream variables like cout and cin and operators like << and >>.

177. An object of a *derived class* is said to have an "**isA**" relationship with its *base class* if the derived class object can properly be substituted for a base class object. In C++, objects of publicly derived classes should have this relationship with their base classes.

178. An **istream** is a *stream* used for input. For example, cin is a predefined istream that reads characters from the keyboard.

179. A **keyword** is a word defined in the C++ language, such as if and for. It is illegal to define an *identifier* such as a variable or function name that conflicts with a keyword; for example, you cannot create a function or a variable with the name for.

180. A **library** (or library module) contains the object code generated from several *implementation files*, in a form that the *linker* can search when it needs to find general-purpose functions.

181. A **library designer** is a programmer who creates classes for *application programmers* to use in writing application programs.

182. The **linker** is a program that combines information from all of the *object files* for our program, along with some previously prepared files called *libraries*, to produce an *executable program*.

183. **Linking** is the process of creating an executable program from *object files* and *libraries*.

184. A **literal value** is a value that doesn't have a name, but instead represents itself in a literal manner. Some examples are 'x' (a char literal having the ASCII value that represents the letter "x") and 5 (a numeric literal with the value 5).

185. **Local scope** describes the visibility of variables defined within a function; such variables can be accessed only by code in that function.

186. A **local variable** is a variable that has *local scope*.

187. A **logical expression** is an expression that takes on the value true or false rather than a numeric value. Some examples of such an expression are x > y (which will be true if x has a greater value than y and false otherwise) and a == b (which will be true if a has the same value as b, and false otherwise). Also see *bool*.

188. A **long** is a type of *integer variable* that can represent a whole number. With most current C++ compilers, a long occupies 4 bytes of storage and therefore can represent a number in either the range -2147483648 to 2147483647 (if signed) or the range 0 to 4294967295 (if unsigned).

189. A **loop** is a means of executing a *controlled block* a variable number of times depending on some condition. The statement that controls the controlled block is called a loop control statement. This book covers the while and for loop control statements. See *while* and *for* for details.

190. A **loop control statement** is a statement that controls the *controlled block* in a loop.

191. **Machine code** is the combination of *machine instructions* and the data they use. A synonym is *object code.*

192. A **machine instruction** is one of the fundamental operations that a *CPU* can perform. Some examples of these operations are addition, subtraction, or other arithmetic operations; other possibilities include operations that control what instruction will be executed next. All C++ programs must be converted into machine instructions before they can be executed by the CPU.

193. A **machine language program** is a program composed of *machine instructions.*

194. A **magic number** is a number that does not have any obvious relationship to the rest of the code. A good general rule is that numbers other than 0, 1, or other self-evident values should be defined as const or enum values rather than as literal values such as '7'.

195. **Manager object**; see *manager/worker idiom, polymorphic objects.*

196. The **manager/worker idiom** (also known as the "envelope/letter idiom") is a mechanism that allows the effective type of an object to be determined at run time without requiring the user of the object to be concerned with pointers. It is used to implement *polymorphic objects* in C++.

197. A **manipulator** is a member function of one of the iostream classes that controls how output will be formatted without necessarily producing any output of its own. Manipulators operate on *fields*; a field can be defined as the result of one << operator.

198. A **member function** is a function defined in a *class interface.* It is viewed as "belonging" to the class, which is the reason for the adjective "member".

199. A **member initialization expression** is the preferred method of specifying how a *member variable* is to be initialized in a *constructor.* Also see *inheritance.*

200. A **member initialization list** specifies how *member variables* are to be initialized in a *constructor.* It includes two types of expressions : *base class initializers* and *member initialization expressions.* Also see *inheritance.*

201. A **member variable** is a variable defined in a *class interface.* It is viewed as "belonging" to the class, which is the reason for the adjective "member".

202. **Memberwise copy** means to copy every *member variable* from the source object to the destination object. If we don't define our own *copy constructor* or *assignment operator* for a particular class, the *compiler-generated* versions will use memberwise copy.

203. A **memory address** is a unique number identifying a particular byte of *RAM.*

204. A **memory hierarchy** is the particular arrangement of the different kinds of storage devices in a given computer. The purpose of using storage devices having different performance characteristics is to provide the best overall performance at the lowest cost.

205. A **memory leak** is a programming error in which the programmer forgot to delete something that had been dynamically allocated. Such an error is very insidious because the program appears to work correctly when tested casually. When such errors exist in a program, they are usually found only after the program runs apparently correctly for a (possibly long) time and then fails because it runs out of available memory.

206. A **modification expression** is the part of a for statement executed after every execution of the *controlled block*. It is often used to increment an *index variable* to refer to the next element of an *array* or vector; see *for statement* for an example.

207. **Modulus operator**; see %.

208. A **month number** is an integer value representing the number of months between two dates.

209. A **nanosecond** is one-billionth of a second.

210. A **native data type** is one defined in the C++ language, as opposed to a *user-defined data type* (class).

211. The **new operator** is used to allocate memory for variables of the *dynamic storage class*; these are usually variables whose storage requirements aren't known until the program is executing.

212. The **newline** character is the C++ character used to indicate the end of a line of text.

213. **Nondisplay character**; see *nonprinting character*.

214. A **nonmember function** is one that is not a member of a particular class being discussed, although it may be a *member function* of another class.

215. A **nonnumeric variable** is a variable that is not used in calculations like adding, multiplying, or subtracting. Such variables might represent names, addresses, telephone numbers, Social Security numbers, bank account numbers, or driver's license numbers. Note that even a data item referred to as a number and composed entirely of the digits 0 through 9 may be a nonnumeric variable by this definition; the question is how the item is used. No one adds, multiplies, or subtracts driver's license numbers, for example; these numbers serve solely as identifiers and could just as easily have letters in them, as indeed some of them do.

216. A **nonprinting character** is used to control the format of our displayed or printed information, rather than to represent a particular letter, digit, or other special character. The *space* is one of the more important nonprinting characters.

217. A **non-virtual** function is one that is not declared with the virtual keyword either in the class in question or any base class of that class. This means that the compiler can decide at compile time the exact version of the function to be executed when it is referred to via a *base class pointer* or *base class reference*.

218. A **normal constructor** is a *constructor* whose arguments supply enough information to initialize all of the member fields in the object being created.

219. A **null byte** is a byte with the value 0, commonly used to indicate the end of a *C string*. Note that this is not the same as the character "0", which is a normal printable character having the ASCII code 48.

220. A **null object** is an object of some (specified) class whose purpose is to indicate that a "real" object of that class does not exist. It is analogous to a *null pointer*. One common use for a null object is as a *return value* from a *member function* that is supposed to return an object with some specified properties but cannot find such an object. For example, a null StockItem object might be used to indicate that an item with a specified UPC cannot be found in the inventory of a store.

221. A **null pointer** is a *pointer* with the value 0. This value is particularly suited to indicate that a pointer isn't pointing to anything at the moment, because of some special treatment of zero-valued pointers built into the C++ language.

222. A **null string** is a string or *C string* with the value "".

223. A **numeric digit** is one of the digits 0 through 9.

224. A **numeric variable** is a variable that represents a quantity that can be expressed as a number, whether a whole number (an *integer variable*) or a number with a fractional part (a *floating-point variable*), and that can be used in calculations such as addition, subtraction, multiplication, or division. The integer variable types in C++ are char, short, int, and long. Each of these can be further subdivided into signed and unsigned versions. The signed versions can represent both negative and positive values (and 0), whereas the unsigned versions can represent only positive values (and 0) but provide greater ranges of positive values than the corresponding signed versions do. The floating-point variable types are float and double, which differ in their range and precision. Unlike the integer variable types, the floating-point types are not divided into signed and unsigned versions; all floating-point variables can represent either positive or negative numbers as well as 0. See *float* and *double* for details on range and precision.

225. An **object** is a variable of a class type, as distinct from a variable of a *native type*. The behavior of an object is defined by the code that implements the class to which the object belongs. For example, a variable of type string is an object whose behavior is controlled by the definition of the string class.

226. **Object code**; see *machine code*. This term is unrelated to C++ objects.

227. An **object code module** is the result of compiling an *implementation file* into *object code*. A number of object code modules are combined to form an *executable program*. This term is unrelated to C++ objects.

228. **Object file**; see *object code module*. This term is unrelated to C++ *objects*.

229. **Object-oriented programming**, in a broad sense, is an approach to solving programming problems by creating *objects* to represent the entities being handled by the program, rather than by relying solely on *native data types*. This has the advantage that you can match the language to the needs of the problem you're trying to solve. For example, if you were writing a nurse's station program in C++, you would have objects that represent nurses, doctors, patients, various sorts of equipment, and so on. Each of these objects would display the behavior appropriate to the thing or person it represents.

     In a more specific sense, object-oriented programming is the use of *encapsulation*, *inheritance*, and *polymorphism* to organize programs.

230. **Off-by-one error**; see *fencepost error*.

231. An **ofstream** (pronounced "o f stream") is a *stream* used for output to a file.

232. An **op code** is the part of a *machine instruction* that tells the *CPU* what kind of instruction it is and sometimes also specifies a *register* to be operated on.

233. An **operating system** is a program that deals with the actual *hardware* of your computer. It supplies the lowest level of the software infrastructure needed to run a program. The most common operating system for Intel CPUs, at present, is some form of Windows, followed by Linux.

234. The keyword **operator** is used to indicate that the following symbol is the name of a C++ operator we are *overloading* to handle the particular requirements of a specific class. For example, to define our own version of =, we have to specify operator = as the name of the function we are writing, rather than just =, so that the compiler does not object to seeing an operator when it expects an identifier.

235. An **ostream** is a *stream* used for *output*. For example, cout is a predefined ostream that displays characters on the screen.

236. **Output** is the process of sending data from the computer to the outside world. The most commonly used destination of output for most programs is the screen.

237. A member function in a derived class is said to **override** the base class *member function* if the derived class function has the same *signature* (name and argument types) as that of the base class member function. The derived class member function will be called instead of the base class member function when the member function is referred to via an object of the derived class. A member function in a derived class with the same name but a different signature from that of a member function in the base class does not override the base class member function. Instead, it "hides" that base class member function, which is no longer accessible as a member function in the derived class.

238. **Overloading** a function means to create several functions with the same name and different argument lists. The compiler will pick the function to be executed based on the match between the function call and the available argument lists.

239. **Parent class**; see *inheritance*.

240. A **pointer** is essentially the same as a *memory address*. The main difference is that a memory address is "untyped" (*i.e.*, it can refer to any sort of variable) whereas a pointer always has an associated data type. For example, char* (pronounced "char star") means "pointer to a char". To say "a variable points to a memory location" is almost the same as saying "a variable's value is the address of a memory location". In the specific case of a variable of type char*, to say "the char* x points to a *C string*" is essentially equivalent to saying "x contains the address of the first byte of the C string". Also see *array*.

241. A **polymorphic object** is a C++ *object* that behaves polymorphically without exposing the user of the object to the hazards of pointers. The user does not have to know any of the details of the implementation, but merely instantiates an object of the single visible class (the *manager class*). That object does what the user wants with the help of an object of a *worker class*, which is derived from the manager class. Also see *manager/worker idiom*.

242. **Polymorphism** is the major organizing principle in C++ that allows us to implement several classes with the same interface and to treat objects of all these classes as though they were of the same class. Polymorphism is a variety of *dynamic typing* that maintains the safety factor of *static type checking*, because the compiler can determine at compile time whether a function call is legal even if it does not know the exact type of the object that will receive that function call at run time. "Polymorphism" is derived from the Greek *poly*, meaning "many", and *morph*, meaning "form". In other words, the same behavior is implemented in different forms.

243. To **pop** is to remove the top value from a stack.

244. The **preprocessor** is a part of the C++ compiler that deals with the source code of a program before the rest of the compiler ever sees that source code.

245. A **preprocessor directive** is a command telling the preprocessor to handle the following source code in a special manner.

246. A **preprocessor symbol** is a constant value similar to a const, but it is known only to the preprocessor, not to the rest of the compiler. The rules for naming preprocessor symbols are the same as those for other identifiers, but it is customary to use all upper-case letters in preprocessor symbols so that they can be readily distinguished from other identifiers.

247. The keyword **private** is an *access specifier* that denies *nonmember functions* access to *member functions* and *member variables* of its class.

248. Creating a class via **private inheritance** means that we are not going to allow outside functions to treat an object of the derived class as an object of the base class. That is, functions that take a base class object as a parameter will not accept a derived class object in its place. None of the public *member functions* and public data items (if there are any) in the base class will be accessible to the outside world via a privately derived class object. Contrast with *public inheritance*.

249. A **program** is a set of instructions specifying the solution to a set of problems, along with the data used by those instructions.

250. The **program counter** is a *dedicated register* that holds the address of the next instruction to be executed. During a *function call*, a *call instruction* pushes the contents of the program counter on the stack. This enables the *called function* to return to the *calling function* when finished.

251. **Program failure** can be defined as a situation in which a program does not behave as intended. The causes of this are legion, ranging from incorrect input data to improper specification of the problem to be solved.

252. **Program maintenance** is the process of updating and correcting a program once it has entered service.

253. **Programming** is the art and science of solving problems by the following procedure :

1. Find or invent a general solution to a set of problems.
2. Express this solution as an algorithm or set of algorithms.
3. Translate the algorithm(s) into terms so simple that a stupid machine like a computer can follow them to calculate the specific answer for any specific problem in the set.

Warning : This definition may be somewhat misleading, since it implies that the development of a program is straightforward and linear, with no revision. This is known as the "waterfall model" of programming, since water going over a waterfall follows a preordained course in one direction. However, real-life programming doesn't usually work this way; rather, most programs are written in an incremental process as assumptions are changed and errors are found and corrected.

254. The keyword **protected** is an *access specifier*. When present in a *base class* definition, it allows *derived class* functions access to member variables and functions in the *base class part* of a derived class object, while preventing access by other functions outside the base class.

255. The keyword **public** is an *access specifier* that allows *nonmember functions* access to *member functions* and *member variables* of its class.

256. Creating a class via **public inheritance** means that we are going to let outside functions treat an object of the derived class as an object of the base class. That is, any function that takes a base class object as a parameter will accept a derived class object in its place. All of the public *member functions* and public data items (if there are any) in the base class are accessible to the outside world via a derived class object as well. Contrast with *private inheritance*.

257. **Push** means to add another value to a stack.

258. A **put pointer** holds the address of the next byte in the output area of an *ostream* - that is, where the next byte will be stored if we use << to write data into the stream.

259. **RAM** is an acronym for Random Access Memory. This is the working storage of a computer, where data and programs are stored while we're using them.

260. **Recursion** : see *recursion.*

261. A **reference** is an identifier that acts as another name for an existing variable rather than as an independent variable. Changing a reference therefore affects the corresponding variable. In this book, we use references only for passing arguments to functions.

262. A **reference argument** is another name for a variable from a *calling function* rather than an independent variable in the *called function*. Changing a reference argument therefore affects the corresponding variable in the calling function. Compare with *value argument*.

263. The **reference-counting idiom** is a mechanism that allows one object (the "reference-counted object") to be shared by several other objects (the "client objects") rather than requiring a separate copy for each of the client objects.

264. A **register** is a storage area that is on the same chip as the *CPU* itself. Programs use registers to hold data items that are actively in use; data in registers can be accessed within the time allocated to instruction execution rather than the much longer times needed to access data in *RAM*.

265. **Regression testing** means running a modified program and verifying whether previously working functionality is still working.

266. A **regular member function** is any member function that is not in any of the following categories :

1. constructor,
2. destructor,
3. the assignment operator, operator =.

267. A *derived class* inherits all regular member functions from its *base class*.

268. A **retrieval function** is a function that retrieves data that may have been previously stored by a **storage function** or that may be generated when needed by some other method such as calculation according to a formula.

269. A **return address** is the *memory address* of the next *machine instruction* in a *calling function*. It is used during execution of a *return statement* in a *called function* to transfer execution back to the correct place in the calling function.

270. A **return statement** is used by a *called function* to transfer execution back to the *calling function*. The return statement can also specify a value of the correct *return type* for the called function. This value is made available to the calling function to be used for further calculation. An example of a return statement is return 0;, which returns the value 0 to the calling function.

271. A **return type** tells the compiler what sort of data a *called function* returns to the calling function when the *called function* finishes executing. The return value from main is a special case; it can be used to determine what action a *batch file* should take next.

272. A **return value** is the value returned from a *called function* to its *calling function*.

ROM is an abbreviation for *Read-Only Memory*. This is the permanent internal storage of a computer, where the programs needed to start up the computer are stored. As this suggests, ROM does not lose its contents when the power is turned off, as contrasted with RAM.

273. **Run time** means "while a (previously compiled) program is being executed".

274. The **run-time type** of a variable is the type that variable has when the program is being executed. In the presence of *polymorphism*, this type may differ from the type with which the variable was declared at *compile time*.

275. A **scalar variable** has a single value (at any one time); this is contrasted with a vector or an *array*, which contains a number of values, each of which is referred to by its *index*.

276. The **scope** of a variable is the part of the program in which the variable can be accessed. The scopes with which we are concerned are local, global, and class; see *local scope*, *global scope*, and *class scope* for more details.

277. A **selection expression** is the part of a switch statement that specifies an expression used to select an alternative section of code.

278. A **selection sort** is a sorting algorithm that selects the highest (or lowest) element from a set of elements (the "input list") and moves that selected element to another set of elements (the "output list"); the next highest (or lowest) element is then treated in the same manner. This operation is repeated until as many elements as desired have been moved to the output list.

279. A **short** is a type of *integer variable* that can represent a whole number. With most current C++ compilers, a short occupies 2 bytes of storage and therefore can represent a number in either the range -32768 to 32767 (if signed) or the range 0 to 65535 (if unsigned).

280. The **short-circuit evaluation rule** governs the execution of the || and && operators. See || and && for details.

281. A **side effect** is any result of calling a function that persists beyond the execution of that function other than its returning a *return value*. For example, writing data to a file is a side effect.

282. The **signature** of a function consists of its name and the types of its *arguments*. In the case of a *member function*, the class to which the function belongs is also part of its signature. Every function is uniquely identified by its signature, which is what makes it possible to have more than one function with the same name. This is called *function overloading*.

283. A **signed char** is a type of *integer variable*. See char for details.

284. A **signed int** is a type of *integer variable*. See int for details.

285. A **signed long** is a type of *integer variable*. See long for details.

286. A **signed short** is a type of *integer variable*. See short for details.

287. A **signed variable** can represent either negative or positive values. See char, short, int, or long for details.

288. **Slicing** is the partial assignment that occurs when a derived class object is assigned to a base class variable. This term is used because in such an assignment only the base class part of the derived class object is assigned while the other fields are "sliced off".

289. **Software** refers to the nonphysical components of a computer, the ones you cannot touch. If you can install it on your hard disk, it's software. Examples include a spreadsheet, a word processor, and a database program.

290. **Source code** is a program in a form suitable for reading and writing by a human being.

291. **Source code file**; see *implementation file*.

292. **Source code module**; see *implementation file*.

293. The **space character** is one of the *nonprinting characters* (or nondisplay characters) that control the format of displayed or printed information.

294. **Special constructor**; a constructor used in the implementation of a *polymorphic object* to prevent an infinite *recursion* during construction of that object.

295. The **square brackets**, [and], are used to enclose an *array* or *vector index*, which selects an individual element of the array or vector. Also see [ ].

296. A **stack** is a data structure with characteristics similar to those of a spring-loaded plate holder such as you might see in a cafeteria. The last plate deposited on the stack of plates will be the first one removed when a customer needs a fresh plate; similarly, the last value deposited (pushed) onto a stack is the first value retrieved (popped).

297. The **stack pointer** is a *dedicated register*. It is used to keep track of the address of the most recently pushed value on the stack.

298. **Standard library** : See *C++ standard library, C standard library*.

299. A **starting expression** is the part of a for statement that is executed once before the *controlled block* of the for statement is first executed. It is often used to initialize an *index variable* to 0 so that the index variable can be used to refer to the first element of an array or vector. See *for statement* for an example.

300. A **statement** is a complete operation understood by the C++ compiler. Each statement ends with a semicolon (;).

301. A **static member function** is a *member function* of a class that can be called without reference to an object of that class. Such a function has no *this pointer* passed to it on entry and therefore cannot refer to normal (non-static) member variables of the class.

302. A **static member variable** is a *member variable* of a class that is shared among all objects of that class. This is distinct from the treatment of the normal (non-static) member variables of the class. Each object of a class has its own set of normal member variables.

303. The **static storage class** is the simplest of the three *storage classes* in C++; variables of this storage class are assigned memory addresses in the *executable program* when the program is *linked*. This use of the term "static" is distinct from but related to the keyword static.

304. **Static type checking** refers to the practice of checking the correct usage of variables of different types during compilation of a program rather than during execution. C++ uses static type checking. See *type system* for further discussion. Note that this has no particular relation to the keyword static.

305. **Static typing** means determining the exact type of a variable when the program is compiled. It is the default typing mechanism in C++. Note that this has no particular relation to the keyword static, nor is it exactly the same as static type checking. See *type system* for further discussion.

306. **std : :** is the name of the standard C++ library namespace. This namespace contains the names of all of the functions and variables declared in the standard library.

307. **Stepwise refinement** is the process of developing an algorithm by starting out with a "coarse" solution and "refining" it until the steps are within the capability of the programming language you are using to write a program.

308. **Storage**; synonym for *memory*.

309. A **storage class** is the characteristic of a variable that determines how and when a memory address is assigned to that variable. C++ has three storage classes : static, auto, and dynamic. Please note that the term *storage class* has nothing to do with the C++ term class. See *static storage class*, *auto storage class*, and *dynamic storage class* for more details.

310. A **storage function** is a function that stores data for later retrieval by a *retrieval function*.

311. A **stream** is a place to put (in the case of an ostream) or get (in the case of an istream) characters. Two predefined streams are *cin* and *cout*.

312. A **stream buffer** is the area of memory where the characters put into a stream are stored.

313. The **string class** defines a type of object that contains a group of chars; the chars in a string can be treated as one unit for purposes of assignment, I/O, and comparison.

314. A **stringstream** is a type of *stream* that exists only in memory rather than being attached to an input or output device. It is often used for formatting of data that is to be further manipulated within the program.

315. The **switch** statement is effectively equivalent to a number of if/else statements in a row, but is easier to read and modify. The keyword switch is followed by a *selection expression* (in parentheses), which specifies an expression that is used to select an alternative section of code. The various alternatives to be considered are enclosed in a set of curly braces following the selection expression. Each alternative is marked off by the keyword case followed by the (constant) value to be matched and a colon.

316. **Temporary**; see *temporary variable*.

317. A **temporary variable** is automatically created by the *compiler* for use during a particular operation, such as a *function call* with an *argument* that has to be converted to a different type.

318. The keyword **this** represents a hidden argument automatically supplied by the compiler in every (non-static) *member function* call. Its value during the execution of any member function is the address of the class object for which the member function call was made.

319. To **throw** an *exception* means to cause an interruption in the normal flow control of a program, usually due to an error condition. An exception can be handled via a ***catch*** statement in a function that directly or indirectly called the function that threw the exception.

320. A **token** is a part of a program that the compiler treats as a separate unit. It's analogous to a word in English, while a *statement* is more like a sentence. For example, string is a token, as are : : and (, whereas x = 5; is a statement.

321. The keyword **true** is a predefined value representing the result of a conditional expression whose condition is satisfied. For example, in the conditional expression x < y, if x is less than y, the result of the expression will be true.

322. The keyword **try** is used to control a block from which an *exception* may be generated. If an exception occurs during execution of that block or any functions within that block, the following *catch* statement will be invited to handle the exception, assuming that the specification of the catch statement indicates that it is willing to handle such an exception.

323. The **type** of an *object* is the class to which it belongs. The type of a *native variable* is one of the predefined variable types in C++. See *integer variable, floating-point variable,* and *bool* for details on the native types.

324. The **type system** refers to the set of rules the language uses to decide how a variable of a given type may be employed. In C++, these determinations are made by the compiler (*static type checking*). This makes it easier to prevent type errors than it is in languages where type checking is done during execution of the program (*dynamic type checking*). Please note that C++ has both static type checking and *dynamic typing*. This is possible because the set of types that is acceptable in any given situation can be determined at *compile time*, even though the exact type of a given variable may not be known until *run time*.

325. An **uninitialized variable** is one that has never been set to a known value. Attempting to use such a variable is a logical error that can cause a program to act very oddly.

326. An **unqualified name** is a reference to a *member variable* that doesn't specify which object the member variable belongs to. When we use an unqualified name in a *member function*, the *compiler* assumes that the object we are referring to is the object for which that member function has been called.

327. An **unsigned char** is a type of *integer variable.* See *char* for details.

328. An **unsigned int** is a type of *integer variable.* See *int* for details.

329. An **unsigned long** is a type of *integer variable.* See *long* for details.

330. An **unsigned short** is a type of *integer variable.* See *short* for details.

331. An **unsigned** variable is an *integer variable* that represents only positive values (and 0). See *char, short, int,* and *long* for details.

332. The term **user** has several meanings in programming. The primary usage in this book is *application programmer*; however, it can also mean *library designer* (in the phrase *user-defined data type*) or even *end user*.

333. A **user-defined data type** is one that is defined by the user. In this context, user means "someone using language facilities to extend the range of variable types in the language", or *library designer*. The primary mechanism for defining a user-defined type is the *class*.

334. A **using declaration** tells the compiler to import one or more names from a particular namespace into the current namespace. This allows the use of such names without having to explicitly specify the namespace from which they come.

335. A **value argument** is a variable of *local scope* created when a *function* begins execution. Its initial value is set to the value of the corresponding *argument* in the *calling function*. Changing a value argument does not affect any variable in the calling function. Compare with *reference argument*.

336. A **variable** is a programming construct that uses a certain part of *RAM* to represent a specific item of data we wish to keep track of in a program. Some examples are the weight of a pumpkin or the number of cartons of milk in the inventory of a store.

337. A **vector** is a group of variables, each of which can be addressed by its position in the group; each of these variables is called an *element*. A vector has a name, just as a regular variable does, but the elements do not. Instead, each element has an *index* that represents its position in the vector.

338. A **Vec** is exactly like a vector except that it checks the validity of the index of an element before allowing access to that element.

339. Declaring a function to be **virtual** means that it is a member of a set of functions having the same *signatures* and belonging to classes related by *inheritance*. The actual function to be executed as the result of a given function call is selected from this set of functions dynamically (*i.e.*, at run time) based on the actual type of an object referred to via a base class pointer (or base class reference). This is the C++ *dynamic typing* mechanism used to implement polymorphism, in contrast to the *static typing* used for non-virtual functions, where the exact function to be called can be determined at compile time.

340. A **void return type specifier** in a *function declaration* indicates that the function in question does not return any value when it finishes executing.

341. The term **vtable** is an abbreviation for *virtual function address table*. It is where the addresses of all of the *virtual functions* for a given class are stored; every object of that class contains the address of the vtable for that class.

342. A **while statement** is a *loop control statement* that causes its *controlled block* to be executed while a specified logical expression is true.

343. **Worker class** : see *polymorphic object*.

344. A **year number** is an integer value representing the number of years between two dates.

345. **Zero-based indexing** refers to the practice of numbering the elements of an *array* or vector starting at 0 rather than 1.

(a) As is often the case in C++, this operator (and the corresponding stream input operator, >>) have other almost completely unrelated meanings besides the ones defined here. I'm only bringing this up so that you won't be too surprised if and when you run into these other meanings in another textbook.

(b) Actually, a char can be larger than 8 bits. However, it is required by the C++ standard to be at least 8 bits, and the most common compilers and machines indeed do have 8-bit chars.

(c) In fact, a variable can be declared in any block, not just in a function. In that case, its scope is from the point where it is declared until the end of the block where it is defined.

(d) You can also declare such a variable as unsigned without a size specifier.

(e) Note that the compiler is not required by the standard to use a vtable to implement virtual functions. However, that is the typical way of implementing such functions.

APPENDIX 2

QUESTIONS ASKED IN TECHNICAL INTERVIEWS

- Explain the Concept of Data Abstraction and Data Encapsulation in Object Oriented Programming (OOPS).
- What are classes ? How are they defined ?
- What are objects ? What is common between all objects of a class ?
- State all the class access modifiers and explain each one of them.
- What are Vectors in C++ (Object Oriented Programming) and how are they used ?
- What are containers in C++ and in Object Oriented Programming ? Which objects are available as containers ?
- What are Iterators in C++ and Object Oriented Programming ? Explain where we use them.
- What are the Algorithms namespace used for ?
- What are Enumerations in C++ and Object Oriented Programming ? Explain with an example ?
- What are References in C++ and OOPS ? How are they used ?
- Explain the Rules for using Default Arguments with an example in C++.
- What do you mean by "Pointers to Function" ? What are Function Pointers ?
- What are NameSpaces in C++ ? How do we use namespaces in C++ ?
- What is the Exception Handling mechanism in C++ ? What is Try and Catch in C++ ?
- What is Operator Overloading in C++ ?
- What are Friend Functions and Friend Classes in C++ ?
- What are Constructors and Destructors in C++ ?
- What is Inheritance ? How is a Class Inherited in C++ ?
- What are Virtual Functions ? Why do we need Virtual Functions ? Explain with an example.

- What are Templates in C++ ? How are Templates declared and used ?
- What is Polymorphism ? How is Polymorphism achieved in C++ ?
- What are the Standard Exceptions in C++ ?
- What is Multiple Inheritance in C++ ? Explain with an example.
- What is the significance of dynamic_cast (Dynamic Cast) in C++ ?
- What is Streaming in C++ ? What are the Stream Types in C++ ?
- How are functions with variable number of arguments implemented ?
- What are the ways for displaying formatted output in C++ ?
- How is memory allocation and deallocation done in C++ ?
- What is a Copy Constructor in C++ ? Give an example.
- What is Static Binding and Dynamic Binding in Object Oriented Programming (C++) ?
- Which are the different ways of function calls in C++ ?
- What is procedural programming ?
- Which are the Different Structures for controlling the program flow ?
- Which are the Different types of Constructors ?
- Why Should Destructors be Virtual ? What is the Significance of having Virtual Destructor ?
- What is Function Overloading in C++ ?
- What are Pointers in C++ (Object Oriented Programming) ?
- What are volatile variables ? Explain Volatile variables.
- What is the Difference between Overloaded Functions and Overridden Functions ?
- What are Inline Functions ? When are Inline Functions used ?
- What are Mutable and Const in C++ ?
- What is 'this' Pointer (object) in C++ ?
- What is Scope Resolution Operator in C++ ?
- What are the Storage Types for Variables in C++ ?
- What are Const Member Functions in C++ ?
- Explain Composition in C++ with an example.
- What do you mean by 'Return by Reference' in C++ ?
- What are static Data and Static Member Functions in C++ ?
- What is a Pure Virtual Member Function ?
- What are Preprocessor Directives ?
- What is a class ?
- What is an object ?
- What is the difference between an object and a class ?
- What is the difference between class and structure ?
- What is public, protected, and private ?
- What are virtual functions ?
- What is friend function ?

- What is a scope resolution operator ?
- What do you mean by inheritance ?
- What is abstraction ?
- What is polymorphism ? Explain with an example.
- What is encapsulation ?
- What do you mean by binding of data and functions ?
- What is function overloading and operator overloading ?
- What is virtual class and friend class ?
- What do you mean by inline function ?
- What do you mean by public, private, protected and friendly ?
- When is an object created and what is its lifetime ?
- What do you mean by multiple inheritance and multilevel inheritance ? Differentiate between them.
- Difference between realloc () and free ?
- What is a template ?
- What are the main differences between procedure oriented languages and object oriented languages ?
- What is R T T I ?
- What are generic functions and generic classes ?
- What is namespace ?
- What is the difference between pass by reference and pass by value ?
- Why do we use virtual functions ?
- What do you mean by pure virtual functions ?
- What are virtual classes ?
- Does c++ support multilevel and multiple inheritances ?
- What are the advantages of inheritance ?
- When is a memory allocated to a class ?
- What is the difference between declaration and definition ?
- What are virtual constructors/destructors ?
- In c++ there is only virtual destructors, no constructors. Why ?
- What is late bound function call and early bound function call ? Differentiate.
- How is exception handling carried out in c++ ?
- When will a constructor executed ?
- What is Dynamic Polymorphism ?
- Write a macro for swapping integers.

❑❑❑

REFERENCES

There are few direct references in the text, but here is a short list of books and papers that are mentioned directly or indirectly.

1. [Barton, 1994] John J. Barton and Lee R. Nackman : *Scientific and Engineering C++*. Addison-Wesley. Reading, Mass. 1994. ISBN 0-201-53393-6.
2. [Berg, 1995] William Berg, Marshall Cline, and Mike Girou : *Lessons Learned from the OS/400 OO Project*. CACM. Vol. 38 No. 10. October 1995.
3. [Booch,1994] Grady Booch : *Object-Oriented Analysis and Design*. Benjamin/Cummings. Menlo Park, Calif. 1994. ISBN 0-8053-5340-2.
4. [Budge, 1992] Kent Budge, J. S. Perry, and A. C. Robinson : *High-Performance Scientific Computation using C++*, Proc. USENIX C++ Conference. Portland, Oregon. August 1992.
5. [C, 1990] X3 Secretariats : *Standard – The C Language*. X3J11/90-013. ISO Standard ISO/IEC 9899. Computer and Business Equipment Manufacturers Association.Washington, DC, USA.
6. [C++, 1998] X3 Secretariat : *International Standard – The C++ Language*. X3J16-14882. Information Technology Council (NSITC). Washington, DC, USA.
7. [Campbell,1987] Roy Campbell, et al. : *The Design of a Multiprocessor Operating System*. Proc. USENIX C++ Conference. Santa Fe, New Mexico. November 1987.
8. [Dahl, 1970] O-J. Dahl, B. Myrhaug, and K. Nygaard : *SIMULA Common Base Language*. Norwegian Computing Center S-22. Oslo, Norway. 1970.
9. [Dahl, 1972] O-J. Dahl and C. A. R. Hoare : *Hierarchical Program Construction* in *Structured Programming*. Academic Press, New York. 1972.
10. [Ellis, 1989] Margaret A. Ellis and Bjarne Stroustrup : *The Annotated C++ Reference Manual*.Addison-Wesley. Reading, Mass. 1990. ISBN 0-201-51459-1.
11. [Gamma, 1995] Erich Gamma, et al. : *Design Patterns*. Addison-Wesley. Reading, Mass. 1995. ISBN 0-201-63361-2.
12. [Goldberg, 1983] A. Goldberg and D. Robson : *SMALLTALK-80 – The Language and Its Implementation*. Addison-Wesley. Reading, Mass. 1983.

13. [Griswold, 1970] R. E. Griswold, et al. : *The Snobol4 Programming Language.* Prentice-Hall. Englewood Cliffs, New Jersey. 1970.

14. [Griswold, 1983] R. E. Griswold and M. T. Griswold : *The ICON Programming Language.* Prentice-Hall. Englewood Cliffs, New Jersey. 1983.

15. [Hamilton, 1993] G. Hamilton and P. Kougiouris : *The Spring Nucleus : A Microkernel forObjects.* Proc. 1993 Summer USENIX Conference. USENIX.

16. [Henricson, 1997] Mats Henricson and Erik Nyquist : *Industrial Strength C++ : Rules and Recommendations.* Prentice-Hall. Englewood Cliffs, New Jersey. 1997. ISBN 0-13-120965-5.

17. [Ichbiah, 1979] Jean D. Ichbiah, et al. : *Rationale for the Design of the ADA Programming Language.*SIGPLAN Notices. Vol. 14 No. 6. June 1979.

18. [Kamath, 1993] Yogeesh H. Kamath, Ruth E. Smilan, and Jean G. Smith : *Reaping Benefits with Object-Oriented Technology.* AT&T Technical Journal. Vol. 72 No. 5. September/October 1993.

19. [Kernighan, 1978] Brian W. Kernighan and Dennis M. Ritchie : *The C Programming Language.* Prentice-Hall. Englewood Cliffs, New Jersey. 1978.

20. [Kernighan, 1988] Brian W. Kernighan and Dennis M. Ritchie : *The C Programming Language (Second Edition).* Prentice-Hall. Englewood Cliffs, New Jersey. 1988. ISBN0-13-110362-8.

21. [Koenig, 1989] Andrew Koenig and Bjarne Stroustrup : *C++ : As close to C as possible – but no closer.* The C++ Report. Vol. 1 No. 7. July 1989.

22. [Koenig, 1997] Andrew Koenig and Barbara Moo : *Ruminations on C++.* Addison Wesley Longman. Reading, Mass. 1997. ISBN 0-201-42339-1.

23. [Knuth, 1968] Donald Knuth : *The Art of Computer Programming.* Addison-Wesley. Reading, Mass.

24. [Liskov, 1979] Barbara Liskov et al. : *Clu Reference Manual.* MIT/LCS/TR-225. MIT Cambridge.Mass. 1979.

25. [Martin, 1995] Robert C. Martin : *Designing Object-Oriented C++ Applications Using the Booch Method.* Prentice-Hall. Englewood Cliffs, New Jersey. 1995. ISBN0-13-203837-4.

26. [Orwell, 1949] George Orwell : *1984.* Secker and Warburg. London. 1949.

27. [Richards, 1980] Martin Richards and Colin Whitby-Strevens : *BCPL – The Language and Its Compiler.* Cambridge University Press, Cambridge. England. 1980. ISBN 0-521-21965-5.

28. [Rosler, 1984] L. Rosler : *The Evolution of C – Past and Future.* AT&T Bell Laboratories Technical Journal. Vol. 63 No. 8. Part 2. October 1984.

29. [Rozier, 1988] M. Rozier, et al. : *CHORUS Distributed Operating Systems.* Computing Systems. Vol. 1 No. 4. Fall 1988.

30. [Sethi, 1981] Ravi Sethi : *Uniform Syntax for Type Expressions and Declarations.* Software Practice & Experience. Vol. 11. 1981.

31. [Stepanov, 1994] Alexander Stepanov and Meng Lee : *The Standard Template Library.* HP Labs Technical Report HPL-94-34 (R. 1). August, 1994.

32. [Stroustrup, 1986] Bjarne Stroustrup : *The C++ Programming Language*. Addison-Wesley. Reading, Mass. 1986. ISBN 0-201-12078-X.

33. [Stroustrup, 1987] Bjarne Stroustrup and Jonathan Shopiro : *A Set of C Classes for Co-Routine Style Programming*. Proc. USENIX C++ Conference. Santa Fe, New Mexico. November 1987.

34. [Stroustrup, 1991] Bjarne Stroustrup : *The C++ Programming Language (Second Edition)*. Addison-Wesley. Reading, Mass. 1991. ISBN 0-201-53992-6.

35. [Stroustrup, 1994] Bjarne Stroustrup : *The Design and Evolution of C++*. Addison-Wesley. Reading, Mass. 1994. ISBN 0-201-54330-3.

36. [Tarjan, 1983] Robert E. Tarjan : *Data Structures and Network Algorithms*. Society for Industrial and Applied Mathematics. Philadelphia, Penn. 1983. ISBN 0-898-71187-8.

37. [Unicode, 1996] The Unicode Consortium : *The Unicode Standard, Version 2.0*. Addison-Wesley Developers Press. Reading, Mass. 1996. ISBN 0-201-48345-9.

38. [UNIX, 1985] *UNIX Time-Sharing System : Programmer's Manual. Research Version, Tenth Edition*. AT&T Bell Laboratories, Murray Hill, New Jersey. February 1985.

Index

Symbol

A

B

C

D

E

F

G

P

Q

R

S

❑❑❑